Staging the Pastoral

Tasso's *Aminta* and the Emergence of Modern Western Theater

MEDIEVAL AND RENAISSANCE
TEXTS AND STUDIES
VOLUME 280

Staging the Pastoral

Tasso's *Aminta* and the Emergence of Modern Western Theater

by
Maria Galli Stampino

ACMRS
(Arizona Center for Medieval and Renaissance Studies)
Tempe, Arizona
2005

© Copyright 2005
Arizona Board of Regents for Arizona State University

Library of Congress Cataloging-in-Publication Data

Stampino, Maria Galli.
  Staging the pastoral : Tasso's Aminta and the emergence of modern Western theater / by Maria Galli Stampino.
    p. cm. -- (Medieval and Renaissance texts and studies ; v. 280)
  Includes bibliographical references and index.
  ISBN-13: 978-0-86698-323-5 (alk. paper)
  ISBN-10: 0-86698-323-6 (alk. paper)
 1. Tasso, Torquato, 1544-1595. Aminta. 2. Tasso, Torquato, 1544-1595--Influence. 3. Tasso, Torquato, 1544-1595--Stage history. 4. Theater--History. 5. Pastoral drama. I. Title. II. Series: Medieval & Renaissance Texts & Studies (Series) ; v. 280.

PQ4639.A3S73 2005
792.9'5--dc22

2005027846

∞
This book is made to last.
It is set in Adobe Caslon,
smyth-sewn and printed on acid-free paper
to library specifications.
Printed in the United States of America

Table of Contents

Acknowledgements — vii
List of Figures — ix
Introduction — xi

Chapter One
Aminta as Printed Text and Performed Event: — 1
Critical History, Failures, and Perspectives
   1. Critical Assessments of *Aminta* — 4
   2. *Aminta*'s Printing and Staging History: An Overview — 17
   3. Re-Presentation — 25

Chapter Two
Pesaro, 1574: *Carnevale* — 51
   1. Pesaro in 1574 — 51
   2. *Carnevale* Festivities at Pesaro — 55
   3. 1574 Reconstructed, 1785–1986 — 61
   4. *Aminta* at Pesaro, *Carnevale* 1574 — 66

Chapter Three
Parma, 1627–28: Before the Medici-Farnese Wedding — 97
   1. The Occasion — 98
   2. Preparations: The Theater — 106
   3. Preparations: Music and Performers — 120

Chapter Four
Parma, 13 December 1628: the Medici-Farnese Wedding Celebration — 165
   1. Sources — 165
   2. The Couple's Arrival — 167
   3. The Setting — 170

4. The Prologue	180
5. Act I	182
6. First *Intermezzo*	184
7. Second *Intermezzo*	188
8. Act III	192
9. Third *Intermezzo*	193
10. Fourth *Intermezzo*	197
11. Act V	200
12. Fifth *Intermezzo*	201
13. Afterwards	208

CHAPTER FIVE
Elements of Meaning Formation: *Aminta* and the Emergence of New Staged Expressions (Western Modern Theater and Opera) — 235

1. Space and Meaning Formation	235
2. Bodies and Meaning Formation	245
3. Rhetoric and Meaning Formation	251
4. Novelty and Meaning Formation	256
5. Emergence of Modern Western Theater and Opera?	261

Works Cited — *285*
Index — *305*

Acknowledgements

It is customary to state at the beginning of a monograph such as the present one that the author has incurred many debts. I will not prove to be the exception to this rule. My own tortuous course leading me to early modern performances started with a rather intellectually lively childhood, during which my parents, Anna and Carlo, and my elementary school teacher, Luciana Galli, offered me plenty of books to read and challenges to think about. In middle school I enjoyed two years under the guide of the extraordinary Beatrice Napodano, too soon departed. My *liceo classico* years were among the most fun and most energizing a teen-ager could have, thanks to teachers as Alberto Colombo, Stefano Crespi, and Mariolino Turri, and to the inspiring theatrical productions traveling to the Gallarate's beloved "Teatro delle arti" under the ægis of the talented and self-effacing don Alberto dell'Orto. At Università cattolica in Milan, Francesca Balestra offered her time, wisdom and mentorship, and after graduation her friendship. When my "American experience" began, two people at the University of Kansas were instrumental to my decision to pursue a Ph.D.: Dr. Elizabeth Schultz, who directed my Master's thesis; and Mike Bodin, who introduced me to the joys of teaching. Afterwards, at Stanford, my thinking on this particular topic would not have even started if it had not been for Sepp Gumbrecht's teaching, in the classroom and out, his encouragement and friendship. Still at Stanford, Professor Karl Maurer gave me the kind of attention and support that a graduate student (particularly one from Italy) does not dare to hope for from a senior faculty member. At the University of Miami, my former chair, David Ellison, supported my research in various ways: this book would not have seen the light without his mentorship. My colleagues at Miami have made my teaching and researching life interesting, stimulating and I dare say even fun. Valeria Finucci and Jane Tylus have supported and mentored me in countless ways throughout the years. The persons who have taken the brunt of my lack of time and attention during the writing process are my parents and sister, Luisa, and my husband, Robert L. Strain, Jr. He has taught me to appreciate those qualities I possess and to strive to acquire those that I do not. This book is dedicated to him.

Some of the arguments of this study have appeared before in print. In particular, I debated the issue of printing versus staging history of Aminta in "Performance, Text, and Canon: The Case of *Aminta*" (*Romance Languages Annual* 1997).

Part of the argument regarding an epideictic reading of pastoral plays is in "Epideictic Pastoral: Rhetorical Tensions in the Staging of Torquato Tasso's *Aminta*" (*Theatre Symposium* 1997), and a more detailed case about the origin of opera and its relationship with courtly performances appears in "Classical Antecedents and Teleological Narratives: On the Contamination between Opera and Courtly Sung Entertainment in the Early Seventeenth Century" (*Italica* 2000). Lastly, an earlier version of the argument about space and meaning formation can be read in "The Space of the Performance: *Aminta*, the Court, and the Theater" (*Romance Review* 1996). I also gratefully acknowledge financial support from the University of Miami in 1997 and 1998 in the form of two Max Orovitz Summer Awards in the Arts and Humanities.

Lastly, all citations from sixteenth- and seventeenth-century documents wholly follow the original documents, including spelling and punctuation. When I have broken down shortened forms, I have indicated additions between brackets ([]); and when I have transcribed struck words or phrases, I have enclosed them between greater than and less than (<>) symbols.

List of Figures

1. Black-and-white etching from manuscript at Biblioteca Apostolica Vaticana, Rome: Barb. Lat. 4434, page 9 — 50

2. Black-and-white ink drawing from manuscript at Biblioteca Comunale Ariostea, Ferrara: MS Antonelli 660, from letter of 8 December 1627 — 115

3. Black-and-white ink drawing from manuscript at Biblioteca Comunale Ariostea, Ferrara: MS Antonelli 660, from letter of 7 September 1627 — 116

Front Cover
   Titian, *Landscape with Nymphs and Satyrs*, Musée Bonnat, Bayonne, France.

Introduction

What is theater? Scholars have traditionally proposed many different answers to this deceptively simple question. Opinions have become even more numerous and varied in the course of the second half of the twentieth century, as a reaction and response to ideological challenges to naturalist theater (such as Brecht's, Artaud's, or Grotowsky's, just to name a few) first, and later as a consequence of technological novelties that made notions such as "presence," "representation," "performance," and "body" open to interpretation, if not downright controversial.

There seems little disagreement, however, over the fact that modern Western theater as we know it (and as, despite countless experimental attempts, is still largely practiced in most Western theater houses) originated in the decades straddling the sixteenth and seventeenth centuries, almost simultaneously in England, France, Italy, and Spain. The events leading to (or, according to some scholars, outright causing) this "birth" are largely shrouded in mystery; they can perhaps be reconstructed after the facts, in a manner that is best described as philological, on the basis of what had the good fortune of being written or somehow reported, and of being extant to this day. Generalizations are often based on scant documents, written, and at times visual (though the latter are not necessarily more trustworthy than the latter, as Thomas Heck's edited volume *Picturing Performance* clarifies in theoretical and practical terms). The further back we go in the past, the more limited (and perhaps less reliable) contemporary documents seem to become.

What we do know can be summarized as follows. In 1545, in the northeastern Italian city of Padua, a troupe of traveling performers went to a notary public to record and make official its existence as well as the relationship between its components and their mutual responsibilities.[1] Some time around then, too, women started performing, in Italian professional troupes first. Troupes were becoming organized in the second half of the sixteenth century in France and England, too. The first covered spaces devoted solely (or at least primarily) to performance also date from the second half of the 1570s to the 1590s: the Hôtel de Bourgogne, Paris;[2] the Theatre (1576), the Curtain (1577), the Rose (1587), the Swan (1595), and the Globe (1599), in London; the Teatro di Baldracca (1576), in Florence; the Corral de la Cruz (1579) and the Corral del Príncipe (1583), in Madrid.[3] During the same decades courtly and academy-associated performative spaces appeared in France, England, and Italy: the Teatro Olimpico in Vicenza,

1580–1585; the *teatro* in Sabbioneta, 1588–1590; the Uffizi theater in Florence, 1595; the Whitefriars and the Blackfriars (built in 1576 and rebuilt in 1597) in London. A process had started by which performances started employing certain people (that is, it was slowly becoming a profession, a trade, or an *arte*) and occupying specific spaces within and outside city limits.

Important as these traits are, they constitute only some of those that we regard as crucial and distinctive to Western theater. Others go entirely unnoticed. Western theater is notable for its referentiality, that is, for the habit and ability on the audience's part to operate a knowing distinction between the body of the performer and his/her role on stage. We applaud an actor's rendition of Iago, though we do not agree with the character's choices and attitudes. Conversely, we frown upon those who boo a competent tenor having just completed a performance as Pinkerton in Puccini's *Madama Butterfly*: though the character may be deemed morally reprehensible, we judge the tenor's abilities from a technical standpoint, as we separate performer from character. This fundamental trait seems to have been missing from medieval stagings. Thus the transition from these to modern Western theater is crucial, yet exceedingly hard to assess. Audiences' expectations and habits are fundamental to theater practices, as Susan Bennett's study *Theatre Audiences* shows. However, they are also very hard to reconstruct, historically: they are fleeting and impermanent, rarely committed to paper (in diaries, letters, or other documents), and at times highly individual. The concept of "audience" is, after all, an abstraction, which makes generalizations all too hard.

Together with the audience's expectations regarding the referentiality (or lack thereof) of the bodies of the performers, the meaning that performers themselves attribute to their bodies while on stage is also exceptionally difficult to assess. The stereotype of professional performers as skilled but unlearned has recently been rejected, even for those more closely associated with it, the Italian *commedia dell'arte* players.[4] Nevertheless, scant traces remain of any self-reflection in written form upon which we could elaborate a sense of the performers' sense of referentiality of their bodies on stage.

There are other elements that we take for granted in a traditional, Western theater-going experience. A corollary of on-stage referentiality is the fact that while events may be "based on a true story" or entirely fictional, audiences perceive them as wholly self-contained. Though we might be moved, even called to action by staged events, we are fully aware that they do not fall within the frame of the everyday, but rather in that of make-believe. This trait is highly problematic as far as early modern stagings are concerned, as the present study indicates.

A further crucial element in Western audience members' theater-going experience is what I call "willing suspension of foreknowledge." We might have seen many different stagings of *Hamlet*, but each time we willingly and automatically revert to a state of ignorance vis-à-vis the events on stage: news of Ophelia's death by drowning shakes us. We may even discuss prior to curtain time whether the ghost of Hamlet's father will be visible, and if so, how. Yet once the curtain opens, we learn all over again the importance of Hamlet's father's ghost for the plot and for character development.

All these traits are constitutive to the Western theater tradition, but not all came into existence in the crucial decades between 1580 and 1630. This study concentrates on two performances of Torquato Tasso's pastoral play *Aminta* that were separated by fifty-five years; through micro-reconstructions of these stagings, I indicate how the emergence of modern Western theater as we know it was far less linear and simple than subsequent teleological narratives have led us to believe. Indeed, this study shows that not all questions can find an answer, even after extensive archival research and with the help of the most current theoretical tools: in certain cases, we can only reach partial, and partially satisfying, hypotheses, since crucial elements have vanished along with the performances and the performers themselves.

By concentrating on Italian events, I have singled out one geographical area whose contributions are usually deemed crucial to the emergence of Western theater. Nevertheless, within the field of Italian studies little attention has been devoted to the various elements that constitute a staged performance. Indeed, the present work reacts against a long-standing literary tradition in Italian letters whereby dramas are solely considered as written texts. The use of non-literary sources to increase our understanding of literary texts is well established in other national traditions, notably the British one. Nevertheless, a bias against impermanent stagings continues to this day in Italian studies, despite the newly-found awareness of the cultural import of communal and private celebrations in early modern times, the increased attention to various forms of performance arts on both sides of the Atlantic, the theoretical questions raised by new media, and the subsequent popularity of performance studies in the United States and the United Kingdom.

Concurrently, in this study I have exploited the traditional attention to dramatic works belonging to the literary canon by choosing one such play: Torquato Tasso's pastoral *Aminta*. Its canonical status within Italian letters — seemingly, from its very first performance — promised that a wealth of contemporary documents had been written about it and, more importantly, had been preserved. Upon research, some turned up; most had been known, but few had been analyzed in some detail. In addition, other factors prompted me to choose *Aminta*: its popularity, both on courtly and "popular" stages; its place in a new genre like the pastoral (still not codified in 1573, hence more adaptable to stage needs); its quick fame in other European locales;[5] and, more importantly, the period when it was originally written and gained fame on stage, at the beginning of the decades in which Western theater is usually said to have emerged.

Specifically, on the basis of various contemporary documents (such as diaries, letters, official descriptions, and so on) in the present work I have reconstructed two *Aminta* performances: the first took place at Pesaro in 1574, the second at Parma in 1628. Separated as they are by fifty-five years, the events leading to and surrounding these two performances, as well as the goings-on on and off stage during the performances themselves, bring to light some elements of modern Western theater and opera then coming into existence. Not surprisingly, my conclusions belie the teleological narratives that histories of the theater have accustomed us to. By studying two performances taking place in such relevant circumstances, the present work calls into question notions relative to the history of performance, the origins of Western theater, and the emergence of opera: the teleological nature of their origin, the primacy of music over words in the so-called *seconda prattica*, the centrality of the written text, and the causal relationship among pastoral, court, and modern Western theater.

The aforementioned attention to performance on both sides of the Atlantic in recent years, prompted by a renewed interest in the construction of social and stage identity, by an explosion in "alternative" performance styles, and by innovative means of recording impermanent events, has resulted in a number of studies devoted to various performance issues, including the relationship between staged events and their reproduction on film, in still photographs, digitally, and otherwise. When I set out on this project, I was therefore well aware that the problems posed by any attempt to make sense of (that it, draw meaning from) and analyze performance only increase when we deal with events of the earlier times. The chronological, spatial, and cultural divides that separate us from past occurrences make it harder to gather first-hand information, and (even if they posed little theoretical problem) rule out photographic evidence at least before the early twentieth century, and video documentation before the 1950s or '60s.

Nevertheless, in the course of the present work I have come to realize that historical performance is so far removed from our expectations and habits that it is paradoxically easier to study: to use an ethnographic analogy, we are more aware of elements, motives, and rationales when immersed in a culture foreign to us, than in ours. Further, as Mark Franko and Annette Richards have recently pointed out in the introduction to their collection *Acting on the Past*, studies in historical performance stand in stark contrast with what they term the "presentism" of the performance studies field. Thus they constitute "a challenge to the field to conceptualize the past and thus also to historicize itself" (Franko and Richards, *Acting on the Past*, 3). Past performances emphasize that they "are always in a state of appearing and vanishing; by definition transient, they are immediate yet quickly become historical" (1).

Through the necessary mediation of the written word (a necessity for both contemporary documents and subsequent reconstruction), past events must be reconstructed, so that we might understand how they produced meaning for their original, intended audience. But as Andrea Gareffi has stated, "[l]o stile del racconto consente per analogia un restauro congetturale dell'avvenimento [i.e., any staged performance], . . . che avrà ben poco a che fare con la pur possibile ricostruzione filologica. . . . [B]isogna far affidamento su di una diversa maniera di comprendere, più bisognosa d'immaginazione, con le sue oscillazioni e le sue incertezze, poiché lo spettacolo è comunque un passo nel reame dell'immaginario e l'ambiguità non gli fa torto."[6] If we push Gareffi's argument further, we can conclude that historical performances such as the two under scrutiny here demand a non-hermeneutic approach, one that belies the scientific pretense of literary and cultural studies, but that is also the most suitable for embodied events such as staged performances.

Consequently, and as is often the case with cultural studies projects like the present one, I have availed myself of a theoretically eclectic approach. In fact, literary criticism plays only an ancillary role with respect to other theoretical tools. Those drawn from ethnography, anthropology, sociology, social and cultural history, semiotics and history of the theater, performance studies and musicology have proved priceless in this endeavor. As Gay McAuley has recently written, performance scholars acknowledge various sources of inspirations and intellectual antecedents, yet their studies are "not for all that . . . semiotic, phenomenological, ethnographic, or sociological . . . , and indeed specialists in any of these disciplines may refuse to acknowledge the paternity" that we allege (*Space In Performance*, 17). The very nature of performance, in its impermanence and embodied immediacy, defeats all attempts at restricting one's approach, or at pigeon-holing a specific event. In other words, I harbor no illusion that this study will bring past events back to life. I am fully aware that my textual and verbal tools are necessarily inadequate to the task of reconstructing a series of embodied occurrences. Nevertheless, this is still the only device available to us, one that can be used with excellent results, as James M. Saslow's splendid 1996 monograph devoted to *The Medici Wedding of 1589: Florentine Festival as* Theatrum Mundi shows.

My goal is different from Saslow's illustrative one. Rather than reconstruct one set of events in its entirety, I have compared two stagings of the same play that are fifty-five years apart in order to analyze the manners in which meaning was then constructed and perceived on stage, and to explore one way in which modern theater emerged in the same period. In the case of the Pesaro and Parma *Aminta* performances, we do not have the same materials available as for the 1589 Medici wedding. My reconstructions are different to reflect these circumstances. Lastly, the present work echoes the fact that at its core lies a work belonging to the Italian literary canon. Thus, in chapter 1 I have first placed *Aminta* in its literary and critical tradition. I have then proceeded to outline my theoretical goals: a thorough re-construction aimed at highlighting staging practices, audience expectations and reactions, and meaning-making strategies utilized by both festivities' organizers and theater-goers.

In order to reach these goals, chapters 2, 3, and 4 are based on extensive archival and library research. They are based on extant letters, diaries, semi-official or official descriptions, account books, and other similar material. Chapter 2 concentrates on the 1574 *Aminta* staging, which took place in Pesaro during *carnevale* season, and after a period of intense civil unrest. Tasso's pastoral was one of three public shows that highlighted the pre-Lenten season. My reconstruction of the staging starts with contemporary decrees regarding which behaviors and celebrations were permissible during *carnevale* in Pesaro in the years immediately preceding and following 1574. This indicates the intellectual climate, expectation, and behavior then prevailing, and contextualizes extant documents regarding the *Aminta* performance proper. With the help of additional archival documents, I have been able to question the traditional notion regarding the location of the temporary theater where *Aminta* took place, and this has interesting consequences as to the play's public relevance and meaning for its contemporary Pesaro audience.

Chapters 3 and 4 are both devoted to the 1628 Parma *Aminta*. This performance was one of many festivities celebrating the arrival in town of the Farnese family scion and his bride, a Medici princess. Far more lavish than the Pesaro staging, the Parma one is also far better documented. The two chapters reconstruct two different aspects of the festivities. Chapter 3 follows the organizers' choices and dilemmas in the many months preceding the performance. Chapter 4, instead, is fully devoted to a detailed descriptive reconstruction of the *Aminta* staging itself, which took place on the evening of 13 December 1628. In both chapters contemporary documents regarding the events leading to the wedding celebrations and the festivities themselves are supplemented by other sources detailing Parma's tradition of civic pageantry, its laws, and so on. Further, I have highlighted differences between the organizational and staging practices associated with spoken and sung performance, as they are integral to both the staging and meaning-formation processes in Parma and elsewhere in this period.

Lastly, in chapter 5 I have compared the two previously reconstructed events to underscore continuities and differences. Specifically, I have highlighted various processes of meaning formation in both Pesaro and Parma audiences. They include spatial relationships, the perceived significance of bodies on and off stage, the underlying rhetorical strategies prevailing at the time in literary texts and on stage, and the to us mysterious (yet crucial) element of novelty. In conclusion, I argue that the processes leading to the origin of modern Western theater, far from being linear or teleological, were at time serendipitous and haphazard, even when a staging was organized by a central authority. Some elements that constitute Western theater and opera emerge in the two courtly stagings at hand; nevertheless, testimonies on the part of audience members and extant documents

Introduction   xvii

by festivity organizers point at a complex process that was essentially non-linear, even unanticipated. Thus, I believe that the reasons for selecting a non-hermeneutic approach as the most appropriate theoretical tool in dealing with embodied, impermanent, non-textual events such as staged performances is amply justified in and by this study.

Finally, it is telling that historical performance has been analyzed in depth by non-performance studies scholars (such as the art historian James Saslow, who follows Aby Warburg's trailblazing influence; or literature scholars like Stephen Orgel). While Franko and Richards point out that in recent years historical performance has elicited a limited amount of attention (*Acting on the Past*, 2), they also indicate that due to historical reasons, early modern performance is still largely neglected by scholars in this field. Yet historical performance showcases the most important trace of embodied events: their being based on absence. Critically and theoretically, therefore, studies of past performances lie at the very core of the field. And while it was never my intention in this study to make the past come alive, historical processes of meaning formations, especially those based on embodied events, demand a reconstructive effort, as they illuminate our historical biases and indicate a fruitful path for performance and literary studies at large.

Notes

[1] A short description of this event and of its import is in M. Pieri, *La nascita del teatro moderno in Italia tra XV e XVI secolo* (Torino: Bollati Boringhieri, 1989), 202. N. D. Shergold asserts that "[t]he first records of the existence of [professional] companies are found in the 1530's [*sic*] and 1540's [*sic*]": *A History of the Spanish Stage from Medieval Times until the End of the Seventeenth century* (Oxford: Clarendon Press, 1967), 175–76; specifically the first reference to a group of players goes back to 1543 (152).

[2] Though the building goes back to 1548, the first extant contract for the Hôtel de Bourgogne is dated 25 March 1598: S. Wilma Deierkauf-Holsboer, *Le Théâtre de l'Hôtel de Bourgogne*, 2 vols. (Paris: Nizet, 1968–1970), 1: 17–18.

[3] A detailed overview of these spaces can be read in the section devoted to "Lo spazio dei professionisti" in F. Cruciani, *Lo spazio del teatro* (Bari: Laterza, 1998), 61–72. On the development of the Parisian *théâtre de l'hôtel de Bourgogne* the most complete study is still Deierkauf-Holsboer. Much attention has been devoted to British performative spaces, especially after the successful endeavor to reconstruct Shakespeare's Globe theater, described in A. Gurr and S. Orell, *Rebuilding Shakespeare's Globe* (New York: Routledge, 1989). Further, many sketches of the Globe and the Rose can be found in J. Wilson, *The Archeology of Shakespeare* (Phoenix Mills: Sutton, 1995), which is less interested in rebuilding a practicable performative space, and therefore philologically more precise. Lastly, on the Spanish *corrales* the classic study is chap. 7 of Shergold, *History of the Spanish Stage*. Chap. 2 of H. A. Rennert, *The Spanish Stage in the Time of Lope de Vega* (New York: Hispanic Society of America, 1909) covers the origin, location and staging practices of the *corrales* in Madrid,

while specifically devoted to the Corral del Príncipe is J. J. Allen, *The Reconstruction of a Spanish Golden Age Playhouse* (Gainesville: University Press of Florida, 1983).

[4] See for example Pieri's chapter devoted to "Il teatro da vendere" in *La nascita*; F. Taviani "Bella d'Asia. Torquato Tasso, gli attori e l'immortalità," *Paragone* 408–10 (1984): 3–76; and the primary documents collected in the third part of Ferruccio Marotti and Giovanna Romei, *La commedia dell'arte e la società barocca. La professione del teatro* (Roma: Bulzoni, 1991).

[5] Mario Praz mentions that *Aminta* might have been staged in Reading, England, in July 1574, that is, barely a year after the traditional date of its Ferrara opening, though he does not fully endorse this hypothesis: "Tasso in Inghilterra," in *Torquato Tasso* (Milan: Marzorati, 1957), 673–709, here 673–74. However, the first English translation of Tasso's pastoral dates from 1591: A. Harbage, *Annals of English Drama 975–1700*, 3rd ed. (London: Routledge, 1989), 56–57; four more translations followed, in 1628, 1635, 1660, and 1698 (Harbage, *Annals of English Drama*, 346), making it the second most translated contemporary play (after Guarini's *Il pastor fido*) (Harbage, *Annals of English Drama*, 347). Interestingly, the first four English versions were not meant for staging, but only for reading, as Harbage's indication "closet" shows (56–57; 126–27; 136–37; 158–59). The 1698 one was awarded a performance patent, and is only extant in its first printing (Harbage, *Annals of English Drama*, 202–3). The situation is harder to assess in France, as Chandler B. Beall's thorough monograph devoted to *La Fortune du Tasse en France* (Eugene: University of Oregon Press, 1942) does not separate translations for the stage from the literary influence *Aminta* exerted there. Nevertheless, it is noteworthy that Tasso's pastoral was printed in Paris in 1584, the same year when its first translation appeared, in Bordeaux (Beall, *La Fortune du Tasse*, 15). Further, the 1591 prose translation was reprinted in 1593 and 1597 (23), while the 1596 one by Guillaume Belliard had three more press runs within thirteen years (1598, 1603, 1609) (30).

[6] "The style of a tale allows for a hypothetical restoration of any [theatrical] event that has little to do with a possible philological reconstruction. We need to rely on a different way of understanding, one that requires more imagination with its oscillations and uncertainties, since a show is a step into the realm of imagination and ambiguity suits it fine": A. Gareffi, *La scrittura e la festa* (Bologna, Il Mulino, 1991), 91.

Chapter One

❧

Aminta as Printed Text and Performed Event: Critical History, Failures, and Perspectives

Anybody who makes it through the fourth year of high school in Italy will have some memory, however faint, of a literary work entitled *Aminta*. Though most will not recall much (and some will take the ending of the name of the play's namesake to designate a female, instead of a male, protagonist), even so trifling a trace indicates beyond the shadow of a doubt that *Aminta* still fully belongs to the canon of Italian literary history. Even in other European traditions, *Aminta* is present as the inspiration or model for various pastoral expressions: from Sir Philip Sidney's *Arcadia* to the French courtly *bergeries*.[1]

However, as Ferdinando Taviani has put it, "[l]'*Aminta* è un classico, ma strano: sembra che tutti sappiano prenderlo alla leggera, senza troppo accaldarsi attorno a problemi che per opere consimili inducono invece a discussioni accademiche serrate."[2] Many questions therefore remain unanswered, or at least only partially explained: what is *Aminta*? In other words, what kind of text is it? And consequently: what are the conditions under which we can best comprehend it? But more importantly: why was it famed and praised? How did it make sense to its intended, original audience? In order to contextualize my answers (and this study), in this chapter I will first attempt briefly to situate Tasso's pastoral in the context of his life and time and of the rest of his literary production. Second, I will survey the traditional critical responses to these issues. Third, I will provide a necessary expansion to the reception to the text of *Aminta*, by sketching its printing and staging history. Last, I will outline the criteria of the present study.

Let us then turn to a brief outline of Tasso's biography and literary production.[3] Born in Sorrento in 1544, Torquato belonged to a family of the lesser nobility; his father, Bernardo, was a courtier for the Sanseverino family and a poet of some fame. The younger Tasso was exposed to the traditional *cursus studiorum* from his childhood, studying under the Jesuits in Salerno and Naples. Later, his education continued in Rome and Bergamo, and at the della Rovere court in Urbino. By 1559, in Venice, he was dabbling in poetry; his first attempt at an epic poem on religious subject matter, entitled *Gierusalemme*, remained unfinished. After a year at the University of Padua, where he studied Aristotle's *Poetics* under the guidance of the best known (and most dogmatic) Aristotelian philosophers of his time, he traveled to Mantua and Bologna, and wrote lyrical poems in the Petrarchan vein (dedicated to Lucrezia Bendidio, a lady in waiting to Eleonora d'Este, duchess of Ferrara, and to Laura Peperara) and another epic poem, *Rinaldo*, published in 1562 with dedication to Cardinal Luigi d'Este.

In 1565, the eighteen-year-old Torquato was retained by the court of the same Cardinal Luigi d'Este. For twelve years, he was to live in Ferrara, at a court still resplendent with artistic genius, yet more and more politically and militarily irrelevant, indeed close to its demise (which took place in 1598, with the devolution of the fiefdom of Ferrara back to the Papacy, after Alfonso II's death without a legitimate heir). Under Cardinal Luigi, and later (from 1572 on) under Duke Alfonso himself, Torquato played many different roles, from accompanying the duke to foreign expeditions (like the one to Rome in 1572–1573) to teaching geometry at the local university (from 1572 onwards). Nevertheless, he enjoyed plenty of time to write: from *Aminta* (composed in 1573) to the tragedy *Galealto, re di Norvegia*, to the elaboration and completion of his first attempt at the epic form, under the title of *Goffredo* (but better known as *Gerusalemme liberata*) (1575), and many lyrical and encomiastic poems.

The composition of his *magnum opus* provoked in Tasso deeply-felt anxiety and doubts stemming from two separate, yet related, sources. On the one hand, Torquato felt that his rhetorical skills were unequal to the task. On the other, he questioned his religious orthodoxy, manifested in the inclusion of numerous love episodes. Aristotelianism and post-Tridentine Counter-Reformation spirituality were closely linked both in Tasso's mind and in the culture of the times, specifically in the group of writers to whose criticism he subjected himself and his epic poem. In 1576, after the "trial" of *Goffredo* in Rome, Tasso wrote an *Allegoria* to accompany and explain the epic poem, aimed at manifesting its orthodoxy in both Aristotelian and Catholic terms.

The period following 1575–1576 has traditionally attracted the most attention on the part of critics and historians trying to explain Tasso's literary production as a mirror of his mind or, alternatively, attempting to find inklings of his later phobias in his earlier production. In 1577, still unsure of his adherence to the tenets of the Roman Catholic Church, Tasso submitted himself to an examination on the part of Ferrara's inquisitor, and was absolved. Soon afterwards, after threatening a servant (supposedly spying on him) with a knife, he was confined to a convent. After he managed to escape, his peregrinations took him first to Sorrento, where he visited his sister, and then to Mantua, Urbino, and Turin. In 1579, back at the Este court, then celebrating Duke Alfonso II's third wedding (to Margherita Gonzaga), he violently protested, feeling neglected, and ended up at Sant'Anna hospital, where he lived until 1586.

The strict isolation of Tasso's first fourteen months at Sant'Anna later gave way to a looser regime; for the better part of these seven years, Tasso was able to correspond with and receive whomever he chose to. He composed almost all his *Dialoghi*, many lyrical poems, and countless letters. Still, he suffered from his isolation, and repeatedly pleaded his cause with Duke Alfonso and many other noblemen and women, as a great many letters attest. Yet other sources of anguish during his confinement to Sant'Anna were the various pirated editions of his works (*Aminta* in 1580, *Gerusalemme liberata* the following year, among others), and the *querelle* on the excellence and superiority of Ludovico Ariosto's *Orlando furioso* as against Tasso's own epic poem. Additionally, the Este court kept its distance from the poet: Duke Alfonso was afraid that Torquato's perceived unorthodox beliefs might further endanger his standing with the papal court, at a time when the Este hold on Ferrara was tenuous for lack of a legitimate heir.

In 1586 Tasso was released to Vincenzo Gonzaga and went to live in Mantua. There he completed revisions to *Galealto*, renamed *Re Torrismondo*, and the new version of his epic poem, published in 1593 as *Gerusalemme conquistata*. His residence there proved short-lived: he escaped to Loreto and from then moved to Rome, where he found protection under Pope Sixtus V. In 1588 he spent a few months in Naples, at the Monte Oliveto monastery, in honor of whose monks he wrote the poem *Il monte Oliveto*, printed posthumously. After a short period in Rome, first with Scipione Gonzaga and later at the convent of Santa Maria Nuova degli Olivetani, he moved to Florence in 1590, where he attended to revising the *Gerusalemme liberata*.

Until 1592, when he settled in Rome for two years, he traveled to and lived in Mantua and Naples (where he met Giovan Battista Manso, his first biographer); meanwhile, he reworked and published his lyrical poems (in two parts: 1590 and 1592), and started composing *Il mondo creato*. Once in Rome, he attempted to secure protection on the part of the newly elected pope, Clement VIII. The first edition of *Gerusalemme conquistata*, dated 1593, is in fact dedicated to one of Clement's nephews, Cinzio Passeri Aldobrandini. During these two years, he also wrote and published *Lacrime di Maria Vergine* and *Lacrime di Gesù Cristo*. After spending the summer of 1594 in Naples, where he published his *Discorsi dell'arte poetica*, he returned to Rome, where Clement VIII gave him a yearly pension and promised him poetic laurels. The following year, while waiting for his coronation, he fell ill again, and died on 25 March at the Sant'Onofrio convent, in whose church he is still buried.

Tasso's own secretive temper, his circumstances during the last years of his life, and (more importantly) rapidly changing social and institutional conditions soon gave rise to a myth of Tasso as romantic hero which still inescapably permeates any reconstruction or understanding of his life experience and his works. As Pier Vincenzo Mengaldo has written regarding Franco Fortini's appreciation for *Gerusalemme liberata*, "se [Fortini] . . . sente e dichiara che Tasso è per sempre legato all'interpretazione romantica e lui stesso ne riconosce più volte la legittimità, ciò avviene perché egli ritiene che la sua individualità e la sua statura stessa siano, almeno in parte, inseparabili dal grande cono d'ombra ch'egli ha proiettato sui secoli a venire."[4]

1. Critical Assessments of *Aminta*

The "cono d'ombra" [long shadow] to which Mengaldo refers darkens *Aminta* in various ways. First, Tasso's pastoral is often seen as ancillary to *Gerusalemme liberata*. Further, even during Tasso's lifetime, his pastoral elicited interest as a literary (that is, immutable, because written) text rather than as a performed event.[5] While it is relatively easy to postulate various legitimate reasons for this situation — the fact that Tasso belonged to courtly circles steeped in academism; his very training at Padua under strictly Aristotelian teachers; the appropriation of *Aminta* on the part of Guarini and his supporters against those theoreticians who denied value to the new genre of pastoral drama[6] — the predominance of a text-based approach over a performance-oriented one continued throughout the centuries, until very recently, with very few exceptions.[7] There have been, moreover, approaches in which the distinction between theatrical and literary analysis is fluid and blurred. Generally speaking, however, a short examination of *Aminta* criticism will suffice to reveal its bias towards a literary approach.

I do not wish to deny the importance of any of these critical stances. Rather than concentrating on various interpretations of the meaning of *Aminta*, my goal is to focus on the process through and by which meaning was produced for the writer, the performers, and the audience of specific stagings. Thus the following analysis of past critical interpretations aims to establish a fundamental difference between the present endeavor and anterior approaches, not to deny their relevance within a different frame of reference. Further, it underscores that numerous insights can be gained by expanding our viewpoint from a strictly literary to a performance one.

It is easy to identify three general and rather inclusive domains into which most *Aminta* literary criticism neatly falls. First, there are those who interpret Tasso's pastoral in biographical terms. These critics can count on a very influential precursor, Tasso's first biographer, Giovan Battista Manso, whom Goethe and Byron knew. According to Manso, while *Aminta* was undoubtedly written at the request of Duke Alfonso II,[8] it became in Tasso's hands a carrier to express in hidden terms his love for Alfonso's sister, Leonora.[9] For Manso and his followers, at this point in his life Torquato had not yet succumbed to the desperation and gloom of his later years. Therefore, *Aminta* shines as a perfect example of Tasso's unimpeded genius: he had not yet been disappointed in his affection; he had recently been accepted in Alfonso's service, harboring high expectations and hopes for his advancement; and he relished his newly found *otium* and appreciation on the part of the courtly audience. For some critics, the pastoral's hasty yet refined composition bears testimony to these circumstances: for Carducci, *Aminta* is "un portento: portento vivo d'armonia tra l'ispirazione e l'espressione e l'impressione rispondentisi negli effetti, che è il sommo dell'arte della poesia riflessa,"[10] one that was composed "in due mesi dell'inverno 1573" [in two months in the winter of 1573] (228) — an assessment that he presumably derived from Tasso's second biographer, Pierantonio Serassi.[11] Umberto Bosco repeats this myth: "si ricordi che la favola fu composta di getto," he notes incidentally, "in una breve parentesi di serenità."[12] Eugenio Donadoni goes even further: *Aminta* is "forse una delle opere sue, a cui dette meno importanza: e che certo gli costò meno fatica. La compose leggermente: in due mesi, pare. Fu una di quelle opere, che ai poeti vengono fatte come da se stesse, in rari momenti di felicità creativa."[13] This assessment of the pastoral as the work that Tasso viewed as his least important depends in all probability on the fact that, contrary to *Gerusalemme liberata*, *Aminta* was not printed under Tasso's close supervision. However, no consideration is given to the fact that publication might not have been as crucial to *Aminta* as to the epic poem, since its privileged means of diffusion was the stage rather than the printed page, as I will underscore in the following section. It is also hard to believe that the twenty-nine-year-old Tasso could have been so utterly unconcerned with the success of the first piece he wrote in the duke's service. Overall, Donadoni espouses an "organic" view of the text: as the pastoral spontaneously created itself, the text shows its felicity at every turn, created with ease and by itself; its artistry is present and can be felt, but not seen.[14]

While for Donadoni the effortlessness on the part of Tasso is evident in the artistry of the end result, for Giuseppe Petronio the importance of the pastoral resides solely in its biographical elements. Contrary to more elaborate, less spontaneous writings, "l'operetta [i.e., *Aminta*], scritta tumultuosamente e con pieno abbandono in due mesi, può aprire uno spiraglio su abissi meno conosciuti, forse anche più profondi dell'animo del poeta."[15] Petronio is also trying to counter a critical tradition that relegates the pastoral to a secondary role vis-à-vis Tasso's epic poem *Gerusalemme liberata* — while yielding to it in using the diminutive (and diminishing) term "operetta" to refer to the pastoral. Petronio assumes that the impulsive poetic birth of *Aminta* affords its readers a glimpse of the "real" Torquato, thus proving pivotal for understanding the poet's *animus*.

Even Claudio Varese, the one critic who openly opposes the notion that Tasso's pastoral was more spontaneous than his other works, falls into the same teleological trap. It has a specific place in Tasso's production, juxtaposed chronologically to his epic poem.[16] Further, Varese denies the possibility of *Aminta* having been written hurriedly (or, as Carducci implies, on the basis of Tasso's readings of Theocritus's *Idylls* ["Su l'*Aminta*," 228]), and envisions it within the entire literary production of Tasso. Although he shuns Petronio's and Donadoni's "organic" view of the text, Varese nevertheless fails to recognize the peculiarity of *Aminta* with respect to Tasso's other works, as it is the only pastoral and one of the two[17] plays he ever wrote. We should always remember that for any strict Aristotelian writer, as (to put it with Fortini), "in un poeta di ricca sebbene disordinata capacità di elaborazione intellettuale e di robusta formazione retorica quale il Tasso fu, la separazione dei generi e degli stili aveva un ruolo decisivo."[18]

Another central element of *Aminta* that has attracted critical attention only with respect to Tasso's own state of mind, but entirely disregarded as a source of meaning for the creation and reception of the play, is its courtly setting, specifically, the influence on it from the milieu in which it was created. Donadoni is of the opinion that Tasso's position in *Aminta* is that of a courtier, serene and at ease with his milieu, with no other goal than to enjoy his position.[19] In other words, according to Donadoni, while writing *Aminta* Tasso was so completely imbued with the courtly ideal that his entire life and production was a reflection of it. Further, the young Torquato harbored no reserve towards the courtly milieu and had entirely espoused its ideals and standards. Petronio, however, disputes this view. In his opinion, *Aminta* follows the earlier pastorals in staging numerous "riferimenti al tempo attuale, ai personaggi assistenti alla recita"[20] — a trait that curtails the artistic relevance of this play as it had stunted its predecessors in the pastoral genre, since the text "più che vivere di una sua autonoma vita artistica, viveva di quella [cortese] soltanto."[21] Instead of exploiting this insight in the performance domain, Petronio continues on the psychological terrain. For Tasso, the court was an ideal to which he had to refer himself and his work, despite his wavering attitude towards it.[22] In other words, Tasso is caught in a double bind: he is a member of the court yet aware of its shortcomings. After the brief, happy period during which the pastoral was composed, Torquato would become more and more sensitive to the divergence between ideal and reality. Indeed, according to Petronio the loss of the tenuous balance to be found in *Aminta* is evident in Tasso's later works. For Raffaello Ramat *Aminta* itself presents psychological and stylistic indications of how precarious this balance was. The pastoral is marked by what he calls "nostalgia del presente" [nostalgia for the present], as "il Tasso sente — per intuizione dolorosa più che per consapevolezza critica — dentro di sé i problemi che minano la saldezza delle fiducie [*sic*] rinascimentali"[23] and resolves them "in una invenzione stilistica" [a stylistic invention] (129).

For one critic trying to underscore the potential for a meaningful tension (psychological or otherwise) in Tasso's pastoral, another resists this reading as betraying the calm composure emerging from *Aminta* and, in general, any work of the Renaissance. Gaetano Trombatore tries to refute Petronio's argument in order to reinscribe Tasso's work in general and *Aminta* in particular within the boundaries of a courtly culture and atmosphere accepted in its concrete existence, without any idealization and subsequent disappointment: "parlare di un'opposizione tra il mondo della corte e quello della natura, con il trionfo di quest'ultima; dell'urto di due opposte concezioni nell'animo del poeta, che le obbiettava in personaggi differenti; è alterare e svisare l'anima stessa della 'favola'."[24] Trombatore's use of the term "favola," though not unusual with respect to pastorals, is telling: *Aminta* is imbued with a fable-like quality. Instead of creating tensions, the discrepancy between real and ideal brings about an idyllic feeling, in *Aminta* as well as in "i versi del Poliziano e del Pontano e, alla fine, il *Pastor fido*:"[25] Pastoralism, for Trombatore, corresponded to Tasso's intellectual desire to escape an ideal-deprived social life.[26] His opinion is, in effect, the exact opposite of Leopardi's, for whom Tasso was the prime example of a sensitive human being seduced first, and deceived later, by appearances and illusions.[27]

The same issue of idealization and idyllic depiction of life at court lies at the core of Umberto Bosco's criticism. *Aminta*'s novelty is to be found in the fact that "il Tasso non vuole già abbassare le corti al livello delle selve, sibbene innalzar queste sino alla linea di quelle."[28] Consequently, a tone of *medietas* permeates courtly "relazioni sociali" [social relations] (143), and *Aminta* itself: "Per tono 'medio' intendo il continuo controllo così della propria espressione, come dello stesso sentire; il non abbandonarsi mai al fluire di questo: lo scorgere un'altra realtà dietro a quella che si vive o a cui si aspira" (143).[29] Implicitly, Bosco contradicts his own earlier assertion regarding the "serenità" [serenity] (142) of Tasso's spirit that he surmises from the text. More importantly, and explicitly, he undermines his opinion vis-à-vis Tasso's identification with the court and its ideals: his work, written for the court, had to correspond to its intended audience's culture as well as mood. Tasso therefore was barred from abandoning himself to his true feelings.[30] We are thus confronted with a double bind: does *Aminta* embody the court and its ideals? Does Tasso avoid the "concessioni" that would have marred his poetry? Or does he espouse courtly *medietas*, the awareness of two levels in each act and event?

Ramat explicitly denies the possibility of reconciliation between real and ideal in *Aminta*. In his opinion, Tasso was aware of these two levels of courtly existence, and of the concurring facts that the court "rappresenta la vita armoniosamente razionale, capolavoro dell'uomo del rinascimento" and that it "è anche il luogo della dissoluzione di tale sogno, il luogo che lo fa sentire come sogno perché ne è l'antitesi."[31] Once again, different opinions stem from a similar approach. *Aminta* is of interest to Petronio and Trombatore both (and, to a smaller extent, to Bosco as well) exclusively as evidence for Tasso's frame of mind while composing the pastoral and, more in general, while at the Este court. Such a viewpoint is condemned to remaining entirely speculative, given the dearth of evidence regarding Tasso's thoughts and feelings in this period (such as letters or diary entries). Moreover, no attention is devoted to the conventional aspect of *Aminta* and, in general, of courtly texts. Such an attempt at searching for straightforward biographical evidence in literature naïvely postulates a direct reflection of the author's psyche and emotions in his/her production, while ignoring the formal and stylistic imposition of the genre and the setting on them. Finally, and more importantly for the scope of the present study, it does not add to our understanding of *Aminta* as a performed work, as it entirely disregards the theatrical and public aspects of the text.

If we move away from biographical interpretations of *Aminta*, we encounter a vast domain of criticism that considers Tasso's pastoral along the rest of his poetical production, specifically his lyric poetry. This approach gives a privileged place to an in-depth analysis of Tasso's poetry, and aims at showing the continuities between what he wrote for the stage and his intertext. This position could prove extremely fruitful, as Tasso's lyric poetry of the mid-1570s was composed for the same audience as the pastoral, that is, the Este court at Ferrara. However, the critics examining *Aminta* in this context largely limit their remarks to the stylistic aspect, while once again neglecting to analyze its reception and the influence of its intended audience.

At the intersection between psychological and lyrical approaches to Tasso's pastoral I would place Benedetto Croce, who tellingly dedicates to *Aminta* only two pages in his essay on "Poesia pastorale" in *Poeti e scrittori del pieno e tardo Rinascimento*. Fundamentally, he espouses Carducci's idea that in the pastoral Tasso's "spirit" shines the brightest, unfettered by any constraints or limitations. Further, he defines the tone and content of *Aminta* on the basis of the emotions animating its characters:

> nell'*Aminta* domina l'amore-passione, non quello filosoficamente sublimato e risolubile nell'idea di Dio, ma non piú l'erotismo puramente sensuale; l'amore che come passione vuole il consenso d'anima della persona amata, e come passione umana, non soprumana né animale, rispettando l'essere che ama e ammira, protegge la propria purezza e nobiltà.[32]

Although Croce does not read these emotions in strictly biographical terms, he does avail himself of the Romantic phrase "amore-passione" that implies an emphasis on the author's intention rather than on the external pressures and interference shaping the work itself and its reception. In fact, a similar opinion echoes more than fifty years later in Umberto Bosco's 1970 biography-prone essay: in *Aminta*, "l'amore che si consiglia e si vagheggia è l'unica possibile estrinsecazione delle forze della vita, perfetta conquista di sé stessi [*sic*], pura gioia."[33]

At the other end of the spectrum, I would place Mario Apollonio's remarks in his history of Italian theater. Instead of emphasizing the emotions conveyed by the characters on stage, Apollonio concentrates on the manner in which the content is expressed, therefore highlighting the lyrical aspect of the play. In his opinion, "la favola è, nonché permeata, intrisa di musica," as each word is utterly musical, to the point that a new, freer stanza form enters Italian literature.[34] Thus Apollonio differentiates among parts of the text according to a lyrical division, not a performance one. If *Aminta* is a part of his theater history, it belongs to it more for important yet extrinsic reasons, rather than for its intrinsic theatricality.[35] For Apollonio, Tasso's pastoral is eminent in so much that it prepares and anticipates later developments on the Italian stage, especially the unfolding of melodrama, that is, staged sung performances, of which *Aminta* is a precursor by virtue of its language.[36]

The other pre-eminent Italian theater historian, Silvio d'Amico, in his *Storia del teatro drammatico* of 1950, reveals the shortcomings of *Aminta* once it is performed on stage: "i cinque atti . . . non sono che effusioni liriche, e narrazioni più o meno dialogate" [its five acts are nothing but lyrical effusions or narrations more or less set to dialog]; yet he dubs the text a "capolavoro del genere" [masterpiece of the genre] of the pastoral (2: 14). He continues:

> Forse, al lettore moderno non pare che la suprema leggiadria della favola tragga il suo fascino dalla drammatica progressione, e dalla felice conclusione, di cotesta vicenda; piuttosto, dall'onda di melodia che la incanta, e le crea tutt'intorno l'alone trasfiguratore. Quelli che pronunciano Silvia e Aminta e i loro amici, sono i più bei versi sciolti del secolo, tra i bellissimi della letteratura nostra in ogni tempo; ondeggiamenti e abbandoni e sconforti e smarrimenti e riprese murmure d'elegia petrarchesca, e, a momenti, anche presentimenti d'una castità d'espressione quasi leopardiana. (2: 14)[37]

It is indicative that d'Amico, within a history of Italian theater, singles out the reactions and critical perspective of a "reader." Consequently, it is not surprising that here *Aminta* is notable for its role in the development of a poetic genre and as a precursor of a whole lineage of Italian poetry.[38] Nowhere does d'Amico examine the impact of the staging on its earliest audiences; all the senses except for hearing are excluded from consideration.[39] Essentially, he is closer to an opinion like Umberto Bosco's, according to whom *Aminta* is "il più bel madrigale della letteratura italiana" (*Saggi sul rinascimento*, 115) [the best madrigal in Italian poetry],[40] than to a genuine theatrical assessment of the play. The stylistic aspect is what allows Tasso to achieve excellence through his pastoral. According to d'Amico, the author does maneuver the plot with dexterity, provoking a sense of catharsis in his audience, but in a mechanical fashion — a concept that negates d'Amico's interest in how drama works, on stage and *qua* text. In his opinion, it is the language of the play that assures its place in theater history.[41]

We should not yield to the notion that such judgments stem from a mindset belonging to the distant past. Take the case of Riccardo Scrivano, a theater historian writing in the 1980s and well aware of the multifarious nature of "theater" in early modern times: "credo che difficilmente si possa fare a meno, nel cercare di definire, insomma di capire quello che chiamiamo Rinascimento, di calcolare i dati che di esso può fornire il teatro in tutte le sue manifestazioni e in tutta l'estensione di fatti in cui è colto dai contemporanei un senso teatrale,"[42] such as church ceremonies, triumphal entries, and so on. His opinion of *Aminta* clearly takes into consideration its earliest audience, but still emphasizes the written text, rather than what was performed: "nell'*Aminta*, dramma . . . tutto di parola, lo spazio è una quasi totale immobilità nella quale si trasferisce il movimento avvenuto altrove,"[43] that is, off stage. Words are important as they build an imaginary space, for Scrivano; stage movements, gestures, even voice inflection and modulations remain outside his critical consideration.

If theater historians take this is approach, is it surprising that Giovanni Getto, a literary critic, falls into a similar pitfall? For him, *Aminta* is notable for its power of lyrical evocation. Consider for example his assessment of landscape, which he deems completely absent from *Aminta*, except for a few suggestions here and there — differently from *Gerusalemme liberata*.[44]

Because these texts belong to different genres, Getto's juxtaposition of *Aminta* and Tasso's epic poems can be pursued only to a certain extent. Indeed, what has to be suggested openly, even forcefully in a text designed for silent reading or recitation can simply be left understood in a text meant to be staged. Other elements, such as the stage set and props, would effectively complement the simple touches and the shades to which Getto alludes. By reducing the pastoral play to a written work, Getto fails to include and understand a host of details and traits that are a part (and an important one at that) of the finished product as Tasso himself devised it.[45]

The critic who most explicitly assigns *Aminta* to the lyric domain is Gaetano Trombatore. He postulates a link between theatrical achievement and characters' psychological stage development, which in Tasso's pastoral is lacking: "riesce vano cercare nei personaggi qualche cosa di più di una facile e superficiale coerenza" ("L'*Aminta*," 119) [it is useless looking for something more than a facile, superficial coherence in the characters]. Tasso's are "intuizioni, e cioè note episodiche ed isolate, non fortemente enucleate nei personaggi, non organizzate in un processo di sviluppo psicologico" (120).[46] The foremost problem with *Aminta* is not with the lack of events happening on stage, to preserve the unity of place and the *decorum* prescribed by Aristotle; it is rather the fact that *Aminta*'s episodes are deprived of dramatic strength, so that they are rather the equivalent to lyrical tableaux.[47] For Trombatore *Aminta* is but a collection of bright lyrical moments, enclosed in themselves and therefore failing to constitute a whole. Because of this emphasis on the individual staged events, rather than on the development of a longer plot, Trombatore ascribes Tasso's pastoral to the domain of the lyric. He considers *Aminta* only as a printed text, and fails to consider if and to what extent the poet was following any theatrical conventions of the times. What he attributes to the influence of lyric poetry could, I believe, be ascribed instead to a tradition of courtly entertainment, in which a sequence of highly spectacular moments was more important than the whole, or rather, than a series of events creating a continuum, as we expect in the naturalist, Western theatrical tradition. The festivities that form the subject of chapters 3 and 4 of the present study give ample evidence to this "disjointed" habit in Italian courtly entertainment. It is not far-fetched to speculate that one of the reasons for the popularity of *Aminta* in courtly circles during the late sixteenth and early seventeenth centuries was precisely the fact that it was conceived as a series of momentary *tableaux*, rather than a continuous (and consequently less ostentatious) text.

The dangers of viewing *Aminta* solely as a written or printed text emerge in a particularly forceful manner in Bartolo Tommaso Sozzi, whose critical edition of the text of Tasso's pastoral lies at the root of much subsequent criticism. However, his opinions are more fruitfully considered in the next section, devoted to *Aminta*'s printing and staging history. For now, I turn to a third critical domain, that considers *Aminta* within the development of Italian literature, more than theater, casting on the pastoral a decidedly historicist, if not flatly teleological, light. Once again, Giovan Battista Manso's apology of Torquato proves a very influential precursor. In his opinion, Tasso was able to gather some crucial elements from antiquity, while transcending them, reaching a more perfect state: "coloro fra gli antichi, che introdussero nelle scene boschereccie le Buccolice rappresentationi, e le persone de' pastori, e delle ninfe, come furono tra Greci Teocrito, e tra Latini Vergilio, e tra nostrali il Sannazaro, & alcuni altri scrittori d'Egloghe"[48] did little more than assemble some pastoral characters on stage in order for them to "favellare quel che loro veniva à grado senza sottoporsi ad altra regola, ch'all'osservanza del costume (onde i loro componimenti si potrebbero più tosto una raunanza di molte scene, che una favola scenica chiamare)"[49] (*Vita di Torquato Tasso*, 48). Tasso was instead aware of the rules governing the stage, and he followed them closely, therefore achieving higher results:

> facendosi Scena de' boschi, e ritenendo le persone pastorali, si sottopose non men'al costume dell'Egloghe, ch'alle regole della Comedia, e della Tragedia parimente, facendo di tutte, & tre una maravigliosa, vaghissima, e regolatissima compositione. Percioche dall'Egloga prese come hora dicevamo la Scena, le persone pastorali, e'l costume; dalla Tragedia le persone divine, l'heroiche, i chori, il numero del verso, e gravità della sentenza; dalla Comedia le persone comunali, il sale de' motti, e la felicità del fine più proprio alla Comedia, ch'all'altre due. La composition poi di questo mescolamento quanto all'unità, & integrità della favola, & al suo circuito, e quanto alla Protesi, & alla Catastrofe, & all'altre parti quali, e quante elleno deono essere disposte egli secondo le regole, & alla Tragedia, & alla Comedia ugualmente comuni, delle quali fu così diligente osservatore, che in tutto quel Poema non ha potuto l'invidia stessa ritrovare mancamento alcuno. (Manso, *Vita di Torquato Tasso*, 49)[50]

Tasso's contemporaries, according to Manso, found no flaw in his pastoral, and hailed it as a contemporary classic. Although Manso mentions the rules associated with works written for the stage — rules that by his first edition of Tasso's biography (1621) had become stricter and more authoritative — nowhere does he mention the popularity of the actual performances. What matters is to prove that Tasso followed the rules of the various genres he summarized in *Aminta*; the rest is irrelevant.

If a century was sensitive to claims of chronological primacy, it is the nineteenth. Indeed, the most thorough investigation to date of the antecedents of Tasso's pastoral is Carducci's series of three essays originally printed in 1895–1896 to celebrate the third centennial of Torquato's death. Carducci's main objective in the first and especially second essay is to explore the field of theatrical texts with a more or less remote pastoral motif, in order to establish Tasso's originality and excellence. Indeed, for him *Aminta* constitutes a watershed, the pivotal moment in the development of Italian literature between the Renaissance on the one hand, and melodrama and Baroque on the other: *Aminta* came at the right time, bringing Renaissance imitation to a close and opening up the time of idealization and melancholy in music.[51] According to Carducci, there is a teleological progression in artistic forms: in his opinion, the historical trajectory of the pastoral genre begins in classical times, but comes to completion only at Ferrara in the sixteenth century. In particular, Tasso exploited various preceding examples of staged pastorals (namely, Giraldi Cinzio's, Beccari's ["Su l'*Aminta*," 206–15] and Lollio's ["Su l'*Aminta*," 224–25]) and managed to surpass them due to his excellent versification. Indeed, *Aminta* and what followed are the consummate fruit of erudition and specific circumstances: the fact that Ferrara offered an outstanding tradition of staged comedies and tragedies from which pastoral tragicomedy could spring.[52] Because Carducci emphasizes the teleological development of this genre, he fails to recognize the importance of an element he otherwise underscores: the role of the court and of courtly entertainment in the emergence of such a new genre.[53]

According to Giuseppe Toffanin, who also gives a privileged place to the development of literary genres, it is precisely on the commonalty of intellectual knowledge and expectations that the success of *Aminta* rests: while Tasso was not a humor-inclined poet, he and his audience share a complicit smile.[54] Though Toffanin does not identify Tasso's intended audience, his opinion has the merit of identifying an intellectual understanding between Tasso and his audience, which unfolds in a theatrical setting; he ignores any shadowing of a political or personal nature in the text and its staging.

Toffanin and Carducci agree in finding *Aminta* far superior to all previous attempts at the same genre. Toffanin further asserts that Tasso was able to transcend all the Aristotelian teaching he had received at Padua ("Il teatro del rinascimento," 75), and thus could connect to ancient poetry. In the text of *Aminta* all the necessary elements of Greek tragedy are present, but devoid of strength; thus the play corresponds to Aristotelian rules because it is conceived according to them, and therefore does not have to pay them too much respect.[55] Toffanin's colorful style manifests a considerable amount of enthusiasm for Tasso's pastoral, transcending the influence of academies and *studia*, inspired and shaped by the true tenets of classical times. This contrasts with his aforementioned opinion regarding the popularity of *Aminta* at court. Indeed, the Este entourage was steeped in those rules that, in Toffanin's opinion, Tasso so successfully neglected. Nevertheless, such a move seems central in order to establish the excellence of Tasso's pastoral, independently of antecedent and contemporary models, so that the genius of the author can shine forth unimpeded. Like Toffanin, Raffaello Ramat shows this Romantic disposition: "Il Tasso non portava a perfezione un nuovo genere letterario, ma creava uno stil nuovo" ("L'*Aminta*," 122).[56] In conclusion, the critical emphasis on the chronological and intellectual primacy of *Aminta* with the history of Italian literature cannot but exclude the domain of the performance: interested in permanence, it ignores the short life of individual stagings.

If the preceding survey of literary criticism has not yielded an approach useful to understanding the making of meaning during the *Aminta* event, we need not despair. Occasionally a scholar will make a foray into the realm of performance or at least comment on the specifically theatrical quality of Tasso's pastoral. Undoubtedly the starting point is Francesco de Sanctis, whose criticism is highly controversial, yet inescapable, due to his importance in the history of Italian literary history. At the beginning of a chapter devoted to Giovan Battista Marino, de Sanctis asserts that "l'*Aminta* non è un dramma pastorale e neppure un dramma. Sotto nomi pastorali e sotto forma drammatica è un poemetto lirico, narrazione drammatizzata anziché vera rappresentazione, com'erano le tragedie e le commedie e i così detti 'drammi pastorali' in Italia."[57] He goes on to say that:

> L'*Aminta* è un'azione fuori del teatro, narrata da testimoni o da partecipi, con le impressioni e le passioni in loro suscitate. L'interesse è tutto nella narrazione, sviluppata liricamente e intramessa di cori, il cui concetto è l'apoteosi della vita pastorale e dell'amore: "s'ei piace, ei lice." Il motivo è lirico, sviluppo di sentimenti idillici, anziché di caratteri e di avvenimenti. Abbondano descrizioni vivaci, soliloqui, comparazioni, sentenze, movimenti appassionati. Vi penetra una mollezza musicale, piena di grazia e di delicatezza, che rende voluttuosa anche la lacrima.[58]

What differentiates de Sanctis's opinion from the ones underscoring *Aminta*'s lyrical or musical nature is its premise. Tasso's pastoral is lyrical and musical because it is deprived of the constitutive elements of a dramatic text, such as dialogue (instead of description) and action (instead of narration). If de Sanctis values *Aminta*, it is largely by virtue of the same elements praised by many other critics; however, he makes no pretense as to the theatrical excellence of this text. Tasso's pastoral is a beautiful lyrical piece, far from satisfying when it comes to its staging.

Such an original, forceful statement could not but provoke numerous strong reactions. Giuseppe Petronio, for example, defends the characters in *Aminta* as coming alive through their emotions on stage. He adds that this constitutes their livelier side, unrecognized due to de Sanctis's influence.[59] Gaetano Trombatore, conversely, is disappointed by de Sanctis's unbalanced judgment, provoked by the overarching view of his *Storia della letteratura italiana*: hell-bent on showing the moral corruption of Italian intellectual life, de Sanctis concentrated on *Il pastor fido* and shortchanged Tasso's pastoral.[60] In sum, Petronio's and Trombatore's betray a scandalized reaction to what they perceive as an attack on an established canonical work.

De Sanctis is not the only literary critic to have paid attention to the theatrical aspects of *Aminta*, albeit subordinately. Umberto Bosco has rejected the view that Tasso's pastoral is merely lyrical because it implies the specific Ferrara audience, while in his opinion lyric poetry is devoid of an implied audience.[61] Though the assertion than lyric poetry excludes an implied reader is highly problematic, Bosco at least recognizes that Tasso was writing for a specific audience, the Este court where he himself lived. However, this element is not sufficient to operate a meaningful distinction between the lyrical and the theatrical; one needs well-developed characters, which *Aminta* sorely lacks.[62] Therefore, if Bosco concentrates his attention on the theatrical aspect of this pastoral, it is only to underscore its deficiencies in the domain of character delineation. He fails to provide a characterization for Tasso's text, after ruling out that it is either a lyrical or a dramatic piece.

Claudio Varese tries to strike a balance by introducing a sort of cultural relativism based on the ideas and standards of Tasso's own times: he agrees that *Aminta* does not have a staged plot or well-rounded characters; yet this merely corresponds to the habits and expectations of the age.[63] He unfortunately stops short of wondering how this type of theater in general, and *Aminta* in particular, fascinated and entertained its audience: in essence, why and how it worked. Thus even this position is resolved in a positive assessment of the pastoral as written text.

Raffaello Ramat at least indicates the structural elements that, in his opinion, attracted the attention of *Aminta*'s originally intended audience; indeed, "con la maliziosa invenzione mitologica del *Prologo* e dell'*Epilogo* [Tasso] getta con disinvolta grazia un ponte fra l'invenzione teatrale e l'ambiente cortigiano, fra quel segno e questa realtà" ("L'*Aminta*," 123).[64] In other words, Ramat at least tries to understand why from a theatrical standpoint Tasso's pastoral was so well received. Although not many events take place on stage, he concedes, *Aminta* is permeated by what he calls a "senso teatrale lirico" (125) [a lyrical theatrical sense] — an interesting, although loose and not sufficiently defined, category, which takes into consideration both the lyrical aspect of Tasso's writing and the theatrical aspect of the performance. But like Varese, Ramat does not follow through; rather, he retreats to a standard assessment of *Aminta* in musical terms: Aminta is a melodrama as its words are pure music.[65]

Among all the literary critics and historians, it is unexpectedly Carducci who focuses on an attempt to recreate the circumstances surrounding the first few

Aminta performances. First, he underscores the presence of references to episodes, situations, or people known to the original audience as essential to the pastoral in Italy: "acquistavan grazie e interesse, almeno nelle prime recite, le allusioni alle costumanze e alle idee, alle persone ed ai fatti del giorno e della corte" ("Su l'*Aminta*," 146).[66] Furthermore, in reconstructing the history of the genre, Carducci is careful in establishing a difference between Beccari's *Il sacrificio* (1554) and previous eclogues: the latter were meant to be read, and printed, and not performed on stage ("Su l'*Aminta*," 211–12). In the same vein, he sees continuity between *commedia dell'arte* and pastoral, from the theatrical standpoint:

> Tra le note caratteristiche della favola pastorale fu anche recata questa, dell'esser e dover essere l'opposto della commedia, a soggetto o dell'arte. La commedia a soggetto, fu detto, era il pascolo della plebe: il dramma pastorale fu il trattenimento delle corti, le quali vi trovavano un linguaggio piú castigato e vaghe moralità senz'obbligo d'applicazione pratica; onde, a mano a mano che la commedia piú diveniva licenziosa e plebea, piú il dramma pastorale prendeva aria cortigiana e la raffinatezza degna delle principesse spettatrici. Tutto ciò è detto molto bene, e par proprio il vero, ma non è. Il vero è che l'*Aminta* a suo tempo fu recitata piú volte da commedianti dell'arte. ("Su l'*Aminta*," 225)[67]

In sum, Carducci stands alone in his consideration of the performance aspects of Tasso's pastoral. Although his essays dwell almost exclusively on a historical reconstruction of the antecedents of *Aminta* and of the people and events to which Tasso alludes in his text, Carducci was at least marginally aware of another domain of inquiry, concerning the stagings of the text.[68]

It is only in recent years that theater historians have abandoned the text-bound tradition that preceded them.[69] For example, Adriano Cavicchi in a 1971 article has attempted to demonstrate that the etching accompanying the 1583 and 1590 Aldine editions of *Aminta* depicted the actual stage set for the first performance of the pastoral. Although this hypothesis has been convincingly refuted,[70] Cavicchi's approach has the merit of addressing performance concerns, instead of speculating on the relationship between Tasso's psyche and *Aminta*, to cite one of many previously explored approaches. Virtually all recent theater historians, however, bow in one way or another to the literary tradition preceding them. A case in point is Giovanni Da Pozzo's *L'ambigua armonia*, a book-length study of *Aminta*. Here Da Pozzo analyzes the relationship between the images and characters used by Tasso and the courtly milieu in which he was living and writing. Consequently, the first staging of the pastoral is the only performance worth studying, and even then, the textual aspect attracts the most attention. In his estimation, Tasso spent a month on the island of Belvedere to adapt his text to the acting abilities of the *Gelosi* and to the potentialities of the space of performance.[71] Yet Da Pozzo builds his theory on the absolute lack of documents and corroborating evidence.

His interpretation of Tasso's behavior, intentions, and decisions while at Belvedere amounts to little more than speculation — as evidenced by phrases such as "sembra quanto mai probabile," "non sembra così probabile," "sembra di star vicini al probabile," and "immaginare." Secondly, and perhaps more importantly, this speculation is shaped by an obvious bias in favor of literature and against performance. Indeed, Da Pozzo points to Tasso's auctorial control over his own text, and to his struggle to accommodate himself to a craft unknown to him. Lastly, although it is fascinating to imagine the relationship and tension between *Aminta* as we know it and the setting of its supposed *première*, once again we possess no extant documents regarding the staging or its whereabouts. Consequently the emphasis on the place of the performance is detrimental to other elements, such as the referentiality of the performers on stage and the reactions of the audience.

Alain Godard's interesting article, "La Première représentation de l'*Aminta*," suffers from the same flaws: it directs its attention to the supposed *première* of *Aminta*, without supporting its premise, namely, that this event took place as hypothesized by Solerti and summarized in Section Two below. Godard aims at demonstrating that the pastoral was a secondary genre within the courtly milieu, as the most important genre at the level of display of pomp and magnificence was the tournament. Although this argument is well supported and convincing, it suffers from a constitutive weakness vis-à-vis *Aminta*, examined solely in a performance about which serious historical doubt still exists. Although Godard's effort to reconstruct the atmosphere and ambiance of the supposed original setting of *Aminta* is interesting, novel, and performance-bound, it still suffers, like Da Pozzo's, from the same historicist bias to which Carducci and Solerti succumb: only the first performance deserves critical and historical attention.

Daniela Dalla Valle carries Godard's argument further, thereby undermining her own conclusions. Not only does she take for granted that *Aminta* premiered on the Belvedere island in July 1573, and follow Godard's assessment of the relative importance of the pastoral within the courtly milieu; she also posits that the playful exchange of identities and disguises on stage was to some extent responsible for the popularity of Tasso's pastoral in France. Dalla Valle fails to account for the speedy transmission of Tasso's pastoral and its courtly double entendres in France, as well as for the relevance of the latter in a setting different from the original one. It seems preposterous to locate the reasons for *Aminta*'s popularity in France (or anywhere else, for that matter) on the efficacy of supposed references to people, events, and occasions internal to the Este court. Though Dalla Valle pays more attention than her predecessors to the staged event *per se*, she is still imbued with too strong a historicist bias to shed light on *Aminta* as a repeatable and repeated event, and to the conditions of its success.[72]

Only one theater historian, Fabrizio Cruciani, has devoted extensive attention to *Aminta* with respect to the issue of its *première* in a way that is both original and fruitful. His article "Percorsi critici verso la prima rappresentazione dell'*Aminta*" reconstructs the theatrical atmosphere and tradition prevalent in Ferrara in the early 1570s. On this basis, and keeping in consideration the earliest known performances of Tasso's pastoral, Cruciani concludes that it is indeed possible that *Aminta* was performed for the first time on the Belvedere island in July 1573. However, he strips this date and this occurrence of most historical relevance, as he considers them as one event among many, testifying to the success of this text: they constitute "non una realtà storica e documentaria ma certo una fertile situazione conoscitiva per costruire percorsi critici che non hanno la propria giustificazione in un punto d'arrivo ma per quanto il percorso in sé ci fa conoscere dell'*Aminta* e del teatro di cui è parte" ("Percorsi critici," 189).[73]

The present study follows in general Cruciani's path, but entirely forsakes the issue of the *Aminta première*. Until new evidence comes to light (a rather unlikely possibility, given the amount of research done on this topic, especially in the nineteenth century), we will not be able to ascertain when and where it took place, who performed it, and who was in attendance. Instead, this study strives to offer a micro-reconstruction of two stagings of Tasso's pastoral, on the assumption that every performance can illuminate our understanding of the text, its meaning-producing dynamics, its reception and popularity, and the kind of "theater" that was brought to life on stage. I agree with Siro Ferrone's assertion that "per conoscere bene . . . autori di teatro dovremmo conoscere molto meglio gli attori e gli spazi (i teatri, le scene, le scenografie) in cui operano."[74] I thus contend that an in-depth reconstruction and analysis of some *Aminta* stagings — on the basis precisely of the wealth of documents regarding this text, well received and popular with various kinds of audiences, hence attracting widespread attention in most extant sources — can shed light on numerous central issues linked to the description of past theatrical events that clarify how a text-event made sense for its audience in the last quarter of the sixteenth century and in the first half of the seventeenth. In other words, it is my firm belief that only by approximating (however faintly) the circumstances surrounding a specific staging will we be able to assess the complex dynamics constituting the foundations of the meaning-making process and, in turn, the circumstances accompanying the emergence of modern Western theater as we know it.

2. *Aminta's* Printing and Staging History: An Overview

Given the traditional understanding of *Aminta* as a written and literary text, it is hardly surprising that nobody has ever attempted to reconstruct the history of Tasso's pastoral on stage. Conversely, the various editions of this play have elicited much attention, since establishing its definitive text was of overwhelming importance to literary scholars. Tasso's own biography also fostered this critical approach: a cursory reading of his letters shows an ever-increasing concern with the preservation and printing of his work (especially *Gerusalemme liberata*), the latter seen as instruments to promote his cause with various noblemen and women who could in turn intercede for his liberation from Sant'Anna. From this standpoint it is clear that a single *Aminta* performance would have profited Tasso infinitely less than an accurate, luxurious printing of his epic poem. Nevertheless, critics did not recognize the at least partially contingent nature of such a stance; indeed, it helped promote and crystallize the pastoral's secondary position within Tasso's production.[75]

Conversely, no critic pays much attention to the fact that *Aminta*'s first printing occurred in 1580, seven years after its reputed first performance, except to execrate the loss of an earlier printed text that for some mysterious reason would reflect Tasso's intended *lectio* with greater accuracy. As Bartolo Tommaso Sozzi put it, "L'*Aminta* fu stampata solamente tra la fine del 1580 e l'inizio del 1581: e la ragione del ritardo sarà certo da ricercare . . . nella sua incontentabilità d'artista. . . . Nel lungo spazio di sette anni interposto, la favola corse manoscritta per le mani di molti."[76] Nobody has ever put forth the hypothesis that in the course of these seven years, *Aminta* could well have enjoyed another kind of vogue, in learned and popular circles alike: it was represented on stage frequently, which might have made a printing unnecessary even for the attention-starved Tasso.[77] In a letter to Scipione Gonzaga dated 26 March 1575, Torquato begs his addressee to pay attention to the *canti* of his epic poem, lest "non si divulghino, né vadano in mano d'alcuno, com'avvenne de l'egloga."[78] Sozzi interprets this complaint strictly in terms of pirated transcriptions (and possibly printings), but nothing allows us to exclude that Tasso might have referred to readings and stagings.[79]

The question of the number of early performances of *Aminta* is still largely shrouded in mystery. Recent studies of *commedia dell'arte* troupes have established that it was a *pièce de résistance* for many of them. For one, Ferdinando Taviani writes that *Aminta*:

> probabilmente, entrò nel repertorio delle compagnie [of *commedia dell'arte*], come un testo che quegli attori, che noi immaginiamo recitare solo all'improvviso, impararono più volte a memoria e concertarono, per rappresentarlo quando il loro pubblico avesse loro richiesto uno spettacolo di poesia. Le notizie sul repertorio dei comici dell'Arte sono quasi sempre esigue e sempre casuali, ma l'*Aminta* vi ritorna, come una notizia che il caso o un poeta d'occasione ci può tramandare a proposito, per esempio, di Maria Malloni detta Celia.[80]

Along the same lines, Solerti briefly notes that "Maria Malloni, detta *Celia*, dei *Confidenti*, sulla fine del [sixteenth] secolo e sul principio dell'altro, provocava sotto il velo della ninfa gli entusiasmi degli ammiratori; e i *Confidenti* sappiamo che recitarono l'*Aminta* anche a Torino" probably between 1609 and 1623.[81] Flaminio

Scala, in a letter to Giovanni de' Medici dated 27 October 1618, wrote that an *Aminta* staging had taken place in Florence the night before, and that he had invited Cardinal Carlo de' Medici to it (S. Ferrone et al. eds., *Comici dell'Arte. Corrispondenze*. 2 vols. [Firenze: Le Lettere, 1993], 1: 506). Beyond these scattered testimonies, the very nature of *arte* performances, as well as the bias against them on the part of a text-based, high-culture-prone literary history, make them exceedingly difficult to reconstruct.

Nevertheless, *Aminta* was, from the outset, a literary, canonical text. The attention bestowed on such a text makes it possible for us to explore at least courtly and academic representations, though little attention has been paid to them. Among all the previously cited critics, only Giosuè Carducci states that "L'*Aminta* fu rappresentato più volte nel decorso del secolo decimosesto: dopo la prima di Belvedere, certamente a Pesaro nel febbraio del 1574, presente il Tasso" ("Su l'*Aminta*," 255);[82] "d'una rappresentazione ordinata a Mantova dal duca Guglielmo I (1586?) non abbiamo notizia certa. Magnifica e plaudita anche dal poeta sarebbe stata la rappresentazione fiorentina per ordine del granduca Ferdinando I nel 1590, alla quale lavorò nella scena e per gl'intermezzi il celebrato artista Buontalenti" (256).[83] More recently, Marzia Pieri has written that Tasso's pastoral "conobbe una fortuna scenica eccezionale: per esempio nel carnevale pesarese del 1574, nel maggio 1581 a Verona, ancora a Ferrara nel 1583, probabilmente a Mantova nel 1586, a Firenze nel 1590."[84] Additionally, in the entry dedicated to Ferrara in the *Enciclopedia dello spettacolo*, Elena Povoledo asserts that *Aminta* "una seconda volta [after the Ferrara *début*] fu data 'con intermedi apparenti bellissimi, e di vari animali,' nella residenza di campagna di Cornelio Bentivoglio, probabilmente il 15 novembre 1579."[85] Cruciani mentions two performances in 1581, one by the "Accademici di Mantova" in their own town, the other at the Montagnola wood outside Ferrara ("Percorsi critici" 180). Lastly, a performance took place in Florence in 1616, at the Rinaldi family residence (M. G. Accorsi, "Musicato, per musica, musicale; Riflessioni intorno ad *Aminta*," in *Torquato Tasso e la cultura estense 3*, ed. Venturi, 881–940, here 896). These scant testimonies attest to the primacy of the written text even to our time.

This study attempts to exploit another vision, one repeatedly proposed by distinguished theater critics. In 1980, the semiotician Jurij Lotman wrote that theater is different from other kinds of texts because:

[s]olo il teatro ha bisogno di un destinatario effettivamente presente e accoglie i segnali che il pubblico gli trasmette (silenzio, segni di approvazione o di biasimo), variando il testo a seconda di essi. Proprio alla natura dialogica del testo scenico è legata la possibilità di cambiamenti. Il concetto di "testo canonico" è estraneo allo spettacolo teatrale come al folklore ed è sostituito da quello di invariante che si realizza in una serie di varianti.[86]

According to Lotman, there is no need to establish a *ne varietur*, literary-like text for performance writings, as they are inevitably destined to modification. Marco De Marinis further explains that the phrase "theatrical text" is "no longer meant to indicate the dramatic, literary text but rather the text of the theatrical performance (*testo spettacolare*), the performance text. This is conceived as a complex network of different types of signs, expressive means, or actions, coming back to the etymology of the word 'text' which implies the idea of texture, of something woven together."[87] This "something woven together" includes the audience, as well as the various people involved in a given production, as Joseph Donohue indicates: "the composition of a play for performance is, normally, inherently a collaborative venture involving a range of theatrical practitioners, most notably actors, in addition to the playwright."[88]

Lotman, De Marinis, and Donohue refer largely to contemporary theater, one in which the printed (or soon-to-be-printed) script is protected by copyright law, is normally available to the theater-goers, and therefore can be easily modified, yet exists independently as a non-modifiable text. The situation with respect to a sixteenth-century play such as *Aminta* is even more fluid. As Andrea Gareffi has succinctly put it, "le commedie non sono e non volevano essere letteratura; almeno nel Cinquecento, son fatte per essere recitate e non per essere messe a stampa, nemmeno quando diventano il capolavoro insuperato che fu la *Mandragola*" (*La scrittura e la festa*, 238).[89]

A quick survey of title pages of sixteenth-century pastoral plays confirms it, indeed establishes the primacy of performance over printing. The frontispiece of Giraldi Cinzio's *Egle* asserts that "[f]u rappresentata in casa dell'auttore l'anno MDXLV una volta a XXIII di Febbraio e unaltra [sic] a III di Marzo all'Illustriss. Signore il S. Hercole II da Esti Duca IIII e all'Illustriss. et Reverendiss. Cardinale Hippolito II suo Fratello."[90] For Beccari's *Il sacrificio*, it mentions that "[f]u rapresentata due volte in Ferrara, l'anno 1554 nel palazzo dello Illustrissimo Signor Don Francesco da Este. La prima adì XI Febraro allo Illustrissimo, et Eccellentissimo Signor il Signor Hercole II da Este Duca IV di Ferrara, et allo Illustrissimo figliuolo il Signor Donn'Alvigi. L'altra adì 4 Marzo alla Illustrissima, et Eccellentissima Madamma et alle Illustrissime figliuole."[91] Similarly, Lollio's *Aretusa* title page specifies that "[f]u rappresentata in Ferrara nel Palazzo di Schivanoia l'anno MDLXIII."[92] Agostino Arienti's *Sfortunato* indicates that "[f]u rappresentata in Ferrara l'anno MDLXVII del mese di Maggio;"[93] and the dedication of Borso Argenti's *Prigione* to an anonymous lady avows: "[b]en mi duole, ch'ella m'abbia imposto che io stampi la Comedia, che, pure a instanza sua, ha già tre anni, fu da me composta e fatta recitare."[94] Nor is this phrase limited to Ferrarese pastoral plays: Raimondo Guarino mentions an undated Venetian printing of Bernardo Dovizi's *Calandria* that indicates that it was "recitata ne la famosa et generosa città di Venetia per prete Giovanni Senese Ierosolimitano nel M.D.XXI e nel M.D.XXII."⁹⁵ Guarino considers such stock phrases as one element in "un complesso di indici che definiscono nella loro mobilità la relazione tra due modi di consumo" of performance texts: on stage and in print (*Teatro e mutamenti* 277–78).⁹⁶ Yet it is interesting that none of *Aminta*'s frontispieces include this simple phrase, as Paolo Trovato's list indicates.⁹⁷ Tasso's pastoral is thereby removed from the specific courtly circles of Ferrara, to which previous pastorals proudly proclaimed their allegiance, as well as from the fleeting existence on stage: in other words, by its first printing *Aminta* has already become a canonical literary text.

The various printed editions of Tasso's pastoral nevertheless tell a different story: they testify to *Aminta*'s double existence, simultaneously as a performance and as a printed text. Instead of being a *ne varietur* printed artifact, *Aminta* contains significant textual tensions, usually associated solely with "popular" or improvised theater.⁹⁸ In other words, the contemporary concept of text is far more fluid than later literary editors have admitted: far from having been "abbandonata al suo destino" (Trovato, "Per una nuova edizione," 1027) [abandoned to its fate], *Aminta* is no different from all performance texts, which "[n]on si realizzano in una forma data una volta per tutte, ma in una somma di varianti intorno ad un'invariante che non è data direttamente" (Lotman, "Semiotica della scena," 19).⁹⁹ Thus, there exist countless versions of Tasso's pastoral, falling into three categories: the canonized one, more or less agreed upon by philologists, reprinted to this day, and usually accepted by scholars as what Tasso wrote and intended for performance; the many *lectiones* to be found in the earliest printings, characterized by a series of hesitations over the inclusion or exclusion of specific passages; and the innumerable variations that were put on stage, exemplified by the two I will reconstruct in this study on the basis of contemporary documents.

Since the first two categories have to do with printed artifacts I will analyze them concurrently. The controversy about what rightfully belongs to the canonical, printed *Aminta* text hinges upon four passages: the so-called "Mopso episode" (I.ii.552–648), a tirade uttered by Tirsi (usually considered as a *figura* of Tasso himself) criticizing Mopso (viewed as a *figura* of Sperone Speroni: T. Tasso, *Aminta* [Milan: Rizzoli, 1976] 83); the five choruses at the end of each act; the four *intermedi* or *intermezzi* played between the acts; and the epilogue, a lyric piece entitled "Amor fuggitivo." *Aminta*'s latest critical edition was established in 1954 by Bartolo Tommaso Sozzi for publication in one of the volumes devoted to Tasso in UTET's "Classici italiani" series; a new critical edition is forthcoming, as Paolo Trovato has announced. Sozzi included the Mopso episode and the choruses, but excluded the *intermezzi* and the epilogue. His attitude is undoubtedly informed by a neo-classical concern with Aristotelian rules and a general appreciation for simplicity and linearity, which he projects onto Tasso himself. He resolutely opposes the inclusion of the *intermezzi* in the text of *Aminta*, even as a supplement to a critical edition, since they are but lyrical passages adapted by Tasso to the text of the play "per un fine tutto pratico ed estrinseco, e in via provvisoria" (B. T. Sozzi, "Nota sui cori e sugl' 'intermedi' dell'*Aminta*," *Giornale storico della letteratura italiana* 126 [1949]: 426–31, here 427).[100] Moreover, "non è neppure possibile stabilire per quale rappresentazione il Tasso li abbia composti" ("Nota sui cori," 428 n. 1).[101] Nor is Sozzi alone in this stance. Bruno Maier, in charge of the 1963 edition of Tasso's works, writes in his preface regarding the *intermezzi* that:

> [l]i collochiamo in appendice alla "favola boschereccia," secondo la consuetudine seguita da varii recenti editori, in primo luogo perché mancano nei manoscritti e nelle edizioni dell'*Aminta* uscite mentre il Tasso era in vita e appaiono per la prima volta in un'edizione del 1666 (Roma, Dragomanni), e in secondo luogo perché hanno soltanto una relazione occasionale, pratica ed esteriore col testo del dramma pastorale, di cui costituiscono non più d'una sorta di coreografico e spettacolare completamento. È, anzi, legittimo supporre che gli intermedi, probabilmente adattamento — come già il coro del III atto — di precedenti liriche, siano stati variati nella diverse rappresentazioni dell'*Aminta*. (B. Maier, in Tasso, *Opere*, ed. idem, 5 vols. [Milan: Rizzoli, 1963], 1: 205)[102]

It is evident that Maier's attitude vis-à-vis the *intermezzi* relies primarily on Sozzi's opinion, as the most recent editor of Tasso's pastoral.[103]

Having summary (and authoritatively) dispatched the *intermezzi*, Sozzi faces the more formidable challenge of the choruses, whose presence in the manuscripts and early editions is more widespread,[104] and whose classical antecedents weigh powerfully in the consideration of the text.[105] Although Sozzi is convinced that *Aminta* loses part of its linear charms with the addition of the choruses, he explains the reason for their inclusion in his critical edition in the following terms:

> l'aggiunta dei cori risponde senza dubbio a quella volontà di classicistica e aristotelica nobilitazione letteraria che presiede alla seconda maniera poetica del Tasso; questo infarcito appesantimento, che a noi fa rimpiangere la leggera nudità della spregiudicata stesura giovanile, è tuttavia da serbare in sede filologica, dove s'impone il rispetto per la volontà dell'autore non meno che per l'oggettiva verità dei fatti; basterà denunciarlo, come un aspetto di una più generale involuzione . . . in sede critica. ("Nota sui cori" 430)[106]

This attitude emerges as recently as 1982: "After the first performances in which there were only choruses for the first and for the fifth acts, Tasso added one for each of the remaining acts to resolutely mark throughout the play the reminders of a reasonable order" (Yoch, "Limits of Sensuality," 73), which is ascribed to numerous classical sources. Yoch agrees with Sozzi that Tasso's authorial control is of paramount importance.

Finally, in a subsequent "Nota sull'episodio di Mopso e sull'epilogo dell' *Aminta*," Sozzi summarily dispatches Tasso's short lyric piece "Amor fuggitivo" as epilogue of *Aminta*. He omits almost entirely any reference to the performances of the pastoral in assessing the reasons for the exclusion of "Amor fuggitivo." When he does, he makes a blatant mistake:

> Non è da escludere che il Tasso possa, in qualche occasione, probabilmente per la seconda rappresentazione della favola, che ebbe luogo in Pesaro nel 1574, aver adattato, in via provvisoria, questo componimento a fungere da epilogo al dramma pastorale: ma — come già osservammo per gli Intermedi — non è però dimostrabile che egli l'abbia voluto nelle stampe come parte integrante di essa.[107]

As the evidence in chapter 2 will show, no source mentions an epilogue at the end of the 1574 performance at Pesaro. Rather than insist on this factual mistake, at this point I want to underscore Sozzi's tone, which betrays his role as interpreter of Tasso's authorial intention, solely on the basis of *Aminta*'s earliest printings. Since at least the 1950s, philologists and literary critics have taken this idea of immutable text to task.[108] Most notably, Jerome McGann has convincingly argued (in chapters 5 and 6 of his *A Critique of Modern Textual Criticism*) that the concepts of "final version" and "authorial intentions" do not always coincide. Specifically, McGann has asserted that an autograph manuscript is not always the best source for a critical edition. In the field of texts for which audience consumption is paramount, McGann's point is infinitely more relevant;[109] specifically, Joseph Donohue has argued that for performance texts:

> in cases where more than one text of a given play is extant, it is a mistake simply to assume that one text (perhaps the latest one) represents the author's intentions more fully than any other. Instead, it seems to make much better sense to consider than each separate text may represent a different, independent "intentionality." ("Evidence and Documentation," 182)

In addition to this abstract intuition, in the case of *Aminta* the manuscript copies and earliest printings do not present as univocal a picture as Sozzi proposes. The Mopso episode appears in four out of eight text manuscripts and in eleven out of thirteen printings dated between 1580 (the earliest one) and 1592.[110] The five choruses are present in one manuscript and only in the Aldine printing of 1590; especially the third and fourth are almost consistently absent. The *intermezzi* appear only in a 1666 printing. Finally, the epilogue is to be found in two manuscripts and two printings.[111]

If we compare these elements with the earliest known *Aminta* performances, sketchily known though they are, the discrepancy is stark. As chapter 2 will elucidate, in 1574 choruses were added. By 1579, according to Povoledo, so were *intermezzi* with animals. Additionally, we know that the governor of Garfagnana had been entrusted with finding some young men among his subjects, to perform *Aminta* in 1583 and Guarini's *Il pastor fido* the following year. In a letter to the Este duke's secretary, he states:

> non ho mancato vedere se tra questo Popolo si potevano trovare tre fanciulli et un'huomo della qualità che in dette lettere [that the secretary had sent to the governor] si contiene per esser atti da recitare in scene, et ha fra gli altri trovati tre fanciuli di 16 o 17 anni d'assai bel viso e buon' garbo, et sebene non hanno più recitato altra volta, nondimeno credo che riusciranno assai bene, et saranno atti à fare la parte di Ninfa come mi scrive, poiche nella Pastorale del Tasso che feci mettere all'ordine l'anno passato per farla recitare, sebene l'occasione de rumori con lucchesi l'impedì, li detti fanciulli, nel provare ch'ella si fece molte volte, riuscivano benissimo. (Solerti and Lanza, "Teatro ferrarese," 181)[112]

These young men selected by the Garfagnana governor to perform first *Aminta* and then *Il pastor fido* fall in the tradition of courtly or academic stagings, as they are not professional players. However, the letter writer assures the duke's secretary that they will act "assai bene" and "benissimo," possibly to allay the fears that the entertainment would not meet the high standards that were common at the Este court.[113] But this *Aminta* performance never took place, nor does this letter provide any indication as to what parts were to be performed. The emphasis of the letter is on their physical appearance and behavior: "assai bel viso e buon' garbo."

To go back to the *Aminta* text that was staged, in 1628 a prologue and five *intermezzi* set to music by Claudio Monteverdi and sung by professional singers hired from Rome and other Italian courts attracted the highest degree of attention on the part of the convened audience, as chapters 3 and 4 will show. The extant testimonies indicate beyond a doubt that for the 1628 audience *intermezzi* formed an integral part of the *Aminta* event. We can thus reject Sozzi's idea that "volontà di classicistica e aristotelica nobilitazione letteraria" ("Nota sui cori," 430) [the desire for classic and Aristotelian literary ennoblement] permeates Tasso's pastoral and has therefore to be reflected in its critical edition. Nor does this attitude prevail only in literary circles. As distinguished a theater scholar as Marzia Pieri wrote that Tasso himself, directing the supposed *première* of *Aminta* in 1573 in Ferrara, "si attenne . . . ad un'estrema linearità classicheggiante, rinunziando ai cori e agli intermezzi, aggiunti poi nella versione a stampa" (*La nascita del teatro moderno*, 170).[114] For Pieri, the printed text does not reflect accurately the performed event, thus clouding the author's intentions, which are preeminently important even for a theater, hence constantly variable, text.[115]

The discrepancy between printed and performed text, authorial and actorial control over it, and embalmed and dynamic *lectiones* points toward a reassessment of *Aminta*'s position within the literary canon. In this study, I will carefully examine it as a successful text/event of the late sixteenth and early seventeenth centuries in Italy. Tasso's pastoral affords us a precious glimpse into performances of this period. *Aminta*'s treatment at the hands of different kinds of performers debunks the myth that only *canovacci* belonging to the *commedia dell'arte* tradition were subject to tensions, expansions, reductions, and accommodations. The importance of establishing a "correct," univocal textual *lectio* waxes less important; conversely, the exploitation of the textual material on the part of the performers and the response of the audience acquire paramount relevance.

3. Re-Presentation

In an article originally published in 1905, the great Dutch historian Johan Huizinga wrote that "se [history] vuole raggiungere il suo scopo, che è di far rivivere il passato, deve superare con consapevolezza i confini di ciò che è riconoscibile per mezzo di concetti e far sorgere davanti agli occhi del lettore un complesso chiaro di rappresentazioni, in altre parole un'*immagine*" (emphasis in original).[116] Such historical images, Huizinga argues, are clear, immediate, that is, non-mediated by concepts: they bring history to life and make us understand "quello che rende possibile il realizzarsi di questo complesso" of historical events ("L'elemento estetico," 24) [what makes all these historical events possible]. For scholars trying to break away from a literature- and written-text-centered view of early modern plays, such words yield a powerful charm.

Almost nine decades later, Andrea Gareffi, opening his study of theater and spectacle in early modern Florence, offers a post-modern counterpart to Huizinga's claim:

> le commedie non devono venir lette e non debbono venir giudicate come opere letterarie: furono altro, e pretendevano d'essere altro anche nelle intenzioni dei loro autori. Questo "altro," oggi, non è riscostruibile se non in minima parte . . . mancherà sempre quel grumo di vita che le rese vive, e fare come se non fosse così produce guasti irreparabili. (*La scrittura e la* festa, 7)[117]

Huizinga's images, according to Gareffi, remain deprived of life: such is the unavoidable destiny of theater historians, attempting the impossible, that is, trying to resuscitate something that by definition is fleeting and transitory.

It would be too easy to juxtapose a supposedly naïve early-twentieth-century historian to a sly one from almost a century later. Huizinga was in fact well aware of many pitfalls, including the fact that a researcher's approach is of great consequence to his/her research outcome:

> [e]ven the best and most complete tradition is in itself amorphous and mute. It only yields history once questions have been put to it. And it is not enough of a question to approach it with a general desire to know *wie es eigentlich gewesen*, how it really was.... [T]he *es* in *wie es eigentlich gewesen*, if it is to have "meaning," must be determined beforehand by a conception of a certain historical and logical unity one is attempting to delineate more precisely. That unity can never lie in an arbitrary slice of past reality itself. The mind selects from tradition certain elements it synthesizes into a historically coherent image, which was not realized in the past as it was lived.[118]

Huzinga is well aware that the images we recreate of the past can only approximate it, as the past can under no circumstances be brought back to life. Yet, such images, or re-presentations, are the best approximation, or rendition, of past events from the standpoint to which we are confined.

This is particularly true with performances, the type of artifact that lies at the core of the present study: not supposedly immutable literary ones, but lived, embodied ones. I will reconstruct, or re-present, two specific *Aminta* performances selected on the basis of document availability and of their specific time frame: the carnival season of 1574 as celebrated in Pesaro, and the wedding festivities of Odoardo Farnese and Margherita de' Medici in Parma in 1628. Though archival research has yielded different material with respect to each event, in both cases I will reconstruct: the occasion for the performance; its physical setting; the audience in attendance; the text performed on stage; the identity or at least the status of the players who were seen on stage; and the processes of making and perceiving meaning at work.

Before proceeding with these re-presentations, pride of place must be given to the realization that either *Aminta* performance might be quite different from our (modern) concept of theater, in terms of time sequence of the episodes, realism of the setting, and representativity of the performers' bodies. Instead, we must understand, to use Susan Bennett's cogent formulation, that "theatre audiences bring to any performance a horizon of cultural and ideological expectations. That horizon of expectation is never fixed and is always tested by, among other things, the range of theatre available, the play, and the particular production."[119] This is all the truer in early modern Italy, where each audience member's "horizon of expectation" was to a large extent determined by his or her geographical provenance, as different cities and courts had different (even diverging) performance traditions, hence expectations.[120]

Here lies one of the main challenges of re-presenting or reconstructing past performance events: the available extant documents are unavoidably the product of one person. Thus we need to balance different sources and keep in mind that there was no single point of view (in both the architectural and conceptual senses) of a given event. While official reports emphasize the audience's satisfaction with the performance or the unimpeded view from the privileged seat of the ruler and his entourage, other sources mention stage machinery that did not work properly, comment on the acting abilities of the performers, or dwell on the suggestive quality of the stage set (or lack thereof). Individual audience members bring different expectations, sensibilities, and taste to each performance. We even have to consider that some audience member might not have made much sense of the proceedings: indeed, to cite Bennett again, a "crucial aspect of audience involvement . . . is the degree to which a performance is accessible though the codes audiences are accustomed to utilizing, the conventions they are used to recognizing, at a theatrical event" (*Theatre Audiences*, 104). If a given performance exploits codes that some audience members are not used to, then they might have made no (or a limited) sense of that staging — to the point that they would not strictly be a part of an audience any longer, according to Hare and Blumberg's definition of the four functions that specifically designate it.[121]

The kinds of questions we ask archival sources, to go back to Huizinga's wording, must be carefully selected, to the point of making our expectations as post-modern critics of literature and theater extraneous to our endeavor. Joseph Roach has asserted that "[t]heatre historians typically approach the problem of style by asking how *natural* a performance was. . . . Historians might more profitably ask by what methods the performance signified, how its meanings came to be shared with its audience, and why its success or failure seemed to be rooted in the particular ideological and aesthetic contingencies of the moment" (J. Roach, "Power's Body," in *Interpreting the Theatrical Past*, ed. Postlewait and McConachie, 99–118, here 106). Roach underscores the pervading nature of our expectations and attitudes vis-à-vis staged performances as post-naturalist theater-goers and critics, and helps us overcome them.

At the other end of the (historical) spectrum lies the classicist, typically literary, approach, which in the case of *Aminta* is equally dangerous, as Tasso's pastoral squarely falls within the Aristotelian debates of his period. Most critics have espoused Aristotle's idea of what constitutes a successful plot:

> Of simple plots and actions, the episodic are worst. By "episodic" I mean a plot in which the episodes follow one another without probability or necessity. Such plays are composed by bad poets through their own fault, and by good poets for the sake of the actors: for in composing show pieces, and stretching the plot beyond its capacity, they are often forced to distort the continuity. (*Poetics* 9.11 [1451 b 33–39]; trans Halliwell, 63)

What for Aristotle and neo-classic critics constituted "natural continuity" of the plot was utterly foreign to theater-goers of the late sixteenth and early seventeenth centuries. As the present study will show, the two *Aminta* performances under scrutiny would have been perceived as fragmentary, if not altogether disjointed, by neo-classic and post-naturalist audience members alike. It is remarkable that so deeply classicist, if Romantic, a critic as August Wilhelm von Schlegel was the one to recognize that pastoral in general might simply reflect a different set of expectations on the part of its contemporary audience:

> although, as a whole, [*Aminta* and *Il pastor fido*] have each their plot and catastrophe, the action nevertheless stands still in some scenes. Their popularity, therefore, would lead us to conclude that the spectators, little accustomed to theatrical amusements, were consequently not difficult to please, and patiently followed the progress of a beautiful poem, even though deficient in dramatic development. (Schlegel, *Lectures on Dramatic Art* [1809] [London: Bell, 1879], 214–15)

How naive, and simplistic, an idea of pastoral staging Schlegel harbors! Thinking perhaps about courtly readings of epic poems, he imagines *Aminta* and *Il pastor fido* as static performances that their intended audience appreciated because they corresponded to their expectations and staging traditions. Instead, it is well established in theatrical history that *Aminta* and other pastorals were lavishly staged, with music, singing, costumes, and plentiful stage machinery — they entertained an audience who did not value plot continuity or its logical development. Indeed, I argue that one of the reasons for the fame and popularity of *Aminta* in late-sixteenth- and seventeenth-century playhouses lay in its capability to accommodate other elements within its plot, particularly choruses and *intermezzi*. In other words, Tasso's pastoral was popular on professional and courtly stages alike because it was articulated in discrete units, rather than as a whole. Organizers and performers could therefore eliminate parts of the original text or add some composed *ad hoc* (such as the prologue and *intermezzi* sung in Parma in 1628) without compromising the audience's interest in it, as well as its intelligibility, as meaning formation did not depend on linear plot sequence. If we do not relinquish literary, neo-classical, or naturalist expectations and mind sets, we will fail at reconstructing or re-presenting the *Aminta* stagings of 1574 and 1628, indeed at comprehending early modern performance in general.

In sum, the goal of the present study is both historical and theoretical. On the one hand, it offers a thorough, micro-historical image of two specific *Aminta* stagings. On the other, it reveals how those two performances "made sense" to their audience. Consequently, it unveils differences in staged meaning-making processes in the fifty-five years separating them, which correspond to the period in which modern theater emerged in Western cultures. I do not harbor any "hope that [my] research will have some effect on actual performance" (F. Kermode, "Sound and Fury," *New York Review of Books* [16 February 1995]: 35–36, here

35), as the scope of this study is to re-present past events, not to bring them back to life. My endeavor is "archeological," in a Foucaltian sense,[122] but not "antiquarian" as Frank Kermode has decried; in his opinion, plays should not necessarily be "viewed" under the conditions in which they were first performed, "because plays cannon survive independently of what is made of them in the course of a continuous history of interpretations" ("Sound and Fury," 35). Our understanding of performance texts is indeed influenced, perhaps even radically so, by the history of their past stagings.[123] It is for this very reason that such reconstructive, re-presentational efforts are particularly important. They open to view the discrepancy between "our" understanding of a performance text, "our" meaning-making strategies, and the original circumstances under which the text was understood as meaning-producing.[124] In other words, only by emphasizing a non-teleological approach will scholars of literature and theater be able to shift from a hermeneutic paradigm to one putting in the privileged position it deserves the process through which meaning is produced.

In the end, I am convinced that only a reconstructive, re-presentative endeavor will allow us to approach, however faintly, past performance events. If we agree that *Aminta*, like all staged texts, cannot be fully understood only *qua* written text, but must involve its staging to be properly grasped, then this micro-reconstructive effort is the only tool we possess to this end.

Notes

[1] A regular five-act play, *Aminta* opens with a prologue spoken by Amore dressed as a shepherd, who explains that his mission is to exert his power over the inhabitants of the woods, who will therefore fall in love and become "sweeter" as a result. Act I, scene i introduces the nymphs Silvia and Dafne. The latter tries to convince the former that love is a natural feeling, and that eschewing it will result in later regrets. Scene ii presents their male counterparts: the young Aminta complains to the more experienced Tirsi that his love to Silvia goes unrequited; Tirsi consoles him and urges him to pursue her. A chorus concludes the act praising the golden age in which these shepherds live. Act II opens (scene i) with a monologue by a satyr, who avows his love and plots to abduct and rape the nymph who forms the object of his affection. Scene ii presents Dafne and Tirsi, the older confidants, agreeing to try to bring Silvia and Aminta together. In Scene iii, Tirsi suggests to Aminta to meet Silvia at a spring, but he refuses because he will not resorts to tricks to have her. The Chorus praises Love and asserts that humanity cannot escape his domination. In Act III, scene i, Tirsi recounts to the chorus Aminta's prowess and modesty in saving Silvia from the satyr's attempted rape, and expresses his desperation: Silvia having disappeared, he has forebodings of impending doom. In Scene ii Nerina tells Aminta and Dafne that Silvia, while hunting, was mangled by a pack of wolves; all that remains of her is a bloody scarf. Aminta, his life devoid of any goal, vows to commit suicide; and the Chorus brings the Act to a close singing that love and glory often go hand in hand. In Act IV, scene i, the shaken

Silvia recounts her fortunate escape from the wolves to Dafne and the Chorus. Her confidante then reports Aminta's pledge to commit suicide, and Silvia feels unknown stirrings in her soul. Scene ii opens with the arrival of a messenger who tells of Aminta's jump from a cliff and presumed death. Silvia, overcome with love and pain, asks to be taken to the place where Aminta's body lies, where she will encounter her own death. The Chorus closes the Act praising Love, whose goals are unknown and yet all-powerful. Act V consists of one scene, in which the older shepherd Elpino tells the chorus that Aminta was revived by Silvia's voice and tears; then their love was sealed by a kiss. The play closes with the Chorus singing of the power of Love to instruct human beings to joy and marital bliss.

² "*Aminta* is a strange canonical work: it seems that everybody knows how to take it lightly, without getting too excited about problems that for similar texts would instead generate intense academic discussions": F. Taviani, "Teatro di voci in tempi bui (riflessioni brade su 'Aminta' e pastorale)," *Teatro e storia* 9 (1994): 9–39, here 12. Unless otherwise indicated, all translations are mine.

³ This sketch is based on Tasso's latest biography, the three-volume work *Vita di Torquato Tasso* published in Torino in 1895 by Angelo Solerti. It is an evident indication of the lack of interest in Tasso that not even the fourth centennial of his death (1995) has elicited the publication of many monographs or of an updated biography.

⁴ "If Fortini feels and asserts that Tasso is forever tied to the Romantics' interpretation, if he recognized its legitimacy more than once, this occurs because Fortini believed that Tasso's individual existence and his stature are at least partially inseparable from the long shadow that he cast on future centuries": P. V. Mengaldo, "Premessa," in F. Fortini, *Dialoghi col Tasso*, ed. idem and D. Santarone (Torino: Bollati Boringhieri, 1999), 7–15, here 11–12.

⁵ According to Claudio Varese, "già il Guarini [in a letter dated July 10, 1585] . . . proclamava l'*Aminta* degno di essere molto stimato *quanto alla dicitura*, e il Manso, nella *Vita* del poeta [originally published in 1621], lo chiamava opera perfettissima": "L'*Aminta*," in idem, *Pascoli politico, Tasso e altri saggi* (Milan: Feltrinelli, 1961), 91–151, here 91–92; emphasis Varese's [already Guarini in 1585 proclaimed *Aminta* worthy of esteem *for its language* and Manso's biography called it a most perfect work].

⁶ See for example the long debate between Giovan Battista Guarini and the Aristotelian Giasone Denores on the subject of *Il pastor fido* and pastoral tragicomedy in general. Some of the crucial texts (ranging from 1588 to 1601) are to be found in a luxurious, multi-volume edition of Guarini's collected works published in Verona by Tumermani in 1737. Included are Denores's *Discorso* and *Apologia*, Guarini's two treatises entitled *Verato* and his *Compendio*, Angelo Ingegneri's *Della poesia rappresentativa* and Paolo Beni's *Risposta*. The relatively late date of this collection attests to the continued interest elicited by this issue even in the eighteenth century. The interrelations between staged pastorals and theoretical positions during the second half of the sixteenth century are clarified in chap. 9 of M. Pieri, *La scena boschereccia nel Rinascimento italiano* (Padova: Liviana, 1983). An overview of this controversy is in Jane Tylus "Purloined Passages: Giraldi, Tasso, and the Pastoral Debates," *Modern Language Notes* 99 (1989): 101–24.

⁷ One assessment will clarify this widespread dismissive stance: *Aminta* "was highly successful and effectively established Tasso's reputation. There were probably many other performances in the years that followed [its début] and there must have been a considerable

number of manuscript copies, but there was no printed text until Aldo Manuzio published an edition in Venice early in 1581": C. P. Brand, *Torquato Tasso* (Cambridge, Cambridge University Press, 1965), 38.

[8] The latter had seemingly suggested to Tasso the genre of theatrical entertainment: "fece egli [Tasso] a volontà del Duca Alfonso, e forse ad imitatione de gli antichi compositori dell' Egloghe": G. B. Manso, *Vita di Torquato Tasso* (Rome: Francesco Cavalli, 1634), 49–50 [Tasso prepared it according to the Duke's will, and perhaps imitating ancient eclogue authors].

[9] "[Q]uesto scherzare di Dafne [940–4] fù, ò cagione, ò augurio, ò effetto almeno del vero, e dell'intriseco del cuor di lui, che per Tirsi era figurato, perciò che intorno à quei medesimi tempi cominciò ad esser Torquato acceso d'alto, e nobilissimo amore, e molto più, ch'alla sua conditione, se risaputo fosse, non haverebbe paruto richiesto": Manso, *Vita di Torquato Tasso*, 52 [Dafne's cajoling was caused by or hoped for or a consequence of reality and Tasso's innermost heart; represented in Tirsi, Tasso at that time fell in love with someone much more noble than his condition would allow, so that it had to remain a secret]. Later on: "con questo suo silentio, e dissimulatione pose sì fattamente in dubbio il mondo della verità de' suoi pensieri, che nè in quel primo tempo de gli amori suoi, ne [sic] poi nel seguente de' suoi travagli, nè meno dapoi ch'egli vicino ne fù, se ne potette giamai risaper l'intero, nè almeno la certezza di chi fosse la donna da lui cotanto amata: quantunque in molti luoghi delle sue rime ne palesasse artificiosamente il nome, il qual fu Leonora" (53) [through his silence and dissimulation, the whole world was unsure of his true thoughts. Neither at the beginning of his love, nor later on while in pain, not even his closest associates could know the whole truth or be assured of his beloved's identity. However, in many poems Tasso made her name artfully known: Leonora].

[10] "A wonder, alive with the harmony among inspiration, expression, and impression, all reflected in those effects that are the utmost of the art of reflexive poetry": G. Carducci, "Su l'*Aminta* di Torquato Tasso," in idem, *Opere*, 30 vols. (Bologna: Zanichelli, 1962), 14: 137–275, here 139.

[11] "Si pose dunque a stendere la sua Favola Boschereccia, ch'ei volle intitolare *Aminta*, e vi lavorò intorno con tanto genio, e con sì fortunata felicità, che in meno di due mesi l'ebbe ridotta al suo compimento": P. Serassi, *La vita di Torquato Tasso* (Rome: Pagliarini, 1785), 170 [he started to write his pastoral, which he called *Aminta*, and worked at it with such genius and happy felicity that in less than two months he had completed it]. Francesco Flora in 1934 reiterates Carducci's assessment while moving it from the psychological to the lyrical domain, in keeping with his global judgment: "l'*Aminta* nella sua ispirazione è assai più spontanea ed una" [in its inspiration *Aminta* is much more spontaneous and unified] than *Gerusalemme liberata*: F. Flora, "L'*Aminta*" in Tasso, *Poesie* (Milan: Rizzoli, 1939), 35–42, here 36.

[12] "We must keep in mind that it was written straight off, in a brief serene parenthesis." For Bosco, psychologically Tasso was in a state of "pura gioia" [pure joy] which "non sarà mai più nel nostro poeta" [he would never feel again]: U. Bosco, *Saggi sul rinascimento italiano* (Firenze: Le Monnier, 1970), 142, 147 at the time of the composition of *Aminta*. It was a period in which Tasso forgets the "esigenza religioso-morale" [religious-moral need] which is however "il costitutivo della sua spiritualità" [the constitutive elements of his spiritual life] (146). It is as though the pastoral were an oxymoron in the global production and psychology of its author.

¹³ "It might have been one of those works that had the least importance for him. Certainly it cost him little effort. He put it together lightly, in two months, it seems. It was one of those works that come to a poet by themselves, in rare moments of creative felicity": E. Donadoni, "L'*Aminta*," in *Torquato Tasso. Saggio critico* (1928) (Firenze: La nuova Italia, 1952), 103–25, here 104.

¹⁴ "L'*Aminta* è l'unica opera del Tasso in cui non si sente lo sforzo. Quel mondo poetico è perfettamente proporzionato alla capacità del poeta. L'*Aminta* è come pianta nata da sè: nel proprio terreno: venuta su, come l'amore del protagonista,

Com'erba suol, che per se stessa germini [I.ii, 426]:

d'una maturazione rapida, e tuttavia non anticipata, nè artificiale. L'arte si sente, ma non si vede": Donadoni, "L'*Aminta*," 114 [*Aminta* is the only work by Tasso in which we feel no effort. That poetic world corresponds perfectly to the poet's ability. *Aminta* is like a plant born by itself, in its own terrain, like the poet's love "as grass that grows by itself is wont to do" with a swift ripening that is nevertheless unforeseen and non artificial. We feel its art, but do not see it].

¹⁵ "This small work, written tumultuously and with full abandon in two months, can open a crack on less known abysses of the poet's soul, perhaps the deeper ones": G. Petronio, "Introduzione alla lettura dell'*Aminta*," *Rassegna della letteratura italiana* ser. 4, 41 (1933): 1–17, here 2.

¹⁶ "L'*Aminta* non è stato una folgorazione, una eccezione felice e casuale nella vita e nell'arte del poeta, ma, preparato ed elaborato nella mente del Tasso, prende il suo posto in una ideale cronologia tra il *Rinaldo* e la *Gerusalemme* e dopo le prime liriche, come una meditata alternativa, una soluzione contrapposta, ma insieme contemporanea e interferente, alla *Gerusalemme liberata*": Varese, "L'*Aminta*," 115 [*Aminta* was not a flash, a happy and haphazard exception in Tasso's life and production. Prepared and thought out in his mind, it has its place between *Rinaldo* and *Gerusalemme* and after his earliest poems in an ideal chronology. It is a well-thought alternative, an opposite and yet contemporary and interference-generating solution to *Gerusalemme liberata*].

¹⁷ Or three, depending on the attribution of the comedy *Intrichi d'amore*; on this debate, see Enrico Malato, "Introduzione," in Tasso, *Intrichi d'amore*, ed. idem (Rome: Salerno, 1976), ix–lxxi.

¹⁸ "The separation of genres and styles plays a decisive role for a poet whose intellectual ability was rich though unsystematic and who had a strong rhetorical education": F. Fortini, *Dialoghi col Tasso*, ed. P. V. Mengaldo and D. Santarone (Torino: Bollati Boringhieri, 1999), 53.

¹⁹ "L'atteggiamento del poeta è più che mai quello di un cortigiano — : il che non toglie nulla alla spontaneità della poesia: il Tasso è cortigiano nell'anima, e nella Corte è lui. L'*Aminta* è l'espressione del Tasso giovine: in equilibrio momentaneo con sè e con l'ambiente: che nella Corte si sente dominatore assai più che dominato. Quel poema è un canto che rompe *ex abundantia cordis*: di un cuore soddisfatto, cosciente, superbo. È un canto di serenità e di tripudio, se non di gioia: il canto di un uomo che si sente libero, anche dalle passioni: e che non si propone altro obbietto, che di godere": Donadoni, "L'*Aminta*," 105 [The poet's attitude is more than ever that of a courtier — which of course does not detract from the poem's spontaneity. Tasso is intimately a courtier and he is at court. *Aminta* is the

expression of Tasso as a young man briefly balancing his own self and the court where he dominates. *Aminta* is a song that erupts from the fullness of his heart, then satisfied, aware and superb. It is a serene, exulting song, perhaps even a joyful one, the song of a man who feels free, even from passion, and who has no other objective but to enjoy himself].

[20] "References to his time, to the people in attendance."

[21] "Rather than live of an autonomous artistic life, it lived solely of the courtly one": Petronio, "Introduzione alla lettura dell'*Aminta*," 4.

[22] "Questo mondo della Corte . . . è presente nell'*Aminta* non solo cosí, come la rappresentazione viva ed anche un poco pettegola della Corte di Alfonso II, ma pure in un senso piú profondo e, per il Tasso, piú serio. La Corte per il Tasso non è solo quella concreta realtá fra la quale gli tocca vivere, ma è un ideale assoluto di vita; e la Corte, senza piú determinazioni, la Corte in astratto, è la sua passione piú profonda forse, l'ideale che volta a volta lo affascina o lo spaventa, ch'egli volta a volta ama o aborrisce, ma di cui ad ogni modo non sa mai fare a meno": Petronio, "Introduzione alla lettura dell'*Aminta*," 6 [The world of the court is present in *Aminta* not just as a lively, even gossipy representation of Alfonso II's court. It is there in a more profound and more serious way. For Tasso, the Court is not simply the concrete one in which it is his lot to live; it is also an absolute life ideal. The Court without any further specification, the abstract Court was perhaps his deepest passion, the ideal that at times fascinates, at times scares him, that at times he loves, at times he abhors. Still he can never do without it].

[23] "More out of a painful intuition than critical awareness, Tasso feels within himself the problems that undermine the strength of Renaissance trusts": R. Ramat, "L'*Aminta*," in idem, *Per la storia dello stile rinascimentale* (Messina: D'Anna, 1953), 119–51, here 126.

[24] "Opposing the world of court to that of nature, with the triumph of the latter or making two opposing ideas in the poet's soul (made real in two different characters), means altering and misunderstanding the very soul of the 'fable'": G. Trombatore, "L'*Aminta*," in idem, *Saggi critici* (Firenze: La nuova Italia, 1950), 113–42, here 120.

[25] "Politian's and Pontano's lines and, eventually, in *Pastor fido*."

[26] "L'aspirazione alle bellezze della natura, ai godimenti semplici, ai sentimenti spontanei e ingenui, era sentita semplicemente come evasione da una vita sociale prosaica e vuota di ogni idealità. O meglio, per esser più precisi, non tanto era 'sentita,' quanto era vagheggiata, perché quell'avversione, . . . piuttosto che un profondo e vitale sentimento, era un atteggiamento intellettualistico, e perciò la corrispondente aspirazione si risolveva di necessità in un vagheggiamento idillico, che di se stesso si nutriva e si appagava, senza, cioè, neanche quella nota di malinconia, che poteva derivargli dalla consapevolezza che mai quel sogno si sarebbe avverato, mai, tranne che nelle illusorie visioni della poesia": Trombatore, "L'*Aminta*," 121 [the desire for natural beauty, for simple enjoyments, for spontaneous and naïve sentiments was simply felt as the evasion from a social life that was pedestrian and devoid of any ideal. Or rather, to be more specific, it was not so much "felt" as hoped for, since his aversion was an intellectual posture rather than a deep, lively feeling. Therefore the corresponding desire necessarily became an idyllic need that fed and contented on itself without an inkling of melancholia that could have arisen from the awareness that the dream would have never become real except in the illusory visions of poetry].

[27] See his 1820 poem "Ad Angelo Mai, quand' ebbe ritrovato i libri di Cicerone della repubblica": *Opere*. 2 vols. (Milan: Riccardi, 1956–1966), 1: 16–23.

²⁸ "Tasso does not want to lower the court to the level of the woods, but rather raise the latter to the level of the former": Bosco, *Saggi sul rinascimento*, 143. Brand echoes this opinion: "Tasso justifies the literary language of his shepherds as being due to the ennobling influence of love": *Torquato Tasso*, 49. And later on: "the conceits and artificialities are comparatively rare in a generally simple, even lowly style" (50). Flora had expressed a similar opinion: "l'*Aminta* solleva a poesia la parlata quotidiana": "Introduzione" in Tasso, *Poesie* [Milan: Ricciardi, 1952], vii–xliii, here xxix) [*Aminta* lifts everyday spoken language to poetry]; and earlier: "Qui non c'è un uso inavvertito e pedestre del comune linguaggio, ma l'assunzione di quel facile linguaggio a lingua poetica": "L'*Aminta*", 37 [there is no unaware or pedestrian use of common language, but the raising of that easy language to a poetic one].

²⁹ "By 'middle tone' I mean a constant control over his words and feelings; he never abandoned himself to their flow or to the perception that there exists another reality behind the one in which we live or to which we tend."

³⁰ "Il Tasso, che scriveva per una festa di corte, come doveva tener conto del grado di cultura e di educazione dei suoi ascoltatori, così non poteva trascurare i loro umori, lo stato d'animo fra essi prevalente, le reazioni che i suoi versi avrebbero suscitate, e che egli era in grado di prevedere perfettamente. Doveva dilettare i nobili e raffinati spettatori, non tormentarli; non gli era lecito, per esempio, abbandonarsi alla sua tristezza e inquietudine, oltre certi limiti. Ma non si tratta di convenienze pratiche, di concessioni che il Tasso avrebbe fatto al gusto della corte: queste avrebbero finito col falsare e annullare la poesia": Bosco, *Saggi sul rinascimento*, 142 [Writing for a court festivity, Tasso had to keep in mind the cultural and educational level of his listeners as well as their moods, the feelings prevailing among them, the reactions that his lines would evoke in them and that he could foresee well. He had to please his noble, refined audience. He could not, for example, yield to his sadness and disquiet, beyond a certain limit. Yet these are not practical advantages, or concessions to the court's tastes; those would have ultimately altered and annulled his poetry].

³¹ It "represents a harmoniously rational life, the masterpiece of a renaissance man" yet "it is also the place where that dream dissolves and is perceived as such because it is its antithesis": Ramat, "L'*Aminta*," 144.

³² "In *Aminta amour-passion* dominates: not the one that is philosophically sublimated and solved in the idea of god, but neither a purely sensual eroticism. This is love that, as passion, looks for the agreement from the beloved's soul, and that, as human (neither superhuman nor animal) passion, protects its very purity and nobility by respecting the being that it loves and admires": B. Croce, "Poesia pastorale," in idem, *Poeti e scrittori del pieno e tardo Rinascimento*, 3 vols. (Bari: Laterza, 1958), 1: 326–37, here 335–36.

³³ "That love that *Aminta* suggests and longs for is the only possible manifestation of life's forces, the perfect triumph over oneself, pure joy": U. Bosco, *Saggi sul rinascimento*, 145.

³⁴ "The fable is not just permeated, but drenched with music." "Ogni parola, ivi, è canora; ma così staccata da un'esperienza direttamente musicale che non solo ogni altra effusione lirica, ma persino i cori si sottraggono volentieri alla struttura tradizionale, che era appunto reminiscenza ritmica di una struttura musicale, e introducono, salvo il primo, quel verseggiar 'a selva' dove la parola ha più libertà d'inventar lei i suoi ritmi e le sue melodie": M. Apollonio, *Storia del teatro italiano*, 2 vols. (Firenze: Sansoni, 1981), 1: 621 [each word

in it is song-like. Yet it is so far removed from a directly musical experience that not just every lyrical expression, but even the choruses freely escape the traditional structure that was the rhythmic memory of a musical structure. Instead they introduce a stanza-like versification in which words are freer to come up with their rhythms and tunes].

[35] In his review of a 1994 staging of *Aminta* Guido Almansi implicitly endorses Apollonio's opinion: he reproaches Luca Ronconi, the director, for not having instructed his performers to insist on the slow delivery of certain lines: "Perché lo spettatore senta quel verso, bisogna che venga compitato e dispiegato, a lentissima velocità, in un ralenti necessitato dall'importanza di quelle sillabe": G. Almansi, "Dov'è la mia fraschetta?" *Panorama* (7 May 1994): 169 [in order for an audience member to hear that line, it has to be spelled and drawn out, very slowly, in slow motion made necessary by the importance of those very syllables].

[36] Bosco had expressed the opposite opinion, when he wrote that in *Aminta*'s "maliosa levità musicale . . . consiste gran parte del fascino della favola boschereccia; non per nulla essa ispirò subito gran numero di musicisti, che la rivestirono di note. Ma non aveva bisogno di note altrui; era già musica; dico musica, non semplice libretto per musica, come qualcuno ha detto": *Saggi sul rinascimento*, 154 [the largest part of *Aminta*'s charm derives from its bewitching musical lightness. This is why it immediately inspired a great many composers that clothed it with notes. Yet it did not need notes; it was already music, and I mean music, not simply a libretto as others have said.] He derives this judgment, but not its polemical tone, from Ramat: "L'*Aminta* è infatti un'opera lirica, opera musicale; e il miglior suo musico, fra quanti la rivestirono in parte o interamente di note, è il Tasso medesimo; ché le sue parole son già musica": "L'*Aminta*," 125 [*Aminta* is indeed an opera, and the best composer among those who clothed it fully or in part with notes is Tasso himself, since his words are already music]; as well as from Flora: "Il tono lieve dell'*Aminta* ha . . . un respiro di alta musica, intimamente elaborata": "L'*Aminta*," 41 [*Aminta*'s light tone has the breath of high, intimately elaborated music]. The myth that Tasso's poetical works were set to music in a significantly higher proportion than his contemporaries' is debunked in Lorenzo Bianconi, "I Fasti musicali del Tasso," in *Torquato Tasso tra letteratura, musica e arti figurative*, ed. A. Buzzoni (Bologna: Nuova Alfa, 1985), 143–50. Andrea Chegai has analyzed the musical pieces based on *Aminta* specifically, and reached similar conclusions: "Musicalità *vs.* musicabilità: l'*Aminta* fra recezione madrigalistica e fortuna critica," *Il saggiatore musicale* 1 (1994): 315–39. Lastly, a list of madrigals based on *Aminta* appears in the appendix to Vassalli, "Il Tasso in musica" in *Tasso, la musica, i musicisti*, ed. M. A. Balsano and T. Walker (Firenze: Olschki, 1988): 45–90, here 59–60.

[37] "Perhaps it might not seem to a modern-day reader that the fable's high beauty derives its charm from the dramatic progression and the happy ending of the plot. Rather, s/he might see it in the melodic wave that charms it and builds a transfiguring halo around it. Silvia's and Aminta's and their friends' lines are among the best non-rhyming ones of that century, indeed among the most beautiful ones of any period of our literature; they are waves and abandons and pains and losses and restarts alive with Petrarchan elegy and, at time, with the foreshadowing of a Leopardi-like expressive chastity."

[38] While d'Amico invokes Leopardi from a linguistic and lyrical standpoint, Bosco believes that Leopardi appropriated Tasso's concept of love in *Aminta*: "I due soli nomi nei quali il Leopardi fissa il suo ideale della donna o dell'amore, Silvia e Nerina, son tratti

ambedue dall'*Aminta*. . . . Questa coincidenza è casuale? Può darsi; e può darsi anche che le ragioni non ne siano che esternamente letterarie. Io però inclino a credere in una più segreta rispondenza; e in verità la concezione dell'amore nell'*Aminta* e quella del Leopardi sono per molti aspetti assai simili": *Saggi sul rinascimento*, 149 [The only two names that Leopardi uses for his ideal woman or love, Silvia and Nerina, both come from *Aminta*. Is this a haphazard occurrence? It might be, and it might also be that the reasons for it might be literary in an external sense. However, I tend to believe in a more covert correspondence; indeed the concepts of love in *Aminta* and in Leopardi are rather similar from many standpoints].

Francesco Flora had already noticed the Tassian derivation of the names of Leopardi's beloved, as well as the recurring usage of the adjective "tenerello": "Introduzione," xxviii; from a historical standpoint, he traces a lineage from *Aminta* to Metastasio to Leopardi: "L'*Aminta*," 41. According to Raffaello Ramat, finally, the parallel between Tasso and Leopardi runs deep: "l'Arcadia del Tasso si configura come una perpetua e mitica stagione umana, non temporale ma spirituale: la giovinezza quale poi la canterà il Leopardi": "L'*Aminta*," 122 [Tasso's Arcadia is set as a perpetual, mythical human season that is not chronological but spiritual: youth as Leopardi will sing it].

[39] d'Amico asserts: "Non duriamo fatica ad immaginarci come dovettero bearsi, di cotesta musicalità leve, le dame e i gentiluomini convenuti dagli Estensi nel nido di delizie cheudì [*sic*] per primo i sospiri del pastore innamorato: l'isoletta di Belvedere sul Po, fiorito rifugio della Corte d'Este, dove la favola fu rappresentata per la prima volta, non da accademici o da studiosi, ma dai comici 'dell'arte' più celebri del tempo, quelli della compagnia dei 'Gelosi'": *Storia del teatro drammatico*, 2: 18 [we had no trouble imagining how happy the ladies and gentlemen must have felt, invited by the Este to the small island of Belvedere, the delight-laden nest where the sighs of the shepherd in love were first heard. Belvedere, the Este court's flowery refuge, was where the fable was first staged, not by members of an academy or by scholars, but by the most famous *arte* performers, the Gelosi troupe].

[40] Alain Godard rightly asserts that "si elle [Bosco's definition] a le mérite de saisir, en une heureuse formule, un des caractères essentiels de l'œuvre du Tasse, [elle] présente cependant le danger de masquer ce qu'elle [i.e., *Aminta*] a de proprement théâtral": "La Première représentation de L'*Aminta*," in *Ville et campagne dans la littérature italienne de la Renaissance 2* (Paris: Université de la Sorbonne nouvelle, 1977), 187–301, here 279 n. 292 [if it has the merit of grasping one of the essential characteristics of Tasso's work in a happy formula, it has the danger of covering up what it contains of fully theatrical]. Even a theatrically inclined critic as Louise Clubb cites Bosco's definition, as she remarks: "Compared with later pastoral plays, for which it was a model of excellence and a quarry for song, sentiment and situation, it seems a lyrical pageant of love, symbolic and stylized into hieroglyph, more tenor than vehicle": *Italian Drama in Shakespeare's Time* (New Haven: Yale University Press, 1989), 96.

[41] Francesco Flora had already espoused this opinion in 1934, when he asserted that "L'*Aminta* crea anche uno schema melodico nuovissimo, mediante il particolare uso dell' endecasillabo e del settenario, distendendo il severo metro di canzone in un ampio recitativo. È questo un fatto di cultura che non si può trascurare": "L'*Aminta*" 41 [*Aminta* creates an utterly new melodic scheme through a specific use of eleven- and seven-syllable lines, so that the *canzone*'s rigid meter could open into a recitative. This is a cultural fact that we cannot ignore].

⁴² "I believe that we cannot easily avoid taking into account the data that theater in all its manifestations and in all the extension of facts in which contemporaries identified something theatrical, if we want to define or understand what we call the Renaissance": R. Scrivano, "Tasso e il teatro," in *La norma e lo scarto* (Rome: Bonacci, 1980), 209–46, here 212.

⁴³ "In *Aminta*, a play fully based on words, space is an almost totally immobile one, to which the movement that took place elsewhere transported itself": R. Scrivano, *Finzioni teatrali da Ariosto a Pirandello* (Messina: D'Anna, 1982), 26.

⁴⁴ Landscape "si può dire che sia ancora assente nell'*Aminta*. Esso invero è sottoposto a un trattamento quanto mai sobrio. Non esistono in quest'opera vere aperture paesistiche, come avverrà nella *Gerusalemme* ed in parte era già avvenuto nel *Rinaldo*. Esiste invece una suggestione vaga di fresca natura, di cieli freschi e di boschi profumati, di limpide acque e di rive fiorite (e, più avanti, di balze dirupate e di folte macchie), ma tale suggestione è raggiunta con tocchi estremamente semplici, con sfumature che potrebbero essere puntualizzate solo con molta difficoltà. Il fascino della bella natura, più che porsi come un elemento preciso che agisca in maniera autonoma e spicchi con preponderante rilievo, vive come uno stato d'animo sottinteso, operante in poetica sintesi con altre disposizioni spirituali": G. Getto, *Interpretazione del Tasso* (1951) (Naples: Edizioni scientifiche italiane, 1966), 130–31 [We could say that landscape is missing in *Aminta*. It does undergo an extremely restrained treatment. There are no true landscape openings, as we will see in *Gerusalemme* and we partially saw in *Rinaldo*. There is, instead, a vague evocation of fresh nature, of cool skies and fragrant woods, of clear waters and flowery banks (later on, of craggy crags and thick forests). This evocation is reached by extremely simple touches, with nuances that could be pinpointed only with great difficulty. The charm of beautiful nature lives as an understood state of mind that works in poetic synthesis with other spiritual dispositions, rather than a precise element that acts autonomously and that is clearly set off].

⁴⁵ It goes without saying that such an approach is open to equally subjective contradictions: in C. P. Brand's opinion, "Nature is more than a background: . . . it is a living participant in the action": *Torquato Tasso*, 46.

⁴⁶ "Intuitions, i.e., episodic and isolated notes, that are not strongly instilled in each characters, and that are not organized according to a process of psychological development."

⁴⁷ "Nè d'altra parte, a negare la drammaticità dell'*Aminta* basta l'ovvia osservazione che la trama non si organizza in vigorosi contrasti ed è tutta affidata alle narrazioni dei personaggi. Bisogna, infatti, notare che questa accusa . . . non intacca la sostanza reale dell'opera; ma riguarda esclusivamente la tecnica. E in tal senso . . . essa è di scarso valore. . . . Bisogna, dunque, dire qualche cosa di più vero e sostanziale; bisogna riconoscere che i racconti dei personaggi dell'*Aminta* sono del tutto esenti di forza drammatica. . . . L'interesse non va allo sviluppo dell'azione, nè in senso drammatico, nè in senso narrativo; ma si volge ai racconti, ognuno in se stesso, che sono come quadri lirici, nei quali via via l'azione si viene disponendo, soste vaghe e incantate della fantasia": Trombatore, "L'*Aminta*," 122–23 [we cannot deny *Aminta*'s dramatic quality with the obvious observation that the plot does not rely on strong contrasts and in fact fully depends upon narration on the part of the characters. We must underscore that this accusation does not alter the work's substance, since it only concerns its technique. Thus it has hardly any value. We must, then, say something truer and more substantial. We must recognize that the characters' tales

are utterly devoid of dramatic strength. Our interest does not flow to plot development, neither in a dramatic nor in a narrative sense. It flows towards each individual tale, as they all are lyrical *tableaux*, vague and charmed stopping points of the imagination in which the plot places itself a little at a time].

⁴⁸ "Those who in antiquity introduced on stage pastoral sets, and shepherds and nymphs (such as the Greek Theocrites, the Latin Virgil, and our Sannazaro and others)."

⁴⁹ "Talk about what they wanted without minding any rule other than their clothing. Therefore their works could be named as collections of scenes, rather than plot or stage."

⁵⁰ "Since he set the plot in the woods, and fashioned his characters as shepherds, he followed the customs of eclogues as well as the rules of comedy and tragedy, and made out of those three a wonderful, most beautiful, and highly regulated work. The latter took set, characters and costumes from the eclogue; gods, heroes, choruses, the length of lines and the weight of style from tragedy; and commoners, facetious wit, and happy endings from comedy. Tasso observed the unity and integrity of the plot, its coming full-circle, its protasis and resolution and all the other parts and rules that must be followed and that are common to tragedy and comedy, and did it so well that envy itself could no find any fault to this poem."

⁵¹ "Venne al momento opportuno, chiudendo il lavoro della imitazione perennemente innovante e trasformante del Rinascimento, e aprendo nella idealizzazione, se può dirsi, della sensualità voluttuosamente malinconica l'età della musica, la quale nel regno della fantasia e dell'arte doveva necessariamente succedere alla poesia": Carducci, "Su l'*Aminta*," 139 [it came at the right time, bringing to a close the perennially innovative and transforming work of imitation of the Renaissance, and opening the age of music, in the idealization (if we can call it that) of melancholic sensuality. Such an age by necessity had to follow poetry in the kingdom of imagination and art].

⁵² "Alla favola pastorale, dunque, nata, cresciuta e venuta alla somma perfezione in Ferrara alla corte estense, diè gli esemplari della sua doppia forma pur il teatro estense: per la mediocrità famigliare e per la giocondità, la commedia: per la passione, per l'elocuzione piú sollevata, per la lirica dei cori, la tragedia. E tra i due generi creduti rinnovare di su l'antico, questo, misto e composito, e per la rispondenza alle idealità dei tempi, e per il valore dei poeti che lo sollevarono, T. Tasso e B. Guarini, apparí e divenne il piú originale e vitale, il piú efficace e fecondo": Carducci, "Su l'*Aminta*," 232 [After giving it birth, nourishing it, and giving it perfection in Ferrara, Este theater gave the pastoral its two-faced exemplary works: comedy as a source of familiar middle nature and of its happiness; tragedy as source of passion, higher elocution, and lyric choruses. This mixed and composite genre, born out of those two that were believed to renew those of classical antiquity, appeared and became the most original and vital, the most effective and fruitful, because it corresponded to the ideals of the time, and due to the value of the two poets that thus lifted it, Tasso and Guarini].

⁵³ Vittorio Rossi, in his review of Carducci's essays, disagrees on the antecedents, but not on the point of view. He recalls a long tradition of "egloghe auliche" [courtly eclogues] (111) preceding *Aminta*, as well as prior and contemporary popular staged entertainment of pastoral subject matter. Tasso's pastoral surpasses them all "in quanto il genio di un grande poeta e il cuore di un uomo innamorato hanno trasformato dei fantocci camuffati da pastori in anime": V. Rossi, review of Carducci, "Su l'*Aminta*," *Giornale storico della letteratura*

italiana 31 (1898): 108–16, here 113 [because the genius of a great poet and the heart of a man in love transformed some puppets dressed as shepherds into souls]. I am indebted to Professor Graziella Parati of Dartmouth College for helping me secure a copy of this review.

[54] "Se c'è poeta non nato all'umorismo è il Tasso: eppure, per tutta l'opera [*Aminta*], fra lui e il pubblico corre l'intesa di un sorriso che non viene poi nè dall'uno nè dall'altro, ma dal continuo e spesso impersuaso specchiarsi la favola pastorale nella tragedia greca per vedere se le somigli": G. Toffanin, "Il teatro del rinascimento," in *Storia del teatro italiano*, ed. S. d'Amico (Milan: Bompiani, 1936), 61–99, here 78 [if there ever was a poet not born for humor, that is Tasso. Yet throughout *Aminta* an understanding smile exists between him and the audience. Said smile does not come from either, but from the continuous and often unconvinced mirroring of the pastoral in Greek tragedy to see if it looks like it].

[55] "Sono tutti in azione quei vecchi mostri, Catarsi, Peripezia, Innocenza colpita; ma così disartigliati e inoppiati che le mancate vittime scappano loro per sotto le zampe e sopra le groppe e, in ultimo, scivolano via contenti per la porticina di una Peripezia aggiunta con un inchino al vecchio Aristotile e al pubblico finalmente contento. Una caricatura? Nemmeno! Dai pure indecifrati enigmi la tragedia greca impone la suggestione della sua lineare architettura, è presente ai primordi stessi dell'ispirazione entro quel particolar ritmo e quella cadenza con cui un'opera dà il primo annuncio di sè al cuore che la porta nascente": Toffanin, "Il teatro del rinascimento," 76 [all the old monsters, Catharsis, Peripeteia, stricken Innocence, are in action. However, they are so wholly devoid of claws and drugged out that their supposed victims sneak through their paws and on their backs, and lastly slip away, through the door of a Peripeteia added in observance to old Aristotle and to the satisfied audience. Is this a joke? Absolutely not! Greek tragedy imposes the example of its linear architecture, though it appears enigmatic and undecipherable. It is present at the very core of inspiration by way of its rhythm and cadence with which a work announces itself to the heart about to generate it].

[56] "Tasso did not perfect a new genre, but created a new style."

[57] "*Aminta* is not a pastoral play; indeed, it is not a play. This is a short lyrical piece hiding under pastoral names and dramatic form. This is a dramatic-like narrative, not a real staging, such as tragedies, comedies, and so-called pastoral dramas in Italy."

[58] "*Aminta* is a plot outside the theater as told by witnesses or participants along with the impressions and passions that it elicited in them. The interest lies entirely in the narration, which is developed lyrically and interspersed with choruses whose ideal is the apotheosis of pastoral life and of love: 'It is possible if you like it.' The motif is lyrical, aiming at developing idyllic feelings, rather than characters and events. There are many lively descriptions, soliloquies, comparisons, witticism, and passionate acts. A certain musical laxity pervades it, full of grace and delicacy that makes even tears voluptuous": F. de Sanctis, *Storia della letteratura italiana*, ed. B. Croce, 2 vols. (Bari: Laterza, 1958), 2: 182–83.

[59] "Il lato più vivo della figura, quello che non sempre i critici hanno visto, per il pregiudizio, derivato dal De Sanctis, dell'assoluta semplicità e liricità dell'*Aminta*, e, quindi, del suo difetto d'intima drammaticità": G. Petronio, "Introduzione alla lettura dell'*Aminta*," 8–9 [the liveliest aspect of the character that went often unnoticed by critics, due to the bias of the absolute simplicity and lyrical quality of *Aminta* and, thus, of its lack of innate dramatic strength, derived from De Sanctis].

⁶⁰ "Siccome egli mirava non tanto a cogliere l'individua poesia dell'*Aminta*, quanto a dimostrare che allora, per la povertà della sua vita morale, la società italiana non poteva produrre il dramma, e che soli vivi potevano essere il sentimento del comico e il sentimento idillico, preferì diffondersi più a lungo sul *Pastor fido*, che meglio dell'*Aminta* si prestava a tale dimostrazione": Trombatore, "L'*Aminta*," 116–17 [He did not aim at assessing the specific poetry of *Aminta*, but rather at demonstrating that at that time Italian society could not produce drama due to its poor moral life, and that only comic and idyllic feelings could live. Thus he preferred to spend more time on *Pastor fido*, which could demonstrate such conditions better than *Aminta*].

⁶¹ "Una lirica non postula di per sé ascoltatori. Sebbene naturalmente ogni poeta si volga a un suo ceto ideale di lettori, la lirica, in sé, ne prescinde: è un puro monologo. Tale invece non è la favola dell'*Aminta*: essa presuppone non solo un uditorio, ma un determinato uditorio: quello della corte estense che il Tasso conosceva bene nei singoli componenti e nel suo complesso": Bosco, *Saggi sul rinascimento*, 141 [a lyrical poem does not imply listeners. Though of course each poet address an ideal class of readers, lyrical poetry in and of itself does without it: it is pure monolog. The *Aminta* fable is not like that: it presupposes not just an audience, but a specific one, that of the Este court that Tasso knew well in its individual components and as a whole].

⁶² "Dramma . . . l'*Aminta* non è. Non solo per il lieto fine annunciato sin dal prologo (vv. 52–67) e costantemente presentito in tutto lo sviluppo dell'azione, ma soprattutto per l'assenza del presupposto stesso di ogni dramma: personaggi individuati profondamente e contrastanti tra loro o in sé stessi [sic]": Bosco, *Saggi sul rinascimento*, 144 [*Aminta* is not a drama, not just because of its happy ending that is announced in the prolog and felt in each plot development, but above all because it lacks the very basis of a drama: deeply individual characters that contrast among or within themselves].

⁶³ "L'*Aminta*, secondo un giudizio molto diffuso e molte volte ribadito, non è teatrale: vi manca l'azione, lo svolgimento, la modificazione progressiva dei caratteri. Ma guardandolo non secondo le abitudini del teatro romantico, ma secondo la tradizione e la pratica del teatro classico, che spesso è fatta di un'azione raccontata e evocata, si dovrà ammettere che i personaggi portano dinanzi allo spettatore un intreccio di avvenimenti e di sentimenti, una modificazione di circostanze, uno svolgimento di carattere": Varese, "L'*Aminta*," 132 [according to a widespread and often repeated opinion, *Aminta* is not theatrical. It lacks plot, development, and progressive modification in the characters. But if we consider it not from the habits of romantic theater, but according to the tradition and practice of classical theater (often consisting of a told or evoked action), we must admit that its characters evoke for the audience a plot made of events and feeling, changing circumstances, character development].

⁶⁴ "With his smart mythological inventions in the prologue and epilogue, Tasso builds a bridge between theater invention and courtly ambiance, that is, between a sign and something concrete; and he does this with grace and poise."

⁶⁵ "Il senso teatrale del Tasso nella favola boschereccia è tutto in questa risoluzione musicale: anche senz'esser rivestita di note, l'*Aminta* è già un melodramma, ché le sue parole sono musica, lo sfondo su cui sorgono i momenti di canto più aperto è un ritmo fra voluttuoso e malizioso e malinconico, la sua azione si svolge secondo un numero e gesto di danza": Ramat, "L'*Aminta*," 150 [Tasso's feel for the theater in the pastoral lies entirely in its musical

solution. Even when it is not dressed up in notes, *Aminta* is already a melodrama, as its words are music. The background against which its most open singing moments emerge is a rhythm that is voluptuous and sensual and melancholic. Its plot develops according to the rhythm and the gestures of dance].

⁶⁶ "Allusions to customs and ideas, to people and events of the day and of the court acquired grace and interest, at least in their earliest performances." He offers a specific example of this vogue in an eclogue to be found in an early sixteenth-century Spanish novel, *Question de amor*: "Su l'*Aminta*," 174.

⁶⁷ "Among the characteristics of the pastoral people also counted the fact that it was (and had to be) the opposite of subject-based or *arte* comedies. It was said that subject-based comedy was fit for the populace, while pastoral drama entertained courts, as they found more restrained language and a vague morality that did not required practical application. Thus, the more comedy became licentious and popular, the more pastoral drama took on courtier airs and the refinement fit for the princesses in the audience. All this is well put, and it seems true, but it is not. What is true is that *Aminta* in its time was often performed by *arte* performers."

⁶⁸ Carducci's tone is unmistakably full of longing for the supposed *première* of *Aminta*, yet his emphasis is again on the theatrical elements: "Nell'isoletta e nel palazzo di Belvedere, a' 31 luglio del 1573, da una compagnia di comici dell'arte che s'intitolavano i Gelosi, famosa poi in Francia e per gli Andreini, allora istrutta e preparata alla recitazione da Torquato Tasso in persona, giovine di ventinove anni, fu rappresentato la prima volta, in cospetto di Alfonso II e della corte, l'*Aminta*. Né altro ne sappiamo, Peccato! Chi sa quale spettacolo di natura e d'arte, di bellezza e di sentimento, dinanzi al sole tramontante o sotto le limpide stelle, su la placida corrente, luccicante tra i pioppi, del fiume d'Italia, eterno nel mito e nella poesia!": "Su l'*Aminta*," 237 [On 31 July 1573, on the island and palace of Belvedere, *Aminta* was put on under the direction of Tasso himself (then a mere 29 years old), acted by an *arte* troupe called the Gelosi that would then become famous in France and through the Andreinis. Alfonso II and his court were in attendance. We know nothing more than this. Too bad! Imagine what a show of nature and art, of beauty and feeling! Imagine if it took place under the setting sun or bright stars! And on the peaceful current of Italy's main river, eternal in myth and poetry, glistening among the poplars].

⁶⁹ For example, in Apollonio's *Storia del teatro italiano*, *Aminta* appears almost exclusively as text, and only marginally as performance — and even then, the reference is to the supposed *première* (1: 619–20) and to the relationship between the actors and the Ferrara court. As recently as 1999, Roberto Alonge, a theater historian, could still devote a short piece to those verbal elements of Tasso's pastoral that identify psychological (specifically, masochist) traits in various characters: R. Alonge, "Riflessioni sull'*Aminta*," *Il castello di Elsinore* 12 (1999): 5–15.

⁷⁰ See the arguments (against A. Cavicchi, "La scenografia dell'*Aminta*," in *Studi sul teatro veneto fra rinascimento ed età barocca*, ed. M. T. Muraro [Firenze: Olschki, 1971], 53–72) in Godard, "La Première représentation de l'*Aminta*," 211–14; and G. Da Pozzo, *Ambigua armonia* (Firenze: Olschki, 1983), 125–26. F. Cruciani praises Cavicchi's attention to visual testimonies ("Percorsi critici verso la prima rappresentazione dell'*Aminta*," in *Torquato Tasso*, ed. Buzzoni, 179–92, here 188 and 192 n. 28). Recently, Cavicchi has reiterated his theory, albeit in a tempered form, in "Ancora sull'*Aminta* del Belvedere," in

Torquato Tasso e la cultura estense, 3: *Il teatro del Tasso* ed. G. Venturi (Firenze: Olschki, 1999), 1151–63. I thank Professor Albert N. Mancini for bringing the collection including Cavicchi's 1999 essay to my attention.

[71] "Sembra quanto mai probabile che il mese trascorso, certo per gran parte almeno, nell'isola, dovette vedere Tasso impegnato a commisurare il testo alla vicina rappresentazione, al luogo in cui essa stava per avvenire, anche se non sembra così probabile, invece, un Tasso disposto ad adattare il tessuto della sua poesia alle caratteristiche, alle capacità naturali degli attori, come sarebbe venuto naturale di fare a uno sperimentato uomo di teatro. Più che attento a far combaciare esigenze del testo con propensioni o possibilità degli artisti della compagnia dei *Gelosi*, sembra di star vicini al probabile se si immagina il Tasso, in quelle settimane, intento soprattutto, non solo probabilmente anche agli ultimi ritocchi formali in senso tecnico-linguistico del testo, ma a sfruttare forse anche al massimo la virtualità illusionista della scena, alla quale lo spazio disponibile e in qualche modo già 'magico' di Belvedere sembrava fornire buon incremento, una ulteriore, straordinaria, cornice": Da Pozzo, *Ambigua armonia*, 126–27 [it seems rather probable that the month that Tasso spent on the island must have been devoted to fitting the text to the upcoming staging and to the place where it was about to happen. It seems less probable, however, that Tasso was willing to adapt the weave of his poetry to the performers' characteristics and natural abilities, as a more expert theater person would have done. It seems that we stay close to what is probable if we imagine Tasso not so much paying attention to fit the needs of the text to the Gelosi performers' inclinations and possibilities. Rather, during those weeks he was probably intent upon the last formal (technical and linguistic) touches on his text, and perhaps also absorbed in exploiting to the utmost the illusion-generating virtual character of the set, to which the available, somehow already "magic" Belvedere space seem to bestow an increase, an additional extraordinary frame].

[72] "Il s'agit d'une relation très étroite [between *Aminta* and the Ferrara court], le texte étant extrêmement riche en allusions au contexte, jusqu'à atteindre le niveau de l'allégorie; on pourrait même parler d'une relation spéculaire, dans ce sens, que le Tasse propose une intrigue dramatique où agissent des personnages qui 'réfléchissent' quelques-uns des membres de cette cour: l'auteur lui-même = Tirsi; Lucrezia Bendidio = Licori; Pigna, le secrétaire du Duc = Elpino; d'autres encore, peut-être, que nous ne reconnaissons plus; mais pour les spectateurs-courtisans l'identification était évidemment plus facile, amusante, l'effet obtenu devant être la sensation d'une implication totale de ce public, non pas dans la pathétique histoire d'Aminta et de Silvia — personnages tout à fait imaginaires —, mais dans le milieu idyllique où cette histoire se déroule, dans ce lieu-non lieu, dans ce pays d'Utopie qui est, en même temps, l'Arcadie classique et la cour de Ferrare, l'éden primitif et l'ile de Belvédère. . . . Il est sûr . . . qu'aucun texte de ce genre [the pastoral] n'eut en France le même succès que l'*Aminta*, et que ce succès fut si immédiat qu'il implique certainement la connaissance de la dimension allégorique de la pièce": D. Dalla Valle, "L'influence en France de l'*Aminta* du Tasse," in *L'âge d'or du mécénat*, ed. R. Mousnier and J. Mesnaid (Paris: CNRS, 1985), 305–14, here 306–7 [There is a tight relation between *Aminta* and the Este court. The text is extremely rich in allusions to the context, to the point that it reaches the level of allegory. We could even talk of a mirror relation, in the sense that Tasso proposes a dramatic intrigue in which characters act who "mirror" some of the members of that court: the author = Tirsi; Lucrezia Bendidio = Licori; Pigna, the duke's secretary =

Elpino; more, perhaps, but we do not recognize them any longer. For the audience members/courtiers the identification was obviously easier, amusing, and it must have elicited the effect of a total implication of that audience, but not in the pathetic story of Aminta and Silvia (wholly imaginary characters), but in the idyllic milieu in which the story takes place, in this place/non-place, in this utopian country that is at the same time the Arcadia of classical antiquity and the Ferrara court, or Eden and Belvedere island. It is certain that no text of this genre has the same success in France as *Aminta*, and that said success was so instantaneous that it undoubtedly implies knowledge of the text's allegorical dimension].

[73] "It is not so much a historical, well-documented reality, but a productive situation for our knowledge, to build critical paths that are not justified by their endpoint but by what the path itself unveils with respect to Aminta and the theater of which it is a part."

[74] "In order to know theater authors well we should know performers and spaces (theaters, stages, sets) in which they work a lot better": S. Ferrone, "Introduzione," in *Seminario sulla drammaturgia*, ed. L. Rustichelli (West Lafayette: Bordighera, 1998): 1–18, here 3.

[75] As recently as 1999, Da Pozzo has remarked upon the discrepancy between Tasso's insistence that his tragedy *Torrismondo* be printed and his seeming neglect of *Aminta*. He asserts: "[s]e un'analoga persistenza di cure non troviamo nell'epistolario anche per il testo dell' *Aminta*, occorrerà ricordare che non è da escludere una consistente perdita di lettere proprio in quell'intorno di tempo, dato che il Guasti ... non riusciva a mettere insieme che una sola lettera ... per tutti i mesi che vanno dal maggio del '72 all'ottobre del '73": G. Da Pozzo, "Forma allusiva e scenario della mente nel teatro tassiano," in *Torquato Tasso e la cultura estense 3*, ed. G. Venturi, 861–79, here 870 [if we do not see a similar constant worry for the *Aminta* text in his letters, we must keep in mind that we cannot exclude that many letters might have gotten lost from that very period of time. Indeed Guasti could not find but one letter for the period from May 1572 to October '73]. By focusing on the loss of relevant letters, Da Pozzo excludes the possibility that Tasso's imprisonment had any influence on his perception of the importance of printed editions to foster the cause of his liberation from the Sant'Anna confinement. Solerti, too, had lamented the lack of extant epistolary testimonies from this period: "in nessun carteggio dei moltissimi veduti, ho trovato cenno della prima recita dell'*Aminta*": A. Solerti, *Vita di Torquato Tasso*, 3 vols. (Torino: Loescher, 1895), 1: 181 [in no letter collection of the many I have looked at did I find a trace of *Aminta*'s first performance]. Similarly, Elisabetta Graziosi's support for Serassi's date (23 July 1573) comes from her dynastic and diplomatic hypothesis, not from archival documents, as she acknowledges: Elisabetta Graziosi, Aminta *1573–1580. Amore e matrimonio in casa d'Este* (Lucca: Maria Pacini Fazzi, 2001), 46–47. Recently, the musicologist Franco Piperno has unearthed documents that place the Gelosi in Bologna at the time of the supposed Aminta performance, thus ruling out one important element of Solerti's hypothesis: Franco Piperno, "Nuovi documenti sulla prima rappresentazione dell'*Aminta*," *Il castello di Elsinore* 13 (2000): 29–40.

[76] "*Aminta* was only printed between the end of 1580 and the beginning of 1581. We must look for the reason behind this delay in Tasso's exacting needs as an artist. In this long seven-year period the fable was held by many in manuscript form": B. T. Sozzi, "Per l'edizione critica dell'Aminta," in idem, *Studi sul Tasso* (Pisa: Nistri-Lischi, 1954), 11–68, here 13.

⁷⁷ As prestigious a precursor as Niccolò Machiavelli never cared for printing what we consider his most important play, namely *Mandragola*: "lo stesso Machiavelli non si preoccupava affatto di curare un'edizione a stampa *ne varietur* della sua pur tanto celebrata *Mandragola*, anzi, le edizioni originali di questa commedia, vivente l'autore, o sono anonime o sono mal abborracciate, tanto da costringere a più d'una perplessità il filologo moderno": Gareffi, *La scrittura e la festa*, 210 [Machiavelli himself did not care to have a *ne varietur* printed edition of his famous *Mandragola*. Indeed its earliest editions, from when Machiavelli was still alive, are either anonymous or badly put together, to the point that modern-day philologists find many perplexing elements in them]. This points to a remarkable discrepancy with the attitude towards printing of *commedia dell'arte* performers, which I have explored in M. G. Stampino, "Publish or Perish: An Early Seventeenth-Century Paradox," *Romance Languages Annual* 10 (1997): 373–79. It is worth mentioning that all early *Aminta* printings were relatively plain: only the 1583 and 1590 Aldine editions were illustrated, and even then, most the 1583 plates were re-used in 1590; these were cheaply bound, and small in size — easily portable even for traveling performers.

⁷⁸ "They might become public or be in someone's possession, as it happened for my eclogue:" quoted in Sozzi, "Per l'edizione critica," 13.

⁷⁹ More recently, Elisabetta Graziosi has put forth the hypothesis that *Aminta*'s goal was primarily political and dynastic, i.e., to further Duke Alfonso II's aim of marrying Alfonsino and Marfisa d'Este, so as to give Ferrara a legitimate male heir. In this vein she also reads *Aminta*'s delayed publication: "[f]ino a quando non fosse giunta l'età matrimoniale di entrambi i fanciulli, il testo era tanto riservato da essere impubblicabile e poteva soltanto correre manoscritto per le corti in cui si sapeva qualcosa dei programmi matrimoniali e successori del Duca": Graziosi, Aminta *1573–1580*, 201 [until the two young people had reached a marriageable age, the text was so confidential that it could not be published; it could only circulate as a manuscript in those courts where the Duke's plans regarding marriages and succession were known]. Graziosi, however, does not consider *Aminta*'s stage fame, which constitutes another vehicle to make it public.

⁸⁰ *Aminta* "probably entered *arte* troupe repertory as a text that those actors learned by heart. We imagine them only acting in improvisatory forms, yet they must have rehearsed and performed *Aminta* when their audiences wanted a play in verse. Our information regarding the repertory of *arte* performers is almost always skimpy and haphazard, yet *Aminta* comes back: as a piece of news that chance or an occasional poet transmit to us for example about Maria Malloni, nicknamed Celia": F. Taviani and M. Schino, *Il segreto della commedia dell'arte* (Firenze: Usher, 1982), 354.

⁸¹ "Maria Malloni, nicknamed Celia, of the Confidenti, elicited her admirers' enthusiasm under the nymph's guise at the end of the sixteenth century and at the beginning of the following one. We further know that the Confidenti staged *Aminta* in Turin, too": Solerti, *Vita di Torquato Tasso*, 1: 191.

⁸² "*Aminta* was staged many times in the sixteenth century: after the Belvedere opening, certainly in Pesaro in 1574, with Tasso in attendance."

⁸³ "We have no firm information about a staging for Duke Guglielmo I in Mantua (perhaps in 1586). In 1590 a staging was done in Florence under Duke Ferdinando I's orders, which was magnificent and supposedly taken in by Tasso himself. Then the famous Buontalenti worked on the stage set and the *intermezzi*."

⁸⁴ *Aminta* "enjoyed an exception fame on stage: for example for the Pesaro *carnevale* of 1574, in Verona in May 1581, again in Ferrara in 1583, probably in Mantua in 1586, in Florence in 1590": M. Pieri, *La scena boschereccia nel Rinascimento italiano*, 213.

⁸⁵ *Aminta* "was performed a second time 'with most beautiful *intermezzi* with animals' at Cornelio Bentivoglio's country house, probably on 15 November 1579": E. Povoledo, "Ferrara," in *Enciclopedia dello spettacolo*, 10 vols. (Rome: Le maschere, 1954–1969), 5: 173–86, here 180.

⁸⁶ "Only theater needs an addressee that is actually in attendance; theater receives the signals that the audience transmits (such as silence and positive or negative reactions) and can change the text in accordance to them. Theater's possibility to make changes is tied to the dialogic nature of the staged text. The concept of 'canonical text' is foreign to staged and folkloric texts. It is replaced by the concept of an unchangeable that becomes real in various variables": J. Lotman, "Semiotica della scena," *Strumenti critici* 15 (1981): 1–45, here 9.

⁸⁷ M. De Marinis, "Dramaturgy of the Spectator," *Drama Review* 31 (1987): 100–14, here 100.

⁸⁸ J. Donohue, "Evidence and Documentation," in *Interpreting the Theatrical Past*, ed. T. Postlewait and B. A. McConachie (Iowa City: University of Iowa Press, 1989), 177–97, here 184.

⁸⁹ "Plays are not and did not want to be literature. At least in the sixteenth century, they were made to be performed, not to be printed, even when they became an unsurpassed masterpiece like *Mandragola*."

⁹⁰ "It was performed once at the author's house on 23 February 1545, and another time on 3 March, while the Duke Ercole II Este and his brother cardinal Ippolito were there": A. Solerti and D. Lanza, "Il teatro ferrarese nella seconda metà del secolo XVI," *Giornale storico della letteratura italiana* 18 (1891): 148–85, here 149 n. 60.

⁹¹ "It was performed twice at Don Francesco Este's residence in Ferrara in 1554. The first time was 11 February, the Duke Ercole II and his son Alvigi in attendance; the second time was 4 March, the duchess and her daughters in attendance": Solerti and Lanza, "Teatro ferrarese," 152.

⁹² "It was performed at Schifanoia Palace in Ferrara in 1563": Solerti and Lanza, "Teatro ferrarese," 153.

⁹³ "It was performed in Ferrara in May 1567": Solerti and Lanza, "Teatro ferrarese," 156–57.

⁹⁴ "It hurts me that you imposed on me that I print my comedy, which I composed and had staged three years ago with your encouragement": Solerti and Lanza, "Teatro ferrarese," 166.

⁹⁵ "Performed in the famous and generous city of Venice by the priest Giovanni from Siena in 1521 and 1522": R. Guarino, *Teatro e mutamenti. Rinascimento e spettacolo a Venezia* (Bologna: Il Mulino, 1995), 277. In performance texts set to music, the primacy of the text is assured until the emergence of opera. As Bianconi cogently clarifies, "è proprio lo sviluppo d'una forma d'istituzione teatrale altamente professionalizzata come quella dell'opera in musica a determinare una forte crisi d'identità nel ceto letterario italiano al cospetto della musica: solo di mal grado il letterato, ridotto a librettista, si piega al rango di prestatore d'opera assegnatogli nella distribuzione delle competenze artistiche dentro

il teatro, e recalcitra all'idea di rinunziare . . . al titolo di 'autore' vero e proprio d'un *opus* artistico che non è più un testo sebbene un con-testo multiplo ed ibrido destinato alla fugacità dell'esibizione teatrale anziché alla riflessiva sedimentazione della lettura": L. Bianconi, "Il Cinquecento e il Seicento," in *Letteratura italiana*, ed. A. Asor Rosa, 7 vols. (Torino: Einaudi, 1982–1989), 6: 319–63, here 357 [It is the very development of such an institutionalized, professional theatrical form as musical opera that provoked a strong identity crisis among Italian literary people vis-à-vis music. It was only reluctantly that they, reduced to librettists, acceded to becoming workers for hire, carrying out one task among the many necessary for the theater. They were loath to give up the title of "author" of an artistic work that is no longer a true text, but a multiple, hybrid con-text destined to a fleeting staging rather than to reflective, sediment-generating reading].

[96] "A series of indices that define, through their very mobility, the relation between two modes of consumption." Conversely, Paolo Bosisio asserts that the primary performance objective of pastorals is what differentiated them from contemporary tragedies and comedies: "tragedie e commedie vengono spesso composte con destinazione eminentemente libraria e solo in qualche caso rappresentate con tempestività, le cosiddette favole pastorali sembrano subire un destino diametralmente opposto, essendo solitamente composte in vista di un allestimento scenico e solo eventualmente date alle stampe in tempi successivi": P. Bosisio, "Teatro e spettacolo nella corte estense," *Il castello di Elsinore* 7 (1994): 51–70, here 60 [tragedies and comedies are often written specifically to become books; only rarely are they staged quickly. The so-called pastoral fables seem to have had the opposite destiny: they were usually written for a staging and only in certain cases they were later printed].

[97] P. Trovato, "Per una nuova edizione dell'*Aminta*," in *Torquato Tasso e la cultura estense* 3, ed. Venturi, 1003–27, here 1011–15.

[98] I prefer the term "tension" to the stronger one utilized by Lotman, who asserts that "[i]l testo scenico è il risultato del *conflitto* che si sviluppa tra un grande numero di fattori": "Semiotica della scena," 19; emphasis added [the staged texts is the result of a conflict among many factors], including the author, the director, and the actors.

[99] They "do not become real once and for all, but as the sum total of variables around an invariable that is not directly present."

[100] "For an entirely practical and extrinsic goal, and provisionally."

[101] "It is not even possible to establish for which performances he wrote them."

[102] "We have placed them in an appendix following the practice established by recent editors, first because they are missing from the manuscript copies and from the printed ones that came out during Tasso's lifetime (they first appear in the 1666 Roman Dragomanni printing); second, because they have an occasional, practical and external relation with the pastoral text. They are no more than a choreographic or spectacular completion of the pastoral text. Indeed it is legitimate to suppose that *intermezzi* (probably the adaptation of previous lyrical poems, like the chorus at the end of Act III) changed in the various *Aminta* stagings."

[103] At the end of his long essay on *Aminta*, Claudio Varese contends that the *intermezzi* were indeed intended by Tasso to complement the pastoral: "Che gli intermedi non siano stati scritti insieme con l'*Aminta* pare oramai dimostrato e sicuro, ma altrettanto sicuro, non confutabile e non confutato, è che il Tasso li abbia scritti e preparati tutti insieme per una recita teatrale": "L'*Aminta*," 149–50 [It has been shown assuredly that *intermezzi* were

not written alongside *Aminta*. It is also sure and certain that Tasso wrote and prepared them all for a staging]. However, he confines his interpretation to the literary realm, while leaving their theatrical relevance aside: "Siano questi versi nati per un'altra occasione o siano stati invece sentiti, pensati e scritti solo per questa favola, resta la precisa intenzione del Tasso di rendere più complesso e più vario non solo lo spettacolo, ma il significato stesso dell'opera" (150) [Whether these lines were born out of another occasion or they were felt, thought out and written just for this fable, Tasso's precise intention remains to make not just the show, but the very meaning of his work more complex]. The emphasis rests unmistakably on the relevance of literary elements, to which the music and dance of the *intermezzi* are ancillary. Even a recent contribution by James Yoch does not go further than a short statement to the effect that "splendid intermedi regularly interrupted the performances, perhaps dwarfed and surrounded them": J. J. Yoch, "The Limits of Sensuality: Pastoral Wildernesses, Tasso's *Aminta* and the Gardens of Ferrara," *Forum Italicum* 16 (1992): 60–81, here 74; he does not raise the question of how such interruptions affected the performance.

[104] See the long list in Sozzi "Per l'edizione," 16–29. Sozzi succinctly explains the situation in the following manner: "Sta di fatto che i cori-eccettuati il I e il V, nati con la favola e connaturati con essa- . . . non appaiono nei manoscritti e nelle edizioni tutti in una volta, ma in numero via via crescente, e taluno in diversa redazione da una ad altra edizione; tutti e cinque completi compaiono per prima volta in A90" ("Per l'edizione, 46) [The fact remains that the choruses (other than the first and fifth, born alongside and of the same nature of the fable) do not appear in the manuscripts or in the printed editions all at once, but little by little, and some in a different lection from one printing to the next. All five complete appear for the first time in A90], that is, in the Aldine edition of 1590.

[105] No mention is made of the fact that *Aminta* was performed with the additions of choruses since its "second" staging, at Pesaro in 1574; chapter 2 of the present study will devote ample attention to this issue.

[106] "The chorus addition undoubtedly corresponds to the desire for classic and Aristotelian literary ennoblement that marks Tasso's second poetic phase. This stuffy burdening makes us wish for the light nakedness of its youthful version. Yet it must be preserved philologically, since we have to respect the author's will as well as objective facts. It will suffice to denounce it critically as one aspect of the writer's involution."

[107] "We cannot exclude the possibility that Tasso might have adapted some poem to serve as conclusion to the pastoral on some occasion, probably for the text's second performance, which took place in Pesaro in 1574. As we already said for *intermezzi*, we cannot demonstrate that Tasso wanted it integrated in printings": B. T. Sozzi, "Nota sull'episodio di Mopso e sull'epilogo dell'*Aminta*," *Giornale storico della letteratura italiana* 127 (1950): 485–85, here 485.

[108] Leah S. Marcus has cogently shown the impact of "nonauthorial forms of authorship" on early modern texts in "Renaissance/Early Modern Studies," in *Redrawing the Boundaries: The Transformation of English and American Literary Studies*, ed. S. Greenblatt and G. Gunn (New York: Modern Language Association of America, 1992), 41–63, here 50.

[109] Morris Eaves has convincingly shown that McGann's ideas are valid in the domain of the visual arts, for example. See M. Eaves, "'Why Don't They Leave It Alone?' Speculations on the Authority of the Audience in Editorial Theory," in *Cultural Artifacts and the Production*

of Meaning, ed. M. Ezell and K. O'B. O'Keefe (Ann Arbor: University of Michigan Press, 1994), 85–99.

[110] It is interesting that Sozzi chooses 1595, the year of Tasso's death, as *terminus ante quem* for acceptable printings, as if the fact that Tasso was still alive had any effect on *Aminta* printings.

[111] Taviani has shown that the act of integrating "Amor fuggitivo" with the text of *Aminta* radically changes the plot outcome ("Teatro di voci," 9–19); thus such editorial issues should be of crucial importance to literary critics, too. Paolo Trovato indeed criticizes Sozzi's critical edition from a strictly textual and philological standpoint ("Per una nuova edizione," 1004–8).

[112] "I did not forget to see if among these people three young ones and a man could be found having the characteristics that your letters point out with respect to staging scenes. So I found three young men aged 16 or 17 with very beautiful faces and good manners; though they have never performed I still believe they will do a good job as nymphs. In the staging of Tasso's pastoral that I intended to have staged last year (though the friction with Lucca did not allow my plan to take place) said young men were very successful in the many rehearsals that we did." On "fanciulli" playing nymphs see Susan McClary, "Gender Ambiguities and Erotic Excess in Seventeenth-Century Venetian Opera," in *Acting on the Past*, ed. Franko and Richards, 177–200, esp. 180–81.

[113] A similar phrase was used ten years before this document, in a letter sent from Lucrezia d'Este at Pesaro to her brother Alfonso at Ferrara, trying to lure him for a visit for the carnival season. For the full citation, see chapter 2 of the present study.

[114] "Kept to an utter classical simplicity, gave up choruses and *intermezzi* that were later added in the printed version."

[115] This does not exclude the possibility that authors might have tried to influence certain stagings: in a famous instance, Giovan Battista Guarini, unable to leave Ferrara, sent his son Alessandro to Mantua to supervise the *première* of *Il pastor fido* in 1595. His ideas regarding an all-encompassing spectacle (his letters to Alessandro are rife with advice in the fields of music and stage decoration) do not exclude his desire to exert some authorial control over the staged text. See for example the letter cited by Cavicchi, "Scenografia dell'*Aminta*," 66–67.

[116] "If history wants to reach its goal, which is to bring the past back to life, it must cross the borders of what can be recognized through concepts, with full awareness. It must generate in front of the reader's eyes a clear series of representations, in other words, an image": J. Huizinga, "L'elemento estetico delle rappresentazioni storiche," in *Le immagini della storia. Scritti 1905–1941*, ed. W. de Boor (Torino: Einaudi, 1993), 5–31, here 23–24.

[117] "Comedies must never be read or judged as literature. They were, and wanted to be, something else even in their author's intentions. This 'something else' can only be reconstructed in minimal part, now. We will always lack that knot of life that made them come alive. Acting as though it were not like that generates irreparable damage."

[118] J. Huizinga, "The Task of Cultural History," in idem, *Men and Ideas* (Princeton: Princeton University Press, 1984), 17–76, here 26.

[119] S. Bennett, *Theatre Audiences* (London: Routledge, 1997), 98.

[120] This also helps explain why efforts at re-staging sixteenth- or seventeenth-century theater works as faithfully as possible to their "original" incarnation are doomed to failure. As producer Jonathan Miller has stated, "chances are that the intended meanings [a past

production] so eloquently expressed at the time would no longer communicate themselves to a modern audience" as "the production would seem quaint and antiquated": J. Miller, "Doing Opera," *New York Review of Books* (11 May 2000): 12–16, here 13.

[121] These four functions are: consensual reality (accepting the performers' enacted roles); cueing (giving performers responses that guide the latter in the enactment); social reinforcement (showing approval or disapproval of the enactment); and finally continual observation (in order to maintain the role behavior of both audience and performers over time): A. P. Hare and H. H. Blumberg, *Dramaturgical Analysis of Social Interaction* (New York: Praeger, 1988), 49.

[122] I refer of course to the definition offered in the "Préface" to *Les Mots et les choses* (Paris: Gallimard, 1966): "il ne sera . . . pas question de connaissances décrites dans leur progrès vers une objectivité dans laquelle notre science d'aujourd'hui pourrait enfin se reconnaître; . . . ce qu'on voudrait mettre au jour, c'est le champ épistémologique, l'épistèmè où les connaissances . . . enfoncent leur positivité et manifestent ainsi une histoire qui n'est pas celle de leur perfection croissante, mais plutôt celle de leurs conditions de possibilité" (13) [These are not pieces of knowledge described in their progress towards the objectivity in which our current science will be able to find itself. What we want to illuminate is the epistemological field, on which these pieces of knowledge base their positive nature and make evident their history — not the history of an ever-growing perfection, but rather the history of their conditions of possibility].

[123] Joseph Roach has recently studied the continuity of certain performance rituals around the Atlantic Ocean along Kermode's line: "[t]he pursuit of performance does not require historians to abandon the archive, but it does encourage them to spend more time in the streets. When students ask about the problems of reconstructing historical performances . . . I now ask them: What evidence do we have that they ever died out?": *Cities of the Dead* (New York: Columbia University Press, 1996), xii. I thank my University of Miami colleagues involved with the Humanities Colloquium for bringing Roach's study to my attention.

[124] Andrea Gareffi agrees: "bisogna fare affidamento su di una diversa maniera di comprendere, più bisognosa di immaginazione, con le sue oscillazioni e le sue incertezze, poiché lo spettacolo è comunque in passo nel reame dell'immaginario e l'ambiguità non gli fa torto": *La scrittura e la festa*, 91 [we must trust a different way to understand, one that needs more imagination with its oscillations and uncertainties, since a show is always a step into the realm of the imaginary and ambiguity does not wrong it].

FIGURE 1.
Villa Imperiale, Pesaro. Black-and-white etching from Mingucci, *Stati, dominii, città, terre e castella dei Serenissimi Duchi, e Prencipi della Rovere tratti dal naturale*, manuscript at Biblioteca Apostolica Vaticana, Rome: Barb. Lat. 4434, page 9.
©Biblioteca Apostolica vaticana.

Chapter Two

Pesaro, 1574: *Carnevale*

Haphazard findings play a central role whenever scholars attempt to reconstruct staged events of the past on the basis of contemporary documents. The February 1574 *Aminta* performance at Pesaro is no exception to this rule. By chance, an important document relating the staging has been preserved. It was found in a library and brought to scholars' attention via journal publication in the late nineteenth century. However, the attention traditionally bestowed on this specific event largely depends on a particular historiographic focus of nineteenth-century researchers in Italy. In the wake of the Romantic emphasis on exceptional individuals first found in writers, scholars concentrated on biographies of so-called geniuses, in whom a period was thought to have found its most accomplished expression. Tasso became part of this paradigm, for better or for worse. Nevertheless, the documents unearthed in the nineteenth century come prominently into play in a quest of utterly different nature like the present reconstructive endeavor.

In the following chapter, I will first offer a short overview of the city and court of Pesaro around 1574. I will then situate *carnevale* festivities in their historical and local context.[1] Third, I will present past reconstructions of the 1574 *Aminta* performance, in order to differentiate between archival documents and their subsequent interpretations. Last, I will reconstruct the *Aminta* performance, using a different frame of reference and exploiting extant documents in a differing way from previous attempts, as I emphasize how meaning was made rather than the teleology of Tasso's biography.

1. Pesaro in 1574

The town of Pesaro, located in the Marches region of central Italy, is a port town on the Adriatic Sea on the estuary of the Foglia river. Founded by the Romans,[2] in 1512 it had become part of the della Rovere family domain, which included (among others) the centers of Urbino and Casteldurante.[3] In 1574, Guidubaldo II was duke. He is usually described as an elderly, harsh man who nevertheless loved the arts and protected numerous artists. His family was powerful, although its domain was not very extensive geographically. Indeed, during Guidubaldo's rule, his brother Giulio was one of the most influential cardinals in Rome,[4] thus guaranteeing further sway to the della Rovere. Guidubaldo's first-born son, Francesco Maria, was then twenty-eight, and had been raised to be an all-encompassing, accomplished Renaissance ruler. Among his teachers we find Gerolamo Muzio and Federico Commandino, one of the most prominent mathematicians of the times (Solerti, *Vita di Torquato Tasso*, 1: 30). Torquato Tasso himself was among the privileged few admitted to partake of this exclusive education; he had spent two years of his life (from 1557 to 1559) at the della Rovere court — typically, at Pesaro during the winter and at Urbino during the summer. On the basis of an extant letter by Bernardo Tasso, Solerti has postulated that Torquato's father had chosen the *roveresca* court for his son's education not simply because of the formal teaching to which his son would be exposed, but for its overall reputation: "egli [i.e., Bernardo] che consigliava di praticare le corti 'dove s'impara la creanza, a fine che la sia ornamento dell'animo,' voleva che anche nelle arti cavalleresche si addestrasse, e riuscisse il perfetto cortigiano dal Castiglione ideato, che all'ornamento delle lettere congiungesse la virtù dell'armi, il gusto della musica e delle arti" (*Vita di Torquato Tasso*, 1: 31).[5] It is not altogether useless to point out that the conversation in Baldassar Castiglione's *Il cortegiano*, the leading manual for the Italian and European courtier, though largely written in Rome and printed in Venice, takes place in the "piccola città d'Urbino" (Castiglione, *Cortigiano*, ed. Carnazzi, 56) [small city of Urbino].[6] It is not surprising, then, that Bernardo considered the della Rovere duchy an utterly fitting locale for training a young man in the liberal arts and in the wiles of living at court.

The interest in the della Rovere court on the part of nineteenth-century scholars looking for elements of Tasso's biography reached beyond the mere personal contact during Torquato and Francesco Maria's formative years. An institutional tie was also in place, since in 1570 the della Rovere heir had married Lucrezia d'Este. The latter was sister to Alfonso d'Este, then ruler of Ferrara, in whose court Tasso served as panegyrist, letter-writer, courtier, and later (starting in 1574 [Solerti, *Vita di Torquato Tasso*, 1: 186]) as university lecturer in geometry. Negotiations between the della Rovere and the Este families regarding this wedding had lasted a long while (according to Solerti, "parecchi anni" [*Vita di Torquato Tasso*, 1: 127] [many years]); Francesco Maria apparently resented getting married to a woman who was approximately ten years his senior. Indeed, it was Cesare Gonzaga who married Lucrezia as his proxy on 18 January 1570; Francesco Maria did not arrive at Ferrara until the 28th of that month (Solerti, *Vita di Torquato Tasso*, 1: 127–28). After the customary celebrations, which included a tournament, Francesco Maria headed back towards Pesaro by himself. It took almost a year before Lucrezia left Ferrara to join her husband:

> Si mosse . . . il 2 di gennaio del 1571 ed arrivò a Pesaro il 9 incontrata a un miglio di distanza dal duca [Guidubaldo II], dal cardinal Giulio della Rovere

e dal principe Francesco Maria. Fece ella l'ingresso nella città seduta in una pomposa lettiga, ricevuta alla porta dal clero e da tutti i gentiluomini che l'accompagnarono al duomo, onde passando sotto 5 archi superbamente decorati fu condotta al palazzo ducale. Erano ivi ad attenderla gentildonne in gran numero, ed ivi si terminò la giornata con una splendida cena che durò fino alle 4 ore di notte. (G. Campori and A. Solerti, *Luigi, Lucrezia e Leonora d'Este* [Torino: Loescher, 1888], 43–44)[7]

The disaffection between Francesco Maria and Lucrezia was apparently mutual, nor did she hide her dislike for the della Rovere court, or at least her nostalgic longing for her native one at Ferrara. In 1572 Lucrezia went back to the Este court for an extensive period of time to help her sister-in-law, Barbara of Hapsburg, who had fallen ill;[8] in 1574, too, she took a trip home, this time without any overt excuse (Campori and Solerti, *Luigi, Lucrezia e Leonora d'Este*, 46). Her ties with the Este court were evidently still very strong. Lucrezia and Francesco Maria's marriage ended in *de facto* separation that became legalized in Ferrara in 1578 (G. Solari, *22 storie dei duchi d'Urbino* [Milan: Mondadori, 1973], 337–40).[9]

Though linked to issues of procreation and therefore of dynastic continuity, these family–circumscribed troubles pale when considered alongside the tensions traversing the duchy in the years 1572–1573. Towards the end of 1572, new and extensive taxations imposed on the cities in the della Rovere domain provoked protests from various members of the noble and merchant families of Urbino.[10] After a brief lull, during which Guidubaldo kept them at bay with various promises and veiled threats, the unrest regained momentum. In February 1573, the city of Urbino sent a delegation to the court at Pesaro; rejected at first, then finally admitted to the duke's presence, it had by then lost most of its external support, most notably the Pope's (to whom the land belonged; the della Rovere had received it from Rome as a fief). Guidubaldo offered them an agreement that was neither generous nor forgiving, but the *urbinati* were forced to sign it. Lastly, having detained the members of the delegation in his castle, Guidubaldo ordered nine of them executed, presumably to send an even stronger message to the other communities under his power.[11] While Urbino is traditionally presented as the only rebellious city in the della Rovere domain ("Pesaro e Senigallia . . . avevano inviato ambascerie a Guidubaldo per dirgli che se quelli di Urbino 'meritavano la cavezza,' loro raddoppiavano in sviscerato amore a Sua Eccellenza" [Solari, *22 storie*, 296]),[12] a manuscript source from Pesaro's Biblioteca Oliveriana points to a contradiction which runs through all the events delineated in this chapter:

> Hebbe il principe Guid'Ubaldo genio cotanto parziale verso la Città di Pesaro, che quasi di continuo con splendida magnificenza, risedendo in essa, la fortifico [*sic*] nel di fuori col recinto di nuove muraglie conforme al disegno delle moderne fortificazioni lasciatogli dal Padre, e nel di dentro la ridusse alla Polizia, et ornamento maggiore ch'ella havesse giammai ed infine havendo

nelle turbolenze d'Urbino sperimentato giornalmente negl'animi de Pesaresi gl'effetti d'una Costantissima Fede, all'hora quando esibitisi eglino pubblicamente di perseverare sotto la devozione di Guid'Ubaldo in qualunque sua fortuna indussero col loro fedelissimo esempio anche l'altre città del Suo Stato à mantenergli in fede, il gratissimo Principe p[er] guiderdonare l'incorrotta fedeltà de benemeriti Pesaresi, concesse loro indono [*sic*] la Quercia Arma della Sua Ser[enissi]ma Casa sostenuta da quattro mani in fede col motto: Perpetua, et firma fidelitas. (G. B. Rinalducci, *Notitie Historiche della Città di Pesaro*, MS oliveriano 380, fol. 242 v)[13]

On the one hand, Rinalducci asserts that Pesaro followed Guidubaldo with "devotion" and "most constant trust" during the Urbino troubles. On the other, by way of pointing out the ruler's beneficial influence on the city, he stresses that under Guidubaldo the city had gained better protection from the outside thanks to new walls, and had become safer and quieter *inter moenia* through the use of police force. As Pesaro was in effect the seat of power, one is left wondering if any behavior other than passivity or superficially enthusiastic support for the ruler was available to its citizens.

Traditionally, the *carnevale* festivities of 1574 at Pesaro have been interpreted as an attempt on Guidubaldo's part to entertain his subjects, specifically to divert their attention both from the gory memories of the past plot and from the heavy taxation still imposed on them.[14] Although no extant document verifies this hypothesis, it is indeed possible that Guidubaldo exploited the coming festivities to show his benevolence to the citizens of Pesaro — who had witnessed the effects of his revenge, but had not directly felt it. He did offer at least two public spaces for some of the performances of the 1574 *carnevale*: the "corte" (probably that of the ducal palace) and a temporary theater that had been built for the festivities accompanying Lucrezia's arrival at Pesaro in 1571. These locations raise the performances to a different status, making them more official and closer to the court than a more or less spontaneous and loosely organized celebration. Still, the time-span of these *carnevale* festivities cannot simply (and reductively) be interpreted as the appropriation of a popular occasion on the part of the ruler and his court. Emmanuel Le Roy Ladurie has pointed out that carnivals included "unbridled masquerades" marking the subversion of the everyday power structure, as well as "Apollonian *formalities* paving the way to a final, violent imposition of order, the return to everyday life" (*Carnival in Romans* [New York: Brazillier, 1979], 307; emphasis in original). The court-sponsored *Aminta* performance at Pesaro can be viewed as part of the transition back to normalcy; as will become clear, its chronology seems to confirm this hypothesis.

The partially courtly nature of the performance of Tasso's pastoral further complicates the issue of its reception, due to the aforementioned connection between the della Rovere and Este families. *Aminta* had been conceived as courtly entertainment for the Este entourage just the year before. Clearly, the 1574 performance of Tasso's pastoral, like those of any other play put on stage, consists of a variety of layers. It involves a wider audience than either an ordinary courtly festivity or *carnevale* entertainment: it aims at the court, at the noble families, and at those in the merchant class that had sparked the uprising in Urbino and their Pesaro counterparts, and to a certain extent, to the populace, by virtue of taking place at a time traditionally devoted to popular celebrations. Poised between the "inner" public sphere, addressing the court, and the "outer" one, geared towards the totality of the subjects and reaching beyond the duchy boundaries, *Aminta* finds a (possibly uncomfortable) niche among the events of the *carnevale* of 1574 at Pesaro. We now turn to the nature of this festivity, traditionally a time when theatrical entertainments were performed,[15] as it was experienced at that historical moment and in that town.

2. *Carnevale* Festivities at Pesaro

Archival sources from the della Rovere domains are scattered throughout central Italy.[16] Some documents, including the *libri dei conti* [account books] (which would offer invaluable insight on how much money the court spent for *carnevale* entertainment) were destroyed in the nineteenth century.[17] Nevertheless, the Archivio di Stato at Pesaro holds three important documents that cast light on *carnevale* revelries: some laws regarding "feste e mercati" [festivities and markets] dated 1568, and a long instruction dated 1576 on the topic of masks during *carnevale*.[18] Both fall in a category that could be broadly defined as "domestic tranquility;" they apparently aim at preventing civil unrest and disturbances, and only to a smaller extent do they define appropriate behaviors, allowed language and clothing, and so on. Even so, they depict a vivid picture of the habitual revelries in town during this eight-year period, which includes the *Aminta* performance.

On 28 January 1568 (that is, not too far from the height of *carnevale* season) Guidubaldo expressed concern about the presence of weapons (both firearms and "armi in asta" [Legazione apostolica di Pesaro-Urbino, decreti 2: 1505–1686, 1535–1651, 1544–1661; decreti dei della Rovere, volume 3, fol. 65 v] such as swords and pikes) in churches, at festivals, and at markets — public places on which many people would converge. He thus commanded that everybody, including members of his own militia, refrain from carrying his own weapons to church, market, or any area where revelries were under way. If the festival took place within the castle walls, then the weapons were to be left at the gate; if it occurred in an area without clear boundaries, then they were to be placed "almeno doicento passa" (fol. 65 v) [at least two hundred steps] from the area itself.[19] The punishment consisted in "tre tratti di corda" [three lashes] and an unspecified "pena pecuniaria" [pecuniary fine] (fol. 65 v) to be divided among the duke, the accuser (whose identity would remain secret), and the executioner (fols. 65 v–66 r).

Barely two weeks later, on 14 February, Guidubaldo promulgated a law designed to protect the space where festivities would take place. The first two lines of the decree make it clear that Guidubaldo had in mind festive entertainment of a private nature held in indoor spaces: "Havendo inteso con molto nostro dispiacere l'insolenze, e mali modi, che da indiscreti, mal creati, e presuntuosi s'usano di continuo nelle Feste, alle Porti, Usci, e finestre, di quelle, che fanno feste, ò altri simili trattenimenti" (fol. 66 v),[20] it had become evident that some law had become necessary in order to avoid this and any other sort of violence. The punishment again consisted of a combination of whipping and pecuniary fine. An even greater crime, punishable with "galera perpetua" (fol. 66 v) [life-long imprisonment], was carrying or using weapons in the *locus* where the festivities were under way. Another interesting notation deserves attention: "non sia lecito ad alcuno di qualunque stato, grado si sia, et Privilegiato di qualunque Privilegio, che in maschera, ò Mascherato, ardischi di portare, ò tenere Armi nelle feste di qualunque sorte sotto la medesima pena della Galera perpetua, et altre à nostro Arbitrio" (fols. 66 v–67 r).[21] Evidently, given that *carnevale* masks could also be used to disguise one's identity to carry out less than legitimate endeavors, a spatial separation had to be enforced between masking and carrying arms. Therefore, the mere possession of a weapon on the part of somebody wearing a mask deserved punishment, no matter what their social status. Further, if some masked people "pongano mano all'Armi in dette feste, ò l'abbassaranno, v'insultaranno alcuno, ò feriranno" (fol. 67 r),[22] they would be punished more harshly than a non-masked person: in addition to the standard whipping, instead of a fine, all their possessions were to be confiscated. From both Guidubaldo's laws the need emerges to separate the space of the revelries from the place of everyday interaction. This essentially unattainable goal indicates the unruly and spatially and socially pervasive nature of the *carnevale* festivities.

The fear and unease with which the established power viewed *carnevale* and, more generally, people in disguise is also palpable in the regulations proclaimed by Francesco Maria II in 1576. The tone of this rather long edict differs markedly from that of the previous ones. It could be argued that it simply reflected the different personality of the new duke vis-à-vis that of his father. One could also perceive in it a sign of the political trend already manifest in the imposition of new taxes that had provoked the Urbino uprising of 1572: a desire on the part of the ruler to gather more and more powers in his hands, according to a well-known direction in European politics in the early modern period.

Rather than concentrate on the punishment of those guilty of violating some law, Francesco Maria II stated the regulations that had to be followed for a harmonious *carnevale* at Pesaro. In other words, the edict offers prescriptive behavior for the future. In fact, from the outset it is plainly the duke himself who graciously bestowed the right to celebrate on his people:

Essendo solito à certo tempo dell'Anno concedersi à Popoli qualche sorte di recreazione pubblica, e particolarmente l'Immascherarsi; Perciò per honesto piacere di Popoli ci contentiamo di dar licenza ale maschere, come per virtù del presente publico Bando diamo, è concediamo à tutte le persone d'Immascherarsi. (Legazione apostolica di Pesaro-Urbino, decreti 2: 1505–1686, 1535–1651, 1544–1661; decreti dei della Rovere, volume 3, fol. 77 v)[23]

Francesco Maria's edict is clear: the tradition of *carnevale* festivities was subject to a particular jurisdiction on the part of the duke, as *carnevale* implied public (not simply private) revelries. Rather than being the time when popular rule (or misrule) gained the upper hand and briefly reversed the social *status quo*, it was presented as a kind concession on the part of the master towards his people, so that they could enjoy themselves. It is within this frame that the duke graciously gave his subjects permission to wear masks.

In order to further the impression of a generous concession on Francesco Maria's part while at same time limiting it, the 1576 law carefully detailed the temporal boundaries within which masking would be allowed. The citizens of Pesaro would be able to regulate their behavior and discern whether or not *carnevale* was still afoot by the presence or absence of a big mask raised on the façade of the "Palazzo de Priori, ò Potestà" (fol. 77 v) [on the Palace of the Priors of or the local representative]. Instead of being merely regulated by the calendar of the Catholic Church, *carnevale* began with the proclamation of the decree at hand and would end "mentre si vedesse levato il detto Mascarone a qualche honestà, e debita cagione s'intenda anche revocata la licenza" (fol. 77 v).[24] Additionally, the duke did not simply impose a time-frame within which these festivities would take place; for the good of his people and the tranquility of the city (so that "chi vuole pigliarsi modestamente questo spasso possa farlo senza essere disturbato; e chi pensasse di fare altrimenti sia tenuto dal timore della pena" [77 v])[25] he carefully determined which behaviors were acceptable and which would encounter his wrath and punishment.

The first conduct to be avoided was wearing masks outside the temporal limit defined at the beginning of the document:

vogliamo, ordiniamo, et commandiamo, che nessuna persona sia di che stato, grado, condizione, ò preminenza possa essere, presuma, ne ardisca farsi maschera in alcuna Città, Torre, e luoghi del nostro stato dove il presente Bando sarà pubblicato se non durante il tempo della presente licenza. (fol. 78 r)[26]

The punishment follows closely that meted out in Guidubaldo's law: a whipping and a fine. Another behavior forbidden at all times was the use of religious habits as *carnevale* masks and disguises. This constitutes a remarkable indication of the respect exacted from and imposed upon common people vis-à-vis religious institutions, in the repressive decades following the council of Trent (1545–1563).

More importantly, it points to the fact that the identification between habit and the person wearing it was total, so much so that the population would be misled by anybody dressed as a monk, priest or nun even at a time when masking was allowed. It is noteworthy that the aforementioned passage eschews phrases such as "wearing" or "putting on" a mask, but uses a stronger verb, "farsi maschera," which implies the transformation of one's being, or nature, beyond one's appearance or surface. One more element underscores the enforcement of a particular respect vis-à-vis religious orders and other boundaries, lay in nature: those in disguise were forbidden to enter or exit city limits as well as "Chiese, ò Conventi di Religiosi, ò Monasterii di Suore, ò Claustri, ò parlatorii, ò altri luoghi Sacri" (fol. 78 v)[27] — a rule that again emphasizes the attention elicited toward the sacred and aims at avoiding any confusion in the rest of the population as to the identity of consecrated people. This rule can also be linked to the spatial provisions in the 1568 decree. Not only was the chronological span of *carnevale* limited (and subject to the duke's jurisdiction, rather than to the religious hierarchy's), but geographical boundaries also had to be respected, indeed reinforced, during the season of revelries. Just as the *carnevale* time-span could not be extended into Lent, so its festivities had to be spatially contained — for reasons of domestic tranquility, supposedly. As in the bound space of the theater, there are two impermeable lines or frames, one separating the space of the performance from the outside or the everyday, the other dividing viewers from players; similarly, during *carnevale* those reveling in masks should be prevented from crossing boundaries easily.

Francesco Maria also duplicated his father's law in prohibiting anybody wearing disguises from carrying weapons, or from having somebody carry them for him. In order to avoid any confusion on this delicate topic, the decree lists what was to be considered as a weapon: "bastone, pugnale, spade di legno lunghe, e grosse, . . . bastoni, e bacchette grosse in modo che siano atte à far offesa" (fol. 78 r),[28] and mentions (but does not define) defensive weapons as well.

Provisions were added regarding the punishment to be administered to those wearing masks and disguises who "parli dishonestamente" or "faccia atto dishonesto ove siano Donne" (fol. 79 r);[29] "percotesse con pugno, ò bastone, ò altrimenti senza effusione di sangue alcuno si mascherato come mascherato" (fols. 79 r–v)[30] (where it is noteworthy that a rule was devised for those situations in which the victim was singled out because of the mask he was wearing); "corresse in qualche casa, ò bottegha per pigliar Armi da offender altri" (fol. 79 v);[31] or, finally, "toranno la robba altrui, ò per forza, ò in altro modo" (fol. 80 r).[32] Francesco Maria allowed his subjects to enjoy a period of celebration and revelries at *carnevale*, yet the provisions of his decree convey a sense of (or potential for) lawlessness that the central authority tried to prevent and curb.

One more category of potential law-breakers is mentioned: people who took to wearing a mask or a disguise in order to perpetrate a crime. Here two possibilities stood out: those who transgressed the law on behalf of somebody else, and those who did so for their own good, so to speak. The punishment is much harsher in the first case, whether or not a crime was carried out:

> E scuoprendosi alcuno, che fosse immascherato per Ammazzar altri, ò per fare qualche altro effetto in qualsivoglia modo ad istanza d'altrui, ancorche non sia proceduto d'atto alcuno, è di volontà, et ordine nostro, che cada nella pena della vita, et della confiscazione de beni, ma che trovandosi semplicemente immascherato per offender altri, e che non procedesse ad altro Atto, habbia la pena d'essersi tagliata una mano, et di scudi cento. (fol. 80 r)[33]

Clearly, the possibility that masks and disguises might be used towards criminal ends loomed large in Francesco Maria's mind. Additionally, although these masks were not necessarily those worn on stage by professional actors and actresses, one can sense that *maschere* in general had profoundly unsettling implications for the viewers, since they effectively prevented the latter from recognizing the men or women wearing them, off and on stage, and changed the wearer's identity altogether.

One passage in this decree helps convey a vivid impression of what it must have been like being in Pesaro during *carnevale*. After sunset, the town was very dark. In the streets, strange figures in outlandish clothes were roaming. Insecurity and fear must have coexisted with the excitement for the festivities under way. Consequently Francesco Maria included some provisions to make the streets safer for the population, or at least, better lit:

> Et passata mezz'ora di notte determiniamo, che non si habbia da porsi Maschera al uscio fuori di Casa, sotto pena di scudi cento d'applicarsi come di sopra, ci contentiamo però, che questi tali entrati, che saranno nelle Case, et anco sopra le feste possono mettere, e tenere la Maschera al volto, sebene fosse di notte; et Sonata la Campana delle tre hore, non vuole, che sia lecito ad alcuno in Mascherato ancorche ei non habbia la Maschera ò barba posticcia alla faccia d'andare à torno se non con lume, non andando però in più di 4 ò 5 sotto un lume, et avertendo che le lanterne, siano tali, che la luce si vegga almeno da 3 bande sotto pena di scudi 25: d'applicarsi come sopra et di 3 tratti di corda. (fol. 78 v)[34]

The duke did not impose a curfew on his subjects; however, he limited their permission to wear masks soon after sunset to enclosed spaces, that is, to dwellings and places where a celebration was under way. Once again, provisions regarding temporal and spatial boundaries were of paramount importance and clearly spelled out. Moreover, the necessity of avoiding ambushes under the cover of darkness and with the help of disguises dictated the rule regarding the number of people sharing a *lume* in the street and the quality of the source of light itself. It is worth noting, additionally, that the decree is very specific as to the difference between being "Mascherato" and having a "Maschera ò barba posticcia" — a difference that is quite obscure to twenty-first-century readers, at least with respect to being *mascherato* versus wearing a *maschera*.

In keeping with the accurate nature of this law, a definition of "persona Immascherata" is offered in closing:

> Con dichiarazione più intelligenda di chi fusse poco avertito, che sempre nel presente Bando si è fatto menzione di persona Immascherata s'intenda per tal nome ciascuno che fosse travestito, ò havesse coperto il volto in altra guisa, che con maschera, ò havesse barba posticcia. (fol. 81 r)[35]

"Masking oneself" involved either wearing a disguise in the form of clothes, or covering one's face with something other than a mask (for example, as little as a false beard), or both.[36] The fact that false beards are mentioned, as well as the aforementioned stipulation regarding the punishment to mete out to those guilty of "atto dishonesto" where women were present, seem to circumscribe the practice of wearing a mask or a disguise largely to men — unless of course women were wont to cross-dress and assume male disguises, a practice which is not mentioned in these documents and on which therefore I must reserve judgment. It is worth pointing out, however, that the decree opens with a non-gender-specific term to describe those at Pesaro who were given permission to wear masks: the phrase "tutte le persone" (fol. 77 v) [all the people] seems to encompass all ages, social strata, and genders.

One could argue that the 1576 decree struck a balance among the limits it set to *carnevale* activities, the punishments it imposed on those who trespassed them, and the freedom it allowed the della Rovere subjects. In fact, Francesco Maria even included a clause protecting those wearing masks and disguises from those who did not. After assigning a punishment to those guilty of verbally abusing others, whether wearing a disguise or not, the decree adds:

> nella qual pena [a fine of 25 *scudi* and three lashes] incorreranno anco quelli Smascherati, che in alcuno di suddetti modi offenderanno quelli, che siano mascherati; intendendo noi, che caschi nella medesima pena, chi cavato haverà, ò vero tentarà di cavare dal Viso la Maschera, ò altro coprimento, ò che entrarà in Scole, ò Botteghe, ò Case d'altri per molestarli, ò ingiuriarli in alcuno de modi sudetti. (fol. 79 r)[37]

Anybody wearing a mask or disguise was considered to be untouchable. Hence, nobody was authorized to rip such a covering off somebody else's "face." It would become an integral part of the disguised person's clothing, indeed even of his identity. Consequently, this clause in Francesco Maria's 1576 legislation on *carnevale* festivities points to a quasi-sacred element embedded in the act of wearing a disguise. This aspect, along with the already mentioned uncertainty regarding a masked person's identity, arguably influenced the atmosphere of the entire *carnevale* celebrations, at court and among the population.

These laws manifest the ruler's desire to subsume the *carnevale* celebrations under his power — a desire that, as already pointed out, pervaded all of Western Europe during the last decades of the sixteenth and the early seventeenth centuries. The aspiration to regulate all aspects of the subjects' life, whether successful or not, is indeed quite different from the attempt to co-opt festivities intrinsically popular in origin, if not in nature,[38] to convey a political message. In other words, this legislation betrays the tension between transgressive and the regulatory impulses, much like current Louisiana laws (J. Roach, *Cities of the Dead*, 269–81). Given that the repression of the Urbino uprising took place during the period normally reserved for *carnevale* entertainment, the remarkable difference between 1573 and 1574 must have been evident to everybody at Pesaro.[39] Yet a univocal, court-dominated interpretation of these events seems reductive and uni-dimensional. As Emmanuel Le Roy Ladurie has successfully argued, *carnevale* cannot simply be viewed as a series of religious, fertility-enhancing, or agricultural festivities; "they also had to do with the changing of seasons. They were specifically connected to the approach of the end of winter, a crucial moment for a society which was still semi-agricultural and thus nature-oriented" (*Carnival in Romans*, 309). If *carnevale* marks the end of the harsh winter season, and the beginning of spring renewal, it is possible that in 1574 the Pesaro population understood these festivities as a (privileged? traditional?) means to sweep away the gory memories of the repression of the Urbino uprising. The sins of the past, including those political in nature, were purged by the revelries of *carnevale*; a new, more harmonious season was going to begin. In this respect, the della Rovere subjects were unlikely to separate courtly influence and popular festivities. In short, *carnevale* was many things at the same time. Thus the *Aminta* performance of 1574 was endowed with a transitional nature, caught between a popular, spontaneous festivity and a regulated, choreographed event, both from the historical and the performative points of view.

3. 1574 Reconstructed, 1785–1986

Before we go on to reconstruct these performed events, it is useful to glance at previous interpretations, to measure the distance between past goals and present endeavor. The fact that *Aminta* had been performed at Pesaro in 1574 was known at least since Serassi's biography of Tasso, printed in 1785. Too many elements conspired to make this event an important point in the development of the popularity of Tasso's pastoral: the author's frequentation of the della Rovere court during his adolescence; the dynastic link between the della Rovere and the Este families, through the marriage of Lucrezia to Francesco Maria; the consecration of *Aminta* as a canonical text by a performance at the court's request so soon after its reputed *première*; and the social *cachet* bestowed on the pastoral by the same request.

Serassi's reconstruction is, as is to be expected, very descriptive yet devoid of any supporting evidence:

> Madama la Principessa d'Urbino, che non avea potuto essere presente alla recita dell'*Aminta* [at Ferrara], sentendo gli encomi e le meraviglie, che se ne facevano, venne in gran desiderio di vedere questa Favola, e di sentirla dalla bocca stessa dell'autore; e perciò lo fece graziosamente invitare a Pesaro, pregando il Duca Alfonso suo fratello a volerglielo concedere per qualche mese. Il Duca ne fu ben contento, e molto più il Tasso, il quale oltre al rivedere una corte, ov'era stato così ben accolto nella sua fanciullezza, desiderava infinitamente di servire e di compiacere una Principessa tanto da lui stimata, alla cui affettuosa protezione si conosceva interamente debitore della grazia, e del grado ch'egli godeva alla Corte di Ferrara. Venne dunque a Pesaro sul principio dell'estate del detto anno 1573, e vi ricevette infinite cortesie, così dai giovani Principi, come dal Duca Guidubaldo, già protettore tanto amorevole del padre, e suo. Quivi dopo l'aver fatto sentire la sua bella Pastorale, con quel diletto di chi la intese, che ben si può immaginare; si pose anche a leggere i Canti già compiuti del suo Poema, che a quella nobile Corte parvero una cosa molto singolare. (Serassi, *La vita di Torquato Tasso*, 177–78)[40]

The most notable aspect of this reconstruction of the events lies in the assertion that *Aminta* was read, and not performed, at Pesaro. Moreover, since Serassi posits a March 1573 opening for the pastoral, in order to stress its quick, indeed phenomenal popularity, he postulates that Tasso went to the della Rovere court during the summer of that same year, a date which Solerti's more fact-based reconstruction rules out.

In general, various elements emerge from this passage that are common to the entire historiography on this episode, at least until Solerti's work. First and foremost, the emphasis and *telos* of Tasso's career and indeed of his entire life reside in the *Gerusalemme liberata*, "il suo Poema." Hence, *Aminta* constitutes only a *divertissement*, a side interest both for the author and for his audience: in the latter, the pastoral elicits "diletto," yet the epic seems "molto singolare," thus stressing the idea that Tasso's originality and outstanding claim to fame lies in the *Liberata*. Secondly, the relationship between the poet and his patrons is presented in such a way to underline the total dependence of the former on the latter from a practical standpoint, but utterly ignores any consequence for Tasso's artistic production or for any staging of *Aminta*. Further, Serassi does not question why Lucrezia might have desired to hear Tasso's pastoral; in his opinion, her request to Alfonso is clearly and solely motivated by the reports coming from

Ferrara vis-à-vis the text of the pastoral, not its staging. In so doing, Serassi once again demonstrates his bias favoring *Aminta* as a text over its performance. He therefore has to postulate an exquisite and refined literary taste at Ferrara, enabling the Este court to recognize a masterpiece *in abstracto*, not as performed on stage. Moreover, the reconstruction of this relationship clearly underscores Tasso's devotion and thankfulness, as well as both courts' generosity and benevolence towards him. Serassi is obviously preparing his readers for the momentous change in Tasso's attitude and personality that will be the cause of much suffering in his later days. For the sake of dramatic effect, he postulates a state of utter accord (reflected in the text of *Aminta* itself, which he calls a "Favola," a fable or fairy tale) that would subsequently come to an abrupt end.[41] Overall, Serassi's description of this episode focuses on Tasso's popularity and his relationship with the della Rovere court, while leaving *Aminta* completely out of the limelight.

A similar approach is present in a slender pamphlet published at Pesaro in 1843, containing the speeches given on the subject of *Bernardo e Torquato Tasso alla corte di Guidubaldo II e Francesco Maria II Duchi d'Urbino* by noblemen and members of the local "Accademia dei Nascenti." Count Luigi Palmaroli writes:

> Lucrezia d'Este moglie a Francesco Maria Duca d'Urbino, che era accesa della brama e di conoscere quella poesia pastorale, e di rivederne l'autore supplicò al fratello Alfonso che volesse far pago questo suo desiderio. Fu condisceso all'onesta domanda della buona Duchessa, e Torquato fu lieto di rivedere quei luoghi, che avevan fatta sì contenta la sua prima giovinezza, e che gli ricordavano tante care memorie dell'affettuoso suo Genitore, e della splendida amorevole cortesia usata verso di loro dal generoso liberalissimo animo del Duca Guidubaldo. (*Bernardo e Torquato Tasso*, 20)[42]

Marquis Ciro Antaldi continues:

> Ma se tutta la Corte onorò con sinceri festeggiamenti l'arrivo di quell'insigne Poeta, sopra tutti ne mostrarono gioja indicibile e il Principe Francesco Maria, che riabbracciava il suo diletto compagno di studi, e la Duchessa Lucrezia, che rivedeva il suo tenero amico. La fama dell'*Aminta* avea precorso Torquato alla corte di Urbino; e quivi eran venuti appunto per ascoltarlo uomini eccellenti per merito e per dottrina. Con tutto ciò la rappresentazione dell'*Aminta* superò i desiderii, compì le speranze di tutti. Nulla si era ancora sentito di più grande ed ammirabile: e tanto fu il giubbilo [*sic*] e lo stupore onde ciascuno fu compreso, che non vi ebbe più ritegno agli applausi, ai donativi e ad ogni onorevole significazione, di cui fu ricolmato il giovine poeta. Talché quel giorno di tanta gioia mi piace di chiamarlo il più lieto della sua vita, e l'immagine vera di quel solennissimo nel quale dovea cingersi in Campidoglio del poetico alloro, preparatogli dalle onorevoli industrie della più fida amicizia, e che la sorte contro di lui sì crudele ed avvelenata gl'impedì di poter conseguire. (21–22)[43]

The intent to glorify the only town in Italy to recognize Tasso's talent during his lifetime and to reward him accordingly emerges forcefully from the last lines of this passage. However, the rest is virtually indistinguishable from Serassi's. Torquato's pastoral was so well received at Ferrara, at the time of its *première*, that Lucrezia asked her brother to "lend" her the poet for a short while; Alfonso agreed; Tasso arrived at Pesaro, where old friends welcomed him. Antaldi's passage nevertheless mentions a "rappresentazione" of *Aminta*; although he does not dwell on any details, the term seems to indicate that the text was performed, not simply read, as in Serassi's description. The pamphlet does not, however, refer to any source for this assertion; nor can we exclude that "rappresentazione" could designate a reading of the text on the part of various people, rather than a full-blown staging. This interpretation is supported by two verbs used in this passage: learned people convened to "ascoltar" *Aminta*; and the play was "sentito" rather than "seen" by them. The audience for this performance of *Aminta* resembles a committee convened to judge a student at an examination rather than a group of people gathered to enjoy a theatrical entertainment. This descriptive emphasis thus clashes somewhat with the conclusion of Antaldi's passage, which emphasizes the complete and utter good will of the della Rovere court towards Tasso. In any case, it is obvious that for Serassi and Antaldi the staging of Tasso's pastoral is utterly devoid of any interest when it comes to its theatrical elements. They can perceive this event only in light of Torquato's access to fame — a blatant anachronism, since for the Este and perhaps the della Rovere court *Aminta*'s appeal was linked to the courtly *ambiance* (as Godard has suggested in "La Première représentation de l'*Aminta*") and to the glorification of its author's patrons, not to Tasso's own fame.

It appears that this critical stance went unchallenged until 1888; further, it seems to have gathered critical currency in other publications. For example, Tasso's biographical sketch included in an 1844 edition of *Gerusalemme liberata* states that "lo straordinario successo delle rappresentazioni dell'*Aminta* invogliò la sorella d'Alfonso, Lucrezia d'Este, di aver Torquato a Pesaro per farla ivi ripetere. Il Tasso partì a questo oggetto per la Corte d'Urbino, ed ivi fu ricevuto con tutta festa dal vecchio duca Guidubaldo che lo aveva fatto educare da giovinetto col figlio suo."[44] This passage is notable only for the hyperbole regarding the multiple stagings of *Aminta* at Ferrara, which contributed to spreading the fame of the play to the della Rovere domain. An anonymous pamphlet printed at Pesaro in 1881 goes as far as to say that "il giovane poeta ... diresse in scena la sua bella favola pastorale, l'*Aminta*, che da vari gentiluomini e dame della corte fu graziosamente recitata" (*L'imperiale castello*, 15).[45] The author asserts that Tasso directed the play, and that noblemen and women acted in it. Again in 1888, when Angelo Solerti reprinted and enlarged Giuseppe Campori's work on Alfonso d'Este's siblings, he did not modify the part regarding Lucrezia; indeed this study does not even mention the *carnevale* entertainment of 1574.

However, that same year, 1888, Alfredo Saviotti published in *Giornale storico della letteratura italiana* a letter that he had found at the Biblioteca Oliveriana at Pesaro. This letter had been written on 28 February 1574 by Tiberio Almerici to his cousin Virginio, then at Padua, with the specific aim of relating the festivities that had taken place in their hometown during the *carnevale* season. It is this same letter that constitutes the main document upon which the present reconstruction is based (cf. above, n. 39).

When Solerti finally published his monumental biography of Tasso, in 1895, he included the recently discovered evidence. He accepted Saviotti's aforementioned idea that the *carnevale* entertainment of 1574 was designed to be especially lavish in order to raise spirits at Pesaro after the Urbino uprising; and repeated the same undocumented (though to a certain extent understandable) depiction of Tasso's welcome at the della Rovere court (*Vita di Torquato Tasso*, 1: 187–88). As far as the performance itself was concerned, Solerti simply gave a short synopsis of Almerici's letter, while dwelling a little longer on the issues of how many choruses were originally part of the pastoral, a matter more appropriately left to the introduction or the footnotes of a critical edition of the text. While one of Solerti's avowed targets was Serassi's biography,[46] his own stance was far from being devoid of similar biases,[47] which render his work quite akin in inspiration to Serassi's.

Since the publication of Solerti's biography, little attention has been devoted to Tasso's life. No comparable work has been published to date, even despite the celebrations for the fourth centenary of Tasso's death in 1995.[48] Whatever little interest the 1574 performance of *Aminta* has elicited, it has been confined to the realm of Pesaro local history or della Rovere family research. Even so, the most recent references to this event are still deeply influenced by previous studies. They nevertheless pick up an element that pertains specifically to the performance and that originally appeared in the anonymous 1881 pamphlet. Giovanna Solari mentions in passing that Tasso's debt towards Lucrezia d'Este was increased by the fact that "a lei Torquato doveva la rappresentazione dell'*Aminta* all'Imperiale" (*22 storie*, 335).[49] Nando Cecini is more specific: "Su espresso invito di Lucrezia, Tasso torna a Pesaro nel carnevale del 1574 per rappresentare, dopo la prima di Ferrara, l'*Aminta*. . . . L'*Aminta* fu recitata nella villa Imperiale da un gruppo di attori dilettanti con la 'regia' dello stesso Tasso, che introdusse i cori tra i vari atti" ("Cultura e letteratura," 343).[50] Both authors, without supporting their assertion, place the performance at an *extra mœnia* villa belonging to the della Rovere family. Cecini (like the anonymous 1881 pamphlet writer) goes as far as to attribute the direction of the play to Tasso, thus justifying the introduction of the choruses in the text. What do contemporary documents assert about these events? It is time to turn to them, and attempt a new reconstruction of the 1574 *carnevale* events.

4. *Aminta* at Pesaro, *Carnevale* 1574

Perhaps the most noteworthy element that all these aforementioned reconstructions have in common is an utter disregard for the preparations leading to the performance, and for the performance itself. Serassi, Solerti, and Antaldi are interested in underscoring the courtly audience's reaction to the reading or staging of Tasso's pastoral. This aspect is certainly very important; indeed, most documents relating to sixteenth- and seventeenth-century performances stress it above many other elements, and *Aminta* is no exception. Nevertheless, other details find room in contemporary documents; it is to those that are extant that we must turn in order to reconstruct these events.

At times, contemporary documents yield details that clash with the imaginative reconstructions offered in later times. For example, Solerti cites a passage from a letter addressed by Lucrezia d'Este to her brother Alfonso, inviting him to Pesaro for the 1574 *carnevale*, when Guidubaldo had arranged some theatrical entertainment: the latter "li farebbe a codesti sudditi recitar alcune comedie che a suo credere non le dispiaceranno, poi che essi in questa sorte di rappresentazione sogliono farle assai bene" (*Vita di Torquato Tasso*, 1: 187).[51] The theatrical entertainment had already been organized; Lucrezia extended an invitation to her brother to come and participate in the festivities. Thus this passage can hardly be taken as an indication that Lucrezia had heard wonders about the *première* of Tasso's pastoral at Ferrara, or that she was asking permission to "borrow" Tasso from the Este court — indeed, *Aminta* is not mentioned in this excerpt.

Similarly, Cecini uses an excerpt from a 1585 letter of Tasso's to Lucrezia as proof that she had invited him to Pesaro: Torquato "in una lettera . . . alla principessa ricorda '[. . .] chiamandomi in Pesaro, giunse favore a favore, cortesia a cortesia, e liberalità a liberalità, donandomi e facendomi donare, onorandomi e facendomi onorare'" ("Cultura e letteratura," 343).[52] Again, there is no reference to *Aminta* or to any of Tasso's works. The emphasis is rather on the honor Lucrezia bestowed on the courtier during his visit to Pesaro, and the quotation offered by Cecini is nothing more than an example among many of Tasso's masterful use of the courtly rhetoric of thankfulness and praise for his betters. Additionally, by 1585 Tasso had already spent six years captive in the Ospedale di Sant'Anna in Ferrara. Most of his correspondence from this period of imprisonment had a twofold goal: first, reminding his patrons and friends of their past familiarity; second, on the strength of these memories, pleading for his freedom. It is entirely possible, then, that the verb "chiamare" that Tasso uses is nothing more than a hyperbole, utilized to remind the princess of past contacts and of her benevolence towards the imprisoned courtier. In sum, it seems ill advised to take a citation from this period of Tasso's life at face value.

To go back to Lucrezia's letter to Alfonso: the short passage cited by Solerti is noteworthy because it mentions the "actors" who will perform the plays on stage:

Lucrezia refers to some "sudditi" of the della Rovere duke, who are accustomed ("sogliono") to playing comedies. The expression is somewhat ambiguous, since we cannot gather from it whether Lucrezia alluded to amateurs who occasionally performed on stage, or to professionals linked to the court by a temporary or permanent contract.[53] In either case, Lucrezia highlighted the performers' ability on the stage, possibly to allay Alfonso's fears that the quality of the entertainment might be substantially lower than at Ferrara, where professional troupes performed regularly.[54] Though Lucrezia's tone might betray her dislike for her new residence, in 1574 Pesaro and the whole della Rovere domain could boast a long tradition of theatrical stagings. Specifically, the first courtly entertainment at Pesaro seems to have taken place in 1475, for the wedding of Costanzo Sforza and Camilla of Aragon; soon afterwards permanent theaters were built, and the duchy produced some of the most distinguished perspective scholars and stage machinery builders of the late sixteenth and seventeenth centuries.[55] The court, as will become apparent, often exploited the talents of architects who had been retained for civil or military projects to set the stage for theatrical entertainments.

Again, Lucrezia's letter to her brother makes no mention of Tasso or of *Aminta*. It is altogether possible that Lucrezia or the della Rovere desired to surprise Alfonso and the other Este guests. On the other hand, perhaps the princess was not involved in the preparations for the festivities. Last, the text(s) to be performed might not have been selected yet. The last hypothesis would be particularly credible if it could be conclusively proven that a professional troupe performed upon this occasion.

Unfortunately, this is one of various issues that must remain undecided, unless new archival evidence is found. The only extant description of the *carnevale* festivities of 1574 is the aforementioned letter that Tiberio Almerici wrote soon after the events to his cousin Virginio. Although this dearth of documentation is lamentable, Almerici's letter is quite relevant to any reconstructive effort. On the one hand, it expresses the opinion and point of view of a member of the nobility of Pesaro; thus it reflects the prevailing taste in town, and it excludes the possibility of basic misunderstanding of the occasion and of the events.[56] On the other hand, it does not present the "official" courtly perspective and intended interpretation of the festivities.

During the *carnevale* season, Almerici explains to his cousin, "si son fatte molte feste, e si son veduti tre spettacoli publici che furono una Sbarra una Comedia et una Egloga" (Saviotti, "Torquato Tasso e le feste," 409; MS oliveriano 390, fol. 92 r).[57] Four elements emerge from this statement. First, there was a clear distinction made between "feste," which in all likelihood were private parties, and "spettacoli publici," which implied a larger audience (although not necessarily a "universal" one comprising all the town dwellers, disregarding their social origin). Moreover, the discrepancy in relevance between the two types of entertainment is underscored by their numerical disparity ("many" versus "three"). Further, the already mentioned public character set the staged entertainment apart from the rest because it could potentially be endowed with additional meanings. Last, Tiberio distinguished the three staged events on the basis of what we could call "genre": there were a tournament, a comedy and a pastoral play. Clearly, the writer and his addressee shared a basic understanding of the differences in staging and in representational relevance among these three genres; identifying them by name was sufficient. This does not allow us to perceive the import of this distinction; it could be derived from the critical, literary tradition, or it could leave understood many other details referring more specifically to their stagings.

It is the knightly tournament that elicits the most attention from Tiberio.[58] It took place on *carnevale* Thursday, in the evening, in the main courtyard of the ducal palace:

> fù bellissimo vedere nel Cortile grande della Corte, loco attissimo à questi spettacoli, la frequenza del populo, la bellezza delle Dame alle finestre e ne i Palchi, il Passeggiare de' Giovani nobili e ben vestiti nello steccato, poi che la nobiltà de' Giovani e d'altri Gentilhuomini era disposta in mille officii ch'appartengono a tal sorte di Cavalleria. (Saviotti, "Torquato Tasso e le feste," 410; MS oliveriano 390, fol. 92 v)[59]

The first spectacle was a show of the audience unto itself: the number of people gathered together, the display of beautiful women, and the bustling activity of well-dressed, handsome young noblemen framed the *locus* of the tournament. The latter took place in an official space, that is, in the main courtyard of the ducal palace, an area that was only partially open and public. It was, indeed, an extension of the building where the duke and his family and court lived; hence it was clearly identified with the political power ruling over the town. Moreover, although structurally this area was outdoors, it was enclosed by at least three (if not four) palace wings, thus furthering the impression of control and domination on the part of the ruling family.[60] The people who comprised the audience for this event were of various social and economic backgrounds, as warranted by Almerici's distinction between "populo" on the one hand and "Dame," "Giovani nobili," and "Gentilhuomini" on the other.

Tiberio and his cousin Virginio clearly belonged to the noble classes; this may be the reason why the letter devotes so much attention to describing the tournament. Over two manuscript pages are occupied by a description of the entrance of the Pesaro knights and of their opponents from Rimini in the designed tournament area (Saviotti, "Torquato Tasso e le feste," 410–11; MS oliveriano 390, fols. 92 v–93 v). Additionally, towards the end of the letter, Tiberio goes back to the tournament to describe some of the emblems carried by the knights (Saviotti, "Torquato Tasso e le feste," 415–16; MS oliveriano 390, fols. 96 r–v). Almerici diplomatically reserved judgment on the performances of each individual knight;

his overall impressions was evidently positive: "E così quella sera con questo torneo si finì il Giovedì grasso che durò fin'a cinque hore se non più, et in verità è stata una delle belle cose che si siano vedute da parecchi anni in qua in questi nostri Paesi, nè io hebbi mai speranza di tal riuscita" (Saviotti, "Torquato Tasso e le feste," 411; MS oliveriano 390, fol. 93 v).[61] Almerici's tone verges upon the triumphant; the tournament was in his opinion a complete success for the participant and for the glorification of the town, the court and the ruling duke; indeed, it surpassed all his expectations.

A few days later, on *Lundi Gras*, the "Comedia" took place: it was *Erofilomachia* by Sforza Oddi:

> fu recitata da nostri di Pesaro una comedia detta *Erofilomachia* cio è Duello d'Amore e d'amicitia che è opera d'uno messer Sforza d'Oddo Dottore Perusino, et è comedia molto affettuosa et è riuscita assai felicemente secondo il solito modo di recitarsi che si fa in questo nostri Paesi, ancora che per dire il vero sia stata assai lunga e conseguentemente tediosa per lo generale, contenendo ella molti soliloquii che se bene riescono piacevoli à leggergli, non riescono però tali in scena. (Saviotti, "Torquato Tasso e le feste," 411–12; MS oliveriano 390, fols. 93 v–94 r)[62]

This passage shows once again that Almerici was knowledgeable enough to be able to pass a judgment both on the text and on the performance. In his opinion, *Erofilomachia*, a 1572 work, was better read out loud than performed on stage, due to its numerous monologues. Furthermore, Tiberio knew the local, customary "modo di recitarsi," and judged the performance positively according to his expectations. Lastly, the passage indicates that the performers were local. The cryptic phrase "nostri di Pesaro" is better explained later in the letter, when Almerici wrote: "Il Cavaglier Claudio nostro ancora qui ha fatto di Vita, e per la parte che rappresentava ha fatto assai convenientemente bene" (Saviotti, "Torquato Tasso e le feste," 412; MS oliveriano 390, fol. 94 r).[63] "Ours from Pesaro" performing Oddi's text were noblemen (or women: the fact that the grammatical gender of "nostri" is masculine does not necessarily mean that women were excluded), as can be gathered by the presence on stage of Claudio Almerici, a relative of both Tiberio and Virginio. For this performance, then, the most likely hypothesis is that the actors engaged in it were non-professional people, who nevertheless were somehow organized in a semi-permanent group (perhaps an *accademia*) in order to perform on stage. It is interesting that the same Claudio Almerici who acted in *Erofilomachia* had taken an active part during the knightly tournament: he was the last Pesaro knight to enter the court on *carnevale* Thursday (Saviotti, "Torquato Tasso e le feste," 411; MS oliveriano 390, fol. 93 r). We can conclude that it was just as dignified for a young nobleman to take part in tournaments as to perform a play on stage.

Tiberio mentions two more details regarding the staging of *Erofilomachia* that are worth underscoring. He praises the setting of the play, "il bellissimo apparato ch'è stato per la lunghezza della sala" (Saviotti, "Torquato Tasso e le feste," 412; MS oliveriano 390, fol. 94 r),[64] in such a way that makes us surmise the lavishness of the production (at least compared to the customs for that town in that period) as well as the fact that there was a specific indoor place at Pesaro dedicated (perhaps not solely, but plainly) to the performing of plays. Almerici referred to "la sala" in implicit terms; he seemed to take for granted that his cousin, familiar with Pesaro customs and places, would understand to which "hall" he was referring.

Secondarily, Tiberio alludes to two *intermedii* that were performed along with *Erofilomachia*. In his opinion, these contributed greatly to the audience's enjoyment. These shorter performances were remarkably different from the main show that was taking place on stage, for a number of reasons:

> Questa comedia poi . . . è stata adornata con due intermedii di Moresca l'uno de' quali è stato il rapimento delle Sabine gia rappresentato altre volte in scena in Pesaro, forse da sedici anni circa, e ve ne dovete ricordare, il qual'intermedio è comparso assai bene, e si può dire che sia riuscito come novo a' spettatori poi ch'è tanto tempo che fu fattò [*sic*].
>
> L'altro intermedio è stato L'arco de' Leali Amanti e della Camera Incantata, dell'Historia d'Amadis di Gaula e d'Oriana, et è comparso benissimo et ancora che quegli che non sapevano l'historia non ne godessero così bene ha però fatta bellissima vista poichè c'intervenivano Cavaglieri e Dame, et incantaggioni, et Combattimenti et altre cose che mirabilmente compariscono in Scena. (Saviotti, "Torquato Tasso e le feste," 412; MS oliveriano 390, fol. 94 r)[65]

Both *intermedi* are qualified as "di Moresca." This definition might imply that a *moresca* dance took place in it; more simply, this phrase could simply suggest that dancing and music were part of the performance. The somewhat violent content of the events staged during these *intermedi* is consistent with the history of this genre, "la regina delle danze armate" (G. Tani, "Moresca," in *Enciclopedia dello spettacolo*, 7: 834–36, here 834) [the queen of fight dances], whose original meaning was to portray a "battaglia tra mori e cristiani" (G. Attolini, *Teatro e spettacolo nel Rinascimento* [Bari: Laterza, 1988], 26) [fight between Moors and Christians].[66] It is evident that the *intermedi* performers are not the same as the comedy ones. Almerici pointed out that knights and ladies took part in them, thus heightening the interest for the convened audience.

Additionally, from the comments regarding the *intermedio* about the rape of the Sabine women, we understand that novelty played an important part in its success. It is a characteristic that will accompany this kind of staged performance well into the seventeenth century. *Intermedi* or *intermezzi* were designed to astonish the audience, to promote comic relief during tragedies or tragicomedies, and to provide another outlet for the imagination and resourcefulness of the artists involved in the staging, as well as for the desire to impress the audience that marks courtly entertainment in this period. The rape of the Sabine women *intermezzo*, although not known at Pesaro, entertained the audience all the same since the latter had presumably forgotten it, "poi ch'è tanto tempo che fu fattò [*sic*]." Sixteenth-century audiences, then, did not practice the unspoken twenty-first-century rule which requires them "to respect the apparent ignorance of the characters as to what will come of them and to wait in felt suspense to see how matters will unfold" (E. Goffman, *Frame Analysis* [Boston: Northeastern University Press, 1986], 137). If onlookers were to be surprised, amazed or left wondering vis-à-vis the outcome of the staged events, the latter must be new, never performed before, or at least not for a long while, as was the case for the first *intermezzo* at Pesaro.

From Almerici's brief comments on the second *intermezzo*, one gathers another essential quality: it was a learned *genre*, one that presupposed some modicum of knowledge on the part of its audience of the events that formed the plot that was being performed (apparently, *Amadis* was still popular). People who were not familiar with the story, Tiberio says, could not enjoy it as much as those who were. However, it was still entertaining, due to the numerous marvels that appeared on stage — and the phrase "mirabilmente compariscono" indicates the intended effect of stage machinery and other props that were in all likelihood already in use at this time. Almerici's remark seems to imply that these *intermezzi* were very different from the comedy they accompanied, from the point of view of the staging and of their theatrical nature. Quite possibly, these *intermezzi* did not include any dialogue, and their symbolism was conveyed by bodily movements (dance, and otherwise). Indeed, they could have been different from later *intermezzi*, which still relied heavily on symbolic meanings and stage machinery, but which included words, although mostly in sung (not spoken) form.[67]

The third and last spectacle in the 1574 *carnevale* season at Pesaro was Tasso's *Aminta*, which actually took place after the onset of Lent, on "Giovedì p[rim]o di quaresima" (Saviotti, "Torquato Tasso e le feste," 413; MS oliveriano 390, fol. 94 r) [the first Lenten Thursday]. This chronological indication is interesting, as it suggests that religious time frames could be ignored and superseded by the lay authorities. As the 1576 laws indicate, *carnevale* was no longer perceived simply as a time of popular misrule allowed by the Catholic Church before the beginning of Lent. Rather, it constituted a concession on the part of the proto-absolutist town ruler, who could then mark its chronological boundaries in any way he saw fit.

Similarly, as we saw, the spatial realm of Pesaro had been circumscribed (and proclaimed) by the completion of new walls. According to Richard Trexler, "The building of the city walls marked an important turning point in the development of worshipful space, for it manifested an impulse toward common experience and protection . . . The walls themselves became the first ritual edifice of the new commune" (*Public Life in Renaissance Florence*, 47). The time-space continuum, therefore, was entirely (and visibly) in the hands of the ruler; this, at least, was the message that the latter wanted to spread within his domain and to his peers abroad. The reader will recall that according to Le Roy Ladurie, carnivals traditionally ended with what he calls "formalities" that signal the return of a "normal" (i.e., repressive) way of life. As the last "public show" offered for the 1574 *carnevale*, the *Aminta* performance fits seamlessly with the twin goal of a proto-absolutist ruler like Guidubaldo: proclaiming the *status quo*, and reasserting his power in an idealized fashion.

It is interesting to underscore that, differently from the Florentine habits so thoroughly researched and eloquently illustrated by Trexler (*Public Life in Renaissance Florence*, esp. 338–40 and 354–61), Guidubaldo did not choose to proclaim the recovered *status quo* with a procession, religious or lay. As Randolph Starn and Loren Partridge have observed, "one could never tell how, or whether, to draw clear lines between broad jokes, serious protest, and grudging deference" (*Arts of Power: Three Halls of State in Italy, 1300–1600* [Berkeley: University of California Press, 1992], 161) during a parade, a procession, or a *trionfo*. Many reasons might have influenced this courtly decision. By bestowing on his subjects the right to celebrate the *carnevale*, Guidubaldo reasserted his primacy and proto-absolutist power. Further, as Stallybrass and White have remarked, "for long periods carnival may be a stable and cyclical ritual with no noticeable politically transformative effects but . . ., given the presence of sharpened political antagonism, it may often act as *catalyst* and *site of actual and symbolic struggle*" (*The Politics and Poetics of Transgression*, 14; emphases in original). Lastly, and perhaps most importantly, the city (particularly its nobility) celebrated by stylizing battle (the tournament), extolling the power of love and concord (*Erofilomachia*), and showing an idealized, normative rendition of courtly life (*Aminta*).

Almerici was not as specific in his description of the *Aminta* staging as with the tournament. Nevertheless, he mentioned two crucial elements. First, he wrote that the pastoral was performed "da alcuni Giovini d'Urbino" (Saviotti, "Torquato Tasso e le feste," 413; MS oliveriano 390, fol. 94 r) [a few young people from Urbino]. This marks a notable difference with respect to both the tournament and the staging of *Erofilomachia*; *Aminta* was performed not by local amateurs but by young men (and possibly women) coming from elsewhere in the duchy. This phrase deserves close analysis. The usage of the masculine plural adjectival form ("giovani") does not imply the exclusion of actresses, because the masculine plural in Italian subsumes both grammatical genders. We must keep in mind that in the pastoral genre it was possible for young men to perform female parts, as witnessed by the 1584 letter cited in chapter 1 regarding the preparations for Guarini's *Pastor fido* in the Garfagnana region of Tuscany. However, in the pastoral genre it was not uncommon for *commedia dell'arte* actresses to perform male parts. Taviani has pointed out that Isabella Andreini was well known for her embodying of Aminta himself, not of Silvia as often reported ("Bella d'Asia," 7).[68] By 1574, women were no strangers to professional Italian troupes: indeed, their presence was one of the defining elements of traveling *commedia dell'arte* companies (Pieri, *La nascita del teatro moderno*, 200).[69] Further, "in the context of the court, women (but not professional actresses) played female parts in the erudite comedies" (Günsberg, *Gender and the Italian Stage*, 59). Thus it is possible that these "giovani" were members of an *accademia*; or this may be the very beginning of a local troupe of performers who engaged solely in this profession. It is impossible to settle this issue conclusively on the basis of Almerici's letter only;[70] however, what emerges clearly from it is the identification of the *Aminta* performers as "others" with respect to the people involved in the tournament and Sforza Oddi's comedy and to the noblemen such as Tiberio and Virginio Almerici. This must have reverberated with the perception of the bodies on stage and on their identification on the part of the audience. In other words, the latter might have been fully involved in the fiction on stage precisely because they were free from any guessing game concerning the identity of performing bodies with whom they were acquainted or related. The staging had become self-enclosed and self-referential — thus potentially curtailing the effect of the oblique allusions to noblemen and women at the Este court that Tasso is said to have embedded in his pastoral,[71] and that could have been effective at Pesaro, too, due to the presence at court of Lucrezia and her retinue.

Furthermore, Almerici's letter identifies (though not conclusively, as will be apparent) the location where the performance took place: *Aminta* was performed "nella sala che fu fatta per la venuta della Principessa" (Saviotti, "Torquato Tasso e le feste," 413; MS oliveriano 390, fol. 94 r) [in the hall built for the princess's entry]. Although this is the only indication provided on the space and its *décor*, it is nevertheless interesting since we possess a brief description of the hall itself in a document now at the Archivio di Stato, Firenze.[72] According to the latter, this was a *locus* specifically devised for performing plays, as opposed to the great hall where the banquet was to take place:

> Vi e, nell'altro salone delle comedie, un'favoloso apparato dove si haverà da recitare una Fabolosa hostiria del Paciotto con molti sollazzevoli, et ingegnosi tramedii <di moresche, danze et altre novità> li quali si potranno ragguagliar' appresso nel fine della festa <che dovrà cominciare> differita fino a Dominica XIIII del primo mese di Genaro <differita in tal giorno> per l'aspettazion dell'Ambas[sa]tor di Venetia che si aspetta di giorno in giorno; con hona di gran pompa. (fol. 654 r)[73]

In the words of the anonymous writer, the hall was notable not for its arrangement, but for the way it was decorated; this "favoloso apparato" was appropriate both for the unidentified *hostiria*[74] and for the *intermezzi* that alternated with it. The entire hall was decorated, according to another passage:

> L'apparato fù vago per li ornamenti della pittura, et della grandezza del suo sito che teneva la longhezza della sala; la quale, era, et è, tutta decorata di pitture à quadri di prospettive di paesaggi d'ogni intorno con alcuni simulacri di stucco bianchi; ma non fù però ricco, come in simil occ[asio]ne aspettar'si poteva, ma supli la vaghezza delle inventioni alla grandezza della spesa. (fols. 659 v–660 r)[75]

It is possible that this theater-hall had been painted and decorated anew for the 1574 occasion, but this hypothesis seems unlikely in light of the recent upheaval in the duchy and of the anonymous writer's comments regarding the scarcity of the expenses for a much more relevant and public event, such as Lucrezia's entrance into her new realm. Presumably, then, the walls within which *Aminta* took place were decorated with realistic *tableaux* of natural scenery, alternating with and framed by three-dimensional stucco moldings.[76] These paintings adorned every wall of this hall, enveloping the convened audience on all sides. The result was that the stage was but one of these *tableaux*, framed by a wider molding but essentially the same as the paintings on the wall; the events on the stage were virtually indistinguishable from the other pictures, painted in a realistic fashion. In other words, the *Aminta* performance was one of many representations offered to the audience's view, though less static.

This setting was far from being unique or even unusual at the time. Cesare Molinari has pointed out that in Castiglione's letter to Ludovico di Canossa regarding the 1513 staging of *La calandria* at Urbino, the hall (tellingly designated by the same term as the one in the anonymous description of 1571: *sala*) "non era affatto concepita come entità autonoma, ma, al contrario, come il prolungamento naturale dello spazio rappresentato sulla scena, o, almeno, come il luogo situato di fronte ad esso."[77] Although over sixty years elapsed between the performance narrated by Castiglione and the one under scrutiny in this study, it is important to point out two elements. First, Urbino and Pesaro were part of the same political domain. Second, changes in the relationship between stage and audience were influenced by architectural advances, themselves linked to the so-called science of perspective. Ferruccio Marotti has identified a pre-Galileian, anthropocentric concept of space that, in what he calls its "renaissance phase":

> vede lo svilupparsi della prospettiva come "tecnica" e quindi il sovrapporsi di un elemento di contrasto alla concezione antropocentrica dello spazio. Ora lo spazio scenico comincerà a scindersi dallo spazio fisico, senza peraltro che si giunga a concepire lo spazio scenico come sostitutivo dello spazio fisico . . . L'impianto prospettico . . . ha . . . la funzione di "amplificare" lo spazio fisico, che è ancora il "dove" della localizzazione scenica o teatrale.[78]

In the hall at Pesaro, it was as if various spaces, or locations, were offered to the convened audience. One, in which the play took place, seems to have been more compelling than the other *tableaux*, static and therefore less attractive. Another element that reinforces this interpretation of the space of the performance are the moldings separating and at the same time linking the various depictions on the wall. These act as a frame, at the same time physical and metaphorical, whose importance has been underscored in Richard Trexler's study (*Public Life in Renaissance Florence*, 91–96). On stage, in particular, architectural frames were common, as James Saslow points out with respect to the performance of *La pellegrina* in Florence in 1589: the Uffizi theater stage's "Corinthian order exactly matched the wall articulation of the theater, forming a single composition uniting stage with auditorium" (*The Medici Wedding of 1589* [New Haven: Yale University Press], 151). At Pesaro, an audience member must have felt surrounded, encircled, and hugged by his/her environment, and all depictions on the wall must have seemed equally important.[79]

Where was this semi-permanent structure built for the 1571 entry of Lucrezia into her new home? Solari and Cecini, followed by a host of scholars in both art and local history, are convinced that the 1574 *Aminta* performance took place at the Villa Imperiale, a della Rovere residence on a hill overlooking Pesaro and the Foglia river plain (fig. 1). Almerici's letter does not specify where the "sala . . . fatta per la venuta della Principessa" [hall made for the princess's entry] stood. The anonymous document relating Lucrezia's entry is similarly devoid of a specific location, although it mentions a few times the "Pallazzo [*sic*] Ducale" (Ducato d'Urbino, classe I divisione B filza X, fols. 654 r and 565 v, for example). In closing the description of the events, the document specifies that the morning after the banquet and play, "la Principessa è andata à messa a san'Dom[eni]co" (fol. 660 r) [the princess attended Mass in San Domenico], a no longer extant church almost facing the Ducal Palace. It is unlikely that she left the Villa Imperiale early in the morning to attend Mass in town. However, the hypothesis cannot be ruled out, and it is in fact highly suggestive.

From the top of Colle S. Bartolo, the Villa Imperiale dominates lands stretching from the Adriatic Sea to Urbino and Casteldurante (now Urbania). When the della Rovere domain incorporated former enemy towns, the strategic importance of this location for Pesaro's defense was severely reduced; at the same time, its symbolic significance increased. The Villa Imperiale was within view of the city, yet geographically, socially, and politically inaccessible. It afforded those allowed into it unimpeded views of places and people, that is, control over the della Rovere subjects.[80] Its very name ("Imperiale") seems to refer to a higher power ruling over and from the hill, the villa and those physically and metaphorically subjugated to it.[81]

Moreover, its striking architectural appearance reinforces the impression of its courtly import. The Villa Imperiale comprises two adjoining buildings, erected at different times and for different purposes. The older part, also referred to as "villa Sforza," was built in the fifteenth century, with "forme tardogotiche di gusto nordico, unite ad elementi rinascimentali"[82] [neo-gothic forms according to the northern taste, together with renaissance elements]. It appears on the left of the depiction in Cod. Vat. Barberini lat. 4434 (fig. 1); it looks like an enclosed three-storied fortress, further protected by a high watchtower over the main entrance. The newer part was commissioned around 1530 from Girolamo Genga by Francesco Maria I della Rovere and his wife Eleonora Gonzaga. Genga had already refurbished the older structure as well as designed the more striking parts of the Ducal Palace in Urbino, thus proving his architectural genius. According to Giorgio Vasari,

> Vedendo dunque il Duca [Francesco Maria] di avere un così raro ingegno, deliberò di fare al detto luogo dell'Imperiale, vicino al palazzo vecchio, un altro palazzo nuovo; e così fece quello che oggi vi si vede, che per esser fabrica bellissima e bene intesa, piena di camere, di colonnati e di cortili, di logge, di fontane e di amenissimi giardini, da quella banda non passano prencipi che non la vadino a vedere; onde meritò che papa Paulo Terzo, andando a Bologna con tutta la sua corte, l'andasse a vedere e ne restasse pienamente sodisfatto. (*Vite*, 5: 349)[83]

All studies on the newer building underscore two elements. First, in Roberta Martufi's words, "la presenza di un'adiacente dimora fa sì che la nuova villa venga a ricoprire esclusivamente funzioni di svago e di divertimento, facendo assolvere alla vecchia costruzione, adeguatamente restaurata, tutti gli oneri e i servizi necessari alla permanenza della corte".[84] The "new" villa seems to have been exploited, if not also conceived, as a *luogo di delizia* for the entertainment of the court and their guests. Second, as a cursory look at the depiction of the new building in the Vatican manuscript makes clear, "il nuovo corpo dell'Imperiale è stato pensato come un organismo chiuso, con mura compatte all'esterno che non lasciano sospettare l'estrema articolazione delle strutture interne."[85] While the original nucleus of the villa was designed to protect its inhabitants from military attacks from the outside, Genga's addition encloses those allowed in it from the curiosity of the outsiders. Marchini and Cecini have remarked that this plan harks back to the medieval tradition of the *hortus conclusus* (*La villa Imperiale*, 34). However, this configuration should also be linked to the enclosed, yet public, spatial articulation of courtyards recurring in the Renaissance that I have already touched upon when discussing the *carnevale* tournament in the courtyard of the Pesaro ducal palace.

It is severely reductive (and naive) to assert, with Pinelli and Rossi, that "non condizionata da funzioni domestiche o strettamente politico-rappresentative, funzioni assolte dalla costruzione degli Sforza, la villa Rovere aveva il solo ruolo di fungere da *teatro* della vita di corte" ("L'Imperiale nuova," 112; emphasis in original).[86]

One cannot assume that the representation of courtly life was not endowed with political value. Indeed, Girolamo Genga, who as we have seen designed the sixteenth-century addition to the Villa Imperiale, had extensive experience as a stage designer for the della Rovere court (Pinelli and Rossi, "L'Imperiale nuova," 103 and 103 n. 9; O. Rossi-Pinelli, "La villa Imperiale di Pesaro come spazio scenico per la corte urbinate," *Bollettino Palladio* 16 [1974], 219–33, here 220–21; and Battistelli, "Teatri storici," 24). Rossi-Pinelli has convincingly argued that Genga's addition to the Villa Imperiale "significa un impegno etico di grande rilievo, il tentativo cioè di rappresentare ancora un polo d'attrazione per le *intellighentzie* più vive del paese, cosí come lo era stato il ducato di Federico e Guidubaldo da Montefeltro" ("La villa Imperiale," 233).[87] In other words, Genga's addition was to link Pesaro and the della Rovere court to its chronological and dynastic predecessor, the court immortalized by Baldassar Castiglione in *Il cortegiano* — a court where, it is worth recalling, each person represents his/her role to fellow courtiers and visitors alike.

The intellectual continuity between Castiglione and Genga emerges also in the field of staged entertainment proper. Interestingly, the author of the *hostiria* performed in 1571, which the anonymous source simply identifies by his last name (Paciotto), can also be linked to the same tradition of architects working for the stage. Saviotti identifies him as "Felice Paciotto, fratello del celebre architetto Francesco" ("Torquato Tasso e le feste," 413 n. 1) [Felice Paciotto, brother to the famous architect, Francesco], who in turn had been a "scolaro" [student] under Girolamo Genga (A. Antaldi, *Notizie*, ed. A. Cerboni Baiardi [Pesaro: Il lavoro editoriale, 1996], 75). Though Francesco is usually described as a military architect,[88] one cannot rule out his having had a part in the festivities for the entry of Lucrezia into Pesaro. Archival documents summarized by the nineteenth-century Parma archivist Ronchini show that on 10 March 1571 Francesco Paciotto was at Urbino, and on 28 February 1572 he was at Pesaro.[89] According to the same source, his brother Felice was studying mathematics in Padua in 1555 (fol. 3 v); he might have been an architect, too, though not as famous as his brother.

Certainly locating the *Aminta* performance at the Villa Imperiale conforms with the prevailing biographical interpretations of Tasso's pastoral as a moment of grace and courtly fame for its author, and, more generally, with the constructions of the pastoral genre as escapist fantasy. Undoubtedly the fact that the 1574 performance cannot be firmly located at the Villa Imperiale undermines this view; I will come back to this genre-related consideration and others in the last chapter.

No matter where the hall had been built, we unfortunately cannot reconstruct it in more detail. For the anonymous writer of the 1571 description, the *locus* of the performance was interesting only so far as it enabled him/her to praise some aspect of the festivities, in this case the "vaghezza" of the wall decorations. Unfortunately, other relevant details (such as the position of the audience vis-à-vis the stage, the dimensions of the theater and of the stage, the designated seats for the duke and his wife) elicited no attention. It may be interesting to note, however, that one of Tasso's own letters in a collection printed in 1588, undated, mentions a theatrical habit of the della Rovere court. Writing to Lorenzo Malpiglio from Ferrara, Torquato begs his friend not to divulge what he had read of *Gerusalemme liberata* in these terms: "sarebbe quasi un rimovere il velo da la scena: & un far cadere le cortine molto prima ch'esca il prologo: ilche [sic] soleva fare il Duca Guido Baldo di felice memoria" (*Lettere familiari* [1588], fol. 57 r).[90] Although this passage does not refer directly to the staging of *Aminta*, I can safely guess that this performance also opened with a curtain falling before the entrance of the person reciting the prologue.

Almerici's judgment of the performance of *Aminta* in his letter is, in general, positive, although not devoid of some negative criticism:

> [è] stata tenuta per una delle vaghe compositioni che siano fin'hora uscite in scena in tal genere perchè ci erano bellissimi e piacevolissimi concetti e l'attione, ancora che semplice, è molto piacevole et affettuosa, è ben vero che per la verità non è stata in alcune parti e principali così ben rappresentata come meritava, massime negli affetti da' quali nasceva il principale diletto dell'Egloga. Pure da quegli che n'hanno gusto è stata giudicata per cosa rara. (Saviotti, "Torquato Tasso e le feste," 413; MS oliveriano 390, fol. 94 r)[91]

The performance, according to Tiberio and possibly to other *savants* at Pesaro, was not so polished as it could have been, yet the excellence of Tasso's work shone through. The plot ("l'attione") is defined as "semplice" and still "piacevole et affettuosa;" and it is precisely from the pathos that it elicited in its viewers that the pastoral derived its efficacy.[92] Moreover, the plot was adorned with beautiful "concetti," which evidently attracted the interest and the praise of the audience. In spite of the uneven quality of the performance on the part of the players, *Aminta* still emerged as "cosa rara" in the opinion of the *cognoscenti*.

Tiberio's last commentary on Tasso's pastoral follows the same line of analysis, while concentrating on the much-debated choruses: "E quel che di gratia s'è aggiunto à quest'Egloga e c'ha piaciuto più che mediocremente è la novità del Coro fra ciascuno atto che rendeva maestà mirabile, e recava con piacevolissimi concetti infinito diletto agli spettatori et ascoltatori (Saviotti, "Torquato Tasso e le feste," 413; MS oliveriano 390, fol. 94 r).[93] It is unfortunate that Almerici did not provide additional information regarding the staging of the choruses, since this would help us understand what provoked this feeling of "majesty" in the audience. It is however remarkable that the presence of five choruses is attested so early in the theatrical history of *Aminta*, given the lengthy debate on this topic in literary circles.[94] Given the fact that Almerici indicated the presence of *intermezzi* in the case of *Erofilomachia*, and that the anonymous source on the 1571 festivities refers specifically to this form of entertainment, I can safely surmise that no such entertainment accompanied the staging of *Aminta*, which was in itself varied by the presence of the aforementioned choruses. Furthermore, Tasso's pastoral differs from Oddi's comedy in one fundamental aspect. While the latter was perceived as static, boring, untheatrical, the former is effective in its very simplicity. For Almerici, then, *Aminta* did not need the addition of the *intermezzi*; the plot was already varied enough.[95]

A short note taken from a now-lost letter addressed to a relative by the Ferrara nobleman Camillo Giordani, then at Pesaro, mentioned by both Saviotti ("Torquato Tasso e le feste," 408 n. 3) and Solerti (*Vita di Torquato Tasso*, 2: 106), has been taken to indicate that Torquato himself was involved in the staging of *Aminta*: "Dirò che 'l Tasso ha dato cura d'attendere a dar piacere a questi Signori che sono quà e doman si faranno cose grandissime."[96] Unfortunately, the letter from which this note was copied is now lost, hence it is impossible to determine how Torquato set about his task to "dar piacere" to his hosts. Moreover, this letter is dated 3 March 1574; it was written after the end of the carnival festivities, and the mysterious "cose grandissime" still to come, to which the nobleman alludes, might be those in which Tasso was involved, rather than the *Aminta* staging.[97]

The most unfortunate occurrence in this episode, perhaps, is that no letter by Tasso himself is extant from this period. His correspondence has not been reprinted since 1852 — a fact that renders it obsolete in its editorial criteria and organization, not to mention exceedingly rare;[98] besides, during this period Torquato had not yet taken to copying (or having someone else copy) his letters before sending them. The likelihood of recovering any is therefore quite remote, especially since many scholars devoted innumerable hours to this endeavor during the nineteenth century. In conclusion, I view this lack of correspondence on Tasso's part as a result of unfortunate circumstances, coincidental and fortuitous, rather than determined by the nature of the event itself.

This performance of *Aminta* at Pesaro was profoundly different from the supposed opening at the Estes' Belvedere. Although it was part of a series of courtly entertainments, it was accessible to a larger audience than the strictly private performance that is said to have taken place in July 1573. Moreover, it was clearly prepared in advance, announced and advertised, as witnessed by Lucrezia's letter of invitation to her brother Alfonso. It seems unlikely that Tasso, if indeed he was personally involved in the staging, did not recount his experience, difficulties, and personal satisfaction in any epistle — unless of course these are lost to us.

Given the relevance of the occasion and the quality of the entertainment, what is particularly perplexing is the lack of more official reports on these carnival festivities.[99] Although one cannot rule out that such a document once existed but does so no longer, this absence largely undermines the traditional interpretation of these festivities as devised by the della Rovere duke to appease his subjects at Pesaro after the bloody solution to the Urbino uprising. If this had been the case, the events would have been glorified and magnified through publication and distribution of descriptions of the festivities — especially when we consider that the unrest at Urbino had been provoked not by the lowest strata of the population, but by the noble and the *notabili*, who would have therefore constituted the main target for the hidden, ideological meaning of these carnival celebrations, and who, moreover, constituted a suitable reading public for such a pamphlet.[100]

Rather, the public entertainment during the 1574 carnival season at Pesaro seems poised between the popular and the courtly spheres, as well as on the brink of the age when any public event would be subject to some form of pre-conceived, endorsed (indeed, forced) interpretation. Guidubaldo II della Rovere celebrated his power, his family, and his domain upon a public, in fact popular, occasion, which he did not (or could not) fully control or deprive of its original characteristics. He juxtaposed the three "public" events and the multitude of private parties that all the town dwellers traditionally relished. Yet at the same time he made his influence on this public entertainment known by hosting it within the physical space of the court. In so doing, he bestowed upon himself the privilege to restrict participation and attendance — thus establishing a paradox between "public" and "private" which goes beyond Almerici's distinction. Furthermore, since the duke apparently did not sponsor the publication of any pamphlet containing the description of the three public events, his influence seems limited to the *hic et nunc* of the performances themselves. There may be historical reasons for this (printed descriptions of festivities became widespread only after around 1590, sixteen years after these events transpired at Pesaro) as well as political ones (Guidubaldo was indifferent to reaching areas outside the town, and word of mouth — much like Almerici's letter to his cousin — would have sufficed for Pesaro and its immediate surroundings) or economic ones (in 1575 the duchy was hit by the plague, so it is possible that the actual tax revenue proved lower than that projected, thus forcing the court to scrap plans for publication). It is also to be borne in mind that a more contingent but equally powerful reason might have caused plans to be modified: Guidubaldo's death, later in 1574, might have deprived the project of its main promoter, or nullified the paramount political reason behind the project.

In her book on seventeenth-century English literature, Anna Nardo tries to resolve this issue of "public" and "private" realms in terms that can be easily applied to the situation at Pesaro:

> Extraordinary times, places and people that fell in between or outside the slots of social order unleashed the folly that could scramble the order and level the hierarchy — temporarily.
>
> Paradoxically, they also helped preserve the social order. By releasing pent-up emotions under controlled conditions, they protected institutions,

serving as safety valves that allowed power structures to marginalize and contain dissidence without accommodating its critique. Furthermore, when carnal appetites are indulged instead of refrained, when fools or children rule instead of being ruled, energy is freed. This energy may be frightening because it tends towards the chaos from which society slowly and painstakingly wrested order. Thus authority can legitimate its power as control over elements deemed harmful to the commonweal. But random energy may also invigorate power by reinfusing it with the vitality that enables it to create order. Without periodic contacts with its primal sources of energy, society stagnates, choked by the structures it has created to channel the potentially destructive and creative powers.[101]

At Pesaro, *Aminta* and all the other carnival events could have been performed with such an end in Guidubaldo's mind. The occasion in itself would warrant such an interpretation, in light of the carnivalesque traditions and of the legislation regarding this period of "misrule." Not only were the citizens eager to shake off the horrible memories of the end of the Urbino uprising; not only was the ruler willing to entertain his subjects and courtiers to renew his image in their minds; the occasion lent itself thoroughly to being exploited from both sides.[102] The populace could enjoy a period of freedom from everyday obligations, while releasing its energy (and possibly rebelliousness) in a mostly indirect and harmless way. The ruler could channel this energy while reasserting his total control over the behavior of the population as well as the entertainment of his courtiers. While, in Bakhtin's words, "the medieval feast had, as it were, the two faces of Janus" (*Rabelais and His World*, 81), the second half of the sixteenth century was even in this respect a period of transition, as remarked by Starn and Partridge (*Arts of Power*, 160–61).

Yet another aspect of the Bakhtinian survey of carnival is difficult to reconcile with the Pesaro events. In his opinion, carnival "does not acknowledge any distinction between actors and spectators.... Carnival is not a spectacle seen by the people; they live in it, and everyone participates because its very idea embraces all the people. While carnival lasts, there is no other life outside it. During carnival life is subject only to its laws, that is, the laws of its own freedom" (*Rabelais and His World*, 7). If we accept Bakhtin's definition, then the 1574 festivities do not constitute a carnival, even though they took place at the time of *carnevale*. By the same token, the staged performances that Almerici called "public" would fall not in the realm of modern-day theater, but in that of games.[103] However, Almerici's letter explicitly differentiates between "fatte" and "veduti" events that took place during the 1574 *carnevale* season. Further, he seems to make a distinction between events that were lived by his peers (the noblemen taking part in the tournament and acting *Erofilomachia*) and those that were merely observed (namely, the *Aminta* performance). Still, noblewomen were certainly excluded from participating in the tournament, and possibly from acting in Sforza Oddi's comedy. For them, these festivities were strictly observed, not lived. Outside Almerici's "class," the common people who had no access to the Ducal Palace courtyard for the tournament or to the hall in which *Aminta* was performed were at an even further distance. They could not observe, much less live, these *carnevale* festivities. It is debatable whether the situation at Pesaro is different from the one posited by Bakhtin because of a chronological and geographical distance, or because what Bakhtin describes is an abstraction, and not concrete and complex circumstances like the ones under scrutiny.

One is left wondering why *Aminta* was selected for performance at Pesaro. It is possible that the success with which the pastoral had been received at Ferrara influenced the della Rovere choice — either by way of Lucrezia's contacts with her native court or, less likely, owing to the strength of the relationship between Tasso and the local court. I favor a twofold hypothesis: on the one hand, *Aminta* offered itself to the della Rovere entourage as a courtly product; therefore, it was more or less implicitly imbued with courtly motifs and ideals. In light of the recent political turmoil in the della Rovere domain, Tasso's pastoral might have taken on an additional veneer of idealization that made it an excellent choice for festivity organizers. On the other, if one endorses the hypothesis that a professional troupe had staged the pastoral at Belvedere the previous year, then the "fame" of the text within theatrical circles (professional and possibly amateur as well) could have spread fast, thus qualifying *Aminta* in the opinion of the actors and "directors" as an excellent text to be performed for learned audiences. In this sense, then, this pastoral text is also somewhat linked to the popular circumstances in which it was performed at Pesaro, that is, *carnevale*. In sum, *Aminta* stands at the convergence among literary, ideological, and theatrical concerns and traditions; it is a play destined to early fame and a unexpected and sudden decline, after literary and ideological conditions change, and possibly because of its very fame — as the events reconstructed in the following chapters seem to warrant.

Notes

[1] Stallybrass and White have remarked that "[o]n the one hand carnival was a specific calendric ritual: carnival proper, for instance, occurred around February each year, ineluctably followed by Lenten fasting and abstinence bound tightly to laws, structures and institutions which had briefly been denied during its reign. On the other hand carnival also refers to a mobile set of symbolic practices, images, and discourses that were employed throughout social revolts and conflicts before the nineteenth century": P. Stallybrass and A. White, *The Politics and the Poetics of Transgression* (Ithaca: Cornell University Press, 1986), 15.

In order to avoid confusing these two aspects of the English word, and to confine my remarks to its stricter (i.e., chronological) meaning, I have used the Italian term *carnevale* throughout this chapter, except of course when citing sources.

² According to the seventeenth-century scholar Marco Antonio Gozze, whose manuscript *Memorie della Città di Pesaro* are kept at the Biblioteca Oliveriana, "L'anno poi 566 dall'istessa edificazione di Roma essendo Consoli P. Claudio Pulchro, e L. Porcio Licinio, e eravi triumviri Q. Fabio Labene, e M. e Q. A Fulvij Flacco, e Nobiliore, la Città di Pesaro, come attestano Livio, e Patercolo, fù dedotta Colonia da Romani essendo assignato à ciascuno dei Coloni sei Jugeri di terra" (fol. 213 r) [in the 566th year since Rome was built, when Claudius Pulcher and Porcius Licinius were consuls and Fabius Labene and M. and Q. A. Fulvius Flaccus were triumvirs, the city of Pesaro was founded as a Roman colony, as Livy and Paterculus attest. Each colonizer was given six land jugera]. Since Rome was traditionally founded in 753 B.C. (*Enciclopedia italiana* 29: 593), according to Gozze the colony of Pisaurum goes back to 187 B.C. The entry for Pesaro in the same encyclopedia places the founding of the Roman colony in 184 B.C. (26: 920).

³ A brief outline of the city's history is in *Enciclopedia italiana* 26, particularly 920–21.

⁴ Born in 1535, Giulio was made cardinal in 1547, when he was just thirteen years of age. He became deacon of the church of San Pietro in Vincoli in Rome and pontifical legate for Perugia and Umbria in 1548. Between 1560 and 1566 he was bishop of Vicenza, and after 1566 of Ravenna. Shortly before his death in 1578 he became archbishop of Urbino. He was close to the Spanish party during the pontifical elections in which he took part, except when family and dynastic reasons pushed him to befriend the French faction (*Dizionario biografico degli italiani* 37: 356–57). The importance of the cardinalate for a newly-established family like the della Rovere is evident in the events surrounding Lorenzo the Magnificent de' Medici's quest on behalf of his second-born son Giovanni, outlined in Trexler's masterly work (455–56).

⁵ "Bernardo advised [Torquato] to mix with courts 'where one learns manners that adorn the soul.' He also wanted him to practice horsemanship and to become the perfect courtier as outlined by Castiglione, who would bring together the adornment of letters, the virtue of arms, and taste for music and arts." Additionally, Solerti provides a short list of the scholars and artists populating the Pesaro court in his biography of Tasso (*Vita di Torquato Tasso*, 1: 32).

⁶ Nando Cecini points out the relationship between the Urbino court and Castiglione's treatise in "Cultura e letteratura nei centri minori e maggiori tra rinascimento e barocco," in *Arte e cultura nella provincia di Pesaro e Urbino*, ed. F. Battistelli (Venice: Marsilio, 1986), 333–59, here 338–39.

⁷ "She left on 2 January 1571 and arrived in Pesaro on the 9th. The Duke, Cardinal Giulio and Prince Francesco Maria met her one mile outside town. She entered the city seated on a lavish litter; the clergy and all the gentlemen welcomed her at the door and then accompanied her to the cathedral. She rode under five richly appointed arches and was taken to the ducal palace. There many gentlewomen were waiting for her. The day ended with a magnificent dinner that lasted until four hours after sunset."

⁸ According to Solerti, she died on 18 September of that year (*Vita di Torquato Tasso*, 1: 178); according to Giovanni Da Pozzo, however, some sources set the date on 18 September, others on the 19th (*Ambigua armonia*, 52). Most recently, Giovanni Ricci asserts that her death occurred on 19 September (G. Ricci, *Il principe e la morte* [Bologna: Il Mulino, 1998], 165); his study provides a brief description of her obsequies and of her funerary monument (166–74).

[9] In Francesco Maria's diary, according to Cecini, "accanto alle citazioni degli avvenimenti esterni che interessano il ducato, si riscontrano notazioni familiari, intime, ma sempre venate da una punta di fatale distacco. Come questa del 15 febbraio 1598 'Intesi come alle 11 la notte seguente era morta in Ferrara madama Lucrezia d'Este mia moglie'" ("Cultura e letteratura," 335) [alongside notes about external events that might have interest for the duchy, we see family-related and intimate notes that are nevertheless veined by some irrepressible detachment. See the following, dated 15 February 1598: I heard the following night that at 11 Lucrezia d'Este, my wife, had died in Ferrara].

[10] In Filippo Ugolini's words, "quando nel medio evo un Comune sottoponevasi alla signoria di qualche principe, il patto principale era sempre quello di non poter mai, sotto qualsiasi titolo, andar soggetto a nuovi balzelli": F. Ugolini, "Diario della ribellione d'Urbino nel 1572 d'ignoto autore," *Archivio storico italiano* n.s. 3 (1856): 37–59, here 45 [when in the Middle Ages a commune yielded to the rule of a prince, the main stipulation was invariably that it would never, for any reason, be subject to new taxes]. Urbino was still ruled by its own laws and the medieval stipulations with a governing family from the thirteenth century, thus forbidding any Montefeltro, first, and later della Rovere duke to impose any taxes. Conversely, Guidubaldo did so on "le carni fresche e salate, le bestie grosse, gli animali suini, il grano e le altre biade" (Ugolini, "Diario della ribellione," 45) [fresh and salted meats, big cattle, swine, wheat and other grains]. Interestingly, a late-eighteenth-century MS at the Biblioteca Oliveriana indicates a precise source of Guidubaldo's need for new taxes: "Chi non sa la ribellione d'Urbino aver avuta origine dall'eccessive spese, che lo forzarono ad aggravare i Popoli con nove gabelle ed imposizioni? Dalle di lui mani scorreva l'oro, come l'aqua delle fonti (al dire di Giacomo Mazzoni suo panegirista in ocasione della di lui morte). Edificj, templj, amenissime Ville erano quelle cose, che continuamente l'occupavano": D. Bonamini, *Abecedario architettonico degli architetti Pesaresi*, MS oliveriano 1009, fol. 80 [who does not know that the Urbino uprising originated from excessive expenses? Those forced him to impose on his people new taxes and dues. Gold flowed from his hands like water from a spring, according to Giacomo Mazzoni who gave his eulogy when he died. Buildings, churches, beautiful villas were his main concern and occupation].

[11] A synopsis of these events opens A. Saviotti, "Torquato Tasso e le feste pesaresi del 1574," *Giornale storico della letteratura italiana* 12 (1888): 404–17. An anonymous manuscript entitled *Diario della ribellione d'Urbino* was reprinted by F. Ugolini in *Archivio storico italiano* (n. 10 above). More recently, Giovanna Solari has offered a highly readable, though source-lacking account in *22 storie dei duchi di Urbino*, 282–302. A decidedly less biographical and tighter narration is to be found in G. G. Scorza, *I della Rovere 1508–1631* (Pesaro: n. p., 1981), 24–27.

[12] "Pesaro and Senigallia had sent Guidubaldo ambassadors to tell him that while the people of Urbino 'deserved the noose,' they redoubled their passionate love to His Excellence."

[13] "Guidubaldo was rather partial to Pesaro. He lived there almost continuously and splendidly; he fortified it on the outside with new walls, following the new design that his father had bequeathed him. Inside he made it more orderly with the intervention of the police and with greater embellishments than it had ever had. Finally, during the Urbino uprising he felt the most constant trust in the inhabitants' souls on a daily basis and when they

publicly showed their devotion to Guidubaldo no matter what the situation and thus convinced the other cities to keep their loyalty. So the thankful prince, in order to reward the open faith of the good people of Pesaro, gave them as a gift the Oak, the arms of his most noble family, supported by four hands with the motto: Everlasting, Unshakable Faith."

[14] "Il duca Guidubaldo II della Rovere aveva stabilito di ravvivare il carnevale di quell'anno 1574 e con le feste far dimenticare ai suoi sudditi le angherie ed i balzelli che avevano provocato la ribellione": Solerti, *Vita di Torquato Tasso*, 1: 187 [Duke Guidubaldo II had decided to revamp the *carnevale* for 1574 and to have his subjects forget the vexation and taxes that had provoked the uprising by way of celebrations]; "A più lieti spettacoli volle nel carnevale del '74 il duca sollevare gli animi": Saviotti, "Torquato Tasso e le feste," 405 [the duke wanted to uplift everybody's soul with happy shows for *carnevale* in 1574].

[15] Even the inauguration of the first permanent theater in Italy, the Olimpico in Vicenza, took place during the *carnevale* season of 1585: G. Nogara, *Cronache degli spettacoli nel teatro Olimpico di Vicenza* (Vicenza: Accademia Olimpica, 1972), 10.

[16] After the devolution of the duchy of Pesaro and Urbino back to the Papacy, in 1631 — when Francesco Maria passed away, preceded in death by his son Federico Ubaldo (1605–1623), the last male descendant of the della Rovere family — his granddaughter Vittoria married Ferdinando II de' Medici, grand duke of Tuscany. Hence most of the *rovereschi* archives were moved to Florence, where they are still kept. Some documents, however, remained at Urbino, others still at Pesaro and other towns in the former della Rovere domain.

[17] At the Archivio di Stato, Firenze, one of the rare extant documents of a financial nature concerns the "entrate et uscite ordinarie di tutto lo stato" [ordinary income and expenses of the whole state] to be expected presumably for 1577, since they are based on "questi ultimi del 1575 et 1576" (Ducato d'Urbino, classe I divisione A filza III parte II, fols. 638 r–652 r) [the most recent ones of 1575 and 1576]. However, this document does not mention any sort of courtly entertainment, since those would be considered as "uscite straordinarie" [extraordinary expenses]. Torquato Tasso's name appears only once in the extant *libri dei conti*, in a note dated December 1588: "A m[es]s[er] Torquato Tasso donati scudi 25" (Archivio di Stato, Firenze; Ducato d'Urbino, classe III filza XXIII, fol. 712 v) [25 *scudi* to Mr. Torquato Tasso as a gift] — an indication that only heightens this scholar's regret that such detailed material is now lost.

[18] Archivio di Stato, Pesaro: Legazione apostolica di Pesaro-Urbino, decreti 2: 1505–1686, 1535–1651, 1544–1661; decreti dei della Rovere, volume 3.

[19] According to John Rudlin, "a masked man had no right to bear arms during Carnival season in medieval Italy because he was considered to have divested himself of his own identity by assuming another persona, for whose actions he was therefore not responsible": J. Rudlin, *Commedia dell'Arte. An Actor's Handbook* (London: Routledge, 1994), 34. It is disappointing that Guidubaldo's laws do not specify the reasons for such a separation of weapons and masks in a clearer way. Still in the seventeenth century similar laws were in place, for example in Bologna, as a letter cited in an article by A. Saviotti shows ("Feste e spettacoli nel Seicento," *Giornale storico della letteratura italiana* 41 [1903]: 42–77, here 67).

[20] "Having heard, with great displeasure, of the insolence and bad behavior that indiscreet, ill-mannered, and conceited people repeatedly carry out at parties, doors, gates, and windows of those places where parties or other similar festivities take place."

[21] "Nobody, of any rank or estate or privileged in any way, must dare to carry or hold weapons of any kind at parties when in a mask or disguised, under the same punishment of life-long imprisonment and others according to our will."

[22] "Grabbed their weapons, or aimed them at anybody, or insulted or wounded anybody at said parties."

[23] "Since it is customary to give the people some public entertainment (specifically wearing masks) during a certain period of the year, to this end for the people's honest pleasure we are satisfied to give permission to masks. With the present proclamation we grant and allow all people to wear masks."

[24] "When this big mask is removed, at the same time the permission is also revoked for good reasons."

[25] "Those who want to enjoy themselves that way and with modesty could do it without being bothered, and those who would like to do it otherwise might be held back by the fear of punishment."

[26] "We wish, order, and command that no person of whatever estate, status, social condition, or reputation take the liberty or make bold to go masked in any city, tower, or place in our state in which this proclamation will be published outside the time of the present authorization."

[27] "Churches, religious convents, nuns' monasteries, cloisters, parlatories, or other sacred places."

[28] "Sticks, daggers, long and thick wooden swords, canes, and thick rods that are capable of hurting."

[29] "Talk or act without honesty where women are in attendance."

[30] "Hit with a fist or a stick or any other way without spilling blood anybody wearing a mask *qua* wearing a mask."

[31] "Run into a home or a store to pick up an offensive weapon."

[32] "Take other people's goods by force or in any other way."

[33] "If anybody is found to have donned a mask to kill someone, or for carrying out something in any way on someone else's behalf, even if he has not done any deed, it is our will and order that he spend his life in jail and lose his goods. Conversely if anyone is wearing a mask to perpetrate an offense on someone else, but he has not done any deed, then he is to have his hand cut off and to pay 100 *scudi*."

[34] "We order that, starting thirty minutes after sunset, nobody put on a mask at the outside door, under penalty of 100 *scudi* to be disposed of as we said before. We are satisfied that those inside homes can put on and wear masks even though it is night. After the bell that rings three hours after sunset, we wish that nobody with a mask go around without a lamp, even if he is not wearing his mask or false beard. No more than four or five people are to share a lamp. The lamp has to cast light from at least three sides, under penalty of 25 *scudi* to be disposed of as mentioned above and three lashes."

[35] "In order to clarify to those who do not understand, in the present proclamation when we have mentioned a masked person we mean anybody who is disguised, or whose face is covered in any way other than a mask or false beard."

[36] With all due historical differences, the fascination with masking emerging from these laws can be likened to the situation described by Terry Castle vis-à-vis masquerades in eighteenth-century England: "The nature of masquerade costume helps to explain

some of the intense symbolic meaning these assemblies held for contemporaries. Theatricality had its formal patterns, and one may detect an underlying system of transformation in the travesties of the age. The masquerade crowd was a shifting, disorienting visual mass, Ovidian in the luxurious proliferation of its forms, but not entirely unregulated": T. Castle, *Masquarade and Civilization* (Stanford: Stanford University Press, 1986), 5. In 1574, when theater was still largely non-codified, there was no clear boundary between a play staging and wearing masques at *carnevale*. However, a similar sense of disorientation is evident, as well as the desire on the part of the ruler to regulate such events.

[37] "Those without a mask will be subject to said punishment who will injure those masked in any of the aforementioned ways. We wish that the same punishment be meted out to those who remove or attempt to remove the mask or any other cover from another person, and to those who enter somebody else's school or home or store in order to annoy or insult them in any of the aforementioned ways."

[38] The almost obvious reference is to Mikhail Bakhtin's seminal study of carnival and misrule in the late medieval and Renaissance periods, *Rabelais and His World* (Bloomington: Indiana University Press, 1984).

[39] Tiberio Almerici for example wrote to his cousin that "Questo carnevale s'è passato piu allegramente che non si credeva, e s'è ricompensato in parte quel tempo che si passò con tanto disgusto di questi popoli quest'anno addietro": Saviotti, "Torquato Tasso e le feste," 409; MS oliveriano 390, fol. 92 r [we spent *carnevale* more happily than we thought, and we partially made up for the period that these people experienced with such displeasure last year]. Notice that Almerici does not suggest (as nineteenth-century critics did) a causal relationship between the courtly organization of the *carnevale* entertainment and the necessity to divert the subjects' minds from the cruelty used to subdue the Urbino rebels. Rather, what emerges from Tiberio's words is his own incredulity for the success of the entertainment, as well as the necessity for the population to leave their worries behind, albeit only temporarily. There could have been a convergence between hidden courtly goals and wishes of the population at large — a convergence that would single out this series of events precisely for its unique position between political and social influences, "popular" desire and courtly wishes.

[40] "The princess of Urbino, who could not have been in attendance at the *Aminta* performance, had heard the praise and wonders that were circulating about it. She thus had great desire to see the fable, indeed to hear it from its author's mouth. She had the latter invited to Pesaro and asked her brother duke Alfonso to lend him to her for a few months. The duke was satisfied, and Tasso even more so, since he had a chance to revisit the court where he had been embraced in his youth, and as he warmly desired to serve and please a princess he esteemed so much and to whose affectionate protection he owed his grace and rank at the Ferrara court. Tasso came to Pesaro at the beginning of the summer of 1573, and he was lavished with attention on the part of the two young princes and of Guidubaldo, who had been his father's and his affectionate protector. Here he first recited his beautiful pastoral, which pleased those who heard it as much as we can imagine. Then he took to reading the completed cantos of his poem, which that noble court found something very special."

[41] For a parallel stance in the realm of literary criticism, refer to the numerous "biographical" interpretations of *Aminta* reviewed in chapter 1 of the present study.

⁴² "Lucrezia d'Este, Duke Francesco Maria's wife, desired passionately to become acquainted with that pastoral poem and to see its writer again. She implored her brother Alfonso to accede to her request. He yielded to the good duchess's honest request, while Torquato was happy to see the place where he had been a happy youth and that would bring back affectionate memories of his dear father and of the splendid, loving courtesy that Guidubaldo's generous soul had bestowed upon them."

⁴³ "The whole court celebrated the famous poet's arrival with sincere celebrations, but nobody was more unspeakably happy than Prince Francesco Maria (who got back his schoolmate) and Duchess Lucrezia (who saw her tender friend again). *Aminta*'s fame had preceded Torquato's arrival at the Urbino court, and well-deserving and well-read men had assembled to hear him. Still, the *Aminta* performance surpassed everybody's wishes and hopes. Nothing greater or more admirable had yet been heard; such were the joy and wonder that everybody felt that there was no stopping the applause, gifts or honorable wishes lavished on the young poet. Therefore I like to call that joyful day the happiest of his life and the foreshadowing of the very solemn day when he would have received the laurel on the Capitol as his closest friends had organized and cruel, poisonous fate denied him."

⁴⁴ "The extraordinary success of the *Aminta* stagings impelled Lucrezia, Alfonso's sister, to have Torquato in Pesaro so that he could repeat it there. Tasso left for this reason for the Urbino court where he was joyfully received by old Duke Guidubaldo, who had him educated alongside his son when he was a young man": Tasso, *Gerusalemme liberata*, ed. G. Sacchi (Milan: L. Sacchi, 1984), lvii.

⁴⁵ "The young poet directed his beautiful pastoral fable *Aminta*, appealingly performed by gentlemen and ladies of the court."

⁴⁶ In his words, "Egli è che nel secolo scorso quel risveglio maraviglioso degli studi storici, che, oltre ai grandi sintetizzatori . . . dette la valorosa falange di eruditi regionali, delle storie e biografie e bibliografie de' quali tuttora ci gioviamo, non fu accompagnato, nè, forse, poteva, da eguale senso critico. La biografia, in particolar modo, era intesa quale elogio, e volentieri assumeva questo nome. . . . Benchè il Serassi, bene adoperando le non molte notizie di fatto che i suoi tempi gli consentirono di raccogliere, avesse cercato di contrapporre la storia alla leggenda, tuttavia la leggenda . . . perdurò e si rafforzò con la critica e con l'arte romantica della prima metà di questo secolo": *Vita di Torquato Tasso*, 1: v–vi [In the last century we witnessed a wonderful reawakening of historical studies, which gave us great synthesizers as well as a valiant crowd of student of local history, of histories, biographies, and bibliographies that are still necessary but that lacked a strong critical awareness. Biography especially was equivalent to praise, often explicitly. Although Serassi had attempted to separate history from legend, exploiting fully the scant factual information that he could gather at the time, still legend persisted, only to become stronger with romantic criticism and art from the first half of this century].

⁴⁷ Among these, first and foremost is the idea that *Aminta*'s opening is particularly significant to Italian literary history due to the excellence of the text: "il fatto [the date of the first staging] era così importante non solo per la biografia del Tasso, ma per la storia del nostro teatro, che io stimai mio dovere di cercare con qualche mezzo di scoprire la verità o almeno di avvicinarmele: *Vita di Torquato Tasso*, 1: 181 [this event was so important not simply for Tasso's biography, but for the history of our theater, that I thought it my duty to try somehow to discover to truth, or at least to get close to it].

⁴⁸ In 1995 a book appeared at Florence, whose very title: *Torquato Tasso. Una psicobiografia*, makes its frame of reference clear. Its author, Giampiero Giampieri, follows Tasso's life events to unearth reasons for his declining mental health. Little attention is devoted to Tasso's literary production, and no sources appear in the book.

⁴⁹ "He owed her the *Aminta* performance at Imperiale."

⁵⁰ "Tasso went back to Pesaro during the 1574 *carnevale* season, invited specifically by Lucrezia, in order to stage *Aminta* after the Ferrara opening. *Aminta* was performed at villa Imperiale by a group of amateurs directed by Tasso himself, who then added the choruses between the acts."

⁵¹ "He would have some subjects perform some comedies that he believes you would not dislike, as they are wont to do a good job at it."

⁵² "In a letter, he reminds the princess 'by calling me to Pesaro, you added favor to favor, kindness to kindness, generosity to generosity, giving me gifts and honors and having others do the same." Here as elsewhere, Cecini merely follows Solerti, who exploited the same passage (*Vita di Torquato Tasso*, 1: 187 n. 5) to make the same point. However, Solerti's assertion is further weakened by his previous conclusion that Tasso "già fin d'allora [1572] non era mai lasciato addietro in nessuna gita che la corte facesse" (1: 179) [from that early date, he was never left behind when the court took a trip]. We could conclude that Lucrezia had invited her brother; the latter had planned a trip, sent his *familiari* (including Tasso) ahead, and subsequently had to modify his plans.

⁵³ An undated contract binding two musici from Siena to entertain Guidubaldo II (Archivio di Stato, Firenze; Ducato d'Urbino, classe I divisione B filza X; the pages in this volume are not numbered, but it is the third document in the second part) testifies to this practice during Guidubaldo's rule. According to Fabrizio Cruciani, the extant documents point to the fact that this performance of *Aminta* undoubtedly availed itself of "la recitazione di giovani non professionisti" ("Percorsi critici," 180) [the acting of young non-professionals].

⁵⁴ Solerti and Lanza sketch the situation at Ferrara in their article "Il teatro ferrarese nella seconda metà del secolo XVI"; Taviani's article on Andreini and Tasso ("Bella d'Asia") offers some interesting insights on this topic as well.

⁵⁵ An outline of the history of local theater building activities is provided by F. Battistelli, "Teatri storici nella provincia di Pesaro e Urbino," in *Teatro delle terre di Pesaro e Urbino*, ed. F. G. Motta (Milan: Electra, 1997), 23–36 (especially, for the period here under scrutiny, 23–25), in a 1997 exhibit catalog that demonstrates the importance of theaters in the area till the beginning of the twentieth century. A quick overview of the contributions of scene- and perspective-building by Pesaro and Urbino practitioners is in E. Gamba and V. Montebelli, *Macchine da Teatro e Teatri di Macchine*, also a catalog for a 1995 exhibit (Urbino: Quattroventi, 1995).

⁵⁶ Cruciani also believes that "L'Almerici parla delle feste da spettatore esperto e partecipe, con giudizi calibrati e informati" ("Percorsi critici," 180) [Almerici talks about the festivities as an expert, involved viewer, whose judgment is thought out and well informed].

⁵⁷ "Many parties took place, and we saw three public spectacles that were a *sbarra*, a comedy, and an eclogue." All citations are from Saviotti's reprint of Almerici's letter in "Torquato Tasso e le feste pesaresi del 1574," as emended by confronting it with the

manuscript of the letter at the Biblioteca Oliveriana at Pesaro (MS oliveriano 390, fols. 92 r–96 v). When discrepancies were detected (mainly in punctuation, accentuation, and capitalization) I have followed the manuscript.

[58] For a brief history of this performed genre, see Elena Povoledo, "Torneo," in *Enciclopedia dello spettacolo*, 9: 991–999, esp. 995–96. Dinko Fabris has pointed out that "[a] mano a mano che le signorie rinascimentali entravano in una crisi irreversibile, gli spettacoli cavallereschi assumevano un ruolo esorcizzante di sopravvivenza dell'ideologia di corte": *Mecenati e musici* (Lucca: Libreria musicale italiana, 1999), 71 [the more Renaissance *signorie* were in crisis, the more knightly spectacles took on the role of exorcism to allow courtly ideology to survive].

[59] "It was very beautiful to see in the big palace courtyard (a most fit place for such spectacles) the crowd of people, the beauty of the ladies in the windows and on the daises, the young well-dressed noblemen walking within the pen. Young noblemen and other gentlemen were involved in a thousand tasks that go with this chivalric exercise."

[60] Trexler has pointed out the ambivalent ("ambiguous" is his term) nature of the Medici *palazzo* in Florence. Clearly in opposition to the Palazzo della Signoria, "the Medici palace cannot be said to have been a domestic or private residence in the modern sense. It was common knowledge that political decisions were made around the dinner table and it was evident that [it was] like a public monument set in a broader ritual space": R. C. Trexler, *Public Life in Renaissance Florence* (Ithaca: Cornell University Press, 1980), 425. "Yet at all times this public house retained its private mystery; in the future absolutistic state, the line between street formalism and domestic intimacy would be thoroughly obscured by the inscrutable prince" (445).

[61] "The tournament brought to a close *carnevale* Thursday at least five hours after sunset, if not later. Truthfully, it was one of the best things we've seen here in many years; I never thought it could come off so successfully."

[62] "Ours from Pesaro performed a comedy entitled *Erifilomachia* (that is, a battle between love and friendship) by the Perugia doctor Sforza d'Oddo. It is a comedy full of feelings and it came off beautifully according to the acting custom of our area. This was despite the fact that, to be honest, it was very long and thus generally boring. It includes many soliloquies that are pleasant when reading, but not on stage."

[63] "Our Sir Claudio had the role of the *vita* and carried it off fittingly well."

[64] "The very beautiful set that covered the entire length of the hall."

[65] "Two *intermedi* with military dances embellished the comedy. One of them was the rape of the Sabine women that was already staged in Pesaro on other occasions, perhaps sixteen years ago. You must remember it! This *intermedio* looked good and we can say that it appeared new to the audience since it was so long since it had been done. The other *intermedio* was the Arch of the Loyal Lovers and of the Enchanted Room, taken from Amadis of Gaule and Oriana. It looked very good; although those who did not know the plot could not enjoy it as well, it still looked good because gentlemen and ladies took part in it and there were magic spells and fights and other things that look good on stage."

[66] Tani, "Moresca" is clear and highly informative. Attolini, *Teatro e spettacolo nel Rinascimento* presents a concise evaluation of the transformation of dances into *intermezzi*. Case studies of the presence of *moresche* in actual staged entertainment are offered in S. M. Newton, *Renaissance Theatre Costume and the Sense of the Historical Past* (London: Rapp and

Whiting, 1975), esp. 55–56, and in J. D. Falvo, "Urbino and the Apotheosis of Power," *Modern Language Notes* 101 (1986): 114–46. Le Roy Ladurie has pointed out a strong link between sword dances ("which ritualized a war-like confrontation" [*Carnival in Romans*, 319]) and *carnevale* celebrations, with four essential meanings (320). Differently from Romans, the setting at Pesaro seems to have been non-confrontational. Still, the stylized violence of the *moresca* might have served as a reminder of the power structure in place at Pesaro at the time, while clashing with the numerous laws against weapons during *carnevale* festivities.

[67] Indeed the *Aminta* performance reconstructed in chapter 4 of this study presents precisely a fully developed series of such *intermezzi*.

[68] On women playing male parts on stage (primarily in opera), see *En Travesti. Women, Gender Subversion, Opera*, ed. Corinne E. Blackmer and Patricia Juliana Smith (New York: Columbia University Press, 1995).

[69] According to M. Günsberg, "[t]here is no doubt that . . . the improvised *commedia dell'arte*, was performed by professional troupes and family companies including actresses from at least 1540": *Gender and the Italian Stage* (Cambridge: Cambridge University Press, 1997), 58.

[70] An additional element is provided in a later passage of the same letter, where Tiberio states that "pur'oggi i recitanti [of *Aminta*] sono partiti per Fossombrone per rappresentarla al Cardinale [Giulio della Rovere] che desidera di sentirla." (Saviotti, "Torquato Tasso e le feste," 413; MS oliveriano 390, fol. 94 v) [the performers left for Fossombrone to stage *Aminta* for the cardinal who wants to hear it]. This brief notation still does not provide us with conclusive evidence, since the Fossombrone performance was to take place in a similar courtly setting, hence it would have been perfectly acceptable for members of an *accademia* to perform under such circumstances.

[71] See for example the identifications provided by Godard, "La Première représentation de l'*Aminta*," 226–36, 271–84.

[72] Ducato d'Urbino, classe I divisione B filza X, fols. 654–60.

[73] "In the other hall, for comedies, there is a fabulous set in which a fabulous *hostiria* by Paciotto will be staged alongside many amusing and ingenious *intermezzi* <of *moresca*, dance, and other novelties>. We will give news of this after the end of the celebration <that will start> postponed to Sunday January 14 <postponed to that day> as we are waiting for the Venetian ambassador who should come any day now, with a great retinue."

[74] Saviotti interpreted and transcribed the rather cryptic term *hostiria* as "historia" ("Torquato Tasso e le feste," 413 n. 1).

[75] "The set was beautiful because it was decorated with paintings and because it was quite large: it was as big as the length of the hall. Said hall was, and still is, entirely adorned with square paintings of perspectival landscapes surrounded by white stucco moldings. It was not as rich as was to be expected upon similar circumstances, yet the beauty of the decoration took the place of the monetary expense."

[76] In following his day's linguistic habit, the anonymous source calls these moldings "simulacri," a term that refers to their three-dimensional quality rather than to a more or less realistic depiction of natural elements.

[77] It "was not at all conceived as an autonomous entity, but rather as the natural extension of the space on stage, or at the very least as the space facing it": C. Molinari, "Gli spettatori e lo spazio scenico nel teatro del cinquecento," *Bollettino Palladio* 16 (1974),

145–54, here 147. Molinari first put forth this argument in "Les Rapports entre la scène et les spectateurs dans le théâtre italien du XVIe siècle," in *Le Lieu théâtral à la Renaissance* (Paris: CNRS, 1964), 61–71.

[78] It "felt the development of perspective as a technique, that is, the superposition of an element in contrast with the anthropocentric theory of space. At this time the space of the stage started to separate from physical space, but it did not yet become a replacement of physical space. The perspectival plan carried out the function of 'amplifying' physical space that still was the place where the stage or the set were situated": F. Marotti, "Teoria e tecnica dello spazio scenico dal Serlio al Palladio nella trattatistica rinascimentale," *Bollettino Palladio* 16 (1974): 257–70, here 259.

[79] In the following chapter, attention will be devoted to the frame of the Parma staging, which was decidedly less subtle than the one at Pesaro.

[80] It is during these very years that cartographers, engravers, and printers were starting to tackle to complex problem of depicting three-dimensional cities on two-dimensional surfaces. In this process, the importance of a spatially elevated, all-encompassing point of view became progressively clearer, as shown by Lucia Nuti, "The Perspective Plan in the Sixteenth Century," *Art Bulletin* 76 (1994): 105–28.

[81] Essentially all sources on the Villa Imperiale record the same legend regarding its naming: "alla sua fondazione intervenne . . . l'imperatore Federigo III d'Asburgo ospite dei signori di Pesaro, gli Sforza, durante il viaggio verso Roma nel 1452, quando si recava laggiù a ricever la corona dalle mani del pontefice Niccolò V": G. Marchini and N. Cecini, *La villa Imperiale di Pesaro* (Pesaro: Cassa di risparmio, 1986), 7 [emperor Frederick III of Augsburg was in attendance when its first stone was lain. He was a guest of the Sforza, then ruling over Pesaro, on his way to Rome to receive his crown from Pope Nicholas V's hands, in 1452]. See also G. Marchini, ed., *La villa Imperiale di Pesaro* (Pesaro: Cassa di risparmio, n.d.), 5–6; A. Pinelli and O. Rossi, "L'Imperiale nuova di Gerolamo Genga," *Storia dell'arte* 6 (1970), 101–19, here 113; and L. Firpo, *Lo stato ideale della controriforma* (Bari: Laterza, 1957), 71.

[82] L. Raimondi, "Villa Imperiale, Pesaro," in *Ville e giardini*, ed. F. Borsi and G. Pampaloni (Novara: De Agostini, 1989), 347–50, here 347.

[83] "Francesco Maria realized Genga was uncommonly gifted, and decided to have a new palace built alongside the old one at Imperiale. Genga then built the one that we now see, a beautiful and well-proportioned building, with many rooms, colonnades, courtyards, loggias, fountains, and delightful gardens. No prince goes by that he does not stop to see it. Even Pope Paul III, on his way to Bologna with his entire court, went to see it and was happy with it."

[84] "The fact that living quarters are nearby means that the new villa only carries out official, entertainment roles. The old building was refurbished and could carry out all the services needed for the court's stay": R. Martufi, *Diletto e meraviglia* (Pesaro: Nobili, 1992), 27.

[85] "The new Imperiale building was conceived as an enclosed body, surrounded on the outside by compact walls that do not let the viewer imagine how the internal structures are articulated": Pinelli and Rossi, "L'Imperiale nuova," 104

[85] "Villa Rovere played the sole role of being a *theater* of courtly life, as the Sforza building carried out the domestic or political and representative ones."

[87] It "is endowed with a relevant ethical commitment: an attempt to going back to being a magnet for the best literati of the land, as the duchy had been under Federico and Guidubaldo of Montefeltro."

[88] See Leone Maggiorotti, "Francesco Paciotto," *Enciclopedia italiana* 25: 288; Maggiorotti was a general in the then Royal Italian Army.

[89] Archivio di Stato, Parma; raccolta Ronchini, busta 4 fascicolo 14a, fol. 4 v.

[90] "It would be like removing the veil from before the stage, like dropping the cloth before the prologue is on stage, which is what the now late Duke Guidubaldo used to do."

[91] "It has been considered as one of the most beautiful pieces thus far staged in this genre. Its concepts were very beautiful and most pleasant. The plot, though simple, was pleasant and affectionate. Truth be told, it was not so well performed as it deserved in some roles, even major ones, especially in its pathos which is the main source of pleasure in this eclogue. Yet people with taste judged it something rare."

[92] This element has rightly been underscored by Cruciani: Almerici "per l'*Aminta* . . . non fa cenno della scena ma solo dei recitatori ed evidenzia che il diletto nasce non tanto dalla storia o dai personaggi quanto dagli 'affetti;' è un giudizio che andrà compreso in quanto definisce ciò che i contemporanei più ammirarono e sentirono del testo del Tasso, e forse anche come indicazione di una qualità drammaturgica non tanto esteticamente quanto tecnicamente diversa e innovativa": "Percorsi critici," 180 [does not mention the set for *Aminta*, but only its performers. He underscores that its pleasure came not so much from the plot or the characters but from 'affects.' This is a judgment that we must understand as it defines what Tasso's contemporaries admired and felt the most in his text. Perhaps we should also take it as an indication of its staging quality, which was different and innovative not from the æsthetic, but from the technical standpoint].

Cruciani's last assertion, however, is problematic in so far that it seems to exclude that *Aminta* could have been both aesthetically and theatrically innovative. Indeed, we could see Tasso's pastoral as an early example of what Barbara Ives Beyer identified as "Baroque Representation." In her words, in this period "the aim of art . . . is not the imitation of accidents of sense-perception, but rather to move the affections by showing character and emotion": B. I. Beyer, "Baroque Representation," *Journal of Aesthetic and Art Criticism* 12 (1953–59): 360–65, here 361. One could then argue that the theater was especially well suited to this task, since it represents "characters" feeling "emotions" directly in front of the audience, that is, in the most direct way possible.

[93] "What was added to the eclogue and that pleased everybody more than a little were the new choruses between the acts that bestowed wonderful magnificence and gave those watching and listening great delight with very pleasing concepts."

[94] In spite of Almerici's letter, Solerti doubts that the third and fourth *cori* had been written before the Pesaro performance (*Vita di Torquato Tasso*, 1: 190). Sozzi offers a complete list of the presence of the text of the choruses in the various manuscripts and editions of *Aminta* ("Per l'edizione critica dell'*Aminta*," 46, 49).

[95] Sozzi cites Solerti (*Vita di Torquato Tasso*, 1: 185 and 190) who believes that the issue of the presence of the *intermezzi* cannot be settled. In any case, Sozzi's own opinion is that they "sono estranei alla favola" ("Per l'edizione critica dell'*Aminta*," 45) [are extraneous to the play] and do not elicit or are worthy of his scholarly interest. The reader will recall that

Sozzi espouses the idea that the *intermezzi* never constituted an integral part of Tasso's text, indeed were a distraction and a disruption of its dramatic unity.

[96] "I will say that Tasso took great care in giving pleasure to these lords in attendance and great things will take place tomorrow."

[97] Solerti interprets this allusion to refer to the learned literary debates between Tasso himself and Jacopo Mazzoni, also mentioned in Almerici's letter (Saviotti, "Torquato Tasso e le feste," 413–15; MS oliveriano 390, fols. 94 v–95 v).

[98] This sad state of affairs has been decried by many, most recently by Lawrence Rhu in his English translation of *Discorsi dell'arte poetica*: *The Genesis of Tasso's Narrative Theory* (Detroit: Wayne State University Press, 1993), 8–9.

[99] The earliest mentioned description of courtly festivities is the one published in 1539 for a Medici wedding: see C. Molinari, *Le nozze degli dei* (Rome: Bulzoni, 1968), 69 n. 24.

[100] Moreover, it appears counterintuitive that Guidubaldo was trying to extinguish the memory of a bloody repression that seems to have had a similar impact to Cesare Borgia's public display of Remirro de Orco's corpse on the main square of Cesena, as presented in Machiavelli's *Il principe* (chap. 7). Since Guidubaldo's goal seems to set an example for other towns in his realm, then he should have wanted to preserve these events in his subjects' minds, rather than trying to distract them with lavish carnival festivities. On the subject of the spectacle of fear in Machiavelli's work, see Wayne Rebhorn, *Foxes and Lions: Machiavelli's Confidence Men* (Ithaca: Cornell University Press, 1988), esp. chap. 3.

[101] A. K. Nardo, *The Ludic Self in Seventeenth-Century English Literature* (Albany: State University of New York Press, 1991), 36.

[102] Attolini's study also goes in this direction, and beyond Bakhtin's position, when he states that a courtly spectacle "si caratterizza in due modi significativamente pregnanti: da un lato la festa è una cerimonia rituale ostentativa, perché consente al signore di mostrarsi al popolo in tutta la sua potenza e magnificenza, dall'altro è anche una cerimonia rituale distruttiva, perché, tramite la festa, il principe può annullare in un solo colpo molti di quei beni prodotti con immane fatica dal lavoro dei sudditi, sfuggendo al destino comune ai più, cui è concesso soltanto di riuscire a sovravvivere": *Teatro e spettacolo*, 27 [has two especially important characters. On the one hand the festivity is a display-heavy ritual ceremony, as it allows the lord to show himself in all his might and magnificence. On the other, it is also a destruction-bound ritual ceremony, because with the festivity the prince can annihilate many goods produced with great effort and work by his subjects, thus escaping the destiny of the masses who are only allowed to manage to survive].

At the same time, "[i]l Carnevale è quella fase temporale durante la quale le libertà quotidianamente represse esplodono in forme ludiche, procurando quella tradizionale 'catarsi' che compensa il popolo ma soddisfa soprattutto il potere, in quanto gli garantisce la ripresa del dominio nel momento in cui lo 'sfogo' si placa" (28) [*carnevale* is the time frame when daily repressed freedoms explode in games. Thus a traditional catharsis takes place that compensates the people but above all satisfies those in power, as it guarantees them that their domination will be back when the "outburst" is over]. Attolini's language betrays his indebtedness to Bakhtin and Gramsci; his assessment is thus markedly more negative than Nardo's, and reflects less accurately the complex, multi-layered situation at Pesaro in 1574.

[103] According to Lotman, "[l]a natura attiva del gioco si oppone per principio alla distinzione tra chi agisce e chi osserva. Nel suo spazio infatti non esiste il pubblico. Tutti vi prendono parte": "Semiotica della scena," 5 [the active nature of play is inherently opposed to a distinction between those who act and those who look. Its space excludes an audience. Everybody participates in it].

Chapter Three

Parma, 1627–1628: Before the Medici-Farnese Wedding

The festivities within which *Aminta* took place in 1628 differ markedly from those of 1574. At Parma, the occasion was the wedding of the heir to the Farnese domain, Odoardo, to a Medici princess, Margherita, daughter and sister of Florentine rulers (respectively Cosimo II and Ferdinando II). Thus the political importance of this alliance and of the events celebrating it far exceeded that of the 1574 occasion; it transcended not just the local borders separating Parma, Piacenza, and other Farnese lands from other Italian realms, but also the geographical and political boundaries between Italy and the rest of Europe. At the same time, these circumstances heighten the tension between private and public domains almost to paradoxical levels. Further, the customs of courtly entertainment had not just evolved greatly in the fifty-five years separating the Pesaro from the Parma events; they had become established and consequently less flexible; thus the 1628 festivities had to come to terms with pre-existing models. Last, as Irving Lavin has remarked,[1] we are uncommonly lucky since many sources are extant that describe, analyze, and comment on the 1628 festivities. Moreover, these sources have different points of view and perspectives; thus the reconstructive task at hand is made easier by exploiting the discrepancies and tensions emerging from them.

Historically, the *Aminta* performance at Parma has elicited little attention on the part of literary or even theater historians. In this respect, too, it differs greatly from the Pesaro events. The 1628 marriage festivities have been studied by historians of the city and domain of Parma, and more briefly by scholars of opera and early theater architecture. This chapter will approach the Farnese-Medici wedding festivities from a different standpoint. As in the case of the 1574 events, I will try to reconstruct the performance of *Aminta* at Parma and the preparations leading to the event itself, while providing some background information on the customs of staged entertainment in the area at the time and the expectations of the audience. The abundance of extant material will enable me to offer a much richer depiction than for the 1574 performance, but the underlying questions that I will try to answer are essentially the same: what was the goal of the performance? How did the audience react? Who was present? Who performed? Where? This chapter opens with a brief overview of the situation in the Farnese domain at the time of the wedding; it then reconstructs the preparations of the festivities, specifically of those for Tasso's pastoral. The next section offers an overview of the performance of *Aminta*, its prologue, and five *intermezzi*.

1. The Occasion

The wedding between Odoardo Farnese and Margherita de' Medici in 1628 was the culmination of a long series of political and diplomatic events dating back from the previous decade. According to Quintavalle (cited in Lavin, "Lettres," 105 n. 2, and idem, *Art and Pageantry*, 548 n. 2), the first Farnese overtures regarding the possibility of a marital alliance went back to 1615, when the groom was a few years old. Paolo Minucci del Rosso was of the opinion that they could be dated to 1619.[2] Either way, by October 1620 a marriage contract had been drafted and signed by all the involved parties.[3] On the second of November of the same year, the Farnese secretary Oratio (or Horatio) Linati received a letter from Florence by Curtio Picchena, one of the Medici secretaries. The contract had been signed, he reported, but abundant care was still in order lest the Pope should find out about it from other sources.[4]

The same month, the groom's mother, Margherita Aldobrandini, sent an envoy to the bride's mother, Maria Maddalena of Hapsburg, to convey to the latter her happiness and *giubilo*.[5] By the time the wedding took place (1628), it was clearly the Farnese court that had the most to gain by linking itself with the Medici. The Farnese had recently traversed a difficult period, due to the unexpected death of Odoardo's father, Ranuccio I, in 1622, when his only son was but ten years of age. Abroad, too, and above all in Rome, the power wielded by the Farnese had considerably dwindled since the zenith reached with the election to the papacy of Alessandro as Paul III, in 1534.[6] The matrimonial alliance with the Medici, a *granducale* family of great wealth and even greater power in Florence and indeed throughout Italy, promised added stability and increased respect on the part of the Farnesian neighbors and subjects.[7]

It goes without saying that, like most politically and dynastically motivated weddings, the one between Odoardo and Margherita was imposed on the two young people involved in the deal. The marriage contract signed on 26 October 1620, mentions Maria Cristina de' Medici as the bride-to-be, and further specifies that:

> in caso però che al detto Ser[enissi]mo Gran Duca piacesse variare, eleggendone un'altra in luogo di esse [*sic*], contentandosi, in tal caso, il Ser[enissi]mo di Parma che al Gran Duca sia permesso variare et che la suddetta facoltà

di nominare et eleggere una dello [*sic*] altre et il tempo della elezione dentro il tempo e termine di sei anni, da hoggi, liberamente resti a detto Ser[enissi]mo Gran Duca. (Minucci del Rosso, "Le nozze," III, 28)[8]

According to Stuart Reiner's well-documented study of the preparations for the Parma events, Maria Cristina was replaced by Margherita after the expiration of the six-year period stipulated in the marriage contract ("Preparations in Parma," *Music Review* 25 [1964]: 273–301, here 291). Consequently, the wedding itself was postponed by about a year, to December 1628. This is how Reiner explains why the Farnese court had started to prepare in the late spring of 1627 for an event that ultimately took place over a year and a half later. Additionally, he thus justifies the lack of clear directions for staged entertainment as well as the frantic tone that emerges from some of the extant sources. The documents he cites do not unequivocally prove the proposed interpretation; rather, they express uncertainty on the part of two people who were involved with the festivity preparation. On 9 January 1628, the composer Monteverdi communicated to Alessandro Striggio that "da Venetia per bocca del Sig[no]r Ecc[ellentissi]mo Contarino mio Sig[no]re per essere procurator di Santo Marco ho ben inteso che teme non solamente credde Sua Ecc[ellen]za che tali nozze non si faranno per questo carnevale ne per questo maggio come mi havea scritto da Ferrara che si faranno all'hora; ma neanche forsi più" (Malipiero, *Claudio Monteverdi* [Milan: Treves, 1929], 284).[9] On 21 January 1628, Antonio Goretti wrote "Del fare poi questa festa si faranno infalibilm[ente] m[a] p[er] le nozze che si sono preparate, ma il quando non si può sapere di certo, e credo che l'istessi prencipi manco loro lo sapiano" (MS Antonelli 660, 21 January 1628, fol. 1 r–v).[10]

Additionally, three documents from the Archivio di Stato, Firenze, neither prove nor disprove Reiner's interpretation of the events. Two of these are similar letters sent by Odoardo and his mother to the Medici court, to accompany and introduce a "dottor Gerolamo Bagarelli" whose task was to mediate the wedding arrangements; both are dated 3 December 1626. The third is by Horatio Linati (the aforementioned Farnese secretary); dated 4 December 1626, it confirms Bagarelli's departure that very morning.[11] These documents could indicate that some unforeseen circumstances had forced a new round of negotiations or, simply, that Maria Cristina had been replaced by Margherita right before the expiration of the six-year period stipulated in the original agreement, and that the time had come for the last arrangements to be discussed. In fact, two additional letters (one by Odoardo, the other by his mother) in the same bound volume express happiness that a proxy wedding had taken place in Florence, shortly before 19 February 1627, when the letters were written.[12] Thus, Reiner's hypothesis is less solid than previously thought, since the chronological frame for the December 1628 celebrations in Parma seems to be supported by extant documents even without a last-minute change of bride.

Interestingly, but not surprisingly, neither the February letters nor the earliest documents congratulating Odoardo and the Farnese on the impending, proxy, or actual marriage mention the name of his bride; if a substitution did take place, it is impossible to date. Still, on 16 February 1627, the Farnese court drafted a list of letters announcing the marriage, to be sent to many courts in Italy and abroad; the name of the bride appears as Margherita, and the date is consistent with the marriage by proxy recorded in the two aforementioned gratulatory letters sent by the groom and his mother to the bride's family. This list[13] truly reads like a seventeenth-century "Who's Who" of European Catholic aristocracy, including among others the archduchess of Flanders, the kings of France, Spain, and Poland, the Pope, the queens (consorts and mothers) of Spain, France and Poland, the emperor of the Holy Roman Empire and his wife, the heads of the Venetian and Genoese republics, and many dukes, princes and viceroys scattered throughout Italy. The document also mentions the Farnese possessions, and gives specific instructions. In the ducal seat of Parma, the news is to be announced on that very day, the "dì di carnevale" Friday 16 February 1627. Elsewhere, namely at Piacenza, Castro, Ronciglione, Busseto, Valli di Nura and Borgovalditaro and in Abruzzo, the letter is meant for a governor or an *autorità* who will then announce the news to the entire population. Far from being a mere gesture of benevolence towards the Farnese subjects, these announcements pursued two separate goals: on the one hand, they aimed at building an initial excitement over this event, to be amplified and perfected at a later time; on the other, they served as a warning for the weighty pecuniary contributions that the court expected on the occasion of the first wedding of a reigning duke. In sum, it is from the first documented decisions regarding the celebrations that the court shows interest and attention for both the domestic and the foreign policy aspects and consequences of such an event.

Indeed, the wedding was an exercise in domestic and foreign policy for both courts; all the official or semi-official documents it spawned reflect these two concurrent concerns. In a manuscript biography of Odoardo now at the Biblioteca Palatina at Parma,[14] Ippolito Calandrini clearly tries to bring together two separate issues in one polished, highly rhetorical exercise:

> Dovevasi ad un Prencipe si qualificato, e grande dalla prudenza del Cardinale, et di Madama procurare proporzionato accasamento, acciò i di lui Popoli vedessero da questo Cielo per gloria di se stessi nascere di nuovo un Sole, Ranutio, che li felicita . . .
>
> Haveva il politico Duca Ranutio passato, e girato con gli occhi della consideratione i meriti de Prencipi Italiani, e vedendo i mondi Ser[enissi]mi de i gran Duca di Toscana, che molti erroneamente chiamano tale, che se tale fossero state, sarebbero piene di vento svanite, e batute da passati accidenti, e sarebbero divenute moli, mà perche sono realmente Mondi, resistetero sempre, divenero forti, e saranno eterni, come per Mondi furono ancor da dotta mano lodati con l'occasione delle nozze, che seguirono tra quelli Prencipi, che le bale

> produr non possono, perche battute cedono, e pugna non rinovano; havevano
> più volte rinovato quelli con i loro felicissimi parti non solo il bellicoso Regno
> di Francia, ma gl'Imperii ancora, che per loro gloria viddero dà [sic] i Mondi
> prudursi le margarite, dono de i più reconditi, che facia la natura alla terra,
> accalori il sole, apprezzino l'aque, e perfetioni con concordanza meravigliosa
> la forza degli elementi, per sodisfare à quei mortali, che hanno in sorte di unire
> il loro merito à merito sì inesplicabile. Quindi fermato l'occhio del pensiero
> il padre del grande Odoardo in quella bramò di ponere in uso ciò, che ad un
> Prencipe suo pari potea somministrare l'intelletto, ò l'arte di un solo negoziato
> donarli; onde con destrezza degna della sua prudenza fece saggiamente to-
> care il Gran Duca, se in caso, che à Dio piacesse di lasciarli ad esso il suo
> Odoardo, et à lui Margherita, havrebbe incontrato 'l suo gusto nell'allegrezza
> di vedere questi duoi Prencipi unirsi in matrimonio insieme in conformità
> del uso Romano, guida del sacro Consiglio di Trenta [i.e., Trento]. Gradi il
> Ser[enissi]mo di Fiorenza l'invito, e stimò che i Stati del Duca di Parma à i
> suoi uniti per mezzo di parentado fossero per apportare maggiori vantagi alle
> di lui grandezze, che però rispose, che quando i Prencipi fossero in essere,
> havrebbe volontieri sentito l'apertura di tal negozio. (fols. 222–24)[15]

Wishing to praise the regents of Parma as well as the deceased duke Ranuccio, Calandrini asserts that the plan for this marriage was originally conceived to further political goals. Those of the Farnese court did not interfere with the Medici's, and the negotiations came to fruition. Furthermore, Calandrini frankly states that the Medici princesses had renewed many noble stocks in Europe through marriage and conception. In other words, not only were the Florentine princesses well placed through marriage; they were also synonymous with procreation, hence presumably sought after by other courts desirous of political alliances with Florence as well as dynastic continuity.[16]

A similar claim surfaces in a printed *Encomio epitalamico* now at the Archivio di Stato, Parma.[17] Its author, Enea Spennacchi (a Florentine and a historian of the Farnese family, as he proudly proclaims towards the end of his dedication to the groom), praises Odoardo's union with the Medici by extolling two separate achievements of the women in that family:

> della PROSAPIA MEDICI . . . è la Regina Madre di Francia, di questa la
> Arciduchessa di Gratz, di questa l'una delle Duchesse vedove di Mantova, e
> di Monferrato, di questa la Duchessa hora di Parma e di Piacenza e di Castro.
> Da MEDICEA Madre è nata la Prencipessa d'Urbino, da lei i Prencipi di
> Modona, da lei la Prencipessa di Piemonte, da lei la Regina d'Inghilterra,
> da lei il rè di Francia, da lei la Regina di Spagna, da lei l'Imperatrice.[18]

Spennacchi, too, makes two claims: Medici princesses sit on the highest thrones of Europe, thanks to a wise matrimonial policy; and they bear ample fruits to their noble husbands, so that the Medici family could be linked by blood to an even higher number of powerful families in the Western world. It is clear that the praise was intended only in a limited way for the female members of the Medici family, and rather concentrated on the wisdom of their male blood relatives.

Weddings were also personal affairs even at a time and in circumstances in which noble brides and grooms had virtually no voice in choosing a mate.[19] Further, the success of this (or any) matrimonial alliance would be measured by the ability to produce a healthy male heir, so the fiction had to be established and maintained that the two young people involved in this transaction were singularly well matched, and in fact had immediately taken to one another. As will become apparent, the festivities accompanying Odoardo and Margherita's arrival in Parma repeatedly underscore the presence of the god of love along the newlyweds. However, there are extant signs that even before the ceremony by proxy the groom's curiosity was allayed through whatever means considered appropriate under the circumstances. Dr. Bagarelli, the Farnese envoy to Florence who had negotiated the last details late in 1626, wrote to Odoardo on 2 January 1627, reassuringly:

> Sono pochi giorni, ch'io non veda la Ser[enissi]ma sposa di V[ostra] A[ltezza], che pero gli do parte, che havendola vista anco hoggi, sta con la solita sua buona salute, e havendola vista heri senza maschera, posso assicurarla, che il pittor non l'ha inganata in far il ritratto, che gia scrissi a V[ostra] A[ltezza]; anzi tengo per certo, che quando vedra l'uno, e l'altra, piu gli piacera questa, che quello, intendendomi ancor per rispetto delli lineamenti, colorito, e bellezza respettivamente.[20]

Though portraits had been exchanged, Odoardo wanted to know (or had to be reassured) that his wife-to-be was physically attractive. Bagarelli had seen her without her mask on,[21] and could personally attest to her beauty. Though the young prince's feelings were entirely subject to the wishes of the court, attempts were made to include him in the process, of which (after all) he would be soon the protagonist. Odoardo's biographer, Ippolito Calandrini, gave a *post ex facto* explanation of the importance of portraits in his pompous style, laden with mythological references:

> Viaggiato havevano i retrati di questi duoi Prencipi, e sebene non erano stati fabricati dalla virtù di quei duoi antichi pittori Fida, e Parasio, che inganarono gli uceli, gli huomini, e le virtù di loro stessi, erano ben però sì di tali maestri, che ne' volti di quello havevano fato comparire la maestà de loro cuori, sì nella fascia [i.e., faccia] di Odoardo si vedeva campeggiare il valore, e in quelle di Margherita quasi in maestoso trono acceso l'honore, quali pervenuti vicendevolmente nelle mani de' sod[det]ti Prencipi nel moto primiero, che aventurarono gli occhi in quelli con l'arte de loro vezzosi vagheggiamenti, accesero entro se stessi il fuocho, col quale sacrificandosi l'uno al'altro il genio, giurarono di eternizzare i di loro amori anco doppo la morte de corpi per le virtù de loro animi, che possono ancora in Cielo con tempo da essi

essere vedute beate; amicò l'uno il compendio della bellezza, che da una grande modestia accompagnata rassembrava l'aurora spirante dal'orizzonte per rendere le opinioni di bianghezza adorno essendo il proprio seme delle geme il comparire delle nevi più illustre, senza far sbagliare chi le mira, perche hanno per proprio del essere contemplate di accrescere il loro valore, mentre l'altro vedendo sotto sembianza di un Marte la maestà di un volto tutto Reggio, giurò al Cielo del suo arbitrio, di non consegnare se stessa in matrimonio ad altro Prencipe accompagnata dalla saviezza del volto, è [sic] un compendio si nobile, che non può nella sua grandezza essere sodisfato, se non trionfa di un cuore simile à quello di Alessandro, Odoardo nè haveva l'effigie, perchè haveva il corraggio, che però ben disse Scipione, che i cuori generosi non erano sodisfati de' i loro spiriti, se non ottenevano quei fini, che li prescriveva il valore,[22] Giacob servì à Laban 14 anni per ottenere la bella Rachel, non curando Lila [sic]; che però non è meraviglia, se i negozii non si concludono subito; furono longhi in tratati, come è solito dei grandi, amore hà i suoi artificii, cosi potenti, per palesarsi potentissimo, frà i numi celesti, che non può se non da una soda pazienza esser capito, facendosi Con il tempo così forte, che rompe con un non voglio le leggi di convenienza per formare con un voglio quella della sua forza, che chiamasi constanza. La forma, che si prende per gli occhi, è l'ardore dello spirito. (*L'Heroe d'Italia*, fols. 226–28)[23]

Calandrini's passage attests to the importance and power attributed to images in the seventeenth century, while perpetuating the cliché (pervading lyrical poetry from the *Stil Novo* on) that eyes were the gateway to the soul. It also provides a romantic, if altogether fictional, explanation for the long time taken up by the marriage negotiations between the Medici and the Farnese. Odoardo's biographer introduces a literary and rhetorical ploy that is present throughout the description of the wedding celebrations: placing the newlyweds at center stage, metaphorically and at times literally, to deflect the reader's (and viewer's) attention away from the political elements underlying the marriage and from the practical, mechanical side of the staged events. The tools of choice were mythological references, rife in this passage, reinforcing the types of the valorous prince and of the beautiful and chaste princess. Other extant documents display the same dazzling familiarity with Greco-Roman mythology and classical history. However, Calandrini in this passage exploits another source of imagery and examples, namely the Bible. Here the episode of Jacob and Rachel (Gen. 29:15–28) is presented as a lesson in faithfulness and patience, the same virtues Odoardo and Margherita showed before their marriage. Additionally, the sacred quality of love sanctioned by matrimony surfaces in this passage when Calandrini asserts that the bond conceived by simply looking at each other's portraits would continue past the lovers' death, into eternal life.

While Calandrini and other writers from the courtly milieu described highly stylized situations and emotions, these documents reveal only a small part of the goings-on, as extant letters make manifest. The nature of early modern Italian courts allows us to peer more closely into the practical side of the wedding and celebrations. Like any early-seventeenth-century court, the Farnese one was at the same time exceedingly interested in the image projected within and outside its social, architectural and geographical boundaries, and amply regulated and bureaucratic. As James Saslow has pointed out in his remarkable reconstruction of the 1589 Medici wedding (*The Medici Wedding of 1589*, 5), it is precisely the attention to details, to the allocation of available funds, and to the identity of those employed at court that allows for the reconstruction of the circumstances leading to the wedding celebrations.

Though the Farnese court was not as minutely regimented as the Medici one,[24] the ducal palace and all personal possessions were kept under constant supervision. On 4 February 1628, the *maggiordomo* or housekeeper Antonio Faelli was charged with constructions and repairs to all ducal buildings in Parma and elsewhere in the Farnese domains,[25] including all the building renovations and alterations associated with the wedding festivities. A system of checks and balances was obviously in place, since the *maggiordomo*'s orders had to be transmitted to the *maggiorente*, or overseer, and in turn to the *computista*, or accountant. Accounts payable, too, had to go through the same chain of command, presumably to avoid any extravagant or unjustified expenditure. Franco Piperno envisions a parallel between "absolutist centralized governments" and court spectacles: the latter "reproduced, on a smaller scale, the nature, structure, and ends of such governments: the new efficiency of the 'state machine' in the realms of warfare, diplomacy, bureaucracy, and taxation was reflected in the persuasiveness and seductiveness of a princely spectacle whose dramatic and musical essence centered on the sole presentation of the character" ("Opera Production to 1780," in *Opera Production and Its Resources*, ed. L. Bianconi and G. Pestelli [Chicago: University of Chicago Press, 1998], 1–79, here 3–4).[26]

The *maggiordomo* was responsible for the upkeep of buildings and all courtly personnel, for bill payments and contract assignments, for crop allocation and account settlements. Those in charge of the wedding celebrations would have had to defer to his judgment, convince him that certain purchases were necessary, and cajole him into granting their requests. It is therefore somewhat surprising that a larger number of documents is not extant. It is particularly unfortunate that we cannot calculate how much money was spent for the Parma celebrations or how much the court extracted from the Farnese domains. It goes without saying that such events were always extremely expensive;[27] in this case, a specific amount cannot be determined. Nevertheless, a few give us glimpses of the situation. For example, a list of the "residui del donativo de S[ignori] Feudatarij p[er] le p[ri]me Nozze del Ser[enissi]mo Sig[nor] Duca Odoardo"[28] itemizes how much each noble family still owed the court.[29] Additionally, it was the feudatory's or the city's responsibility to suggest to the Duke ways to raise the required donation. The city of Piacenza addressed the ducal Chancery a letter to this effect:[30]

Parma, 1627–1628: Before the Medici-Farnese Wedding

> Dovendo la Comunità di Piacenza fare al Serenissimo Signor principe Odoardo il solito donativo delle prime nozze che è di doble sessanta milla di Spagna e ducati sei milla che valutati al corso corrente di £45.c£18 importano a monete di Piacenza due millioni ottocento cinquanta milla lire   £2850000
>
> Si pensa che coll'essempio di Parma, si dovesse anche la Comunità di Piacenza indure a pagar qualche somma di contanti, e cosi che se ne possi sperare almeno la somma di dieci mille doble di Spagna che sarebero   £450000
>
> si che resterebbe il debito di   £2400000
>
> Per sodisfare à questo resto, si crede che la Comunità non havrà dificoltà ad imporre tanti delli Dazij imposti già per altre occasioni, ma puoi aboliti, e questi per la somma annua di lire duecento milla con le quali si estinguerebbe il debito tutto in termine d'anni dodici in punto, e si seguirà in questa parte l'uso praticato altre volte di pagar appunto in questa forma.[31]

The various customs duties listed in the rest of this document cover everything from salt to milled grains to the rights of passage over the Po river to the production and sale of wine and the slaughtering of animals. This letter, along with other documents of a similar nature, helps counterbalance the noble, mythological imagery pervading court-sponsored or -dedicated texts like Calandrini's biography of Odoardo. It is precisely the variety of sources extant that makes the Parma festivities a fortunate anomaly and that allows a rather precise reconstruction of the *Aminta* performance. Although the Farnese did not directly sponsor the writing or printing of any accounts of the wedding festivities, the complex relationship linking the court to the artists working for and within it[32] was the basis for the publication of a detailed report on the part of their creator, Marcello Buttigli. Moreover, the authors of the *intermedi* and the prologue that were played with *Aminta* also had their texts printed. We can rely on the abridged version of the diary of a *parmense* as well as on Calandrini's manuscript biography of Odoardo. Moreover, four letters are extant by Luigi Inghirami, the Medici envoy who accompanied Margherita on her trip and addressed to her mother, Maria Maddalena of Hapsburg. Lastly, the Pesaro nobleman and *letterato* Camillo Giordani related his experiences at Parma to his wife in five letters. These sources differ widely in the degree of precision and thoroughness they offer; however, their sheer number as well as the different backgrounds and allegiances of their authors prove singularly enlightening. Indeed, such standpoints provide a varied picture of the event, based as they are on different expectations and experiences among audience members. Conversely, official or semi-official sources strive for a univocal report and interpretation of the events; reductive though they might be, they are also devoid of misinterpretations or misreading of the staged events. The tension among these documents is a decided advantage to the endeavor at hand.[33]

2. Preparations: The Theater

According to the printers of Marcello Buttigli's report, "il Sig[nor] March[ese] Entio Bentivoglij, ed il Sig[nor] Co[nte] Fabio Scotti" were to be considered as "gli Hercoli, e gli Atlanti di sì gloriose Sfere" (*Descrittione dell'apparato* [1629], iv) [Marquis Entio Bentivoglij and Count Fabio Scotti . . . Hercules and Atlas of these glorious spheres], that is, of the entire production that took place for the Farnese-Medici newlyweds. A similar claim, in a similar style, is in Calandrini's biography of Odoardo:

> erano gionti i Bentivoglii in Parma, e nel gran Cortile della Pilota sod[det]ta havevano con i loro sotilisimi ingegni fato rizzare le più superbe machine, più vaghi edifizii, che da humano intendimento possi essere capito, e formato, per essere indubitato, che per darli la perfetione, che si li diede, altro non vi voleva, che la liberalità di un Odoardo, l'ingegno di uno Ecc[ellentissi]mo Marchese Bentivoglio, l'assistenza di un Duca di Poli, e le virtuose compositioni trà molte altre del Co[nte] Bernardo Morandi. (*L'Heroe d'Italia*, fols. 313–14)[34]

Enzo Bentivoglio was an important figure in early seventeenth-century northern Italian courts, due to his knowledge in the field of theatrical and musical entertainment. He had been among the founders of the Accademia degli Intrepidi at Ferrara in 1601 (T. Ascari, "Bentivoglio, Enzo," in *DBI* 8:610–12, here 611), for which five years later he had a theater built by Giovan Battista Aleotti (Carandini, *Teatro e spettacolo*, 198). According to Janet Southorn, "[u]ntil 1617 . . . Enzo the impresario, Aleotti the designer and for a time Alessandro Guarini the poet collaborated on a spectacular series of dramas-to-music and *intermezzi*, tournaments and quintains, which entertained Ferrara at Carnival and welcomed distinguished visitors" (*Power and Display in the Seventeenth Century: The Arts and their Patrons in Modena and Ferrara* [Cambridge: Cambridge University Press, 1988], 80–81). Fabris considers him an innovator as he assembled a "'squadra ferrarese' specializzata nell'organizzazione di tornei anche fuori dell'ambito cittadino" (72) ['Ferrara team' specializing in putting together tournaments even out of town].[35]

In 1618, the Farnese invited Bentivoglio to Parma to help organize spectacles to celebrate the passage of Cosimo II de' Medici on his way to Milan to venerate the body of Carlo Borromeo, bishop of the city and newly proclaimed saint. For this occasion, which never materialized, Bentivoglio again collaborated with Aleotti for the construction of the precedent-setting Teatro Farnese.[36] Again in 1627, the Farnese appealed to him to organize the festivities to celebrate the newlyweds' arrival in Parma. It seems reductive, though justifiable, to agree with Reiner that "it was natural that the original impresario of the theatre should be thought of; and it surely was for this reason that Bentivoglio was asked to superintend the new preparations" ("Preparations in Parma," 285). Nine years had gone by; if Bentivoglio had not continued to organize spectacles and had not acquired even more fame, the Farnese presumably would not have called him back. In Southorn's words, "Enzo had created for himself a unique rôle as the supplier of a multitude of services and people relied upon him. . . . It was his network of contacts which made Enzo so useful as an agent, and which he could exploit when he acted as entrepreneur. . . . [At Parma in 1627–1628] the artists [painters, architects, and so on] worked for Enzo as much as for the Farnese" (*Power and Display*, 83–84).[37]

Along with Bentivoglio, the other nobleman Buttigli's introduction singles out was the *maggiordomo* of the Farnese duke, Count Fabio Scotti. Evidently, for those who had in some capacity witnessed the preparations for the festivities, the artistic and organizational role played by Bentivoglio was complemented by that of the *maggiordomo*, who — as noted above — authorized all expenses and contracts. If Bentivoglio's role was organizational and creative, Scotti's was bureaucratic and financial, less glamorous perhaps, but equally important.

While Scotti lived at Parma, perhaps even at court, Enzo Bentivoglio was in Ferrara, for most of the time absent from the construction sites. Consequently, instructions were requested and conveyed by mail. The extant letters, all directed to Bentivoglio and soliciting his opinion, were located in a manuscript letter collection at the Biblioteca Comunale at Ferrara by Irving Lavin, who twice printed a selection comprising the letters relevant to the nuptial festivities of 1628.[38] Bentivoglio's main correspondents from Parma fall into two categories: Antonio Goretti was charged with the musical entertainment; Francesco Guitti and his assistant Francesco Mazzi were responsible for the architectural side of the festivities. In essence, Bentivoglio reproduced the hierarchical order of the Farnese court. This in turn allowed him to limit his visits to Parma, while keeping the situation there under his firm control. Guitti designed the plans for the temporary theater in the ducal Palazzo della Pilotta (called "di San Pietro martire" after a pre-existent church in the same courtyard) and was in charge of supervising its construction as well as of refurbishing, adapting and decorating the main stage, the Teatro Farnese.[39] Scotti's first letter to Bentivoglio is dated 10 July 1627; the last one, by Goretti, 15 December 1628. Naturally, since all three correspondents wrote only when Bentivoglio was not present at Parma, the letters tend to concentrate in specific periods; thus we do not possess a complete and continuous documentation. What we do have, however, allowed Lavin to attribute to Guitti the paternity of the project for the temporary theater, which until 1964 had been uncertain.[40] Moreover, these letters constitute a powerful counterbalance to the idealized tone present in most of the other sources; even the ones that were not directly spawned by the Farnese court, such as Giordani's letters, betray a sense of wonder and astonishment at the end result, but do not consider (because they could not have known) the practical aspects of the project. Finally, some of Guitti's and Mazzi's letters contain sketches that help reconstruct the temporary structure in which *Aminta* was performed. These constitute the only contemporary visual testimony available to us, since owing to a series of unfortunate circumstances Buttigli's *Relattione* had to go to print without the planned etchings.[41]

The first letter directly related to the architectural work at hand, dated 19 August 1627,[42] seems to continue a conversation that Guitti and Bentivoglio had begun in person when the latter was present at Parma.[43] Work on the temporary Teatro di San Pietro martire was under way, not without problems.[44] From the very start, the architects were short of hands, and implicitly appealed to Bentivoglio for help. Also, what emerges is the amount of sheer muscular strength necessary to carry out each of these tasks.[45] The hopeful and energetic tone of this letter could blind us to other, more telling, details. Here as everywhere, practical concerns command the highest attention (such as the specific measurements given for the wooden planks used in the temporary structure). Guitti reported these details to Bentivoglio for two reasons: they helped the addressee visualize or imagine the temporary structure, and the building had to fit a certain budget. Practical and financial reasons presumably justify the satisfaction Guitti and his colleagues derived from the unexpected *trouvaille* of ready-made columns that could be easily utilized for this new construction.

The following day, the proscenium was in place: "si sono levati in piede i legni dell'imboccatura della scena" (Lavin, "Lettres," 120; idem, *Art and Pageantry*, 526; MS Antonelli 660, 20 August 1627, fol. 1 r) [we raised the poles for the stage opening]. Even the *maggiordomo* Scotti was aware that more hands were needed, as his letter of 24 August attests.[46] A few days later, on 4 September, the canvas was being readied;[47] and on 7 September, the structure had been erected and the crew was getting ready to hoist the canvas cover above it:

> Di sotto [i. e., in the temporary theater, as opposed to the permanent structure, the Teatro Farnese, which was usually called "superiore" or "di sopra" as it was on the second floor] abbiamo fatto l'orditura per il coperto, e sono già i legni in esecuzione per cominciarlo, essendo ancora segnato, et aggiustato in ogni parte, e dirò à V[ostra] S[ignoria] Ill[ustrissi]ma, come è ordinato; e ne potrà vedere schizzo del profilo fatto nella p[resen]te maniera.
> La l[ette]ra segnata .a. è l'altezza del suo frontespicio.
> La .b. è la cima del coperto per poter riscotere il Tempio p[rim]o che và al Cielo, e per più altezza per il dinanzi, dove seranno i Cavalli; e riscoteremo l'acqua, che viene dal .b. .a. con un Zorno, e con una canna, che la porterà appunto nella Doccia; che se avessimo cominciato il piovere da .a. per andare nell'ult[im]a pendenza, saressimo riusciti tanto bassi, che niente più. (Lavin, "Lettres," 121–22; idem, *Art and Pageantry*, 527; MS Antonelli 660, 7 September 1627, fol. 2 r)[48]

The *Aminta* show performed in this temporary structure did not include any effect of artificial rain. This points to an important element that has so far been largely neglected: Bentivoglio, Mazzi, Guitti, and all the workers under their orders were in the process of building a theater without knowing exactly how it would be used. There was a serendipitous quality to this endeavor, since the final product required a high degree of adaptability to elements pertaining to entertainment that had not yet been decided. There were other imponderables, such as the weather. At least one member of the 1628 audience was of the opinion that the canvas cover was not meant to shelter the theater and its occupants from the rain. Camillo Giordani in fact wrote that "L'*Aminta*, che si recita con intramezzi reali, se piove non si può fare, poi che s'ha da rappresentare in un teatro, cui fa tetto una tela incerata" (Saviotti, "Feste e spettacoli," 47)[49]. Giordani's opinion seems to be confirmed by the fact that the canvas did not cover the entire temporary structure, but just the area where the audience would sit. In any case, from a practical standpoint the wooden poles supporting the canvas cover, although necessary, added another challenge to the architects in that they interfered with the audience's line of vision towards the stage. No extant document touches on this subject, which was possibly broached directly with Bentivoglio during one of his trips to the construction site.

Guitti had probably been overly optimistic, since eight days later, on 15 September, no progress had been made and the canvas cover had not yet been put into place. As a way to explain and justify the delay, Guitti pointed out adverse weather conditions.[50] His frustration is palpable: what had been built was ravaged by inclement weather, which in turn delayed the placing of the protective cover. A week later, on 22 September, Guitti's tone is remarkably lighter: "Saremo sabbato a coperto, et essendo questo un gran lavoro all'ordine per ridurlo in opera, spero che ad un tratto si farà gran fracasso" (Lavin, "Lettres," 123; idem, *Art and Pageantry*, 528; MS Antonelli 660, 22 September 1627, fol. 1 r).[51]

Guitti's ensuing letter is dated 24 October: left without clear instructions, he requested an assistant and further advice.[52] Guitti must have been convinced that Bentivoglio was shirking his responsibilities or at the very least that he needed help. Two days later, on 26 October, the Farnese *maggiordomo*, the aforementioned Fabio Scotti, sent a note to Bentivoglio via a special dispatcher: in no uncertain terms, he summoned Bentivoglio to Parma, to carry out his duties as organizer and supervisor (MS Antonelli 660, 26 October 1627, fol. 1 r). It was, in effect, a call to order uttered by the courtier closest to the festivity preparations. The import of this letter is heightened by the fact that it is the first of only a handful of explicit dispatches.

Scotti's summons did not produce the intended results: starting on 28 October, it was Mazzi who wrote to Bentivoglio, until January 1628. His first letter gives us the impression that he felt somewhat overwhelmed by all he had to familiarize himself with; nevertheless Mazzi wanted to convey to Bentivoglio that he had jumped right into his task.[53] He had met and talked to all the people who were collaborating on the celebrations: Goretti, Scotti, and above all Francesco Guitti, who had been sick. He might also have ordered a list of workers employed in the *fabbrica*, which was composed by a Giovanni Andrea Cattanio and is extant in the Archivio di Stato, Parma.[54] Though this document and others do not substantially help the reconstruction of the festivities, they give us a sense of the multitude of unskilled and skilled workers and materials employed in this project. The fact that workers are all called "Messer" (an honorary title loosely equivalent to "master") is presumably to be taken as an indication that these men were skilled masons. Further, they remind us how pervasive court bureaucracy was.[55]

Mazzi's following letter, dated 16 November, is extremely rich in practical details. By then the wooden structure of the temporary theater was in place, but a few technical elements needed tending to, specifically the movement of the wings and backdrops.[56] Work was also beginning on the scenery and the stage machinery that would be used during the performance itself.[57] Mazzi again comes across as extremely active and engaged in his work; interestingly, in this letter he did not inform Bentivoglio only about the building and decoration progress, but also about how various artists and craftsmen were employed. Perhaps Mazzi merely wanted to show Bentivoglio that he knew how best to make use of the skills of various men; or a more practical reason was also at play, since Mazzi would eventually respond to Bentivoglio (and the latter to Count Scotti) as to the cost and timeliness of the finished product, so to speak.[58]

Building props out of sketches was difficult enough, but the architects' endeavor was made more difficult by the fact that they often had to proceed without a clear understanding of exactly what kind of entertainment would take place in this newly built theater. Guitti's letter dated 7 September, in which reference was made to the effect of artificial rain, provides an early example. Mazzi's letter of 16 November, however, is even more striking. At the same time when specific decorations and stage machines were under way, the architect in charge did not know what was going to be performed there. Here, Mazzi mentioned seven pieces of stage machinery. A temple, on which Riboni had started to work, could be identified with the three-dimensional and flying piece dedicated to the god of marriage, Hymen, in Achillini's prologue. A garden, cited twice, on which knights would stand, was a large platform (Mazzi tellingly calls it "il palco che và sù e giù") that presumably was utilized in Pio di Savoia's first printed *intermezzo*.[59] Bradamante and Melissa's horse, as well as Atlas's, also appear in the first *intermezzo*. The heavenly city could be the machinery on which Jupiter and most of the gods and goddesses of Greco-Roman mythology appeared in the fifth printed *intermezzo*. The "Machina de Cavali" is probably the moving platform on which the knights appeared for the final tournament at the end of the fifth *intermezzo*. We can thus surmise that thirteen months before the festivities the plots (if not the texts) of the *intermezzi* had been established.[60] What about the play, though? Interestingly Mazzi thought that a pastoral would be performed not in this temporary structure, but in the *salone*, that is, in the Teatro Farnese. At the beginning of this same letter, he wrote that he would start talking "prima del salone" (Lavin, "Lettres," 129; idem, *Art and Pageantry*, 531; MS Antonelli 660, 16 November 1627, fol. 1 r); and he went on to say: "Vi era natta una difficoltà grandiss[i]ma in esse scene, che nel tempo che dovea sorgere la Città di Dite, vi si ritrovava sopra, di quelle che traversa una scena, la quale à bisognato levar via, è [sic] farla venir presso la Boscarecia" (Lavin, "Lettres," 129–30; idem, *Art and Pageantry*, 531; MS Antonelli 660, 16 November 1627, fol. 1 r).[61] The "Boscarecia" does not univocally identify Tasso's pastoral; however, it seems unlikely that two plays would be performed with a similar topic and setting. Additionally, Mazzi's letter betrays a lack of consideration for the play (to whichever genre it belonged) within which the *intermezzi* were to take place. While it is true that for an architect and stage decorator the latter constituted a formidable task and therefore demanded more attention, the same attitude emerges in the extant audience members' reports, as we will see in the following chapter.

The temporary theater of San Pietro martire, much like the Farnese itself, was built for the performance of *intermezzi*, and only secondarily for other sorts of plays. Additionally, serendipity played a significant role in the end result, both in the architectural and the performative realm. Lavin has suggested that "le théâtre de Guitti semble annoncer le théâtre à loges, où les balcons sont en effet divisés en cellules spatiales distinctes, reliées par les couloirs qui passent derrière, en des chaînes flexibles auxquelles on peut donner toute une variété de formes" ("Lettres," 113).[62] Further, in his opinion "[s]o far as I know, this is the first time in a theatre of this kind that two of these elements occur, namely the polygonal shape, and the corridors with stairways that give access to the galleries" (*Perspecta*, 12; idem, *Art and Pageantry*, 522). For Lavin, in other words, the theater of San Pietro martire is the first baroque theater. In the process of translating concepts and sketches into practice, the situation seems a little more complex — and a lot less linear.[63]

On 23 November, Mazzi again wrote to Bentivoglio offering a list of accomplishments.[64] As work progressed, certain previously unforeseen needs arose: for example, strengthening the temporary wooden structure, in order to avoid its collapse under the weight of the stage machinery. Mazzi and Guitti's task seems to have been to coordinate the various craftsmen and artists to insure the completion of a satisfactory whole; each worker had a specific skill: Riboni was (still) busy with Hymen's temple for the prologue, while Pareschi was getting the ropes and gear ready to lower and raise it. Painters from Bologna busied themselves with the heavenly city, perhaps for the fifth *intermezzo*; though it was flat, three-dimensional touches were to be added to it in the form of (imitation) precious stones fashioned by a Jewish craftsman whose name remains unknown.

Three days later, on 26 November, Riboni was still "atorno al tempio" [busy with the temple], Mazzi reported, and "si assera di dietro la scena da Basso Verso San Domenico è verso la Guardarobba" [we are working on the back of the stage downstairs, on the San Domenico side]. Additionally, work had begun on "castello d'Atlante" [Atlas's castle] and the two missing waves mentioned in the previous letter (either for the third or fourth printed *intermezzo*): "Si fanno due onde, con non poca difficoltà . . . per dover poi esse sparirsi per la Calata della Machine [*sic*] de Cavali" (Lavin, "Lettres," 135; idem, *Art and Pageantry*, 535; MS Antonelli 660, 26 November 1627, fol. 1 v);[65] painters too were busy.[66] Why this letter, when

Mazzi had nothing special to report? It is possible, even likely, that Mazzi never failed to communicate with Bentivoglio with every "ordinary" (that is, scheduled) mail run. Though he had written just three days earlier, he did not want his supervisor or *impresario* to miss the customary mail news. Further, Bentivoglio's opinion was solicited with respect to the decorations (statues, in all likelihood) to be placed in the niches of the frontispiece. It is evident that the Ferrarese nobleman was in charge both of architectural and of iconographic decisions, so that Mazzi and Guitti could not rule on these issues without consulting him.

The following letter, dated 30 November, brings this relationship into sharp relief. Mazzi appears caught between Count Scotti, the *maggiordomo*, and the absent Bentivoglio, because he could not answer the former without consulting the latter. The issue tackled in this letter is how to light the theater; the term "teatro" without any additional specification makes it impossible to decide if the query regarded the Farnese or the temporary structure (or both). Nevertheless, it is a typical (and interesting) passage that deserves to be cited:

> Il sig[no]r Co[nte] Fabio mi disse che cosa havea pensato per Iluminar il teatro gli risposi che gli direi il mio pensiero quando havessi fatto far una lume per mostra, è cosi glielà mostrai è sì restò che con lochasione della venuta di V[ostra] S[ignoria] Ill[ustrissi]ma si sentirebbe il suo pensiero: il mio parere erra questo, di far doi ordini di lumi atorno a doi cornisoni che sonno uno sopra l'altro, come V[ostra] S[ignoria] Ill[ustrissi]ma hà visto. Sopra gli sentali mà però certi lumi di poco spatio è d'assai stupini, che mi parebbe mandassero un gran lume, è seguitar anco ordinatam[en]te sopra i pogioli dove sonno le statue à Cavalo; che accompagnati con le due lampade e i doi gili che si trata apendere al suolo, crederei che fosse assai iluminato, vi restarebbe sollo due dificoltà, l'uno che i lumi non spandessero è rovinasse quelli dei sentali, l'altra come s'avessa à impinzare, alla p[ri]ma segli rimedia col provarle ad'una per una avanti si mettessa alle suoi lochi à l'altri, chi facesse un stupino atificiato, che torcendolo da un cappo girasse attorno atorno per tutti gli stupini impizandoli, credo che farebbe l'effetto. (Lavin, "Lettres," 136–37; idem, *Art and Pageantry*, 535; MS Antonelli 660, 30 November 1627, fol. 1 r–v)[67]

Scotti evidently had asked a relatively technical, but straightforward, question. Mazzi, for his part, had to run his idea by Bentivoglio, while buying himself time with the *maggiordomo* by saying that this question would have a definite answer upon Bentivoglio's visit to the construction site. Incidentally, Mazzi was obviously making the point that Bentivoglio should soon visit Parma to answer this and other questions in person. The issue at hand was not aesthetic, but practical: where to place the numerous candles that would give light to the theater, without interfering with the stage set, the audience, or the structure itself; and how to light them all not at the same time (the term "effetto" is not the equivalent of "effect," even less of "special effect;" it merely means "result" or "outcome"), but without sending workers around to set each wick on fire individually. Mazzi's ingenious solution had to be approved by the superintendent to the festivities; since Bentivoglio's letters are not extant, we cannot know if Mazzi was merely expecting a hurried approval or if the two would engage in protracted conversations over this and other similar issues.

After the letter dated 30 November, a list is bound in entitled: "notta delle cose che si sono fatte dalla Scena da basso per conto delle fatture de' Marangoni" [list of things carried out in the downstairs theater by bricklayers] that also includes some "Fatture de Pittori" [painters' invoices]. Here the term "fattura" has two concurrent meanings: it refers to "what has been carried out" by construction workers and painters, but also to their "invoices" to the court in order to receive their payment.[68] Though this note is undated, and in a different hand from Mazzi's letter, its position in the bound volume seems chronologically accurate. By late November 1627, over a year before the festivities were to take place, not only had the temporary structure been built, but much of its stage setting and machinery was completed or well under way.

First and foremost, the incredible number of pieces of stage machinery deserves to be stressed. Second, this list reflects the aforementioned bureaucratic order reigning at court: everybody's contribution to the project had to be accounted for, in order for it to receive its payment. Third, the word "tellaro" or "telero" used here in reference to Atlas's castle calls for specific attention. Lavin has pointed out that "[n]umerous painted and moveable 'tellari' are mentioned in the documents of the 1618 productions for the Teatro Farnese, and Aleotti has been credited with the creation of the flat wing stage. We cannot be quite certain of the meaning of the term *tellaro* at this period, however, nor that the 1618 were to have *only* flat wings" (Lavin, "Lettres," 114–15; idem, *Perspecta*, 18; idem, *Art and Pageantry*, 523). We might add that no staging took place in 1618, so what had been planned might have never gone beyond the conceptual stage. Additionally, this list and previously cited letters make it clear that *tellaro* referred to any painted cloth, such as those draped around a presumably wooden scaffold that "built" three-dimensional stage structures such as Hymen's temple and Atlas's castle. Lavin thus correctly cautions us against drawing hasty conclusions based solely on linguistic evidence. Similarly, the designation of "temporary" given to the structure in the San Pietro martire courtyard is somewhat misleading, though essentially accurate. Though conceived to house only one performance, it was in existence a full year before the event itself, so it was meant to "last" for a much longer time than that of the evening on which it would come to fruition. One might wonder why a second theater was deemed necessary for the wedding festivities of 1628. If the Farnese decided to have another performative space built, it was evidently to "contain" a different sort of spectacle, to exhibit their wealth, and also to respond to the practical impossibility of removing all the stage machinery for the *Aminta* and its *intermedi* overnight, so that the *Mercurio e Marte* tournament could have taken place the following night.[69] While the location of this structure might have responded to practical needs, it carried some powerful meanings with it. André Chastel has studied the relationship between the space of the *palazzo* and the space of the courtyard in an earlier period (1470–1540/1550), when they were being examined, codified, and built.[70] The courtyard, like the courtly space devoted to the theater (Ruffini, *Teatri prima del teatro* [Rome: Bulzoni, 1983], 180–85), is at the center of the *palazzo*, which in turn lies at the center of the town, and of the ruler's domain.[71] It is worth noting that the Teatro di San Pietro martire might have had a longer life span than what had originally been planned.[72]

With the beginning of December 1627, a new issue surfaced: how to build the seating for the audience in the temporary theater. This constituted another reason for Mazzi to renew his pleas to convince Bentivoglio to come to Parma in person. On 4 December, he wrote to report that he had devised a sketch;[73] evidently Mazzi was proposing some modification to a plan conceived by Guitti that Bentivoglio had seen and presumably approved. At this point, he had elaborated a design, which he would sketch and send to the Ferrarese nobleman with the following mail run. Again, Bentivoglio's approval emerges as necessary for anything to be built. Four days later the sketch was ready and on its way to Ferrara:

> non si manca di lavorare atorno alla scena da basso è si comincia à meter all'ordine i legnami per cominciar gli sentali, il disegno delli quali mando à V[ostra] S[ignoria] Ill[ustrissi]ma acciò comandi quello gli pare; il quale quanto alla prima figura non è diferente in altro à quelo del sig[no]r Fran[ces]co se non, che la linea D che dovrebbe venir inanzi à quadra si ritira nel punto i è questo fo perche gli spetatori si sfugiono l'uno con l'altro et habiano ocasione di meglio vedere. Fò poi per ogni palco un coritore H che gira atorno atorno per ogni ordine di Palco, per la comodità d'entrarvi dentro; Le quatro F sonno le scale, l'una preso all'altra, che anderà, dal fondo in Cima alla fabrica. Le tre E sono tre strade che lascio, da poter andar nell'arena in Caso di bisogno. il C è il palco de seren[issi]mi Prencipi, il quale hò fatto di questa forma per darli più gratia se cosi parerà à V[ostra] S[ignoria] Ill[ustrissi]ma, il quale si tirerà poi nel caso di far il Torneo si tirerà sino nel drito de Palchi. (Lavin, "Lettres," 138–39; idem, *Art and Pageantry*, 537; MS Antonelli 660, 8 December 1627, fol. 1 r) (fig. 2)[74]

Mazzi was again asking for permission to modify a plan already agreed upon, and gave Bentivoglio an important reason for his proposed change: he was concerned that as many audience members as possible would enjoy the show. In order to provide the audience with good sight lines, Mazzi wanted the angle of the wings to be altered. Another modification, which according to Lavin is much more important for the development of baroque theaters and, later, opera houses, is the

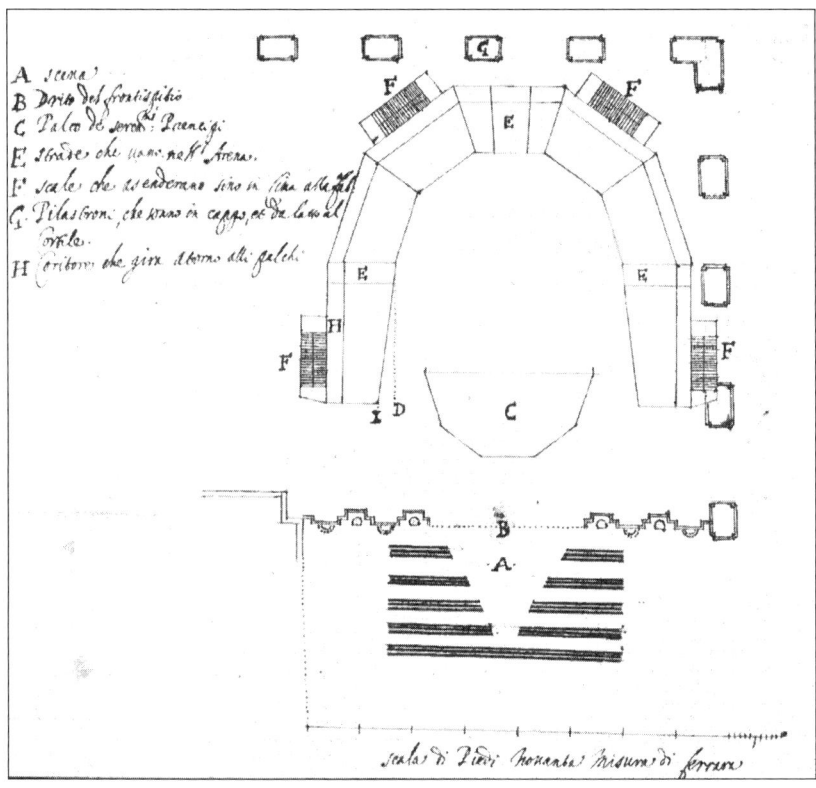

FIGURE 2.
Black-and-white ink drawing from manuscript at Biblioteca Comunale Ariostea, Ferrara: MS Antonelli 660, from letter of 8 December 1627

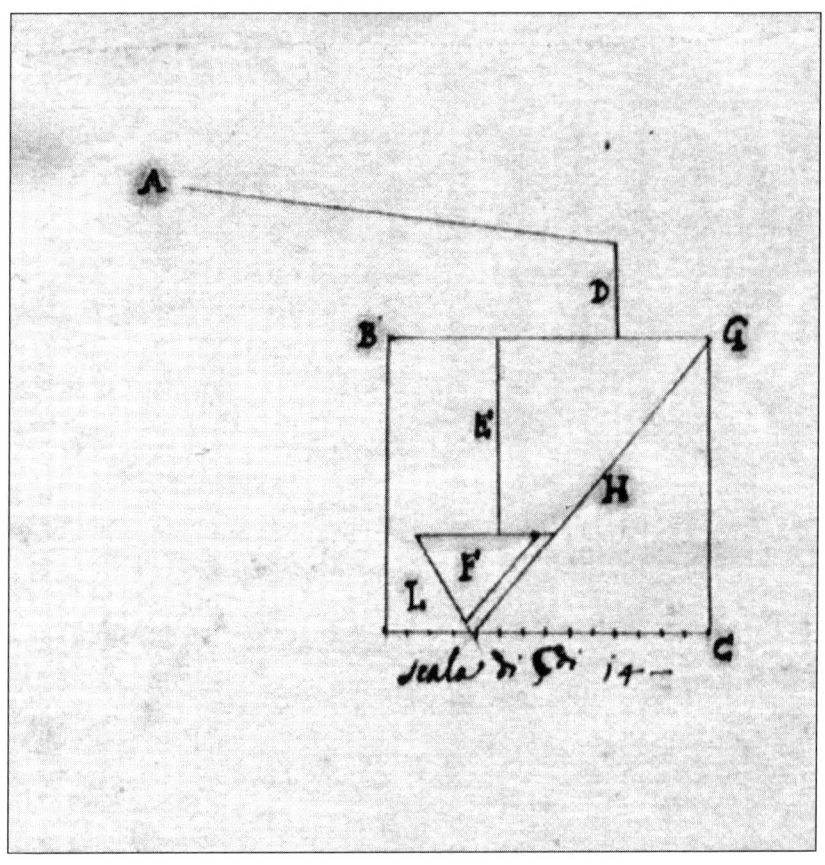

FIGURE 3.
Black-and-white ink drawing from manuscript at Biblioteca Comunale Ariostea, Ferrara: MS Antonelli 660, from letter of 7 September 1627

addition of the corridors running on the outside of the boxes and linking them. Mazzi writes that his intent was merely to make access to the boxes more expedient. While Mazzi's tone is meant to express deference both to Bentivoglio's judgment and to Guitti's plan, it also shows that this innovation came about serendipitously, that is, to accommodate the audience more comfortably and without modifying the existing plan too severely. Another element that deserves attention in Mazzi's revised sketch is the special place where the newlyweds and their retinues were going to sit. This does not correspond to the *palco reale* of later opera houses. Instead, it is placed seemingly in the middle of the empty space between the boxes and the stage, in an eminent and privileged position.

His keen eye always attentive to practical details, Mazzi added:

> Ho pensato quanto ò potuto è secondo i miei conti posso far capire più di 3500 persone in d[et]ti palchi; ne paia poco à V[ostra] S[ignoria] Ill[ustrissi]ma p[er]che nel teatro di sopra non vi ne caperà solo che 2400: è nondimeno pigliano assai più luoco che non pigliaremo noi. è sene farebbe capir assai più ma non vederebbono. è non vedendo gli palchi sarebbono fati senza il suo fine. (Lavin, "Lettres," 139; idem, *Art and Pageantry*, 537; MS Antonelli 660, 8 December 1627, fol. 1 r)[75]

The architect's pride is evident in these lines: his plan would be able to accommodate a greater number of people in a smaller area, and everybody would be able to see. Again, Mazzi made it clear that unimpeded lines of vision were of the utmost concern, even to the detriment of the occupancy of the structure.

With this momentous issue essentially settled, another one would soon come up, concerning the stage rather than the audience. On 9 December Mazzi took advantage of an envoy from Bentivoglio to address the issue of the stage entry of one of the knights taking part in the tournament with which the fifth *intermezzo* ended, specifically the Infernal Knight, who had to emerge from under the stage as if from the nether regions of the earth.[76] The plan proposed by Mazzi had to be approved by Bentivoglio before construction would begin. The task at hand was far from simple: Mazzi had to make sure that the knight could be astride his horse in full costume, including the towering helm. Further, he could not run the risk that the audience would be able to see or even surmise the knight's presence before its time, or else the effect of surprise would be ruined. Also, Mazzi had to take into consideration all the other pieces of stage machinery that had already been devised and that would be in place during the performance: the sea for the fourth *intermezzo*, and more generally the grooves in which ropes would be placed to move the various pieces of stage machinery. Lastly, care had to be exerted in order not to break the planks of the stage or anything else during the performance itself. While Mazzi's tone is, as usual, deferential vis-à-vis Bentivoglio, by the end of the passage his imagination was racing: he proposed a bas-relief scene to be carved into the knight's support, in order to enhance the audience's *amiratione* for the machinery.

At the very end of this letter, reality resurfaces: "Vi sono di questi maestri che vorebbono venir à casa a far le feste" (Lavin, "Lettres," 140; idem, *Art and Pageantry*, 538; MS Antonelli 660, 9 December 1627, fol. 1 v); approximately two weeks before Christmas, workers evidently had started to clamor to take leave to go spend the holidays with their families. Nor is this the only complication into which Mazzi's plan for the infernal knight ran, as the following letter (dated 14 December) explains:

> Il Cavagliere che viene dall'inferno non piace à questi sig[no]ri che venghi nel moddo mostrato a V[ostra] S[ignoria] Ill[ustrissi]ma giudicandolo di troppa spesa; è vorebbono che venisse per le prospetive, mà gliò fatto vedere che la scena serà piena da quatro Cari per le quatro parti del Mondo; è la sortita di Plutone con gli personaggi infernali, Mà il tamera procura di sodisfarli, ma credo che vi serà che fare à non concertar l'intram[ez]zo. (Lavin, "Lettres," 140–41; idem, *Art and Pageantry*, 538; MS Antonelli 660, 14 December 1627, fol. 1 r)[77]

Mazzi's plan for the last entry of the evening was deemed too expensive by the court — the letter does not specify if "questi sig[no]ri" are to be identified with the duke himself or with an emissary of his; given the issue, Scotti might have been the one to object to the plan. Mazzi expresses here his displeasure at the court's counterproposal that the infernal knight should come on stage from the wings, since those ways were already crowded with other pieces of machinery; nor is he thrilled that Tamera, a mason (hence a subordinate), has assured the court that he would find a way to accommodate the knight's stage entry from the wings.

Christmas, meanwhile, was approaching; on 14 December, Mazzi invoked Bentivoglio's help to extending Mazzi's credit with the bakers, so that he would be able to feed himself even after the term of what must have been his original engagement had expired.[78] Evidently, Bentivoglio's extensive network encompassed all the crafts essential for building and staging a performance, as well as those necessary for the physical and material means of support of all the workers.

Five days later, on 19 December, Mazzi was still trying to solve two problems: the stage entrance of the infernal knight and the boxes for the audience. As to the first, it is unclear if the Farnese court (especially the *maggiordomo*) had criticized the expense linked to the stage machinery necessary to lift the infernal knight to the stage, or to the knight's outfit.[79] Since Mazzi's plan had been rejected, he had stopped working on a model for the knight; when Bentivoglio asked to see it, Mazzi evidently sent it (at the hands of Alfonso Chenda, who was going back to his hometown of Ferrara for the Christmas holidays)[80] but profusely apologized for its incomplete state.[81]

The other problem that surfaces in this letter involved the structure of the temporary theater, in particular the area reserved to the audience:

> Son à torno al Modello de Palchi del Cortile, nel quale hò quei riguardi che mi par segli devono; è di buona veduta, e di capacità di gente assai, e di fortezza, è di sito proportionato alla scena è quando ò mostrato il disegno al sig[no]r Conte Fabio simile à quello che mandai à V[ostra] S[ignoria] Ill[ustrissi]ma subito cominciò à torcersi con dire che le spese sonno grandiss[i]me è che bisogna atender alla brevità è pure questi palchi, sonno l'istesa brevità, perche non si trata d'altro che drizar legni in piedi, quali vi sonno, i piani dove si zappano asse ò di pelto ò di pioppa puntate tale quale sonno i parapeti dinanzi, doi legni solo à traverso, con sopra i suoi tapeti, la seraglia atorno asse distese puntate così come sonno, gli coridori à torno dei legni che faciano mantegno è via; si che non mi saprei imaginare, cosa più facile è più comoda. Finito che avro il modelo glielo mostrarò à [sic] procurarò di farli capire questo. (Lavin, "Lettres," 141–42; idem, *Art and Pageantry*, 539; MS Antonelli 660, 19 December 1627, fol. 1 v)[82]

It is an unfortunate occurrence that the model promised by Mazzi is not extant.[83] However, the letter clearly reveals that in Mazzi's opinion, the architectural structure he proposes for the *palchi* was the most expedient both from the point of view of building it and of offering plenty of room and good viewing to the audience. At the same time, he could not disregard the issue of building costs, since Scotti seems to have examined each proposal carefully, as was the nature of his job. Mazzi's uneasy position, between the absent Bentivoglio and the ever-present Scotti, emerges forcefully a little later in the same letter.[84]

After the holiday season, Mazzi wrote on 31 December, briefly, and with the understanding that "mentre questa mia sene viene à Ferrara, V[ostra] S[ignoria] Ill[ustrissi]ma nello stesso tempo venghi Costà" (Lavin, "Lettres," 142; idem, *Art and Pageantry*, 539; MS Antonelli 660, 31 December 1627, fol. 1 r) [as this letter comes to Ferrara, your excellence arrives here]. Bentivoglio's visit to Parma might explain why two whole weeks go by before Mazzi wrote another letter, on 14 January 1628. The latter is mostly devoted to preparations for the Teatro Farnese, but it mentions that painters were working on the backdrops for the first and fourth printed *intermezzi* and on the waves for the fourth one. This is Mazzi's last extant letter; the following one, dated 18 February, is by Guitti,[85] in it he informed Bentivoglio that "È fatto l'Iride nella Scena da basso, e provaremo presto la Machina co' Cavalli, perche saranno domani fatte le taglie" (Lavin, "Lettres," 126; idem, *Art and Pageantry*, 529; MS Antonelli 660, 18 February 1628, fol. 1 r).[86] Iris appears at the very end of the second printed *intermezzo*, while the horse machinery is probably from the last one. It appears that the architectural work had been completed by then, and that most stage sets and machines were advanced enough that rehearsals were possible.

Still, much work remained to be done, and time was wasted on other tasks. On 3 March, after a hiatus of two full weeks (which again might be easily explained by the fact that Guitti felt more authoritative and empowered to settle matters than Mazzi had been), with evident disappointment the architect wrote: "Dall'ultimo ch'io scrissi à V[ostra] S[ignoria] Ill[ustrissi]ma in quà, poco si è lavorato, e quasi niente, perche s'è atteso à servire il s[igno]re Prencipe Fran[ces]co Maria per Mascherate" (Lavin, "Lettres," 126; idem, *Art and Pageantry*, 529; MS Antonelli 660, 3 March 1628, fol. 1 r).[87] It is apparent that for the Farnese court the craftsmen and workers employed for the wedding festivities were salaried like anyone else; they could be ordered like anyone else, in this case to build a chariot and a ship for *carnevale* entertainment. Guitti, though unhappy, had no choice but to comply; still he reported to Bentivoglio in Ferrara, perhaps to prevent being criticized for his slow pace later on. This confirms Southorn's opinion that Guitti worked for Bentivoglio as much as for the Farnese.

Guitti's last extant letter, dated 18 April, again underscores the added tasks devised by the Farnese court for the Grand Duke's arrival, at Easter time. The tone here is regretful, when Guitti asserts that he would not be able to go to Ferrara for the holiday, but also self-assured, when he explains to Bentivoglio the knightly tournament he had devised for the occasion.[88] His rhetorical strategy in this letter is to juxtapose the honor bestowed on him through this new task with his limited abilities and utter lack of experience. Bentivoglio could then simultaneously rejoice in his choice of a trusted, able collaborator and be reassured that the latter still deferred to his judgment and practice in matters of entertainment.

No letter is extant on the part of the architects charged to build the new structure and stage machinery after April 1628. Their role evidently was complete. Still, even as the temporary theater was being built, other crucial elements of the future performance attracted Bentivoglio's attention; to these we now turn: music and performance.

3. Preparations: Music and Performers

Long before the building of the theater of San Pietro martire was completed, preparations had started on the performances that would take place in it. This section will attempt to reconstruct the various aspects involved in this process: selecting the texts, the composer, the performers; adapting the music to the theater; and rehearsing.

Before venturing a reconstruction, it is necessary to understand what sort of performance is identified by the term *intermezzo* or *intermedio*, what role it had at the time, and how it has been traditionally explained. This will help set up contemporary expectations and measure the Parma events against those. According to Nagler, "musical interludes, or intermezzi, serv[ed] as intermission features" (*Theatre Festivals of the Medici*, 2) in court plays. Its origin, shrouded in mystery, is linked by Elena Povoledo "allo sviluppo della commedia erudita" ("Intermezzo," in *Enciclopedia dello spettacolo*, 6: 572–76, here 572) [to the development of learned comedy]. David Nutter agrees: "Staged *intermedi* first occur between the acts of Latin comedies by Plautus and Terence performed in translation at Ferrara in the late 15th century" ("Intermedio," in *New Grove* [1980], 9: 258–69, here 260). Later, when Aristotelian rules influenced the structure of all "regular" plays, "the intervals between the acts, and therefore the *intermedi*, suspended but did not break the action, while allowing an artificial compression of time necessary to indicate the passage of hours between one act and the next" (Nutter, "Intermedio," 261). According to Povoledo, *intermezzi* can be construed as "un abile accorgimento per sfuggire alla rigorosa applicazione del sistema [aristotelico], senza intaccarne la validità: la rappresentazione drammatica rispetta le regole ma alterna l'azione a quella degli intermezzi" ("Intermezzo," 574).[89] By 1586 in Florence, *intermezzi* were routinely linked among each other in theme, if not overtly in plot (Nagler, *Theatre Festivals of the Medici*, 61); Karen Newman has convincingly argued that "the production of *La Pellegrina* and its intermezzi [for the Medici wedding of 1589] was a unified effort with political significance to the marriage at which it was performed;"[90] more recently, Saslow has pointed out that "the six [1589 Florentine] intermedi were unified by the theme of the power of music to influence both the human soul and the gods" (*The Medici Wedding of 1589*, 30).

Since *intermezzi* were set to music and utilized lavish stage sets, they have often been teleologically linked to the hazy period in which opera was born: "In theatrical and artistic terms, these presentations united humanist antiquarianism and far-reaching musical-dramatic innovation with important advances in architecture, mechanics, and stage design to lay the foundations for theater and opera as we know them today" (Saslow, *The Medici Wedding of 1589*, 2). While Thomas Walker prudently asserts that one "antecedent of opera was the *intermedio*, episodes or tableaux performed between the acts of plays (mostly comedies) with music and often with machines" ("Opera," in *New Grove* [1980], 13: 544–647, here 550), Povoledo contends that "il melodramma, fiorito a Firenze sulle esercitazioni della Camerata de' Bardi e del cenacolo di J. Corsi, riconoscerà nelle scene mutevoli degli intermezzi il proprio naturale apparato" ("Intermezzo," 575).[91] Even as distinguished a musicologist as F. W. Sternfeld believes that "the main difference between opera and *intermedio* (though not the only one) is one of time-scale: hence opera enjoys the prominence associated with being the principal business of an afternoon's or evening's entertainment" (*The Birth of Opera* [Oxford: Clarendon Press, 1993], 33). In a similar fashion, David Kimbell's monograph *Italian Opera* (1991) opens with a chapter devoted to "The Renaissance *intermedi*" that does not delineate any specific difference between the two genres.

Given the position attributed to *intermezzi* in opera history, it is hardly surprising that they attract no attention after 1607, that is, after the event considered as the first full-fledged opera: Monteverdi's *Orfeo*. The only exception in musicological research is to be found in David Nutter's entry devoted to "Intermedio" in *The New Grove Dictionary of Music and Musicians* [1980]: "*Intermedi* did not disappear after the birth of opera but became interwoven with it. *Intermedio* traditions furnished many of the themes and conventions of early opera." If proof were needed that we are faced with genres felt to be separate and distinct, Nutter adds: "As well as absorbing much from the *intermedio* tradition, operas, like spoken plays, were felt to need their own *intermedi* for contrast" ("Intermedio," 267; *New Grove* [2001], 486).

Another consequence of this teleological interpretation of *intermezzi* and opera is the almost total lack of attention bestowed on the music composed for the Parma festivities by none other than Claudio Monteverdi. Nino Pirrotta, possibly the most knowledgeable musicologist on the topic, interrupts his research with the Florence *intermezzi* of 1589, and comes to the following conclusion:

> The history of the courtly *intermedi* is simply the history of a colossal, as well as multifaceted, handicraft. We can evaluate its single achievements, but hardly give a comprehensive judgment of their worth. They are a conglomerate of diverse elements held together by some thread of logic (although we have seen how tenuous such logic could be), but hardly susceptible to being turned by this alone into a single work of art. It is pointless to praise or belittle their artistic merit, though from a practical standpoint or historical point of view they can be admired for the very large amount of effort put into them. ("Studies in the Music of Renaissance Theatre," in idem and E. Povoledo, *Music and Theatre from Poliziano to Monteverdi* [Cambridge: Cambridge University Press: 1982], 1–280, here 236)

Pirrotta's judgment is clear-cut, and rather unkind to *intermezzi*: they are not art, but merely craftsmanship. Thus, though they can be considered as precursors of opera, they cannot (and should not) be analyzed and studied as one of many concurrent musical genres straddling the sixteenth and the seventeenth century. The only musicologist to underscore how various genres set to music coexisted in this period is Kimbell, who openly states: "For some years after 1600 opera was one of several musico-dramatic genres that might grace a festival. *Intermedi, mascherate* and dramatic ballets continued to flourish for many years, and may well have been more popular with the larger part of the audience" (*Italian Opera*, 54). Still, musicological research on the 1628 *intermezzi* is scarce; as Reiner's work shows, many documents are extant that clarify the events leading to the actual performance.

At a time when the final composition of the festivities was far from being settled, one of Bentivoglio's first decisions was to appoint a musician to compose the *armonie* for the event. We see confirmed here something that already emerged in the letters regarding the architectural preparations and that will come to the forefront in the actual staging: the performance set to music was by far more complex and important than that merely "said" or recited. Other, important decisions could be reached more serendipitously,[92] but the presence of music was a given for this kind of celebration at the time; thus the choice of a composer was serious business.

It is in conjunction with this momentous decision that Antonio Goretti's name first surfaces. Reiner explains that little is known about this composer from Ferrara ("Preparations in Parma," 288); according to Bianconi, his "collection of instruments, portraits of musicians, musical manuscripts and prints" was "extolled in the various early seventeenth-century guide-books of Ferrara" and was later transferred to the Innsbruck court (*Music in the Seventeenth Century*, 80; and see A. Newcomb, "Antonio Goretti," in *New Grove* [2001]). The extant documents regarding the Parma events describe him as Bentivoglio's right hand in matters of music. On 13 August 1627 Goretti wrote him a letter recommending that Sigismondo d'India not be hired for the "Parma music and festivals" (Reiner, "Preparations in Parma," 287).[93] While his music was notable, his attitude vis-à-vis the singers charged with performing it was lamentable, due to his perfectionism and stubbornness. Whether Bentivoglio had elicited other opinions or not, Sigismondo's letter dated 26 August (Reiner, "Preparations in Parma," 286)[94] must have fallen on deaf ears; around the time of Goretti's letter, the Ferrarese nobleman had approached Claudio Monteverdi in Venice, as the latter explains in a letter dated 10 September 1627:

> Il Sig[no]r Marchese Bentivogli molto mio Sig[no]re per molti anni passati, mi scrisse già un mese fa adimandandomi; se io gli haverei posto un musica certe sue parole fatte da sua Eccellenza per servirsene in una certa principalissima comedia che si saria fatta per servitio di nozze da prencipe, et sarebbero statti intermedi; et non comedia cantata; essendo molto mio particolar signore gli risposi che haverei fatto ogni possibile maggiore per servire alli comandi di S[ua] E[ccellenza] Ill[ustrissi]ma mi replicò un particolar ringratiamento et mi disse che se ne haveva da servire nelle nozze del Seren[issi]mo di Parma, gli risposi che haverei fatto ciò si fosse degnato comandarmi. (Malipiero, *Monteverdi*, 267–68)[95]

In the course of a month, it appears, numerous contacts had occurred. First Bentivoglio asked Monteverdi to work on *intermezzi* based on a text of his own for a princely event. At this stage, according to Monteverdi's letter, no details were specified; however, after the composer had agreed to offering his services, Bentivoglio explained the occasion for which they were needed.

It is evident from Monteverdi's letter that he was somehow beholden to Bentivoglio. Even if we take into consideration that it is addressed to another of Monteverdi's patrons, Alessandro Striggio (who might have needed convincing that the musician could not easily escape this commission), this reinforces Southorn's and

Fabris's opinion that Bentivoglio's network of artists and craftsmen was wide and far-reaching, and that his authority in matters of festivity organization was well recognized. Further, Monteverdi discriminated between "intermedi" and "comedia cantata." The former constituted, in his opinion, a much lighter task, as a letter dated 1 May of the same year makes clear.[96] Perhaps Monteverdi took on the Parma commission hoping that it could be dispatched quickly and painlessly; indeed, at the beginning he proceeded with great speed, so much so that in the aforementioned letter to Striggio dated 10 September, Monteverdi wrote that Bentivoglio "di subitto mi mandò il primo intermedio et di già l'ho fatto quasi mezzo, et lo farò con facilità perchè sono quasi tutti soliloqui" (Malipiero, *Monteverdi*, 268).[97] Further, this commission promised a high return of fame: "le quali Altezze [the Farnese] mi honorarno molto con tal comando havendo io inteso che vi erano da sei o sette che facevano instanza per haver tal carico, non [sic] moto proprio si sono voluti dignare questi Sig[no]ri di eleggere la persona mia" (Malipiero, *Monteverdi*, 268).[98] Sigismondo d'India's letter to Bentivoglio can surely be counted among these.

The second contact between Bentivoglio and Monteverdi had legal as well as practical relevance.[99] The document with which Margherita Aldobrandini Farnese (Ranuccio's widow and Odoardo's mother) had given Enzo Bentivoglio the power to hire anyone he deemed suitable for the festivities had been copied and transmitted to Monteverdi. Additionally, one *intermezzo* had traveled, specifically the one written by Ascanio Pio di Savoia that would eventually be performed after the third act of *Aminta*. According to Monteverdi, four stages in plot development could be identified, each deserving its own specific tune. Evidently, music was thought to underscore and reinforce the events set forth in the plot.

A few days before Monteverdi's letter, Bentivoglio received one from Guitti at Parma:

> Hò avuto gl'Intramezzi dal s[igno]re Co[nte] Fabio, e gl'hò considerati, i quali sono belliss[i]mi, mà stimo di molta fattura, fatica, e tempo, se bene, quando v'è frapposta V[ostra] S[ignoria] Ill[ustrissi]ma non mi sgomentano, cominciarò a far dipingere la p[rim]a Scena per ord[i]ne, che è quella della Campagne di Roma e così anderò seguendo; mà bisognerebbe, che V[ostra] S[ignoria] Ill[ustrissi]ma mi significasse di que' trà che hà mandati. qual p[rim]o; 2°; e 3°. (Lavin, "Lettres," 121; idem, *Art and Pageantry*, 526; MS Antonelli 660, 7 September 1627, fol. 1 r)[100]

Guitti's reaction to the *intermezzi* he had received from the *maggiordomo* is remarkably less enthusiastic than Monteverdi's. This might be because he had received three simultaneously, and without any indication as to their order. Additionally, Guitti was on site, dealing with the practicalities of stage and machinery building; thus his tasks were less abstract than the composer's, at least at this point. The letter indicates the chain of command: Bentivoglio would receive the texts from the writers charged with composing them; he would then transmit them to the Farnese court, presumably for approval; finally the court, through the *maggiordomo* Scotti, would convey them to the craftsmen charged with building the apparatus for the stage.

One of Bentivoglio's rare extant letters was written on 12 September; in it he brings up three separate issues: "Quando è piaciuto a Dio, è giunto, L'archilino, e siamo à peggio, che mai, perche bisogna rinverdir . . . ogni cosa, p[er] acquistarsi, con le Machine, . . . I pittori bolognesi no[n] sono ancora gionti . . . A quest'ora seria necesario sapersi, che musici si possono avere, perche importa assai, a chi compone" (Archivio di Stato, Parma: Teatri e spettacoli di età farnesiana, busta 1 mazzo 1 fascicolo 20 sottofascicolo 3).[101] "L'archilino" is none other than Claudio Achillini, charged with the tournament for the Farnese; that is why the situation looked dire, because the amount of work needed on the stage machinery built for 1618 had become painfully clear. Moreover, the painters from Bologna who were mentioned in Mazzi's letter had yet to arrive. Lastly, and most importantly, Bentivoglio needed to know from the court who would perform the music and singing; his phrase ("importa assai, a chi compone") seems to indicate that Monteverdi, or someone on his behalf, had asked about it. The importance of the singers' identity is reinforced in a letter by Margherita Aldobrandini, dated 14 September, in which she specified that Bentivoglio would be the first to know once the decision had been reached, "perché il Monte Verde nel fare la musica possi appropriarla alla qualità de cantanti" (Fabris, *Mecenati e musici*, 407).[102] The person who acted as go-between with Bentivoglio and Monteverdi is the aforementioned Antonio Goretti, who on 1 October wrote to Bentivoglio that he had received a text to be set to music; he would have it copied and sent to Monteverdi in Venice.[103] The latter then would know what effects the festivity organizers wanted to elicit in the viewers/listeners.

On 18 September, Monteverdi reassured Bentivoglio that he had almost completed one of the *intermezzi*, having Dido as its heroine and therefore presumably the second one to be performed.[104] On 25 September, again Monteverdi wrote two letters, one to Striggio and the other to Bentivoglio. He justified his tardiness in sending something he had promised to Striggio because "questi canti per Parma molto mi tengono occupato" (Malipiero, *Monteverdi*, 274) [these songs for Parma keep me very busy]. At the same time, he asked Bentivoglio to defer a trip to Parma because his position as musician in San Marco required his presence.[105] In this letter, furthermore, we see the second task that Monteverdi perceived as inherent to his commission: adapting the music to the space in which it would be performed. As other letters will make clear, this process was more complex than our notion of rehearsing, because performative spaces were being developed, acoustics was still being studied, orchestras had not yet found their final makeup, and so forth.[106]

Some time after 1 October, Bentivoglio wrote to Margherita; this letter is interesting because it recapitulates some of the events that had taken place until then, reiterates some previous requests, and advances new ones:[107]

> Io non posso dir il gusto che ho della risolutione presa in valersi del S[igno]r Monte Verde si per la qualità rara del soggetto come ancora per poter meter mano a l'operare, che realm[en]te mi vedevo disperato col non haver risposta e con si far niente, perche so il tempo che ci vuol a voler far bene. Ho spedito con diligenza subito al detto le parole d'un intermezzo, e farò agiustar quelle di Venere, acciò sia più modesta perche i Padri hiesuiti non abbino scrupolo. madama, siamo di noze e non di setemana santa: tutto starà bene.
>
> Le cose belle non sono mai longhe: faciamo noi bene e non dubito di stuffare li spetatori, e l'uno e l'altro starà bene circa il far comedia di bufoni o opera recitata: non è però dubio che avrà più del Nobile una Tragicomedia, e certo la comodità del Principe di Massa non la perderei, perche s'avrà senza fastidio, e so saria recitata bene e con maraveglia che si, [sic] perche aparisca non credono sapino parlare cruschescamente; però tutto starà bene come gustarà alla V[ostra] A[ltez]za e piliando Trag[e]dia, quella de l'odi in publico vuol in scena.[108]

Bentivoglio here reiterates one of Monteverdi's concerns, that is, that a suitable amount of time is necessary to properly organize festivities. He also compliments Margherita on having retained Monteverdi's services; since Bentivoglio was acting on behalf of the court, strictly speaking he had not hired the composer, but only suggested his name to the Farnese.

This letter also contains a unique reference to the religious climate prevailing at the time. Margherita or some emissary must have raised questions about an *intermezzo* in which Venus was among the characters (perhaps the third printed one, which Monteverdi had received on 9 September 1627); Bentivoglio promises here to have it "fixed" and at the same time he reassures her: the Jesuit fathers will be appeased by those changes, nor will they look too deeply into the texts because the occasion is a wedding (for which Venus is appropriate), not the penitential Holy Week preceding Easter.

Last, this relatively early letter contains suggestions for the play to be performed along with the planned *intermezzi*. This remark by Bentivoglio makes it clear that the "spoken" play was deemed of secondary importance, since it could have been either one staged by professional performers or a learned one, without influencing the rest of the staged event.[109] Moreover, Bentivoglio seems aware that time constraints were of the utmost importance (a rather ironic remark, as will become apparent), and that a tragicomedy was nobler than an improvised play.

The period at the end of October 1627 is uncommonly well documented. First, a letter from Margherita Aldobrandini announces to Bentivoglio on 23 October that her son's departure for Florence has been delayed for a few weeks, until St. Martin's Day (11 November) (Fabris, *Mecenati e musici*, 411). It is unclear whether the Parma crew was informed of the change in plan at the same time. On 24 October Guitti asked for textual and practical advice. Evidently the text for what eventually was performed as the fifth *intermezzo* did not contain extensive stage directions. In order to build the machines and set the stage properly, Guitti needed to know how these four characters would enter the stage. It is one of the many details that Bentivoglio's absence from Parma forced on paper, for our benefit.[110] Four days later, on 28 October, the recently arrived Mazzi wrote to Bentivoglio asking a similar, though broader, kind of question. The rather inexperienced and overwhelmed Mazzi, faced with a large number of stage machines, backdrops, and wings, needed to know how they would come on stage, in order to make sure that they would not be in each other's way during the actual performance.[111] It is useful to underscore that the complexity, bulk, and opulence of the stage apparatus made it virtually impossible to solve such issues as brought up in Guitti's and Mazzi's letter at rehearsal time, for at least two reasons: first, the stage machinery was often decorated only on the visible side, hence it was crucial to know at an early stage which side the audience would see; second, its dimensions would prevent easy handling and moving.[112]

On 28 and 29 October, it was Antonio Goretti's turn to bring Bentivoglio up to speed. Monteverdi had arrived at Parma and they had started thinking about who the singers might be: "per conto di done, non si averà altro che la S[igno]ra Setimia che . . . dubito non farà quela riuscita che si crede; il S[igno]r Claudio tiene il medemo pensiero" (Fabris, *Mecenati e musici*, 412).[113] Such a severe judgment is surprising, given that Settimia Caccini (one of Giulio Caccini's two daughters) was one of the most famous sopranos of her time. On 29 October, Goretti reports that he had gone with Goretti to assess the space in which the *intermezzi* music was to be performed. Goretti expressed his marvel at the temporary structure, and even teased Bentivoglio about the amount of wood and work that the new theater had required. All the news was not good, however: it was Goretti's understanding that the courtyard would be closed in order to cover the temporary structure, and this would prove detrimental to the acoustics of the place, particularly for the singers' voices, but also for the instruments.[114] Here we notice how at the time "affetto" and "effetto" were interchangeable words, since the latter only aimed to elicit the former. Far from being a simple slip of the pen, this usage reflects an important element of these festivities (and, in general, of entertainment of the period) that will be analyzed more thoroughly in the next chapter. This visit by Monteverdi seems to have been a quick inspection of the premises, at least on the basis of Goretti's remark that after Bentivoglio's visit to Parma he and the composer would head back to Venice, where the latter's services were needed for the Christmas season. Even at a time when traveling was much slower, two months were an exceedingly long time to plan a trip from Parma to Venice. Perhaps Goretti was merely joking about Bentivoglio's slowness in responding to all requests that he would come to Parma.

The day after Goretti's second letter, on 30 October, Monteverdi wrote to Bentivoglio from Parma, first to reassure him that he had been warmly welcomed at the Farnese court, and secondly to explain how far along he was.[115] The speed at which Monteverdi was composing music for the *intermezzi* is as remarkable as the fact that over a year before the festivities the first and second *intermedio* were already decided upon and in the order in which they would be performed. As Monteverdi was composing, he would also rehearse; at this point the only missing *intermedio* was the last one, though the third and fourth are not identified in the letter and thus might have been different from those that were eventually performed.

The missing *intermezzo* was delivered soon after Monteverdi's letter, since Goretti wrote Bentivoglio on 2 November that "Per un'altra mia V[ostra] S[ignoria] Ill[ustrissi]ma havrà inteso quanto mi occorre dirle ora di meno le dico che si è havuto sì il quinto intermedi [*sic*] come anco le parole mandate dal s[igno]r D[on] Ascanio al S[igno]r Monteverdi p[er] agiustare uno intermedi" (MS Antonelli 660, 2 November 1627, fol. 1 r).[116] Here for the first time in the extant documents the name of the *intermezzi* writer is mentioned: Ascanio Pio di Savoia (whose family, as the name suggests, came from Savoy or Piedmont) was a poet whose "genius was revealed less in his invention of themes (for these were drawn usually from the stock of mythology, the poetry of Tasso or the time-honoured forms of combat) than in his imaginative interpretation of character and in the dramatic effect of his poetry for performance" (Southorn, *Power and Display*, 134). He was also related to Enzo Bentivoglio, having married his daughter Beatrice in the summer of 1627.[117] Whether he was called to participate in the Parma festivities on the strength of his poetry or on the basis of this relation with Enzo Bentivoglio, he ultimately contributed the texts for the five *intermezzi* for entertainment that took place in the temporary theater. Further, the commission included also "fixing" or adapting the *intermezzi* to any need that would arise in the meantime. Goretti's passage does not make clear why one of the four pieces needed "agiustare," whether it was at Monteverdi's request or Scotti's or perhaps a religious censor's. Pio evidently complied, and Goretti informed Bentivoglio that all the texts were available and about to be set to music.

The letter continues: "La lista delli cantori che dicono dover venire da Roma non si è ancora potuta vedere, abbiamo però fato elezione d'un basso eminente che si ritrova in Italia e li deve al S[igno]r Co[nte] Fabio, et ancora p[er] un pur p[utto] d'amore il quale si trova a Ravenna presso il S[igno]r Card[inale] Caponi" (MS Antonelli 660, 2 November 1627, fol. 1 r).[118] While Monteverdi's and Goretti's tasks did not include the selection of the singers (presumably reserved for the court or *maggiordomo* Scotti), they were obviously very interested in their identity and abilities. This passage also reveals the practice of retaining singers from anywhere in Italy, as well as Rome's fame as a center and reservoir of good singing talent.[119] If the *intermezzi* were considered to be the high point of the festivities, then no expense (or influence: Goretti explicitly mentions that Scotti reminded a famous bass that the latter owed him) would be spared to secure the best singers on the market.[120]

On 8 November, Monteverdi had to write to a *procuratore* of the Venetian Republic (one of his institutional bosses) explaining what his situation at Parma was like: the three-week period that Monteverdi had anticipated spending in Parma quickly became longer, though not substantially (on 30 October Monteverdi wrote that he had just reached Parma, so the intended return was a mere ten days earlier than this letter projects); more work was necessary than previously thought.[121]

The following day, Goretti complained that Bentivoglio was not helpful in the decision process. Many singers had arrived at Parma, including some notable ones like Loreto Vittori,[122] Gregorio Chianchi, Ugolino,[123] and the young man Goretti had already mentioned a week before as suitable for the part of Amore, presumably for the third *intermedio*. Many more were still to come, and at this point rehearsals might have been close at hand, except for a crucial detail: Goretti and Monteverdi essentially refused to attribute parts to singers. Goretti in no uncertain terms specified here that Bentivoglio's presence was needed to settle this momentous issue. It is worth underscoring that, differently from professional actors and actresses, seventeenth-century singers "belonged" to noble patrons. Thus, "[e]ven when they moved from one court to another, such moves were a reflection of political and diplomatic events and of the patron's need to show a prestigious image to the outside world" (Durante, "The Opera Singer," 351). Assigning parts to singers was a delicate endeavor from both the performance and courtly standpoints.[124]

The following week, Monteverdi finally went to assess the temporary structure, as two letters dated 16 November indicate. Goretti's is more explicit: he judged the temporary structure as worse than the Farnese, because it did not offer more space (presumably for the musicians) and it was still under construction. Goretti's tone betrays his disappointment; his words manifest that his patience (and Monteverdi's, presumably) was running out.[125] Mazzi's letter is also filled with frustration, not with Bentivoglio but with those in charge of the music, as he did not appreciate Monteverdi's immediate dissatisfaction with the San Pietro martire theater; however, he assured Bentivoglio that he would do anything to try to assuage the composer.[126] This state of affairs could well have been a consequence of the serendipitous nature of the building process; if Mazzi and Guitti (and indeed, Bentivoglio) had known from the start exactly what sort of entertainment was to have taken place in this new theater, they could have proceeded differently. At the same time, Monteverdi had a specific and precise idea ("il suo pensiero") of what the final "product" would look and sound like; thus, he was understandably loath to compromise. Bentivoglio's absence also contributed to complicating the situation, as a passage later in Mazzi's letter indicates: "il Sig[no]r Co[nte] Fabio tutavia tien detto quale machine vogliamo mostrar alli Musici, e non ristringendole, malamente segli puo dar sadisfatione" (Lavin, "Lettres," 131–32; idem, *Art and Pageantry*, 533; MS Antonelli 660, 16 November 1627, fols. 3 v–4 r).[127] This passage implies that not all stage machines were ready to be shown to those in charge of the musical part of the entertainment;

thus the *maggiordomo* was free to decide how to proceed, rather than the architects, because Bentivoglio was not there to overrule Scotti's decisions.[128]

Bentivoglio, however, could not be persuaded to come to Parma; on 19 November, Scotti informed him again of the singers on hand (Fabris, *Mecenati e musici*, 418), and Goretti on the following day Goretti suggested that the role of Mercury (presumably from the second printed *intermezzo*) be given to Grimani, Monsignor Ciampoli's alto (Fabris, *Mecenati e musici*, 418).[129] By 26 November Goretti and Monteverdi felt that they had to attribute parts to the singers:

> Alla s[igno]ra Setimia Didone Europa Aurora Giunone e la Musa.
> Al S[ignor] Loreto Venere, Asia Venere prima Musa Belona
> Al S[ignor] Gregorio Diana, America età dell'oro, seconda musa e Bericintia
> All'angiola e dedicato la parte di Giunone nella Comedia, e nel torneo la Discordia, molte parte sono bene à propriate ma come sono alcune parte de cantori di Parma e uno di Roma che è un soprano di S[a]n Pietro, che l'isperienza e la prova farà conoscere se è huomo ò nò e così quelli di Parma et il contralti, di Modona. (MS Antonelli 660, 26 November 1627, fol. 1 r–v)[130]

Among the characters mentioned in this passage, none are from the first printed *intermedio*; Dido, attributed to Settimia Caccini, and Juno, given to Angiola Zanibelli, belong to the second one. Venus and Diana, to be played respectively by Loreto Vittori and Gregorio Chianchi, belong to the third printed *intermedio*, while Europa, Asia, and America are undoubtedly part of the fifth one. The other characters (the other Juno, the three muses, Bellona — the Italic goddess of war —, and Berecynthia or Cybele — the mother goddess) cannot be placed in any extant piece, except for Discordia, who was a part of the tournament that took place in the Teatro Farnese. Nevertheless, it is important to underscore that both men and women would sing in the *intermezzi*;[131] since male singers like Lorenzo and Gregorio were cast in female roles, we surmise that they were *castrati*. Mixing men, boys, and women on stage does not seem to have been a problem for Goretti; their different provenance, however, worried him a little. Some were from Rome, some from Parma, and a contralto was from Modena; according to Goretti, only the rehearsal process would reveal their worth[132] and how compatible they would be.[133]

While Goretti's letter dated 27 November contains only a passing reference to the preparations for the festivities,[134] Mazzi's of 30 November brings up a more basic concern: "Siè atorno ora à consultar il teatro che si deve fare, è mi pare che secondo la pianta dell sig[no]r Fran[ces]co si piglia troppo luoco per rispeto, del recitare è della musica, è state che se bene si asserà, la voce però si svanirà molto più che non farebbe nelle Muraglie. è per l'atezza [*sic*] che serà grande" (Lavin, "Lettres," 137; idem, *Art and Pageantry*, 535–36; MS Antonelli 660, 30 November 1627, fol. 1 v).[135] Mazzi criticized Guitti's plan as bestowing too much of a precious resource, space, on the performers, presumably to the detriment of the audience. In order to avoid too direct a confrontation both with the mentioned Guitti and the unmentioned Monteverdi and Goretti (who, as we have seen, complained that there was not enough room for the musicians in the temporary structure), Mazzi professed to be worried precisely by how the sound would travel in a structure in which the stage took up an inordinate amount of space. What is also notable in Mazzi's passage is the discrepancy between the progress in building the theater and in putting together the performance side of the festivities. This again points to the somewhat casual nature of both the final structure and the events that eventually transpired on stage.

The flurry of activity documented in November subsided in December; this lull could be at least partially motivated by the Christmas holiday, requiring Monteverdi's presence in Venice and prodding the various workers and artists at Parma to return to their hometowns. The first of two extant letters dated from December 1627, is by Goretti, written on the seventh. Rehearsing has not yet been completed, as work progressed on the temporary structure, and at least some musical sessions were taking place elsewhere ("in camera").[136] Goretti cautioned Bentivoglio that the acoustic adjustment had to be space-specific and tailored to the place in which the performance would actually occur. As Goretti was originally from Ferrara, he expected to see Bentivoglio in person on the occasion of his return for the holidays. Later on in the same letter he wrote that "[i]l Mazzi mi a mostrato molte cose in modello della quale [sic] ne hò avisato V[ostra] S[ignoria] Ill[ustrissi]ma e aboca li dirò quanto mi ocorerà" (Lavin, "Lettres," 147; idem, *Art and Pageantry*, 541; MS Antonelli 660, 7 December 1627, fol. 1 r).[137] The discussions between architects and musicians regarding the performative space had continued; unfortunately, Mazzi's models are not extant, and Goretti planned on discussing them in person with Bentivoglio after his return to Ferrara.

The other extant letter from this month is dated Venice, 18 December, and addressed by Monteverdi to Alessandro Striggio. In it he discussed a commission by Striggio, and considers who might sing this work in progress, presumably because his patron had asked him for his professional opinion.[138] Gregorio (already cited in Goretti's letter of 26 November) and Antonio Grimano (whose name had not been mentioned previously) were good singers; the former was in service to a powerful Roman cardinal, but both were impossible to wrest from their patron's service. The other two, the singer in St. Peter's (who also had surfaced in Goretti's letter of 9 November, where his name was specified as Vincenzo Ugolino) and the eleven-year-old *putto* (for whom Goretti thought the role of Amore was tailor-made), had failed to impress Monteverdi with their singing abilities. Ugolino's voice was unclear, colorless and laden with catarrh; the boy's was dull, though not devoid of some value. Overall, Monteverdi tried to dissuade Striggio from trying to hire these four singers for his own performance: the first two were under contract elsewhere, and the other two were not worth the effort. We could conclude that Monteverdi was not thrilled to have to work with these singers at Parma, for he harbored serious doubts as to the caliber of their singing voices.

By early February 1628 Monteverdi was back in Parma, ready to rehearse: the music was finished and the singers and musicians were all at Parma; but evidently the theaters were not ready, since the rehearsals took place "in piassa." According to Monteverdi, the reason for this situation was that nobody, even at court, was sure when the wedding would take place: some said May, others September.[139] However, the Farnese were satisfied with what they saw at the rehearsals; so the composer predicted that in a few days rehearsals would be complete and everybody would go back to their regular place of employment, to come back to Parma when a date would be in place for the wedding and, consequently, for the festivities.

Monteverdi went on to explain that the festivities would involve a "comedia recitata" and a tournament.[140] Like his contemporary, the composer was aware that the two events differed in nature and genre; moreover, in his opinion the tournament was much harder to set to music than the *intermezzi*.[141] Reiner has pointed out that "in the published version of Pio di Savoia's five *intermedii* only the second and the third have as many as 300 lines; and Achillini's *Mercurio e Marte*, as published, consists of 891 lines, plus two strophic repetitions amounting to eleven lines" ("Preparations in Parma," 293); in his opinion, consequently, after 4 February the texts underwent considerable changes to reflect the different identity of the bride (293). Specifically, the tournament was divided into two texts: one still called *Mercurio e Marte*, the other serving as prologue to the spoken drama and published as *Teti e Flora* (293 n. 88). Since extant documents regarding the identity of the bride as Margherita date precisely to this period in early February, it is more likely that Monteverdi was somewhat exaggerating the magnitude of his task with Striggio, who had acted as go-between with the court of Mantua and had accepted an already composed piece in lieu of the new one originally promised (286 n. 63).

On 8 February, Ascanio Pio wrote a letter to Bentivoglio accompanying the last of the five *intermedi* to be composed.[142] Since this piece came much later than the others, clearly Ascanio Pio was concerned that stage machinery already built could be utilized for this new text:

> Spero, che p[er] la musica non sarà cattivo; le macchine sono le medesime poiche il carro di Venere puo servire à Febo; solo hò cangiata l'agitazione della furia in una turbazione di aria, e di fiumi, parendomi questa e più naturale, e che farà effetto molto magg[io]re, né questa novità apporta alterazione alcuna di macchina, che occupi luogo, onde ne venga impedita alcuna dell'altre, oltre che ove sono tante divinità in altre macchine in nuvole p[er] p[er]fetione anche un'oscuramento ed un rasserenam[en]to di cielo, in che l'ingegno di

V[ostra] S[ignoria] Ill[ustrissi]ma s'eserciti con eminenza. (Lavin, "Lettres," 145; idem, *Art and Pageantry*, 540)[143]

Well aware that the architectural and engineering aspects of the entertainment were infinitely more complex to carry out than the textual ones, Pio di Savoia was quick to point out that he had given consideration to modifying as little as possible in the required stage machinery, both for building and staging purposes. Further, he tried to ingratiate his father-in-law by flattering him for his ingenuity in staging matters, as the end of the cited passage makes clear.

As the texts to all five *intermezzi* were presumably completed, Pio di Savoia offered also his advice as to the order in which they would be staged.[144] While ultimate authority rested with Bentivoglio, Pio di Savoia had to modify somewhat the previous order of *intermezzi* because the one centering on Aeneas and Lavinia was being replaced by the one he was enclosing, which had Bacchus as its protagonist. As it happens, not only was the final order different from either of those proposed in this letter, but one of the *intermezzi* was still replaced — ironically, the one about Bacchus that Pio di Savoia had just written and that Scotti received a week later.[145] He wrote to Bentivoglio to inform him that "Ho ric[evu]to l'intermedio di Bacco inviatomi da V[ostra] S[ignoria] Ill[ustrissi]ma e doppo havendo mostrato al ser[enissi]mo Duca, lò datto à Madama ser[enissi]ma laquale mi hà detto che lò vedrà e legerà, e se occorrerà cosa alc[un]a n'avisarò V[ostra] S[ignoria] Ill[ustrissi]ma" (Lavin, "Lettres," 144; idem, *Art and Pageantry*, 540; MS Antonelli 660, 15 February 1628, fol. 1 r).[146] Scotti, the *maggiordomo*, gives here the impression of acting merely as a go-between in the transactions of Bentivoglio and the Farnese. His role was to convey to the dowager duchess textual, performative, and technical suggestions, to receive the court's opinion, and to transmit it to whomever necessary. In spite of Pio di Savoia's care for pre-existing stage machinery and its movement during the performance, the *intermedio* centering around Bacchus was discarded; maybe the reason behind it was, as Reiner suggests, that Odoardo's choice of a new bride required it ("Preparations in Parma," 300), or maybe that the court did not approve it, as implied in Scotti's letter.

Meanwhile, Monteverdi, Goretti, and Guitti were still busy adapting the music to the performance place and the latter to the need of the musicians. Two letters dated 18 February agree that a solution has been reached in the Teatro Farnese (one by Guitti: Lavin, "Lettres," 126; idem, *Art and Pageantry*, 529; MS Antonelli 660, 18 February 1628, fol. 1 r–v; the other by Goretti: Lavin, "Lettres," 147; idem, *Art and Pageantry*, 541; MS Antonelli 660, 18 February 1628, fol. 1 r–v). As for the temporary structure, Goretti merely wrote that they had reached a partial solution. Since all the structural problems had not yet been solved, and since the *intermezzi* were being chosen still, the musical side of the entertainment could not be completed either.[147]

The last letter strictly pertaining to this phase of the festivities is dated 15 March 1628; addressed by Guitti to Bentivoglio, it informs the latter of the rehearsals under way and conveys the architect's exasperation.[148] After many changes in plot and music, the rehearsal process was still in its earliest stage. The complexity of this phase can hardly be imagined: inexperienced musicians led in newly-composed music by as important a figure as Monteverdi, and occasionally in the Duke's very presence; architects and workers trying to synchronize the movements of bulky and delicate stage machinery with the music; plenty of verbal banter to go along with the process . . . No wonder the entire exercise felt to Guitti rather like an occasion to spoil the machines than anything constructive.

What happened after mid-March 1628 is virtually impossible to reconstruct because only a handful of documents are extant from this period. Perhaps Bentivoglio took frequent trips to Parma;[149] perhaps the Farnese understood that the wedding would not take place until the fall, and let all the artists, workers, and craftsmen return home to avoid too hefty a bill. In any case, on 2 October Odoardo left Parma to go wed Margherita;[150] by mid-October some additional details of the impending festivities received attention. The rough draft of a letter sent by Margherita, Odoardo's mother, to Barsotti, governor of Piacenza, remains,[151] and it is of extraordinary interest:

> Volendo noi far recitar quà, <come sapete,> una Pastorale, come sapete alla venuta della <S[igno]ra Duchessa> sposa <del Duca mio figlio,> haviamo fatta elettione del S[ign]or Cesare Bernardini, dandoli <perche habbia à recitar> una parte principaliss[im]a come quello, che et p[er] presenza, habilità, pronuntia et per altre bone parti sue, <et p[er] la pronuntia,> la rapresenterà ottimamente <in bene>; et havendovi egli con molta modestia risposto <che> di esser pronto ad accettarla, mentre <che> il S[igno]r suo P[ad]re se ne contenti et che di più habbiano accompagnato alla buona nascita loro, l'inteligenza presupponendosi forse, che gli altri recitanti non siano gentilhuomini. <Mà hora udendo noi havendo noi havuta q[ue]sta considerat[io]ne haviamo non solo haviamo eletti gli altri recitanti che sono gentilhuomini mà feudatarij anche, et frà gli altri il Conte Molla, che hà ancor lui una parte, noi ordiniamo, dunque che ritroviate il> Hora desiderando noi infinitam[en]te che detto S[igno]re, si contenti, che il S[igno]r Cesari accetti la parte destinatali e reciti vi ordiniamo che diate habito da lui P[ad]re del Cesari et <facciate ogni offitio, con spendere> riccam[en]te off[ti]o <dello> anche in n[ost]ro nome p[er]che se ne contenti <che egli suo figlio vi reciti, atteso che> assicurandolo che tutti gli altri che hanno da recitare <sono> non solo sono gentilhuomini, ma anche feudatarij come lo è il Conte Molla che è frà essi et però, che non ci nieghi q[ue]sta cortesia nella q[ua]le premiamo oltremodo,
> <gli altri recitanti sono della qualità che vi haremmo detto,> ne gli dia serapale che <esso suo> il figlio sia Prete, p[er]che vi recitano de <q[ue]lli

che sono> sacerdoti, et che hanno titoli di Dignità, <rappresentandoli> riscatatesi dunque grandem[en]te in q[ue]sto partic[ola]re significandoli di più, che dove non ricorriamo, si accetto piacere da S[ua] S[igno]ria, ci ritroviamo in malissimo termine, si p[er] essere vicine [sic] il tempo della venuta della S[igno]ra Sposa, come per non <saper> veggiamo in chi altri metter le mani, che sia più habile del S[ignor] Cesari suo figlio, per <recitare> la parte che gli haviamo destinata. <però riscaldatemi quanto potete, p[er]che si contenti di darci gusto di concedergliene la, . . . ^{152} assicurandolo, che gli è ne [sic] saremo> et assicurate esso S[igno]re che come no[n] ci può dar maggior segno di corrispondere alla buona disposit[io]ne n[ost]ra, verso di lui, che col promettere al S[igno]r suo figlio che accetti d[ett]a parte, cosi gli è [sic] saremo sempre m[ol]to obblig[ati] et Dio vi contenti.^{153}

By 16 October, Tasso's *Aminta* had been chosen as the *commedia* to be spoken on stage; though it is not identified in this letter, it is unlikely that it would be replaced barely two months before the festivities.^{154} Cesare Bernardini, a nobleman and priest, had been selected as one of its main performers, but his father had objected to his presence on stage. Margherita Aldobrandini hence had to write to Barsotti, to convince Cesare's father to agree to his acting in the pastoral. Three strategies are suggested. First, it must be made clear that there was no social stigma attached to performing *Aminta*, as testified by the numerous noblemen who had agreed to this task — even to the gentleman in question, who happened to be a man of the cloth. Second, Barsotti could sway Bernardini's father through lavish gifts and personal attention. Third, Barsotti could plead the court's case by pointing out that time was of the essence, and that Cesare could be replaced only with great risk for the production. Though the stage still elicited moral and social repugnance among noblemen like Bernardini,^{155} the letter suggests that pastorals were more acceptable, unfortunately without offering any rationale for the reasons behind it. At the same time, it is almost unnecessary to point out that the spoken *commedia* required much less organizing than the sung *intermezzi*, as the late date of this letter manifests.

In early November rehearsals were afoot in the Teatro Farnese but not in the teatro di San Pietro martire, as a letter by Goretti dated 3 November attests (Fabris, *Mecenati e musici*, 432); by the end of the month, rehearsing had begun anew,^{156} but the main difficulty was in having music and machinery proceed at the same pace;^{157} to this end rehearsals continued, even though Goretti, ever outspoken, was looking forward to the actual event so that, after over a year, he could leave Parma for good and go back to Ferrara. He got his wish, the following month, when the newly married Odoardo and Margherita finally reached the city and the festivities took place.

Notes

[1] See I. Lavin, "Lettres de Parme (1618, 1627–28) et débuts du théâtre baroque," in *Le Lieu Théâtral à la Renaissance*, ed. Jacquot, 105–58, here 106; idem, "On the Unity of the Arts and the Early Baroque Opera House," in *Art and Pageantry in the Renaissance and Baroque*, ed. B. Wisch and S. S. Munshower (University Park: Pennsylvania State University Press, 1990), 518–79, here 521; and idem, same title, *Perspecta* 26 (1990), 1–20, here 11. I cite the identically-titled articles by giving those of the publications in which they appeared, *Perspecta* and *Art and Pageantry*.

[2] See P. Minucci del Rosso, "Le nozze di Margherita de' Medici con Odoardo Farnese duca di Parma e Piacenza, I-II-III," *Rassegna nazionale* 21 (16 February 1885): 551–71, 22 (16 April 1885): 550–70, 23 (1 May 1885): 19–45, here I, 551.

[3] This contract, now at the Archivio di Stato, Firenze, is reprinted in Minucci del Rosso, "Le nozze," III, 27–29.

[4] "Il Gran Duca scrisse una lettera al S[ign]or Cardinale [Odoardo] Farnese, mettendoli in consideratione, che l'indugio di andare à Roma, potrebbe trovare il Papa già avvisato da altri del Parentado stabilito. L'Ambasciatore Guicciardini hà ordine espresso, di non ne parlare fin che il S[ign]or Cardinale non arrivi à Roma, et di governarsi nel modo, che da S[ua] S[ignoria] Ill[ustrissi]ma gli sarà commandato. che è quanto m'occorre dire à V[ostra] S[ignoria] in risposta della sua": Archivio di Stato, Parma: Carteggio farnesiano e borbonico estero, busta 475 [the grand duke wrote to Cardinal Farnese indicating that his delay in going to Rome could result in the Pope finding out the concluded marriage from someone else. Ambassador Guicciardini is under explicit orders not to talk about it until the cardinal arrives in Rome and to behave according to your highness's commands. This is what I wanted to tell you as a reply to your letter].

[5] Archivio di Stato, Firenze: Mediceo del Principato, filza 6088.

[6] Roberto Ciancarelli points out that in 1611 a group of noblemen had attempted to murder Duke Ranuccio Farnese; several of them were executed, thus damaging relations with the many noble families to which they were related elsewhere: *Il progetto di una festa barocca. Alle origini del Teatro Farnese di Parma (1618–1629)* (Rome: Bulzoni, 1987), 21–22.

[7] A concise description of the history of the Farnese is to be found in Letizia Arcangeli, "Atlante genealogico della famiglia Farnese," in *I Farnese. Arte e collezionismo*, ed. L. Fornari Schianchi and N. Spinosa (Milan: Electa, 1995), 25–48. A fictionalized, yet essentially accurate, account of the situation in Parma before Ranuccio's death can be read in the third chapter of E. Paglioli, *La breve festa del Cardinale Francesco Maria Farnese* (Parma: PPS, 1998). The cardinal was Odoardo's brother.

[8] "If the grand duke would like to change and select another daughter in her stead, then the Parma prince is happy to give him that privilege within six years from today."

[9] "I heard from lord Contarini who is my boss and *procuratore* at St. Mark's that his excellence is afraid that the wedding will not take place at *carnevale* or in May as he had written me; perhaps it will not take place at all."

[10] "The festivities will undoubtedly take place for the wedding, but we cannot know when, and perhaps the princes themselves do not know." Dinko Fabris has identified the recipient of this letter as Caterina Martinengo, Enzo Bentivoglio's wife, rather than Enzo himself: *Mecenati e musici*, 425.

¹¹ Archivio di Stato, Firenze: Mediceo del Principato, filza 6087.

¹² On 3 February 1628, the secretary to Francesco I of Este duke of Modena noted: "Parte da Mod[e]na S[ignor] Seg[reta]rio per andar à Parma mandato da S[ua] A[ltezza] con ordine di . . . partecipar loro [i.e., to Margherita Aldobrandini and Odoardo Farnese], come s'è già fatto altre volte certi nuovi avvisi spettanti il matrim[oni]o di S[ua] Alt[ezz]a con la S[ignor]a Margh[erit]a Medici" (Archivio di Stato, Modena: cancelleria ducale, ambasciatori Parma busta 5) [our secretary is leaving Modena to go to Parma under orders to share with the Farnese some new regarding his highness's wedding with Margherita de' Medici]. By the beginning of the month, then, the Estes were already making provisions for Odoardo and Margherita's passage through Modena on their way to Parma. The proxy wedding had not yet taken place, but for the Estes the identity of the bride was certain.

¹³ Both the gratulatory letters and the list of Farnese announcements are now at Archivio di Stato, Parma: Casa e corte farnesiane, serie II busta 28 fascicolo 5.

¹⁴ MS parmense 737. The work is entitled *L'Heroe d'Italia*.

¹⁵ "Such a great prince had to get an adequate match, and the Cardinal and his mother saw to it that his people would see a new sun, Ranutio, shining on them. The politically savy Duke Ranutio considered the merits of all Italian prices. Many think that the Grand Duke of Tuscany's world would disappear or fold when encountering any difficulty. But this is a world, so it becomes stronger and will live on eternally. It was praised as a world on the occasion of the wedding; this is not just a story! The Medici had renewed the kingdom of France and even some empires, thanks to heirs born to them. This world put forth a daisy, the most hidden gift that nature bestows on to the earth, in comparison with the sun's warmth, water's appreciation, and the wonderful concordance of the elements. Odoardo's father chose her as the one that high intellect or a negotiation could give him. Deftly and prudently he had the Grand Duke sounded: would he like to see these two noble people get married in the church, according to the rules of the Council of Trent? The Florentine Excellence liked this invitation, thinking that he would have profited from this alliance with Parma; so he replied that he would have gladly opened negotiations once the two young people reached the right age." Note that "daisy" in Italian is "Margherita."

¹⁶ This aspect was underscored in Florence, too, at least since Eleonora di Toledo's entrance of 1539; in 1565, the god Hymen (the first character on stage in Achillini's prologue, as we will see) was part of the iconography for Giovanna d'Austria's festivities: M. Casini, *I gesti del principe* (Venice: Marsilio, 1996), 230. Also, a 1628 poem celebrating the wedding explicitly refers to the bride's role to produce an heir to Odoardo: "Tù, bella MARGHERITA, al casto Amante / Lieta rivolgi, e baldanzosa, il piede; / Si che, prodotto un pargoletto infante, / Del paterno valor si chiami herede" H. Persiani, *Contesa d'Apollo e di Amore* (1628), 28 [Beautiful Margherita, walk happy and proud to your chaste lover, so that you may produce a baby boy, heir to his father's valor].

¹⁷ This document can be found in Comune, busta 625, among many manuscript documents attesting to the various activities planned and carried out by the elders of the municipality to celebrate the wedding, particularly for Margherita's triumphal entry into Parma.

¹⁸ "The French queen mother, the archduchess of Graz, one of the dowager duchesses of Mantua and Monferrato, the duchess of Parma, Piacenza and Castro all come from Medici stock. The princess of Urbino, the princes of Modena, the princess of Piedmont,

the queen of England, the king of France, the queen of Spain, and the empress were all born of a Medici mother."

[19] This point has been most recently emphasized by Stephen Orgel, who asserts that "alliances were normally arranged for sons just as for daughters; the distinction here is between fathers or guardians and children, not between sexes": *Impersonations* (Cambridge: Cambridge University Press, 1996), 13. Though his assertion concerns early modern (Protestant) England, Catholic Italy in the same period was as much a patriarchal society as the British Isles. It is in this key that Graziosi interprets *Aminta*'s ending, for the wedding between Aminta and Silvia are predicated upon her father Montano's assent: Graziosi, Aminta *1573–1580*, 123–24.

[20] "It had been a few days since I had seen your bride. I will tell you, however, that I saw her today. She is in good health. I saw her without her mask and I can assure you that the painter who did her portrait did not deceive you. As I already wrote you, I am sure that when you see both the portrait and the princess, you will like the latter better, especially for her features, colors, and beauty": Archivio di Stato, Parma: Carteggio farnesiano e borbonico estero, busta 475.

[21] Readers will recall that the season of *carnevale* started immediately after Christmas, New Year's Eve, or the feast of Epiphany (6 January). Since Bagarelli's letter is dated 2 January, it is likely that Margherita's wearing of a mask was linked to *carnevale* festivities rather than a sign of modesty.

[22] This is taken from Macrobius, *Commentary on the Dream of Scipio*, 2.17.

[23] "The portraits of the two princes had been exchanged. Though they had not been painted by Phidias or Parrhasius, who deceived birds and men and their own virtue, their authors managed to have their sitters' majestic souls show. In Odoardo's face valor prevailed, in Margherita's honor as though seated in a throne. When these portraits reached their intended recipients, at the very moment when they first set eyes on them, they were ablaze and promised to sacrifice themselves to the other and to make their love eternal even after their bodily deaths, as their blessed souls can still be seen in the heavens. One felt liking for the epitome of beauty, accompanied by modesty, looking like dawn peering from the horizon to signify whiteness. Buds do look whiter than snow when they first appear, but there is no mistaking them, as their value increases as we contemplate them. The other saw the majesty of a royal face under the guise of Mars, and she gave the heavens her promise that she would not marry another prince than that one with such a wise face and a such noble countenance, that cannot be happy in his greatness unless he conquers a heart like Alexander. Odoardo looked like Alexander because he was as courageous as he — as Scipio said, noble hearts are not satisfied with their spirit unless they achieved those goals that valor imposed on them. Jacob worked as a servant to Laban for fourteen years in order to marry Rachel, and did not care for Leah; thus it is not surprising that agreements are not reached right away and that they spent a long time negotiating, as noble people do. Love has such powerful tricks that make him the most powerful of the gods. Only a very patient person can understand love, as it becomes so strong with time that it easily breaks the laws of convenience and creates the law of love, that is, perseverance. Its form, acquired through the eyes, is the soul's passion."

[24] Or, perhaps, some documents have not been preserved to this day, for example those of financial nature, as is the case for the della Rovere court of Pesaro and Urbino.

²⁵ "Il Maggiordomo hà d'havere il pensiero di tutte le fabriche intra, et extra, et quando ci sarà bisogno d'alcuna reparatione di fuori, il Mag[gioren]te ne manderà poliza à Guglielmo Rossi Comp[utis]ta delle fabriche. Li conti si devono vedere alla presenza del Magg[iordo]mo con parte del Mag[gioren]te, et da saldanti conforme la Constitutione": Archivio di Stato, Parma: Casa e corte farnesiane, serie VII busta 51 fascicolo 23 [the *maggiordomo* oversees all buildings inside and outside the wall. When repairs are needed outside, the overseer will send a request to Guglielmo Rossi, building accountant. Accounts must be reviewed in the maggiordomo's, overseer's, and payees' presence according to the rules].

²⁶ Another document presents an even larger picture of the *maggiordomo*'s duties, and is therefore worth quoting extensively:

1 Cura principale del Magiordomo sarà il procurare che ciascuno officiale di Corte faccia l'ufficio suo in fede e diligenza che devono partecipando con noi le cose più gravi

2 Ordinarà al Computista tutti li mandati per pagare li sallariati et tutti quelli che sarano altresi creditori in Computist[eri]a et di tutte le spese ordinarie della Casa et delle straordinarie che li saranno incaricate da noi, et sottoscriverà tutti i mandati, et quelli ch'havrà ordinato il medesimo Magistrato al Med[esi]mo Comp[utis]ta cosi per li Deviti [i.e., debiti] et sentenze del Presidente come per tutte le spese straord[ina]rie attinenti alla coltura dei beni della Camera conserationi del raccolti, per riconoscere et misurare il sod[det]ti beni, per far compositioni con i delinquenti copie di scritture, viaggi in simili et altr occasioni concernenti l'interesse della Cam[e]ra et finalmente per le monitioni del vivere de i Castelli non volendo che il Tesor[ie]ro gnante [i.e., niente] riceva ò faccia pagare altri mandati che li fermati dal Comp[utis]ta et sottoscritti dal D[ett]o Maggiordomo, eccetto però quelli, che parrà di riservare a noi med[esim]a

Conforme all'ordine già dato dal Sig[no]r Cav[alie]re haverà cura delle fabbriche de i Pallazzi del Duca nella Città et delle Case et Molini fuori della Città et nello stato di Par[m]a mà per rispetto delle fabbriche fuori della Città non farà metter mano a cosa alcuna prima che dal Magistrato sia stato avisato il Comp[utis]ta delle fabriche. (Archivio di Stato, Parma: Casa e corte farnesiane, serie VII busta 51 fascicolo 23)

[1 The highest priority for the *maggiordomo* will be to make sure that each court official will carry out his duty with faith and devotion and share with us the most important things.

2 He will give our accountant all the invoices to pay those who are hired and all those who are owed money, including the ordinary and extraordinary expenses that we will require. He will sign all invoices: those sent from the justices to the accountant for the debts and sentences of the jury; those for extraordinary expenses having to do with our goods, our chamber, and our harvest, so that such goods be measured; those having to do with those who break the law; those regarding copies of documents, trips, and other occasions concerning the

Chamber; and finally those necessary to feed those in the castles. The Treasure does not wish that anything be received or paid unless signed by the accountant and the aforementioned *maggiordomo*, other than those that we will reserve for ourselves.

Following the previously issued orders, the *maggiordomo* will take care of the palaces inside and outside of town as well as the homes and mills outside and in the state. Out of respect for the buildings outside he will not start anything before the building accountant is informed.]

[27] As Lisa Jardine has pointed out, "[d]ynastic marriages were a formal part of Renaissance power politics, and the expenditure on the dowry, the trousseau and the betrothal and wedding celebrations was included in the calculations of the cost of the occasion versus the value of the contract to the families involved": *Worldly Goods* (London: Norton, 1996), 408. Piperno agrees: "[t]he enormous monetary expenditures involved were calculated in terms of political and diplomatic affirmation rather than profit and loss": "Opera Production," 2.

[28] "Rest of the feudatories' gifts upon Odoardo's first marriage."

[29] Archivio di Stato, Parma: Casa e corte farnesiane, serie II busta 2 fascicolo 2. This *fascicolo* and the following (3) contain many similar documents attesting to the monetary contributions of various Farnese communities.

[30] Archivio di Stato, Parma: Casa e corte farnesiane, serie II busta 6 fascicolo 2.

[31] "The city of Piacenza has to give duke Odoardo the customary gift for his first marriage, which amounts to sixty thousand Spanish *doble*. At the current exchange rate of £45.18 it amounts to £2,850,000. We believe that, following Parma's example, at least part should be paid in cash, we hope at least ten thousand Spanish *doble*, which are equivalent to £450,000. The rest of what we owe would be £2,400,000. In order to raise this sum, we believe that the city will have no trouble imposing many of the customs duties already imposed upon other occasions and then removed. Raising this way £200,000 yearly, we would pay our debt in twelve years, as has been done before."

[32] "A volte è difficile stabilire all'interno di complesse manifestazioni pubbliche una principale sfera di committenza. Spesso gli eventi si sovrappongono e a diversi livelli committenti e promotori risultano molteplici": Carandini, *Teatro e spettacolo*, 34 [sometimes it is difficult to figure out who the main patron was, within complex public festivities. Often events are superimposed one upon another and there are many sponsors at different levels]. This is not the case with the staged entertainment at Parma (ordered and financed by a single patron, the Farnese themselves), though other events such as Margherita's entry saw the direct participation of other local authorities. However, Carandini's statement is rather suitable for illustrating the printing of "official" descriptions.

[33] Franco Ruffini, in his study of the 1513 performance of *La Calandria* in Urbino, similarly juxtaposes two sources: one coming from inside the court, the other penned by a member of the audience. He states: "se la restituzione filologica si appoggerà anche sulle concordanze, l'indagine ermeneutica dovrà far perno sulle discordanze": *Commedia e festa nel Rinascimento:* La Calandria *alla corte di Urbino* (Bologna: Il Mulino, 1986), 211 [philological reconstruction will rest partly on concordances, while hermeneutical investigations must exploit discrepancies]. The present work rests on the awareness that no single reading or interpretation of this (or any) event is possible. Rather than opposing philological

and hermeneutic endeavors, I will try to integrate them to offer as complete a micro-reconstruction as possible.

[34] "The Bentivoglio have arrived in Parma, and have raised the most amazing machinery, the most beautiful buildings that our human intellect can comprehend and conceive, through their subtle ingenuity. There is no doubt that that perfection only be achieved thanks to Odoardo's munificence, Bentivoglio's genius, Poli's assistance, and Morandi's compositions, among others."

[35] I was unable to read Maria Grazia Borazzo, "Musica, scenotecnica, illusione nel grande apparato farnesiano del 1628 a Parma" (*laurea* thesis, Università degli studi di Parma, 1982).

[36] It is ironic that this theater indirectly owes its existence to a man of the cloth who vehemently opposed theatrical entertainment like Carlo Borromeo; a nuanced judgment of his opinion toward the stage is in L. Vignati, *Storia delle filodrammatiche negli oratori milanesi* (Milan: FOM, 1991), 14–19.

[37] Bentivoglio had numerous contacts with professional performers belonging to *arte* troupes, as attested to letters addressed to him by Giovan Battista Andreini (S. Ferrone et al., *Comici dell'arte, Corrispondenze*, 1: 107), Nicolò Barbieri (1: 185), Pier Maria Cecchini (1: 270–73 and 1: 274), and Silvio Fiorillo (1: 331–36). Though *impresari* typically "aimed at making money" (Piperno, "Opera Production," 22), Bentivoglio's activities fall squarely within those normally attributed to an *impresario*. No extant document mentions a payment to Enzo for his services in 1627 and 1628. Though such document might have been lost, it is conceivable that no cash was exchanged, as the Ferrara nobleman stood to reap a generous reward of success and reputation.

[38] The selected letters from MS Antonelli 660 can be read in "Lettres," 119–51 and *Art and Pageantry*, 525–43. All citations will be from these two printed sources, as emended by comparing them with the originals. When discrepancies were detected, I have followed the manuscript. It should be noted that Lavin concentrated on the architectural aspect of the festivities, to the detriment of the musical one. In "Lettres" he justified this omission because "le Professeur Pirrotta m'apprend qu'une étude complète des aspects musicaux des représentations de 1628 a été entreprise" (108 n. 16) [Pirrotta tells me that a complete study of the musical side of the 1628 festivities is under way]. The same reason is given in *Art and Pageantry*, 550 n. 16, published twenty-six years after the original essay in French. In 1999 Dinko Fabris published *Mecenati e musici*, which explores the Bentivoglio family's patronage of musicians; it includes countless documents about the Parma events.

[39] Not surprisingly, nineteenth-century archivists and scholars were more interested in the Teatro Farnese than in the temporary structure on which the present study focuses. For example, the Parma scholar and librarian Amadio Ronchini selected letters and passages on theaters and festivities, but the documents concerning this period (Archivio di Stato, Parma: Raccolta Ronchini, busta 2 fascicolo 2a) cover only the Farnese and exclude the theater of San Pietro martire.

[40] Paolo-Emilio Ferrari (*Spettacoli drammatico-musicali e coreografici in Parma dall'anno 1628 all'anno 1883* [Bologna: Forni, 1884, repr. 1969], 9), followed by Saviotti ("Feste e spettacoli," 49 n. 1) and Lodovico Gambara ("I teatri minori," in *I teatri di Parma*, ed. I. Allodi [Milan: Nuove edizioni, 1969], 205–20, here 206), followed by Marco De Grazia

("Per una storia del Palazzo della Pilotta," *Parma dell'arte* 4 [1972]: 101–49, here 136), both attributed the Teatro di San Pietro martire to Girolamo Rainaldi, without however justifying their assertion. Irène Mamczarz (*Le Théâtre Farnèse à Parme* [Firenze: Olschki, 1988], 77 n. 1) instead shares Minucci del Rosso's opinion ("Le nozze," III, 24 n. 56), for whom the temporary theater was due to another architect, whose last name was Magnani. Lastly, A. M. Nagler offers both views; first, he asserts that Rainaldi had built it (*Theatre Festivals of the Medici* [New Haven: Yale University Press, 1964], 142) but that Magnani "was the architect of the cortile theatre" (143).

[41] "Dieci mesi sono, questa Relatione sarebbe uscita dalla Stampa, ornata di quegli ornamenti, colli quali un Real Apparato, e molte Imperiali Feste comparvero in faccia del Mondo; se per fatal disgrazia sua alcuni, che tolsero l'affronto d'intagliare in rame gli Archi trionfali, i Proscenij, e le Scene, parte da lunga infermità aggravati, parte da inaspettata Morte oppressi, non havessero prima per molti mesi prolungata, e poi alla fine lasciata l'Opera imperfetta": Buttigli, *Descrittione dell'apparato*, i [Ten months ago this account would have appeared with those decorations that they had when this royal celebration and imperial festivities saw the light. Yet out of adverse fate some who were to carve the triumphal arches, the proscenia, and the sets in copper fell seriously ill, and others died. Work was delayed by many months and finally left unfinished].

[42] Guitti's first extant letter is dated a mere six days after one that Bentivoglio addressed to Francesco I d'Este in Modena from Parma: "Con l'occasione, ch'in servizio di questa A[ltezza] di Parma son venuto à lavorare nel suo Teatro, havendo ritrovato in questo Mare certi Gambari, non hò voluto mancare di mandargli all'A[ltezza] V[ostra] gli quali consacrole con ogni più divoto affetto. Di Parma li 13 Ag[o]sto 1627": Archivio di Stato, Modena: Cancelleria ducale, particolari filza 123 [Upon my trip to Parma, where I am to work on his highness's theater, I found a few salt-water shrimp that I want to send to your highness to whom I am affectionately devoted].

[43] According to Reiner, Bentivoglio's visit lasted from 11 to 17 August, on the basis of a letter to Ferrara dated 16 August, in which he "announc[ed] his intention of returning the next day": "Preparations in Parma," 295 n. 93. Another letter by Bentivoglio, dated 12 September (Archivio di Stato, Parma: Teatri e spettacoli di età farnesiana, busta 1 mazzo 1 fascicolo 20 sottofascicolo 3), does not indicate where it was written, but can be safely assigned to Parma. We also have a letter by Goretti in Ferrara addressed to Bentivoglio at Parma, dated 3 August 1627 (Fabris, *Mecenati e musici*, 399). Reiner's hypothesis seems disproved, at least as far as Enzo's arrival date to Parma is concerned.

[44] "Prima con fatica intollerabile si sono condotte quelle Piane, che sono necess[a]rie per il letto della fabrica, e M[ast]ro Pareschi, e Tavano v'hanno avuto à lasciar le braccia, che non avevano homini; quando Dio hà voluto per tanto cridar m'hanno dato 12 falegnami, e 12 fachini, che per ora sono sufficienti": Lavin, "Lettres," 119; idem, *Art and Pageantry*, 525; MS Antonelli 660, 19 August 1627, fol. 1 r [First, with great effort, we brought in those planks that are necessary for the floor of the building. Pareschi and Tavano worked themselves to death, as they did not have enough men. Finally, after much complaining, I was given twelve carpenters and twelve porters, enough for now].

[45] "Abbiamo posto gli scaloni sù i dritti di quelli, che vanno piantati in piede per il Coperto, e per li Gargami, et abbiamogli livellati, e distesi tutti, e cominciato à legare insieme il letto ... Cominciaremo, à Dio piacendo, à levar legni in piede, et abbiamo

legni di 34, e più piedi, per la luce, e per il mezzo, trà gli scaloni di mezzo, che sono di 32 p[ie]di larghi l'uno dall'altro per la scena, et imboccat[u]ra. Abbiamo cominciato con gran furia la facciata, cioè. Si fanno le cornici, e con molto avvantaggio di fattura, e si fanno gli Piedistalli, et abbiamo trovate certe colonne fatte, che fanno per noi, con un poco d'aiuto seranno à proposito": Lavin, "Lettres," 119; idem, *Art and Pageantry*, 525–26; MS Antonelli 660, 19 August 1627, fol. 1 r–v [We placed the staircases on the planks that are to be raised for the cover and the ropes. We planed them and set them down and we have started to tie them together. God willing, we will start to raise planks, some of which (those for the light, for the center and for the middle staircase) are 34 and more *piedi* long, while others (those for the stage and its opening) are 32 *piedi* long. We are preparing the frames, with ease, and the pedestals. We also found some ready-made columns that can fit, and with a little help they will work fine].

⁴⁶ "[H]o fatto venire da Piacenza 12 maestri . . . al suo arivo faro una scelta d'huomini buoni a Parma . . . ed ocorendo mandarne a pigliar delli altri a Piacenza": Fabris, *Mecenati e musici*, 402 [I sent for twelve masons from Piacenza; when you get here I will pick a few handy ones from Parma and if necessary I'll send for more from Piacenza].

⁴⁷ "Nella nova scena siamo a termine, che già cominciamo a preparare il coperto": Fabris, *Mecenati e musici*, 404 [we are well advanced for the new stage, and we are readying its cover].

⁴⁸ "Downstairs, we have prepared the scaffolding for the cover and the poles to position it are in place. The cover is marked and fitted. Let me tell your excellence how it is set, as you can see in this sketch of the profile. The letter 'a' designates the frontispiece height. The letter 'b' stands for the peak of the cover. It is necessary for the temple raised to the sky. It is higher in the front as we need more room for the horses. We will sprinkle the water from 'b' to 'a' with a horn and a line that will gather it in a gutter. If we had started the rain from 'a' we would have ended too low."

⁴⁹ "*Aminta*, to be staged with royal *intermezzi*, cannot take place if it rains, since it is housed in a theater covered with an oilskin."

⁵⁰ "I tempi sono tanto impetuosi, e contrari, che fanno danni grandi per la fabbrica nova, la q[u]ale (se le giornate seranno buone) q[ues]ta sett[ima]na sarà coperta; e certo assicuro V[ostra] S[ignoria] Ill[ustrissi]ma, che non si poteva far più": Lavin, "Lettres," 122; idem, *Art and Pageantry*, 527; MS Antonelli 660, 15 September 1627, fol. 1 r [The weather is so stormy and adverse that it greatly damages our new building, which (if the weather is good) next week will be covered. I assure you that we could not have done more].

⁵¹ "We will have a cover by Saturday; this is a job that requires a lot of preparation, so I hope that at a stroke a lot will be accomplished."

⁵² "Non havendo ricevuto da V[ostra] S[ignoria] Ill[ustrissi]ma sin hora letera alcuna resto tutavia con maggiore desiderio che ella mandi il Sig[no]r Mazzi a Parma poi che non basta ch'io voglia sforzarmi di star sul opera poi che la prova mi riesce malle [i.e., male]": Lavin, "Lettres," 124; idem, *Art and Pageantry*, 528; MS Antonelli 660, 24 October 1627, fol. 1 r [I have not received any letter from your highness. I still hope that you will send Mazzi to Parma, because it is not enough for me to try to stay on top of things, since they come out bad].

⁵³ "Son gionto con questi sig[no]ri piacendo a Iddio salvo è sano à Parma; nel qual arrivo ò trovato il sig[no]r Francesco Guitti amalato che desiderarebbe da V[ostra] S[ignoria] Ill[ustrissi]ma licenza per potersene andare à Casa, essendo anco il parere del sig[no]r

Medico... Il sig[no]r Goretti mià [sic] presentato al sig[no]r Co[nte] Fabio, il quale mià Inanimato alle facende, et alle solecitudine del lavoriero. Non manco è non hò mancato in questo doi giorni di sempre andare discorrendo con il sig[no]r Fran[ces]co per maggiorm[en]te informarmi dell'opere e di quelo fà bisogno e piacia al sig[no]r Dio di darmi tal spirito quanto bisogna all'impresa è quanto è il desiderio che ò di servir a da V[ostra] S[ignoria] Ill[ustrissi]ma sempre": Lavin, "Lettres," 129; idem, *Art and Pageantry*, 531; MS Antonelli 660, 28 October 1627, fol. 1 r [I arrived safe and sound at Parma, God willing, with these people. I found Guitti sick and wishing to have permission from you to go home. The doctor agrees. Goretti introduced me to Scotti who let me in to the job and to its tasks. In these two days I have not neglected to talk to Guitti to find out the work and what is necessary. I hope God will give me enough strength as is necessary to the job and as I desire to be of service to you always].

[54] "Adi 28 di ottob[re] 1627. M[esse]r Bartolome lodisano M[esse]r Pietro drago M[esse]r Bartolome Bolarico M[esse]r Antonio M[ari]a Cattanio M[esse]r Ruccolina M[esse]r Gio[vanni] Bula M[esse]r Gio[vanni] Maria firari M[esse]r laberoroso jo: Gio[vanni] Andrea Cattanio" (Teatri e spettacoli di età farnesiana, busta 1 mazzo 1 fascicolo 18 sottofascicolo 1) [28 October 1627. Master Bartolomeo from Lodi, master Pietro Drago, Master Bartolome Bolarico, Master Antonio Maria Cattaneo, Master Ruccolina, Master Giovanni Bula, Master Giovanni Maria Firari, Master Laberoroso signed by me Giovanni Andrea Cattanio].

[55] This is particularly evident in three subsequent documents to be found in Archivio di Stato, Parma: Teatri e spettacoli di età farnesiana, busta 1 mazzo 1 fascicolo 18 sottofascicoli 3, 4, and 5. The first is a "Liste dela feramenta che fa bisognio [sic] per fare il teatro cioe chioderia" [list of hardware, that is nails, needed to build the theater], which gives the exact number of various kinds of nails to be used and is signed on the bottom by Bartolome Tamaro (whose name appears in some of Guitti and Mazzi's letters). The second is a "lista delli legnami di Piopa che fano bisogno p[er] il servizio della scena che si fà nel Cortile di S[ua] A[ltezza] Ser[enissi]ma" [list of poplar wood necessary for the stage set being built in his highness's courtyard] and specifies the number and dimensions of the necessary poplar wood planks. The third and last is a "Lista di legnami, di Piella, che fanno bisogno per la scena over teatro, che si fà nel Cortille di S[ua] A[ltezza] S[erenissi]ma avanti S[an]to Pietro Martire" [list of planed planks needed for the stage or the theater that is being built in his highness's courtyard previously called San Pietro martire]. The last two are also signed by one Giuseppe Salladio. The signatures are a testimony to the fact that such lists carried a specific bureaucratic and administrative weight, and consequently, responsibility on the part of the signer.

[56] "Quanto ale scene le dico che non pasarano quatro giorni al più che sarrano agiustate, per poter far il suo effetto al suo tempo ordinatamente. Vi era natta una dificoltà grandiss[i]ma in esse scene, che nel tempo che dovea sorgere la Città di Dite, vi si ritrovava sopra, di quelle che traversa una scena, la quale à bisognato levar via, è farla venir presso la Boscarecia, con certe animelle fatte alla traversa de telari, e con rodelete sotto caminando sopra il piano della scena; se gli è agionto del peso è crederei, si come ò visto nella Tragica, che tutte facessero il suo Affetto bene": Lavin, "Lettres," 129–30; idem, *Art and Pageantry*, 531; MS Antonelli 660, 16 November 1627, fol. 1 r [As far as the sets are concerned, in no more than four days they will be ready, so that when the time comes they will produce their effect as they should.

We had great difficulty with the sets: at the same time as the city of Dis was supposed to emerge, another one was on top that runs across the whole stage. So we had to remove it and bring it closer to the pastoral set, with the help of small lines that go through the *telari* and small wheel that run above the planks. We added some weight to it and I believe that all sets will produce their effect well, as is the case with those for the tragedy].

[57] "Il Riboni Comincierà Domatina a far il Tempio. Il Pitor da Carara è atorno alli telari, che anno gli Nichi. Si mette in opera il pezzo di Solaro, che va davanti il Proscenio. Si lumezza le Bataglie d'oro, che sono nei telari del proscenio. Siè [sic] fatto il Giardino, cioe il palco che và sù è giù per gli Cavalieri. Sie [sic] tirata sù la Machina de Cavali, è il Tamera dice finirla ivi. Mi dà però fastidio in detta Machina quel doverla Calare con doi mangani, perche score pericolo di non andar giù para. Il Tamara à fatto gli Doi Modeli de feri, per il Cavalo di Bradamante è Melissa, e quello di Atlante mà non sonno ancora forniti, ne posso dir à V[ostra] S[ignoria] Ill[ustrissi]ma il suo effetto. Gli Bolognesi sonno atorno alla Città Celeste, gli telari della quali à bisognato scavezare, non potendo, quando la Machina è in cielo capire sin sotto il Coperto, ma però serà così facile il congiungervi quei pezzi, che parerà tutta intiera, ne si potea farla incasata in sieme, per rispetto dei risalti overo azeti che fano le base è Capitali è le cornici. M[esser] Alfonso à disegnato il Giardino è restarà meterlo in pianta quando si serà sbrigato dalle Machine di sopra": Lavin, "Lettres," 131; idem, *Art and Pageantry*, 532; MS Antonelli 660, 16 November 1627, fol. 3 r–v [Tomorrow morning Riboni will start work in the temple. The Carrara painter is busy with the cloths that have niches. We are putting in place a piece of the top that is before the frontispiece. We are gilding the battles that are on the proscenium cloths. We built the garden, that is, the platform that rises and falls with the knights. We lifted the horses, and Tamera says he will finish it there. What bothers me about that piece of stage machinery is that it moves downward thanks to two mangles, so there is a risk that it might not descent in a straight line. Tamera prepared two iron models (one for Melissa and Bradamante's horse, the other for Atlas), but they are not yet finished and thus I cannot tell your highness what effect they have. Those from Bologna are busy with the heavenly city. We had to separate those cloths as it cannot fit under the cover when it is high up. Putting the pieces together will be easy, so that it will look whole. Another reason why we could not make it in one piece are the abutting bases and capitols and frames. Alfonso sketched the garden and now we have to design it, which we will do when the machinery for upstairs will be out of the way].

[58] Though this report is largely positive, Mazzi brings to Bentivoglio's attention a few practical difficulties, as he and Guitti do in almost every letter. First, Mazzi was skeptical that the two ropes guiding the horse machine could be handled at the same speed; hence the final effect could be ruined. Second, and more importantly, a structural problem had arisen with respect to the heavenly city machinery, since it had proven too big to remain hidden over the stage before and after it was needed. In this instance Mazzi gave Bentivoglio many reasons and reference points, so that the latter could visualize the problem and the effected changes. We witness a moment in the long and complex process of turning concepts and drawings into three-dimensional stage properties.

[59] We will see in the next chapter that the treatment of this episode goes beyond its source, Ariosto's *Orlando furioso*.

[60] This is not equivalent to saying that they could not modified afterwards, as we will see. The last *intermedio*, in particular, was inextricably linked to the occasion then cele-

brated, as a letter by Alfonso Pozzo regarding the aborted festivities of 1618 indicates: "It never will be possible for me to do the final intermedio until the occasion of the festival shall arrive, on which the conclusion of the work depends; for I cannot know what it behooves me to make happen at that point" (Reiner, "Preparations in Parma," 283).

[61] "We had a major problem with the set. When the city of Dis comes up, one of those that takes up the whole space is there. So we had to move it closer to the pastoral.

[62] "Guitti's theater seems to announce that built with boxes, in which balconies are divided in separate spatial cells connected by a corridor behind them — flexible chains to which one can give many shapes."

[63] This does not imply agreement with Reiner's opinion that "the [temporary] theatre . . . could not well be left idle if — as was the case — the tourney came to be performed in the salon; for the necessarily conspicuous presence of a large, new theatre in the palace courtyard was bound to induce in the guests at the festivities an expectation of seeing some sort of performance staged there" (297).

[64] "Il Riboni à cominciato a far il Tempio per da basso. Il Pareschi con un'altr'huomo mette le Girele per tirar sù il sud[det]to Tempio. Si metono in opera li telari della Battaglie del frontispitio p[er] dà basso. S'atende al fortificar la scena, da basso verso al Guardaroba poiche si è giudicato star bene cosi, accio la fabrica non stramazasse havanti per il gran peso che havrà per la Machina de Cavali. La sortita del Mar da basso con il gioco delle regognole è fornito salva però le due ultim'onde verso il frontispicio, che si fano, le quali vi và fatura assai per doversi quelle Calare mentre deve Calar la Machina de Cavali come V[ostra] S[ignoria] Ill[ustrissi]ma sà. Si fano le sale per portar gli cari è de sassi è de Mostri per la comparsa de Cavaglieri. Gli Bolognesi atendono alla Città Celeste la quale la voglione [sic] far Belliss[i]ma, et anno pensiero, che così siè discorso di adornar le colone, che serano finte, con certe filze di Gioie, che gli farà l'ebreo, che serà una Cosa belliss[i]ma": Lavin, "Lettres," 132–33; idem, *Art and Pageantry*, 533; MS Antonelli 660, 23 November 1627, fol. r [Riboni started working on the downstairs temple. Pareschi and another man are placing the wheels to raise it. We are putting in place the cloths with battle scenes for the downstairs frontispiece. We are strengthening the stage from the bottom towards the backstage. We decided we had to do it so that the building would not collapse towards the front, due to the weight of the horse machinery. The sea appearing downstairs is finished, with the play of strings, except for the two waves that are closer to the front. These are being built with great care as they enter at the same time as the horse machinery, as you know. We are building ramps for the carts with stones and for the knights' entrance. Those from Bologna are busy with the heavenly city, which they want to make extra beautiful. To this end we have discussed decorating the (fake) columns with strings to jewels prepared by the Jew, which will be most attractive."

[65] "We are building two waves with some difficulty because they have to disappear when the horse stage machinery descends."

[66] "M. Alfonso atende al Caro, et Furora di Giunone. Quel da Carrara è atorno à finir gli Nichi gli quali bisognarà che V[ostra] S[ignoria] Ill[ustrissi]ma stabilisca che figure gli vano dentro. Tre ò quatro altri di quei giovini atendono adorare [*sic*] è dipingere il friso del Cornisone": Lavin, "Lettres," 136; idem, *Art and Pageantry*, 535; MS Antonelli 660, 26 November 1627, fol. v [Master Alfonso is busy with Juno's chariot. The painter from Carrara is bringing to completion the niches, but your excellence has to decide which figures

they will house. Three or four of the young painters are gilding and painting the frieze on the cornice]. Lavin has identified "M. Alfonso" as Alfonso Chenda (Lavin, "Lettres," 113, *Perspecta*, 17; idem, *Art and Pageantry*, 523); far from his being a simple "scene painter," this letter testifies that his skills were exploited for three-dimensional pieces as well.

[67] "Count Fabio asked me how I was going to illuminate the theater. I answered that I would communicate him my thoughts when I had prepared a lamp prototype. I showed it to him and we concluded that we would hear your opinion when you come. My idea was as follows: to build two rows of lights on the two cornices that you saw, one on top of the other. Above the seats we could put lamps that take up little room but have long wicks, which in my opinion would send forth a lot of light. We could put more in a row on the ledge where the equestrian statues are. Together with the two lamps and the two lilies that we have to hang from the ceiling, I would think that the theater would have enough light. There would be but two difficulties: the first is that the lights be not too bright and ruin those above the seats; the second is how to light them up. We can solve the first by trying each one ahead of time; the second by preparing a wick in such a way that it would touch on all the individual ones. Thus when that one is lighted, it would then set the other ones on fire and I believe it would create the proper effect."

[68] "P[rim]o si e fatto tutti li Carri delle scene. Si sono fatto li fusi alli Mangani per tirarli inanti è indietro. Si è quasi fatto il Mare, e finto che Ondeggia, è che sorga. Si è fatto i mangani, è le rode per mandar giù la Machina de Cavalli. Si è fatto il letto, e la parte di dietro di detta Machina. Si è fatto il Pavimento, e ordito, che si tira innanti e indietro. Si sono messo tutte le girele per ordir le scene. Si è fatto il letto del Giardino per portar sù i Cavaglieri è le Damme. Si è fatto l'orditura per il Cavallo di Melissa e Bradamante e per l'Hippogriffo. Si è fatto dodici Caretti con le sue anime per calare, da portar Machine nel'Aria al traverso la scena con tutti li suoi Mangani, che le devono tirare. Si sono fatto quattro letti per portar Machine per Mare, con suoi mangani, e caretti. Si sono fatti li tellari per il Castello d'Attlante [*sic*]. Il tempio è, come finito.

Fatture de Pittori

Si è fatto il Sfondato sotto la Gronda fuori del Frontespitio. Si sono dipinto le Battaglie, che vanno al di sopra del cornisone, e meze. Si è dipinto il Cornisone. Si è dipinto tre Nicchie. Si sono fatto tutte le scene, fuori, che la Reggia di Nettuno, la quale è principiata. Si sono fatto tutte le foglie, che vanno alli capitelli delle collone. Li pittori Bolognesi dano a dietro alla citta celeste": Lavin, "Lettres," 137; idem, *Art and Pageantry*, 536; MS Antonelli 660, between 30 November 1627 and 4 December 1627, fol. r–v [First we built all the stage machinery. We constructed the handles for the mangle to move it back and forth. We are almost done with the artificial sea, which has waves and can rise on stage. We prepared the mangles and wheels to drop the horse machinery from above. We built the bottom and back side of this same piece of machinery. We took care of all the pulleys for the sets. We built the bottom of the garden that lifts ladies and gentlemen. We built the scaffolding for Melissa and Bradamante's horse and for the flying hippogriff. We prepared twelve carts to move the machinery in the air across the stage, along with the necessary ropes for dropping them and the mangles to move them. We prepared four bottoms to move the sea stage machinery, complete with mangles and carts. We prepared the drops for Atlas's castle. The temple is essentially done. Painters' invoices. The backdrop outside the frontispiece is done. The battle scenes that go above the cornice have been painted and put in place. The cornice is painted, as are three niches. All sets are done, except for Neptune's palace that is begun. We have done all the leaves that go on the column capitals. The painters from Bologna are busy with the heavenly city].

[69] Gambara oversimplifies the issue by stating that the building of the teatro di San Pietro martire was arranged "riuscendo troppo ampio e costoso il Teatro Farnese per gli spettacoli ordinari" ("Teatri minori," 206) [because the Farnese was too big and expensive for ordinary stagings]. Gambara obviously overlooks the fact that the Farnese was the *sala* where the most prestigious entertainment was to take place; no extant document indicates that the *teatro inferiore* was meant to replace the Farnese in any permanent way. Kristiaan Aercke has emphasized the link between a previously unstaged performance and new space where it occurs: "In the sacred play of ritual as well as for the splendid performance, setting is of primordial importance: establishing the locus actually initiates the ritual and is the first playful act": *Gods of Play* (Albany: State University of New York Press, 1994), 104. Michael Anderson has further remarked that "the impermanence of [these] theatres was not merely a powerful demonstration of the prodigality of princely patronage, but an aspect of the idealized time and place [which lay] at the center of these festivals.... It is significant that even when permanent or semi-permanent theatres were constructed, they were not put to regular use, but simply left standing until the next festive occasion on which they were required": "The Changing Scene: Plays and Playhouses in the Italian Renaissance," in *Theatre of the English and Italian Renaissance*, ed. J. R. Mulryne and M. Shewring (London: Macmillan, 1991), 3–20, here 14–15. On the strength of extant documents as well as on these interpretations Reiner's opinion should be rejected, according to which "this second theatre . . . was created as a potential substitute for the older theatre and, consequently, as a virtual copy of it" ("Preparations in Parma," 297) and that "the courtyard theatre appears to have been intended as a second embodiment of the scenic requisites of Achillini's tourney — which is to say that its design and equipment were to be essentially like those of the older theater in the salon of the Farnese palace" (299). These documents suggest instead that, while at first considerable uncertainty on the usage of the *teatro inferiore* existed, ultimately it played a specific purpose within the entirety of the wedding entertainment.

[70] A. Chastel, "Cortile et théâtre," in *Le Lieu théâtral à la Renaissance*, ed. Jacquot, 41–47.

[71] Starn and Partridge have identified the same dynamics at play in Florence in the second half of the sixteenth century (*Arts of Power*, 174–75).

[72] A 1909 study by Lina Balestrieri asserts instead that the temporary theater "fu subito dopo [the festivities] demolito": *Feste e spettacoli alla corte dei Farnesi* (Parma: Donati, 1909), 26 [demolished right after]; however, she does not provide any evidence for her assertion. Similarly, according to Marco De Grazia, it was torn down only around 1687, "quando Ranuccio II fece costruire il Teatro Ducale" ("Palazzo della Pilotta," 136) [when Ranuccio II had the Teatro Ducale built].

[73] "Hò fatto il Disegno de palchi, il quale è quasi come quelo che V[ostra] S[ignoria] Ill[ustrissi]ma ha visto del sig[no]r Fran[ces]co, ò mutato certe cose, della quali ne renderò conto à V[ostra] S[ignoria] Ill[ustrissi]ma per quest'altro ordinario è gli Mandarò un disegneto, è non si farà nisuna risoluzione se V[ostra] S[ignoria] Ill[ustrissi]mo [*sic*], non presterà il Consenso. Non sò che dir altro à V[ostra] S[ignoria] Ill[ustrissi]ma per ora, solo che se venesse non sarebbe se non bene, e per la solecitudine de Maestri è per l'agiustamento

di molte cose che stano in dubio": Lavin, "Lettres," 138; idem, *Art and Pageantry*, 536; MS Antonelli 660, 4 December 1627, fol. r [I drew the boxes almost in the same way as you saw drawn by Master Francesco. I did change a few things that I will tell you about with the next mail run. I will send a little sketch but no change will take place unless your excellence approves. For now I have nothing else to tell you, other than your arrival would be good both for the masters' worries and for figuring out many things that are undecided at this point].

[74] "We continue working on the stage downstairs; specifically we are considering the planks for the seating area. I am sending you a drawing so that you can tell us what you think. With respect to Master Francesco's drawing, it only differs in the line coming down from point D. It was at a right angle but I am drawing it to point 'i' so that the audience avoid being in the way of each other and can see better. I also drew a corridor H that runs around each row of boxes so that each box can be easily reached. The four Fs designate staircases close to each other that will go from the bottom to the top of the building. The three Es designate the openings that I devise to reach the pit if necessary. C is the box for the princes, shaped in this way to be prettier, if your excellence agrees. If there is a tournament, it can be pushed back to the line where the boxes begin." In Mazzi's letter, the sketch is accompanied by the following caption: "A scena — B aria [i.e., area] del frontespicio — C Palco de seren[issi]mi Principi — E strade che vanno nell'arena — F scale che ascenderano sino in cima alla fab[rica] — G Pilastroni, che sono in cappo, et da lato al Cortile — H Coritore che gira atorno alli palchi."

[75] "I thought about occupancy as much as I could and according to my calculations these boxes will accomodate over 3500 people. Your excellence might think it too little, but the theater upstairs only accommodates 2400 in more space. We could fit more people downstairs but they would not be able to see, and if they cannot see the boxes do not carry out their goal."

[76] "Gli mando questa [i.e., sketch] nella quale vedrà meglio il mio pensiero di far venire il Cavalier dall'Inferno, di quello abi visto, nella mia quando gliene significai, con pensiero che V[ostra] S[ignoria] Ill[ustrissi]ma havisi particolarm[en]te se gli piace, perche l'incaminaressimo.

La linea A del qui congionto disegno è il pavim[en]to, la D il parapeto della scena; voglio dunque cavare una buca di larghezza, cinque ò sei piedi, di longhezza 14 di profondità 14, che sarebbe la figura B C mà però che salti quatro piedi fuori del parapeto della scena, sino all'angolo G, si che stando questa profondità il Cavaliere può stare con Ciemiero intesta a cavallo sotto il piano di terra B G, esendo sopra il palco è sodo della Machina F, con l'altezza del Ciemiero è cavalo che è la linea E, è stando questo può facilm[en]te tirarsi al piano di terra G, per la linea diagonale H, con ruote poste nel vano della Buca L à cò doppio essendo gli gireloni al piano di terra G, et à questo modo mi pare che si dia poco fastidio, ne al Mare, ne à gargami che abbiamo sotto la scena come V[ostra] S[ignoria] Ill[ustrissi]ma sà, non si può pero far manco che il Cimiero non cominci à sorgere dal piano di terra in sù lontano al parapeto meno di cinque piedi è da quì al sud[det]to parapeto vi serà à potervi far l'onda che v'andarebbe, per la buca che bisogna vi resti, pura quando V[ostra] S[ignoria] Ill[ustrissi]ma comandarà così s'ingegneremo poi: si che mentre sorgesse si spezzarebbe, in quel drito il parapeto è il pezzo di pavim[en]to che vi soprastasse, è la buca delli quatro piedi fuori della scena, è usito che fosse si profondarebbe giù la machina, è con fiame di fuoco è fumo si chiuderebbe questo buchi; <anzi> è per render maggior amiratione della Machina si potrebbe in luoco di stare atorno atorno al palco dove stasse il Cavalo, finger di basso rilevo, demoni avitichiati l'uno con l'altro; che con vari modi mostrasse, portar sù il Cavaliere": Lavin, "Lettres," 139–40; idem, *Art and Pageantry*, 537; MS Antonelli 660, 9 December 1627, fol. r–v (figure 3) [I am sending you this sketch so that my idea of how to have the infernal knight enter is clearer. I already explained it in another letter but I specifically need to know if you like it so that we can get started. In the enclosed, line A designates the stage and D its parapet. I would like to build a hole 5 or 6 *piedi* wide, 14 long and 14 deep, corresponding to C D in the sketch. This area would project four *piedi* from the stage plane, to the angle G. When the knight is on the bottom, even wearing his helm he would be below the line B G, standing on the machinery (designated by F), as the height of the horse, knight and helm is equivalent to E. From this position it would be easy to get the machinery on stage using the diagonal H, thanks to wheels place in the hole at L corresponding to those at ground level (G). In this manner it seems to me that this machinery would not interfere much with the sea or with the ropes under the stage, as your excellence knows. However the helm would be seen from the ground if the hole is fewer than five *piedi* from the parapet. Then we would have to build a wave to fit where the hole is. If your excellence wishes it to be so, we will work so that it will be done. We could make it so that when the machinery is rising, the parapet in front of this spot and the piece of floor above the hole would break; and when the knight is on stage the machinery could drop and the hole could close amid flames and smoke. To make the machinery even more amazing we could carve demons intertwined that would seem to lift the knight, on the front of the stage].

Bentivoglio had already gotten wind of this particular problem on 26 November, from Goretti, who wrote: "Se V[ostra] S[ignoria] Ill[ustrissi]ma fusse venuto qua havrebbe . . . facilitate molte cose che si ritrova d'affare nella sena da basso e imparticolare il comparve del Cavagl[iere]": Lavin, "Lettres," 147; idem, *Art and Pageantry*, 541; MS Antonelli 660, 26 November 1627, fol. v [If your excellence had come, you would have made many things easier in the downstairs theater, especially the knight's entrance].

[77] "Their lordships do not like that the infernal knight enter in the way I showed your excellence. They think it too expensive and would like for him to enter from the wings. I showed them that the stage will be filled with the four pieces of machinery for the four parts of the world and Pluto and the infernal characters' entrance. Tamera yet tries to satisfies them but I believe that we have no other solution than to modify the *intermezzo*." An extant letter by Tamera to Bentivoglio is in Fabris, *Mecenati e musici*, 421; it is dated 29 November 1627 and it provides a few additional details on the issue of the emerging infernal knight.

[78] "Se V[ostra] S[ignoria] Ill[ustrissi]ma comanda ch'io mi tratenghi qui dall'San[tissi]mo Natale, inanzi, è necessario che mi facci gratia di farmi prorogar il termine da fornari": Lavin, "Lettres," 141; idem, *Art and Pageantry*, 538; MS Antonelli 660, 14 December 1627, fol. r [If your excellence orders me to stay from Christmas on, it is necessary that you act on my behalf to have the bakers continue to provide my food].

[79] "Mando à V[ostra] S[ignoria] Ill[ustrissi]ma il Modello del Cavaliere che dimanda, sotto la custodia di M[esser] Alfonso; il quale se non à quella perfetione che doverebbe, mi scusi, perche quando lo feci fare ebbi pensiero, se la maniera piaceva à V[ostra] S[ignoria] Ill[ustrissi]ma è a questi sig[no]ri farne poi uno formalmente con tutte le sue circostanze; mà quando lo mostrai qui è fra l'altri al sig[no]r Magiordomo, parse che proponessi una cosa imposibile, e sentito questo, lo messi da parte, e non ne tratai più": Lavin, "Lettres,"

141; idem, *Art and Pageantry*, 538; MS Antonelli 660, 19 December 1627, fol. v [Via Master Alfonso I am sending your excellence the model for the knight as you asked me. It is not as polished as it should, and I apologize, but when I had it made I thought that if your excellence and these lords here liked him I would have one made with all the bells and whistles. Then when I showed it here, to the *maggiordomo* among others, it looked as if I was putting forth something impossible. Once I heard this, I set it aside and did not pay it any mind].

⁸⁰ A letter addressed by the *maggiordomo* Scotti to Bentivoglio confirms this: "A M[esser] Alfonso Pittore come anche à tutti li altri si e dato la licenza p[er] venire à far le feste à Ferrara in conformità di q[uel]lo che V[ostra] S[ignoria] Ill[ustrissi]ma mi scrive, et il simile si è fatto alli falegnami, eccetti che al Tamara con trè o quatri altri che restano qui": Lavin, "Lettres," 144; idem, *Art and Pageantry*, 540; MS Antonelli 660, 19 December 1627, fol. r [we allow the painter Master Alfonso to come and celebrate the holidays in Ferrara according to what your excellence writes. We gave similar permission to the carpenters, except for Tamara and three or four more who are to stay]. Evidently Bentivoglio had asked their release, the court had authorized it, and Scotti was writing to confirm it.

⁸¹ At the end of the letter, Mazzi went back to this issue, and his irritation was still unabated from the five days before: "Io ò deto molte volte al Tamera che è impossibile il Cavaliere venghi dalle prospettive, anco riguardo al Intramezzo, che ricerca in quel punto le quatro parti del Mondo in scena sopra gli suoi Cari à la sortita di Plutone, con il coro, esendo ocupato il palco da questi, che devono vicendevolm[en]te parlar in sieme, è con Giove, pura sta saldo in questa opinione, la quale come ò detto non sollo è dificile mà imposibile, però se V[ostra] S[ignoria] Ill[ustrissi]ma verà come spero vedrà infati il tuto": Lavin, "Lettres," 142; idem, *Art and Pageantry*, 539; MS Antonelli 660, 19 December 1627, fol. r [I told Tamera repeatedly that it is impossible for the knight to enter from the wings in the *intermezzo* in which the four parts of the world are then on stage on their machinery and Pluto enters the stage with the chorus. The stage is taken up by all these characters who have to speak together and by Jupiter. Yet he will not budge, but as I told you such a solution is not difficult, but rather impossible. If your excellence comes, as I hope, you will see everything].

Mazzi considered this issue of such importance, and his disagreement with Tamera so deep, that nothing else but Bentivoglio's own presence could have solved it.

⁸² "I am busy with the models of the boxes in the courtyard, with respect to which I have all the aspects that I think necessary: it looks good, it holds quite a few people, it is strong, it is built in proportion to the stage. When I showed Count Fabio a drawing similar to the one I sent you, he immediately started to make a scene: he said that the expense is high and we need to pay attention to the speed [with which these boxes can be put together]. However these boxes are swift to build. All that is needed it to raise the poles that we already have; put in place the planes on which *pelto* or poplar planks are to be nailed to become the parapets to the front (two poles crossing each other covered by tapestries); the walls around are straight planks simply nailed; and the corridors around are poles to hold together, that is all. So I cannot imagine anything easier or more comfortable. As soon as I finish the model I will show it to him and I will manage to make him understand."

⁸³ This is far from being an uncommon occurrence. Henry Millon states that "centinaia, se non migliaia dei modelli architettonici per edifici e parti di edifici, costruiti in

Italia durante il periodo rinascimentale sono andate perdute. Se ne è conservata solo una piccola parte, composta per lo più da modelli realizzati per strutture religiose": "I modelli architettonici nel Rinascimento," in *Rinascimento da Brunelleschi a Michelangelo*, ed. idem and V. M. Lampugnani (Milan: Bompiani, 1994), 19–73, here 19 [hundreds or thousands of architectural models, for whole buildings or parts thereof, built in Italy during the Renaissance have gotten lost. Only a small part remains, comprising mostly models of religious buildings].

[84] "Certo sig[no]r Ill[ustrissi]mo io stò in mezzo al timore è la speranza, la speranza che lei mi dà con le sue letere, e il timore di non gradir à questi sig[no]ri con le mie fatiche, vedendone qualche effetto contrario e se mi fosse lecito pregarei V[ostra] S[ignoria] Ill[ustrissi]ma di qualche rimedio con ogni caldezza": Lavin, "Lettres," 142; idem, *Art and Pageantry*, 538–39; MS Antonelli 660, 19 December 1627, fol. v [for sure, your excellence, I am torn between fear and hope: the hope you give me with your letters, and the fear that these lordships will not like my work if their see some contrary effect. If I could I would warmly pray your excellency to share some remedy].

[85] The hiatus is explained by Guitti's reference to a visit by Bentivoglio that lasted approximately two weeks, since one of Monteverdi's letters, dated 4 February 1628, announced that the Marchese had arrived soon before he started writing it (Malipiero, *Monteverdi*, 285).

[86] "We finished Iris for downstairs, and we will soon try out the horse machinery, as the planks cut to measure will be ready by tomorrow."

[87] "Since I last wrote your excellence we have worked little, almost nothing, because we have been busy serving Francesco Maria with masked entertainment."

[88] "Io sperava di venire a fare le feste della Sant[issi]ma Pasqua à Ferr[ar]a; Mà perche aspettano il ser[enissi]mo Gran Duca vogliono, che gli si prepari una Quintanata, e se gli facciano le seguenti Machine, le quali per loro comandam[en]to, io gli proposi, e che furono da S[ua] A[ltezza] S[ovrana] accettate, il quale volle, ch'io glie le dicessi, e mostrò di restarne sodisfatto. Mà veram[en]te l'inesperienza mia mi fà lento, e'l non essere avvezzo co' pari suoi mi tiene guardingo": Lavin, "Lettres," 128; idem, *Art and Pageantry*, 530; MS Antonelli 660, 18 April 1628, fol. 1 r [I had hoped to come and spend Easter in Ferrara. But here they are expecting the duke and therefore asked me to prepare a knightly tournament and build some pieces of stage machinery as his ruling highness ordered me and I proposed him. He accepted them and showed his pleasure for them. But to tell the truth my lack of experience slows me down and my lack of familiarity with his peers makes me cautious].

[89] "A nifty device to escape a rigorous application of the [Aristotelian] system without sapping its validity: dramatic stagings follow the rules but alternate their actions to that of the *intermedi*."

[90] "The Politics of Spectacle: *La Pellegrina* and the Intermezzi of 1589," *Modern Language Notes* 101 (1986): 95–111, here 96–97.

[91] "Melodrama, blossomed in Florence on the basis of the exercises of the Camerata de' Bardi and J. Corsi's circle, found its natural apparatus in *intermezzi*'s changing sets."

[92] For example, in Reiner's opinion one of the two writers involved in the festivities, Claudio Achillini, was ordered to follow as closely as possible the text written by Alfonso Pozzo for the 1618 festivities that were to inaugurate the Teatro Farnese but never took place. In this manner, many of the already built pieces of stage machinery could be restored

and exploited ("Preparations in Parma," 295–96). Whether or not this hypothesis can be proven, it corresponds to two impulses we have observed at work in Guitti's and Mazzi's letters: achieve the best, most amazing, and lavish results possible without undue monetary expenses or technical efforts.

[93] The letter is transcribed in Fabris, *Mecenati e musici*, 400. It is worth noting that Goretti was then in Ferrara and wrote to Bentivoglio in Parma.

[94] The letter is transcribed in Fabris, *Mecenati e musici*, 402.

[95] "Marchese Bentivoglio, for many years my lord, wrote a month ago to ask me if I would set to music lyrics set to music by his excellence. These were to be used in the main comedy staged for a prince's wedding celebration, in the form of *intermedi* and not a sung comedy. Since he is my lord, I answered that I would do anything possible to obey his commands. He replied with singular thanks and told me that these pieces were to be used at the wedding of the ruler of Parma. I answered that I would do what he deigned to bid me."

[96] When under time constraints, "se l'operatione vertesse intorno ad intermedi per comedia grande ne cosi faticoso ne cosi lungo sarebbe il parto; ma una comedia cantata che tanto vol dire come un poema in breve tempo mi credda V[ostra] S[ignoria] Ill[ustrissi]ma che non si può fare senza incorrere in uno dei due errori o far male o amalarsi": Malipiero, *Monteverdi*, 250 [if it were *intermedi* for a major comedy giving birth would not be either tiring nor long. But believe me, your excellence, when under time constraints if we are talking about a sung comedy, which is like a [narrative] poem, the outcome is one of two mistakes: doing it poorly or falling ill].

[97] "Immediately sent the first *intermedio* and I have completed almost half of it, and I'll do it easily because it consists almost entirely of soliloquies." Monteverdi's assertion directly contradicts the anonymous author of the treatise *Il corago*, written after 1628, who unequivocally states that the composer "procurerà di avere in mano tutta l'azione se sarà finita, intenderla bene in quanto all'universale invenzione e anche verso per verso nell'elocuzione" [will manage to have the whole plot in his possession so that he can understand it well in its generality and also line by line in its elocution] so that he will not "waste" his talents in the wrong places of the score: P. Fabbri and A. Pompilio, eds., *Il corago* (Firenze: Olschki, 1983), 80.

[98] "Their highnesses honored me highly with this command since I understand that there were six or seven begging for this task. Of their own volition these highnesses deigned to select me."

[99] "Heri che fu alli 9 del presente dal curriere ricevei un plicco di V[ostra] E[ccellenza] Ill[ustrissi]ma nel quale vi era un Intermedio et una lettera di V[ostra] E[ccellenza] Ill[ustrissi]ma piena d'infinita humanità et honore verso la persona mia, et insieme una copia d'un capitolo di una lettera della Sere[nissi]ma Sig[no]ra Duchessa di Parma scritta a V[ostra] E[ccellenza] Ill[ustrissi]ma nel quale si degna honorarmi di comandarmi con il mezzo di V[ostra] E[ccellenza] Ill[ustrissi]ma ch'io ponga in musica quello che da V[ostra] E[ccellenza] Ill[ustrissi]ma mi sarà comandato.... Et si ben è statto poco il tempo, non per questo son statto indarno in tutto, perchè di già gli ho datto principio come ben ne farò vedere qualche poco d'effetto p[er] mercore venturo a V[ostra] E[ccellenza] Ill[ustrissi]ma havendo di già visto che quattro generi di armonie saranno quelli che anderanno adoperati dal principio, e seguita sino al principio delle ire, tra Venere e Diana, et tra le loro discordie, l'altro dal principio delle ire sino finite le discordie, l'altro quando

entra Plutone a metter ordine et quiete, durante sino dove Diana s'incomincia a innamorare d'Endimione, et il quarto et ultimo dal principio di detto innamoramento sino alla fine": Malipiero, *Monteverdi*, 270–71 [Yesterday, on the 9th of the current month, I received from the mail carrier an envelope from your excellence containing one *intermedio*, one letter from your highness filled with infinite kindness and honor toward me, and the copy of a letter from her highness the Duchess of Parma written to your excellence in which she deigns honoring me that you command me to set to music what you will bid me to. Though little time has passed, it has not been wholly in vain, since I have already started as I will show you next Wednesday. I have already noticed that four types of tune will have to be used: one from the beginning to the start of the disagreement and fight between Diana and Venus; the second from the beginning to the end of their disagreement; the third when Pluto comes in to impose order and quiet until Diana starts falling for Endymion; the fourth and last from the beginning to the end of said falling in love].

[100] "Count Fabio gave me the *intermezzi* and I studied them. They are most beautiful but I believe they will require much work, toil, and time. Yet if your excellence is involved they do not intimidate me. I will start by having the first set (the Roman countryside) painted in the order I have them in and I will proceed in the same manner. I would like for your excellence to tell me which one of those you sent is the first, which the second, and which the third."

[101] "God willing, Achillini arrived. Yet we are in the worst shape ever, since we have to restore everything to achieve the stage machinery. The painters from Bologna still have not arrived. At this point it should also be necessary to know which musicians are to be had, as this is most important to the composer."

[102] "So that Monteverdi might fit the music to the singers' quality as he writes it."

[103] "Faccio sapere a V[ostra] S[ignoria] Ill[ustrissi]ma come ebbe l'Intermedi, et libretto. L'Intermedi lì mandato a Venetia al S[igno]r Monteverdi conforme all'ordine di V[ostra] S[ignoria] Ill[ustrissi]ma, del libreto, il . . .[illegible name: presumably that of the transcriber] era fuori si aspeta questa matina gionto che serà sub[it]o li faro coppiare, e farò p[er] apunto quanto V[ostra] S[ignoria] Ill[ustrissi]ma mi hà comandato": MS Antonelli 660, 1 October 1627, fol. r [I want your excellence to know that I received the *intermedi* and *libretto*. I sent the *intermedi* to Monteverdi in Venice as you ordered. As far as the *libretto* is concerned, Mr. [illegible] was out and is expected this morning. As soon as he arrives I will have it copied, as your excellence bade me to do]. The difference between the *intermezzi* and the *libretto* is unclear; while the former undoubtedly referred to the text that Monteverdi had to set to music, perhaps the latter was a description of the events that would be handed out to the audience, or an explanation of what the organizers intended to achieve.

[104] "Spererò senz'altro, per lo venturo ordinario di Sabato, mandar a V[ostra] E[ccellenza] Ill[ustrissi]ma fatto tutto l'intermedio di Didone": Fabris, *Mecenati e musici*, 408 [with Saturday's mail run I hope to send to your excellence the completed Dido *intermezzo*].

[105] "Vorrei supplicar V[ostra] E[ccellenza] Ill[ustrissi]ma che si degnasse farmi gratia ch'io possi restar in Venetia sino alli 7 del venturo mese possiachè il Ser[enissi]mo Doge, in tal giorno processionalmente se ne va a Santa Justina per rendere gratie a Dio N[ostro] S[ignore] de la felice vittoria navale [at Lepanto in 1571], et vi va con tutto il Senato insieme et si canta solenne musica, che subbito fatto tal funtione mi porrò in barca col Corriere et verrò ad ubbidire ai comandi di V[ostra] E[ccellenza] Ill[ustrissi]ma et sarà cosa cauta

l'andar a vedere il Theatro in Parma per poterli applicare più che sia possibile le proprie armonie decenti al gran sito, che non sarà così facil cosa (secondo me) il concertar le molte et variate orationi che veggo in tali Intermedii, frattanto anderò facendo et scrivendo, per poter mostrare a V[ostra] E[ccellenza] Ill[ustrissi]ma altra cosa e maggiore che mi ritrovo": Malipiero, *Monteverdi*, 275 [I would like to beg your excellence to allow me to stay in Venice until the 7th of next month. On that day the most serene Doge goes with a procession to Santa Giustina to thank the Lord for the naval victory [at Lepanto], with the whole senate, and they sing solemn music. As soon as this ceremony is over I will embark with the dispatch carrier and I will come to obey your excellence's commands. It would be good to go take a look at the theater in Parma in order to adapt the tunes as much as possible to this great place. It will not be easy, in my opinion, to harmonize the many various parts that I see in these *intermedi*. In the meantime, I will work and write, so that I will be able to show to your excellence something greater than what I have now].

[106] Solerti has pointed out that a similar arrangement to Monteverdi's at Parma befell to Emilio de' Cavalieri for the Florentine *Rappresentazione di Anima e Corpo* in 1600: the composer "aveva calcolato la capacità e l'acustica del salone ove doveva avvenire la recita e voleva che anche le parole fossero bene intese, senza di che 'l'effetto scema, e la tanta musica, mancando all'udito la parola, viene noiosa'": *Albori del melodramma*, 3 vols. (Torino: Forni, 1903), 1: 56 [had calculated the capacity and acoustics of the hall in which the staging was to take place. He also wanted words to be understood, because without this "the effect diminishes and all that music becomes boring since hearing cannot understand words"]. Guidotti's text was reprinted in *Le origini del melodramma*, ed. Solerti (Torino: Bocca, 1903), 1–39. On the position of instruments on or off stage for *intermezzi*, see Nino Pirrotta, "The Orchestra and Stage in Renaissance *Intermedi* and Early Opera," in *Music and Culture in Italy from the Middle Ages to the Baroque* (Cambridge, MA: Harvard University Press, 1984), 210–16.

[107] This letter is now extant in a nineteenth-century transcription that does not include its date. However, a letter dated 1 October is now extant (Archivio di Stato, Parma: Teatri e spettacoli di età farnesiana, busta 1 mazzo 1 fascicolo 20 sottofascicolo 4), addressed to Margherita Aldobrandini and requesting an answer to the same question broached here. Reiner cites ("Preparations in Parma," 288 n. 73) a translated passage from a letter by Bentivoglio to Margherita dated 4 September 1627; he locates it at the Archivio di Stato, Parma: Carteggio farnesiano inedito. It might be the original of the one cited here.

[108] "I cannot tell you how pleased I am with your decision to retain Mr. Monteverdi, both for his rare qualities and so that I can start working. I was truly despondent that I had no answers and therefore could do nothing, for I know how long it takes to do a good job. I immediately sent to the aforementioned the lyrics to an *intermezzo* and I will have the Venus one fixed so that it is more modest and the Jesuit fathers have no problems with it. Dear lady, this is for a wedding, not for Holy Week: everything will be fine. Good things never take too long: if we do well we will not bore the audience, whether we have *buffoni* perform a comedy or someone perform an opera. There is no doubt that a tragicomedy will be nobler and I would not give up the Prince of Massa's offer. I know it would be performed well and with wonder because they do not seem to be able to speak properly. Anything will be good according to your highness's taste, even if it is a tragedy that the audience wants." Archivio di Stato, Parma: Teatri e spettacoli di età farnesiana, busta 1 mazzo 1 fascicolo 20 sottofascicolo 5.

[109] That the spoken play was not as important as the *intermezzi* is not unique to the Parma festivities. Andrea Gareffi has pointed out that the celebrations of the wedding of Francesco de' Medici with Giovanna of Hapsburg (1566) utilized an old comedy, Francesco D'Ambra's *Cofanaria*: "l'ordito letterario . . . diventa solo pretesto per la trama scenica, e trama scenica vuol dire intermezzi" (*La scrittura e la festa*, 303) [the literary plot is but a pretext for the one on stage, that is, for the *intermezzi*].

[110] "Desidero che V[ostra] A[ltezza] Ill[ustrissi]ma si compiaccia d'avisarmi in che maniera comanda che venghino le quatro parti dell'mondo sul palchoncino sè usciranno tutte quatro da una parte o overo due di qua e due di la . . . la vedutta di Plutone non sia poi tolta a' spettatori però n'aspetto l'ordine": Lavin, "Lettres," 125; idem, *Art and Pageantry*, 528; MS Antonelli 660, 24 October 1627, fol. 1 r [I wish that your excellence do me the honor of letting me know how the four parts of the world are to come on stage, if they are all four to come from one side or two from each . . . Pluto's view might not be shielded from the audience. I am waiting for your order]. The dots indicate a tear in the sheet that makes the word(s) illegible.

[111] "Par à mè che non sarebbe se non di gran giovam[en]to à restar pienamente inform[a]to, haver una informatione, over instrutione della comparsa delle machine, con le scene specificate che le devono accompagnare, et in sieme il tempo di esse, per l'inventione dà Basso, acciò che dipote [*sic*; i.e., disposte] che fosse le scene è machine l'una non impedisse all'altra": Lavin, "Lettres," 129; idem, *Art and Pageantry*, 531; MS Antonelli 660, 28 October 1627, fol. r [It seems to me that it would only help me a lot if I had some information or full instructions regarding how the machinery is to enter on stage with its individual stage sets and its timing for the performance downstairs, so that once the set and the machinery are both on stage, one would not be in the other's way].

[112] During the preparations for the 1589 wedding celebrations in Florence, Saslow points out, Bastiano de' Rossi (who wrote the official *descrizione* of the staged events: *The Medici Wedding of 1589*, 29) "goes into detail about the painted design on Necessity's throne, but the sides of her seat are invisible in this drawing; another *modello* must have provided instructions for the prop painters. (That such decorative details would have been nearly as invisible to the audience as they are to a viewer of the drawing seems not to have deterred Bardi's desire for iconographic elaboration)" (63). Saslow assumes that Rossi, who had taken part in the preparations (like Buttigli at Parma), describes events as the audience had seen them, without filling in the blanks with his additional knowledge. Conversely, "Bardi's desire for iconographic elaboration" might have been mere verbal virtuosity, not corresponding to actual painted props.

[113] "As far as women are concerned, we will only have Ms. Setimia, but I do not think she will manage as well as it is believed; Mr. Claudio is of the same opinion."

[114] "Son rimasto maravigliato del nuovo teatro, e della nova sena, e ci siamo andati con s[igno]r Claudio, e tutto anderà bene. Quando però sera coperto e serato a proportione il cortile che in altra maniera le voce non fariano afeto alcuno. e con dificulta li strumenti. Io credo certo che V[ostra] S[ignoria] Ill[ustrissi]ma si serà cavato lo voglia di far fare machine e far ponere legname in opera, la staremo aspetando p[er] poter dare una volta alla patria p[er] le feste di natale che così ne fà ancora istanza il s[igno]r Claudio p[er] dover poi tornare sub[it]o dopo le feste, che co[n] servi poi anco sempre, lo fine": Lavin, "Lettres," 146; idem, *Art and Pageantry*, 541; MS Antonelli 660, 29 October 1627, fols.

1 v–2 r [I marveled at the new theater and stage, which I saw with Mr. Claudio. Everything will work out great. When the courtyard is covered and closed in, voices will have no effect, and the instruments little. I believe that your excellence has satisfied his desire to have stage machinery built and wood planks set up. We are waiting for you to go back home for the Christmas holidays and Mr. Claudio himself begs you for it; he would be back immediately after the holidays, to continue to be in your service].

[115] "Mi trovo haver fatto il primo intermedio, qual è quello di Melissa et Bradamante, et non quello di Didone, ma sarà il secondo. Son dietro al terzo, il qual finito, comincierò a provar qualche cosa. Fra il qual tempo de le prime prove finirò piacendo a Dio anco il quarto. Il quinto per anco non l'ho hauto, ma creddo che mi sarà dato quanto prima": Malipiero, *Monteverdi*, 277 [I have finished the first *intermedio*, the one of Melissa and Bradamante, not the one of Dido, which is the second. I am busy with the third, and once I finish it, I will start to rehearse something. During the first rehearsal period, God willing, I will also finish the fourth one. I still have not received the first one, but I believe I will soon].

[116] "Through another letter of mine your excellence must have learned what I am about to say. Nevertheless let me tell you that I have received the fifth *intermedio* and the lyrics that don Ascanio sent to fix another one."

[117] According to Irène Mamczarz, Pio di Savoia likely moved to Ferrara "au moment de son mariage avec Porzia Mattei qui eut lieu vers 1620. Par ce mariage Ascanio Pio se lia avec la puissante et célèbre famille aristocratique des Bentivoglio en devenant le gendre d'Enzo": *Le Théâtre Farnèse*, 124 [when he married Porzia Mattei, around 1620. With this marriage Ascanio Pio married into the powerful and famous Bentivoglio noble family, as he became Enzo's son-in-law]. Though it is possible that Ascanio Pio moved to Ferrara around the time suggested by Mamczarz, extant letters at the Archivio di Stato, Modena, testify that he married Beatrice Bentivoglio, not Porzia Mattei, between 27 July and 1 August 1627. Two letters by Enzo Bentivoglio (Archivio di Stato, Modena: Cancelleria ducale, particolari filza 123) addressed to Francesco d'Este, Modena's ruler at the time, on 25 and 27 July 1627, ask him for advice over the proposed match; a third one, dated 1 August, announces the concluded marriage.

[118] "We still have not seen the list of the singers that are supposed to come from Rome. However, we selected a great bass who is in Italy, after Count Fabio's suggestion, and a 'love *putto*' [i.e., a specialist in roles of this type] who is currently at Ravenna with Cardinal Capponi."

[119] Kimbell has explained this point clearly: Rome "was the home of great singing, the central source from which flowed an enormous number of performing artists who were instrumental in taking opera to most corners of the Italian peninsula. The excellence of Roman singers must have been due in large part to the Church. The city had innumerable churches which offered professional employment to musicians" (*Italian Opera*, 110). Four extant letters related to the Parma festivities attest to Rome's pre-eminent position: Cardinal Scipione Borghese wrote a letter to Bentivoglio on 30 October 1627 accompanying Gregorio Chianchi to Parma (Fabris, *Mecenati e musici*, 414); Monsignor Giovanni Ciampoli and Cardinal Guido Bentivoglio (Enzo's brother) respectively on 30 and 31 October to accompany Antonio Grimani (Fabris, *Mecenati e musici*, 414 and 414–15); and again Cardinal Bentivoglio on 23 December to accompany Nicolini, "musico della cappella di Sua Santità" [musician in the Pope's chapel] (Fabris, *Mecenati e musici*, 424).

[120] As Sergio Durante has pointed out, "[a]lthough descriptions and 'librettos' gave little information on the performers, contemporary letters show that they were recruited with great care": "The Opera Singer," in *Opera Production and Its Resources*, ed. L. Bianconi and G. Pestelli (Chicago: University of Chicago Press, 1998), 345–417, here 347.

[121] "Venni da V[ostra] E[ccellenza] Ill[ustrissi]ma a pigliar licenza per qualche venti giorni per potermi trasferire sino a Parma addimandato da queste Ser[enissi]me Altezze . . . credendo, veduto il Theatro e datto conto alle loro Altezze dell'ordine che tenevo in mettere in canto le dette parole, potermene di subito ritornare, ma quando sono stato giunto, l'Ill[ustrissi]mo Sig[no]r Majordomo mi ha fatto molta istanza che io resti fino a tanto che gli habbi fatto gli detti cinque intermedii per la detta commedia; essendovi altre parole da compire: gli risposi che no haveva licenza da le V[ostre] E[ccellenze] Ill[ustrissi]me che per vinti giorni: esso Sig[no]re mi rispose che queste Ser[enissi]me Altezze havrebbero scritto per la licenza almeno per tutto il presente mese, nel qual tempo promisi de darlo fatto: et avrebbe scritto a V[ostre] Ecc[ellenze] Ill[ustrissi]me a Sua Serenità: gli risposi che più saria stato di necessario che mi fossi potuto partire alla fine del presente mese per potermi trovare a tempo per la messa della notte di Natale a Venetia: mi rispose che si certamente": Malipiero, *Monteverdi*, 278–79 [I came to your excellence to ask to be allowed to go for twenty days to Parma, having been called there by their highnesses. I believed that I could come back as soon as I had seen the theater and explained to their highnesses how I was going to set those lyrics to music. When I arrived, however, the *maggiordomo* begged me time and time again that I stay until I have written the five *intermezzi* for the aforementioned comedy, since there are more lyrics to be completed. I answered that your excellence had allowed me to come only for twenty days. He replied that the Parma highnesses would write to ask your highness and his Serenity [the Doge] that I be allowed to stay at least the entire month, in which time I promised I would be done. I answered that the most necessary thing was that I should be allowed to leave at the end of the current month so that I can be in Venice in time for Christmas Eve's Mass, and he replied that there would be no problem].

[122] Vittori, "author of comedies and a mock-heroic poem, [was] more highly extolled for his abilities as a virtuoso castrato" (Bianconi, *Music in the Seventeenth Century*, 83). Among his performances, he also "sang the leading role in Gagliano's *Flora*" (Durante, "The Opera Singer," 359) during the Medici-Farnese wedding celebrations in Florence.

[123] That Ugolino was indeed in Parma is confirmed by Vincenzo Giustiniani's "Discorso sopra la musica de' suoi tempi" of 1628, in which he wrote: "Vincenzo Ugolino d'età in anni 40 in circa, che fu Maestro di Cappella in S. Pietro per alcuni anni, et ora si trova in Parma chiamato con l'occasione delle nozze di quel Duca Serenissimo con la Serenissima Margarita de' Medici sorella del Gran Duca di Toscana": *Le origini del melodramma*, ed. Solerti, 98–128, here 123 [Vincenzo Ugolino, approximately forty years old, was *maestro di cappella* in St. Peter's for some years, and is now in Parma, having been called for the wedding of the Duke with Margherita de' Medici, sister to the Grand Duke of Tuscany]. The wording seems to indicate that the festivities had not yet taken place when Giustiniani wrote this passage.

[124] "Siamo qui senza mai haver sentito pure un minimo ceno di V[ostra] S[ignoria] Ill[ustrissi]ma Ci andiamo però afaticando in torno a queste musiche. Questa sera è gionto di Roma il Caval[ier] Loreto Il S[ignor] Gregori, et un putin che credo serà buono p[er] la

parte d'Amore, e con quelli è venuto il S[igno]r Vincenzo Ugolino già maestro di Capela di S. Pietro a Roma, e dicono che ne aspettano un'altra caravana. Si starà aspettando ancora V[ostra] S[ignoria] Ill[ustrissi]ma p[er] molte cose, e imparticolare p[er] li nostri afari avendo determinato il S[igno]r Claudio et io che V[ostra] S[ignoria] Ill[ustrissi]ma sarà quela che faccia la distributione delle parte à questi cantori, se si darà pur parte alcuna sarà alla sua presenza": MS Antonelli 660, 9 November 1627, fol. r [We are here, deprived of any sign from your excellence. Yet we are busy with the music. Tonight Loreto, Gregori, and a young boy (suitable for the role of Love) arrived from Rome, together with Vincenzo Ugolino, former *maestro di cappella* in St. Peter's. Rumor has it that another big group is to come. We still wait for your excellence for many things, especially for our equipment. Mr. Monteverdi and I have determined that you will distribute the parts to the singers, and if we distribute them it will be in your presence].

[125] "Sperava che in questo novo teatro ci avesse haver maggiore comodità, ma è tutto alo posito, e pegio delli saloni sì che tocherà a V[ostra] S[ignoria] Ill[ustrissi]ma à trovarli il suo luoco che noi non ne da l'animo di trovarlo, acio debba fare la musica quella riuscita che desideriamo": Lavin, "Lettres," 147; idem, *Art and Pageantry*, 541; MS Antonelli 660, 16 November 1627, fol. r–v [I hoped that this theater would be more comfortable, but all is messy, more so than in the big halls. Since we do not have the strength to do so, it will be your excellence's task to find us a place, so that the music will come out as we desire]. Elena Povoledo has pointed out that the 1628 Parma festivities offers a rare glimpse of the space where Monteverdi's music would be performed: "Controversie monteverdiane: spazi teatrali e immagini presunte," in *Claudio Monteverdi: studi e prospettive* (Firenze: Olschki, 1998), 357–89.

[126] "Il Sig[no]r Monteverde è stato a veder i luochi per la Musica è viè una buona dificoltà a darli sadisfatione conforme il suo pensiero, et alla prima à cominciato a dire, che non può capirvi, però non mancharemo in ogni maniera di procurar di sodisfarlo": Lavin, "Lettres," 131; idem, *Art and Pageantry*, 532; MS Antonelli 660, 16 November 1627, fol. 3 r [Mr. Monteverdi went to see the spaces for music and it is difficult to satisfy his thoughts. From the beginning he said that they cannot fit, but we will try in every way to satisfy him].

[127] "Count Fabio still has not told us which pieces of machinery to show to the musicians, and if we do not know, we can hardly satisfy them."

[128] Mazzi's *istrutione* bound after his letter of 23 November seems to attest that the latter crisis was being solved: among the things to be done, he listed "agiustar li palchi della musica" [fix the boxes for music] and added just below: "Il s[igno]r Monte Verde et io li agiustaremo, e di gia habbiamo dato pre[n]cipio": Lavin, "Lettres," 134; idem, *Art and Pageantry*, 534; MS Antonelli 660, 23 November 1627, fol. 2 v [Mr. Monteverdi and I will fix them, indeed we have already started]. Mazzi now agreed with Monteverdi that there was a need for "boxes" for the musicians, and had already started to work with the composer to locate them in the theater. These problems contradict Adriano Cavicchi's generalized assertion that "[i]l nascente melodramma . . . non avrà bisogno di inventarsi un *suo* spazio scenico ma si approprierà dell'esperienza maturata in oltre mezzo secolo di prassi rappresentativa pastorale": "Immagini e forme dello spazio scenico nella pastorale ferrarese," in *Sviluppi della drammaturgia pastorale nell'Europa del Cinque-Seicento*, ed. M. Chiabò and F. Doglio (Viterbo: Union, 1991), 45–85, here 45; emphasis in original [the

burgeoning melodrama does not need to create *its own* stage space as it take advantage of the experience accumulated in fifty years' worth of staging pastorals].

[129] Ciampoli was Urbano VIII's secretary of the breves and *cameriere segreto*; he was part of the patronage net set in place by the Barberini family during the Urbano VIII's papacy (1623–1644), thoroughly examined in Frederick Hammond, *Music & Spectacle in Baroque Rome. Barberini Patronage under Urban VIII* (New Haven: Yale University Press, 1994). Sung entertainment formed a conspicuous part of the Barberini patronage system.

[130] "Dido, Europa, Dawn, Juno and the Muse to Mrs. Setimia. Venus, Asia, Venus [again], the first Muse, and Bellona to Mr. Loreto. Diana, America, the Golden Age, the second Muse, and Berecynthia to Mr. Gregorio. Juno in the comedy and Discord in the tournament are for Angiola. Many parts fit well, yet some are given to singers from Parma and one to a Roman who is a soprano in St. Peter's. Experience and rehearsal will say if he is a man or not, as well as the one from Parma and the alto from Modena."

[131] On male and female roles in Monteverdi's music in general, see S. McClary, "Construction of Gender in Monteverdi's Dramatic Music," in eadem, *Feminine Endings* (Minneapolis: University of Minnesota Press, 1991), 35–52.

[132] Goretti used an interesting phrase, and we have no way of knowing if he did that ironically or not: "l'isperienza e la prova farà conoscere se è huomo ò nò" means, of course, that only experience and rehearsal would ascertain their worth as singers, but literally what would become clear was whether they were men or not. Given their status as *castrati*, this conventional phrase sounds ironic to twenty-first-century ears, but was likely to have been taken at face value in 1627.

[133] Loreto Vittori's presence is somewhat puzzling, because after Goretti announced his arrival on 9 November, a week later it took the news back: "il S[igno]r Loreto è a Fiorenza, e non verà qui sino che non sarà finita quella festa": Fabris, *Mecenati e musici*, 417 [Mr. Loreto is in Florence and will not be here until the festivities there are over].

[134] "Si sta aspettando chiamando la venuta del S[igno]r D[on] Ascanio" [we are waiting and calling for Don Ascanio] presumably to help with parts of the *intermedi* that needed to be modified (MS Antonelli 660, 27 November 1627, fol. r).

[135] "We are consulting over the theater that has to be built, and it seems to me that Mr. Francesco's plan devotes too much space to the staging and the music. Even if we fix it, voices will fade out much more than against walls because it is very high."

[136] "Ma ci voria ancora qualche giorno, che una cosa e provare in camera, e altra cosa provare in sena, e le bisog' prima concertarla bene con li strum[en]ti in camera e poi in sena": Lavin, "Lettres," 147; idem, *Art and Pageantry*, 541; MS Antonelli 660, 7 December 1627, fol. 1 v [but it will take a few extra days, as rehearsing in a room is different from doing it on the stage, and we need to adjust the instruments well, first in the room and then on stage].

[137] "Mazzi showed me many things in his model, of which I have already informed your excellence and I will personally tell you all that I need."

[138] Regarding singers, "in Parma si trova il migliore essere il Sig[no]r Gregorio che serve il Sig[no]r Ill[ustrissi]mo Cardinal Borghese qual con fatica grandissima a mio credere si potria rimovere vi è anco il Sign[no]r Antonio Grimano et questo manco si potria sperare di havere, ve ne sono duoi altri pervenuti da Roma che sono un tal castrato che canta in San Pietro, ma non mi par cosa troppo bona perché ha voce che tira al catarro non troppo

chiara e gorgia durotta et poco trillo, vi è ancora un putto di qualche undici anni, ne questo mi par haver voce grata, ha qualche gorgietta et qualche trillo ma il tutto pronuntiato con una certa voce alquanto ottusa": Malipiero, *Monteverdi*, 280 [the best one in Parma is Gregorio who is at Cardinal Borghese's court. It would be extremely hard to pry him from there. There is also Antonio Grimano, who is also impossible to get. Then there are two more from Rome: a castrato who sings in St. Peter's, but he does not seem too good to me as his voice is marred by catarrh and is not clear, his throat is rather hard and does not have any trill. Then there is a young boy aged eleven who does not have a pleasant voice either: he does possess some throat voice and some trill but everything is pronounced in a rather dull voice]. According to Hammond, the eleven-year-old boy was Marc'Antonio Pasqualini, a singer at San Luigi dei Francesi in Rome and a student of Vincenzo Ugolini (*Music and Spectacle in Baroque Rome*, 86).

[139] "Si provano le musiche da me composte in piassa credendo questo Ser[enissi]me Altezze che loro Ser[enissi]me Nozze si havessero a fare di gran lunga un pezzo prima di quello si tiene anderanno et tali prove si fanno per trovarsi in Parma cantori Romani et Modenesi et sonatori Piacentini et altri che havendo visto queste Ser[enissi]me Altezze come rieschino per li loro bisogni et la riuscita che fanno et la sicura speranza al occasione in brevi giorni si metteranno al ordine si tiene che tutti se ne anderemo alle case nostre, sino al sicuro aviso del effeto qual si dice potrebbe essere a questo Maggio et altri tengono a questo Settembre": Malipiero, *Monteverdi*, 286 [We are rehearsing the music I composed in a square, since their highnesses think that their wedding will take place much later than it is thought. We are rehearsing because there are Roman and Modenese singers and Piacenza musicians in Parma, along with others who have seen how their highnesses succeed in their needs. Along with this success there is the hope that we will be done in a few days and go home until we get sure news that the effect will take place; some say it could be next May, others next September].

[140] "Saranno due bellissime feste l'una tutta comedia recitata con gli intermedi apparenti in musica et non vi è intermedio che non sij longo almeno tre cento versi et tutti variati d'affetto le parole le quali le ha fatte il Sig[no]r Ill[ustrissi]mo D[on] Ascanio Pii Genero del Sig[no]r Marchese Entio Cavaglier dignissimo et virtuosissimo: l'altra sarà un *torneo* nel quale interverranno quattro squadriglie di Cavaglieri, et il mantenitore sarà il Seren[issi]mo stesso. Le parole di esso *Torneo* le ha fatte il Sig[no]r Aquilini, et sono più di mille versi, belle si per il *Torneo* ma per musica assai lontane, mi hanno datto estremo da fare": Malipiero, *Monteverdi*, 286–87 [there will be two magnificent festivities. One will be a spoken comedy with staged *intermezzi* set to music; no *intermezzo* is shorter than 300 lines and their effects are varied; the lyrics have been written by Don Ascanio Pio, son-in-law of Enzo, most dignified and virtuous knight. The other will be a tournament in which four groups of knights will participate, with the duke himself as *mantenitore*. Achillini wrote the words to the tournament and they are more than a thousand verses. They are very beautiful for a tournament but very far from musical and gave me a lot of work].

[141] Monteverdi uses a common phrase to describe what kind of *intermezzi* would take place at Parma; in David Nutter's words, "In some instances only instrumental music was used, played out of sight of the audience (*intermedio non apparente* or 'invisible'). Far more popular, however, was the staged or 'visible' type (*intermedio apparente*), performed by costumed singers, actors and dancers who enacted a pastoral or mythological story through pantomime and rhythmic movement" ("Intermedio," 258).

[142] "Con la fretta, che mi diede la l[ette]ra del s[igno]r Co[nte] Fabio, e la voce di V[ostra] S[ignoria] Ill[ustrissi]ma mi posi attorno all'Intramezzo, che mancava, e'l feci oggi appunto sono otto giorni; che p[er] essere stato composto p[er] la posta, porta seco de suoi errori la scusa": Lavin, "Lettres," 145; idem, *Art and Pageantry*, 540 [with the haste that Count Fabio's letter and your voice conveyed, I started working on the missing *intermezzo*, and I finished it eight days ago. Since it was composed in haste, it contains the reason for its mistakes].

[143] "I hope that it will not be inappropriate for the music. It uses the same machinery: Venus's chariot could be Phoebus's, since I changed only the motion into a turbulence of the air and of the river, which appeared to me more natural and more effective. This change does not modify the space of any machinery so that the movement of others might be impeded. There are so many gods in as many machines in the air that a darkening or clearing of the sky elicits the work of your excellence's genius."

[144] "Non lasciarò di dire, che l'ordine degli intramezzi voleva, che 'l quarto fosse quello di Enea con lavinia, p[er] allontanarlo dall'altro di Enea e didone, il che cessando di presente, io cangiarei, e porrei p[er] lo p[rim]o Atlante, 2° questo che mando, 3° Venere, 4° Enea e didone, 5° il campo aperto e cosi andrebbono intramezzandosi un'alegro ed un grave sino al 4°, poiche in ogni modo l'ultimo deve essere il campo aperto, ovvero p[rim]o didone ed enea, 2° Venere, 3° Bacco, 4° Atlante; ed in ogni caso non vorrei, che questo di Bacco, e quello del campo aperto si seguissero l'uno immediatam[en]te dopo l'altro. Sia però tutto detto p[er] semplice consideratione, e rimettendomi affatto alla sua prudenza": Lavin, "Lettres," 145–46; idem, *Art and Pageantry*, 540–41 [let me also say that I would like the order of the *intermezzi* to be as follows: Aeneas and Lavinia's as fourth, to separate it from Aeneas and Dido's. But if this one is taken out, I would change it: first Atlas, second the one enclosed, third Venus, fourth Aeneas and Dido, fifth the open field, so that we would alternate happy and sad ones till the fourth one, since the last one has to be the tournament. Alternatively, the order could be: 1st Dido and Aeneas, 2nd Venus, 3rd Bacchus, 4th Atlas. In any case I would not want the Bacchus one and the tournament to be back-to-back. I offer all this to your consideration, since I trust your judgment].

[145] A description of the stage machinery and movements for this projected piece is extant under the heading "Si vorebbe fare per ult[im]o Intermedio la Deifficazione di Bacco à questo modo" [as the last *intermedio* we would like to stage Bacchus's deification in the following manner] in Archivio di Stato, Modena: Cancelleria ducale, particolari filza 123.

[146] "I received the Bacchus *intermezzo* that you sent me, which I showed to the duke and then to his mother. She told me that she will read it; if anything is needed I will let your excellence know."

[147] "Si siamo afaticati, si infinire l'opera del salone come anco nel scrivere e far formare quatro libri p[er] le parte da sonare, come si è fatta scelta p[er] apunto, e ancora della Comedia sie sono formati quatro libri, pure p[er] sonare del Primo et Secondo Intermedii. Più inanti non si può passare p[er] le dificultà che V[ostra] S[ignoria] Ill[ustrissi]ma deve sapere": MS Antonelli 660, 18 February 1628, fol. 1 r [We toiled to finish the work in the theater and to write and put together four books for the musical parts as we decided. For the comedy too there are four books, and also to play the first and second *intermezzo*. We cannot go any further due to the difficulties that your excellence has to learn about].

[148] "Dopo le cose, che hò già à V[ostra] S[ignoria] Ill[ustrissi]ma scritto, resta ch'io le dia avviso delle prove, alle quali si siamo ridotti, e credo quanto al mio giudizio dell'istessa fatta, che prima; Poiche si sono mutate le parti de Musici, e sono inesperti, e sono anco

impauriti, e queste armonie del s[igno]re Monteverde non accordanno affatto, e hò veduto il ser[enissi]mo s[ignor] Duca con meno, che mediocre gusto quanto alla Musica, che più e ridotta in discorsi, che in fatti, e q[u]ando comandano, che si provi, non s'aggiustano i tempi, per movere, e fermare la Machine, si che è quasi, che non prova, e senza frutto s'affatica, perche giammai si fà cosa di mom[en]to; e le machine si guastano più ch'altro": Lavin, "Lettres," 127; idem, *Art and Pageantry*, 530 [In addition to all that I have already communicated to you, your excellence has to hear about the rehearsals. We are at the same point and in the same situation as before. The music parts have been changed; the musicians are green and fearful; Monteverdi's tunes do not fit together; and I saw that the duke likes the music less than well. So we talk about the music rather than act on it, and when we are ordered to rehearse we cannot settle the times when stage machinery moves and stops. So it is almost a non-rehearsal and we are plugging away for nothing, since nothing important comes out of it and the stage machinery gets ruined more than anything else].

[149] It is hard to document his movements in these months. The rough draft of a letter dated 8 June 1628, addressed to Bentivoglio by an anonymous writer presumably at Modena (Archivio di Stato, Modena: Cancelleria ducale, particolari filza 121) seems to indicate that Enzo was then in Ferrara. It states: "I musici son già incaminati per venir a servir cotesta confraternita di S. Spirito conforme alla richiesta fatta da V[ostra] S[ignoria]" [the musicians started to come and play to the *confraternita* of S. Spirito as your excellence asked]; it is unlikely that Bentivoglio would have hired a group of musicians for a religious group outside his hometown of Ferrara.

[150] A description of his departure and progress is in a loose leaf extant in Archivio di Stato, Parma: Casa e corte farnesiane, serie II busta 28 fascicolo 5.

[151] Archivio di Stato, Parma: Casa e corte farnesiane, serie II busta 28 fascicolo 5.

[152] The ink here has corroded the paper, making the word(s) illegible.

[153] "As you know, we have decided to have a pastoral performed when my son's bride arrives. We selected Mr. Cesare Bernardini to play a main character because he will perform it very well due to his physical presence, ability, pronunciation, and other qualities. He modestly replied that he is ready to take the part on as long as his father agrees and as long as the other performers are from the nobility. We truly want this gentleman to act his chosen part and therefore order that you prevail on his father, sparing no expense, so that he is convinced that the other performers are not simply noblemen, but even feudatories like Count Molla. Nor should he be worried because his son is a priest, because other performers are and this should cause him no apprehension. You should also make it clear that if he does not agree we would find ourselves in a predicament as the bride's coming is near and we do not know who else to tap who is as good as his son. You should let him know that this would be the best way to have us beholden to them. May God bless you."

[154] Paola Besutti agrees: "le procedure di scelta di testi drammatici per eventi rappresentativi complessi, quali l'allestimento di una commedia con intermedi, il più delle volte venivano condotte in tempi rapidi, con una buona dose di casualità, ma soprattutto con attenzione all' *auctoritas* letteraria": "Tasso contra Guarini: una rappresentazione con intermedi degli *Intrichi d'amore*," in *Torquato Tasso e la cultura estense 3*, ed. Venturi, 1197–1220, here 1200 [the process of choosing dramatic texts for complex stagings such as a comedy with *intermezzi* mostly took place quickly, with lots left to chance, but above all paying attention to literary authority figures].

[155] This should come as no surprise, given the social and moral atmosphere of the time. The seminal and extensive study of the stigma attached to theater in Western cultures across the centuries is Jonas Barish, *The Antitheatrical Prejudice* (Berkeley: University of California Press, 1981).

[156] Rehearsals were imperative since Goretti reported twice on 17 November, to Antonio Ciavernelli and Caterina Martinengo Bentivoglio, that the festivities would take place on 2 December (Fabris, *Mecenati e musici*, 433 and 434).

[157] Goretti to Bentivoglio: "Siamo sul fine del mese e siamo ancora al tempo di fare queste feste, le abbiamo provate e p[er] parte nostra le musiche riescono beniss[im]o le Machine sono belle e mirabile, mà ancora non vano à tempo, si va però tutti sperando aciò le machine e la musica dovendo andare di concerto e necessario che tutte due vadino bene si che si andiamo travagliando, e io non vego l'ora di vederne il fine p[er] potermene venire": Lavin, "Lettres," 148; idem, *Art and Pageantry*, 542; MS Antonelli 660, 28 November 1628, fol. r [it is the end of the month and we are close to the festivities. After all that rehearsing we believe that the music comes off beautifully and that the stage machinery is fine and admirable. Still they do not move in unison, so we all hope that music and machinery will proceed at the same time and well. We are worried and I look forward to the end so that I can come home].

Chapter Four

Parma, 13 December 1628: The Medici-Farnese Wedding Celebration

1. Sources

While letters of a personal nature testify to the preparatory stage of the Parma festivities, the stagings can be reconstructed on the basis of documents that vary greatly as far as their intended readers, style, and scope are concerned. Readers will recall that the texts of the prologue and *intermezzi* were printed after the event; that we have two manuscript sources written years after the fact; that a number of letters by two different witnesses are extant; that Goretti reported his impressions to Bentivoglio soon after the performance; and finally, that a printed description of the events is available. What is remarkably (and regrettably) missing is Monteverdi's score for the *intermezzi*.[1]

Of all extant sources, Marcello Buttigli's *Descrittione dell'apparato fatto per honorare la prima solenne entrata in Parma della Serenissima Principessa Margherita di Toscana, Duchessa di Parma, Piacenza, . . .* is, from its very title, the bulkiest and the most thorough.[2] Buttigli seems to have played an important role in the preparation of the entertainment; according to Paolo-Emilio Ferrari, he had been "incaricato dagli Anziani e Consiglio della Città di Parma di inventare l'apparato per ricevere la Principessa Margherita" (*Spettacoli*, 4).[3] Buttigli, to cite Franco Ruffini, presents to us the "visione del dentro e del prima" [view from within and before]; letter writers who witnessed the events and reported about them were "delegat[i] allo sguardo del dopo e del fuori" (*Teatri prima del teatro*, 220) [relegated to afterwards and from outside]. These texts thus offer a fundamental discrepancy. How could have Buttigli not described the events as they should have been, rather than as they actually were, so as to better glorify his patrons and his own work?

The publishers of Buttigli's *Relattione* broached this topic in their customary address to the readers, aware that the latter would be suspicious of the relationship between event and text. They felt it necessary to defend Buttigli's work on a number of counts. Interestingly, they chose to open with the avowal that no description can be absolutely complete. Thus, in order to understand Buttigli's description, a reader must fulfill one of two requirements: s/he must have been present at the events, so as to be able to "fill in the blanks" where the author was necessarily incomplete; or, s/he must be an expert in any field implied in the description, and therefore capable of imagining what is not directly mentioned.[4] This passage, like most addresses to the reader, exploits the classical cliché of *captatio benevolentiæ*, praising the reader for his/her knowledge. At the same time, it reveals a keen awareness that no description, no matter how specific and detailed, can make the events present again, and to this end imagination can play an important part. Reading is not the same as experiencing by being present.[5] Indeed, the purpose of the *Descrittione* is not to provide a complete treatise on all the *arti* involved in the building of the theaters and their stages as well as in their decoration. Thus the publishers want to defend Buttigli from the charges of superficiality and oversimplification: the aim of the text is to make the events known, not to explain technically how stage machinery moved, for example.

The sources of the description are two: its author's presence at the entertainment and other reports whose sources and nature go unexplained:

> Comporteranno gli Historici ch'egli habbia, facendo un misto morale, accoppiato le Poetiche favole colla verità Historica, e non ricuseranno di far testimonianza, che quando egli ha trattato di cose antiche, non habbia loro aggiunto cosa benche minima del suo, assicurando esso in oltre, che quando egli ha descritto le cose moderne, non si è partito punto, ne dalle cose vedute, ne dalle relationi ricevute. (*Descrittione dell'apparato*, iii)[6]

It is evident that Buttigli's text implies two distinct objects of description. On the one hand, he depicts the events of the festivities, what the publishers call "le cose moderne." On the other, however, he also has to refer to "cose antiche," that is, those examples after which the celebration was modeled.[7] It is over the contemporaneous events that Buttigli could exert a greater power, modifying them, describing them in a different manner from what they were in reality. While this passage seems to discount the possibility of any interference on the part of the author, as if he were a completely transparent medium, another paragraph bestows on him a privileged point of view and, consequently, a better understanding and a more thorough capability of describing the events:

> Quei, che furono Spettatori non s'altereranno, se talhora abbondante, talhora deficiente loro paresse la Descrittione. Delle cose vedute frà lume, e scuro non dovranno accertar meglio, di chi le osservò innanzi il fatto, nel fatto, e dopò [*sic*] il fatto; e se gli essecutori mancarono in qualche cosuccia, non deve risultarne biasimo, a chi le cose percio haveva a compimento stabilite. (*Descrittione dell'apparato*, iv)[8]

Buttigli, according to his publishers, achieved a better understanding of the festivities precisely because of his involvement in them. Since he was able to "observe" them "before, during, and after" the performance, he could describe them as they were or as they should have been, in case "the performers fell somewhat short" at the moment of the event itself.⁹ Luckily, this admittedly idealized text can be counterbalanced with other descriptions (at times crude, and certainly not disinterested) presented by the remaining sources.¹⁰

2. The Couple's Arrival

Odoardo and Margherita were married in Florence on 11 October (Minucci del Rosso, "Le nozze," I, 557–59), with great fanfare and amid majestic celebrations; their departure for Parma did not take place until 30 November. A curious letter now at the Archivio di Stato, Firenze, indicates that Parma and Florence were not the only cities involved in preparations and celebrations.¹¹ The Este ruler of Modena asked his peer in Urbino for all the silver he could spare, in the redundant, formal style so common in seventeenth-century Italy.¹² The urgency of this letter is unmistakable: the duke of Modena feared the competition with the luxurious ostentation of his neighbors, as well as the high expectations of his guests; consequently, he had no choice but to ask for help from somebody whose domains would not be crossed by the newlywed couple, so as to be provided with enough pieces of silver flatware and platters.

The Este duke was not the only person anxious about the outcome of the festivities. Even detached, external witnesses give their readers the impression the occasion was, by all accounts, momentous. Andrea Pugolotti, a *notabile* from Parma, left us the most succinct description, quite helpful in providing the date of the events:

> 1628. Due Ottobre. Il Duca Odoardo con molti Cavalieri partì per Firenze, onde sposare l'Infanta Margherita Sorella del Gran Duca. Il giorno 14 Ottobre Venne un Corriere colla nuova dello Sposalizio. Si fece lo sparo dell'artiglieria con suono di campane, e fuochi d'allegrezza. Il giorno 24 giunse il Duca a Parma incognito, e andò a smontare al Palazzo del Cardinale suo Zio, e fu a visitarlo la Ser[enissi]ma Madre, e molti della Città.
>
> 1628. 6 Dicembre Alle ore 18, giunse a Parma la Sposa con tempo assai cattivo. (Morì questa li 7 Febbraio 1679, e fu sepolta nella Chiesa delle Teresiane). Il giorno 9 Dicembre fece l'entrata solenne circa 2 ore di notte con grande illuminazione. Venne dalla Porta S. Michele alla piazza, indi al Duomo, poi al Palazzo. (*Diario parmigiano*, 10–11)¹³

Pugolotti's *Diario* (as abridged by the nineteenth-century Palatina librarian Ireneo Affò) is exceedingly brief, yet it reveals the importance of this occasion. The duke left with "molti Cavalieri" on 2 October;¹⁴ the news of the Florence wedding was publicly celebrated with fireworks, the ringing of the church bells and an artillery salute. When Margherita arrived in town, in spite of bad weather conditions, she was greeted by the *apparato* of a triumphal entry, which comprised a display of lights shining in the night.[15]

Or was she? The first letter from Camillo Giordani to his wife Felice in Pesaro (sent from Parma on 8 December 1628) depicts a much more disappointing situation:

> Dopo che giugnemmo a Parma s'è voltato un tempo così dirotto, che non fa altro che piovere e che nevare, nè si può praticare. La S[igno]ra Duchessa venne, e per non poter far l'entrata, venne privata e non ha ancora potuto farla... Doveva detta entrata farsi di notte a lume di torcie, per lo che S[ua] A[ltezza] aveva fatto fare un'infinità di lumiere, e queste non si useranno, poiché si farà di giorno. Nè l'accompagnamento delle carrozze e delle Dame e dei Cavalieri e delle livree, che sono numerosissime e bellissime, faranno pompa. Pensi poi quanto abbiano patito tanti archi trionfali ed un casone di legno fatto in forma d'un sontuosissimo Palagio un quarto di miglio fuori della città, nel quale si sono spesi più di sedici mila scudi e dove sono quattro appartamenti, sale, logge e gallerie, tutto dipinto ed abbigliato preziosissimamente. (Saviotti, "Feste e spettacoli," 46–47)[16]

According to Giordani, the princess's arrival in her new domain was far from dazzling, due to adverse weather conditions; no night entrance, no display of lights, no numerous train of knights and damsels were possible, at least at their scheduled time. Giordani had heard rumors about, and quite possibly seen, the temporary buildings to which he refers in the aforementioned passage. He himself, although an outsider at the Farnese court, was under the spell of the magnificence and luster of the complex display that Parma had been readying for the *ingresso trionfale* of its new duchess.

Adverse weather conditions emerge also in a letter, dated 9 December, that the Este ambassador to Parma sent to Modena: there was snow on the ground, and the triumphal entry could not take place as planned.[17] Yet Pugolotti's diary mentions that very day for Margherita's entrance, and Giordani's second letter, dated 12 December, confirms it:

> la S[igno]ra Duchessa Sposa fece la sua entrata a Parma li 9 del corrente. La fece di notte al lume di 600 torcie. Fu incontrata da quantità di Dame superbissimamente vestite e con tante gioie, ch'è una meraviglia. Ad un casone di legno si fece una superbissima colezione, una salva terribile, incontro di Cavalieri con livree di grandissimo valore, tre compagnie di cavalli, lettiga di brocato d'argento avanti e poi la S[igno]ra Duchessa in una lettiga discoverta tutta di brocato d'argento raccamato, ella aveva un cappello con piuma bianca, cappotto e veste di concerto bianco, non corona, non gloria in testa. Il Vescovo e Clero l'andò ad incontrare alla porta e le camminò apparato davanti fino al Duomo, ch'era una compassione di vedere quel povero Vescovo

pestar la fanga, che quella sera era abbondantissima, e pioveva e si disfaceva la neve, ch'era finissima. Sei Gentiluomini, vestiti a livrea di bianco con calza a taglio e cappotto bianco, le portavano il baldacchino, che riportato a S[ua] A[ltezza] sono stati regalati di 500 doble. Madama [the groom's mother] e le Principesse [his sisters] l'andarono ad incontrare a piedi delle scale. (Saviotti, "Feste e spettacoli," 48)[18]

The discrepancy might be easily explained if one considers that Odoardo and Margherita had actually reached Parma on 6 December (Minucci del Rosso, "Le nozze," II, 554). The Este ambassador and Giordani had certainly heard rumors of their arrival and, seeing the bad weather, assumed that the entry had been postponed. When it did occur, it involved the participation of the whole city: ladies and knights welcomed her first, then the bishop and the priests, and finally her mother- and sisters-in-law. Giordani's reference to the latter's welcome of Margherita "a piedi delle scale" is more than a quirky detail. As Richard Trexler has pointed out in his work on Florentine Renaissance ritual, "stairs were critical locations for measuring the relations between powers" (*Public Life in Renaissance Florence*, 319). Meeting someone at the foot of the stairs was a signal honor; in this case, it indicates the desire of the Farnese princesses to welcome Margherita and include her in their household.

It would be naïve to assume that the participation of Parma's nobility and clergy was spontaneous. Before the festivities, in November, many letters were sent to Farnese subjects requiring their presence and explaining what their appearance and role was going to be.[19] In December, four lists were penned, both descriptive and prescriptive in nature. They name respectively the "Cav[alie]ri, et Gentilhuomini che hanno servito il S[ign]or Duca Ser[enissi]mo nella sua andata à Fiorenza p[er] le sue Nozze" [knights and gentlemen who served the duke on his wedding trip to Florence]; the noblemen "che hanno incontrato la Ser[enissi]ma Duchessa sposa, nel suo ingresso in Parma" [who met the duchess bride on her entry into Parma]; the "Dame, che hanno incontrato la Ser[enissi]ma Duchessa sposa, nel suo ingresso in Parma" [ladies who met the duchess bride on her entry into Parma]; and finally, "quelli di compagnia del Ser[enissi]mo di Parma Odoardo nel suo viaggio a Firenze, con l'ordine della tavola" [those accompanying Odoardo on his Florence trip, in their order at the table], noblemen and commoners alike.[20] Certainly these lists were conceived as reminders to the Farnese court of the services rendered by their subjects; the honor of being included in some official capacity in the festivities could not, however, be refused without some consequence. Additionally, these lists point at a division based on gender and at a social stratification of the people involved in the events.

Extant sources are hardly helpful in establishing who came to Parma from elsewhere to celebrate Margherita's arrival. While the aforementioned list of letters sent all over Europe and the Farnese domain attests to the desire of spreading the news as widely as possible, it does not constitute an index of who was invited to attend the festivities. Giordani's first letter, dated 8 December, mentions that "il concorso de' forestieri è grandissimo e tutti stiamo con disgusto di tempo così perverso, poi che ne impedisce tanti gusti. Vi sono molti di questi Principotti incogniti e la Città tutta è pienissima" (Saviotti, "Feste e spettacoli," 47).[21] Until that date, Giordani had failed to see any prince of high renown. Indeed, with the phrase "principotti incogniti" he stresses their mediocre social status.[22] Still, he could not attend any festivity, and given that he himself was not from a particularly important family, he might not have encountered whoever was socially his superior until the public events that followed. Nevertheless, the audience taking part in the festivities constituted a relatively homogenous group, within which differences in gender and age yielded to local expectations and social stratification.

After Margherita and Odoardo's triumphal entry, the Farnese celebrated them and entertained their guests for many days and in various ways, among which was *Aminta*.

3. The Setting

The one element on which all sources agree is the date on which *Aminta* was performed along with its prologue and *intermezzi*. Giordani wrote to his wife, on 15 December 1628: "Mercoledì si fece l'*Aminta* del Tasso" (Saviotti, "Feste e spettacoli," 49) [Tasso's *Aminta* was done on Wednesday]; Inghirami informed Maria Maddalena on 14 December: "Hiersera mercoledì à 13, giorno di Santa Lucia, si fece la Commedia" (Minucci del Rosso, "Le nozze," II, 562; Mediceo del Principato, filza 6075, 14 December 1628, fol. 1 r) [Last night, St. Lucy's day, the 13th, a comedy took place].[23] Lastly, Buttigli asserts:

> Furono intermediate le feste di ballo, colla rappresentatione della Favola boschereccia, intitolata Aminta, Poema singolare del Signor Torquato Tasso, che fù accompagnata dagli Intermedij dell'Illustriss[imo] Sig[nor] D[on] Ascanio Pij, e da un Prologo dell'Eccellentiss[issimo] Sig[nor] Dottor Achillini.
>
> Fù recitata la notte del mercore, venendo il giovedi, dopò l'entrata della Serenissima, nel primo cortile del palagio nuovo. (*Descrittione dell'apparato*, 148)[24]

Buttigli's passage gives an early indication of the relatively secondary importance of the *Aminta* performance vis-à-vis the rest of the festivities. By stating that the balls were "intermediati" by the theatrical entertainment, Buttigli places the emphasis on the former, not on the latter. Overall the impression is that *Aminta* did not elicit any special attention, but rather that it was at most as important as many other forms of entertainment organized and performed on this occasion.

It was clearly subordinate to the tournament *Mercurio e Marte* which ended and crowned the festivities, and which inaugurated the Teatro Farnese almost a decade after its inception.

According to Buttigli, the crowd assembled "avanti le due hore di notte" (*Descrittione dell'apparato*, 154) [before two hours after sunset], which in Ferrari's computations correspond to 6:55 P.M. The only mention of a closing time comes instead from Inghirami: "si diede fine allo spettacolo sonate le 10" (Minucci del Rosso, "Le nozze," II, 564; Mediceo del Principato, filza 6075, 14 December 1628, fol. 4 r) [the show ended after ten hours past sunset], that is, about 3 A.M. The show seems to have lasted eight hours. At the time, this was the normal length of staged entertainment.[25] However, other elements conspired to make this particular evening feel too long to the convened audience.

The location of these events was, in Buttigli's words, the "primo cortile del palagio nuovo, nel quale S[ua] A[ltezza] aveva fatto fabbricare Theatro, Proscenio, Scene, e Machine particolari" (*Descrittione dell'apparato*, 148) [in the first courtyard of the new palace, where his highness had a theater, a stage, sets and stage machinery built solely for this purpose]. This sentence alerts us to a recurrent linguistic feature: whenever Buttigli uses the term "theatro" (capitalized or not) he etymologically designates the area reserved to the audience.[26] While many pieces of stage machinery had been built ten years earlier and never utilized, or had been designed without a clear knowledge of how they would be used on stage, the phrase "Machine particolari" indicates that the *Aminta* stage machinery was not to be re-used for any other event during the wedding festivities. Inghirami succinctly describes the location of the stage: "Il luogo dove si rappresentò è un Cortile così grande che la metà ne fù lasciata; nell'altra la prospettiva, lo spazio dove si giostrò, il teatro di legno, dove stette la gente, molto commodam[ent]e, benche fosse numerosiss[im]a, si viddero" (Minucci del Rosso, "Le nozze," II, 562; Mediceo del Principato, filza 6075, 14 December 1628, fol. 1 r).[27] For Inghirami, too, "teatro" refers to the area destined to accommodate the audience. He refers to the stage as "la prospettiva," the space arranged according to the rules of central perspective (for the benefit of the audience).

Inghirami's letter describes the theater in plentiful detail. His passage, and the corresponding one in Buttigli's text, should be compared to Mazzi's sketch in the letter of 8 December 1627 to Bentivoglio. Readers will recall that this drawing constituted merely a proposal; Bentivoglio and then the Farnese court had to approve it. The final product, that is, the theater in which *Aminta* took place, might have looked relatively or even considerably different from what the architect had originally proposed and designed. According to Inghirami, "Il teatro non era di forma sferica, ma alzandosi dal piano della terra con trenta gradi, arrivava molto in sù, et da grossis[sim]e travi e ben commessi tavoloni si formava, ricorrendogli di sopra intorno intorno due ordini di logge, sostenute da finte colonne di misti, con i capitelli di bronzo dorato e con li loro balaustri, che abbellivano con il popolo che vi era, nobilissimam[en]te il luogo" (Minucci del Rosso, "Le nozze," II, 562; Mediceo del Principato, filza 6075, 14 December 1628, fol. 1 r).[28] His overall impression is evidently positive: wooden planks were well set, the boxes were convincingly decorated, and the convened audience contributed to a noble ensemble. More importantly, Inghirami's passage indicates that some modifications had been made to Mazzi's plan: the fact that the area reserved to the audience was not "sferica," or round, does not refer to Mazzi's proposed modification to Guitti's original design (which he justified with his concern for the viewers' lines of vision), or to the fact that either Guitti's or Mazzi's proposal articulated that space through straight segments and not along a semi-circle. Rather, Inghirami indicates that the area within the boxes had been filled with "gradi" or steps on which people could sit. Specifically, there were thirty of these steps, and two rows of boxes about them.[29]

Buttigli's description is far richer in style and details. He is more specific, but also less reliable when it comes to events, since he describes them as they should have been rather than as they were. Buttigli confirms Inghirami's perception that the temporary structure took up only half of the courtyard, and specifies the orientation of this structure and how far the stage and the pit were from each other.[30] He also gives measurements for the temporary building.[31] The area reserved for the audience was deeper than it was wide and than the stage. Also, according to Buttigli, the boxes and corridors behind them only took up 6 *braccia*, that is, less than three and a half meters or 129 inches, considerably less than the boxes in an opera house. Buttigli's description agrees with Mazzi's plan as it indicates that the area reserved for the audience was articulated in cells; however, in the architect's letter seven sides were projected, while Buttigli refers to a hexagon. Further, Buttigli specifies the arrangements for the steps and gives their measurements. Inghirami's count of thirty seems excessive, since each step was a *braccio* high and all of them took up ten *braccia*. Lastly, while Inghirami simply described the temporary theater, Buttigli compared it to the Farnese and indicated how they differed; he clearly marks himself as a narrator in the know, and consequently also increases the implicit praise for the Farnese, the festivity organizers, and the architects.

Though Buttigli points out that the steps held a considerable number of audience members, from what follows in his description we detect an additional detail, which in turn constitutes another discrepancy with Mazzi's plan of December 1627: "Nel mezo di quei gradi risaltava un verone, largo braccio sei, lungo dodici, nel cui mezo sporgeva in fuori un mez'ovato di braccia sei, che formava luogo appartato per li Sereniss[imi] Prencipi" (*Descrittione dell'apparato*, 149).[32] It is worth pointing out that Buttigli used the verb "risaltare" in reference to the space reserved to the newlyweds and their retinue, both in its literal and in its metaphorical meanings:

the ducal balcony stood out both architecturally (as it projected towards the stage) and figuratively (as it drew attention to itself). Buttigli is not the only one to underscore this particular arrangement. Inghirami notes:

> Nel centro di questo [i.e., the theater] rimaneva un capac[issim]o piano di assi, nel mezzo del quale fù eretta la sessione per i Card[inal]i L[oro] A[ltezze] Pr[inci]pesse e Dame, coperta pur d'asse, . . . foderata di teletta d'oro; di quà e di là sedevano le Dame, et daman manca hebbero ricetto i Cav[alie]ri di Tosc[an]a dietro alla sessione di Principi vi fecero uno stanzino sopra il quale come in terrazzo stettero molti che godevano per linea retta della prospettiva. (Minucci del Rosso, "Le nozze," II, 562; Mediceo del Principato, filza 6075, 14 December 1628, fol. 1 r–v)[33]

The position of the ducal balcony was meant to be central, so that whoever sat there enjoyed an unimpeded and direct view. Inghirami openly refers to *prospettiva*, using it in its technical meaning as well as metaphorically. On the one hand, we can assume that the stage was designed so as to provide the best vision to a central observer placed in the middle of the *cavea*; on the other, the people on the terrace above the ducal couple enjoyed the best *prospettiva* in the theater, that is the best view, with no reference to how it was achieved, but only to its results.

Buttigli mentions another interesting detail, at the end of his verbose description of the ducal *verone*, or balcony (semantically related to Inghirami's *terrazzo*), which he calls "luogo appartato per li Sereniss[imi] Prencipi" — thus stressing its separateness from the rest of the audience:

> Ne' fianchi poi, quel poggio era aperto, ne haveva altro ornamento, che di altre due colonne quadre, incontranti le descritte, in distanza di quattro braccia, e mezo, le quali colligate colla ballaustrata, sostenevano il raggirante cornicione, e per lo vano di quell'intercolonnio, davano commodità alli Prencipi, e di vedere, e di essere veduti dalli circostanti. (*Descrittione dell'apparato*, 149)[34]

There was more than one spectacle going on at the same time: the stage; the princes offering themselves to view to the court and invitees; and the court displaying itself for the benefit of the duke and duchess. This is by no means an uncommon occurrence;[35] indeed the very fact that Buttigli makes it explicit could imply that his readers need to be alerted about it, lest they overlook an obvious, ordinary feature.

Throughout the extant documents regarding the festivities for Odoardo and Margherita, Valeri's opinion is confirmed: "da spettatori di se stessi nelle feste, i popoli diventano spettatori dei loro principi; il codice della festa ciclica sparisce per lasciar posto a invenzioni nuove e sempre diverse."[36] The audience's presence was nevertheless crucial as no festivity could take place without somebody to take it in.[37] The audience's attitude is also important; the Parma celebrations are linked to specific literary genres but also to a set of expectations. Far from being mere entertainment, they celebrated a ritual, in which "l'elemento di anticipazione e proiezione diventa preponderante rispetto a ciò che è effettivamente recepito. Ciò è dovuto all'assenza di un processo di comunicazione vero e proprio" in the sense that "coloro che li [i.e., the shows] producono utilizzano deliberatamente l'unilateralità comunicativa per stimolare al massimo le proiezioni dello spettatore."[38] The audience converged on Parma and at court expecting to take part in an event marking a change in the Farnese present and future, through the hoped-for progeny. At the same time, the audience was not prepared to make sense of this event and its celebrations: the meaning was already decided and set by the festivity organizers.

This obviously affected the performers' ability to create meaning on stage. McAuley, in *Space in Performance*, emphasizes that in Western theater "through the agency of the actor . . . objects are brought to the attention of the audience, and it is the actor who creates the mobility that is characteristic of the theatrical function of the object: the actor can, with a gesture or an act, transform a walking stick into a machine gun, a bundle of rags into a baby, a chair into a table into a mountain" (91). Conversely, the over-determination of characters and objects on stage implies that at the Parma performance little mobility of signifiers was tolerated, indeed possible. Objects, like bodies on stage, had a specific meaning that the festivity organizers had imposed upon them; the audience's role was to understand that meaning through explicit (that is, verbal) or implicit references, but little negotiation was possible.

Further, for the Farnese wedding it is hardly appropriate to follow Aercke's assertion that "the advent of perspective with a single vantage point coincides with the withdrawal of the sponsor-ruler as an active participant [in the performance]: the whole stage is arranged in perspective from his or her vantage point in perfect symmetry — the world is ordered, the ruler is the fixed point of reference, the embodiment of stability heads the state" (*Gods of Play*, 34). For one thing, the ruler's participation in staged entertainment seems to have been far more rare in Italy than north of the Alps. For another thing, the political situation in the various Italian courts was less stable and established than in those where the process of absolutization had begun more successfully. However, Aercke's statement can be seen as an ideal towards which the Farnese (and other Italian courts) strove. This is what Alessandro Fontana means when he asserts that baroque spectacles are blazons: "il desiderio di questo sogno [taking place on stage] è negli individui di abolire la differenza, identificandosi con l'ideale immaginario della persona utopistica e teatrale."[39] At the same time, they are also rituals, referring to the present and centrally located ruler for their meaning: "in ogni situazione rituale, la comunicazione tra gli 'attori' reali avviene riferendosi a un 'attore' immaginario, ma che serve a sanzionare il contenuto della comunicazione, e gli dà una forma specifica."[40] The newlyweds had thus to be present, visible and yet detached from the performance itself and the rest of the audience.

Readers will recall that Mazzi's letter of 8 December 1627 referred to the fact that the ducal balcony-seat was planned as retractable away from the stage to free room "nel caso di far il Torneo" (Lavin, "Lettres," 139; idem, *Art and Pageantry*, 537; MS Antonelli 660, 8 December 1628, fol. 1 r) [if there is a tournament]. This points to the fact that Guitti and Mazzi were sometimes uncertain about the usage intended for the space they were building; it could also refer to the possibility of a multiple exploitation of this temporary theater. It was, however, the Farnese theater that was better suited for the performance of tournaments. These required plenty of room between the stage and the boxes and seats of the audience, and the Teatro inferiore did not provide it, owing to the fact that the steps for the audience partially filled the area between the boxes.

The existence of these steps helps explain another discrepancy between Mazzi's letter and the written testimonies that exist of the *Aminta* performance. Mazzi asserted that "secondo i miei conti posso far capire più di 3500 persone in d[et]ti palchi; ne paia poco à V[ostra] S[ignoria] Ill[ustrissi]ma p[er]che nel teatro di sopra non vi ne caperà solo che 2400" (Lavin, "Lettres," 138; idem, *Art and Pageantry*, 537; MS Antonelli 660, 8 December 1628, fol. 1 r);[41] he was referring to those who could fit in the two rows of boxes. Inghirami, it is worth repeating, simply wrote that "stette la gente, molto commodam[ent]e, benche fosse numerosiss[im]a" (Minucci del Rosso, "Le nozze," II, 562; Mediceo dei Principato, filza 6075, 14 December 1627, fol. 1 r) [people fit comfortably, though they were many]. Conversely, Buttigli estimated that the attendance was "non . . . meno di se milla" (*Descrittione dell'apparato*, 154) [no fewer than six thousand], an assertion that has attracted the bemused remarks of many later commentators.[42] Though it is likely that Buttigli exaggerated, if Mazzi's estimation of three thousand five hundred people in the boxes was correct, then it is possible that over five thousand audience members could fit in the temporary structure with the addition of the steps between the boxes.

There are three more discrepancies between Mazzi's floor plan and Buttigli's description. The latter does not mention the corridors, or the staircases leading to the boxes, or the three passages accessing the *cavea*. However, it refers to two side entrances located between the frontispiece and the area reserved for the audience.[43] Mamczarz offers two possible explanations for these discrepancies: either Buttigli was more interested in the decorations and the staged performances than in the technical details, or Mazzi's original plan suffered some changes while going through the building process (*Le Théâtre Farnèse*, 87). These suggestions are not mutually exclusive, especially given the tone and goals of Buttigli's text.

Though Buttigli spends a page and a half describing the decorations of the two box tiers, he devotes over two and a half to illustrating the fourth side of the temporary structure, which he call the "proscenio" [proscenium] or "frontespicio" [frontispiece]. This was elevated by one *braccio* and "compartito in due parti, la metà pieno, e la metà vacuo" [divided in two: one open, one full] of the same dimension (27 *braccia*). The open part was obviously placed in the middle, flanked by two wings. On top, linking all the columns and pillars and extending "ben'anche sopra il vacuo del Proscenio," ran a cornice, "nel cui mezo veniva ornato d'un Arme grande di rilievo de' Serenissimi Sposi, accompagnata da quattro festoni di varij frutti, e fiori, e sei cascate di trofei, le quali sotto l'architrave, facevano bellissima vista" (Buttigli, *Descrittione dell'apparato*, 152).[44] Not only did those escutcheons produce a handsome view; placed as they were in the "space at the top center of the proscenium arch, its visual focus architecturally,"[45] they also reminded the audience, subtly but constantly, of whom they had come to celebrate. In essence, by enclosing the proscenium with such a structure, the architects and decorators had devised a way to frame the events on stage — a physical frame as well as a metaphorical one (in Goffman's sense). In a sense, to follow Richard Schechner's suggestion,[46] a frame defines and constrains whatever takes place inside. Additionally, whatever would happen within this frame was highlighted — in the case of *Aminta*, doubly so, due to the performance of framing events like the *intermezzi*, as we will see.[47] Though partially redundant, this frame was also made necessary by a well-known trend in early modern absolutist courts. To use Saslow's wording, it consisted of "the theatricalization of the whole spatial environment, in which the natural world was physically built (or rebuilt) in theatrical terms, as a stage set for human actions in the broadest sense" (*The Medici Wedding of 1589*, 15). Theaters, specifically courtly ones like the temporary structure in the San Pietro martire courtyard, were *loci* "where the apparatus of state presentation could operate at a more contained and private — but correspondingly intensified — level" (15). Within this theater setting, the frame directs the audience's gaze and bestows particular resonance on the goings-on inside: "La cornice psicologica comunica che ciò che essa include è un'azione rappresentativa o una 'finzione,' cioè un'azione che non sta sullo stesso piano ontologico di ciò che essa rappresenta o di ciò cui è opposta" (Valeri, "Rito," 238).[48] Thus, "paradossalmente, la cornice assume due funzioni contraddittorie: l'una segnala che ciò che essa contiene è fittizio; l'altra fa dimenticare che lo è" (238).[49] Thus the frame, as Anna Nardo has pointed out, is inherently paradoxical, because as a self-referential element "the definition of the class of actions is itself one of the actions being defined" (*The Ludic Self*, 10).

The frame did not only depict the escutcheons of the Farnese and Medici families; statues representing War, Peace, the rivers Arno and Parma, Conjugal Love, Marital Faithfulness, Victory, and Abundance also found room on it. So-called baroque *horror vacui* is also an attempt at layering meanings to underscore the event's significance to the convened audience. Buttigli and Inghirami, who both describe the proscenium, do not emphasize its ideological underpinning, but lavishly praise its richness and imagination.[50] While the structure was floored with wooden planks, as the earliest extant letters attest, Guitti had also sketched a cover for this theater. According to Buttigli, three ropes "sostenevano un tendone, che composto di ben trè milla, e sei cento braccia di tela, copriva tutto il Theatro non solo, ma ben'anche quello spatio, che restava frà il Proscenio, e Theatro" (*Descrittione dell'apparato*, 154).[51] Buttigli makes it clear that the canvas hoisted over the temporary structure covered only the area reserved for the audience and that separating the latter from the stage. Giordani had seen the theater di San Pietro martire before the *Aminta* performance or heard about it, as he wrote his wife on 8 December that the show would have to be postponed "poi che s'ha da rappresentare in un teatro, cui fa tetto una tela incerata" (Saviotti, "Feste e spettacoli," 47) [as it has to take place in a theater whose roof is an oilcloth]. On 15 December, he reiterated that the theater in the courtyard was "coperto da una tenda" (Saviotti, "Feste e spettacoli," 49) [covered by canvas]. Inghirami, however, complained about this arrangement: the temporary structure "era per disopra coperto con una tenda, ma perché dalla parte della scena rimaneva di sopra una grand'apertura, vi si hebbe, doppo nella notte, un sottiliss[im]o freddo, che ricercò la testa e tutta la persona" (Minucci del Rosso, "Le nozze," II, 562; Mediceo del Principato, filza 6075, 14 December 1628, fol. 1 r).[52] We encounter here an early example of Inghirami's critical attitude toward the festivities;[53] it is of course impossible to know if he genuinely disliked whatever he criticizes or if he took on the attitude expected of him as a courtier. There was an eminently practical reason for the lack of cover over the stage area: the necessity to leave as much room as possible to move the stage machinery needed for the performance. Obviously Inghirami shows no concern for any technical element, as his letter conveys the impressions of a (partisan) observer, not of an (equally partisan) organizer.

Another concern of Mazzi's, manifested in his letter of 30 November 1627, had been the lighting of the *teatro inferiore*. In the sixteenth and seventeenth centuries, "the auditorium was usually lighted just as the stage was, meaning that the actors could see the audience as well as the audience could see the actors" (Aercke, *Gods of Play*, 79). Buttigli emphasizes the final effect and the artistry involved in placing lights on and off stage: "Illuminavano il Theatro, Proscenio, e Scena, trecento, e più doppieri di cera bianca, oltre a mille altri minori lumi, i quali artificiosamente disposti in modo, che non si vedevano, sbandeggiavano da sì grande apparato le tenebre della notte" (*Descrittione dell'apparato*, 154).[54] The magically charming effect derives from the fact that candles were hidden from view; light poured onto the scene and the viewers, but its source remained hidden. Conversely, Inghirami compares what he saw at the Teatro di San Pietro martire with his expectations and with Florentine custom. In his words, "[era] già ripiena ogni cosa con torci bianchi ed ogni colonna intorno al teatro, e da canti della prospettiva con due lumiere à uso di coteste di Firenze, diversificando solam[ent]e nelle lucerne, che dove costà sono con due lumi, qui con uno, e sono fatte come quelle dei cappuccini, le quali non durarono però finanzi all'ultimo" (Minucci del Rosso, "Le nozze," II, 562; Mediceo del Principato, filza 6075, 14 December 1628, fol. 1 v).[55] According to this testimony, there were torches as well as lamps. The latter were similar to those is use in Florence, except for having one wick instead of two. Unfortunately, these lamps died out prematurely; the effect, Inghirami seems to imply, was ruined, though Buttigli leaves this detail unmentioned.

While the etymologically termed "theatro" is richly described by all extant sources, we are much less well informed about the stage and the scenery that occupied it. Giordani and Inghirami, who were part of the 13 December audience, could only describe their experiences from the physical standpoint of their seats; everything that was backstage was hidden and unknown to them. Conversely, Buttigli ignored the technical details, because, as his publishers suggested in their letter to the readers, he intended for his point of view to identify either with that of the readers or with that of the audience members, but never with that of the organizers. In other words, Buttigli is interested in the effect that the goings-on on stage elicited in the audience, not in how they were arrived at.[56] While the letters addressed to Bentivoglio are concerned with the final product as much as with the provisions to achieve them, Buttigli wants his readers to overlook the fact that he has reverted to a state of ignorance about the preparation stage, even though he might occasionally refer to it to explain the intended effects better. This rhetorical stance achieves two concurrent results: it promotes the readers' identification with the narrator's point of view; and it reinforces the programmatic illusion that everything on stage took place effortlessly, by magic, almost with *sprezzatura*. The festivity organizers, workers, craftsmen, and artists who had spent countless months devising these effects and building whatever was necessary to make them come alive would be absent, transparent to us like they were supposed to be to the 1628 audience and to Buttigli's readers, if it were not for Bentivoglio's absence from Parma that brought about the letter exchange testifying to the earlier phases of this enterprise.

To ensure that the complexity of the evening's events would be open to the audience's understanding, printed descriptions were made available. Giordani sent one home along with his letters of 15 and 18 December. In the former, he wrote: "Mando un ristretto del Torneo, e gl'intramezzi gli porterò meco, che farebbono troppo volume; desidero che si faccia vedere a tutti, acciò ammirino lontani tanto spettacolo" (Saviotti, "Feste e spettacoli," 49).[57] In the latter, "Invio questi ristretti de gl'intermedi, acciò si prendano un poco di gusto, fin ch'io potrò poi più distintamente raccontargli: faccia loro aver cura, acciò non si perdano, perchè io non n'ho d'altri" (Saviotti, "Feste e spettacoli," 49).[58] Evidently for the Pesaro nobleman such printed summaries were the best possible approximation of the event for those who had missed it, until at least his own description *viva voce*. Inghirami, too, was sending along a summary. Referring to the prologue, he mentions a "libbretto, che le invio" (Minucci del Rosso, "Le nozze," II, 562–63; Mediceo del Principato, filza 6075, 14 December 1628, fol. 2 v) [small book that I am sending].[59] Also, when writing about the first *intermezzo*, he mentions in passing that "di questo, come degli altri, viene [to Florence, with the letter] il ristretto" [I am sending the summary of this *intermezzo* and of the others]. These summaries carried out two separate functions. They helped those present to make sense of what they were about to see or had seen on stage. At the same time, they constituted a powerful tool in the hands of the organizers to spread the word about the excellence and novelty of the celebration itself. In sum, they presented the official meaning of the festivities; to use Starn and Partridge's formulation, these printed précis were "one way of assuring that something intended would not be missed. Conversely, and even more importantly perhaps, the written program meant that nothing unintended could be added" (*Arts of Power*, 166). We do not know, since no extant document mentions this detail, when these printed summaries were distributed to the audience. However, they were easily obtainable, since not only Inghirami, but also Giordani (who attended in no public capacity) could get hold of one.[60]

What the audience could see upon entering the temporary theater was limited to the two-tiered boxes, the steps, the ducal balcony, and the proscenium. The scenes were not visible, as two sources agree in placing a curtain that closed the stage to view until the beginning of the entertainment.[61] Unfortunately, neither describes it, but both mention that it disappeared at the appropriate moment. In Inghirami's words, "essendo la scena coperta da una tela all'uso di costà, si alzò, ma adagissimo" (Minucci del Rosso, "Le nozze," II, 562; Mediceo del Principato, filza 6075, 14 December 1628, fol. 1 v).[62] According to Inghirami, this habit was adopted at Parma from a Florentine tradition;[63] yet it was not carried out properly, since the effect was marred by the slow speed at which the curtain rose. Not surprisingly, this detail is again missing in Buttigli's text, which instead emphasizes the placement of the guests and the sweet music.[64] The liminal function of the curtain is paired with the music that likewise establishes and reinforces the transition from the frame of the everyday to that of the event. Further, similarly to the custom at masques at the British court, the event that signaled the beginning of the entertainment was neither the raising of the curtain nor the music emanating from the stage. Rather, it was the fact that the ducal family had taken their seats, as we gather from Buttigli's description. Then and only then could the theatrical entertainment begin,[65] further underscoring that "performance" and "social event" were one and the same thing.[66] The spectacle of the court and of the ducal family displaying themselves can help explain the *décalage* between the time reported by Buttigli for the beginning of the entertainment: "avanti le due hore di notte" (*Descrittione dell'apparato*, 154) [before two hours after sunset]; and that given by Inghirami: "alle tre hore di notte" (Minucci del Rosso, "Le nozze," II, 562; Mediceo del Principato, filza 6075, 14 December 1628, fol. 1 v) [three hours after sunset].

According to Buttigli, the convened viewers were assigned seating based on their noble status; men were segregated from women, except on the ducal balcony.

This was not unprecedented: for example, for the Medici wedding of 1589 "[u]nlike the rest of the hall, here [on the *palco* reserved to the newlyweds and their retinues] men and women sat together; at this symbolic level, royal rank somewhat superseded gender divisions" (Saslow, *The Medici Wedding of 1589*, 151). In Florence in 1589, as at Parma in 1628, the festivities were organized and staged to celebrate a wedding, and the union of the sexes had to be physically and metaphorically placed at the center of the events. It is possible that by the third decade of the seventeenth century this arrangement had become commonplace when celebrating weddings; and that Buttigli underscored it precisely by making reference to it.

The staged entertainment was about to begin. With everybody in place (on and off stage), after the *sinfonia* and the rising of the curtain, it was time for the Prologue to start.

4. The Prologue

Finally, the audience was able to see what the curtain had hidden until then. The innumerable hours of work at the hands of craftsmen and painters produced a remarkable effect, according to Buttigli: "comparve il vacuo del Proscenio riguardevole per la positura del Tempio d'Himeneo nel mezo, e da ambe le parti per l'apparenza di varie prospettive formate da' piani giardini, fontane, colli, vigne, monti, boschi, grotte, dirupi con sue lontananze tanto ben compartite, che ingannandosi l'occhio, la pittura era tenuta per rilievo" (*Descrittione dell'apparato*, 154).[67] Buttigli's text is rife with similar expressions, which simultaneously reinforce the narrator's point of view (identical with the audience's); underscore the marvelous effects produced on the senses of the witnesses; and celebrate the artists involved in the preparations and, indirectly, the court who had hired them.

To complete the illusion, even the sky was reproduced on stage.[68] A three-dimensional piece of machinery stood at center stage: Hymen's temple. Inghirami enjoyed what he saw after the curtain rose: "Quest'ornam[en]to tutto [of the proscenium arch], arricchiva la scena beniss[im]o alluminata et esquisitamente fatta, dove si vidde il tempio d'Imeneo, macchina grande, e molto bene intesa" (Minucci del Rosso, "Le nozze," II, 562; Mediceo del Principato, filza 6075, 14 December 1628, fol. 2 r).[69] Everything in the temple façade alluded to the deity to which the temple was dedicated.[70] Buttigli describes elements and details that the audience could see with difficulty. However, such an abundance of signs invited those convened to understand the set and to relate it to the couple being celebrated.

If the visual details had not given enough hints, Hymen's stage appearance certainly did. His brief introductory passage is laden with deictics and other elements aiming at identifying both the speaker and his privileged audience. The newlyweds are directly addressed as "earthly demi-gods" (Achillini, *Teti e Flora*, vi; Buttigli; *Descrittione dell'apparato*, 157; Solerti, *Musica ballo e drammatica*, 416), the first of many Virgilian references scattered through the *intermezzi*. In this case, it refers to Aeneas's nature as son of Venus, thus establishing a direct link between Rome, its founder, its empire, and the Farnese domain, as well as the newlywed couple proper. After an explicit self-identification, Hymen explains what the entertainment, and particularly the *intermezzi*, was meant to produce: a glorification of the newly married couple. Hymen was going to ascend into heaven so as to ensconce the Medici-Farnese couple securely in the empyrean, where they would forever dwell in glory. These lines also reinforce the ritual in which the audience is participating: having first addressed the guests of honor, the god of marriage could then turn to introducing the spectacle about to take place to the audience at large. A direct address ensued to all the people present in the *sala* (who, interestingly, are designated both as viewers and listeners) and an explanation of what was immediately to follow: two "blessed tongues" singing the well-deserved praise of the royal couple (Achillini, *Teti e Flora*, vi; Buttigli; *Descrittione dell'apparato*, 157; Solerti, *Musica ballo e drammatica*, 416).

As had been anticipated in his words: "Finito il canto d'Himeneo, con soavissimo moto salirono al Cielo le [*sic*] Deità, ed il Tempio" (Buttigli, *Descrittione dell'apparato*, 157),[71] a "scena boscareccia" [pastoral set] became visible, enhanced "alla destra da una fiorita spiaggia, alla sinistra da un braccio di mare" (157).[72] This backdrop was a compromise, presumably dictated by practical concerns, between the one required for *Aminta* and the other necessary to the mythic dialogue that was to take place.[73]

This eclectic split of the scenery reflected and designated the two deities on stage: Tethys and Flora. Inghirami asserts that both sang "con musiche rare e voci esquisite, essendo questa composizione di Monteverdi, e questi li migliori d'Italia" (Minucci del Rosso, "Le nozze," II, 563; Mediceo del Principato, filza 6075, 14 December 1628, fol. 2 r).[74] Buttigli conversely emphasizes the lavish stage set and actions. Throughout the prologue Tethys and Flora sang in counterpoint, the former praising Margherita and the Medici, the latter Odoardo and the Farnese. Structurally, this division furthers the didactic and commemorative intents of the performance, as well as adapts to the fact that these stanzas are set to music. The rest of the prologue alternates Tethys and Flora's praise of Margherita (likened to a pearl, following the name's Latin etymology) and of Odoardo (consistently represented as a lily, the Farnese heraldic symbol), as well as of their families. Only rarely in the first part of their melody did Tethys and Flora address the audience directly. However, their words concerned humanity at large, at least those who were learned enough to recognize the designations of *vita attiva* (exemplified by the curious explorers mentioned in Tethys's lines) and of *vita contemplativa* (the scholars referred to in Flora's passage). The geographical and scientific exploration of the adventurous and the learned attest to the fact that Margherita and Odoardo represent the highest example of beauty and wisdom of the present and of the past. For this reason, they deserve eternal mutual love, as "La famiglia del mare" and "La famiglia de fiori" (Achillini, *Teti e Flora*, xvi–xv; Buttigli; *Descrittione dell'apparato*, 165–66; Solerti, *Musica ballo e drammatica*, 424–25) implored Jove on behalf of the newlyweds towards the end of their songs.

The last lines of the prologue point even more directly at the framed entertainment, in a remarkable display of self-referentiality:

> Ma, poiche sù quest'hora,
> Per far' honore à si felice coppia
> Si drizzano Teatri
> A spettacoli scelti,
> E corrono torrenti
> D'anime pellegrine
> A questo mar di gioie, e di stupori,
> Quinci convien homai
> Portar' altrove, e le parole, e 'l piede. (Achillini, *Teti e Flora*, xv–xvi; Buttigli;
>   *Descrittione dell'apparato*, 166; Solerti, *Musica ballo e drammatica*, 425)[75]

These deictics indicate both the time of the utterance and the events taking place then, while the last line then acts as a transitional device to the first act of A*minta*.

The abundant references to the main actants of the ceremonial, Margherita and Odoardo, and the profusion of deictics pointing to the *hic et nunc* of the performance and embracing both the audience and the singers on stage, render this prologue more akin to the format and type of representation of a masque than to that of modern theater. No hermeneutic effort is required of the audience, since meaning is constantly re-emphasized by stage appearance and in words. Additionally, this text can be represented only once, that is, within the frame of these nuptial ceremonies; any attempt at re-staging it under different circumstances would require an extensive rewriting of the text (and, consequently, modification of the music, of costumes, and of stage machinery).[76]

5. Act I

If the extant documents regarding these events are indicative of the audience's attitudes and reactions, one quickly comes to the conclusion that nobody really cared for the staging of *Aminta* at Parma in 1628. Only very few scattered clues remain, a situation that is all the more remarkable considering Buttigli's long-winded and extremely detailed description of the rest of the staged entertainment.

The question comes almost naturally: why this *décalage*? First, in Inghirami's words, "la Commedia . . . riuscì . . . cognita per essere l'Aminta è per q[ue]sto non fù con attenzione ascoltata" (Minucci del Rosso, "Le nozze," II, 562; Mediceo del Principato, filza 6075, 14 December 1628, fol. 1 r).[77] Inghirami's simple and direct remark points to the fact that the audience thirsted for novelty, the only tool available to organizers to elicit admiration and surprise in early seventeenth-century viewers, who (contrary to our habits as theater-goers) did not suspend their foreknowledge of staged events. It was of course possible, notwithstanding the popularity of Tasso's pastoral, that not all those convened in the Teatro di San Pietro martire had seen it before. However, *Aminta* is clearly part of a long tradition of pastoral plays, dating back to the fifteenth century.[78] Thus it is conceivable that even those who had not seen it before harbored some specific expectations as to the nature and development of its plot and the types of characters involved in it.

Second, *Aminta* might have been chosen precisely for its status as an established text in a genre firmly anchored to the court. Readers will recall that Enzo Bentivoglio wrote to Margherita Aldobrandini some time in September or October 1627, asserting that tragicomedies were nobler spectacles than improvised comedies. Further, the history of the genre indicates the intimate connection with courtly settings and specifically with private stagings. In Marzia Pieri's words, at Ferrara (where staged pastorals were born) "[l]a scelta di comporre una pastorale . . . scaturisce sempre da occasioni immediate di rappresentazione . . . almeno fino ad una certa altezza cronologica, questi spettacoli si organizzano privatamente, di solito a spese dello Studio, in case di semplici cittadini e in palazzi di alcuni membri della famiglia ducale per intrattenimenti pressocché intimi" ("La scena pastorale," *Biblioteca teatrale* 5 [1980]: 3–30, here 6).[79] While the Parma celebrations had extensive public and political relevance, they centered upon an individual event that concerned the Farnese family and was celebrated in the presence of a few choice noblemen and women. Their staging was much more important than the printing of the texts.[80] What Mamczarz has termed *Aminta*'s "climat particulier de rêve" [specific dream-like climate] that should allow to "sublimer la réalité, . . . savourer le bonheur" (*Le Théâtre Farnèse*, 116) [sublimate reality, savor happiness] was perceived as lending an additional aura of nobility to the events, even if it failed to entertain the audience.

Third, Tasso's pastoral was not explicitly linked to the nuptial event lying at the heart of these celebrations. Buttigli, the most thorough writer, might have considered it unworthy of attention (at least in printed form) precisely because it was a play that did not carry specific meanings to be explained to the reading public.

For at least these reasons, we have very few elements with which to reconstruct the first act of *Aminta*. It is doubtful that Tasso's prologue, which should be performed by "Amore in abito pastorale" (Tasso, *Aminta*, 51) [Love dressed as a shepherd] and introducing the setting and the plot, took place, since Achillini's sung prologue served to open the staging. Further, neither Buttigli, nor Inghirami, nor Giordani mentions it. The lack of *Aminta*'s own prologue might have further weakened its impact: those viewers who were not familiar with it would have been left in a state of incertitude as to the events of Act I.

Buttigli is uncharacteristically laconic about the first act; all he writes is "ritornò la Scena boschereccia, e si diede principio dalli Pastori, e ninfe al recitare l'Aminta" (*Descrittione dell'apparato*, 166).[81] Since he had already described the pastoral setting, after the rising of Hymen's temple, all he reports is the presence on stage of shepherds and nymphs. It is noteworthy that he does not distinguish between the persons or the performers and their parts or characters. Inghirami conversely alludes to them in their professional guise: "Uscirono dipoi i Comici a dir i loro versi" (Minucci del Rosso, "Le nozze," II, 563; Mediceo del Principato, filza 6075, 14 December 1628, fol. 3 r) [the actors came our to say their lines]. His choice of the word "Comici" seems to indicate that he identified them as professional performers, though the only extant document on this issue (Margherita Aldobrandini's letter to Barsotti at Piacenza) seems to indicate that amateurs were considered for this staging. Given the lack of records regarding contacts with or payment to any professional troupe, it seems indeed likely that amateurs performed *Aminta*. Perhaps Inghirami projects his Florentine expectations onto the Parma festivities; we know that the *arte* company of the Gelosi was called to Florence and took to the stage for the 1589 wedding (Saslow, *The Medici Wedding of 1589*, 37). At any rate, Giordani's attitude sums up that of the audience at large. His praise is boundless: it was a "spettacolo tanto meraviglioso, che meritava che vi stessero gli anni intieri" (Saviotti, "Feste e spettacoli," 49) [such a marvelous spectacle that it deserved whole years], but he never mentions *Aminta*, only the *intermezzi* and their machinery. Things were bound to get worse for the *comici* that evening, as we shall see.

6. First *Intermezzo*

After the first act of *Aminta*, according to Buttigli, a "ben concertata sinfonia" (*Descrittione dell'apparato*, 166) [well-composed symphony] marked the transition to the following piece. This customary boundary seems particularly appropriate, since it marked the transition from spoken to sung representation. While this musical piece was being played, the scenery for the pastoral disappeared and was replaced by many steep mountains and moving clouds "di vario colore, e di diversa forma" (166) [varied in color and shape]; then a castle appeared.[82] If the convened courtiers were familiar with epic poetry, then a reference might have come to mind: Atlas's castle in the third and fourth *canti* of Ludovico Ariosto's *Orlando Furioso*. Well suited to accompany *Aminta*, since both works were conceived and composed within Ferrara courtly circles, Ariosto's epic poem devotes considerable time to depicting the whereabouts of its episodes. Atlas's castle is no exception: its recurring features are the unusual building material, steel, and its ability to reflect light.[83]

Buttigli claims the contemporaneity of the stage appearance of the castle and of the first of the flying stage machines: a monstrous black horse, with bat-like wings, throwing flames out of its mouth, nostrils, eyes and ears, and carrying on its back two women, one old and haggard, the other young and beautiful (*Descrittione dell'apparato*, 168). Though their physical appearances might have helped the audience's identification, the fact that they were astride a flying horse did not coincide with Ariosto's tale.[84]

The dialogue set to music began immediately. The first part of the *intermezzo* consists of a dialogue between Melissa and Bradamante in which names emerge as though casually, much like at the beginning of a modern play. After they dismounted from the horse,[85] Melissa launched into a prediction of the feats she would accomplish: the defeat of Atlas and the freeing of Ruggiero. This passage constitutes a radical abridgment of Melissa's long speech in *Orlando Furioso*, where it takes up 8 octaves (III, 66–74). Further, a secondary male character of Ariosto's epic poem disappears here altogether: the Moor Brunello, whose magic ring plays an important role (III, 76–77; IV, 2–10). While the simplification of the plot and reduction of the number of bodies on stage is well suited to this already complex *intermezzo*, it also bestows increased importance on the female protagonist, Bradamante, now wholly unaided by men in her lover's quest. Thus this simplification corresponds to the occasion and goals of the Parma staged entertainment: celebrating the power of love and, consequently, women's strength when their beloved is in danger.

In the second part of the *intermezzo* Bradamante issued her challenge to Atlas, who entered astride "un Hippogrifo di color bianco, macchiato di morello in sembiante, e forma di cavallo, dal capo, ale, e zanne in poi, che lo rendevano somigliante all'aquila" (Buttigli, *Descrittione dell'apparato*, 169).[86] After a short fight, Atlas tricked Bradamante into believing that he was going to free all the prisoners by removing the stepping stone to the castle. Yet "col muovere una pietra dalla porta della Rocca, deludendo il Mago Bradamante, sparve il Castello, e seco gli alpestri, e dirupati monti, e restò Ruggiero, con altri Cavaglieri, e Dame nel mezo della scena in deliciosissimo Giardino" (169).[87] Much like Bradamante, the audience and Buttigli's readers were taken in: not by Atlas's magic, but by the craft of the event organizers. Even Inghirami marveled at the sudden change of scene: "Il Castello era beniss[im]o formato, sparì à suo tempo in un punto, e rimase un belliss[im]o Giardino pieno di Cav[alier]i che era cosa vaghissi[m]a fra quei mezzi" (Minucci del Rosso, "Le nozze," II, 563; Mediceo del Principato, filza 6075, 16 December 1628, fol. 2 v).[88] The overall effect was that of a passage from a "horrido" [horrid] place to one "amenissimo" (Buttigli, *Descrittione dell'apparato*, 173) [most agreeable]; technically this was complicated by the fact that the castle walls did not break "per retta linea, ma con varie tortuosità, volarono quei spezzamenti alla destra, e sinistra della scena" (173).[89] The scenery unveiling before the spectator's eyes was such as to allay all his or her fears. This garden, Buttigli tells us, occupied all the width of the *proscenio* and almost all of its depth. That this was an extraordinarily complex staging is confirmed by the frequent mention of a "giardino" in three of Mazzi's letters to Bentivoglio (respectively on 16 and 30 November 1627, and 14 January 1628).

From the visual standpoint, this *hortus conclusus* could not have been more different from Atlas's castle. Further, instead of a relatively difficult identification, here indices were numerous. This luscious garden was the setting for a love dialogue between Ruggiero and Bradamante.[90] Neither the garden nor the conversation between Bradamante and Ruggiero are in the episode's source, *Orlando Furioso*. In Ariosto's epic poem, after Atlas's castle disappeared:

> Le donne e i cavallier si trovâr fuora
> de le superbe stanze alla campagna:
> e furon de lor molte a chi ne dolse;
> che tal franchezza un gran piacer lor tolse. (IV, 39)[91]

Further, Ruggiero immediately recognizes his benefactor and feels gratitude (IV, 42), but his calling is to fight against the Moors. To this effect he escapes on the *ippogrifo* (IV, 44), and Bradamante is left trying to catch up with him once again (IV, 47–48). In the *intermezzo*, instead, soon the references to Ruggiero's imprisonment are metaphorized in a different realm: he was now physically free but more than ever entangled in a "tenace nodo" [tenacious knot] of love and ready to revere another master. At the same time the valiant Bradamante was wounded in her heart and willing to give herself up in marriage. After Ruggiero pronounced the marital vows, as he kissed the bride to seal them (Buttigli, *Descrittione dell'apparato*, 176–77; Pio di Savoia, *Intermedii*, 7–8; Solerti, *Musica ballo e spettacolo*, 434–35), Atlas appeared on stage anew "in aria dentro d'una nuvola, circondato da un cerchio con carateri, e fiori [sic] del cerchio molti spiriti in forma di mostri diversi" (Pio di Savoia, *Intermedii*, 9).[92]

This cloud, which Inghirami calls a "carro . . . nobiliss[im]o" (Minucci del Rosso, "Le nozze," II, 563; Mediceo del Principato, filza 6075, 14 December 1628, fol. 2 v) [most noble piece of machinery] and which constituted the fifth piece of stage machinery of the *intermezzo*, kept changing shape as it moved over the stage.[93] Challenged by Atlas to free herself, Ruggiero, and the other knights and ladies from the enchanted garden, Bradamante replied that she had no desire to leave it since she and Ruggiero both were held there by the chains of love. These chains were a fruit of his illusion: Atlas had retained Ruggiero in that garden to save him from an untimely death (Buttigli, *Descrittione dell'apparato*, 178–79; Pio di Savoia, *Intermedii*, 9–10; Solerti, *Musica ballo e spettacolo*, 435–36).[94] Bradamante's ruse, therefore, had only accomplished the reunion with her beloved, but had not vanquished Atlas's power or his plan to protect Ruggiero's life. With a few words, Atlas made the next change of scenery take place: he commanded his demons to carry the garden elsewhere, where he intended to build

> un palagio . . .
> Sontuoso, magnifico, stupendo. (Buttigli, *Descrittione dell'apparato*, 179; Pio di Savoia, *Intermedii*, 10; Solerti, *Musica ballo e spettacolo*, 436)[95]

At that point, the entire garden rose heavenward, "con tutti quei Cavalieri, e Dame sopra" (Pio di Savoia, *Intermedii*, 10) [carrying all the knights and ladies]. Inghirami was obviously impressed: "fù cosa maravigliosa il moto del giardino innanzi e all'insù e lo svanimento di esso" (Minucci del Rosso, "Le nozze," II, 563; Mediceo del Principato, filza 6075, 14 December 1628, fol. 2 v).[96] Simultaneously, Atlas's cloud started disappearing as well, and as the garden moved upwards, Ruggiero and Bradamante thanked Atlas for their newly-found place of happiness, as the magician invited all the damsels and the knights in the garden to join him in his "grandissimo palagio" [very large palace] where they will "star senza prigion lieti prigioni" [happy prisoners without a prison] — a paradox reinforced by a polyptoton. It is noteworthy that Atlas addressed his invitation to "nobilissimi Baroni" (Buttigli, *Descrittione dell'apparato*, 179–80; Pio di Savoia, *Intermedii*, 10–11; Solerti, *Musica ballo e spettacolo*, 436–37) [most noble barons], implicitly including the noble audience: his luxurious castle becomes, by implication, the Farnese *palazzo* next to which the performance is taking place.

Though the last part of the *intermezzo* plot differs greatly from its source, it is remarkably suited to the occasion then celebrated. Love conquers all; even women are capable of valiant deeds to achieve it, and men know when to give up worldly pursuits to delight in it. This pedagogical goal appears to be a counterpart of that conveyed by *Aminta*'s Act I, where love rules over everything that lives and breathes (213–255), but its young female protagonist, Silvia, has to be pushed to abandon her devotion to Diana, goddess of hunting and chastity (I.i). Conversely, Aminta is a lovelorn young man who does not know how to bring his emotions to fruition, and who could stand being rescued by a strong female character like Bradamante (I.ii).

The closing chorus expresses the desire to follow Atlas, Ruggiero, and Bradamante to the new palace and praises the generosity of their master (hence, by implication, of the most important person ruling over the ceremony, Odoardo himself) and the power of love, "desiderabil prigionia" (214) [desirable captivity]. Everything in this piece refers to the ducal couple's new status: love, marriage, and, ironically, the utter unavailability of choices or escapes. However, the 1628 audience seems to have experienced the show at face value, according to the over-determined staged bodies and properties. Even the critical Inghirami could not find much wrong with this *intermezzo*: "Le scene erano benissimo intese e dipinte, però nel mutarle che ad ogni intermedio si faceva andavano adagio" (Minucci del Rosso, "Le nozze," II, 563; Mediceo del Principato, filza 6075, 14 December 1628, fol. 2 v).[97] The lengthy rehearsing process, so tedious to Monteverdi, Goretti, and Mazzi, had evidently paid off.

7. Second *Intermezzo*

Neither Giordani nor Inghirami have left any trace of *Aminta*'s second act. No only do they not specify how it took place; their letters do not indicate that it did. Buttigli, conversely, writes that it was "recitato" (*Descrittione dell'apparato*, 181), but does not dwell on it at all.[98] However, "una dolcissima harmonia di angeliche voci, e di musicali stromenti" (181)[99] marked the boundary between the play and the *intermezzo*, while the pastoral scenery was replaced.

When the setting finally became visible to the audience, it satisfied even Inghirami: "Nel secondo intermezzo di singolare era la scena, bella sopra modo" (Minucci del Rosso, "Le nozze," II, 563; Mediceo del Principato, filza 6075, 14 December 1628, fol. 2 v).[100] It displayed a city on the left, a pine grove on the right, a plain in the middle, and at the back a harbor filled with tall ships. The seascape elicited Inghirami's criticism: "Il mare mancò e non arrivò all'esquisitezza di Toscana, come ne anche la tempesta" (Minucci del Rosso, "Le nozze," II, 563; Mediceo del Principato, filza 6075, 14 December 1628, fol. 2 v).[101] Upstage, a city was being built:[102] "Cartagine, poco avanti l'arrivo d'Enea, cominciata a fabbricarsi, e però non rappresentante cosa di perfettione" (Buttigli, *Descrittione dell'apparato*, 182).[103] Well-read noblemen and women steeped in classical lore would have probably recognized the stage set, rather faithfully based on *Aeneid* 1.420–40. The singers, Buttigli explains, performed in the area at center stage, which represented "una bella, ed amena pianura" (182) [a beautiful, pleasant plain] and extended all the way to the back, where the harbor was depicted according to the geometrical rules of perspective.[104]

The action started with two men entering the stage "dalla porta di Cartagine" (Pio di Savoia, *Intermedii*, 12) [from Carthage's door] discussing their situation: one is in love with Queen Dido, while the other reminds him of the lofty goal and destiny that the gods had assigned him after the fall of Troy. Their identities emerge as in the first *intermezzo*. While the source of this episode, *Aeneid* 4, underscores Dido's deep love but only obliquely refers to Aeneas's,[105] this *intermezzo* develops the episode so as to stress the power of love, a topic well suited for the occasion the Farnese were celebrating and in ironic contrast with *Aminta*'s Act II. There, the male protagonist had to be pushed to love Silvia by his older companion (I.iii), as Aminta is far too shy and respectful to do so.

With an eye on the message to be conveyed to the audience and another on how best to entertain them, Pio di Savoia made Aeneas's companion ineffective;

divine intervention was required. Thus, "ecco Mercurio attorniato da molte, e varie nubi, discendendo dalla seconda a lui propria sfera comparve sopra un carro tutto argentato" (Buttigli, *Descrittione dell'apparato*, 183),[106] wearing a silver suit of armor and carrying his defining attributes: talaria, caduceus, and winged hat. While the *intermezzo* simplifies the plot with respect to Virgil's epic poem (which includes Jove ordering Mercury to earth to convey his message to Aeneas: 4.219–37), the decoration is much more lavish. Mercury's role is to reproach Aeneas for his lapse from his destiny and into effeminacy (Buttigli, *Descrittione dell'apparato*, 183–84; Pio di Savoia, *Intermedii*, 13; Solerti, *Musica ballo e spettacolo*, 438–39). Aeneas assures him that he would follow "quanto 'l Ciel commanda" (Buttigli, *Descrittione dell'apparato*, 184; Pio di Savoia, *Intermedii*, 13; Solerti, *Musica ballo e spettacolo*, 439) [what the heavens order] — but only after bidding the queen adieu.

From the point of view of the staging, by introducing Aeneas's companion, Achates, Pio di Savoia managed to make manifest the two tendencies harbored in Aeneas: his love for Dido, and the need to follow his destiny. In the *Aeneid* Mercury is depicted as leaving "medio sermone" (4.277) [in the middle of his speech]; Aeneas reacts with guilt at having forgotten his appointed fate (4.279–282), but immediately afterwards reacts with decision and calls his companions to implement the escape plan he has devised (4.283–294). In this *intermezzo*, however, he depends on his companions and divine intervention for everything.

Mercury's disappearance coincided with the entry of Ascanius, Aeneas's son; puzzled by Achates's actions, he had come to ask his father whether he should stay in Carthage with him, or depart with the Trojan fleet (Buttigli, *Descrittione dell'apparato*, 185; Pio di Savoia, *Intermedii*, 15; Solerti, *Musica ballo e spettacolo*, 441). The tone of this episode is profoundly different from the previous one: there are no supernatural or divine elements, and the emphasis is on the relationship between the two characters, in a familiar and everyday manner. Further, the boy served as a living example or reminder to Odoardo, the young duke, of his duties and fate. Aeneas urged Ascanius to leave with the fleet, and the child (the embodiment of another aspect of Aeneas's character in the *Aeneid*) lifted a thankful song to the heavens for bringing him back to action, so that in the future he would be able to cover himself with glory, scorning love (Buttigli, *Descrittione dell'apparato*, 185–86; Pio di Savoia, *Intermedii*, 15–17; Solerti, *Musica ballo e spettacolo*, 441–42). The content of this *aria* might seem ill suited to the occasion of the festivities. However, it expresses a deeper intent that goes beyond the marriage celebration itself: it reinforces the role of the young in carrying on the legacy (variously called "destiny" or "fate" in this aria) of the preceding generations. In other words, it reiterates that the marriage is subordinate to a patriarchal structure firmly in place and in control of the future of the young.

As Ascanius was leaving the stage, another *macchina* entered: Fame (Fama), whose "volar . . . fù cosa mirabile" [flight was admirable] in Inghirami's words

(Minucci del Rosso, "Le nozze," II, 563; Mediceo del Principato, filza 6075, 14 December 1628, fol. 2 v). According to Buttigli, she entered from stage left and, upon reaching the middle, advanced toward the audience to utter her lines (*Descrittione dell'apparato*, 187).[107] She made a profound impression on the audience, as her appearance was striking from a technical standpoint (since the machine's supports were invisible). According to Buttigli, Fama was an old woman dressed "d'habito di sottilissimo velo" (187) [with the thinnest of veils] with feathers, eyes, mouths and ears sewed on it[108] and carrying two trumpets in her hands.

Addressing an unspecified "tu" directly, Fame announced Aeneas's betrayal of Dido, openly siding with the queen (Buttigli, *Descrittione dell'apparato*, 187; Pio di Savoia, *Intermedii*, 17–18; Solerti, *Musica ballo e spettacolo*, 442). This aria obviously targeted the audience to further clarify the plot. As Fame left the stage, Dido entered, calling Aeneas "Amante traditore, marito infido" (Buttigli, *Descrittione dell'apparato*, 188; Pio di Savoia, *Intermedii*, 18; Solerti, *Musica ballo e spettacolo*, 443) [treacherous lover, unfaithful husband]. The following aria alternates accusations and excuses between the two lovers, and ends with Aeneas directing the queen's attention to the harbor, whence the Trojans' ships were departing. Deprived of her revenge on the whole people of Troy, Dido swore to make at least Aeneas pay, as he was devoid of means of escape. As the two exited the stage, Juno entered.[109] The sky to the back of the stage underwent a series of color changes.[110] The emotion conveyed by her entry was further underscored by a "dolentissima sinfonia" (Buttigli, *Descrittione dell'apparato*, 190) [most mournful symphony] played on wind instruments by Juno's train, fourteen nymphs dressed in gold changing to red, while the clouds opened up to make room for the goddess's arrival in a *Gloria*, a piece of stage machinery in the shape of a cloud. Interestingly, her name is never mentioned. Her utterance bemoaned Dido's foreseen fate and manifested her inability to avert it (Buttigli, *Descrittione dell'apparato*, 191; Pio di Savoia, *Intermedii*, 20–21; Solerti, *Musica ballo e spettacolo*, 445).

Soon Dido re-entered the stage, furious and carrying a sword: she explained that she was looking for Aeneas in a homicidal fit (Buttigli, *Descrittione dell'apparato*, 192; Pio di Savoia, *Intermedii*, 21; Solerti, *Musica ballo e spettacolo*, 445).[111] He appeared, too, out of Dido's reach as he was astride the dragon whose intervention had been promised by Mercury. It is highly unlikely that this monster was the same *ippogrifo* that had appeared during the first *intermezzo*: it would have been impossible to modify this piece of machinery so quickly and in the small room available to the crew backstage. Aeneas sat on it while it flew over the stage from left to right "con sì bell'artificio, che spiccato da tutte le parti dalli sostegni, e da gli appoggi pareva vero mostro volante, e non finta machina pendente" (Buttigli, *Descrittione dell'apparato*, 192).[112] The monster continued its flight during the entire exchange between Dido and Aeneas, which is based on recurring lines ("Ferma, ferma la mano," 242, 247; "Cangia, cangia consiglio," 243, 248; and "O core del mio cor, riedi, deh riedi," 255, 264, 275, 286).[113] These lines serve primarily a musical purpose, constituting as many refrains; semantically they contribute to underscoring the inescapability of the situation. On the one hand, Dido is presented as in love with Aeneas; on the other, Aeneas by then had realized that he needed to pay heed to his destiny and to the gods' calling. The second of these refrains ("Cangia, cangia consiglio") is the first (and only) direct citation from Tasso's *Aminta* in all five *intermezzi*. However, in the pastoral this line was frivolous and slightly ironic in meaning (I.i; precisely 96–97, 129, and 256); here, conversely, it acquires a dramatic tone that all but alters its original meaning. Given the scant attention the audience bestowed on the *Aminta* performance, it is indeed possible that they missed this isolated verbal echo. However, the *intermedio* shares the same pedagogical and epideictic goals with Tasso's pastoral, which nevertheless differs from it as it ends on a happy note.

By the end of their exchange, Aeneas asserts his faith in the gods and in their designs, not merely in the power of human love as Dido believed (Buttigli, *Descrittione dell'apparato*, 193; Pio di Savoia, *Intermedii*, 23; Solerti, *Musica ballo e spettacolo*, 447). Alone on stage, she launched into an aria also based on two refrains. The first one, "Tanto t'agitarò, quanto t'amai" recurs four times (300, 306, 312, and, with a small variation, 318)[114] and marks the first part of the tirade, aimed against Aeneas (Buttigli, *Descrittione dell'apparato*, 193–94; Pio di Savoia, *Intermedii*, 23–24; Solerti, *Musica ballo e spettacolo*, 447–48). The second one, "Che più tardo à morire?" is used twice (324 and 330) to refer to Dido herself (Buttigli, *Descrittione dell'apparato*, 194; Pio di Savoia, *Intermedii*, 24–25; Solerti, *Musica ballo e spettacolo*, 448), and twice again (342 and 351)[115] to address her hand and her sword (Buttigli, *Descrittione dell'apparato*, 194–95; Pio di Savoia, *Intermedii*, 25–26; Solerti, *Musica ballo e spettacolo*, 448–49). The last section is filled with the paradoxes typical of love poetry, though reversed: instead of love chaining while setting free, as in the first *intermezzo*, here the sword cures the wound by inflicting another one, more fatal.

The ending of the *intermezzo* follows the Virgilian plot while improving it. Dido could not commit suicide on stage: this would violate Aristotelian *decorum*, and would be inconsistent with the happy occasion for the festivities. Additionally, by removing the queen to the wings, the occasion was at hand for another piece of stage machinery. Iris, the messenger of the gods, arrived on stage to announce Dido's death. Juno moreover had asked her to warn the ladies in the theater of the dangers of love:

> Messaggera non men l'alma Giunone,
> O bellissime Dame, à voi m'invia,
> E vuol che specchio à l'alme vostre sia
> Il caso de la misera Didone. (Buttigli, *Descrittione dell'apparato*, 196; Pio di Savoia, *Intermedii*, 26; Solerti, *Musica ballo e spettacolo*, 449)[116]

This episode thus is presented as a warning for women against the power of unbridled passion, rather than as an example of courageous behavior for men. Like the first *intermezzo*, the conclusion addresses the audience, thus breaking the theatrical frame and making the events just performed on stage relevant to the viewers — a ready-made interpretation to conform with the occasion of the festivities and the goals of their organizers. However, while in the first instance the hint to the audience was implicit, in this occurrence it was made explicit. With each subsequent piece the commemorative and didactic intent becomes progressively more evident.

8. Act III

Buttigli's text consistently gives just one indication about *Aminta*'s acts: they took place. Again for the third one, he writes "recitato il terzo atto" (*Descrittione dell'apparato*, 197) [the third act having been performed], and adds that "concerti musicali di voci angeliche" [musical concerts of angelic voices] enacted the marking devices between *intermezzo* and act. Buttigli also mentions that the pastoral stage set was introduced and then removed very swiftly (197), while music distracted the audience.

Conversely, Inghirami, with his already noted tendency to underscore every mishap, provides a rather colorful description of what happened during the third act. Since his own attention (and, as he remarks, that of the entire audience) wandered from the Tasso's work because it had been recognized, he focused instead on the behavior and reactions of those convened in the temporary theater. Inghirami's letter, therefore, offers a unique testimony because it underscores the receiving end of the spectacle. During Act III, then, the performers (whom he labels "istrioni," a term again implying their professional status) were altogether drowned out by the noise provoked by the people in the boxes and in the *cavea*: "nessuno li sentiva essendovi un sordo rumore che ognuno batteva i piedi e non facevano gran fracasso perché tutti i tavoli erano coperti di tappeti" (Minucci del Rosso, "Le nozze," II, 563; Mediceo del Principato, filza 6075, 14 December 1628, fol. 3 r).[117] Minucci heavily edited his sentence, by adding the parenthetical remark "per iscaldarsi" [to warm up] to explain why the audience were stamping their feet. The text is more ambiguous: perhaps the audience was protesting the quality of the performance and at the same time trying to keep warm in an outdoor theater in the dead of winter. The basic irony of the situation is intact, though: the partial and incomplete canvas cover could not keep the cold air out of the "eternal springtime" setting suggested by the pastoral play. A violently extraneous element found its way into the frame of the performance, breaking it and thus exacerbating the audience's distraction.

Some audience members were luckier than others: "I Principi andarono nella stanzina di sopra accennato [behind the ducal box] à far collazione;" while others decidedly less so: "mentre il Card[inale] Ludovisi stava per bere, fù profumato, con acqua humana da chi stava di sopra."[118] It is not surprising that the audience paid so little attention to the staged pastoral, as something truly amusing was taking place among them. Odoardo and Margherita offered the ladies some refreshments, "ma v'era bisogno di fuoco" [we needed fire].

The actors' performance went almost entirely unnoticed, because of the text that had been entrusted to them, and because of external circumstances.[119] More and more in the course of the evening, everybody's attention became riveted to the *intermezzi*, much to the detriment of the *pastorale*.

9. Third *Intermezzo*

Inghirami's tone becomes downright enthusiastic when he describes the third *intermezzo*: "Finito l'atto, il terzo intermedio ranimò tutti, perché fù mirabiliss[im]o" (Minucci del Rosso, "Le nozze," II, 563; Mediceo del Principato, filza 6075, 14 December 1628, fol. 3 r)[120] for two specific reasons: the stage machinery, and the music. For starters, when the stage set for *Aminta* disappeared, the stage floor was removed as well.[121] To the right, there was a "pianura ornata di verde manto, riccamato di varij fiori," then hills "piene di vigne" and with "molti boschetti di nociuoli, . . . alcune spalliere di fichi, . . . qualche pergolato di melegranate" among which stood "molti casini" of various shapes (Buttigli, *Descrittione dell'apparato*, 197).[122] To the left, the set imitated "campagne ben coltivate" [well cultivated fields] and between the fields "canali di acque correnti" [canals with running water]; on the hills fewer vineyards, and more olive groves and "boschi di castagne" [chestnut tree woods] and "selve di quercie" [oak copses] (198).[123] In the unrelenting quest for marvels, this pastoral stage set is different from the one accompanying *Aminta*. Since Buttigli's description always takes on the audience's physical point of view, the discrepancy between the cultivation on the left and right of the stage set was, at least in his opinion, obvious: the right was to the east and south, the left the west and north. The fiction is complete: for Buttigli the temporary theater was a self-contained, but complete, universe, with its geographical (and metaphorical) points of reference.

The *intermezzo* opened with a technical feat: "sorsero all'improvviso dal fondo del calmeggiante golfo trè Sirene" (198)[124], lifted from under the stage area. The mermaids were "finte ignude" [pretending to be naked] from the waist up; the fact that Buttigli specifies this detail is an apt reminder of the strict moral code enforced after the Council of Trent in sacred as well as lay representations (in painting and sculpture, and on stage).[125] Singing, they identify Venus then entering the stage, floating on a silver shell resembling a triumphal chariot (199). Since the mermaids identified Venus as soon as she entered the stage, the moving shell supporting her and all additional elements were strictly redundant. While she was still coming into full view, according to Buttigli, "nella soprema regione dell'aere cominciò a comparirle incontro una lucida nube" (199)[126] carrying yet another goddess. As the mermaids saw her, they called her "Dea di Delo" (Buttigli, *Descrittione dell'apparato*, 199; Pio di Savoia, *Intermedii*, 27; Solerti, *Musica ballo e spettacolo*, 450) [goddess from Delos]. The plot of this *intermezzo* originates in the mermaids' erroneous assumption that Diana had come to pay her respects to Venus. A rather trite classical cliché found room on stage as appropriate to the celebrations and as fitting to display the technical prowess of the Farnese (or rather, Bentivoglio) staff.

While Diana and Venus were quarreling about their respective merits, "comparve nella soprema parte del Cielo una luminosa, e molto artificiosa nube" (Buttigli, *Descrittione dell'apparato*, 201).[127] This fourth piece of stage machinery seems to have been even more complex, as "quanto più s'avvicinava al mezo della scena, tanto più dilatandosi" (201).[128] This cloud was in the process of opening up, only to reveal another chariot, "tirato da due gran Civette" (201) [drawn by two owls]. This element alone would probably have sufficed to identify the seated goddess as Pallas.[129]

Her words sung to Diana manifested that in the quarrel at hand she sided with her, and that she despised Venus as being "impudica" (Buttigli, *Descrittione dell'apparato*, 202; Pio di Savoia, *Intermedii*, 30; Solerti, *Musica ballo e spettacolo*, 452) [immodest]. To further complicate matters, a fifth *macchina* came into play: "comparve una terza nube alla sinistra della scena" (Buttigli, *Descrittione dell'apparato*, 203)[130] on which a chariot and a god stood. His identity could again be gleaned from various elements in his appearance, his conveyance, and his words.[131] Inghirami indicates that the back of the three flying machines could have been seen, since "Tre nuvoli Diana, Pallade e Marte, e q[ue]sto era belliss[im]o; però quel che di straordinario fu considerato in loro che le nuvole, oltre al moto trasversale, ne havevano un'altro di voltarsi tutte in faccia" (Minucci del Rosso, "Le nozze," II, 563; Mediceo del Principato, filza 6075, 14 December 1628, fol. 3 r).[132] The Florentine envoy underscores a technical feat that he considered extraordinary, novel, and daring.[133]

Beside being the god of war, Mars was also Venus's lover; his sung words made it evident that he had come to defend the goddess of love, since with her "soavi baci / Anche in mezzo à le guerre hò le mie paci" (Buttigli, *Descrittione dell'apparato*, 204; Pio di Savoia, *Intermedii*, 31; Solerti, *Musica ballo e spettacolo*, 453).[134] As the three gods continued their mutual banter, yet another change of stage set took place: "s'aprì alle radici d'una montagna remota là nel mezo della scena, un'horrida voraggine, nel profondo della quale vedevasi la Città di Dite tutta piena di fiamme" (Buttigli, *Descrittione dell'apparato*, 204).[135]

The hoped-for spectacle was more horrifying than precise, since Buttigli acknowledges that the audience could not clearly perceive the stage set due to the distance as well as to the effect of fire (205).[136] The display of the City of Dis was necessary to introduce and identify Pluto, coming on stage with a small retinue and entirely dressed in black and gold.[137] He complained that such quarrel was unfit for heaven, and that it would be equivalent to "portare in Ciel l'Inferno" (Buttigli, *Descrittione dell'apparato*, 206; Pio di Savoia, *Intermedii*, 32; Solerti, *Musica ballo e spettacolo*, 453) [move hell to heaven]. This phrase, a good example of what Jean Rousset in *La Littérature de l'âge baroque en France* called the baroque tendency to depict the world upside down, reinforces the identification of the convened audience, and of the Farnese court at large, with heaven. Aiming to reach peace, Pluto sang that he had come "Non come Pluto, ò dell'Inferno il Dio, / Mà, come frate à Giove, e vostro Zio" (Buttigli, *Descrittione dell'apparato*, 206; Pio di Savoia, *Intermedii*, 33; Solerti, *Musica ballo e spettacolo*, 454).[138] Along with the self-deixis, these two lines establish the tone of the rest of the *intermezzo*, emphasizing family ties over sheer power — not unlike the behavior advisable for the young members of a politically powerful family.

Pallas and Mars having exited the stage, Pluto proposed a challenge to solve the argument pitting Diana against Venus. A beautiful virgin was to be chosen; Venus was to try "di farsela seguace" [to make her into a follower], Diana "Di tenerla lontana / Da lascivi pensieri" (Buttigli, *Descrittione dell'apparato*, 207; Pio di Savoia, *Intermedii*, 34; Solerti, *Musica ballo e spettacolo*, 455) [to keep her away from lustful thoughts]. Immediately a young man entered the stage, a "pastore" [shepherd] according to Buttigli to indicate his humble station in life. He is a hunter, short of breath, tired, and looking for rest after a long day of fruitless pursuit (Buttigli, *Descrittione dell'apparato*, 208–9; Pio di Savoia, *Intermedii*, 36; Solerti, *Musica ballo e spettacolo*, 457). As his identity is not important to plot development, he remains nameless both in Buttigli's description and in Pio di Savoia's text. Diana then chanced upon the same clearing; at first attracted to the handsome youth, she recognized Venus's trick and woke the shepherd up urging him to leave (Buttigli, *Descrittione dell'apparato*, 209–10; Pio di Savoia, *Intermedii*, 36–37; Solerti, *Musica ballo e spettacolo*, 457–58). The young man was puzzled and in love with her and therefore tried to retain her. Unshakable in her resolve, Diana left the stage leaving the young man to adore the very ground on which she had walked. The challenge is concluded: Pallas's chariot re-entered the stage from the left[139] to announce Diana's victory over Venus to the audience and to her city, Athens (Buttigli, *Descrittione dell'apparato*, 211–12; Pio di Savoia, *Intermedii*, 38–40; Solerti, *Musica ballo e spettacolo*, 459–60).

The hunter, expressing his puzzlement in song (Buttigli, *Descrittione dell'apparato*, 212; Pio di Savoia, *Intermedii*, 40–41; Solerti, *Musica ballo e spettacolo*, 460–61), indicates that his character does not partake of the frame of the magical and sacred to which the deities belong. Rather, he belongs to the frame of the everyday. It is the awareness of this *décalage* that makes the hunter's passionate outburst different (in nature, if not in emotion) from those uttered by Aminta in Tasso's pastoral. While the *intermezzo* juxtaposes these two frames, *Aminta* utilizes but one. Yet another reason emerges as to why the convened audience responded favorably to the occasional sung pieces; by representing two separate frames, the *intermezzi* approximate the audience's situation closely, and generate a sense of alienation from the make-believe of Tasso's pastoral.

Before the close of the *intermezzo*, the stage machinery was exploited one last time. Venus reappeared "dal mare" (Buttigli, *Descrittione dell'apparato*, 212) [from the sea], accompanied by "Amore disarmato" (212) [unarmed Love]. Upset over her loss to Diana, Venus reproached Cupid for having failed her (Buttigli, *Descrittione dell'apparato*, 213; Pio di Savoia, *Intermedii*, 41; Solerti, *Musica ballo e spettacolo*, 461). He nevertheless offered a good reason for his failure: a woman had stolen all his charms, so he could not utilize them:

> Questa Sposa reale,
> M'hà tolte tutte l'armi
> Madre non hò più face,
> Essa l'ha ne begli occhi.
> Madre non hò più lacci,
> Essa gli hà ne capelli.
> Madre non hò più strali,
> Poichè rimasta è vota,
> Tutta la mia faretra in quel bel volto.
> E chè far potev'io contro Diana? (Buttigli, *Descrittione dell'apparato*, 213–14;
>   Pio di Savoia, *Intermedii*, 42; Solerti, *Musica ballo e spettacolo*, 461–62)[140]

Although Margherita is not directly mentioned, there was but one royal bride in the temporary theater. The enumeration of her charms follows the traditional Petrarchan representation of the beloved, though shortened; to each feature that Cupid mentioned corresponded one of his lost weapons. Venus yielded to the *status quo*; having lost to Diana she was now ready to give in to a mortal — who, by implication, rises to the status of a goddess.

While the topic of this piece originates from classical mythology, its exploitation is probably more surprising to twenty-first-century readers than to a seventeenth-century audience.[141] Indeed Inghirami, extremely impressed that "in un tempo erano fuori cinque machine," also praises the musical component of this *intermezzo*: "Le musiche quì certam[en]te, furono divine, e non voleva meno à sostenere gli spettatori morti di freddo" (Minucci del Rosso, "Le nozze," II, 563; Mediceo del Principato, filza 6075, 14 December 1628, fol. 3r).[142] He must have been more accustomed to manipulating classical myths to praise a nobleman or woman, than to sitting in the cold for hours on end.

10. Fourth *Intermezzo*

Inghirami evidently thought that he was not the only one in the audience who was uninterested in the acts of *Aminta*. After the end of the third *intermezzo*, he writes, "Uscirono i pastori à dir i lor versi, ma li dissero per se, che niuno li sentì, tutti picchiando e soffiando" (Minucci del Rosso, "Le nozze," II, 563; Mediceo del Principato, filza 6075, 14 December 1628, fol. 3 r).[143] Buttigli again reports two swift set changes, one after the third *intermedio* and the other after the fourth act of the pastoral (*Descrittione dell'apparato*, 215). It is noteworthy that *Aminta*'s acts III, IV, and V differ from the first two as they concentrate on narration rather than action. In order to respect the unity of space, Silvia's and Aminta's dramatic events take place off-stage, and are recounted by Tirsi (III.i), Nerina (III.ii), Silvia (IV.i), and a nameless announcer (IV.ii). The juxtaposition with the *intermezzi* thus becomes progressively more pronounced: not only are their respective performance frames different, but the quality and pace of the action differ as well.

The stage set for the fourth *intermezzo* was a "scena marittima"[144] [sea set] with a palace on stage right, which Buttigli identifies as Neptune's, that was "superbissimo" [quite superb] and endowed with a "bizara facciata" (215) [bizarre façade]. On stage left, a mountain was visible, "grande, alpestre, dirupato, pieno di alberi infruttiferi, ed haveva nel mezo, sul pelo dell'acqua, una profonda caverna" (217).[145] Music again marked the boundary between the pastoral and the *intermezzo*; and after its ending a character emerged from the sea, seated on a throne placed on an island. His provenance as well as his accoutrements showed his identity. If his appearance had not sufficed, his words identified him: "lo mio Regno" [my kingdom], "La Reggia di Nettun" [Neptune's palace], were threatened by the human race's "temerario ingegno" [rash genius]. To repel man's first foray on the high seas, he ordered that "Eolo conturbi il regno di Giunone, / E le fiere del mar chiami Tritone" (Buttigli, *Descrittione dell'apparato*, 217; Pio di Savoia, *Intermedii*, 43–44; Solerti, *Musica ballo e spettacolo*, 463).[146] With that, he dove back in the sea, leaving just one of his followers behind. If the story that was about to unfurl on stage was still unclear to some audience members, the words of the Triton would have unmistakably identified it: it summoned all marine monsters "per combattere / L'umano ardire, e gli Argonauti abbattere" (Buttigli, *Descrittione dell'apparato*, 218; Pio di Savoia, *Intermedii*, 44; Solerti, *Musica ballo e spettacolo*, 463) [to fight human daring, and defeat the Argonauts].

Four creatures emerged: "un Delfino, un'Orca, una Focca, ed una Balena. Erano questi mostri tanto ben formati, e sì bene condotti al naturale, che niente più" (Buttigli, *Descrittione dell'apparato*, 218).[147] Each of these pieces of stage machinery was three-dimensional (though no extant document indicates if a person was inside it, or if a system of pulleys and ropes made its movement possible), monstrous in appearance, and lavishly appointed with gold and silver. They came into view along with Eolus, the god of the winds. From the cave on stage left, "vestito di sottilissimi veli, tutti vergati di lamme d'argento, havendo manto, corona, e scettro regali, e superbi" (218),[148] Eolus's identity must have been obvious to the audience thanks to his attributes. Singing, he ordered the winds to wreak havoc in the sky and the other elements (Buttigli, *Descrittione dell'apparato*, 218; Pio di Savoia, *Intermedii*, 44–45; Solerti, *Musica ballo e spettacolo*, 464), then retreated to his cave.

Were the winds going to enter the stage? Yes, but not embodied by performers: "non si videro già i venti, ma si sentirono bene a soffiare per la scena con tanto empito, che s'innalzarono le onde, si condensarono le nubi, s'oscurò il Cielo, si videro folgori, s'udirono tuoni naturalissimi" (Buttigli, *Descrittione dell'apparato*, 219).[149] In the midst of this whirlwind, another three-dimensional machine entered the stage: the ship of the Argonauts. Buttigli devotes over three pages to describing it in the most minute detail (219–22). It was certainly imposing, at least in its dimensions: according to Buttigli, it was "lungo quasi, quanto s'estendeva la larghezza della scena" (219).[150] All around its sides, bow, and stern, harpies decorated it to protect the seamen from the dangers of the deep. This machine was practicable; the bow offered "luogo competente al nocchiero, e di poter stando reggere il timone, e d'osservare sedendo il bussolo" (220),[151] and a balustrade higher up "forniva il luogo, in cui sedeva il Capitano degli Argonauti" (221).[152] The reason behind the *intermezzo* was reinforced by the presence of the escutcheons of the Farnese and Medici families prominently displayed on stage;[153] it was as if the Argonauts were dedicating their feat to the newlyweds.

Buttigli's description assumes that the Parma audience was well versed in classical mythology and, more specifically, conversant with the story of the Argonauts.[154] It seems that the audience did not have much time to observe the ship; soon, as a direct consequence of the Triton's entreaty and of Eolus's command, a storm rose, and one could:

> vede[re] all'improvviso dal turbine de' venti innalzate montagne di onde sino al Cielo, ed aprirsi voragini di acque sino al fondo del mare; ud[ire] lo stridore delle sarte, il fragor de' remi: il ripercuotersi delle antenne vede[re] il gonfiar delle vele, mentre le nuvole ingombrando l'aere rapivano a gli occhi de gli Argonauti la luce del giorno, e l'oscurità sovragiuntasi pareggiava colle tenebre della notte: mentre intonando i poli, il Cielo per i replicati folgori di quando in quando con minacciosi lumi lampeggiava: mentre in fiamma ogni cosa minacciava morte ai naviganti. (222)[155]

This seems to have been a *tour de force* for the performance organizers, and Buttigli describes it as if it were carried out without a glitch. Inghirami, however, is a little less convinced: "Il quarto intermedio rincorò l'auditorio con la Nave Argonautica e col mare, però à me non parve che la Nave, il mare, e la tempesta, andassero come dovevano" (Minucci del Rosso, "Le nozze," II, 563–64; Mediceo del Principato, filza 6075, 14 December 1628, fol. 3 r–v).[156] The fury of the elements was the first effect riveting the audience's attention, then the sailors' fight against enraged nature and the four monsters. Only one of them has power over nature: Orpheus.[157]

Accompanied by his lyre, Orpheus sang a prayer to the gods "con sovrhumana armonia" (Buttigli, *Descrittione dell'apparato*, 224) [with superhuman harmony]: the Argonauts had taken to the sea not to challenge Neptune, but to accomplish a noble deed (Buttigli, *Descrittione dell'apparato*, 224; Pio di Savoia, *Intermedii*, 47; Solerti, *Musica ballo e spettacolo*, 466). As suddenly as the storm had begun, it ceased, prompting Hercules to express his wonder, followed by a chorus (presumably the entire crew) (Buttigli, *Descrittione dell'apparato*, 225; Pio di Savoia, *Intermedii*, 48; Solerti, *Musica ballo e spettacolo*, 466). To emphasize the events that the audience had just witnessed on stage, Pio di Savoia resorted to a common stratagem: the helmsman enumerates the various natural elements now calm and serene, and each' line is followed by an echo effect (Buttigli, *Descrittione dell'apparato*, 225; Pio di Savoia, *Intermedii*, 48; Solerti, *Musica ballo e spettacolo*, 466–67). As harmony returned on stage, the sun reappeared, in the guise of Apollo.[158] Inghirami was favorably impressed by this piece of stage machinery: "il Carro del sole sì fu macchina degna, come anche la Conchiglia di Nettuno; però le musiche davano lo spirito, e l'anima à tutto" (Minucci del Rosso, "Le nozze," II, 564; Mediceo del Principato, filza 6075, 14 December 1628, fol. 3 v).[159] The appearance of sunrays and the dazzling luminosity of the three-dimensional chariot were indicators of the god's identity, emphasized by his clothes and accoutrements.

Entering from stage left, as soon as he was visible he started singing, rebuking the winds and urging Neptune to hold the sea in check (Buttigli, *Descrittione dell'apparato*, 227; Pio di Savoia, *Intermedii*, 49; Solerti, *Musica ballo e spettacolo*, 467). Addressed directly, Neptune again surfaced from under the stage, this time not on an island, but in a chariot, drawn by seahorses and shaped like a shell resting on wheels formed by golden eels. Neptune expressed his displeasure at the ship's encroaching on his kingdom, but convinced by Apollo he accepted this single intrusion in his realm (Buttigli, *Descrittione dell'apparato*, 228; Pio di Savoia, *Intermedii*, 49–50; Solerti, *Musica ballo e spettacolo*, 468). Apollo predicted that from Etruscan (that is, Tuscan) ports ships bearing "Le'nsegne felicissime Reali" would go forth to help sailors in distress and to fight oriental enemies (Buttigli, *Descrittione dell'apparato*, 229; Pio di Savoia, *Intermedii*, 51; Solerti, *Musica ballo e spettacolo*, 469). Another reference to the Medici is clearly present when Neptune sang about a "Mano Medica" which would come to rescue ships in distress, an obvious pun on "medico / mediceo" [hand of a doctor / of the Medici]. Navigation, then, is ordained by the gods for the everlasting fame of the Tuscan ruling family.

As Apollo and Neptune blessed Argo in its maiden trip to Colchis, the ship started to move (Buttigli, *Descrittione dell'apparato*, 229), while the Argonauts sang to urge the mortals to confide in the gods (Buttigli, *Descrittione dell'apparato*, 229–30; Pio di Savoia, *Intermedii*, 51–52; Solerti, *Musica ballo e spettacolo*, 469–70).

The didactic intent of this *intermedio*, evident in its concluding lines, targets humanity in general, rather than the whole audience (like the second one) or just the newlyweds. Further, the commemorative goal is not directly linked to the identity of the main protagonists of the festivities (as was the case in the third); still, it is political in nature. As the scope of the *intermezzo*'s celebratory intent widened, the glorification of the families involved in the festivities became more obvious; yet the audience was seemingly unaware, awed as they were by the display of virtuoso singing and of dazzling machinery, or perhaps accustomed to such treatment of classical myth for similar occasions.[160]

11. Act V

One last time, after the end of the fourth *intermezzo*, the pastoral set reappeared. Buttigli, as is his custom, provides no indication in addition to the short phrase: "recitato che fù il quinto atto dell'Aminta" (*Descrittione dell'apparato*, 231). Inghirami does not dwell on the last act of Tasso's pastoral, but his wording is interesting: "Al quint'atto, i comici accortisi di non haver udienza l'arrostirono presto, presto" (Minucci del Rosso, "Le nozze," II, 564; Mediceo del Principato, filza 6075, 14 December 1628, fol. 3 v).[161] In his opinion, the performers were by then well aware that the audience had no interest in the pastoral; consequently, they sped through it, whether by saying their lines faster or by omitting some of them we cannot assess.

Such behavior would strike a twenty-first-century audience as bizarre at the very least, because our expectations and behaviors differ widely from those of a seventeenth-century play viewer. Given the circumstances of this specific performance, the latter did not have the opportunity to leave the temporary theater, unless s/he wanted to create a stir and offend the hosts. Furthermore, audience members wanted to be entertained, and the performers responded to this desire, as well as to the practical circumstances that stood in the way of a pleasant evening. Extant documents indicate that the audience was neither entertained nor satisfied with *Aminta*, through no fault of the performers, but rather due to external circumstances (cold weather and insufficient insulation of the theater) and the dazzling nature of the *intermezzi*.

Additionally, the *Aminta* performers might have taken liberties with the text, but brought the run-through to completion. They had either received clear instructions to this effect or they considered the text as a unit to be performed in its entirety. Whether their behavior depended on internal or external constraints, it would be extremely interesting to know whether the ending of Tasso's pastoral was acted on stage in its scripted form. Since the plot of *Aminta* comes to a manifest conclusion, emphasized by a chorus, if the actors performed it more or less the way we read it the contention that the text was perceived as inalterable (especially in its key moments) would be strengthened. Additionally, one could decide the issue whether the performance of the pastoral was completely separated from that of the *intermezzi*, and on the same level of relevance as they, and justify it by the fact that the "main" plot had to come to a conclusion before the entire entertainment ended (which is what happened with each individual *intermezzo*). Unfortunately, the lack of evidence on this point does not allow us to settle it in either direction. What is evident is that the rest of the show could not go on unless the pastoral went on as well.

12. Fifth *Intermezzo*

While the customary "sinfonia" (Buttigli, *Descrittione dell'apparato*, 231) was playing, a new stage set appeared: "una campagna piena di horridi monti, di scoscesi rupi, di balze dirupate, toccanti colla cima il Cielo, e tanti difficili di salita, che facevano spaventevole prospettiva" (231).[162] Then, four lavishly dressed singers entered, each on a piece of stage machinery. Even Inghirami was impressed: "Gli animali sui quali le parti del Mondo vennero, sicome erano ottimam[en]te fabricati, essi caminarono naturalm[en]te" (Minucci del Rosso, "Le nozze," II, 564; Mediceo del Principato, filza 6075, 14 December 1628, fol. 3 v).[163] These pieces of machinery were not simple platforms, but three-dimensional chariots built in the semblance of animals, whose limbs moved to give the illusion that they walked on stage supporting the characters. Two entered from stage left, and two from stage right.

Who were these four young women? Buttigli describes both their costumes and their machinery in detail, but the beginning of the aria makes it clear that identification was in order:

> Fermiamo i passi erranti
> O della Terra Imperatrici Altere.
> Quì l'America e l'Asia,
> E l'Africa, e l'Europa
> Faccian del Mondo il general consiglio. (Buttigli, *Descrittione dell'apparato*,
>   232; Pio di Savoia, *Intermedii*, 53; Solerti, *Musica ballo e spettacolo*, 471)[164]

The plot of this *intermedio* differs from the previous ones inasmuch as it is not the reworking of a classical myth or of a literary episode. More importantly, it is qualitatively different from the others because references to the newlyweds are the very core of the plot. This means that references are direct, not implicit, and surface early on in the plot. Why did the four parts of the world converge on stage? Europa referred to a "generale oltraggio" [general affront], which Asia and Africa explained immediately afterwards: Jove had singled out Florence by filling it with beautiful women; the four parts of the world were, therefore, indignant.[165] America, proud and strong, proposed to take up arms; the rest agreed, including Europa, despite Florence's lying in her domain (Buttigli, *Descrittione dell'apparato*, 232–33; Pio di Savoia, *Intermedii*, 53–55; Solerti, *Musica ballo e spettacolo*, 471–72).[166] As mere mortals, they were powerless against the king of the gods; Europa thus proposed to ask Pluto for help while Africa and America together invoked "il gran signor de la Città di Dite" [the great lord of the city of Dis], then separately, singing two lines apiece, all four prayed him to take heed to their request (Buttigli, *Descrittione dell'apparato*, 233; Pio di Savoia, *Intermedii*, 55; Solerti, *Musica ballo e spettacolo*, 472–73).

Pluto emerged while the four sang together lines filled with deictics that reiterated his identity (Buttigli, *Descrittione dell'apparato*, 233–34; Pio di Savoia, *Intermedii*, 55–56; Solerti, *Musica ballo e spettacolo*, 473). According to Buttigli, the stage set was thoroughly changed, "poiche subito quei sassi spezzandosi mandarono fuori fiamme, ed in un subito nella remota, ed ultima parte della scena s'aprì una gran caverna infuocata, fuori della quale sorse Plutone colle Furie, ed alcune altre deità infernali sopra d'un Carro trionfale" (Buttigli, *Descrittione dell'apparato*, 234).[167] Plenty of visual elements would have helped the audience: the chariot was of "Ebano negrissimo" (234) [the darkest ebony], drawn by Cerberus (the three-headed dog placed at hell's entrance), and decorated by Harpies, witches, and other infernal characters.

From the plot's standpoint, Pluto's aria (Buttigli, *Descrittione dell'apparato*, 234; Pio di Savoia, *Intermedii*, 56; Solerti, *Musica ballo e spettacolo*, 473) is inconsequential; metaphorically, though, the learned audience would have made the association between "il die" [the day] and "l'odiata luce" [hated light] on one hand and Margherita's eyes, according to a well-known *topos* of Petrarchan lyrical poetry. Further, the stage is set for the ultimate triumph of the newlyweds, this time over a god; they themselves were scarcely human, but quasi-divine if not altogether godlike.

Pluto imposed a different solution: matters of love and beauty could only be solved "In singolar duello" [in single combat]. Thus he would call "della mia Corte / . . . un Cavaliero" [a knight from my court], if the four parts of the world were amenable to such a solution. In quick succession, they individually agreed, then together urged Pluto to send this knight to heaven to fight Jove (Buttigli, *Descrittione dell'apparato*, 236; Pio di Savoia, *Intermedii*, 57–58; Solerti, *Musica ballo e spettacolo*, 474–75). The god then ordered:

Parti ò guerrier da l'infernal baratro
Ad esser meta de gli umani sguardi
In questo nobilissimo Teatro. (Buttigli, *Descrittione dell'apparato*, 236; Pio di Savoia, *Intermedii*, 58; Solerti, *Musica ballo e spettacolo*, 475)[168]

This is the very first time in the *intermezzi* that a character acknowledges the fact that these events take place on a stage, and under the gaze of an audience. Furthermore, these lines are a remarkably direct statement of the goal of the impending events: the plot is but an excuse to display the beauty and power of the infernal knight to those convened in the "nobilissimo Teatro." Thus, this utterance chips away at the boundary between stage and audience, players and onlookers, which will before long disappear altogether.

For the duel to take place, the challenge had to be announced to and accepted by Jove. Pluto therefore ordered the Furies to go up to heaven, the gods' seat (Buttigli, *Descrittione dell'apparato*, 236–37; Pio di Savoia, *Intermedii*, 58–59; Solerti, *Musica ballo e spettacolo*, 476). Presumably during this action a mistake occurred that Inghirami reports: "Vi fù errore nel salir le furie al Cielo, che si vide un pezzo della trave, che le conduceva" (Minucci del Rosso, "Le nozze," II, 564; Mediceo del Principato, filza 6075, 14 December 1628, fol. 3 v).[169] By becoming visible to the audience, the beam supporting the Furies broke the illusion of flight and thus damaged the effect of the stage action. Considering the number of set changes and of moving stage machinery, it is surprising that more similar mishaps did not take place. This last *intermezzo* was obviously designed to surpass all the previous ones; indeed, the extant documents indicate that technically challenging actions were taking place in short succession, and Inghirami opens his recollection of this piece with the following: "il quinto et ultimo intermedio fu notabiliss[im]o e lasciò à bocca dolce tutta la gente."[170] After the flight of the Furies, first Pluto, then the four continents (Buttigli, *Descrittione dell'apparato*, 237; Pio di Savoia, *Intermedii*, 59; Solerti, *Musica ballo e spettacolo*, 476) indicated the stage entrance of the infernal knight. If the direct identification had not been enough, the place whence he entered the stage would have made it unambiguous.[171] This stage effect seems to have been spectacular: "La voragine dell'inferno era belliss[im]a e rendeva una lontananza immensa" (Minucci del Rosso, "Le nozze," II, 564; Mediceo del Principato, filza 6075, 14 December 1628, fol. 3 v).[172]

Flames accompanied this stage change, then "si sentì l'annitrir d'un Cavallo" (Buttigli, *Descrittione dell'apparato*, 238) [the whinny of a horse was heard] and a human figure started to emerge from the back of the stage. This stage entrance, which had created so many problems to the festivity organizers, constituted a turning point in the staging, as both Buttigli's and Inghirami's texts make clear. The audience could have identified the newly entered character without any ambiguity, as the plot and the stage effect accompanying him converged; his costume reinforced these two elements, and he was "accompagnato da diversi mostri infernali" (238) [accompanied by several infernal monsters]. Here for the first time the identity of the stage character is not as important as that of the performer, also unmistakable: "uscì il mantenitore della giostra il sig[nor] Cornelio Bentivoglio armato à cavallo belliss[im]a machina" (Minucci del Rosso, "Le nozze," II, 564; Mediceo del Principato, filza 6075, 14 December 1628, fol. 3 v); "l'Illustrissimo Signor Marchese Cornelio Bentivoglio Cavaliero mantenitore, armato di tutte armi, con lancia impugnata, e stocco cinto, . . . sorgendo s'avanzò" (Buttigli, *Descrittione dell'apparato*, 238).[173] As during the *carnevale* festivities at Pesaro in 1574, the tournament at Parma was performed by noblemen of the court, whose identity was recognized by audience members, even those (like Inghirami) who did not belong to the local court. Cornelio Bentivoglio, Enzo's son, had evidently inherited his father's passion for and ability in knightly displays.[174]

Inghirami's reference to the infernal knight's horse as a "belliss[im]a machina" has two concurrent meanings. First, though the horse was not a piece of machinery, it was part of the stage effects designed for the *intermezzo* and therefore almost artificial. Second, it was one element in a highly complex stage set, whose movement must have favorably impressed the audience.[175] This moving platform on which the mounted knight entered the stage could move vertically and horizontally. As the knight advanced, the boundary separating the stage from the viewers was broken: spatially, the knight had descended from the stage, crossed the metaphorical (but until then all important) line of the proscenium, and paced across the area between stage and audience; representationally, he was no longer a character but a nobleman whose identity was clear even under the guise of the Infernal Knight.

The tournament obviously required an opponent; while Cornelio Bentivoglio was reconnoitering the field, another character entered the stage on yet another stage machine: "dal più remoto della Scena videsi venire per linea horizontale Mercurio volante, il quale spicco da tutte le parti della Scena, aggirandosi hora alla destra, hora alla sinistra con tutta la vita, fatta vaga, e riguardevole mostra d'armatura dorata, di talari, caduceo, e capello [*sic*] alato, ricchi d'argento, e di manto riccamato" (238).[176] Mercury was easily recognizable by his traditional attributes, and by the fact that he had already appeared in the second *intermezzo*. Having arrived "alli due terzi della Scena" (238) [two-thirds downstage], he stopped and addressed Pluto and the four continents, still on stage, as well as the audience ("voi che dimorate / Nella Reggia del Giglio" [Buttigli, *Descrittione dell'apparato*, 238; Pio di Savoia, *Intermedii*, 60; Solerti, *Musica ballo e spettacolo*, 477]),[177] and identified himself as "di Giove il messaggiero, e figlio" [messenger and son of Jove]. On the strength of his assignment and of his ruler, he announced that no law commanded that beauty be equitably distributed in the heavens, on earth, or in hell. Jove had therefore ordered that the knightly battle take place. Mercury's aria carried out three separate functions. It identified him directly; it advanced the plot by introducing the knights defending Jove's rule of law; and it underscored the explicit connection between staging and festivities by mentioning the audience convened at Parma, Florence's superiority over other cities and domains, and Margherita's beauty as manifested in her eyes ("Il lume sopr'umano / Che d'un Sole Toscano / Ne raggi lucidissimi risplende" [Buttigli, *Descrittione dell'apparato*, 238–39; Pio di Savoia, *Intermedii*, 60–61; Solerti, *Musica ballo e spettacolo*, 477]).[178]

As Mercury's speech was ending, "Il Cielo s'aprì, con lontananza stupenda, e venne innanzi Giove con un corteggio degli Dei" (Minucci del Rosso, "Le nozze," II, 564; Mediceo del Principato, filza 6075, 14 December 1628, fol. 3 v).[179] Buttigli also specifies that this piece of stage machinery entered from "l'ultimo della scena" (*Descrittione dell'apparato*, 239) [the furthest part of the stage]; he calls this a "maestosa Gloria" (239) [majestic machine], whose size and complexity were remarkable.[180] Jove's appearance was dazzling, and his throne was appropriate for such majesty. More importantly from the staging standpoint, the rest of the "gloria" was impressive: this moving platform supported the weight of approximately seventy people, according to Buttigli, since Jove was flanked by Juno, Mars, Apollo, and Venus on one side, and by Pallas, Diana, Hercules, and Bacchus on the other, plus the choruses.[181]

The size and mass of this platform were not to the detriment of its mobility: "cominciò a moversi dall'ultimo della scena per linea horizontale la Regia Celeste, ed avanzandosi con moto equabile, e slargandosi a poco, a poco, quanto era tutto il vacuo della scena, fermossi al mezo di quella, ed abbassossi ad un terzo dell'altezza" (240).[182] This platform seems to have been made up of various parts that could open up and move horizontally (toward the proscenium) as well as vertically (from the top of the temporary theater down). Perhaps because this structure was so dazzling and complex, Buttigli refers to some technical details that made such feats possible: irrespective of the position of the piece of stage machinery vis-à-vis the audience, its scaffolding and structure were always hidden and the performers always in full view.[183]

That the audience would pay attention to the arias then being sung is scarcely comprehensible; however, first the four continents together, then Pluto alone briefly belittled Jove and his knight. Finally the irate Jove sang, restraining his anger, so that his knights could undertake to defend his rule (Buttigli, *Descrittione dell'apparato*, 240–41; Pio di Savoia, *Intermedii*, 61–62; Solerti, *Musica ballo e spettacolo*, 477–78). Indeed the last two lines directly addressed these knights, whose stage entrance constituted the last piece of stage machinery of the evening. Inghirami was impressed: "Stupenda fù l'ultima machina dei tre Cav[alie]ri i quali con i Cavalli armati e loro in sella, e con i loro staffieri per tener i cavalli scesero dal Cielo fino in terra" (Minucci del Rosso, "Le nozze," II, 564; Mediceo del Principato, filza 6075, 14 December 1628, fol. 3 v).[184] Interestingly, the Tuscan secretary adopted the stage as his spatial point of reference in this description, since he uses "Cielo" to designate the back of the stage and "terra" to refer to the front of the stage.

Giordani took the same perspective with respect to the back of the stage and the area below it: "vennero dal cielo tre cavalieri sopra cavalli, che fu il condimento ogni cosa e fecero una giostra a campo aperto contro un cavaliere c'era [sic] venuto dall'Inferno ed era mantenitore" (Saviotti, "Feste e spettacoli," 49).[185]

Buttigli devotes over two pages (*Descrittione dell'apparato*, 242–44) to describing this new piece of machinery, which represented a "Città Celeste" [heavenly city]. Again the appearance of this *macchina* is accompanied by a "celeste Sinfonia dal Cielo" (241) [celestial symphony from the heavens] to mark a new event taking place on stage. The knights, richly clad and mounted, stood in the central square of this moving heavenly city. Along with surprise and astonishment, this stage machinery provoked some worry, as Buttigli reports:

> A tale vista restarono, altri ammirati della bellezza dell'ingegnosa machina, altri oppressi da timore, parendo loro, che tali Cavalieri, poggianti sulla nube si trovassero in gran pericolo, se quei bizzarri corsieri fossero saltati da basso, non vedendosi alcuni gran perni di ferro, che cingendo d'ogni intorno i cavalli, impedivano loro il moversi, non che il precipitarsi. (242)[186]

Inghirami relates that, despite the organizers' precautions, a mishap came very close to taking place: "Il cavallo del conte Troilo Sansecondo cominciò à rallegrarsi e fece rimescolare tutta la gente, dubitando nonostante che fosse con forti lacci legato che non facesse qualche burla, ma il suo servitore lo tenne quieto" (Minucci del Rosso, "Le nozze," II, 564; Mediceo del Principato, filza 6075, 14 December 1628, fol. 3 v–r).[187]

This last piece of stage machinery was also capable of moving horizontally and vertically; the mounted knights "col Padrino usciti dalla nube callata sino al piano del campo, havendo ceduto il pavimento della scena, slargandosi a destra, e sinistra, corbettando, e rapettando passeggiarono con gratia il campo, e fatta riverenza alli Serenissimi Sposi, ed a gli altri Prencipi, con abbassar le lancie, conforme al fatto dal Mantenitore, se ne andarono del pari a collocarsi dirimpetto all'Inimico" (Buttigli, *Descrittione dell'apparato*, 242).[188] At that point the knights had taken their places; however, rules had to be agreed upon: "i Padrini, fatta elettione de' Giudici, accertavano i Capitoli, coll'osservanza de' quali s'haveva a combattere, e si facevano altre diligenze, per esseguir felicemente, e gloriosamente l'abbattimento" (242)[189]; and the heavenly characters on Jove's *gloria* sang an aria: they urged their knights on; asked Margherita Aldobrandini to graciously watch the impending duel; begged the bride, groom, and cardinals to do the same; and emphasized the prowess of the knights about to battle (Buttigli, *Descrittione dell'apparato*, 244; Pio di Savoia, *Intermedii*, 62–63; Solerti, *Musica ballo e spettacolo*, 478–79).

The ground master, Rhò, assisted by the two seconds, "Il Sig[nor] Marchese Odoardo Scotti, e il Sig[nor] Cavalier Giulio Baiardi" (Buttigli, *Descrittione dell' apparato*, 244) oversaw the fight, which started with a flourish. Buttigli, knowing that his readers knew how a tournament would proceed, simply writes: "si continuò hora unitamente, hora separatamente, talhora con chiamate, talhora con risposte, conforme a ciò, che richiedeva la rappresentatione del Campo aperto" (244).[190] This military stage action had to follow strict rules, as Inghirami's letter also manifests: "La prima lancia si ruppe dall'uno e dall'altro, il giuoco degli stocchi andò beniss[im]o serrandosi bravam[en]te i cavalli insieme, come anco fecero i due sussequenti, seben con le lance non s'investirono" (Minucci del Rosso, "Le nozze," II, 564; Mediceo del Principato, filza 6075, 14 December 1628, fol. 3 r).[191] The result was also preordained, and the fact that no extant source refers to winners and losers only confirms it.

Buttigli's final assessment is that the tournament took place "con molto honore de' Cavalieri, e sodisfattione de' Spettatori" [with great honor to the knights and satisfaction of the audience] to bring the evening to a close: "fù terminata la Pastorale, ed Heroica festa" (244) [the pastoral and heroic festivity were done]. It is striking that Buttigli, who pays scant attention to *Aminta* in his verbose description, juxtaposes the terms "Pastorale" with "Heroica" to describe the events. Whether it helped set the tone for the evening, or associated the court with an idealized and idealizing genre, the pastoral deserves to be mentioned at the beginning and at the end of Buttigli's description. The phrase serves to underscore the gap between the two types of entertainment: one lavish, set to music, requiring the efforts of countless craftsmen and eliciting the praise of those convened; the other humbler, easier to stage, and performed hurriedly owing to the audience's lack of attention. The juxtaposition could not be starker; yet Buttigli subsumes both aspects of the evening in his positive assessment.

Among those convened at Parma, Enzo Bentivoglio was conspicuously absent. Two days after the *Aminta* performance, a relieved Antonio Goretti wrote to him excitedly:

> Lodato Iddio habbiamo fatto una festa la quale è stata la comedia con l'Intramedii del S[igno]r Do[n] Ascanio la quale è riuscita stupendamente à segno che tutti sono restati gustati e consolati, e li Prencipi con tanta consolazione che niente più, e ne hanno regalati di mandarci a ralegrare del felice successo . . . Il s[igno]r Corneglio si è diportato tanto regiam[en]te e con tanto bel modo e garbo che certo mi creda s[igno]r Ma[estro] che non si poteva vedere la più bella cosa e la più maravigliosa che il veder questo cavaliero, venire à cavalo con la lancia, e venire dal punto della sena, e poi scendere dal cielo una liza con 3 cavaglieri à Cavalo con la lor lanza. (Lavin, "Lettres," 148; idem, *Art and Pageantry*, 542; MS Antonelli 660, 15 December 1628, fol. 1 r–v)[192]

Even though some of the praise should be discounted (Goretti was writing to his direct superior about the latter's son), obviously the Farnese court was satisfied with the evening's events. The failure of *Aminta* to entertain the audience, evident from Inghirami's letter, did not mar the evening as a whole.

Given the focus of the evening, we wonder why *Aminta* was chosen at all. Bentivoglio's opinion that a tragicomedy would bestow a higher degree of nobility refers to the pastoral genre. It is important to underscore that it thematizes idealized (and ideal) circumstances that were central to the Parma wedding celebrations and to the message conveyed to the audience in general and the newlyweds in particular. With respect to *Aminta*, furthermore, the juxtaposition of nature and court lies at the center of the controversial Mopso episode (I.ii). Tasso's very text contemplates the tension between nature and nurture, or court as it should be and court as it might exist. It celebrates love, in keeping with the events being celebrated, by placing the love between two young people at the plot's center. Differently from *Il pastor fido*, *Aminta*'s one-couple plot indirectly underscores the uniqueness of the couple whose wedding lies at the center of the Parma performance. Additionally, through the satyr's monologue (II.i) and the recounted attempted rape (III.i), love is juxtaposed to lust, a message that would reinforce the patriarchal structure at the basis of this dynastic wedding. Despite this, and *Aminta*'s poetic language, various elements prevented Tasso's pastoral from gaining attention and being appreciated on 13 December 1628.

13. Afterwards

Ippolito Calandrini's biography of Odoardo is, of all extant contemporary texts, the most open and the frankest, though not the most detailed. Interestingly, he mentions only the temporary theater built by Guitti and Mazzi for the festivities, and completely overlooks the tournament *Mercurio e Marte*, which inaugurated the Teatro Farnese itself. These are his reasons:

> Io non stò particolarizzando le bellezze formate dal'ingegno dell'Ill[ustrissi]mo et Ecc[ellentissi]mo Sig[no]r Marchese Bentivoglio, et altre superbe rappresentazioni, perché furono dotamente cantate dalle Muse di diversi poeti, molto nelle rime versati, et misteriosamente rapresentate nel famoso coro dal famoso ingegno del sod[det]to Co[nte] Bernardo Morando intitolato gareggiamento d'amore, e Parma acquistò tanto onore in questo solennissimo ricevimento con le sue divozioni à Margherita, quanto facesse mai per altro tempo con la spada, soccorrendo, abbattendo, e superando Reggi, esserciti, e Potenze con generose vittorie. (*L'Heroe d'Italia*, 334–35)[193]

Calandrini's role is not to describe the wedding festivities or to praise their organizers; better writers had already seen to that. However, he must point out that through these spectacles the name of the city of Parma and of its rulers gained honor: more honor, indeed, and more lasting than that gained through military actions.

One could argue that Calandrini, in his official capacity of biographer, could not have written anything less than boundless praise. Nevertheless, two details are worth underlining. First, the excitement and expectation at Parma seems to have been pervasive, as Giordani wrote on 15 December 1628: "Domenica o martedì si farà il Torneo regale di S[ua] A[ltezza], che supererà quanti mai ne sono stati fatti" (Saviotti, "Feste e spettacoli," 49)[194]. After having seen *Aminta* and its *intermezzi*, the Pesaro nobleman expected to be thoroughly amazed by the *pièce de résistance* of the whole event. The excitement and perhaps tension at Parma held sway even over such an outsider as Giordani. Second, though the Farnese were not the first to exploit festivities for political and dynastic advantage, they certainly were not the last. Later in the century, the French court put this lesson to work, and Félibien could explicitly assert with respect to the 1668 Versailles entertainment that:

> Così come non vi è che il Re capace di mettere in piedi in così poco tempo delle grandi armate e di portare a termine delle conquiste con la rapidità che si è vista . . . , allo stesso modo non appartiene che a questo grande Principe il riunire con la medesima rapidità così tanti musicisti, danzatori, strumentisti e tante bellezze così diverse. Un condottiero romano affermava anticamente che il saper bene allestire un piacevole festino per gli amici non qualifica meno un grande uomo del saper organizzare un'armata capace d'intimorire i suoi nemici. (*Le feste di Versailles*, 63–64)[195]

Rhetorically, Félibien's passage is similar to Calandrini's. Both authors want to praise their ruler and neutralize criticism that such lavish spectacles were wasteful. Further, they also wanted to stress the power exerted by the king or duke over human beings as well as nature, as James Yoch writes: through stagings, "the court and the academy showed their control over the stuff of even the grandest romances as well as the simple lives of the peasants."[196] However, in practice the discrepancy could hardly be more remarkable. For the Farnese were not absolute rulers over a large and strong domain as were the Bourbons in France in the 1660s. What politics did not allow, spectacles had to supply.

Notes

[1] This is unfortunately a common occurrence, as Franco Piperno has pointed out: "for the sovereigns who had financed the entertainment, the score, which only a few persons endowed with special skills could read, was of much less importance than descriptions of the performances in letters, diplomatic dispatches, and printed reports (at times with an accompanying engraving depicting the scenery) that told courts near and far of the magnificence and splendor of the spectacle and — by implication — of its sponsor" ("Opera Production," 4). Bianconi agrees with Piperno on this point (*Music in the Seventeenth*

Century, 170–71); nevertheless he asserts that "the complete score of several Italian court operas" were printed at the court's expense and are extant (74). This apparent discrepancy deserves attention on the part of musicologists.

[2] To borrow James Saslow's wording, Buttigli's text "forms part of an established genre of sumptuous festival books, . . . which were published to describe almost all the royal festivals" (*The Medici Wedding of 1589*, 23) in the second half of the sixteenth and during the seventeenth century. He continues: "The majority were published after the fact, serving mainly to fix these transitory events in permanent memory; they were a form of souvenir, to be distributed to those who had been present and, perhaps more importantly, sent abroad for propaganda for the magnificence and sophistication of the sponsoring court" (23–24).

[3] "He had been charged by the Parma elders and city to come up with the *apparato* to welcome Margherita." Minucci del Rosso essentially agrees with Ferrari: "Gio. Batta Magnani architetto, e Marcello Buttigli, letterato piacentino, riceverono dagli Anziani di Parma, l'incarico di preparare e disporre le decorazioni e gli addobbi per l'ingresso solenne della Duchessa": "Le nozze," II, 555 [The architect G. B. Magnani and the Piacenza scholar Marcello Buttigli were charged by the Parma elders to prepare and set up the decorations and ornaments for the Duchess's solemn entry].

[4] "Se frà gli Armigeri qualche novizzo nell'Arte militare notasse per mancamento, che nella Descrittione de' due Campi [the tournament bringing the *Aminta* evening to a close, and the one entitled *Mercurio e Marte* at the Farnese] non si fosse espressa la quantità geometrica de' squadroni, colle misure, e forme del terreno, ne l'aritmetica, non moltiplicandosi i fianchi per le fronti de' medesimi squadroni, e non accusandosi il numero particolare de' Picchieri, Moschettieri, ed Archibuggieri con Scimetrica proportione concertati; in tal caso i provetti risponderebbono per l'Autore, dicendo: Altro è l'Ufficio del Sergente Maggiore, altro lo dell'Historico, il quale descrivendo due Esserciti, coll'istessa quantità di Soldati in varie ordinanze giudiciosamente disposti, allhora si crederà, c'habbia compitamente sodisfatto al debito suo, quando havrà colla sua Descrittione rappresentata in modo la seguita attione, che, chi la vidde, la riconoscerà senza difficoltà per quella, che fù fatta, e chi non la vidde, la intendendo il mestiero delle Armi, conoscerà dalla quantità de' Squadroni, sì dell'uno come dell'altro Campo, quanto à proportione fosse ogni sorte di soldati ben compartita": Buttigli, *Descrittione dell'apparato*, ii [if someone who is a beginning military expert were to notice that the geometry or arithmetic of the squads is not expressed in the description of the tournament, along with the measurement and conditions of the terrain, or the specific numbers of pikemen, swordsmen, and gunmen, the experts would reply on the author's behalf. They would say that a sergeant and a historian play different roles. When the historian describes two armies with the same quantity of soldiers with various specialties well arranged, then everybody believes that he has done his job, as long as he has described the action in such a way that those who saw it can recognize it easily, and those who know only military matters can figure out how the various types of soldiers were arranged on both sides by reading how many squads were there.]

[5] This is exactly the situation described by Tracy Davis when she wrote: "If it were possible to 'score' a theatrical performance the way music is scored, and to account for all the components of stage expression (costume, decor, music, lighting, furnishings, action, words, line, color, intonation, rhythm, etc.), the experience of reading the mise-en-scène could be the same experience as being in the audience. But this is not possible, for however

complete the score is, it is only a partial rendering of a real and immediate experience": "Questions for a Feminist Methodology in Theatre History," in *Interpreting the Theatrical Past*, ed. Postelwait and McConachie, 59–81, here 73. André Félibien, describing the celebrations at Versailles in July 1668, avows as much: he felt "un sentimento di sorpresa che si può conoscere solamente provandolo": *Le feste di Versailles*, ed. A. Ausoni (Rome: Salerno, 1997), 60 [a feeling of surprise that we can only know if we feel it].

[6] "Historians will understand that he put together historical and poetical truth in a moral mixture. They will testify that when he deals with things from antiquity he does not add anything personal. They will be assured that when he describes things from our times he does not depart at all from what he saw or from the descriptions he received."

[7] That the concept of imitation is of overwhelming importance in this text is underscored by other instances in this same introduction to the readers. Linguistically, "Tolereranno i Signori Toscani di buona voglia, ch'un Vecchio Lombardo, descrivendo con semplice frase Italiana cose grandi, fatte in honore d'una Gran Principessa di Toscana, non si sia ristretto all'osservanza delle regole della Sapientissima Academia della Crusca; poiche chiaramente conosceranno, che non già ch'egli non habbia in pregio le cose loro, ma si bene per evitar quel biasimo, che meritamente ridonda ne' vecchi, i quali per parer giovini si tingono la barba, egli non si è partito dal suo ordinario methodo di scrivere" (ii) [Tuscan gentlemen will willingly accept that an old Lombard describing the great things done in honor of a Tuscan princess with simple words does not follow the rules of the most wise Academia della Crusca. They will recognize that, far from not praising their language, he wants to avoid the blame that we bestow on old men when they dye their beards to look younger. Similarly, he did not change his customary way of writing].

Vis-à-vis the authorities of the past in the artistic field, also: "Non lo riprenderanno tam poco gli Antiquarij, poiche s'accorgeranno, che s'egli trasgredì le Leggi dell'Antichità, ornando i rovesci de gli Archi, a tanto fare fù necessitato, e dalla coppia de gli Heroi, e dalla maestà de i luoghi, i quali richiedevano, che s'ornassero non meno i rovescij, che i diritti": *Descrittione dell'apparato*, iii [Antiquarians will not scold him, as they will realize that if he did not follow the rules of Antiquity, he was made to act thus by the two heroes and the majestic quality of the place that required that both front and back be decorated].

It is obvious that any transgression from the rule needs to be justified. In the first passage, the excuse is certainly weaker than in the second, where the authority of the noble couple and the place itself simply "required" (i.e., imposed) some infringements on the rules.

[8] "Those who were in attendance will not be disappointed if this description will appear at times profuse and at times insufficient to them. They cannot be more certain of what they see in darkness and light than someone who observed them before, during, and after the fact. If those in charge of bringing the show to life missed something, those who had fully devised them should not be blamed."

[9] The author of *Il corago* for example mentions a mishap whose presence would simply be inconceivable in Buttigli's text: "è grande sconvenevolezza il vedere un uomo andare nel mezzo a manovrare una macchina come seguì nelle nozze del serenissimo di Parma": Fabbri and Pompilio, eds., *Il corago*, 125 [it is highly improper for a man to go to the middle of the stage to move a piece of stage machinery as it happened during the wedding [celebration] of the duke of Parma].

¹⁰ It is worthwhile pointing out the difference between Buttigli's *Descrittione* and scholarly studies of performance spaces. According to Gay McAuley, the latter "are . . . concerned with the building as aesthetic object, rather than with its function in a complex social process": *Space in Performance*, 9. Buttigli's text, conversely, always emphasizes some socio-political elements, but it is highly selective: he stresses the "official," courtly aspects, to the detriment of those linked with the performers and musicians.

¹¹ Synopses of the Florence wedding festivities are in A. Solerti, *Musica ballo e drammatica alla corte dei medicea* (Firenze: n. p., 1905), 189–93; Reiner, "Preparations in Parma," 294 and 294 n. 91; and Nagler, *Theatre Festivals of the Medici*, 139–42.

¹² "Il passaggio che farà per questi miei Stati il sig[no]r Duca di Parma con la Ser[enissi]ma sua sposa mi fà con la mia solita confidenza ricorrere a i favori di V[ostra] A[ltezza]. La supplico con ogni efficacia maggiore ad accomodarmi di quella maggiore quantità d'Argenti che potrà, assicurandola che io gliene sentirò sing[olarissi]ma obbligazione, e che passata l'occasione di valermene glieli rimanderò senz'alcuna interposizione di tempo. Non fastidirei V[ostra] A[ltezza] se il bisogno non mi necessitasse; oltre ch'io non posso darle argomenti maggiori del mio ardent[issi]mo desiderio di servirla che la fiducia con che mi meno a pregarla nell'occorrenze mie. Guardi Dio lunghiss[i]mo tempo la persona di V[ostra] A[ltezza] alla quale bacio perfino affet[ionatament]e le mani. Di Modana il 9 Agosto 1628": Ducato d'Urbino, classe I divisione G filza CCXLII carta 1133 r [I am asking your highness for a favor due to the fact that the Parma duke and his bride will soon pass through here. I beg you as well as I can to lend me as many silver goods as you can. I will be indebted to you and I will return everything promptly. I would not bother your highness if I did not have a tremendous need. I can assure you that it is my desire to be of trusted service to you that makes me ask. May God bless your highness as I kiss your hand. From Modena on 9 August 1628].

¹³ "2 October 1628. Duke Odoardo left for Florence with many knights to marry Margherita, daughter and sister to Grand Dukes. On 14 October a dispatch carrier brought news of the wedding: a salvo was fired, bells rang, and fireworks went off. On 24 October the Duke arrived back incognito and went to stay at his uncle the Cardinal's, where his mother and many others visited him. 6 December 1628. At midday the bride arrived in Parma; horrible weather (she died on 7 February 1679, and was buried in the Church of the Teresiane). On 9 December at around 7P.M. we had the grand entry with many lights. She came in from S. Michele's door to the square to the cathedral to the palace."

¹⁴ This date is confirmed in a document at Archivio di Stato, Parma: Casa e corte farnesiane, serie II busta 28 fascicolo 5.

¹⁵ A succinct description of the newlyweds' trip from Florence to Parma is in Minucci del Rosso, "Le nozze," specifically I, 559–60 and II, 550–54.

¹⁶ "Since we have arrived in Parma the weather has been foul: it keeps raining and snowing and we cannot go out. The [new] duchess has arrived but since she cannot make her entry she has come as a private citizen. She was supposed to make her entry at night, by the light of many torches that were specially built and that will not be used as the entry will now take place during the day. The accompanying chariots, ladies and gentlemen with their numerous and lavish liveries will not be shown. Imagine also how much the triumphal arches and a big building in the shape of a rich palace a quarter mile outside town must have suffered in this weather. They spent over sixteen thousand *scudi* on it and it has four apartments, halls, balconies, and galleries, all painted and lavishly appointed."

[17] Archivio di Stato, Modena: Cancelleria ducale, ambasciatori Parma busta 5.

[18] "The duchess bride made her entry into Parma on the 9th of this month. She came at night, with six hundred torches shedding light. A large number of ladies met her, who were so lavishly dressed and with some many jewels that it was marvelous. They ate at a wooden building. Then we had a tremendous volley, a meeting of gentlemen with the richest liveries, three horse groups, and a litter embroidered with silver brocade carrying the duchess. She was wearing a hat with a white plume, dress and overcoat of white fabric, no crown or ornamental headdress on her head. The bishop and clergy went to meet her at the door and preceded her in procession to the cathedral. It was pitiful to see the poor bishop walking in the mud (that night abundant); it was raining and fine snow was melting. Six gentlemen wearing white liveries, cut-to-measure hoses, and white overcoats carried the canopy; when they brought it back to his highness they received 500 *doble* as a gift. The groom's mother and his sisters went to meet her at the foot of the stairs."

[19] Archivio di Stato, Parma: Casa e corte farnesiane, serie II busta 28 fascicolo 5.

[20] Archivio di Stato, Parma: Casa e corte farnesiane, serie II busta 28 fascicolo 5.

[21] "Very many foreigners have come and we are all disgusted by this abominable weather which stands in the way of so much fun. There are many unknown little princes and the whole city is filled with them."

[22] A letter by Goretti to Caterina Martinengo Bentivoglio dated 12 December shows that at least one important set of guests left before the festivities: "la morte del S[igno]r Duca di Modena ha fatto partire di quei Principi che era venuti a vedere queste feste": Fabris, *Mecenati e musici*, 434 [the Duke of Modena's death provoked the departure of some of the princes who had come to see these festivities].

[23] I have checked the manuscript of Inghirami's letter at Archivio di Stato, Firenze (Mediceo del Principato, filza 6075) against the printed version. Minucci's transcription is rather free, perhaps because Inghirami's text is often elliptical and grammatically imprecise, though always fully intelligible. Here, too, when discrepancies were detected, I have followed the manuscript.

[24] "The dancing festivities were interspersed with the staging of the pastoral titled *Aminta*, a great poem by Torquato Tasso, accompanied by the *intermedi* by Ascanio Pio and a prologue by Achillini. It took place on the night of the Wednesday after the duchess's entry in the first courtyard of the new palace."

[25] Solerti and Lanza, in "Il teatro ferrarese nella seconda metà del secolo XVI," cite a passage from a letter dated 22 February 1578, written by the Medici *corrispondente* at the Este court Bernardo Canigiani, where he asserts that "Si recitò il Lunedì sera la Commedia rincrescevole e sazievole straordinariamente, che durò senza intermedi aparenti 7 ore" (170) [on Monday night an exceedingly stuffy and boring comedy took place; it lasted seven hours without *intermezzi*]. Although Canigiani aimed at impressing on his addressee the awkwardness and platitude of this unmentioned *commedia*, it was evidently possible that a single performance lasted seven hours — all the more so in the case at hand, where the text of *Aminta* was accompanied by five *intermezzi*. The anonymous writer of the treatise *Il corago* agrees: "una azione piena e compita sì come non deve durar meno di tre ore, così non deve ecceder di molto le cinque, se bene alcuni pensano che se l'azione è ripiena d'altro che di recitamento possi arrivare fino alle sette": Fabbri and Pompilio, eds., *Il corago*, 25 [a full, complete staging should last no less than three hours and no more than five, though some believe that if a staging contains more than play acting then it could last up to seven].

²⁶ Nor was this usage rare: in Angelo Ingegneri's treatise of 1598 "teatro" is clearly labeled as "il luoco per gli spettatori": *Della poesia rappresentativa*, in *Lo spettacolo dall'Umanesimo al Manierismo*, ed. F. Marotti (Milan: Feltrinelli, 1974), 271–308, here 299 [place for the audience].

²⁷ "The place of the staging was such a large courtyard that half of it was not taken up. In the other half you saw the stage, the space for the tournament, and the wooden area for the audience, where people fit comfortably, though they were many."

²⁸ "The area for the audience was not circular. It rose from the ground with thirty steps and reached high. It was built of large beams and well-fitted planks. Above it there ran two orders of boxes raised by imitation mixed-style columns with gilt bronze capitals and balustrades. All this, along with the people in attendance, made the place beautiful in a noble manner."

²⁹ While Guitti and Mazzi solved the problem of preserving the audience's lines of vision by elevating the steps, Inghirami does not remark on the difference between this solution and the Florentine one, which was to slope the floor towards the stage (in 1589, by "about 4 feet" according to Saslow [*The Medici Wedding of 1589*, 79]). Perhaps the 1589 innovation had not found wide application in the seventeenth century; or perhaps Inghirami was not accustomed to considering the line of vision from the floor, given his position at court.

³⁰ "Haveva l'Architetto preso la metà del cortile, detto di San Pietro Martire, da Tramontana a Mezzogiorno, verso quella parte collocando il Theatro, e verso quella il Proscenio, e Scena, e lasciando frà l'una, e l'altra distanza di braccia 18": Buttigli, *Descrittione dell'apparato*, 148 [architects had taken over half of the San Pietro martire courtyard; they placed the area for the audience to the south and the proscenium and stage to the north. Between them lay a distance of 18 *braccia*]. Mamczarz (*Le Théâtre Farnèse*, 77 n. 4) has persuasively argued that Buttigli referred to "braccia di Parma" throughout his description. Each one was about 55 centimeters or 21 ½ inches long.

³¹ "Il Theatro, cominciando dalli pilastri della loggia verso mezogiorno, e stendendosi col destro, e sinistro corno vero Tramontana, occupava in larghezza braccia 48 in lunghezza comprendendo i gradi, e li due ordini di loggie sopraeretto a' gradi da Levante a Ponente tirava braccia 54. Altretanta lunghezza haveva il Proscenio, il quale occupava, colla sua profondità, quanto tirava la facciata della Chiesa di S. Pietro Martire, cioè braccia 48. Il Theatro nel vano de' gradi era largo da un corno all'altro braccia 42, e profondo sino al verone de' prencipi braccia 18. Girava il Theatro in sembiante di mez'ovato esagono, e fondava sopra un basamento, alto braccia trè, sul quale cominciando i primi gradi, s'elevavano braccia dieci, e ciaschedun grado haveva un braccio d'alzato, ed altretanto di larghezza. Non era il vacuo di mezzo libero, come nel Theatro superiore, che si descriverà con occasione del Torneo; ma la metà del concavo di quello era libera, l'altra metà era ripiena di gradi, i quali tirati per linea retta da un corno all'altro, davano luogo a non poco numero di Spettatori": Buttigli, *Descrittione dell'apparato*, 148 [the area for the audience was 48 *braccia* wide from the balcony pillars to the other end, to the south. It was 54 *braccia* long, including the steps and the two rows of boxes above them, measured from east to west. The stage was as long and 48 *braccia* deep, that is, as deep as the façade of the San Pietro martire church. Where the steps were, the area for the audience was 42 *braccia* wide from one end to the other, and 18 deep to the prince's balcony. It was shaped like a six-sided half egg and was built on a 3-*braccio* base. The steps were 10 *braccia* high and each step was one *braccio*

high and as wide. The space in between was not empty (as in the theater above, which I will describe with the tournament); half of it was empty, the other taken up by steps that were in a straight line from end to end and allowed not a few to be in attendance."

Elena Povoledo describes a typical tournament setting in the following manner: "Si trattava generalmente di un vasto anfiteatro provvisorio all'aperto, con pianta ovata o poligonale, e più raramente rettangolare. Le assise erano risolte con ampie gradinate a cavea, oppure venivano organizzate verticalmente": "Torneo," 997 [generally it consisted of a large open-air temporary amphitheater, oval or polygonal, or more rarely rectangular. Seats were on large pit-like steps or arranged vertically]. Both the temporary and the Farnese theaters were essentially compromises on the basis of the needs of the tournament and of staged performances.

[32] "In the middle of the steps a balcony stood out; it was six *braccia* wide and 12 long, and it accommodated a six-*braccio* half-egg-shaped area that was set aside for the princes."

[33] "In the middle there was a spacious floor, in the middle of which the seats for the cardinal, princes and ladies was built. Then it was covered with planks and upholstered with thin gold cloth. The ladies were sitting on both sides, while the Tuscan gentlemen sat on the left. Behind the princes' seats a little room was built above which sat many who enjoyed the perspective in a straight line."

[34] "That balcony was open on the sides. Its only ornament were two square columns that met with those we have already described and that were four and a half *braccia* apart. They were linked to the balustrade and held up the running cornice. The empty spaces between columns made it easy for the princes to see and to be seen."

[35] Readers will recall that a similar remark appeared in Almerici's letter regarding the tournament at Pesaro in 1574. Starn and Partridge point out that the importance of the audience's gaze, particularly of a privileged member, can be linked to Baldassar Castiglione's *Cortigiano* and was exploited both in Mantegna's *Camera picta* at Mantua (1465–1474) (*Arts of Power*, 120) and in the Florentine festivities for Giovanna d'Austria's entry into Florence in 1565 (181). A similar development had been under way at the British court since 1605, when Inigo Jones devised the setting for his first work there: *The Masque of Blackness*. In Stephen Orgel's words, "Jones's theater transformed its audience into a living and visible emblem of the aristocratic hierarchy: the closer one sat to the King, the 'better' one's place was, and only the King's seat was perfect": "The Poetics of Spectacle," *New Literary History* 2 [1971]: 367–89, here 378.

[36] "People no longer watch themselves in festivities, but their rulers; cyclical festivities disappear and novel, ever-changing inventions replace them": V. Valeri, "Festa," in *Enciclopedia*, ed. R. Romano, 16 vols. (Torino: Einaudi, 1977–1989), 6: 87–99, here 94.

[37] In this respect José Antonio Maravall's analysis of Spanish baroque theater falls woefully short of its mark. First, he naïvely compares the courtly manipulation of the stage in the sixteenth century with the one during the Enlightenment, and differentiates them according to their respective goals: "Anche il XVIII secolo è spettatore di un teatro altamente contrassegnato dalla preoccupazione dirigista. Ma qui si tratta — salvo alcuni retaggi del Barocco che si trascineranno fino a Settecento inoltrato — di un dirigismo in certo qual modo di segno opposto: un dirigismo *riformatore*, che reclama partecipazione per compiere l'impresa di educare la gente in vista di un futuro modello di vita più raccomandabile, un dirigismo istruttivo e stimolante": *Teatro e letteratura nella Spagna barocca,*

(Bologna: Il Mulino, 1995), 23; emphasis in original [The 18th century, too, had theater marked by high dirigist desires. Here, however (other than for some baroque remains that drag on to the 18th century), we have a *dirigisme* of the opposite political mark: it is a *reforming*, educational, stimulating one that calls for people's participation to educate them, to point them to a future, more commendable way of life].

Secondly, and for my argument more importantly, he opposes two kinds of festivities, one in which the audience participates, the other in which it observes: "Ritengo fondato chiamare la festa innestata sulla mentalità barocca *festa contemplativa*. È proprio questo infatti l'aspetto che la differenzia dalla *festa partecipativa*, nella quale tutto è predisposto per coloro che vi intervengono" (36; emphases in original) [I believe it justified to call the festivities of the baroque frame of mind *contemplative*. This is what makes them different from *participatory* ones, where all is set for those who participate in them]. In baroque festivities, the audience "guarda, prova stupore, paura, ma rimane fermo al suo posto. Non facendo parte del ristretto numero di coloro che si occupano della riuscita dello spettacolo, il popolo non illustre è costretto a un atteggiamento di assoluta passività" (37) [look, are astonished and afraid, but stay in their places. Since they do not belong to the small number of those who are concerned with the festivity outcome, non-noble people are forced into absolute passivity]. Maravall equates participation with physical movement, and discounts the possibility of emotional involvement (38). Conversely, in Western theater audience members are usually physically still, yet "the live presence of both performers and spectators creates complex flows of energy between both groups": McAuley, *Space in Performance*, 247. Further, ceremonials, in Goffman's words, "often provide for a clear division between professional officiators, who work at this sort of thing and can expect to perform it many times, and the officiated, who have the right and the duty to *participate* a few times at most" (*Frame analysis*, 58; emphasis added). For example, Arizona's Yaqui dances, according to Schechner, "do not have an independent life: they are related to the audience that hears them, the spectators who see them. The force of the performance is in the very specific relationship between performers and those-for-whom-the-performance-exists": R. Schechner, *Between Theater and Anthropology* (Philadelphia: University of Pennsylvania Press, 1985), 5–6. Specifically for the period at hand Guarino writes about Renaissance Venice that "[a]ssistere a una cerimonia civica, o allo spettacolo che ambisce ad assumerne o imitarne i valori e la sensibilità, è un'esperienza attiva, in cui si riconosce l'efficacia emotiva e simbolica dell'azione rappresentativa": R. Guarino, *Teatro e mutamenti*, 292 [being in attendance at a civic ceremony or at a spectacle that wants to take on or imitate its values is an active experience, recognizing the emotional and symbolic effectiveness of the representational act]. Further, Cesare Segre, in a semiotic analysis of renaissance theater, has asserted that "[a]lmeno come testimone, lo spettatore si trova entro il sistema modellizzante" of the stage: "Il teatro italiano del Rinascimento e la semiotica," in *Il teatro italiano del Rinascimento*, ed. Lorch, 389–401, here 395 [audience members are inside the model system at least as witnesses]. From a more practical standpoint, Saslow has brilliantly shown how the number of those who were concerned with the success of the 1589 Florentine staged events was far from small (*The Medici Wedding of 1589*, 142, 146). In the case at hand, the Parma festivities had relevance for the nobility and commoners alike, as attested in the archival sources referring to various monetary and in-kind contributions from all the Farnese subjects. Indeed, as Ruffini points out, at times spectators did not have a choice, since a frame was cast around them: "Che gli spettatori non siano 'coloro che guardano' ma una componente della festa è implicito nel fatto che essi sono dentro la cornice": *Teatri prima del teatro*, 19 [audience members are not "those who look on" but a component of the festivities, as is implicit in the fact that they are within the frame]. With respect specifically to court spectacles set to music, Piperno adds: "[o]ften, the prime function of the spectators of court opera was as an integral part of the ceremony, for which they provided a frame and an ornamental complement": "Opera Production," 6.

[38] "What is anticipated and projected overpowers what is actually perceived. This is a consequence of the absence of a true communication process, as the show's producers deliberately exploit one-sided communication to maximize the stimulus to the audience's projections": V. Valeri, "Rito," in *Enciclopedia*, ed. Romano, 12:210–43, here 229.

[39] "Individuals want in this dream to eliminate differences so that they can identify with the imagined ideal of a utopian, dramatized person": A. Fontana, "La scena," in *Storia d'Italia. I caratteri originari*, ed. R. Romani and C. Vivanti (Torino: Einaudi, 1972), 791–866, here 841.

[40] "In every ritual situation, communication among 'real' performers takes place in reference to an imaginary 'performer' whose role is to sanction and to shape that communication specifically": V. Valeri, "Cerimoniale," in *Enciclopedia*, ed. Romano, 2:955–67, here 959.

[41] "According to my calculations these boxes will take over 3500 people. Your excellence might think it too little, but the theater upstairs accommodates only 2400."

[42] "Cifra senz'altro esagerata" [undoubtedly an inflated number] according to Gambara ("Teatri minori," 206); "ce qui est une exagération grossière" [a glaring exaggeration] according to Lavin ("Lettres," 110 n. 23); "une grosse exagération" [a big exaggeration] in Mamczarz's opinion (*Le Théâtre Farnèse*, 113).

[43] "Entravasi nel descritto Theatro per due porte, collocate l'una dirimpetto all'altra, ad oriente, ed occidente, in quello spatio, che restava frà il Theatro, ed il Proscenio": Buttigli, *Descrittione dell'apparato*, 150 [one entered the theater through two doors, one to the east facing the other to the west, placed in the space between the stage and the pit], much like those still extant in the Teatro Farnese itself.

[44] A cornice ran "on top of the empty part of the proscenium. In the middle it was adorned with the carved arms of the newlyweds with four garlands of fruit and flowers and six cascades of trophies that produced a handsome view under the architrave."

[45] M. Carlson, *Places of Performance* (Ithaca: Cornell University Press, 1989), 178.

[46] "As soon as you define something, you are framing it. . . . I think theater is a set of perceptual transformations and elaborations on behavior; it is where we become aware of our behavior. Theater is also interactive": R. Schechner, "Behavior, Performance, and Performance Space," *Perspecta* 26 (1990): 97–102, here 97.

[47] On the social and cultural import of the frame for courtly stagings, please refer to the discussion in chapter 2. That Bentivoglio understood the importance of a frame around the proscenium emerges in an example cited in Southorn's study: in 1610, he placed a tournament "onstage, and through the central opening of the Corinthian *scaenae frons* (a vestige of the 'academic' theaters) decorated, on this occasion, with fictive reliefs of other jousts organised by Enzo": *Power and Display*, 81. In 1618, the Intrepidi theater proscenium arch (built in Ferrara by Aleotti and under Bentivoglio's supervision) was decorated

with two escutcheons (Cavicchi, "Immagini" 82, plate 26). His example proved lasting: in 1631, for *carnevale* entertainment, "the proscenium arch designed by Francesco Guitti complimented . . . the [papal] Legate Sacchetti, whose *stemma* was seen here to hold firm in a world falling into ruin": Southorn, *Power and Display*, 134. Interestingly, the same feature first appeared in France in a courtly setting in 1641, specifically, "the handsomely ornate *salle* in Richelieu's Palais Cardinal": W. L. Wiley, "The Hotel de Bourgogne," *Studies in Philology* 70 (1973): 1–109, here 94. Its proscenium arch had "Richelieu's arms lavishly embossed on the center." Later on, this feature occurred twice at Versailles, according to Félibien: in 1668, the stage on which the comedy took place was crowned by "una grande cornice . . . al centro della quale si vedevano le insegne del Re su uno stemma dorato accompagnato da trofei": *Le feste di Versailles*, 30 [in the middle of the great cornice you saw the king's arms on a golden escutcheon flanked by trophies]. In 1674, the area in which Molière's *Le Malade imaginaire* took place was topped by "un frontone, il cui timpano era interamente decorato con le insegne del Re" (79) [a frontispiece whose tympanum was wholly decorated with the king's arms]. Bentivoglio and Guitti did not originate this architectural element. According to Saslow (who understands the practical value of this innovation, but does not dwell on its implications), in Florence in 1589 "[a]t the front of the house was the most innovative and influential feature, the framed proscenium" which "served to visually define the stage area and mask the complex machinery and movements of performers and crew": *The Medici Wedding of 1589*, 81. Commercial opera theaters in Venice retained this feature: "[t]he civic nature of the performance was . . . explicitly stated on the middle of the proscenium arch, which was emblazoned with the insignia of the city authorities rather than the noble crest usually found at a court performance": Piperno, "Opera Production," 8.

[48] "The psychological frame indicates that what it includes is a staged action, a 'fiction,' that is, an action that ontologically does not lie on the same plane as what it stages or as what it opposes."

[49] "Paradoxically the frame has two contradictory functions: it signals that what it contains is fictional, and it makes us forget that it is such." Ortega y Gasset's famous "Meditations on the Frame" are hardly relevant here, as he was concerned with a concept of art that cannot be applied to the Parma festivities. Additionally, he defined the frame as the "neutral object" that "serves to neutralize a brief strip of wall" (in the case of a painting) (repr. in *Perspecta* 26 [1990]: 185–90, here 189); but the architectonic frame in Parma's temporary structure can hardly be termed neutral, as we have seen.

[50] According to Inghirami, the scene "fece belliss[im]a veduta perché, dalla banda di fuori haveva una belliss[im]a facciata le cui arcate con molte colonne toccate d'argento e d'oro in ordine composto, che piantate sopra alto imbasam[en]to s'ergevano in alto, e sostenevano un grand'architrave e sopra, una larghiss[im]a fascia piena di buone figure à chiaroscuro, che ricovrevano tutta la facciata. Ne vani degli archi erano Nicchie con figure di rilievo toccate similm[en]te d'argento. Quest'ornam[en]to tutto, arricchiva la scena beniss[im]o alluminata et esquisitam[en]te fatta": Minucci del Rosso, "Le nozze," II, 562; Mediceo del Principato, filza 6075, 14 December 1628, fol. 1 v–r [produced a most handsome view, as it had on the outside a beautiful façade with arches on gold- and silver-painted columns in various styles soaring high from a high base. These columns held a large architrave and above it an area covered with good images in chiaroscuro for the entire façade. All this decoration enriched the well-lighted, exquisitely-built stage].

Inghirami, like Buttigli, emphasizes the dimensions of the structure and its elements, as well as the amount of decorations and the profusion of gold and silver.

⁵¹ "Held a canvas made up of 3600 *braccia* of cloth that covered the stage and the area between the proscenium and the pit."

⁵² "It was covered above with canvas, but on the side of the stage there was still a gaping hole, and therefore after dark we suffered from piercing cold that bit into our heads and our whole bodies."

⁵³ Lina Balestrieri exaggerates when she writes that "con una malizia tutta cortigiana [Inghirami] si affretta a comunicare all'arciduchessa anche le più lievi critiche fatte allo spettacolo": *Feste e spettacoli*, 26 [Inghirami with courtly cunning hastens to tell the archduchess even the smallest criticism against the show]. Let us recall that the Medici had staged some theatrical entertainment in Florence right after the wedding of Margherita with Odoardo Farnese merely two months before — although, in Nagler's opinion, "for this celebration the Medici did not greatly exert themselves": *Theatre Festivals of the Medici*, 140. Thus, by criticizing the festivities at Parma, Inghirami implicitly asserts the superiority of the Florentine celebrations. It might be helpful to bear in mind, additionally, that Inghirami's attitude was far from being unique: the Florentines believed sung theater their invention, and already in 1608, according to Solerti, "par difficile che Firenze volesse rinunciare [to staging a *spettacolo in musica* for Cosimo's wedding] avendone avuto fino allora quasi il vanto esclusivo": *Albori*, 1: 104 [it is hard to believe that Florence might have wanted to give up staging a *spettacolo in musica* for Cosimo's wedding since till then they had been the only ones to do so]. Giordani's letters contain some criticism, too, but of a different nature. For example, he regrets that the *teatro inferiore* is only a temporary structure: "Si rappresentò [*Aminta*] in un grandissimo cortile coperto da una tenda e fu ridotto in forma di augustissimo Teatro, nel quale S[ua] A[ltezza] non puote avere speso meno di 30 mila scudi: e va guasto": Saviotti, "Feste e spettacoli," 49 [*Aminta* was staged in a courtyard covered by an awning that his highness had made into a noble theater. They must have spent at least thirty thousand *scudi* on it and it will be ruined soon].

⁵⁴ "The area for the audience, the proscenium, and the stage were lighted by over three hundred two-branched candelabra with candles of white wax and by a thousand or so smaller sources of light. They had been placed with so much artifice that they could not be seen and yet they banished the darkness of night from the whole place."

⁵⁵ "Everything was filled with white torches as was every column around the theater. On the side of the stage there were two lamps in the Florentine manner. What was different were the oil-lamps, for in Florence they have two wicks and here only one; and they did not last till the end."

⁵⁶ This is common in official or semi-official festivity descriptions: "[a]ll'eloquenza puntigliosa e ridondante che caratterizza le cronache ufficiali dell'evento spettacolare si contrappone sempre il nascondimento delle fasi e delle tecniche della sua preparazione, in modo che a ogni spettatore — fisico o mentale — la meraviglia del prodotto compiuto giungesse in tutta la sua magica levità, epurata dalla zavorra delle sue concrete componenti artigianali": C. Burattelli, *Spettacoli di corte a Mantova tra Cinque e Seicento* (Firenze: Le Lettere, 1999), 142 [There is a constant juxtaposition between the detailed and redundant rhetoric marking the official chronicles of a spectacle and their hiding of the phases and techniques of its preparation. This is done so that each viewer (whether physically present

or imagining it in his/her mind) could feel the marvel of the finished product in all its magic lightness, freed from the ballast of concrete craft-based components].

[57] "I am sending a summary of the tournament; that of the *intermezzi* I will bring back myself, as it is too bulky. I want everybody to see it, so that they can admire this spectacle, even from far away."

[58] "I am sending the summaries of the *intermezzi* so that you can enjoy them a little until I can recount them to you with further details. Make sure you do not lose them, as I have no others."

[59] We do not know whether the audience were given the same printing of the text of the prologue which is extant (indeed a slim booklet, or "libbretto"), or another one. The fact that Achillini's dedication to Lorenzo de' Medici is left without a date (the text has: "Di Parma il Decembre 1628" [Achillini. *Teti e Flora*, iv]) could be a consequence of the many postponements of the festivities due to inclement weather.

[60] These publications explaining the plot and meaning of the staged entertainment went on to become absolutely necessary to the audience: for example at the imperial court in Vienna, in 1668, "the fact the most spectators of the première had already read the libretto and knew the outcome . . . strengthens the power of [the author's] epideictic rhetoric — for in this type of argument, the audience is not presented with 'new' information but with the *auxeisis* of a well-known 'fact,' which the allegorical lavishness of the representation of its architectural framework made even more memorable": Aercke, *Gods of Play*, 236. This is not the case at Parma, as will become clear from the rest of the chapter.

[61] Mazzi's letter dated 16 November 1627, mentions a "tela dinanzi" (Lavin, "Lettres," 130; idem, *Art and Pageantry*, 532; MS Antonelli 660, 16 November 1627, fol. 2 r) without specifying how or where it is to be used; however, it is likely that it was a curtain to close the stage to view before the beginning of the performance.

[62] "The stage was covered as we do in Florence; the curtain lifted, but very slowly."

[63] The phrase "all'uso di costà" confirms recent findings indicating that curtains had been used in Florence since at least 1565: "Per la *Cofanaria* di Francesco D'Ambra, rappresentata nel 1565 per le nozze del principe Francesco con Giovanna d'Austria, si utilizza una scena che figura una prospettiva fiorentina di piazza e di strada . . . È una delle prime volte che abbiamo notizia dell'esistenza di un sipario dipinto (di mano di Francesco Zuccari) destinato ad occultare la vista della scenografia agli spettatori nei giorni precedenti la festa, accrescendone l'aspettativa e il mistero": Pieri, *La nascita del teatro moderno*, 92–3. The reader will recall Tasso's letter regarding the use of a curtain at Guidubaldo II's courtly entertainment cited in chapter 2; such a practice can be dated to the decade after the Florentine event to which Pieri makes reference.

[64] "Essendo pieni di Dame i gradi tirati per retta linea a destra, e sinistra del verone de' Prencipi, pieni li raggiranti fuori delle loggie di Cavaglieri, piene le prime, e seconde loggie di Prencipi incogniti, e di personaggi forastieri, comparvero gli illustriss[imi] Sig[nori] Cardinali, colla Sereniss[ima] Madama, Sposi, Prencipi, e Prencipesse, i quali dopo di haver salutato le circostanti Dame, e Cavaglieri, s'assisero a suoi luoghi, e subito s'udì una dolcissima sinfonia di stromenti, sì da mano, come da fiato, nel finir della quale in un balleno d'occhi sparve la cortina, e comparve il vacuo del Proscenio": Buttigli, *Descrittione dell'apparato*, 154 [when the steps to the right and left of the princes' balcony were filled with ladies and gentlemen; the steps on the outside with knights; the two rows of boxes with unknown princes and foreign people, then the Cardinals, the dowager duchess, the

newlyweds, princes and princesses appeared. They said hello to the ladies and gentlemen around and sat in their seats. Immediately a highly sweet tune was heard, played by handheld and wind instruments. At the end of this tune in the blink of an eye the curtain disappeared and the open part of the proscenium appeared].

65 See for example lines 1 and 2 opening the description of the masque *Love Freed from Ignorance and Folly* by Ben Jonson and Inigo Jones: "So soon as the King's majesty was set and in expectation, there was heard a strange music of wild instruments": S. Orgel and R. Strong, *Inigo Jones: The Theatre of the Stuart Court*, 2 vols. (Berkeley: University of California Press, 1973), 1: 231; as well as line 107 in the *Middle Temple and Lincoln's Inn Masque* by George Chapman and Inigo Jones: "The King being come forth, the masquers ascended": Orgel and Strong, *Inigo Jones*, 1: 257.

66 This is indeed quite different from Western theater as we conceive it. For it, McAuley feels the need to underscore that "spectators in the theatre are not just witnessing the performance, they are also experiencing the social event in the audience space": *Space in Performance*, 273.

67 "The empty part of the proscenium appeared. It was notable for the position of Hymen's temple in the middle; on both sides there were various scenes set in perspective and depicting gardens, fountains, hills, vineyards, mountains, woods, grottoes, and precipices in the distance. They were so well devised that the eyes were taken in and the painting was believed to be three-dimensional."

68 "Vedevasi nella parte superiore della Scena, l'aere tanto ben illustrato, colla finta del riflesso del sole, e le nuvole in varie forme tanto ben figurate, che non era facile il giudicare, se più belle, e gratiose le facesse l'Arte, o la natura": Buttigli, *Descrittione dell'apparato*, 154 [in the upper parts of the stage you could see the air so well depicted (including the imitation of the reflection of the sun and the clouds reproduced in various shapes) that it was not easy to judge if art or nature made them more beautiful and pretty].

69 "The whole decoration enriched the well-lighted, well-built stage; on it we saw Hymen's temple, a big piece of machinery, and well put together."

70 In the pedestals "si vedevano la Face d'Himeneo, ed il Pillo di Thalassione, colligate col drappo nuziale": Buttigli, *Descrittione dell'apparato*, 155 [one saw Hymen's torch and Thalassio's designated object, linked by the marriage cloth]. Thalassio, or Talassio, was an obscure Sabine deity whose presence was invoked during marriage ceremonies ("Talassio," in *Harper's Dictionary of Classical Literature and Antiquities*, ed. Harry Thurston Peck [New York: Cooper Square, 1962], 1521). In the cornice frieze "si vedevano dui Amori, involti in varij fogliami d'oro, tessere ghirlandette di poma d'oro, e di celesti Giglij": Buttigli, *Descrittione dell'apparato*, 155 [one saw two Loves wrapped in golden leaves in the act of weaving garlands with golden apples and light blue lilies]. On top of the three domes, three statues showed a woman's virtues: Juno, Virginity, and Chastity (156). The two side domes also were decorated by "bei cartelloni dorati, una la Virtù, c'haveva per mano l'Amor Divino; l'altra la Buona Fortuna, che conduceva a mano l'Amor Humano" (156) [beautiful gilt posters: one with virtue holding hands with divine love; the other with good luck holding hands with human love]. Finally, the central intercolumniation comprised a door, on whose molding "si vedevano impresse due mani, che si stringevano l'una coll'altra, proprio Geroglifico della Fede maritale" (157) [one saw two hands holding each other, the true hieroglyph of married faithfulness]. This last, the clasped-hand motif, comes directly from late antiquity.

⁷¹ "Hymen's song concluded, the god and his temple rose into the heaven with a most sweet motion." Inghirami agrees: the temple "s'alzò al Cielo con sicuro e ben compartito moto" (Minucci del Rosso, "Le nozze," II, 562; Mediceo del Principato, filza 6075, 14 December 1628, fol. 2 r) [rose to the sky with sure, well-devised motion], that is, without any perceivable jolt.

⁷² "On the right by a flowery plain, on the left by a sound [lit. "an arm of the sea"]." Nagler's description of the setting as "a coastal landscape" (*Theatre Festivals of the Medici* 145) considers only Tethys's half, entirely neglecting Flora's.

⁷³ On the right, the painted lawn was covered by "varij colori, azzurri, dorati, incarnati, rossi, gialli, e quanti erano i colori, tanti erano i fiori. Fioriti erano ben'anche gli alberi, e questi di cedri, di naranzi, di palme, di lauri rappresentavano una ridente Primavera": Buttigli, *Descrittione dell'apparato*, 157 [various colors: blue, gold, pink, red, yellow. There were as many flowers as there were colors. The trees, too, were in blossom: cedars, oranges, palms, laurels represented sweet spring]. On the left, the scene reproduced a beach with waves; the latter elicited the most wonder, since they were constantly moving, from right to left and vice versa, and from away far to up close and vice versa. Mamczarz maintains that "après la scène d'Hyménée... deux autres décors se succédèrent: un champ printanier... puis, les plages et la mer": *Le Théâtre Farnèse*, 123 [after Hymen's scene, two sets followed one another: a springtime field, then sea and beach]. Buttigli clearly indicates rather that these two scenes appeared simultaneously, not sequentially.

⁷⁴ "With rare and exquisite music; the music had been written by Monteverdi, and the voices are the best in Italy."

⁷⁵ "Since at this time theaters are being built for choice spectacles to honor this most happy couple, and since rivers of visitors run towards this sea of joy and marvel, it behooves us to take our words and feet there."

⁷⁶ Achillini himself was aware that his poetry was only relevant because it had been staged, indeed "alla presenza della Sereniss[ima] Principessa Margherita in Parma" [in the presence of the most serene princess Margherita of Parma]; therefore, all that was possible now for the dedicatee Lorenzo de' Medici was to "legger volentieri, in questa breve fatica, alcuni cenni delle lodi regali delle due Sereniss[ime] Case": Achillini, *Teti e Flora*, iii [read some elements praising those two most serene families in this short piece].

⁷⁷ "The comedy was recognized as *Aminta* and therefore nobody paid it any attention."

⁷⁸ A thorough reconstruction of the development of the pastoral tradition on stage is in Marzia Pieri, *La scena boschereccia*.

⁷⁹ "The choice of putting together a pastoral always comes from specific staging needs. Up to a certain period these are privately organized shows paid for by the Studio and performed in the dwellings of citizens or in the palaces of members of the ducal family for almost intimate entertainment."

⁸⁰ The headings of the extant copies of the prologue and *intermezzi* underscore this: "Teti e Flora Prologo Della Gran Pastorale recitata in Parma Nel maraviglioso Teatro fabricato quest'anno Dal Serenissimo Signor Duca Per honorar l'arrivo della Serenissima Principessa Margherita di Toscana Sua Moglie": Achillini, *Teti e Flora*, i [Tethys and Flora, prologue to the great pastoral performed in Parma in the marvelous theater built by the duke this year to honor the arrival of Princess Margherita of Tuscany, his wife]; "Intermedii Recitati In musica Dalle più Eccellenti Voci del nostro Secolo In uno

dei superbissimi Teatri Di Parma Fabricato dall'Heroica Magnificenza del S[erenissi]mo Duca Odoardo Farnese Per honorar l'arrivo della Ser[enissi]ma Prencipessa Margherita di Toscana Sua Consorte": Pio di Savoia, *Intermedii* (1629), i [*intermezzi* sung to music by the most excellent voices of our century in one of the superb theaters of Parma, built by the heroic magnificence of Duke Odoardo Farnese to honor the arrival of Princess Margherita of Tuscany, his consort]. Similar, verbose headings were traditional in printed pastoral plays, as mentioned in chapter 1.

[81] "The pastoral set came back and shepherds and nymphs started performing *Aminta*."

[82] "Un vago non meno, che forte Castello, fabricato d'ordine del Mago Atlante da gli Spiriti Infernali, finto col talco quasi d'acciaio, tanto risplendente, che non era possibile, per lo riflesso de gli occulti lumi, l'affissarlo con gli occhi": Buttigli, *Descrittione dell'apparato*, 167 [a castle as beautiful as it was strong. It had been built at the wizard Atlas's order by infernal spirits, with talc as if it were steel. It was so shiny that it was not possible to look at it because it reflected hidden lights]. In this introduction to the full-fledged description of the castle, Buttigli clearly speaks from his knowledge of the preparations that made the *intermezzo* possible. First, he elucidates both the mythical origin of the castle and the name of its maker. The epic-poetry-loving audience in attendance would have likely identified these elements correctly and quickly, once the plot had begun, but no identifying clues were immediately apparent on stage. Further, he reveals the material with which the castle itself was built. Félibien's description of the 1668 festivities at Versailles is remarkably different from Buttigli's text: the French chronicler avoids all references to humble materials taking on the appearance of precious ones. Alberto Ausoni, the Italian translator and editor of Félibien's text, feels compelled to explain: "Félibien, a proposito di tali decorazioni provvisorie, nomina il bronzo, il marmo o il lapislazzulo, non precisando che si trattava, in realtà, di legno o di cartapesta trattati illusionisticamente con l'intervento della pittura": *Le feste di Versailles*, 29 n. 3 [Félibien mentions bronze, marble, lapis with respect to temporary decorations; he never specifies that they were actually made of wood or paper mâché and then painted over]. Thus Buttigli's description concurrently fulfills two (sometimes conflicting) goals: he describes the events as they were supposed to be, while glorifying the craft and ability of those involved in the preparations. This very passage offers a good example, in the phrase "finto col talco quasi d'acciaio." A notoriously frail material, which has come to occupy the lowest spot on the hardness scale, talc here takes on the appearance of steel, emblematic then as now of some of the most important and defining qualities of metal: permanence, strength, and rigidity. The effect is all the more remarkable because the original material was so lowly. This is an example of what Saslow has rightly called "control over nature" (*The Medici Wedding of 1589*, 11) on the part of the festivity organizers and of the court. Its effects were similar to those described at Florence in 1589: "commentators are fond of describing audience reaction with such adjectives as *stupiti* (astounded, overwhelmed), and the causes of their amazement are often termed *meraviglie*, marvels or wonders — a central term throughout Mannerist criticism to figure a fascination with all that pushes beyond the bounds of the normally possible" (11).

[83] For example: "Da lungi par che come fiamma lustri, / né sia di terra cotta, né di marmi" (II, 42) [From far away it seemed to glow like flame / No glaze, no marble, has such radiance (trans. Reynolds, 1: 148)]; "i demoni industri, / . . . / tutto d'acciaio avean cinto il bel loco, / temprato all'onda et allo stigio foco" (II, 42) [demon masons of ill fame

/ . . . / had clad the castle with finest steel, / Forged in the fires and tempered in streams of Hell (trans. Reynolds, 1: 148)]; "Di sì forbito acciar luce ogni torre, / che non vi può né ruggine né macchia" (II, 43) [The steel of every tower shines so bright, / no rust disfigures it, or any stain (trans. Reynolds, 1: 148)]; "lucente castel d'acciai'" (III, 63) [castle built of steel (trans. Reynolds, 1: 173)]; "d'acciar murata" (III, 67) [walls of steel (trans. Reynolds, 1: 174)]; "un castello / . . . fatto per incanto, / tutto d'acciaio, e sì lucente e bello" (IV, 7) [a castle . . . / . . . / built by magic art of shining steel; / so beautiful it is (trans. Reynolds, 1: 179)]; "la cima / d'un bel muro d'acciar tutta si fascia" (IV, 12) [its top encircled by / a wall of steel (trans. Reynolds, 1: 181)]; "Da quattro canti era tagliato, e tale / che parea dritto a fil de la sinopia" (IV, 13) [The walls on every side as steeply drop / as if by line and plummet built, four-square (trans. Reynolds, 1: 181)].

[84] In the *Furioso*, the two women walk together, and in order to while away the boredom of the trip and their tiredness, they talk about the young one's impending feat (III, 64–75).

[85] "Il Cavallo di Melissa e Bradam[an]te scese per traverso, e girò perchè elle smontassero al Castello, e rivoltò per levarle di scena": Minucci del Rosso, "Le nozze," II, 563; Mediceo del Principato, filza 6075, 14 December 1628, fol. 2 v [Melissa and Bradamante's horse came down diagonally and turned so that they could dismount by the castle. Then it turned again to take them away from the stage].

[86] "A white hippogriff with a brown spot on its nose. It was shaped like a horse but from the wings down it looked like an eagle." In *Orlando Furioso*, Ariosto feels compelled to summon some witnesses for the *ippogrifo*'s appearance (the innkeeper and his family, IV, 4) and to give a pseudo-scientific genetic explanation of its nature (IV, 18–19). The *meraviglia* that Buttigli registers in the convened audience for the benefit of his readers does not fall in the natural realm, but rather in the mechanical one: nature has already been domesticated by technology, so only the latter, not the former, can show off.

[87] "When the wizard moved a stone from the castle door, he tricked Bradamante and made the castle and jagged mountains disappear. Ruggiero and the other knights and ladies were left in the middle of the stage in a delightful garden."

[88] "The castle was well put together. It disappeared at once to reveal a beautiful garden filled with knights that was most pleasant."

[89] "In a straight line. The pieces flew to the left and right of the stage in jagged pieces and with crooked motion."

[90] Jo Ann Cavallo has underscored the pervasive nature of the tradition of the garden setting in Ferrarese epic poems, as the place where knights are enticed by beautiful and wily women: "Tasso's Armida and the Victory of Romance," in *Renaissance Transactions: Ariosto and Tasso*, ed. V. Finucci (Durham: Duke University Press, 1999), 77–111, here 78–82. Though this cliché emerges in a different genre, it comes to a complete reversal in this *intermezzo*, where the praise of love crushes the desire for glory on the part of the male character.

[91] ". . . setting free anew / The knights and ladies; some of these (I mean / The ladies) being from superb apartment to / The countryside transferred, in no small measure / Were disappointed by such loss of pleasure" (trans. Reynolds, 1: 187).

[92] "In a cloud in the air, circled by symbols, and outside these symbols many sprites shaped like various monsters."

[93] "Hora colla lunghezza sembrava una piramide, hora col dilatarsi nel mezo, e ristringendosi nella pianta, pareva un rombo: talhora gettando fuori varie quasi ale, fingeva un volatile, talhora crescendo da tutte le parti, rassembrava figura mostruosa, il cui capo non corrispondeva al piede, il cui petto non confrontava colle braccia, ed in somma dopò di haver variamente delusi gli spettatori con varie, e strane forme, apertasi mostrò il mago Atlante": Buttigli, *Descrittione dell'apparato*, 177–78 [at times it looked like a pyramid, at times it grew in the middle and shrank on the bottom as if a rhomboid. At times it seemed to grow wings as if it were a bird. At times it grew on all sides and looked like a monster whose head did not fit its feet, whose chest did not measure up to its arms. In the end after it took the audience in with many strange shapes it opened up and showed Atlas].

[94] On the issue of illusion in Ariosto's and Tasso's epic poems, Sergio Zatti, *L'ombra del Tasso* (Milan: B. Mondadori, 1996) is particularly relevant. In chapter four (translated in English as "Epic in the Age of Dissimulation") he differentiates between Ariosto's treatment of the seductress's garden from Tasso's. Ironically, this *intermezzo* is much closer to Ariosto's position than to Tasso's.

[95] "A luxurious, magnificent, marvelous palace."

[96] "The onward and upward motion of the garden was marvelous as was its disappearance."

[97] "The sets were very well put together and painted but they moved slowly when they were changed at each *intermezzo*."

[98] The phrase "Recitato il second atto" [the second act having been performed] that Buttigli employs here (and, modified, for all the other acts) is not unique to his *Descrittione*. From the earliest printed documents, attention is devoted to the *intermezzi* while the regular play is barely mentioned. For an early example, see the documents cited in Thomas Ault, "Classical Humanist Theatre in Transition," *Theatre Annual* 50 (1997): 17–39, esp. 29–34.

[99] "A most sweet harmony of angelic voices and musical instruments."

[100] "The set was singular and most beautiful in the second *intermezzo*."

[101] "The sea came up short; it was not as exquisite as in Tuscany, and neither was the storm."

[102] Buttigli mentions that "non finite torri," "imperfette cortine," "ponti pensili, fatti per sostentare i fabri, pieni d'ulubre, argani, taglie, viti perpetue, ed altri strumenti meccanici," "monti d'arena," and "mazze di quadrelli" [unfinished towers, incomplete walls, scaffolding supporting workers and all manners of tools, sand mounds, and brick piles] were depicted: *Descrittione dell'apparato*, 181. It is again doubtful that the audience could see all the details mentioned by Buttigli, who exploits his knowledge of the festivity preparations. However, this particular stage set depicted *in fieri* is an interesting, if hidden, reference to the countless hours of work on the part of masons, woodcarvers, and craftsmen of all kinds, that had made the performance possible.

[103] "Carthage was begun shortly before Aeneas's arrival; therefore it was not perfect on stage."

[104] "Con varij ravvolgimenti in proportionata distanza, dal porto s'andava distendendo sino all'interiore profondità della scena": Buttigli, *Descrittione dell'apparato*, 182 [becoming smaller at the right distance it extended from the harbor to the deepest part of the set].

[105] Even when Jove orders Mercury to remind Aeneas of his destiny, the emphasis is placed on time wasted rather than on love (4.225).

[106] "Here appeared Mercury flanked by many various clouds, coming down from his second sphere on a silver chariot." Note that in the Ptolemaic universe the second sphere is appropriate to Mercury's planet.

[107] According to Inghirami, however, Fame entered from stage right: "Venne per diritto dal proscenio innanzi, passeggiò per traverso e poi obliquo essendo sola e senza Carro sostenuta con ingegno non veduto" (Minucci del Rosso, "Le nozze," II, 563; Mediceo del Principato, filza 6075, 14 December 1628, fol. 2 v) [it came from the right of the proscenium straight ahead, waltzed across it and then diagonally without machinery and supported by an unseen trick].

[108] Here Pio di Savoia followed Virgil's own description in the *Aeneid*: "Monstrum horrendum, ingens, cui, quot sunt corpore plumae, / Tot vigiles oculi subter (mirabile dictu) / Tot linguae, totidem ora sonant, tot subrigit auris" (4.181–183) [Monstrous, deformed, titanic. Pinioned, with / an eye beneath for every body feather, / and, strange to say, as many tongues and buzzing / mouths as eyes, as many pricked-up ears (trans. Fitzgerald, 102)].

[109] Inghirami mentions a "Carro di Nettuno belliss[im]o" [Neptune's most beautiful piece of machinery] for this *intermezzo* (Minucci del Rosso, "Le nozze," II, 563; Mediceo del Principato, filza 6075, 14 December 1628, fol. 2 v). However, no such prop occurs here, yet Juno is never named, thus leading to Inghirami's mistake.

[110] "Si vestì d'oro, d'argento, di torchino, di giallo, di fosco, di trasparente, con tanta vaghezza, e con tanta varietà, che non è possibile, che mente humana lo possa imaginare, non che lingua, o penna mortale vaglia spiegare, o descrivere sì meravigliosa concorrenza, e mescolanza di colori": Buttigli, *Descrittione dell'apparato*, 190 [it was covered in gold, silver, turquoise, yellow, gray, and luminescence with such beauty and variety that it is not possible for a human mind to imagine it, let along for mortal tongue or pen to explain or describe such marvelous agreement and mingling of colors].

[111] Here Pio di Savoia departs substantially from the Virgilian plot, where Dido's reactions immediately consider suicide but never homicide (*Aeneid* 4.408–503).

[112] "With such artifice that it looked like a real flying monster, unconnected to supports from all sides, rather than a fake flying machine."

[113] "Stop, stop your hand;" "Change, change your mind;" and "Come back, come back, heart of my heart."

[114] "I will bother you as much as I loved you."

[115] "Why do I delay my death?"

[116] "No less powerful a god than Juno sends me as messenger to you, most beautiful ladies. She wishes that poor Dido's story be a mirror to your souls."

[117] "No one heard them due to a dull sound: everybody stamped their feet but it was not too noisy because there were carpets on the planks."

[118] "The princes went to the small room I mentioned before to eat;" "while Cardinal Ludovisi was about to drink he was perfumed with human water by someone above him."

[119] Documents pertaining to sixteenth- and seventeenth-century staged entertainment occasionally point out the audience's displeasure with a specific performance, usually due to a particularly bothersome detail (like the cold at Parma in 1628). In 1571, for Lucrezia d'Este's entry into Pesaro, an anonymous writer reported that "La comedia In se per

esser'stata fredda di soggetto, colpa dell'Autore causa anche prolissità poco salsa ne i recitanti . . . no[n] pote alleviar il fastidio à circonstanti del spatio di cinque hore che duro la favola, co[n] no[n] poco detrim[en]to de calca": Archivio di Stato, Firenze: Ducato d'Urbino, classe I divisione B filza X [the comedy itself had an uninspiring subject matter and its author had been long-winded, not to mention that the performers had little stamina. Nothing relieved the annoyance of those in attendance for the five hours of the plot, and the crowded conditions did not help]. In February 1578, according to the Florentine envoy to Ferrara, "Si recitò il Lunedì sera la Commedia rincrescevole e sazievole straordinariamente, che durò senza intermedi apparenti 7 ore d'una prosa dura, maledica e assai mal pronunziata": Solerti and Lanza, "Il teatro ferrarese," 170 [Monday night an extraordinarily sorry, stuffy comedy was performed. It lasted without *intermezzi* seven hours and its prose was tough, uncouth, and badly uttered]. Overcrowding and bad writing were replaced at Mantua in 1608 by bad performing: "fu bella la comedia del Cav[alie]re Guarini [*La idropica*], assai piena di motti et sentenze, ma recitata da persone per lo più parte sgarbate, et era così grassa che faceva arrossire": Solerti, *Albori* 1: 100–101 [Guarini's comedy was beautiful, full of puns and witticisms, but it was acted by people who were largely without grace, and it was so rude that people blushed].

[120] "After the act, the third *intermezzo* revived everybody, since it was most marvelous."

[121] "Portando seco il pavimento, lasciò la scena ornata in faccia d'un mare, cinto di campagne, sì alla destra, come alla sinistra piene di colli, vigne, monti, e boschi, con tal varietà di nobili, e rustici edificij, che pareva un Paradiso terrestre": Buttigli, *Descrittione dell'apparato*, 197 [the floor was taken away. On the front of the stage there was a sea flanked by fields on both sides: there were hills, vineyards, mountains, and woods, such variety of noble and rustic buildings, that it seemed an earthly paradise].

[122] "A plain covered with green and many flowers;" hills "covered with vineyards, hazelnut coppices, rows of fig trees, pergolas of pomegranates" and "many little buildings."

[123] On the copy of Buttigli's text from which I cite, this page and the next are incorrectly numbered 200 and 201, followed by two pages bearing the same numbers. To avoid ambiguity, I have normalized the numbering, referring to them as 198 and 199.

[124] "Three mermaids rose all of a sudden from the bottom of the calm gulf."

[125] It is worth mentioning that the printed versions of the Prologue and of the *intermezzi* open with a disclaimer regarding the usage of pagan language in the texts, placed before the *imprimatur* bestowed by Parma's inquisitor: "Si protesta, che le parole Dio d'Amore, Dea d'Amore, Deità, Divinità, Paradiso, Adorare, Beato, & altre simili s'intendono conforme all'uso de' Poeti, & non mai in senso, che offenda in parte alcuna immaginabile i sensi, e i Dogmi purissimi della Religione Cattolica": Achillini, *Teti e Flora*, ii [we assert that the phrases "god of love," "goddess of love," "divinity," "paradise," "adore," "blessed," and others are used according to poets' habits, and never in a way that could in any way offend the meanings and the purest dogmas of the Catholic religion]; "Si protesta, che le parole Dio d'Amore, Dea d'Amore, Deità, Divinità, Paradiso, Adorare, Beato, & altre simili s'intendono conforme all'uso de' Poeti, & non mai in senso, che offenda in parte alcuna imaginabile i sensi, e i Dogmi purissimi della Religione Cattolica": Pio di Savoia, *Intermedii*, ii [we assert that the phrases "god of love," "goddess of love," "divinity," "paradise," "adore," "blessed," and others are used according to poets' habits, and never in a way that could in any way offend the meanings and the purest dogmas of the Catholic religion].

[126] "In the highest area a shining cloud started advancing towards her."

[127] "A luminous, highly wrought cloud appeared in the highest part of the sky."

[128] "The closer it got to center stage, the larger it became."

[129] Her appearance was nevertheless overdetermined: "Armata di lucentissimo usbergo, di scudo non meno risplendente, che spaventoso . . . [h]aveva in testa elmo fornito di cimiero ricchissimo, . . . e colla destra stringeva l'invincibil'hasta" (202) [She wore a most shining armor, carried a no less resplendent than frightening shield, had a helmet with a very rich plume on her head, and carried in her right hand an invincible spear].

[130] "A third cloud appeared stage left."

[131] Two she-wolves adorned the front of his chariot, while the sides were decorated "da varij picchi, e scaravaggi, uccelli dedicati a Marte" [many woodpeckers and black beetles, devoted to Mars] along with "elmi, usberghi, e bracciali ricevevano la forma posteriore" (203) [helmets, armors, and arm-covers on the rear].

[132] "There were three clouds, with Diana, Pallas, and Mars, which were quite beautiful. What was extraordinary was the fact that the clouds move horizontally as well as around."

[133] Frank Mohler has unveiled the technical complexity of seventeenth-century aerial stage machinery in "A Brief Shining Moment," *Theatre Symposium* 4 (1996): 83–90: an effect which at this point in the *intermezzo* had to be multiplied by five (the number then on stage).

[134] "Blessed kisses, even at war I enjoy peace."

[135] "In the middle of the stage, by the foot of a faraway mountain, a frightening hole opened up; in it you could see the city of Dis in flames."

[136] He also avows that a certain amount of classical erudition was necessary to properly and assuredly identify the whole. However, Virgil's description of hell (*Aeneid* 4.548–632) is far less detailed and colorful than Buttigli's. The reference is more prescriptive than descriptive, in essence.

[137] Inghirami writes that Pluto entered "in un carro di fuoco" (Minucci del Rosso, "Le nozze," II, 563; Mediceo del Principato, filza 6075, 14 December 1628, fol. 3 r) [a chariot of fire]. It is therefore possible that Pluto did not walk on stage with his retinue, but that the whole infernal setting moved closer to the front of the stage.

[138] "I am not here as Pluto, god of hell, but as Jupiter's brother, and your uncle."

[139] Buttigli claims that it provoked the same awed response of its first appearance: "lasciando non minor ammiratione della seconda veduta, di quello facesse nella prima colla varietà delle forme, nelle quali si mutava la nuvola, col girare delle ruote, e col mostrarsi da ogni parte spicca dalla Terra, e dall'Aere": *Descrittione dell'apparato*, 211 [it drew no less admiration the second time than the first: the cloud's shapes varied, the wheels turned, and it seemed separated from land and air on all sides].

[140] "This royal bride took all my arms. Mother, I no longer have my torch: she has it in her beautiful eyes. Mother, I no longer have my laces: she has them in her hair. Mother, I no longer have my arrows: my quiver is emptied in her beautiful face. What could I do against Diana?"

[141] Horazio Persiani's poem written for the wedding exploits the same classical *topos*, that is, the struggle between love and valor to claim the newlyweds' allegiance. Persiani does not juxtapose Venus and Diana, but rather Apollo and Love; further, his poem does not embody this contest like Pio di Savoia's *intermezzo*. However, the conclusion is

remarkably similar, down to Love's request to Venus to yield to Margherita's beauty and power (*Contesa*, 27).

[142] "On stage were five pieces of stage machinery at one time. The music was divine, and we needed no less than that, since the audience was dying of cold."

[143] "The shepherds came on stage to say their lines, but they did so for themselves, as everybody was stamping their feet and breathing on their hands."

[144] "Era il piano di mezo della scena tutto mare, che alla destra poco distante dal lito, haveva la Regia di Nettuno alla sinistra un'altissimo scoglio, nel quale percotevano le onde marine" (215) [the middle of the stage was all sea. On the right, not far from the shore, there stood Neptune's palace. On the left, there stood a very high cliff against which waves beat]. The last phrase seems to indicate that, as for the third *intermezzo*, the stage floor had been at least partially removed, so that moving props could depict waves beating on the shore. Interestingly, Buttigli devotes just a few lines to the middle part of the stage. The imitation sea differed from the one in *intermezzo* three in color and motion; further, "non sempre servava l'istessa maniera di moto" (217) [did not always move in the same way], thus providing an additional source of surprise for the audience.

[145] "Large, alpine, craggy, covered with non-fruit-bearing trees, with a big cave in the middle, at water level."

[146] "Eolus will wreak havoc on Juno's kingdom, and Triton call forth the monsters of the sea."

[147] "A dolphin, a killer whale, a seal, and a whale. These monsters were so well put together and nature-like that nothing came close."

[148] "Wearing the thinnest veils, all decorated with silver flakes, carrying a superb and royal cloak, crown, and scepter."

[149] "One could not see the winds, but could hear them: they blew on stage so hard that waves rose, clouds gathered, the sky darkened, lightning was seen, and most natural thunder was heard."

[150] "Almost as long as the width of the stage."

[151] "The proper place for the helmsman where he could stand and steer the rudder or sit and see the compass."

[152] "Offered a spot for the Argonauts' captain to sit."

[153] "Le vele erano di lamma d'oro, cangiante in azzurro. Gli stendardi di tele, altre d'oro, altre d'argento, riccamate colle arme de' Serenissimi Sposi" (221) [the sails were of golden cloth changing to light blue. The flags were some of gold, others of silver cloth, embroidered with the newlyweds' arms].

[154] At the bow, "vedevasi un'armato, che per la pelle del Nemeo pendentegli dalle spalle, e per la noderosa mazza, ch'ei teneva vicino, stringendo l'arco colla sinistra mano era tenuto per Hercole" (221) [one could see a man carrying weapons who was recognized as Hercules because the skin of the Nemean lion was on his shoulders, he had a knotty club nearby, and he carried his bow with his left hand]. Close to the main mast, "vedevasi un laureato inerme, il quale vestito con habito di broccato d'oro, e ornato di cintola gioiellata, ... dalla lira ch'ei stringeva colla destra, e dall'arco, che teneva nella sinistra, si credeva, che fosse Orfeo" (221) [one saw an unarmed man crowned with laurel, wearing gold brocade and a bejeweled belt. From the lyre in his right hand and the bow in the left one believed that he was Orpheus]. Close to the stern "sedeva un vecchio, vestito con habito sacerdotale con una bacchetta in mano, che si giudicava, fosse Mopso" (221) [there sat an

old man dressed as a priest, a wand in his hand, who was believed to be Mopsus]. On the stern, in a privileged position, "sedeva un'armato, con sopraveste, e manto di broccato, tempestato di perle, colla spada cinta, con lo scudo imbracciato, con l'elmo in testa dorato, e con l'hasta impugnata, che tutti tenevano per Giasone" (221) [there sat an armed man, with an overgarment and cloak covered with pearls, wearing his sword, shield, golden helmet, and spear, whom everybody believed to be Jason]. In this case, the gilding of the helm as well as the conspicuous position on the ship seem to have helped the identification of the character. Lastly, below him "Sedeva . . . un vecchio, succintamente vestito d'argentino, colla barba lunga, con picciola brivola in testa, colle braccia ignude, il quale maneggiava il temone" (221–22) [there sat an old man scantily clad in silver, with a long beard, a small hat on his head and naked arms, who was at the helm]. Though the helmsman had an important role to play in the plot of the *intermezzo*, and despite the fact that both Buttigli's and Pio di Savoia's text mention him, he remained nameless.

[155] "Suddenly we could see huge waves lifted by the winds to the sky, and gaping holes opening up to the bottom of the sea. One could hear the noise of the rigging and of the oars. The masts' motion caused the sails to billow, while the clouds gathered in the sky and deprived the Argonauts of the light of day: it was then as dark as night. When the skies were thundering, the sky at times was lit up with the menacing glow of threatening lightning. Everything aflame put the sailors in danger of dying."

[156] "The fourth *intermezzo* revived everybody with the ship of the Argonauts and the sea. However I did not think that the ship, the sea, and the storm proceeded as they should." Mamczarz points out that the theme of Jason and the Argonauts had been exploited in a lavish celebration in Florence in 1608, when it was represented as a naval battle on the Arno (*Le Théâtre Farnèse*, 142–43). It is possible that Inghirami's criticism may be based on a memory (albeit largely idealized) of the Florence festivities, in comparison to which the Parma staging might have indeed paled.

[157] The first chapter of F. W. Sternfeld, *The Birth of Opera* (Oxford: Clarendon Press, 1993), is a well-argued, in-depth analysis of the importance of the myth of Orpheus for the beginning of opera proper. Though this *intermezzo* at Parma deals with this mythic figure only tangentially, and not in the usual setting of the myth of Eurydice's liberation from and return to hell, it is clear that at least one element shows continuity: "the hero's mastery of music" (8) and the power of music over humanity and nature alike. The "magical" frame of the festivities is thus reinforced by the presence of the mythic Greek musician on stage.

[158] "Cominciarono a poco a poco a slargarsi le nubi, e dileguandosi altre a settentrione, altre ad occidente, si videro i raggi del Sole prima rari, e poi uniti, e finalmente a mez'aere comparvero quattro destrieri bianchi, i quali tiravano un lucentissimo Carro": Buttigli, *Descrittione dell'apparato*, 225 [the clouds started opening up: some went away to the north, some to the west. We saw first a few sunrays, then a lot, and lastly four white horses appeared in mid-air, drawing a brightly shining chariot]. On the copy of Buttigli's text from which I cite, this page is incorrectly numbered 252, an obvious transposition for 225. I have regularized the numeration of this page.

[159] "The chariot of the sun was a great machine, like Neptune's shell, but it was music that gave soul to everything."

[160] In a printed sheet wrongfully filed among the celebratory papers regarding Ranuccio's wedding to Margherita Aldobrandini (Odoardo's parents) at the Archivio di Stato, Parma

(Comune, busta 625), an anonymous writer dedicated a poem to Margherita de' Medici entitled "Giasone in nove" [sic]. Here, Jason praises the princess as having found "più ricco tesoro, / Del vello, ond'io sospiro, / Bella perla Tirena" [a richer treasure than the fleece that I sigh for: a beautiful pearls from the Tyrrenian sea]. The same mythological figure is obviously exploited in a very different manner from Pio di Savoia's fourth *intermezzo*.

[161] "By the fifth act the performers had realized that the audience was not following them and so dispatched [their work] very quickly."

[162] "An area filled with rugged mountains, steep cliffs, precipitous, as high as the sky and so hard to climb that they made for a frightening-looking set."

[163] "The animals on which the parts of the world entered were well put together and walked naturally."

[164] "Let us stop our wandering feet, noble empresses of the earth. Here America, Asia, Africa and Europe will have a general council of the world." Asia, on stage left, rode a crocodile and wore a gold gown adorned with "foglie, fiori, e frutti, di cassia, di peppe, e di garofani": Buttigli, *Descrittione dell'apparato*, 231 [leaves, flowers, and fruits of cassia, pepper, and cloves]. Her identity was manifested and reinforced by depictions of the spices that traditionally came from the Orient. Africa, on a lion, was dressed in dark gray cloth adorned by snakes and scorpions embroidered in gold. Her head was "armato colla spoglia d'una testa d'Eleffante, la cui proboscide le faceva zuffo" (231) [covered with the skin of an elephant head, with its trunk as a forelock]. America, the fourth and last part of the then-known world, sat on a silver turtle; proud in demeanor, with motley feathers on her head, she wore a veil with gold threads. Barefooted, she carried an arrow in her right hand and a bow in the left one. It is evident that with these characters, the festivity organizers wanted to impress and surprise the audience with their exotic garb together with their display of luxury.

[165] "ASIA Troppo si scopre / Giove parziale, e sembra / Sol di Firenze Dio / E del resto Tiranno ingiusto, e rio. / AFRICA Perche fuori di lei togliere affatto / I leggiadri sembianti?": Buttigli, *Descrittione dell'apparato*, 232; Pio di Savoia, *Intermedii*, 53–54; Solerti, *Musica ballo e spettacolo*, 471 [ASIA: Jove is too partial and he seems to be god only to Florence and unjust and cruel tyrant to the rest. AFRICA: Why remove beautiful faces from every other place?].

[166] In these lines, Europa reiterated some of the praise heaped on the Medici princesses in Calandrini's and Spennacchi's texts; she found it unfair "Che da la sola stirpe d'Everardo / Debbano uscir Reine / Non solo à dominar nel suol Lombardo, / Mà in tutti i Regni miei, / E i Prencipi proddurvi, e i Semidei": Buttigli, *Descrittione dell'apparato*, 233; Pio di Savoia, *Intermedii*, 54; Solerti, *Musica ballo e spettacolo*, 472 [Only from Everard's seed queens must come, to rule not only over Lombard soil but also over all my kingdoms, to produce princes and demigods].

[167] "Those rocks breaking immediately sent forth flames. All of a sudden in the furthest part of the stage a big flaming cave opened up, and Pluto, the Furies, and some other infernal deities came out of it on a triumphal chariot."

[168] "Depart, O knight, from the infernal abyss, to be the object of human gazes in this most noble of theaters."

[169] "A mistake occurred as the Furies left for the sky: we saw a piece of the plank that supported them."

[170] "The fifth and last *intermezzo* was highly notable and left everybody with a good impression."

[171] "Udissi un gran terremoto, e videsi, aperta la Terra in un istante, formarsi in largo, e profondo circolo trè ordini di gradi discendenti, da' quali si poteva presumere, che gradatamente si continoasse sino al centro, luogo dell'Inferno": Buttigli, *Descrittione dell'apparato*, 237 [a great earthquake was heard, and after the earth opened up in an instant, a large circle was seen to form, going down three steps, from which one could conclude that it went all the way down to hell].

[172] "The infernal pit was very beautiful and gave the impression of an immense distance."

[173] "The tournament champion, Cornelio Bentivoglio, entered fully armed on a horse, a great piece of stage machinery;" "The famous Sir Cornelio Bentivoglio champion knight of the tournament, ascended and came forth with all his weapons, his spear in hand and his sword around his waist."

[174] According to Ascari, Enzo Bentivoglio "fu amantissimo . . . dei tornei cavallereschi": "Bentivoglio, Enzo," 612 [loved chivalric tournaments a great deal] and he took on the role of *mantenitore* or costumed champion during the performance of Maffeo Venieri's *Idalba* at Ferrara in 1614 (Southorn, *Power and Display*, 81). Reiner cites a letter written in January 1627 by Alfonso d'Este to Enzo in which he rejoices "that the young people yonder continue in the employment of those knightly practices" ("Preparations in Parma," 281 n. 51) which had been the hallmark of Ferrara and of the Bentivoglio family.

[175] The infernal knight "sorgendo s'avanzò sopra d'un cavallo nero bardato, sino al piano del pavimento della Scena, al pari del quale s'alzò con meraviglia de' circonstanti la terra contigua, facendogli commodo ponte, per discendere dal palco, e dopò di essere disceso, e di haver passeggiato il campo, mostrando non minor peritia nel cavalcare di quello facesse fierezza il destriero nel maneggiare, si fermò alla parte verso oriente, innanti all'Arco sitoato frà 'l Theatro, e Proscenio, in luogo a lui destinato": Buttigli, *Descrittione dell'apparato*, 238 [ascended and came forth on a caparisoned black horse to the floor of the stage. At the same time the area around it rose with great marvel to those in attendance so as to create a comfortable bridge for him to come down from the stage. Having done so, he paced across the field and showed no less expertise in riding than the horse showed pride in moving. He stopped in his specific spot to the east, in front of the arch between the area for the audience and the proscenium].

[176] "From the furthest part of the stage one could see Mercury advancing horizontally, flying detached from any set part. He wandered stage right and stage left and he showed off his gilt weapons, his silver-rich winged sandals, caduceus, and winged hat, and his embroidered cape."

[177] "You who live in the palace of the lilies."

[178] "The superhuman light shining in shimmering rays from a Tuscan sun."

[179] "The sky parted with amazing distance and Jove with a divine court came forth."

[180] Readers will recall that a *Gloria* is a piece of stage machinery in the shape of a cloud.

[181] "Era attorniato da molti chori di fanciulli, i quali, ricevendo dal di lui volto lume, e gloria, facevano in Theatro bellissima prospettiva. Erano sessanta, e più tali fanciulli, vestiti di drappo di color di carne, rappresentanti l'ignudo, e sedevano sulla machina della Gloria in modo tale, che i più piccioli sopra la testa di Giove, crescendo di mano in mano i maggiori formavano sino a nove semicircoli, i quali recingevano il Trono di Giove, e le

Sedi degli Dei" (239–40) [many children's choruses were around him. They received light and glory from his face and thus presented a most beautiful sight to the theater. These children, sixty or more, were wearing skin-colored cloth that imitated nudity. They sat on the *Gloria* machinery in such a way that the smallest were above Jove's head; arranged by size they formed nine half-circles around Jove's throne and the seats of the gods].

[182] "The heavenly palace began advancing horizontally starting from the furthest part of the stage. It came forth with constant speed, opening up little by little to the width of the open part of the stage. Then it stopped in the middle and came down by a third."

[183] "Essendo tutti i Chori de' puttini, e tutto lo stuolo de' celesti Numi assentati sopra occulte staffe di ferro, che giravano sulli poli, quando s'abbassavano le nubi, che comprendevano la Gloria, s'elevavano i personaggi, e s'abbassavano, quando le nubi s'elevavano, e sempre si mostravano perpendicolari all'horizzonte della scena" (240) [the children's choruses and the crowd of heavenly gods were seated on hidden iron bars turning on a hinge. When the clouds of the machinery lowered, the characters rose and vice versa, so that they always looked perpendicular to the stage horizon].

[184] "The last piece of machinery, that of the knights, with which the three of them, astride their armed horses and with grooms holding the horses, descended from the sky to earth was magnificent."

[185] "Three knights astride their horses came down from the sky and this crowned everything. They fought an open tournament against a knight who had come from hell and was the champion."

[186] "When the audience saw all this, some were awed by the beauty of the ingenious machinery, while others were frightened, for it seemed to them that the knights on the cloud could have been in danger if the horses jumped down. They could not see the big iron clamps that went around each horse and prevented them from moving and from jumping headlong."

[187] "Count Troilo Sansecondo's horse got a little too happy and had everybody all roiled up. They feared that it would do something silly, despite being all tied down; but the servant kept him calm."

[188] "They came with the second down from the cloud, now descended to the ground. The stage floor had opened up to the right and left. They gracefully walked across the field, then bowed to the newlyweds and other princes. They lowered their spears, following what the champion was doing, and placed themselves facing the enemy."

[189] "Judges having been elected, the seconds made sure the principals knew what combat observances they had to follow, and made sure they would pay attention, so as to carry out the combat happily and with glory."

[190] "They continued at times together, at times separately, sometimes with calls, sometimes with answers, according to what was necessary to performing an open field."

[191] "They both broke their first spear, and the game of swords went very well as the horses came together courageously, as was true of the two following, though they did not draw their lances."

[192] "Blessed be the Lord, we had the festivity which was a comedy with Don Ascanio's *intermezzi*. It came out wonderfully to the point that everybody was satisfied, especially the princes who were the most content of all. They honored us by sending their congratulations for our success. Mr. Cornelio behaved in a manner fit for a king, with such courtesy

that, you must believe me, we could not have possibly seen anything more beautiful or noble than this knight astride his horse with his spear from the end of the stage, and then a group of three knights from the sky with their spears."

[193] "I do not want to give many details on the beauty put together by Marchese Bentivoglio's genius or on other performances, since they have been fittingly sung by other and better poets. They were also adumbrated in Count Bernardo Morandi's famous chorus entitled 'Love's Competition.' Parma acquired so much honor in these celebrations of and devotions to Margherita as it did upon other occasions with the sword, helping or winning or defeating other kings and powers with deserved victories."

[194] "A royal tournament will take place Sunday or Tuesday. His highness will perform in it and it will exceed all those before."

[195] "The king is the only man capable of putting together great armies in so little time and of conquering lands so quickly. Similarly it behooves only this great prince to gather so many musicians, dancers, players and different beauties so quickly. A Roman general said that putting together a party for one's friends is no less qualification for a man than organizing an army capable of instilling fear in their enemy."

[196] J. Yoch, "'A Greater Power than We Can Contradict': The Voice of Authority in the Staging of Italian Pastorals," in *The Elizabethan Theatre* 8, ed. G. Hibbard (Toronto: P. D. Meany, 1982), 164–87, here 181.

Chapter Five

Elements of Meaning Formation: *Aminta* and the Emergence of New Staged Expressions (Western Modern Theater and Opera)

As I pointed out at the end of chapter 1, the value of reconstructing past theatrical events goes well beyond the flatly historical or the antiquarian. The 1574 and 1628 *Aminta* performances allow for a detailed view of the processes of meaning formation on the stage that, in turn, yields precious indications about the conditions that made modern Western theater and opera possible in the decades spanning the sixteenth and the seventeenth centuries. In this chapter, micro-history gives way to a theoretical line of inquiry that emphasizes the convergence of the organizers' goals with the audience's expectations and reception from the standpoints of space, courtly theatricality, referentiality, rhetorical strategies, and finally (and perhaps obviously) novelty, or *meraviglia*. As is often the case with lived (i.e., embodied) experiences (as opposed to theoretical ones), teleology plays a marginal role in this chapter. Serendipity did not prevent the 1628 *intermezzi* from being a resounding success with the convened audience, and a mark of glory and distinction for the Farnese court for many years afterward.

1. Space and Meaning Formation

The traditional emphasis on the linguistic and non-dramatic aspects of theatrical events in the field of Italian studies has resulted, among other things, in the marginalization of studies dealing with the space of performance. Theater historians have dealt with the development of theoretical studies regarding theater building, acoustics, and perspective in the late sixteenth and early seventeenth centuries,[1] but their research has had virtually no impact on literary scholars.

Nevertheless, as Gay McAuley's book *Space in Performance* emphasizes, space is central to performance, as it constitutes "the condition that alone makes possible the simultaneous presence of performer and watcher" (3). It is also an exceedingly complex and multi-faceted concept: we have a textual and a physical space, a concrete space (the stage), one that is represented, and at times one that is evoked (a feature that has central import in *Aminta*). In this section, I will consider space's representative and architectural aspects, and secondarily the topographical aspect.

Crucial to any consideration of early modern theater is whether (and if so, to what extent), spaces were representative, that is, if they could "stand for" something else. I have already indicated that both *Aminta* performances of 1574 and 1628 were public occasions, to the extent that they took place in a public space such as the court. While we might take the concept of "public" for granted, as Jürgen Habermas has shown, it acquired its origin, variable meanings, and connotations at a time only shortly following the two performances under scrutiny here. We tend to forget, for starters, that "public" is not equivalent to "open to everybody:"

> [w]e call events and occasions "public" when they are open to all, in contrast to closed or exclusive affairs — as when we speak of public places or public houses. But as in the expression "public building," the term need not refer to general accessibility; the building does not even have to be open to public traffic. "Public buildings" simply house state institutions and as such are "public." (*The Structural Transformation of the Public Sphere* [Cambridge, MA: MIT Press, 1989], 1–2)

Both *Aminta* performances were in this respect both public and not accessible to everybody. Further, they were public in another of Habermas's senses: "The word has yet another meaning when one speaks of a 'public [official] reception;' on such occasions a powerful display of representation is staged whose 'publicity' contains an element of public recognition" (*Structural Transformation*, 2). Thus these two *Aminta* stagings also displayed the type of representation associated with public recognition.

Nevertheless, they differ in the degree of restriction to and contamination with non-courtly events. At Pesaro, Tasso's pastoral was framed within *carnevale* festivities, and socio-political conditions traditionally deemed favorable to their appropriation on the ruler's part. Furthermore, though as we saw in chapter 2 the evidence is not conclusive as regards its topographical location, *Aminta* took place in a temporary structure that was endowed with the public recognition and political relevance of the ducal family. Therefore the Pesaro staging maintains an uneasy balance among popular occasion, restricted admission, city-wide import, and courtly attempt to endow this occasion and the specific performance with identifiable, political meanings (as past critics have maintained).

Fifty-four years later, the public relevance of the wedding celebrations within which *Aminta* took place at Parma was prominently featured, starting with the earliest actions of the Farnese, both within and outside their domain borders. The degrees of accessibility varied depending on each individual event: the whole town turned out to witness Margherita's entry into Parma on 9 December, despite the cold, damp weather. Conversely, only selected guests were admitted to the apex of the festivities, the *Aminta* and *Mercurio e Marte* performances. Still, even in the case of the performance at the Teatro di S. Pietro martire, there may have been more people in attendance than historians seem willing to concede, if we believe the figures offered by contemporary sources. In other words, while Buttigli's claim that over six thousand people were present is likely exaggerated (in keeping with the overall tone of his *Descrittione*), we must avoid imagining an exceedingly small performance hall, or a sparsely populated theater. Since the Farnese were keen on offering a spectacle for the world to remember and recount, they simultaneously needed to restrict those admitted, to create a sense of exclusion (and therefore exclusivity) in the audience, but also to assure that enough witnesses would then describe, praise, and explain what they had seen to those that had been literally left out. As Calandrini's manuscript biography of Odoardo makes clear, through entertainment such as this the Farnese hoped to become famous, honored, and respected among both their peers and their subjects.[2]

Such an attitude towards public yet restricted events is entirely consistent with the ritual character with which the 1628 festivities were endowed. Stanley Longman has put forth the useful category of the "exoteric" to explain the appeal of spectacles on their courtly audience. He asserts that "[l]'esoterismo, di solito, si riferisce ad un sapere riservato ai privilegiati o agli iniziati. Così, il raggiungimento della verità richiede un contatto mistico attraverso la magia, il rito, o i misteri. Per estensione, quest'idea si può applicare tanto al sapere quanto al potere."[3] Courtly entertainment provides the necessary point of contact in this partaking of power on the part of the courtiers, excluding everybody else not just from a lavish spectacle, but from a defining occasion. Furthermore, it was of paramount importance for the festivity organizers that those in attendance understood the events on stage and the celebration on and off stage. Selecting the audience therefore played many relevant roles.[4]

Further, Calandrini's verbose work reveals what was for centuries the most important paradox of the 1628 festivities and those akin to it: that such a momentous and public event be celebrated in such a fleeting, impermanent manner. Still, tools were available to insure that these festivities would be long remembered: printed or manuscript works (such as Buttigli's *Descrittione* and Calandrini's *L'Heroe d'Italia*) were powerful tools in the hands of the organizers and of the court, serving the purpose of immortalizing, or re-presenting (in Louis Marin's first sense) what had taken place.[5] The overabundance of details and the excited tone of these works also correspond to their semi-official capacity. However, the fact that the authority and legitimacy of the court can be represented, in Marin's second sense, in a published description points to an evolution taking place in the concept of the embodiment of power. In the Middle Ages, according to Habermas:

> in itself the status of manorial lord, on whatever level, was neutral in relation to the criteria of "public" and "private," but its incumbent represented

it publicly. He displayed himself, presented himself as an embodiment of some sort of "higher" power . . . Representation in the sense in which the members of a national assembly represent a nation or a lawyer represents his clients had nothing to do with this publicity of representation inseparable from the lord's concrete existence, that, as an "aura," surrounded and endowed his authority. (*Structural Transformation*, 7)

From early modernity onward, however, "the independent provincial nobility based in the feudal rights attached to the land lost its power to represent; publicity of representation was concentrated at the prince's court" (9). Although the sociological concept of the "public" continued to exist, more and more its representation retreated to the enclosed domain of the court. As power did not have to be embodied in a single human being any longer, the ruler could retreat to this privileged dwelling place and display himself more rarely, but more lavishly, and only in specific circumstances. Such displays were carefully concerted and their audience highly selected, but "representation must still depend on the presence on people before whom it was displayed" (10). Both *Aminta* performances under our scrutiny were simultaneously restricted to a small part of the population, yet also open to the public due to their relevance to the town and by virtue of the fame they acquired.[6]

Far from being merely external or secondary, limited or enclosed space is of crucial import in early modern culture, as Richard Trexler has shown: "[i]nhabitants created worshipful [i.e., ritualized and common] space by enclosing it" (*Public Life in Renaissance Florence*, 47). Within city limits, each event and occurrence acquired a specific meaning within the network of spatial (and therefore social) relationships in which it took place. Yet this contradicts one of the most common interpretations of pastoral texts, especially *Aminta*: that such plays were strictly courtly entertainment, performed either within the limits of the ruler's *palazzo*, or outside city limits in country estates, precisely to underscore the pastoral's links to a less corrupt and more private state.

It is impossible to overstate that at the core of such interpretation lies Solerti's hypothesis that the first performance of *Aminta* took place on the Este retreat of Belvedere, an island in the Po river just outside Ferrara's city limits. Thus Giovanni Da Pozzo juxtaposes "spettacoli pubblici" [public spectacles] to "forme alternative di spettacolo" (*Ambigua armonia*, 31) [alternative forms of spectacle] that include pastoral plays, devoted to *otium* and carefree enjoyment.[7] *Extra moenia*, Alfonso II can divest himself of the "funzione rappresentativa" [representative function] with which he is invested at court. *Extra moenia*, Alfonso II enjoys an intimate, private enjoyment ("spasso"). While Da Pozzo's judgment is nuanced and implicit, Godard's explicitly involves *Aminta*, interpreted as corresponding to the harmonious, unofficial life possible on Belvedere.[8] For Godard, in essence, the spatial setting on a private, exclusive island is eminently suited to the idealized court that

Tasso seemingly put before the courtiers' eyes. I will return to the ideological elements implied by Godard's interpretation later on in this chapter, since escapist interpretations of *Aminta* and of pastoral in general have long been popular, but, in my opinion, have also hindered a thorough analysis of the process of meaning formation on stage. From the spatial standpoint, it is important to avoid the symbolic distinction between court and garden that Da Pozzo and Godard postulate. Gardens stood within a noble family's realm: they were thus steeped in what I would call the public self-display that permeated the courts. Daniela Dalla Valle rightly remarks that the garden in which pastoral plays took place or were staged is not a post-romantic glade in the woods, beautiful in its unkempt, wild state; it is instead an emanation of the court, a space made safe by the presence of the ruler, therefore vested with his representativity and authority.[9] Traditionally, however, this aspect has gone largely undetected; even perceptive critics, like Gianni Venturi and Giovanni Da Pozzo, emphasize the alterity between the space of daily courtly interaction and the spatial setting of *Aminta*, i.e., the garden. Da Pozzo for example writes that

> il presupposto che permette la simulazione [of the staging] è che lo spazio del teatro sia diverso da quello della corte. Nel caso particolare [of the opening performance of Tasso's pastoral], è sempre apparso come motivo di singolarità il fatto che il luogo stesso su cui poggia lo spazio teatrale è altrove, rispetto al consueto spazio della stessa città, è l'isola di Belvedere, per arrivare alla quale gli spettatori dovevano attraversare l'acqua del fiume.
> . . . Nell'*Aminta* il luogo rappresentato sulla scena non è l'Arcadia della consueta finzione e nemmeno la corte, che sta oltre il fiume, ridisegnata nello spazio scenico. Il luogo deputato è il posto stesso in cui si rappresenta la favola, il "luogo di passo" di cui parla il Coro al verso 1211, esteso e allargato a tutto il resto. (*Ambigua armonia*, 146)[10]

The alterity of the space of the island as against that of the city and of the court is made manifest, according to Da Pozzo, by the water that the spectators need to cross in order to attend the performance. The Po river, in other words, functions as a liminal device, much like the wall encircling the city (or the curtain that separates the stage from the viewers before a staging begins). This, in turn, allows the convened audience to identify this location with that of the *Aminta* plot. Da Pozzo nevertheless fails to notice the continuity between the island-garden and the court. To follow Dalla Valle, while the atmosphere at Belvedere was different from the one at court (since the former was the space of *otium*, while the courtly palace was devoted to the endeavors of *negotium*), both spaces were rigidly separated from that occupied by those who did not have access to the court, and equally public, since they were clearly associated with the space of the ruler. By limiting his analysis to literary elements (and undocumented ones, as I have remarked before),

Da Pozzo ignores the issue of accessibility: for most residents of Ferrara, the ducal palace was as off-limits as was the island of Belvedere, and for the members of the court admitted to both spaces, these were obviously the ruler's *loci*.[11]

The pull of a traditional interpretation of the garden *qua* idealized retreat from the court proves too powerful to resist even for a historian of architecture and gardens like Gianni Venturi. In a collection of essays dedicated to Tasso's works, he states that Belvedere is a frame conceived by the ruler to make possible the artistic expression of a sign-based power structure.[12] If Belvedere is the place of utopia, it is also highly ideological; far from being "natural," it is endowed with the marks of the ruler's domination and power, indeed it is one of these signs on the structure of the very space of the city — and consequently on its citizens.[13] In James Yoch's opinion, "[i]n such gardens it would have been difficult to forget even for a moment the authority that controlled the scene by means of talent, learning, money and tricks" ("Limits of Sensuality," 66).[14] Nevertheless, in an earlier work, Venturi has asserted that in Tasso specifically, Belvedere is the mirror of the court: the latter aspires to a golden age of innocence, but cannot conceive it apart from itself.[15] Venturi emphasizes the "antitetico" and "speculare" nature of Belvedere vis-à-vis the court, which directly contradicts his other interpretation. What has shifted here is the emphasis: Tasso's own idealized aspirations prove more important than the cultural and spatial backdrop within which *Aminta* was conceived. Thus, a conflicted Tasso could only have written a text that yearns for a space other than the ruler's official one, but irrevocably (and inherently) marked by the presence of the court as source of "cultura" and "onore."[16]

If the implied space of the text elicits such sustained attention, it is evident that the explicit space of performance, in both its topographical and its architectural connotations, is of paramount importance to the process of meaning formation. For the 1574 and 1628 *Aminta* stagings no member of the convened audience could release him/herself from the specific spatial setting. At Pesaro, the performance took place in a temporary hall built for the 1571 festivities accompanying the entry of the new duchess, Lucrezia d'Este. Whether such a theater was situated outside the city limits at the Villa Imperiale, or (as is far more likely) within the confines of the ducal palace itself, the *Aminta* setting was firmly rooted in a courtly atmosphere. Similarly, at Parma the temporary "teatro inferiore" was ensconced inside the ducal Palazzo della Pilotta. Beyond this topographical resemblance, however, these two stagings had virtually nothing in common from the architectural standpoint — not surprisingly, since the intervening fifty-four years had seen various changes in courtly staging traditions.

The "sala . . . fatta per la venuta della principessa" (Saviotti, "Torquato Tasso e le feste," 413; MS oliveriano 390, fol. 94 r) [the hall built for the princess's entry] where the 1574 performance took place was rectangular in shape, and (as the painted scenes that adorned all sides indicate) non-perspectival in nature. Though it is possible, indeed even likely, for a privileged seat to be established in a central position in the pit so as to provide a privileged viewer (or a group of them) with the best geometrical view, the existence of painted scenes on all hall walls indicates that the stage was one of many pictures surrounding each audience member. Furthermore, as already stressed, the "simulacri di stucco bianchi" (fol. 659 v)[17] [white stucco moldings] separating the paintings and the stage front from each other insist on the representational unity of each element, whether bi-dimensional (the paintings) or embodied (the performers on stage). The stage, then, is one of many competing foci of attention, and subsumed into the totality of the hall itself (and, by extension, of the wider space in which it takes place, a ducal palace).

Before the 1628 *Aminta* performance, conversely, architects, festivity organizers, and court deputies spent long hours considering how best to build a comfortable and lavish, but quick and inexpensive, temporary hall, in which as many people as possible could view the various shows that would take place at the same time: both on stage and off. Though the result was reached somewhat serendipitously, the "teatro inferiore" represented quite a different space from the "sala" of the 1574 *Aminta*. Though the latter was distinct in its destination from the banquet hall that was also built for Lucrezia d'Este's 1571 Pesaro entry, its architectural configuration indicates that the reflection on and practice of building theater structures was still in its infancy. How well each of the convened spectators would be able to see elicited little or no attention. Conversely, as Mazzi's letter to Bentivoglio dated 8 December 1627 indicates, one of the principal concerns during the preparations for the Parma staging was that as many audience members as possible be able to see the various events unfolding: "perche gli spetatori si sfugiono l'uno con l'altro et habiano ocasione di meglio vedere" (Lavin, "Lettres" 138; idem, *Art and Pageantry* 537; MS Antonelli 660, 8 December 1627, fol. 1 r) [so that the audience avoid being in one another's way and can see better]. While at Pesaro the staged performance was one of many concurrent visual elements vying for the audience's attention, at Parma the concomitant occurrences (the *Aminta* performance with its *intermezzi*; the display of the newlyweds and their retinue to the convened courtiers and guests; the corresponding parade of the court for the benefit of Margherita and Odoardo) were subordinate to the occasion then being celebrated, as the liminal indication of Margherita and Odoardo's entrance into the hall makes clear. Thus the 1628 Parma events show the confluence of two transformations that took place in the fifty-four years separating them from the events in Pesaro. First, the location of a privileged viewing point emerged as crucial to conceiving and building a performative space. Second, and perhaps in relationship with the first, the space of the performance became more specialized: still fully endowed with courtly connotations (indeed more than before, as the description of the "teatro inferiore" indicates beyond the shadow of a doubt), it acquired a character that clearly set it apart from the rest of the courtly building, in order to emphasize its ritualistic elements and separate it from the theatricalized everyday at court.

It is in this vein that *Aminta* emerges as the far from casual centerpiece of the Pesaro *carnevale* and one of the most important events of the Parma wedding celebrations. Rhetorically, Tasso's pastoral play is epideictic, as I will show later on in this chapter; representationally, it expresses the early modern court's defining ideology, that is, the need for everything within the spatial and symbolic boundaries of the court to stand for, that is to represent, something else. These *Aminta* performances (especially the one at Parma) simultaneously formed a part of the continuous staging that life at court is and yet managed to distinguish themselves from this theatrical continuum, thus establishing themselves as a staged play closer to the modern sense of the term.

That early modern courts were spaces where everyday life became fully theatricalized is a topic that has been extensively studied. Clifford Geertz's famous anthropological study of nineteenth-century Balinese culture offers a description that best adapts to this early modern situation, perhaps because it situates its readers in a reality "other" than his/her own. He characterizes the state in the following terms:

> Court ceremonialism was the driving force of court politics; and mass ritual was not a device to shore up the state, but rather the state, even in its final gasp, was a device for the enactment of mass ritual. Power served pomp, not pomp power.
>
> Behind this, to us, strangely reversed relationship between the substance and the trappings of rule lies a general conception of the nature and basis of sovereignty that, merely for simplicity, we may call the doctrine of the exemplary center. This is the theory that the court-and-capital is at once a microcosm of the supernatural order — "an image of . . . the universe on a smaller scale" — and the material embodiment of the political order. It is not just the nucleus, the engine, or the pivot of the state, it *is* the state.[18]

Needless to say, late-sixteenth- and early-seventeenth-century European courts show specific characteristics that differ in part from the details that Geertz offers. Early modern courts were busy setting up centralized means of control over the various activities of the state (embodied in a all-pervading, unwieldy bureaucracy). They also wanted to establish an "exemplary center" through symbolic means, such as staged events taking place at court. In this respect, too, it is evident that performances such as those under scrutiny here were profoundly public, though access to them might have been restricted. They reverberated through the court, the city and its population, and outside the domain boundaries.[19]

Nevertheless, Geertz's approach is fruitful inasmuch as it is predicated upon our estrangement from contemporary categories, such as representativity and the dualism between form and content (or appearance and substance).[20] Within courtly performances, contamination was the rule, as Aercke has rightly pointed out.[21]

Though "work" (or, perhaps more appropriately, "serious behavior") and "play" did not exclude each other, there existed a fluid, yet evident, boundary separating the event of staging proper from the continuum of everyday, all-pervasive court theatricality. Difficult to conceptualize (as it falls in the Goffmanian keying of ceremonials, where the playful and the momentous coexist), this boundary made it possible for courtly stagings to be at the same time self-referential and heteroreferential — to refer to their plot, but also to courtiers and to the representative foundation of the court's patterns of action and behavior. Such interferences, in Anna Nardo's words, "create logical paradoxes because the definition of the class of actions is itself one of the actions being defined. Although theoretically invalid, this confusion of logical types — of the defining frame with what is inside the frame — pervades human life and can provide great pleasure" (*The Ludic Self*, 10). The success of the 1628 *intermezzi*, and of many other such stagings, indicates unequivocally that such paradoxes greatly appealed to early modern Italian audiences. Further, the tension between self-referentiality and external reference brings about a keen awareness of both in the audience.[22] The frame is emphasized by the constant insistence on the *décalage* between what it contains and what it excludes.[23]

This is a first sense in which performances are set apart from the "ordinary theatricality" of courtly life, even as its frame helps to contain it within its appropriate boundaries.[24] In this respect, the spatial frames that surrounded both *Aminta* performances under scrutiny, though different in nature (as noted above), exert the same role: setting the staging apart from the everyday court theatricality, so that they are clearly separated from it (while belonging firmly to the courtly milieu). Both architectural frames were devised in such a way to insist on themselves, so that they could not be ignored. At Pesaro, this frame was overabundant: in the anonymous reporter's words, "l'apparato . . . teneva la longhezza della sala" which was itself "tutta decorata di pitture à quadri di prospettive di paesaggi" (Ducato d'Urbino, classe I divisione B filza X, fol. 659 v) [the stage was as big as the length of the hall. Said hall was entirely adorned with paintings of perspectival landscapes]. At Parma, instead, the three-dimensional cornice framed the staging while insisting on the occasion being celebrated by displaying the escutcheons of the newlyweds' families.

In addition to this imposing architectural frame, the 1628 *Aminta* performance also enjoyed a temporal lag marking a boundary between ordinary courtly theatricality and the staged events. Thus at Parma there were three distinct liminal indications: the rising of the curtain; an orchestral melody; and the arrival of the newlyweds and dignitaries in the theater. The court and the invitees were already present in the theater for a period of time preceding these three events; this waiting phase emphasizes the difference between the two degrees of theatricalization, as well as the different social and political relevance of the newlyweds and those convened to celebrate them.

The *Aminta* text itself provided audiences with a reinforcement of this spatial and temporal frame. Tasso's pastoral opens with a prologue, which aims at constituting the time and space of the performance as separate and different from the rest by insisting on self-deixis and other explicit liminal indications. Unfortunately on the basis of extant testimonies the issue of whether Tasso's prologue (or another one, perhaps written specifically for that performance) was staged in 1574 cannot be decided. Conversely, Achillini's prologue for the 1628 staging underscored the events celebrated with the Parma festivities, thus simultaneously distancing the performance from and linking it with ordinary courtly theatricality.

It bears repeating that such courtly festivities did not fall into the category of make-believe. In other words, though frames separated different degrees of theatricalization of the everyday, they did not divide "reality" from "pretense." Once again we are confronted with notions that do not easily fall into our categories. Nevertheless, if we refer to the concepts of ritual and ceremonial, we will make sense of a seemingly puzzling trait shared by both lay and religious early modern representations: the participation of the audience. I have already observed, in chapter 4, the inadequacy of José Antonio Maravall's analysis of baroque theater in Spain, based on the utter alterity between staged events on the part of performers and passive observation on the part of the audience. The theoretical foundation for Maravall's thesis lies in a later idea of theater, one in which onlookers enjoy specific rights (such as expressing their approval or disapproval of the performers' acting abilities) but also are firmly aware of the make-believe status of what transpires on stage between the rising of the curtain and the last line. Thus the audience's participation, though crucial for any staged event, is codified and limited from the standpoint of interaction with and participation in the proceedings.[25]

Furthermore, within the Italian critical tradition, a long-lasting negative view of the mannerist and baroque periods has contributed to a disparaging view of festivities like the 1628 *Aminta*, based on their supposedly gratuitous and self-serving nature. Mamone writes, for example, that in Florence, at least since 1537, "[o]gni avvenimento spettacolare . . . non aveva altro valore in sé, ma fungeva da termine di riscontro con altre prestazioni, e la magnificenza di ogni allestimento valeva, oltre che per il pregio intrinseco, per quello che essa fruttava di prestigio e di risonanza presso i sovrani e i maggiorenti delle grandi corti d'Europa" (*Il teatro nella Firenze medicea*, 32).[26] It is worth noting the paradoxical juxtaposition of intrinsic "valore" [value] and "pregio" [merit]: the former is important, but utterly missing in Florentine sixteenth- and seventeenth-century festivities, the latter negligible, yet possibly present. The present study indicates, conversely, that the lavishness and magnificence of such festivities were deeply endowed with values and relevance, for the convened audiences as well as for those excluded from them within and outside city limits. William Butler Yeats aspired to the formation of an Irish National Theatre, because he saw in it an important tool to build "a community bound together by imaginative possessions."[27] This sense of inclusion for all members of the community was undoubtedly a goal of early modern festivity planners, but such "imaginative possessions" went beyond those imposed from above. As the Pesaro *carnevale* celebrations indicate, contamination was possible, even likely. The process of meaning formation was not limited to the intended connotations bestowed upon the festivity planners — theater had outgrown its function "as a means of violent but eminently useful socialization" that early humanists envisioned for it, according to Tylus ("Colonizing Peasants," 116). Space was important, as was the continuum of courtly theatricality. Within the space of performance, however, there were bodies. How did they contribute to meaning formation?

2. Bodies and Meaning Formation

When we consider the category of bodies within festive and performative spaces, there are two concurrent sorts that are of the utmost importance. The first is the (degree of) presence of the body of the ruler(s). The second is the presence of the bodies of the performers on stage, and its status. Neither one can be ignored, as both were central to the process of meaning formation in early modern stagings. Traditionally, the presence of the ruler has attracted the most critical attention; more recently, with the emergence of scholarly fields such as performance studies, the issues surrounding the status and possible meanings of the performing bodies have elicited sustained study.

Undoubtedly there existed a staging tradition, from medieval times, hinging upon the absent presence of the divine: as Georges Bataille has stated it, "Christianity has made the sacred *substantial*,"[28] that is, thanks to the Incarnation it has embodied it and therefore made it an object of depiction and representation. Simultaneously, the very possibility of representation depends upon an absence, or invisible presence, of its object, as remarked by Marin. The absent-present ruler (always a "he" in early modern Italy) occupied a similar position in late-sixteenth- and early-seventeenth-century courtly stagings. From an organizational standpoint, the ruler was ultimately responsible for the organization of the events, as attested in the chain of command emerging from the documents regarding the preparations for the Parma events. In a perspectively built hall, such as the "teatro inferiore" of 1628, he occupies the geometrical point of view from which the staging is meant to be observed. Lastly, he (or a member of his family) is the ultimate subject of the performance, that is, of the ritual being celebrated.

The geometrical and metaphorical centrality of the ruler does not necessarily imply that he has to display himself on stage. In this respect, the situation delineated by Geertz vis-à-vis nineteenth-century Balinese culture is profoundly different.[29] There, the physical central presence of the ruler was necessary for the event to take place and be socially and politically relevant. In late-sixteenth-century

Western Europe, on the contrary, the presence of the ruler, albeit necessary, did not have to be at the center. As we saw in chapter 4, Aercke has postulated that the transition to an absolute regime results in the removal of the ruler from active participation in the staging.[30] The situation in early modern Italian courts was nevertheless different from the one Aercke described in England. Virtually all Italian rulers, including the Pope, never enjoyed as developed an absolute control over their domain as did the kings or queens of England, France, and Spain. So the withdrawal from the stage in Italy is a way to mark a wish, an ideal towards which to strive, rather than the mark of the accomplishment of absolute rule. Furthermore, in at least one genre northern Italian rulers participated more often in the seventeenth century than before: precisely in those courtly ballets from which Louis XIV retreated in France (Burattelli, *Spettacoli di corte*, 66).

The geometrical and architectural position in which the ruler installs himself at Parma indicates beyond a doubt his will to control (optically and metaphorically) a vast portion of the audience as well as the goings-on on stage. In a post-Tridentine, absolutism-oriented culture, control over the object of vision and the point of view was of paramount importance to both lay and sacred authorities. While the ruler is not at the center of attention on stage, he occupies the most prominent position in the *sala*, displays himself for the benefit of the convened audience, and makes the events possible in practical and symbolic terms. In other words, the ruler's absence from the stage creates an aura of effectiveness and control around him, all the more powerful because he is disembodied and invisible. The absolute monarch does not assert his power through presence, because — as we have already noticed — his rights to it are perennial, untouchable and unchangeable, whether or not they are embodied in a specific human being.[31]

Louis Marin has underscored the parallelism between the overarching absence of the ruler from the stage and the one figured in the Eucharist: "the body present here of him who speaks now [saying, "l'Etat, c'est moi"] is none other than one body everywhere and always. Now a body at once local and translocal is precisely what the sacramental host realizes for Jesus Christ in the universal community of the church" (*Portrait of the King*, 10). Like the Eucharist, the body of the king becomes a sacrament. Here lies the ultimate paradox of early modern courtly stagings: they constitute privileged moments of courtly theatricalization and of representation of disembodied power in an embodied text.[32]

The ambiguous situation existing in early modern Italian courts with respect to the ruler's role on stage (or lack thereof) is evident in the Parma events of 1628. Odoardo, the groom and heir to the Farnese domain, was the *cavaliere mantenitore* of the tournament that closed the wedding festivities, entitled *Mercurio e Marte*. Yet neither he nor Margherita performed a role in the *intermezzi* that accompanied the *Aminta* staging. On the most obvious (and superficial) level, the fact that the *intermezzi* were set to music might be considered as an ultimately insuperable obstacle. However, the presence on stage of professional singers might have been perceived as contaminating for the groom, and in general, for noblemen. Margherita Aldobrandini's letter to Barsotti to convince Cesare Bernardini's father that it was perfectly acceptable and dignified for his priest son to perform in a pastoral is a clear indication that the stage was still perceived as dangerous in 1628, as the many treatises against theater by such influential figures as San Carlo Borromeo attest.[33] This stands in stark contrast with the Medici's participation in the Florentine *Aminta* performance, accompanied by music written by Emilio de' Cavalieri, in 1590 (Accorsi, "Musicato, per musica, musicale," 896, 916; Fenlon, "Staged *Ballo*," 32). Odoardo and Margherita are constantly referred to as viewers and reasons for the festivities, thus making their direct participation impossible.

Another element might have come into play: the fact that most of the professional singers were *castrati*. The contaminating effect of their bodies on the groom's thus acquires another layer of significance: it might have jeopardized the primary goal of the wedding itself, the continuation of the Farnese through Margherita and Odoardo's plentiful offspring. Conversely, in the *Mercurio e Marte* tournament all the participants were noblemen, and they engaged in a military show that displayed their prowess in skills suitable to young male scions of noble families. Readers will recall that for Tiberio Almerici, too, the identity of the tournament participants, their ability, and their appearance during the 1574 Pesaro festivities was far more important to pass along to his cousin than the identity, ability, and appearance of non-courtly performers of the contemporary *Aminta*. Whether or not Tasso's pastoral was performed by professionals at Pesaro, the juxtaposition of the relevance of the performers for Almerici could not be starker.

This element is directly at variance with the often postulated teleological development of modern Western theater with respect to referentiality, one of its fundamental traits. In Northern Italy in the decades spanning the fifteenth and sixteenth centuries, according to Giulio Ferroni, the basis for the all-encompassing nature of the court is the identity between what happens on and off stage; no referentiality is possible, except for the fact that some truly incomparable intellectuals, such as Ariosto, transcend their age and its prevailing customs — thus setting the path for subsequent developments.[34] With this slightly Burckhardtian assertion, Ferroni emphasizes the all-pervasive and literalizing influence of the ruler over courtly stagings. Yet seemingly by magic, by the time Tasso composes *Aminta*, the situation is profoundly different, according to most scholars. For example, Jane Tylus has asserted that Tasso "challenges the prerogative of the court to invade the pastoral space and appropriate it as its own. His theater firmly and implicitly rejects an analogy between an innocent audience and innocent viewers, between purity offstage and purity onstage" (*Writing and Vulnerability in the Renaissance*, 92). From the identification and lack of referentiality described by Ferroni, we have now moved to a complete juxtaposition and opposition predicated upon referentiality: when Alfonso d'Este and his court watch *Aminta*, they are made aware that the characters on stage refer to something other than their own bodies and other than the court.

Judging from the testimonies referring to the two *Aminta* performances of 1574 and 1628, we must avoid imagining a linear, teleological development of the performers' referentiality, and we cannot conclude that the transition from non-referential to referential theater had occurred by 1628. The 1576 Pesaro edict concerning *carnevale* celebrations indicates, through its word choice, that the act of putting on a mask implied a substantial change of identity, albeit temporarily. It was not simply a disguise, but rather "farsi maschera," making a different identity for oneself. Wearing masks is thus a potentially dangerous activity, from the standpoint of city rulers, and therefore has to be regulated and limited.[35] Conversely, in 1634 the *commedia dell'arte* performer Nicolò Barbieri writes in his defense of his profession:

> qual è colui così sciocco che non sappia che differenza sia dall'esser al finger? Il buffone è realmente buffone, ma il comico che rappresenta la parte ridicola, finge il buffone, e perciò porta la maschera al viso, o barba rimessa, o tintura alla faccia, per mostrar d'essere un'altra persona; e la maschera istessa si chiama *persona* in latino, e la licenza delle arme al mascherato il carnevale si rende invalida, poiché un mascherato si fa col grado d'altr'uomo, spogliandosi per quel tempo del suo; e per ciò i comici fuori scena sono altre persone, si chiamano con altro nome, mutano abiti e professano altri costumi. (*La supplica*, ed. Taviani, 24)[36]

For Barbieri, there is an obvious difference between make-believe, however effective, and reality, or (to use his own, sharp word choice) between pretending and being. The outward trappings of the performers' profession, such as false beards, masks, and make-up, are limited to a human being's surface, and cannot penetrate into his/her inner nature. It would therefore appear that between 1576 and 1634 this trait of Western theater was acquired. But at Parma in 1628, the *intermezzi* singers participated in a ritual relevant to everyday life, not in a situation of make-believe. They were professionals, hired and retained as such; yet differently from their *arte* colleagues, their gendered bodies were non-hetero-referential: for the ritual to be valid, the *castrato* Gregori (or Gregorio) was simultaneously the physical originator of the sung melody and Diana, in the third *intermezzo*.

It is precisely this fundamental discrepancy between the representational modes of *Aminta* and its *intermezzi* that justifies the different reactions to them on the part of the convened audience. Tasso's pastoral uses the tools that are to be found in modern Western theater, as far as the introduction and identification of the characters are concerned. Even a cursory analysis of the two scenes of Act I shows that characters are introduced *in medias res*, as though the playwright (and the audience) had caught them in the middle of an activity or of a situation that had already begun. Moreover, their names emerge from the flow of their verbal exchange: in I.i Dafne mentions Silvia's name in her first line, but she goes unidentified until line 205; in I.ii Aminta is identified in the twentieth line (356), while his interlocutor Tirsi's name is never pronounced. In sum, the audience's participation is required to make sense of the events happening on stage and to link them with the information offered in the first scenes.

Of the 1628 *intermezzi*, only the first and the second share this representational approach. In the prologue and the third, fourth, and fifth *intermezzi*, the strategy is profoundly different, as noted in chapter 4. There, characters appear on stage with the clear intent to identify themselves first, and only secondarily (if at all) to advance a plot or a story line. The ritualized context of this staging curtails the performers' ability to acquire a different identity and to exert this power over other objects on stage. As their agency is curtailed, the performers' bodies gain almost hieratical traits — traits that are only emphasized by their frequent stillness. Mostly, the performers' bodies do not move on stage, since they appear, disappear, and move about on stage machinery.[37] This feature again strips the performers of their ability to mean, while indirectly pointing at what (or rather, who) has made the performance possible. Furthermore, the characters' self-deixis goes hand in hand with a direct and explicit identification of the whereabouts of the action in these particular circumstances. During the *intermezzi*, the audience's role therefore is much more passive than in *Aminta*, since (as is the case in rituals) they are not required to make sense of (or to extract meaning from) the staged events. A considerable jump was required of the *Aminta* audience at Parma, one that increased after the second *intermezzo*. Even if one is to assume that the audience recognized these different representational strategies (that is, that they were not left puzzled and confused by these sudden changes), they did not have to conform to them: they simply refused to make the jump, and became utterly uninterested in the representation of *Aminta*.

Differently from the prologue and *intermezzi*, moreover, *Aminta* required the audience to sustain the same representational mode for the duration of the entire play. While we would find the continuous interruptions annoying and distracting, in 1628 the variety that *intermezzi* conferred on the evening was welcome; *Aminta* proved boring because it demanded sustained attention and one representational mode of the audience for its entire duration.

A paradox emerges here. On the one hand, for all these reasons *Aminta* proved boring at Parma; the extant testimonies leave no doubt on this point. On the other, however, Tasso's pastoral is otherwise eminently suited for a ritual celebration of the present, but removed, ruler. This performance text has often been decried for its lack of action, as most events take place off stage and become known to onstage characters and audience members alike through informative speeches. This allows for the location of the action never to move away from the "luogo di passo," in conformity with one of Aristotle's unities. Because very few actions take place on stage, characters and viewers are obliged to imagine those occurring elsewhere. Consequently, from the standpoint of representational strategies, *Aminta* is filled with instances in which a different place must be imagined, conjured up, that is, referred to. Riccardo Scrivano has come the closest to making this point, if we discount his use of the term "finzione" as too vague:

> Tasso . . . crea per la sua giovanile opera teatrale un codice generale che è appunto teatrale, dando materialità di gesto alla parola, che dunque va decifrata nel suo valore spaziale, che sarà anche sonoro e gestuale. . . . il teatro come finzione ha chiarito il suo vero ruolo intellettuale proprio in questa costituzione di un universo alternativo a quello della realtà e alla costituzione conseguente di modi di conoscenza finti, senza oggetto, deliberatamente paradossali ma parfettamente giustificabili . . . In questa vicenda una concezione alternativa dello spazio ha una funzione portante, larga e impegnativa.[38]

If by "finzione" we mean referentiality, then *Aminta* emerges as a liminal text in the transition to modern Western theater, based on building a reality "other" than that of the everyday. Ferdinando Taviani has perceptively noted that this representational strategy emerges from the prologue of the play, which "detta subito allo spettatore le regole della visualizzazione attraverso la quale l'opera gli apparirà in tutta la vividezza delle sue immagini seconde: una semplice verga [in Cupid's hand] dev'essere pensata come una pericolosissima face 'che tutta spira d'invisibili fiamme'" ("Teatro di voci," 25).[39] By the end of the play, therefore, "la scena culminante della storia, il congiungersi dopo infinite pene di Aminta ferito e Silvia pietosa, sta tutta dentro l'intreccio delle parole, viene luminosamente visualizzata e quindi mai materialmente vista dagli spettatori" (25).[40] In sum, with respect to representational strategies, Tasso's pastoral is eminently suited, albeit in a paradoxical fashion, to a celebration based on the removed presence of the ruler and his ability to endow the events with a set of meanings to which the audience refers to make sense of the proceedings.[41]

As a pastoral, *Aminta* differs from comedies that had preceded it, as it hides any sexually charged event by placing it off stage. Thus it does not contain the stock homoerotic situations created through the cross-dressing of female characters as found in learned theater.[42] Nevertheless, desire is present, as the scene with Tirsi and Dafne in II.ii illustrates. Thus the gender identity of the performers must be considered, as *Aminta* was performed both at court and on *commedia dell'arte* stages. At court, young men embodied all characters, but for *arte* troupes the appeal of women performers was undeniable (as well as financially crucial).[43] It is likely that the referentiality of the bodies on stage differed in various performance situations:

Margherita Aldobrandini had to spell out the opinion that it was perfectly suitable for a nobleman and priest to perform in a pastoral at court, but gender identity was subject to manipulations, as the presence on stage of *castrati* makes clear.

Aristotelian *decorum* proves central to the *Aminta* plot, as a rule to be followed, but also as a handy tool to remove from stage what was offensive, while inviting the audience to imagine what could not be staged and embodied. What did Tasso deem indecorous? In addition to anything even remotely sexual, anything bloody and encounters with power and rulers (in keeping with the pastoral fiction, seemingly) take place off stage and are later recounted on stage. While the stricter moral code in place after the Council of Trent is likely to have influenced Tasso's plot, the latter corresponds well to Aristotelian *decorum*, since "the greater the subject, the more powerful the emotions the speaker or writer may decorously solicit" in his readers or audience.[44] As the writer of a pastoral play dealing with humble men and women, the author aimed at emotions of love, rather than the horror of catharsis. Most events disappear from the stage, reminding this reader of a well-known trick of painters in post-Tridentine Western Europe: nudity being strictly forbidden as a subject matter for its own sake, it resurfaced in biblical stories, such as the bathing Susannah and the elders, or a scantily clad Mary Magdalene meditating over her past sins. On stage, where events are embodied, this invisible quality carries out an important function: training the audience's imagination and expectations to recognize the sort of referentiality that marks modern Western theater. Thus this element can be added to the growing list of those making *Aminta* eminently suited for performance in the crucial decades spanning the sixteenth and seventeenth centuries, both at court and on professional stages.

In the 1574 and 1628 courtly performances, *Aminta* emerges both as the intellectual progenitor of referential stagings, and as essentially old-fashioned, as it relies on one privileged creator of meaning (hence, one privileged meaning). Courtly ambiances did not stifle artists' imagination, as Burckhardt would have us believe; they promoted a self-serving representational strategy that had more far-reaching consequences than they could have possibly imagined. But what "ideology" lay under this strategy?

3. Rhetoric and Meaning Formation

Precisely because the *Aminta* text relies so essentially on a referential, "other" reality, for decades a debate has raged over the ideology that lies at its basis. Most scholars subscribe to the view that Tasso aimed at conjuring up in the intended audience's mind an idealized reality, different from that of the court. But at this point two tendencies emerge: one sees this idealization as sanctioned by the court, the other interprets it as a candid indictment of the court, its inhabitants, and the relations among them. While all subsequent interpretations are equally plausible, the present work is concerned with the process of meaning formation in its earliest audiences; it therefore restricts itself to those intellectual tools and categories that were available and widespread in the period of the two *Aminta* performances and immediately preceding them.[45]

Scholars have devoted very little attention to an intellectual tool the use of which was of the utmost importance for early modern learned people (by which I mean not just intellectuals per se, but anybody who had been schooled beyond the threshold of literacy): classical rhetoric.[46] Brian Vickers has forcefully asserted the need for subsequent scholars to realize that in early modern times "not only works of literature but modes of reading literature were shaped by rhetoric, and this in ways which may surprise us."[47] Although Vickers's study is concerned with how "the Renaissance *reader* approached his *books*" (499; emphases added), classical rhetoric also illuminates how early modern viewers endowed what they saw on stage with meaning.

Only Dante Della Terza has linked *Aminta* to its effects on its audience, and then only in passing: Tasso's pastoral "mira, in prima istanza alla persuasione e all'edificazione di uno spettatore insieme ferrarese e cortigiano" ("La corte e il teatro: il mondo del Tasso," in *Teatro italiano del Rinascimento*, ed. Lorch, 51–63, here 51) [aims, above all, at persuading and edifying a viewer who is both from Ferrara and at the court]. By referring to "persuasione" and "edificazione" of Tasso's implied audience, Della Terza hints that *Aminta* can be cast in the light of epideictic rhetoric. One of the three branches described by Aristotle, according to the latter it "has for its subject praise and blame" (*Rhetoric* 1358 b 3) projected on "the present, for it is the existing condition of things that all those who praise and blame have in view. It is not uncommon, however, for epideictic speakers to avail themselves of other times, of the past by way of recalling it, or of the future by way of anticipating it" (*Rhetoric* 1358 b 4). Though Della Terza has the merit of pointing out this fundamental trait, he attributes a limited scope to it, by linking it to *Aminta*'s local (i.e., Ferrara) court, which (as noted in chapter 1) might have never seen the play performed.

Aminta's popularity in courtly circles (at times, as at Parma in 1628, to its detriment) nevertheless provides a privileged point of departure for an epideixis-informed process of meaning formation, if we recall that early modern courts were given the continual representations of their inhabitants, their social place and position. As Frank Whigham has asserted, in early modern courts "[i]dentity comes close to becoming a pure commodity generated (however self-consciously) for conversational consumption."[48] In short, "the ideal courtier is never offstage" (634) because s/he is under the constant gaze of his/her fellow noblemen and women, as well of his/her underlings and the commoners (632). Life at court, in sum, *is* epideictic.[49]

On specific occasions, such as courtly entertainment, this epideictic spirit was especially heightened. Moreover, given their public, yet restricted, nature, courtly performances constituted one of the tools in the ruler's hand to influence the public at large (as might have been the case at Pesaro during the 1574 *carnevale*); they also tend to (literally) embody ideals in which the court would recognize itself.

Further, due to its patent lack of reference to everyday existence, even in the pampered lives of the courtiers, the pastoral genre lies at the convergence between Neoplatonic inclinations and Aristotelian rules. Because of Aristotle's wording regarding the preferred topic of an epideictic speech, "much of Renaissance literature . . . suffers from being divided into . . . sharply opposed binary categories. Virtue or vice, praise or blame, are instantly recognizable, since the whole of human experience is polarized into these extremes" (Vickers, "Epideictic and Rhetoric," 507). Such a stance fits well with the Neoplatonic ideals permeating humanism, and it becomes particularly concrete in the pastoral genre. Yet the Aristotelian debt is obvious in the practical turn that literature takes in this period. Virtually no text from any genre is devoid of the goal of showing the path to, or examples of, virtue to its audience.[50] Staged performances are especially susceptible to the same moralizing and didactic concerns, as evidenced in texts written by two stage practitioners and authors of the period. Writing presumably in the 1560s, Leone de' Sommi defines a play as "non . . . altro che una imitazione overo essemplar ritratto de la vita umana, dove si hanno a tassar i vizii per fuggirli, et ad approvar le virtù per imitarle."[51] Though epideixis is not explicitly mentioned in this definition, it is strongly implied. At the end of the sixteenth century, in 1598, Angelo Ingegneri more specifically linked the need for a play to adhere to the truth ("verità") with the effects that it elicits from its audience: "quanto più le dette cose s'avvicinano alla verità, tanto sono elleno di maggior efficacia nella . . . commozione."[52] In sum, an approach that pays attention to epideixis has the advantage of not imposing later categories on the reconstruction of early modern events.

Moreover, in historical terms epideixis plays a crucial role in this period. I have already remarked how religious and lay authority imposed stricter rules on what topics and subject matters were acceptable in the arts (in literature as well as the visual arts) in the period following the Council of Trent.[53] Because the other two Aristotelian rhetorical forms (the deliberative and the forensic) had lost their import in a progressively more centralized and controlled society, and because of the "confident belief in the power of literature to reach its audience and change it" (Vickers, "Epideictic and Rhetoric," 510), rhetorically shaped texts became both a rare tool to counsel rulers and an important means of influence over peers and subjects. It would be simplistic to see pastoral plays solely as a way to impose an interpretation or an alternative view on commoners and courtiers alike. The tension created by and within court staged pastorals ran in both directions, making their impact more cogent.[54]

In this respect, we can better understand how *Aminta*, a static (or, to use Louise Clubb's adjective, "undramatic" [*Italian Drama in Shakespeare's Time*, 96]) play in which wooden characters do little more than refer on stage to events that have taken place elsewhere,[55] was greeted with immediate success. Its characters[56] are not meant to reproduce human beings or imitate their behavior; rather, they are intended as embodiments of ideas and virtues: "[t]he Renaissance reader was accustomed, in theory at least, to seeing each character not as a complex, autonomous personality but as an illustration of a virtue.... Secondly, ... the Renaissance reader saw only the virtue represented in the character [and] looked through him, as if using an X-ray, to the moral quality and ignored other, less essential aspects of his or her behavior" (Vickers, "Epideictic and Rhetoric," 522). Maria Grazia Accorsi has even noted in passing that the rhetorical nature of the pastoral was an outstanding target of Giasone De Nores's criticism in the course of his diatribe with Giovan Battista Guarini. De Nores "vede nelle pastorali la pretesa di sostituirsi alla drammaturgia giustificata classicamente e socialmente conformata, cioè commedia e tragedia, e ... le giudica ... più orientate verso la concettosità e l'argomentazione che verso il diletto" (Accorsi, "Musicato, per musica, musicale," 889).[57] Far from being an accessory element, concepts and argumentation lay at the core of the then new pastoral genre.

In sum, what constitutes a weakness to our eyes (as readers or theatergoers) was indeed an advantage for a Renaissance viewer.[58] *Aminta* therefore falls into the same category as earlier treatises aimed at educating the perfect courtier (such as Castiglione's *Il cortigiano*, written in 1526). Because of its public nature as staged entertainment, its scope went beyond the boundaries of the court to enter the public arena at large. Certainly different social and political conditions required new examples to be set forth for the courtiers; this need accounts for the fact that tracts and printed dialogues were replaced by theatrical performances aiming at instructing while entertaining. It is a recognition of the effectiveness of staged entertainment, thanks to its ability to reach larger audiences (including, if necessary, the illiterate) and its clarity in giving life to, or embodying, moral and behavioral examples. It also highlights the multifaceted ability of contemporary performers, who exploited skills and resources garnered from disparate sources (religious preaching as well as the tenets of classical rhetoric that were drilled into any school pupil)[59] in order to entertain and sway their audience.[60]

The epideictic nature of pastorals, and of *Aminta* in particular, made them well suited to courtly performance, for reasons that differ from the escapist or status-quo-reinforcing ones that have traditionally been associated with them. As Scrivano has claimed, Tasso's "meccanismo teatrale ha come principio e fine se stesso, è l'aspetto teatrale del puro diletto che l'arte può dare, non si rapporta a niente" (*Finzioni teatrali*, 103);[61] within an epideictic mode (one that, to go back to Aristotle's definition, is inextricably linked to the present), this indeterminacy is perhaps the most cogent argument for staging *Aminta* time and time again.[62]

Though in 1574 Tasso's pastoral was still relatively new, having been written only the year before, its staging at Pesaro is remarkable from an epideictic standpoint because there it took place within the *carnevale* festivities, yet firmly ensconced within a courtly setting. The restricted staging, whether it took place at the ducal palace or at the Villa Imperiale, might have served to present a dignified and non-controversial view of social life (even beyond the confines of the court) to noblemen and women recently shocked by the conclusion of the Urbino uprising. The happy ending of Aminta and Silvia's love story, viewed as a bowing of their wills to their respective fates, might have worked to foster Guidubaldo's agenda in organizing *carnevale* festivities. Conversely, the controversial Mopso episode in I.ii goes in the opposite direction, as it criticizes the deceitfulness and corruption of the court, in veiled but uncertain terms. As Quarta has stated, "[s]e nelle parole di Mopso, riferite da Tirsi, la corte è il luogo claustrofobico, d'illusione, di perdita d'identità e di maligne forze . . . la corte vista e narrata da Tirsi è luogo di delizie e di grazia, di bellezza e di arte" ("Spazio scenico," 312): both ideas are suggested on stage, but the latter certainly prevails in the end.[63] The presence of the "novità del Coro fra ciascuno atto" (Saviotti, "Torquato Tasso e le feste," 413; MS oliveriano 390, fol. 94 r) [new phenomenon of choruses between the acts], supporting the notion that Tasso's pastoral was a flexible and adaptable text, additionally indicates that *Aminta* could strengthen a sense of "maestà," dignity, and nobility among audience members, increasing in them an awareness of their privileged status at court and within the city and the whole domain.

At Parma, *Aminta*'s epideictic nature paled in comparison with that of the prologue and five *intermezzi*. In 1628, Tasso's pastoral was perceived as fully self-referential, and apart from the ritual nature of the wedding festivities. Therefore it was easily dismissed by the convened audience. The prologue and *intermezzi*, conversely, acted as a bridge between the events on stage and those ritualized in real life. Their didactic nature, which we would find stilted (if not downright annoying and patronizing), indicates that the epideictic moment had simply shifted, but not disappeared; if anything, it had become stronger. Time and time again in chapter 4 I have underscored the teaching of the various episodes staged between the acts of *Aminta* for the newlyweds, and for the entire audience. Courtly theatricality, epideictic nature, and self-referentiality all went hand in hand for the 1628 audience. In order to complete the elements contributing to meaning formation, another trait of these performances deserves consideration: the above-mentioned "novità," "novelty," a mysterious category, to which I now turn.

4. Novelty and Meaning Formation

When in February 1574 Tiberio Almerici wrote to his cousin extolling the *Aminta* performance, and describing the *carnevale* celebrations, he underscored the element of newness at least twice. First, when talking about the *intermezzi* to Sforza Oddi's *Erofilomachia*, he attempts to make his cousin recall the one about the rape of the Sabine women in the following manner: "gia rappresentato altre volte in scena in Pesaro ... e si può dire che sia riuscito come novo a' spettatori poi ch'è tanto tempo che fu fattò" (Saviotti, "Torquato Tasso e le feste," 412; MS oliveriano 390, fol. 94 r).[64] Later, with respect to *Aminta*, he recounts that Tasso's pastoral was performed with the "novità del Coro fra ciascun atto" (Saviotti, "Torquato Tasso e le feste," 413; MS oliveriano 390, fol. 94 r) [new phenomenon of choruses between the acts]. In the first case, the Sabine women *intermezzo* appeared "as if" new, as it had not been performed for years in town. In the second, the chorus was a complete novelty, at least (as I pointed out in chapter 2) in that textual form and in that geographical location.

In December 1628, Inghirami's letter to Maria Maddalena mentions that "la Commedia ... riuscì ... cognita per essere l'Aminta e per q[ue]sto non fù con attenzione ascoltata" (Minucci del Rosso, "Le nozze," II, 562; Mediceo del Principato, filza 6075, 14 December 1628, fol. 1 r).[65] Novelty in this passage is implied, and juxtaposed to knowledge, or rather, to foreknowledge. These testimonies help us understand an added essential difference between modern theater and the 1574 and 1628 performances. Erving Goffman, in his study of twentieth-century social interaction, has pointed out that one central aspect of our experience as modern theatergoers is what I would term "willing suspension of foreknowledge":

> members of the audience in their capacity of onlookers, as official eavesdroppers, are accorded by the playwright a specific information state relative to the inner events of the drama, and this state necessarily is different from the playwright's and in all likelihood different from that of various characters in the play ... Being part of the audience in a theater obliges us to act as if our own knowledge, as well as that of some of the characters, is partial. (Goffman, *Frame Analysis*, 135)

The fact that Goffman's conclusions are evident, yet somehow go undetected because taken for granted, is a clear indication of the widespread (not to say obvious) nature of this behavior on the part of Western theatergoers. Goffman also helpfully indicates that the onlookers' state "is not ordinary ignorance, since we do not make an ordinary effort to dispel it. We willingly sought out the circumstances in which we could be temporarily deceived or at least kept in the dark, in brief, transformed into collaborators in unreality. And we actively collaborate in sustaining this playful unknowingness" (*Frame Analysis*, 135–36).

In 1574 and 1628 this behavior had yet not been established. For an early modern audience fully to enjoy the show, they needed to experience a sense of utter novelty vis-à-vis the staged events. Leone de' Sommi well recognized this need, as he wrote:

> nova la comedia vorrei, se fosse possibile, o almeno poco nota, fuggendo più ch'io potessi le stampate, quantunque più belle, sì perché ogni cosa nova più piace, et sì per esser parer quasi comune che le comedia, delle quali lo spettatore ha notizia, rieschino poco grate, per di molte cagioni, tra le quali principale cred'io sia questa: che, dovendo l'istrione ingegnarsi e sforzarsi quanto più può . . . d'ingannar lo spettatore in tanto che li paiono veri i successi che se gli rappresentano, sapendo l'ascoltante prima quello che ha a dire et a fare il recitante, li par poi troppo aperta e sciocca menzogna, et la favola perde quel suo naturale con che ella ha sempre da esser accompagnata. (*Dialoghi*, ed. Marotti 38)[66]

While he is specifically targeting the comedic genre, and not the pastoral, de' Sommi openly juxtaposes "new" and "printed" texts, and focuses on the effect that performers strive to have on their audiences. The more effortlessly their actions "build" a different reality, the more readily the audience will accept it.[67] The goal of any performance (and thus of each organizer and performer), for de' Sommi, consists in recreating as realistic a set of events as possible. This influences all staging aspects, such as costumes and make-up: "a me basta il trasformarli [i.e., the performers], e non trasfigurarli, ingegnandomi quanto più posso di farli parer tutti persone nove, però che quando lo spettatore conosce il recitante, se gli leva in parte quel dolce inganno in cui devressimo tenerlo, facendoli credere, più che possibile, per vero successo ogni nostra rappresentazione" (*Dialoghi*, ed. Marotti, 50).[68] The crux of any performance, in sum, is to convince the audience of the "vero successo" [actual occurrence] of what takes place on stage. Once a play had been seen once, then it would have been recognized, as was the case for *Aminta* at Parma, and perceived as fictional.

Conversely, *intermezzi* were by definition always new, as they were determined by the occasion then celebrated, and thus non-repeatable. Additionally, they ritualized reality and thus did not belong to make-believe. We are again confronted with events that we cannot easily understand: how can something be understood as new as well as real? Let us turn again to de' Sommi and Ingegneri, whose treatises highlight this paradox and provide us with an explicitly theoretical entry point into this practical and intellectual conundrum.

De' Sommi differentiates *intermezzi visibili* from those that consist solely of music. As far as the former are concerned, in his opinion a genre distinction is paramount. In the case of comedies, "dico che quando sono d'invenzioni che eccedono il naturale, non molto convengono alle comedie, le quali hanno da essere di cose naturalissime ripiene" (*Dialoghi*, ed. Marotti, 68).[69] Indeed, "con la loro novità traviano la mente allo spettatore, in modo che quando torna poi alla favola, le par men bella" (69).[70] Instead:

> [n]elle tragedie ... divise in atti, et così ne i poemi pastorali, saranno senza dubbio concesse cose più inusitate, poiché ne i loro stessi corpi si ammette ancora introdurre ombre, furie, et diverse deità et personaggi estraordinarii; ma se questi intermedii avranno poi qualche proprietà con le favole, senza dubbio si faranno più riguardevoli ... senza però torsi in tutto del soggetto della favola (70–71)[71]

de' Sommi allows for more imaginative *intermezzi* to be performed alongside tragedies (when already divided into acts) and pastorals because their plots are in themselves less linked with everyday reality. The simplicity and linearity of *Aminta*'s plot emerges as a potential drawback from its earliest performances, since few mythic characters appear on stage, thus undermining the aura of non-reality-bound quality that de' Sommi counts on for seamlessly linking the *intermezzi* with the body of the text.

A few decades later, Angelo Ingegneri condemns *intermezzi* in no uncertain terms as disrupting the dramatic tension of tragic plots, but accepts them in comedies and pastorals: "alla pastorale e alla comedia non pure convengono, ma sono di grandissimo ornamento, e simili, over dissimili, ch'essi si sieno dalla favola, sempre arricchiscono lo spettacolo e dilettano gli spettatori" (*Della poesia rappresentativa*, ed. Marotti, 282)[72]. Ingegneri emphasizes a different element from de' Sommi's verisimilitude: dramatic tension, the goal of any performance, is what concerns him the most. A shift occurs in the decades between the 1560s, when de' Sommi wrote his *Dialoghi*, and 1598, when *Della poesia rappresentativa* was composed.

Because *intermezzi* are so different from the modern Western concept of theater, scholars have badly miscast and misunderstood them — partially because of the past limited emphasis on reconstructing actual staged events. Marzia Pieri asserts that in the spectacles taking place in Florence in 1586 and 1589, under Bernardo Buontalenti's direction, stage machinery involved and dazzled all the senses of the convened audience, while foreshadowing self-serving baroque *apparati*.[73] At least in the pre-baroque period of the 1580s the fascination that stage machinery, ever-changing stage sets, and what we would call "special effects" produced in the audience cannot be ignored. Surely there is a different degree of exploitation of these "special effects" between the Pesaro staging of *Aminta*, with its new choruses, and the one at Parma. Yet the goal is the same: enthralling and fascinating the audience, so that the staging would captivate them. This is a first, important sense in which Pieri's assessment of set changes as "fini a se stesse" [an end in themselves] is only partially accurate.[74] Moreover, if the audience is enthralled and held captive by the performance, then its message will be effectively delivered and its epideictic task accomplished. At that moment, the dazzling, bewildering staging of the *intermezzi* will not simply satisfy the audience's desire for novelty; it will also convey the deeper significance of the event. It is worth recalling that, while at Parma the plot of the *intermezzi* was approved by the Farnese court, the ruler was also a part of the audience. As such, he was subject to the same effects as everyone else in attendance. We cannot simply talk of imposition of a privileged meaning on the audience, and even less of straightforward manipulation of the onlookers' reactions.

Elena Povoledo puts forth another inadequate judgment of the *intermezzi*'s nature and object. In her opinion, *intermezzi* play a multifarious role: they aim at "saldare la continuità spettacolare che la riaccesa polemica aristotelica chiama ormai 'unità d'azione;' giustificare la progressione temporale, distrarre il pubblico dalle operazioni dei servi di scena, sollevandolo anche dal fastidio della lunga e obbligatoria permanenza in sala."[75] Yet *intermezzi* do not aim at joining together the various parts of the entertainment; the very fact that they do not share a plot but are free-standing emphasizes this discontinuity.[76] They did respond to the organizers' need and the audience's desire to dazzle those convened with ever-novel and unexpected elements. Moreover, since *intermezzi* performers are on stage, no stagehand could be at work to remove the props needed in one scene and to replace those with others for a subsequent one. Last, early modern audiences did not seem to be bothered by "lunga . . . permanenza in sala" [long presence at the theater]; it was quite ordinary for an evening of theatrical entertainment to last six or seven hours. If Inghirami notes, à propos of the Parma *Aminta*, that audience members were restless, it was only because of the cold surrounding them: they needed solace from weather conditions, not from an eight-hour performance.

By 1628, in sum, *intermezzi* fulfilled various needs. They satisfied the audience's desire for novelty and amazement and carried out the overt epideictic goal of festivity organizers. At the same time, they expressed and acted out the ritualized reality celebrated on stage. From the latter standpoint, they realized a similar cathartic effect as that drawn from verisimilitude in tragedies, according to de' Sommi: "sapendo lo spettatore che la rappresentazione ha origine da la verità, si moverà più a terrore et a compassione ne i successi terribili et essemplari di quella; et essendo maggiormente commosso, purgherà più l'animo da i vizii, traendo più profitto da gli essempi, come cose considerate per vere" (*Dialoghi*, ed. Marotti, 16).[77]

Verisimilitude and novelty could (astonishingly, to us) go hand in hand. Yet this was by no means an isolated occurrence within early modern courtly culture. Novelty is even at the heart of the earliest attempts at scientific inquiry, according to William Eamon: in courtly circles, such as that of the Medici in which Galileo worked, "the idea of scientific inquiry [was] conceived as the discovery of *new* things rather than as attempts to demonstrate the known. The theme of novelty appears repeatedly in the scientific literature of the early modern period" (*Science and the Secrets of Nature*, 271–72; emphasis in original), as the titles of numerous scientific pamphlets and treatises makes clear.[78] So de' Sommi could simultaneously claim that the need for novelty induced him (and other contemporary directors) to stage exotic locales: "perché ogni novità più piace assai, riesce molto piacevole spettacolo veder in scena abiti barbari et astratti dalle nostre usanze, et quindi aviene che riescono per lo più così vaghe le comedie vestite alla greca" (*Dialoghi*, ed. Marotti, 50).[79] More importantly, for de' Sommi the necessity for verisimilitude essentially excluded indoor stage sets: "è . . . tanto fuori del naturale essere la stanza senza il muro dinanzi (il che necessariamente far bisogna), che a me pare non molto convenirsi, oltra che non so se il recitare in quel loco si potrà dire che sia in scena" (68).[79] The fourth wall that any present-day audience takes for granted when watching a performance was entirely unimaginable for de' Sommi and audiences in the 1560s, because it could not have possibly been present and transparent at the same time.

de' Sommi's explicit assertion indicates beyond any doubt that the marvelous stagings of the *intermezzi* were inherently similar to the pomp and self-display of the court to itself and to its subjects. Novelty was required by a contemporary audience's lack of willing suspension of foreknowledge, but also responded to the self-image of the court as deserving of homage and as giver of fame and honor. In other words, it was not inconceivable to courtiers that deities and characters from classical epic poetry would appear on stage to pay homage, through their very presence, to the assembled court, and in particular to the court members being celebrated. In Eamon's words, "[t]o belong to a court, even to a minor one, was to share in the prestige that went with rendering service to an overlord. Honor — that is, the praise and recognition of a prince — was the reward of servitude and the engine of courtly ambition" (*Science* 222).

One additional element deserves our consideration as it constitutes an important link between novelty and staged performances. Indeed, in a fundamental sense, novelty is fully possible only in an embodied form. If we do not emphasize the impossibility of establishing a boundary between what Aercke calls "play" and "work," or what I have called "reality" and "make-believe," we fail to recognize the lack of a fully rational and consequential type of communication that prevailed in courtly circles in early modern Italy. Eamon has opposed it to the previous tradition, when he writes that "[i]n contrast to scholastic argumentation, courtly discourse did not aim to result in necessary logical conclusions, but to present paradoxes and riddles, just as nature continually surprises the observer with its wonders."[81] The embodiments of staged performances foster this a-rational tendency, which deserves a non-hermeneutic investigation on our part. Novelty and wonder can best be elicited by the appearance of bodies on the stage, rather than through the more intellectual medium of written treatises. Again, the epideictic message of courtly pastoral performances emerges forcefully.

Eamon's assertion is nevertheless based on the juxtaposition between past intellectual tradition and habits and a new one. This comparison might be obvious to us, steeped as we are in the "awareness of the present as a future-oriented transitory moment that is diametrically opposed to an orientation to tradition as the basis for a type of civilization."[82] Yet the extant testimonies regarding the audience's reactions to both the 1574 and 1628 *Aminta* stagings suggest that such a clear-cut alternative was not conceptually available to late-sixteenth- and early-seventeenth-century intellectuals. Rather, the emphasis on novelty that runs through these festivity descriptions (and characterizes many of those contemporary to them) suggests an awareness of the transitory nature of the lived or experienced moment (again, underscored by its embodied characteristics) and a projection onto the future, which potentially holds newer, more bedazzling views. At the same time, the attention to past events that emerges in Almerici's and Inghirami's letters and in Buttigli's printed *Descrittione* hints at a conscious effort to link the present to a past tradition, on which it must prevail if it is to be new and marvel-generating. Cruciani has asserted that "lo spettacolo [in Flavio Biondo's treatise, written in the 1450s] non è ripetizione ma, pur quando si muove nell'alveo di una tradizione iterata, è il nuovo, la sorpresa, l'unicità."[83] Little seems to have changed from the 1450s to 1574 and 1628. Yet here we perceive the seed for the development of two of the three senses of the term "modern" that Gumbrecht has identified. The first, attested from the fifth century C. E., is "'present,' to which the concept of 'previous' can be opposed. . . . The second possibility of 'modern' is 'new;' its opposite is 'old.' . . . The third possibility of 'modern' is 'transitory' as opposed to 'eternal'" ("The Concept 'Modern',", 81). Gumbrecht perceptively goes on to note that "[i]t was characteristic of the Renaissance to pattern itself on the classical model, which may be why 'modern' was prevented from entering the self-reflection of the time as a predicate for an independent period" (83). While the term "modern" retained in early modernity a medieval connotation, the emphasis on novelty and newness intimate the future possibility to equate "modern" with "new" and, later on (specifically, according to Gumbrecht, in the nineteenth century [101]), with "transitory."

5. Emergence of Modern Western Theater and Opera?

Space, bodies on stage, epideixis, and novelty contribute to meaning formation for late-sixteenth- and early-seventeenth-century audiences. All these elements indicate the distance between the 1574 and 1628 *Aminta* performances and the current definition of theater. These two reconstructed events belie the linear, teleological development often postulated in histories of Western theater. If modern theater emerged during these decades, it was through a complex interaction between courtly sponsorship and professional (acting and singing) performers, between self-deixis and referentiality of the staged bodies, between demonstrative and commercial intents (such as those of *commedia dell'arte* performers). Novelty is perhaps the most puzzling element, or at least the hardest to rationalize.

Since our theatergoing experiences are largely based on exerting our willing suspension of foreknowledge, we appreciate novelty but find it hard to believe that it was such a crucial feature for early modern courtly audiences. Yet what separates us from "them" is a radically different concept of history, which we largely inherited from the Enlightenment; as Gumbrecht puts it, from the 1680s onward "[i]nstead of the Renaissance's cyclical view of history, which itself had replaced the typological perspective of the Middle Ages, there was once again a progressive historical model" ("The Concept 'Modern'," 84). For all our efforts to overcome modernity and be post-modern, the very fact that we need to "overcome" something existing in the past indicates how deeply teleology still permeates our intellectual outlook.

The conjunction of early modernity's attempt to relate to classical antiquity (and its impossibility to conceive of itself as an independent period) with the subsequent progressive (i.e., teleological) view of history have produced interesting historiographic results. The role of classical antiquity went from being something to be brought back to life to being the logical source for many unprecedented early modern events, from perspective in the visual arts to the *carpe diem* mentality emerging in disparate written works, from Lorenzo de' Medici's *canzoni* to Rabelais's mock-heroic poems.[84] Thus many writings and pronouncements left by the humanists themselves were reinterpreted to verify a teleological intent present in early modern times.

Courtly performances such as those in Pesaro and (even more) Parma had to be reinterpreted along the lines of classical tenets as well as later genres. As rituals, they do not fall in the frame of make-believe. As self-deictic, they are largely non-referential. As courtly, they mark their difference from everyday theatricalization differently from plays performed in spaces permanently devoted to embodied, for-hire, referential, and make-believe performance. Novelty was a largely neglected category, or else viewed as one of the deleterious effects of the baroque era. The distance from modern Western theater emerges rather decisively from a careful reconstruction.

What about the musical pieces accompanying the 1628 *Aminta*? Another interesting historiographic story surrounds *intermezzi* and other pieces like prologues and epilogues. Keen on finding a clear-cut beginning, music historians have attempted to determine how the new genre of opera was born. Thomas Walker, in the entry devoted to opera in the *New Grove Dictionary* of 1980, mentions various "antecedents" to the new genre: *intermedi*, courtly and academic entertainments, and the pastoral ("Opera," 550; see its updated version in *New Grove* [2001], 18: 418–29). Robert Donington refers to its three main "ingredients:" a philosophical, a poetical, and a musical one (*The Rise of Opera* [New York: Scribner's, 1981], 21, 32, 40). Sternfeld writes that "[t]he *intermedi* of the fifteenth and sixteenth centuries [were] one of the main roots out of which opera grew" (*The Birth of Opera*, 32). Even Nino Pirrotta, whose volume deals with a great variety of musical compositions for the stage, opens one of his chapters with the claim that "[f]ew other genres have their beginning as precisely determined as opera" ("Studies in the Music of Renaissance Theatre," 237). After "the first performance of *Euridice*, with music by Iacopo Peri on a text by Ottavio Rinuccini, which took place on the evening of 6 October 1600 in the Pitti palace in Florence" (237), he considers opera a full-blown, mature musical genre.[85]

From the historiographic point of view, with the establishment of opera something utterly unsurprising takes place: a new scholarly field emerged, separate from the study of other spectacular entertainment, as if courtly and academic shows on the one hand and opera on the other ceased influencing each other. Neglect, like dust, accumulates on the "gray zone" that continues well into the seventeenth century during which opera coexisted with other forms of sung, staged entertainment in what Bianconi has called "a kind of multi-coloured promiscuity" (*Music in the Seventeenth Century*, 171). In fact, like most births, the "birth" of opera was a messier affair than we have been led to believe, and its fictional quality emerges when we reconstruct past events, such as the Parma *Aminta* of 1628.

In chapter 3 I have dwelt at length on the secondary part played by music (and musicians) in the preparation of the 1628 festivities. In chapter 4, conversely, the primacy of sung entertainment for the contemporary audience can hardly be emphasized. In one fundamental respect the Parma *intermezzi* (and such musical pieces in general) differ from the earliest extant operas: the latter required some amount of interpretation by their audience. In this respect, they are far more similar to the *Aminta* text than to the Parma *intermezzi*. This constitutive element has elicited no attention on the part of those scholars intent on defining opera and exploring its historical and intellectual origins. Yet perhaps it is by following Buttigli's frequent mention of the liminal quality of instrumental music that it is possible to find a link with the often invoked classical antiquity. According to Vincenzo Galilei, ancient music:

> conservava la pudicizia; faceva mansueti i feroci; inanimiva i pusillanimi; quietava gli spiriti perturbati; inacutiva gli ingegni; empieva gli animi di divino furore; racchetava le discordie nate tra i popoli; generava negli huomini un'habito di buoni costumi; restituiva l'udito à sordi; ravvivava gli spiriti smarriti; scacciava la pestilenza; rendeva gli animi oppressi, lieti & giocondi;

faceva casti i lussuriosi; racchetava i maligni spiriti; curava i morsi de' serpenti; mitigava gli infuriati, & ebbri; scacciava la noia presa per le gravi cure, & fatiche; & con l'essempio di Attione possiamo ultimamente dire (lasciandone da parte molti altri simili) che ella liberava gli huomini dalla morte; oltre alle altre ammirabili sue operationi di che son pieni i libri d'autorità.[86]

This attitude, derived from both Plato and Aristotle, is reiterated by Mei[87] and Giovanni de' Bardi,[88] music archeologists intent on bringing classical music back to life. Later music practitioners, including Caccini (Pirrotta, "Studies in the Music of Renaissance Theatre," 245) and Peri (245–46), also espoused this opinion. More importantly, Monteverdi himself shared the opinion that music could evoke and stir emotions in its listeners, by way of reproducing those very feelings. Both Bianconi (*Music in the Seventeenth Century*, 39) and Sternfeld (*The Birth of Opera*, 36–37) cite a letter to Striggio dated 9 December 1616, in which Monteverdi squarely criticizes the plot of a piece he was to set to music because it included inanimate objects as characters, devoid of feelings and therefore incapable of stirring them through music. Over ten years later (and a few months before taking on the Parma *intermezzi*), Monteverdi detailed how he would "imitate" the feelings and emotions of Licori, a *finta pazza* and the protagonist of a piece he was to set to music: "il mio fine tende che ogni volta che sia per uscire in scena [Licori] sempre habbi ad apportare diletto novo con le variationi nove in tre lochi, bensi penso sortirassi l'effetto" (Malipiero, *Monteverdi*, 256).[89] Like Goretti, Monteverdi aimed at stirring the audience's feelings (*affetti*) through the effectiveness (*effetti*) of music.[90]

Here there emerges an important continuity between the *Aminta* text and Monteverdi's goal when composing. As Franco Croce has pointed out, while Tasso's pastoral is built around the on-stage narration of events taking place elsewhere, in IV.i Dafne's tale of Aminta's first attempt at suicide differs from those preceding it as it "non è più volto a commuovere in platea il pubblico (che è già commosso, già in ansia per le sorti di Aminta da quando alla fine del terzo atto lo ha visto allontanarsi dichiarando: 'io vo per non tornare'). È volto invece a commuovere, sulla scena, la protagonista" ("La teatralità dell'*Aminta*," 147),[91] that is, Silvia. With this seemingly simple staged event, the balance changes: "[s]ulla scena per la prima volta nell'*Aminta*, direttamente davanti agli occhi del pubblico, avviene qualcosa. E non è avvenimento da poco. Bensì una improvvisa e drammatica svolta nel comportamento della protagonista. Sulla scena, davanti agli spettatori, Silvia piange" (147),[92] thus setting the stage, literally, for the play's happy ending. But more importantly, I believe, *Aminta* stages the effect it intends to have on its very audience: emotions, *affetti*. In this respect, the earliest practitioners of stage music viewed Tasso's pastoral as a work akin in inspiration and intended effect to theirs.[93] This element has gone unnoticed by all the scholars of literature and music history that have dwelt on the topic, but not by Angelo Ingegneri, who identified the evoking of "nobili affetti" as one of the advantages of staged pastorals:

> le Pastorali . . . con apparato rustico e di verdura, e con abiti più leggiadri che sontuosi, riescono alla vista vaghissime; . . . co 'l verso soave, e colla sentenza dilicata sono gratissime a gli orecchi e all'intelletto, che, non incapaci di qualche gravità quasi tragica . . . , patiscono acconcissimamente certi ridicoli comici; . . . admettendo le vergini in palco e le donne oneste, quello che alle comedie non lice, danno luoco a nobili affetti, non disdicevoli alle tragedie istesse; e . . . in soma, come mezzane fra l'una e l'altra sorte di poema, dilettano a maraviglia altrui, sieno con i cori, sieno senza, abbiano, o non abbiano, intermedi. (*Della poesia rappresentativa*, 276)[94]

What bears underscoring here is the reason that Ingegneri gives for the effectiveness of pastoral plays: the decorous display of "vergini" and "donne oneste" on stage. The display of affections, and therefore its evocation in the convened audience, occurs more easily and more realistically through female characters, as Franco Croce implies when talking about Silvia. Further, from a practical standpoint, for Ingegneri pastoral plays were also capable of evoking "maraviglia" and "diletto" even without the staging of choruses and *intermezzi*; their form proved flexible and capable of accommodating additions, but their efficacy did not depend on external elements.

Along the same vein, the musicologist Francesco Luisi has proposed that "la pastorale era già un dramma per musica nel 1573" [pastoral was already a drama for music in 1573].[95] In his opinion, the year of *Aminta*'s reputed first performance should be seen "come punto di divisione tra la cultura del pastorale come genere rappresentativo e il dramma pastorale come genere letterario capace di esprimere una nuova drammaturgia" (102)[96] that will later be singled out by the earliest opera practitioners. Luisi identifies this role for *Aminta* as the earliest fully developed pastoral play, a genre that offered two concurrent benefits. On the one hand, it showed "rispetto degli schemi teorici e formali consolidati dalla tradizione;" on the other, it offered "adesione all'urgenza creativa di un nuovo genere che . . . meglio rappresentasse il gusto e le tendenze culturali della corte" (107).[97] More importantly, the pastoral was "un genere rappresentativo non del tutto nuovo ma tuttavia rinnovabile proprio perché aperto alle trasformazioni del gusto e ancora in attesa di teorizzazione" (Croce, "La teatralità dell'*Aminta*," 107).[98] From a theoretical standpoint, then, pastoral plays (though well known and accepted in learned circles) still offered the necessary flexibility to music and lyrics writers for a new-fangled genre such as opera.

Together with this theoretical flexibility, from the staging standpoint too *Aminta* offered a malleable structure; as its meaning did not depend on linear structure, it could be expanded, as pointed out in chapter 1, with the addition of choruses or *intermezzi* more easily than other genres (though, admittedly, not as easily cut). It appealed to theater practitioners for reasons similar to those brought up by late-twentieth-century writers engaging in librettos; as Joyce Carol Oates explains, "[o]pera has a spatial and temporal elasticity you don't get in any other [literary] form."[99] Tasso's pastoral, built on on-stage narration of events taking place in an evoked elsewhere, is by definition flexible and pliable, and furthermore, like post-modern opera, "non-linear," as the writer Manuela Hoelterhoff asserts (Smith, "Freedom of Opera," B2). *Aminta* falls in a pre-modern category, endowed with what Paul Zumthor has called "mouvance";[100] yet it appeals to our visual, post-modern sensibility, as Smith has underscored about opera: "[i]t's not surprising that a generation of writers who grew up immersed in film and television would be drawn to opera's visual spectacle, to its immediacy, to stories told to the accompaniment of music" ("Freedom of Opera," B2).

This very theoretical pliability might indeed help explain why *Aminta* has always been a part of the Italian literary canon, though, as noted, as a "minor" work. For its contemporaries and subsequent critics alike, *Aminta* constituted the perfect fruit of the Renaissance, belonging to a novel genre and to a revitalized literary sphere, linked to classical antiquity and yet fully modern: theater. Even Riccardo Scrivano, uncommonly attuned to the bond between written texts and staged events, writes that "la nascita del teatro moderno . . . si configura da subito come sintesi di una utilizzazione sorvegliata degli enormi magazzini di materiali antichi, sia nel campo dell'architettura teatrale che della realizzazione scenica, ma anche dei meccanismi, dei problemi generali, . . . e di una reinvenzione continua dei singoli pezzi di tale eredità e della loro combinazione e disposizione."[101] The birth of modern theater, then, is the logical intellectual link between the love for classical antiquity of the Renaissance and the desire for novelty and displacement of the baroque: in other words, according to Scrivano, the quintessentially mannerist artistic expression.

If there is an intellectual lesson to be drawn from reconstructing the *Aminta* performances of 1574 and 1628, however, it is certainly that we must exert the utmost caution in this comparison across centuries and cultures. If Scrivano's analogy between theater and mannerism is to be carefully evaluated, we should also resist the temptation to relate (if not equate, though in different media) television and courtly spectacles such as the 1628 *Aminta*. As Robert Hughes succinctly puts it, "[t]elevision is not . . . an art of conceptual memory. Its images are always displacing themselves. It must therefore pump up each one's vividness to keep the millions watching."[102] Conceptual memory seems to have been missing also from the fast-paced, novelty-laden *intermezzi*. Yet they were central to the events celebrated at the Farnese court, as the 1574 *Aminta* was to the *carnevale* entertainment in Pesaro. Conversely, TV entertainment (though, one may venture to hope, not news programming) squarely falls into make-believe: both shows and commercials aim "to create a fictive paradise of desire to which the quotidian reality is merely a backdrop, a world rearranged in such a way that we don't have to experience it" (Hughes, "Why Watch It, Anyway?" 38).

The distance that separates us from past events is insurmountable. Cultural differences and the very nature of staged performance make antiquarian or archeological re-stagings impossible, even undesirable. If the Romantic and post-Romantic pitfall of seeing Tasso and *Aminta* as our contemporaries elicits our criticism, perhaps even a sense of superiority, we must withstand the urge to find parallels between the past and our own experience. In the end, Goethe's and Chateaubriand's figure of Tasso will live next to positivistic reconstructions and post-modern, disenchanted studies — through the opaque, yet inescapable, screen of the written word.

Notes

[1] In particular, Ferruccio Marotti, *Lo spettacolo dall'Umanesimo al Manierismo* (Milan: Feltrinelli, 1974) and *Lo spazio scenico* (Rome: Bulzoni, 1974); and Franco Ruffini, *Teatri prima del teatro* (Rome: Bulzoni, 1983).

[2] Lorenzo Bianconi has made the same point with respect to musical entertainment: "The notions of 'public' and 'publicity' vary widely in accordance with social structure, forms of government and modes of artistic production and consumption. No less variable is the extent — both quantitative and qualitative — of the definition in question": *Music in the Seventeenth Century*, 66.

[3] "Exoterism usually refers to knowledge restricted to the privileged or the initiated. Reaching the truth implies a mystical contact through magic, ritual, or mysteries. We can extend this concept from knowledge to power": S. Longman, "Esoterismo negli spettacoli della corte dei Farnese," in *Il bosco sacro*, ed. E. Zolla and M. M. Siniscalchi (Foggia: Bastogi, 1992), 121–25, here 121.

[4] The restricted access to courtly rituals such as the Parma wedding celebrations underscores the danger that common consumption entailed. Only those who would be able to comprehend the rules of the court could be admitted. A similar hybrid (public yet restricted) space existed in the seventeenth century in England, where the Royal Society wanted to avoid the risk "that experiments might simply bedazzle onlookers instead of enlightening them . . . This is why it was important that the space within which experiments were performed be a *disciplined* and to some extent *restricted* space": W. Eamon, *Science and the Secrets of Nature* (Princeton: Princeton University Press, 1994), 338; emphases in original. Those who could obtain access to this space were "those who gave their assent to the legitimacy of the game being played within its confines": Eamon, *Science*, 338 — a serious game, but play nevertheless, much (as we will see) in the case of courtly performances. I thank my friend Eric Nicholson for bringing Eamon's study to my attention.

[5] "What is re-presenting, if not presenting anew (in the modality of time) or in place of (in the modality of space)? The prefix *re-* introduces into the term the value of substitution.

Something that was present and is no longer is now represented. In the place of something that is present elsewhere, a given is present here. At the place of representation then, there is a thing or person absent in time or space, or rather an other, and a substitution operates with the double of this other in its place": L. Marin, *Portrait of the King* (Minneapolis: University of Minnesota Press, 1988), 5.

[6] Habermas' words: "In comparison to the secular festivities of the Middle Ages and even of the Renaissance the baroque festival had already lost its public character in the literal sense. Joust, dance, and theater retreated from the public places into the enclosures of the park, from the streets into the rooms of the palace. The castle park made its first appearance in the middle of the seventeenth century but then spread rapidly over Europe along with the architecture of the French century. Like the baroque palace itself, which was built around the grand hall in which the festivities were staged, the castle park permitted a courtly life sealed off from the outside world. However, the basic pattern of the representative publicness not only survived but became more prominent": *Structural Transformation*, 9–10, are echoed by Silvia Carandini's: "Per un verso, [in the seventeenth century] agisce ancora lo stimolo a mettere in mostra nelle occasioni festive la sfera personale, a rovesciare all'esterno le superfici interne delle case, ad esibire l'arredo pregiato delle abitazioni di lusso, a trasformare tutta la città in un ambiente prezioso, illuminato e confortevole, e anche a mostrare in pubblico rituali e comportamenti intimi, privati diremmo oggi. Per l'altro verso, allo stesso tempo si precisa una tendenza inversa a circoscrivere il luogo dello spettacolo nel territorio urbano, a chiudere entro recinti il sito di eventi particolari, a ricreare all'aperto una dimensione interna raccolta, controllata e sicura, oppure a trasferire in ambienti chiusi, a stabilmente fissare gli impianti mobili della festa cittadina sempre più specializzando e funzionalizzando le strutture ricettive per il pubblico e per la scena [with the creation of permanent enclosed theaters for hire]": *Teatro e spettacolo nel Seicento*, 182–83 [On the one hand, the seventeenth century still shows the desire to display the personal sphere upon public occasions, to turn the surface of homes inside out, to parade high-quality furniture from luxurious dwellings, to transform the whole city into a precious, lighted and comfortable room, and even to display publicly what we now call private behavior. On the other hand the opposite tendency emerges concurrently. It is the tendency to limit the space of the spectacle within the city, to enclose the area of special events, to re-create an inside, secluded, controlled and safe dimension outdoors, or to move indoors and settle the movable city festival apparatuses by making the space for the audience and the stage more specialized and purpose-specific].

[7] "Tutti i signori d'Este conoscono il soggiorno presso le delizie di campagna, tutti si dilettano di teatro, di commedie come di pastorali, di sfilate trionfali come di tornei fastosamente e fantasiosamente carichi di motivi di meraviglia. Ma Alfonso [II d'Este] sembra, più degli altri predecessori, ritirarsi nei luoghi di delizia per coltivare un conforto, una consolazione della mente, in modo più intimamente privato ambisce al luogo di spasso campagnolo, quasi per una alternativa alla funzione rappresentativa che è tenuto a sostenere in corte; si ritira a riposare con maggior disposizione a lasciarsi convincere della fugacità di quanto assedia la sua mente e a lasciarsi illudere dalla esaltazione che dalla piccola corte che lo segue fuori le mura viene alla sua persona": Da Pozzo, *Ambigua armonia*, 31–32 [all Este lords are familiar with countryside retreats, with pastoral and comedic theater, with triumphal processions and with tournaments loaded with lavish,

fantastic reasons for marvel. Yet more than anyone else, Alfonso seems to retreat into his *délices* to comfort and soothe his mind. He wishes for country enjoyment in an intimate and private way, almost as an alternative to the representative function that he has to play at court. He retreats and rests and is willing to be convinced that what beleaguers his mind is short-lived and to cultivate the illusion that he is to be exalted, the way the small court that follows him *extra moenia* wants him to believe].

[8] "Avec l'*Aminte*, une parfaite correspondance s'établit entre les conditions extérieures de la représentation et la fiction proposée sur scène: à un spectacle strictement réservé — à la différence des grands tournois — au public de la cour, comme l'étaient, en règle générale, les pastorales et comme le fut tout particulièrement l'œuvre du Tasse, répond, sur le plan du contenu, un monde d'Arcadie où les protagonistes, nymphes et bergers, apparaissent comme des représentants de l'élite aristocratique, mais des représentants de cette élite délivrés de tout ce qui pourrait suggérer le poids des soucis et des responsabilités qui leur reviennent en tant que classe dominante, puisque ces personnages sont aussi, aux termes des conventions du genre, les uniques habitants de l'univers fictif, vivant en une harmonie aussi immediate que faire se peut avec la nature": Godard, "La Première représentation de l'*Aminta*," 285 [*Aminta* establishes a perfect correspondence between the conditions exterior to the staging and the fiction on stage. On the level of content, an Arcadian world corresponds to a show strictly reserved (differently from the great tournaments) to a courtly audience, like pastorals and Tasso's work in particular. In this Arcadian world the main characters, nymphs and shepherds, appear as representatives of the aristocratic elite, yet free from the weight of any worry or responsibilities of the ruling class. These characters are also, according to the rules of the genre, the only inhabitants of this fictional world, living in the most immediate harmony with nature as possible].

[9] "Le processus d'interprétation du thème littéraire du jardin a traversé . . . toute la Renaissance italienne, en renouvelant le motif médiéval du jardin-Eden, qui était caractérisé par toute une série de *topoi* d'origine biblique et classique, 'hortus conclusus' et 'locus amœnus' en même temps. Sous l'influence du néoplatonisme, le jardin des humanistes est devenu une sorte de paradis du savoir, lieu privilégié du débat d'amour et de l'idylle, dans une nature chargée de symboles où l'on voit revivre et se charger de nouvelles significations des motifs tels la 'pax naturæ,' l'éternel printemps, l'âge d'or, etc. . . . ces thèmes traditionnels se sont greffés, dans l'Italie de la Renaissance, sur une réalité spatiale et architecturale bien définie: les jardins et les villas que princes et seigneurs se plaisent à disséminer dans leurs états. . . . on vit s'établir un lien direct entre le jardin idéalisé, édénique, et la personne du seigneur-prince-mecène, créateur et propriétaire du jardin, lien qui finit par charger le thème littéraire d'un message politique: le jardin, né par volonté du prince, dans le moment même où il repropose l'éternelle utopie d'un monde parfait, fermé et exclusif, attribue au prince le mérite de la création et la tâche de la conservation de ce lieu idéal. Chanter le jardin, ses qualités topiques et ses caractéristique particulières, devient ainsi un acte d'hommage au prince démiurge et protecteur, et la poésie du jardin se fait poésie de circonstance": Dalla Valle, "L'influence en France de l'*Aminta* du Tasse," 308–9 [the interpretive process of the literary theme of the garden crosses the entire Italian renaissance and renews the medieval garden-Eden with its many classical and biblical *topoi* like the *hortus conclusus* et *locus amœnus*. With the Neoplatonic influence, the humanists' garden became a sort of paradise of knowledge, a privileged space for debating love and idylls, within a symbol-laden

nature where the themes of *pax naturæ*, eternal springtime and the golden age come back to life and become charged with new meanings. In renaissance Italy, these traditional themes latched on to a well-defined spatial and architectural reality: the gardens and villas that the princes and rulers liked to build in their domains. A direct link was established between the idealized, Eden-like garden and the person of the ruler-prince-patron who had created and was the owner of the garden. This link ended up charging the literary theme with a political message: born out of the prince's will, the garden bestows on the prince the merit of having created and the task of keeping up this ideal place, at the same time as it proposed anew the eternal utopia of a perfect, closed, and exclusive world. Singing of the garden, its topical qualities, and its specific qualities became then an act of homage to the patron creator, and the poetry of the garden became linked to specific circumstances].

[10] "What makes the fiction of the staging possible is the supposition that the space of the theater differs from the space of the court. In this specific case [*Aminta*'s opening], what has always seemed peculiar is the fact that the performance space is elsewhere vis-à-vis the usual one of the city: it is Belvedere Island, that could be reached by the audience by crossing the river's water. The space represented on stage in *Aminta* is neither the usual Arcadia of fiction nor the court beyond the river and subsumed in the performance space. It is instead the very space where the fable is being staged, the 'place of passage' mentioned by the chorus at line 1211, made wider so that it can embrace everything else."

[11] Marzia Pieri agrees with Da Pozzo's opinion of pastorals as tools towards an idealized view of the court. In her view, the very development of the pastoral genre depends upon its setting in a courtly garden or on a stage approximating it: "[l]'ambientazione scenografica della favola pastorale in . . . luoghi di meraviglia [i.e., gardens] o in loro ricostruzioni di sala, . . . spiega la svolta idilliaca che il genere assume a Ferrara verso la metà del [16th] secolo e il progressivo attenuarsi, al suo interno, di elementi realistici, comici, gnomici (che non escludevano ad esempio il finale tragico) presenti invece nei testi più arcaici": *La scena boschereccia nel rinascimento italiano*, 196 [the stage set of pastoral in marvelous places or in indoor reconstructions explains why the genre becomes more idyllic in Ferrara halfway through the sixteenth century. It also explains why realistic, comic, and gnomic elements become rarer while they were present in older texts. For example a tragic ending was not impossible before].

[12] "Belvedere, isola come non altri mai designata e destinata ad essere il paradiso del Principe, si prospetta, alla vigilia della recita di *Aminta*, come il luogo voluto dal signore a fungere da cornice, in una proiezione utopistica e ideologica assieme, al dispiegamento del carisma di corte. Belvedere, in altri termini, e l'idea che lo sostiene, si caricano di altissime e complesse valenze emblematiche; si propongono come il referente privilegiato di una situazione mentale e ideologica voluta certamente dal principe, ma, prima di tutto, elaborata dall'immaginario cortigiano che interpreta, codifica, restituisce a livello letterario-artistico un progetto di presa del potere saldamente notificato dai *segni*: la città, i giardini, lo spazio urbano in primo luogo, ma anche nel disegno generale, l'organizzazione stessa dello stato": G. Venturi, "Un'isola tra utopia e realtà," in *Torquato Tasso tra letteratura, musica, teatro e arti figurative*, ed. Buzzoni, 173–78, here 173; emphasis in original [Belvedere was designed and destined to be the prince's paradise. On the eve of *Aminta*'s performance, it is the place that the ruler wanted as a frame to the display of the court's charisma to be projected as a utopia and ideologically. In other words, Belvedere and the idea behind it

are laden with high and complex emblematic values. They are the privileged referent of a mental and ideological situation willed by the prince but above all processed by the courtly imaginary. Thus this project of taking power firmly codified in *signs* is interpreted, codified, and embodied on the literary and artistic levels by the court: the city, its garden, urban space above all, but the general design and organization of the state as well].

¹³ The specific ideological relevance of Belvedere emerges in the events following the devolution of the Ferrara domain back to Rome. First, the buildings and gardens of the island were destroyed to make room for a fortress, as if these signs of the Este domination had to be forcibly erased from the landscape. Consequently, as late as in 1889 the loss of Belvedere was depicted as regrettable, a testimony to the greed and insensitivity of the Papacy, and a source of pride in and yearning for the Este authority: "Tutto [that was built or arranged on Belvedere] scomparve sotto la furia della dominazione papale, che gelosa della nuova pregevole gemma, che per l'acquisto di Ferrara era andata ad ornare la sua corona, atterrò palagi, ville e case per costruire una fortezza, con la quale dominare la città, che prevedeva avrebbe rimpianto il dominio degli antichi signori": A. F. Trotti, "Le delizie di Belvedere illustrate," *Deputazione ferrarese di storia patria. Atti e memorie* 2 (1889): 1–32, here 21 [everything disappeared under the papal fury: it was jealous of the new jewel in its crown (the newly acquired city of Ferrara) and it destroyed palaces, villas, and houses to build a fortress with which it would dominate the city, believed to regret its old rulers].

¹⁴ Claudia Lazzaro's monograph *The Italian Renaissance Garden* (New Haven: Yale University Press, 1990), thoroughly examines the tension between nature and culture, wilderness and court in Renaissance gardens: see especially chaps. 1 and 3.

¹⁵ "Nella poesia del Tasso, Belvedere, luogo di delizia e simbolo edenico, si pone come il corrispettivo antitetico e speculare alla corte: nel giardino-isola e non nella corte, 'in vista' della corte e non nel palazzo si svolge lo pseudoidillio di Silvia e Aminta. Il carattere estremamente costruito del giardino che imita la natura incontaminata e primigenia corrisponde alla poetica e alla poesia del Tasso, il quale aspira ad un'incorrotta innocenza, da età dell'oro, ma non può far a meno della corte come il luogo privilegiato della cultura e dell'onore": G. Venturi, "Picta poësis," in *Storia d'Italia. Annali* 5. *Il paesaggio*, ed. C. de Seta (Torino: Einaudi, 1982), 663–749, here 723 [in Tasso's poetry Belvedere is a *délice* and a symbol of Eden. It is then the antithetical and mirror-like counterpart to the court. The pseudo-idyll between Silvia and Aminta takes place on the garden-island, not at court, within view of the court and not inside the palace. The constructed character of the garden, imitating untouched, primitive nature, corresponds to Tasso's poetics and poetry. He wishes for incorrupt innocence and for a golden age, but cannot do without the court *qua* privileged place of culture and honor].

¹⁶ Similarly, on the textual level, Giovanni Getto asserts that there can be no open opposition between court and nature, as the former "non è fuggita neppure in quell'evasione provvisoria, in quella vacanza lieta che è rappresentata dal sogno della vita pastorale": *Interpretazione del Tasso*, 128 [could not escape into the temporary, happy vacation of the dream of pastoral life]. Indeed, according to Louise Clubb, it is precisely the liminal quality of the pastoral as a genre that constitutes its main advantage and attraction for courtly audiences:

> While these two genres [comedy and tragedy], with their court or city settings and figures could function as mirrors for the spectators, in tricky as well as

straight ways —revealing, distorting, multiplying vistas and images, canceling the clear distinction between the fictive "object" viewed and the real "subject" viewing —, they were limited, as mirrors are, to reflecting; reflecting requires visible things, and what these were for tragedy and comedy was almost equally limited by precedent and by contemporary theater. But theatrical representation in the regular pastoral play was not a *speculum*, and the purely literary nature of its milieu made it a theatrical instrument of great range. It could represent the physically invisible — very specific but veiled in-group relationships, very general psychological states and sexual fantasies, as well as patterns of meaning and design beyond human sight. ("The Pastoral Play: Conflation of Country, Court and City," in *Il teatro italiano del Rinascimento*, ed. Lorch, 65–73, here 68)

For an opposing opinion, see Daniela Quarta, "Spazio scenico, spazio cortigiano, spazio cortese," in *La corte di Ferrara e il suo mecenatismo 1441–1598*, ed. M. Pade et al. (Modena: Panini, 1990), 301–27, esp. 310–11.

[17] Archivio di Stato, Firenze: Ducato di Urbino, classe I divisione B filza X.

[18] *Negara: The Theatre State in Nineteenth-Century Bali* (Princeton: Princeton University Press, 1980), 13; emphasis in original.

[19] It is in this respect that Giulio Ferroni's judgment must be tempered, when he asserts that "l'intera cultura cortigiana cinquecentesca può essere definita come produzione di scena, sistema di rappresentazione, che offre uno spettacolo che si riflette in se stesso, in quanto la corte ne è contemporaneamente produttrice e spettatrice. La 'nascita' o l'"invenzione' del teatro s'inserisce in questa più ampia scena culturale; lo spettacolo teatrale viene a proporsi come incontro e sovrapposizione celebrativa delle diverse forme e dei molteplici strumenti della scena cortigiana, dando luogo ad un'apparenza multipla, che non va confusa con più moderne forme di spettacolo 'totale': in essa emergono, in una simultaneità spaziale e temporale, le forme pure delle diverse arti e tecniche, ciascuna delle quali mantiene però la sua autonomia strutturale": "La scena, l'autore, il signore del teatro delle corti padane," in *Il teatro italiano del Rinascimento*, ed. Lorch, 537–70, here 537 [The whole courtly culture of the sixteenth century can be defined as a stage production, as a representational system, offering a self-mirroring spectacle, for the court is at the same time its producer and audience. The "birth" or "invention" of the theater fits within this larger cultural horizon. Theatrical stagings are the meeting point and the celebratory superposition of the different forms and the many instruments of the courtly stage. Thus a multiple appearance comes into existence that is not to be confused with more modern forms of "total" spectacle. In this spectacle the pure forms of various arts and techniques emerge at the same space and time, yet each art and technique keeps its own structural autonomy].

At the basis of his opinion lies an excessive emphasis on the self-enclosed and self-referential characteristic of courtly performances. Conversely, if we frame them as ritual, and not as make-believe, then their relevance to entities beyond the court becomes evident, as emerges for both the 1574 and the 1628 *Aminta* stagings.

[20] See for example Hare and Blumberg's definition of "three levels of reality that are accepted in the theater [and] also apply to everyday life . . . :

1. The 'pretend' reality of games, sports, parties and ceremonies.
2. The 'alternative' reality of occupational worlds and ritual.

3. The 'overriding' reality concerned with the deliberate efforts to change or defend definitions of the situation or the rules of the game": *Dramaturgical Analysis*, 8. For these sociologists, these three levels are mutually exclusive and can never coexist, other than in a situation of chaos, revolution, or anarchy.

[21] "In [Baroque] feasts and festive performances . . . 'work' and 'play' were still closely related, even intertwined 'categories.' In other words, the splendid festive 'play' performances of the Baroque court constituted a political and philosophical program that was potentially as intense as (and . . . probably more entertaining than) many contemporaneous treatises or tracts on absolutism. But it would be fallacious to assume these feasts were merely so many forms of political discourse; they were also, quite simply, festive celebrations, elaborate games, forms of play for a limited number of players. . . . Together with exuberant perukes and stunning experiments with three-dimensional clothing, the grandiose festive performance was part and parcel of this playful yet serious strategy": Aercke, *Gods of Play*, 8–9.

[22] In this sense, I disagree with Da Pozzo's interpretation of the space of the performance as uniquely self-referential: "se da un lato, ad esempio, comincia ad essere sempre più ammessa una separazione tra la scena e gli spettatori di essa, e di conseguenza la presenza di un luogo ideale che possa indicare soltanto uno spazio deputato senza l'intento di alludere ad un corrispondente reale preciso, lasciando perciò la sua decifrazione in relazione appunto agli elementi che l'azione andrà portando in luce, d'altro canto tutto un gusto sempre più massiccio viene maturando, di forme teatrali pubbliche durante il cui svolgimento pubblico popolare e pubblico ristretto della corte ugualmente si beano, e per le quali il luogo postulato per l'azione non ha bisogno di alcun sottinteso allusivo, ma è esplicitamente e semplicemente un determinato spazio della città che non rinvia a niente altro da sé": *Ambigua armonia*, 82–83 [For example, on the one hand a separation between stage and audience comes to be accepted, and consequently the presence of an ideal place that stands for a selected place without alluding to a specific real correspondent. This space is therefore to be deciphered with respect to those elements disclosed by the plot. On the other hand a taste for public theatrical forms is ripening, during which both the popular and limited courtly audience are happy. The selected space for these forms needs no allusion; it is explicitly and simply a specific space in the city that contains no reference to something other than itself].

The first element that must be pointed out in this assessment derives directly from the physical space represented on the *Aminta* stage. It is not a cityscape, but a "luogo di passo" in a natural setting. If critics such as Ludovico Zorzi have maintained that in the case of the *scena di città* the separation between stage and audience is total and that the former is idealized in a paradigm of classical derivation ("Figurazione pittorica e figurazione teatrale," in *Storia dell'arte italiana*, ed. G. Bollati and P. Fossati, 12 vols. [Torino: Einaudi, 1979], 1.1:419–63, here 444–49), this position is clearly untenable within the pastoral domain due to the lack of an identifiable archetype. Secondly, Da Pozzo's interpretation relies on the identification of *Aminta* with an escapist myth, which later on in this chapter I will show to be woefully inadequate.

[23] Or, to cite Nardo: "because play conflates the defining frame with what is inside the frame, a single play action takes place simultaneously on two levels of reality: the player both participates in his action and stands apart framing the action, whereby gaining distance and perspective on himself": *The Ludic Self*, 10–11.

²⁴ I cannot agree with Jane Tylus when she writes that in the prologue, "by cloaking himself in such a 'velo' (veil), by transforming his potent dart into a mere shepherd's staff, Cupid symbolizes the allure of a courtly theater that attempts to negate its own theatricality, of a force that disguises its invasive potential": *Writing and Vulnerability in the Renaissance* (Stanford: Stanford University Press, 1993), 88. It is precisely in such liminal scenes as the prologue and the epilogue that the frame emerges fully. In particular, in *Aminta* the prologue is remarkably different from the rest of the play in terms of its representational strategy, since it insists on self-deixis to the detriment of the more interpretation-bound tools that are used throughout the rest of the text.

²⁵ Nor is Maravall's position isolated or rare among scholars of Italian theater. For example, describing the Florentine festivities of 1568 to celebrate the baptism of Eleonora de' Medici (Francesco I and Giovanna d'Austria's firstborn daughter), Sara Mamone writes: "[a]gli spettatori non viene più chiesto l'uso delle proprie facoltà critiche, ma solo un assenso all'esibizione, la partecipazione è subordinata all'ammissione diretta da parte del duca, che non si limita ad invitare ma può escludere secondo il proprio arbitrio": *Il teatro nella Firenze medicea* (Milan: Mursia, 1981), 50 [audiences are not required to use their critical abilities, but they have to consent to the show. Participation is subordinate to the duke's permission to attend. Not only does he invite, but also exclude according to his will]. Here Mamone confuses two separate issues: access and participation. While the Medici ruler did oversee the invitations, he also relied on the convened audience to celebrate a public event. Francesco I needed those he had invited in order to carry out the ritual of welcoming his daughter into the community of the baptized, or else such a ceremony could not take place properly.

²⁶ "Each staged event had no intrinsic value but acted as a term of comparison with other spectacular occurrences. The magnificence of each staging had value, other than for its intrinsic merit, for the prestige and resonance it elicited with kings and noblemen at other European courts."

²⁷ Quoted in E. Boland, "When the Spirit Moves," *New York Review of Books* (12 January 1995): 25–28, here 28.

²⁸ *Visions of Excess: Selected Writings, 1927–1939*, ed. A. Stoekl (Minneapolis: University of Minnesota Press, 1985), 242; emphasis in original.

²⁹ "The ritual extravaganzas of the theatre state, its half-divine lord immobile, tranced, or dead at the dramatic center of them, were the symbolic expression less of the peasantry's greatness than of its notion of what greatness was. What the Balinese state did for Balinese society was to cast into sensible form a concept of what, together, they were supposed to make of themselves: an illusion of the power of grandeur to organize the world": Geertz, *Negara*, 102.

³⁰ Aercke's point seems proven within the French context, too: Louis XIV ceased dancing during courtly entertainment on or around 1670, but remained the organizer and main spectator of these occasions: P. Burke, *The Fabrication of Louis XIV* (New Haven: Yale University Press, 1992), 68–69.

³¹ This paradox emerges also from a recent article by Paolo Cherchi regarding the canon of beauty for rulers and its political exploitation. While beauty cannot be taught or could only partially be acquired by artificial means, its effectiveness is remarkable, as a tool in the hands of the prince: "da questa consapevolezza nasce la 'gestione della bellezza del re' come affermazione di potere, gestione che, a sua volta, sfocia nell'estetizzazione

del potere come mezzo di potere stesso": P. Cherchi, "Il re Adone," in *The Sense of Marino*, ed. F. Guardiani (New York: Legas, 1994), 9–33, here 26 [this awareness generates the "management of the king's beauty" as a way to assert power. This management itself leads to the aesthetization of power as a tool of power itself].

[32] According to Georges Bataille, however, theater cannot possibly make reappear the "privileged instants" when the sacred makes itself known, precisely according to the fact that it is exceedingly body-oriented and -based:

> If one now wants to represent, with an initial clarity, the "grail" obstinately pursued through successive, deceptive, and cloudy depths, it is necessary to insist upon the fact that it could never have been a *substantial* reality; on the contrary, it was an element characterized by the impossibility of its enduring. The term *privileged instant* is the only one that, with a certain amount of accuracy, accounts for what can be encountered *at random* in the search; the opposite of a *substance* that withstands the test of time, it is something that flees as soon as it is seen and cannot be grasped. The will to fix such instants, which belong, it is true, to painting or writing is the only way to make them *reappear*, because the painting or the poetic text *evokes* but does not *make substantial* what once appeared. (*Visions of Excess*, ed. Stoekl, 241; emphases in original)

[33] A succinct list of Italian anti-theatrical tracts, along with their ideological conditions and goals, can be found in F. Taviani's introduction to Barbieri's *La supplica* (Milan: Il Polifilo, 1971), xvii–xviii.

[34] "Nella corte, quasi sempre, attore e spettatore coincidono, e chi recita il simulacro ha ben scarse possibilità di straniamento, cade nello stesso inganno in cui viene catturato chi guarda. Soltanto alcuni (molto pochi per la verità, e tra essi certamente l'Ariosto) di quelli che oggi chiamiamo 'intellettuali' riescono a liberarsi, almeno parzialmente, dall'accecamento necessario al sistema del simulacro, suggerendo così, con la loro prospettiva 'da lontano,' con i loro scarti e con le loro contraddizioni, la possibilità di definire il senso di quella struttura. Ma gli altri intellettuali cortigiani (la maggior parte) oscillano tra la piena collaborazione all'edificazione del simulacro e la subalterna, incosciente passività nei suoi confronti, sono integralmente avvinti nella sua illusoria parvenza, tra servilità idealizzante e cieche denunce di malessere": Ferroni, "La scena," 540 [At court actor and spectator almost always coincide. Those who act the fiction have little possibility to become estranged for they fall into the same trap as those who look. Only a few of those we now call intellectuals (very few indeed, and certainly Ariosto was among them) manage to free themselves at least partially of the blinding necessary to the simulacrum system. Through a perspective from far away, with *décalage* and contradictions, they suggest the possibility of defining the meaning of that structure. The rest (the largest part) of courtly intellectuals hesitate between full collaboration in building this simulacrum and a subaltern, non-self-aware passivity in its regard; they are wholly bound up with its illusory appearance, idealizing servility and blind protestations of uneasiness].

[35] In his study on *commedia dell'arte* masks and their use by twentieth-century performers, John Rudlin remarks that a "masked man had no right to bear arms during Carnival season in medieval Italy because he was considered to have divested himself of his own identity by assuming another persona, for whose actions he was therefore not responsible": *Commedia*

dell'Arte, 34. Such regulations indicate that the status of a masked person was ambiguous, as s/he had relinquished his/her identity but could not be said to have fully acquired another.

[36] "Who is so foolish not to know the difference between being and pretending? A buffoon is truly a buffoon, but an actor that takes on a funny part pretends to be a buffoon. That is why he wears a mask or a false beard or colors his face: to pretend to be another person. Masks are called *persona* in Latin. At *carnevale* the license to bear arms is taken away from those wearing masks because they give up their own identity and take on someone else's. That is why actors off stage have a different name, change their clothes, and have other habits."

[37] McAuley has pointed out that in performance "[t]he absence of movement is as important as movement, and the utterly immobile body exerts its own fascination . . . In the theatre, as elsewhere, it is in relation to stillness that movement is defined": *Space in Performance*, 106.

[38] "For his youthful work Tasso creates a general code that is truly of the theater. He gives words the concreteness of gesture, and therefore words must be interpreted in their spatial, aural, and gestural value. Theater *qua* fiction has made its true intellectual role clear specifically because it creates this universe alternative to the real one, and consequently it creates feigned ways of knowing, without object, deliberately paradoxical yet perfectly justifiable. In this development an alternative conception of space carries out a large and momentous key role": R. Scrivano, *Finzioni teatrali*, 105–6.

[39] "Immediately imposes on the audience its rules of visualization. Through them the images of the work will appear as vividly as secondary images: a simple wand must be thought of as a highly dangerous torch 'breathing forth invisible flames'."

[40] "The climactic scene of the plot, the coming together of wounded Aminta and compassionate Silvia after many toils, fits entirely with the words; it is visualized brightly and therefore never concretely seen by the audience."

[41] Franco Croce has identified the theatricality of the *Aminta* text precisely in its "modulo della narrazione" [narration module]: "La teatralità dell'*Aminta*," in *Sviluppi della drammaturgia pastorale*, 131–57, here 134, that is, in the fact that events take place off stage and are simply reported on stage. However, he believes that in this way "il mondo pastorale dell'*Aminta* riflette, tutto quanto, sempre, e con immediatezza, il mondo in cui vive il pubblico": "La teatralità," 135 [*Aminta*'s pastoral world reflects the world in which the audience live, in its entirety, all the time, and immediately], which he strictly identifies with the Ferrara world of the supposed *première*. Such a narrow interpretation presents an evident disadvantage: except for its original intended audience, the theatricality of Tasso's text would prove inadequate. *Aminta*'s popularity on the early modern Italian stage, conversely, belies this interpretation, while pointing at an important reason for its success: the fact that it requires the audience's imaginative efforts.

[42] Sometimes, as recently argued by Maggie Günsberg, three gender identities are superimposed in one staged character: see *Gender and the Italian Stage*, esp. chap, 2, "Gender Deceptions," and the essays in Blackmer and Smith, *En Travesti*.

[43] Fernando Taviani has argued that, given the composition of the Gelosi troupe, Isabella Andreini performed Aminta, a male character, rather than Silvia, as is usually asserted ("Bella d'Asi," 7).

[44] W. Trimpi, "Decorum," in *The New Princeton Encyclopedia of Poetry and Poetics*, ed. A. Preminger et al. (Princeton: Princeton University Press, 1993), 282–83, here 282.

[45] The argument presented here has appeared in a shorter version in M. G. Stampino, "Epideictic Pastoral," *Theatre Symposium* 5 (1997): 36–49.

[46] I do not mean to suggest that scholars have thus far never considered the elements of rhetorical forms. James Yoch, for example, has argued that pastoral stagings, with their "wit, . . . machines, . . . splendid sets and costumes are part of a rhetoric following literary models of irony, symmetry and repetition": "A Greater Power," 183. He refrains from exploring classical rhetoric in order to unearth useful examples as far as audience effects are concerned.

[47] "Epideictic and Rhetoric in the Renaissance," *New Literary History* 14 (1983): 497–537, here 498.

[48] "Interpretation at Court: Courtesy and the Performer-Audience Dialectic," *New Literary History* 14 (1983), 623–39, here 631.

[49] E. R. Curtius has pointed out that Aristotle's third rhetorical *genus* can be called either epideictic or panegyrical: "the term *epídeixis* (*ostentatio*) goes back to its aspect of display, the term *panegurikós* to the outward occasion": *European Literature and the Latin Middle Ages* (Princeton: Princeton University Press, 1983), 69 n. 15.

[50] Vickers asserts that "rhetoric and poetics are thus instrumental faculties which that citizen employs for action, namely, to make his fellow citizens good": "Epideictic and Rhetoric," 509. This wording reflects an idealized image of early Renaissance city-states that clashes with the historical frame of the *Aminta* performances here under scrutiny.

[51] "Nothing other than the imitation or exemplary portrait of human life, in which vices have to be criticized so that they will be avoided and virtues praised so that they will be imitated": L. de' Sommi, *Quattro Dialoghi*, ed. F. Marotti (Milan: Il Polifilo, 1986), 12.

[52] "The closer these things are to the truth, the more effective they are in eliciting emotions:" A. Ingegneri, *Della poesia rappresentativa*, in *Lo spettacolo*, ed. Marotti, 271–308, here 277.

[53] The much-dreaded institution of the *Index librorum prohibitorum* was greatly reinforced by the decrees of the Council (1545–63); indeed, a similar list of inappropriate and indecent images failed to see the light due to external circumstances, among which was the untimely death of one of its most ardent proponents, Bologna's Cardinal Giovanni Paleotti. On these events and their ideological background, see P. Prodi, "Ricerche sulla teorica delle arti figurative nella Riforma cattolica," *Archivio italiano per la storia della pietà* 4 (1965): 121–212, esp. 142–47.

[54] The socio-cultural atmosphere in which *Aminta* was conceived and performed might also explain why its epideictic character has gone undetected, indeed often ignored when compared to the more blatant, but less convincing, *Pastor fido*. In Arnaldo Di Benedetto's opinion, for example, "l'*Aminta* non è una celebrazione del matrimonio, come invece pretende d'essere il *Pastor fido*, ben più carico d'intenti edificanti": "L'*Aminta* e la pastorale cinquecentesca in Italia," in *Torquato Tasso e la cultura estense 3*, ed. G. Venturi, 1121–49, here 1140 [*Aminta* is not a celebration of marriage, as *Pastor fido* wants to be, as it is much more laden with edifying intentions].

[55] Franco Croce offers the following description: "[p]iù spesso sul palcoscenico dell'*Aminta* non c'è azione, ma discussione e commenti sulle azioni che si sono svolte al di fuori della vista del pubblico. Più spesso le vicende della trama sono fatte conoscere attraverso racconti": "La teatralità dell'*Aminta*," 132 [More often than action, on stage with

Aminta we see discussions of and commentaries on the actions that took place outside the audience's gaze. The plot is known through tales most of the time].

[56] Mario Fubini criticizes them as "profili, e profili stilizzati, meglio che . . . caratteri": "*L'Aminta* intermezzo alla tragedia della *Liberata*," in idem, *Studi sulla letteratura del Rinascimento* (Firenze: La nuova Italia, 1971), 200–215, here 211 [stylized profiles rather than personalities]; Donadoni goes further: "[i]l Tasso non sente il bisogno di indagare nella realtà e nel mistero psichico. Nessuna crisi nei personaggi. Ciascuno è sino alla fine quello che appare in principio": "*L'Aminta*," 110 [Tasso feels no need to investigate psychic reality or mystery. No character suffers a crisis. They all are at the end the way they were at the beginning]. The outward appearance of the staging had little impact on the audience's perception of a character's verisimilitude, despite Luigi Ronga's assertion that "[e]ntro la cornice di scene ricolme d'ogni più piacente attrattiva è naturale che i lineamenti drammatici dei personaggi si attenuassero nella statica sommarietà di alcune figure tipizzate": "La nascita del melodramma," in *Teatro del Seicento*, ed. L. Fassò (Milan: Ricciardi, n. d.), xxvii–liii, here xlix–l [within the frame of scenes filled with the most likeable attractions it is natural that the characters' dramatic features are reduced to the static summary of a few types]. There is little "natural" (in both senses of "obvious" and "naturalistic") about these staged characters, as we have seen throughout this study.

[57] "Sees pastorals as an attempt to replace classically justified and socially conformed drama, that is, comedy and tragedy. He judges them as leaning towards concepts and argumentation rather than entertainment."

[58] Nor was this stance restricted to the Italian theatrical situation. Stephen Orgel has cogently argued that Shakespeare's drama creates an argument, not a plot: "[t]his is what critics from Horace to Castelvetro and Sidney mean when they say that mimesis is only the means of drama, not its end. Its end, they assume, is the same as the end of poetry and the other verbal arts — to persuade": "Shakespeare Imagines a Theater," in *Shakespeare, Man of the Theater*, ed. K. Muir (Newark, DE: University of Delaware Press, 1983), 34–46, here 44. With this in mind, the quality of *Aminta*'s characters would have been an advantage, and not a liability, in England as well as in Italy.

[59] See F. Cruciani and D. Seragnoli, eds., *Il teatro italiano nel Rinascimento* (Bologna: Il Mulino, 1987), 18.

[60] It is worth mentioning the deeply split relationship between Catholic Church authorities and the stage: while using it for educational purposes in their *oratoria* and schools (see Vignati, *Storia delle filodrammatiche*, chap. 1), they condemned professional performers for luring viewers to the devil by their Proteus-like ability to change their appearance.

[61] "Theatrical mechanism begins and ends in itself; it is the theater aspect of pure entertainment offered by art, disassociated from everything."

[62] Moreover, the spatial indeterminacy of the *Aminta* events (the unidentified "luogo di passo" where the plot takes place) reinforces the plot's epideictic strength. In *The Myth of the Golden Age in the Renaissance* (Bloomington: Indiana University Press, 1969), Harry Levin has asserted that "Arcadia is oriented toward the immemorial past as Utopia is oriented toward the inscrutable future. Since *never* can be said with more assurance about the past than about the future, Arcadianism represents a purer state of escapism" (99). Tasso's "luogo di passo" can be adapted to many settings (and it has been, particularly to the Po island of Belvedere, as I have pointed out before); the plot relevance to its audience,

hence, emerges as stronger. Giovan Battista Guarini's *Il pastor fido*, whose plot occurs explicitly in Arcadia, should be juxtaposed to *Aminta* with respect to their respective degrees of epideixis or escapism.

[63] "In Mopso's words, as reported by Tirsi, the court is a claustrophobic space, filled with illusion, loss of identity and evil forces. In Tirsi's view and narration the court is the place of delicious grace, of beauty and art." Enrico Fenzi has underscored the same ambivalence on Tasso's part: "pare che esistano . . . due corti, specularmente contrapposte: quella negativa di Mopso . . . e quella positiva di Tirsi, il quale vi trova realizzati nel loro grado più alto i valori che danno un senso alla sua stessa vita": "Il potere, la morte, l'amore. Note sull'*Aminta* di Torquato Tasso," *L'immagine riflessa* 3 (1979): 197–248, here 199 [there seem to be two mirror-like courts: Mopso's negative and Tirsi's positive. Tirsi finds there the realization of the highest degree of those values that bestow meaning on his very life].

[64] "Already staged in Pesaro on other occasions . . . we can say that this *intermezzo* appeared new to the audience since it was so long since it had been done."

[65] "The comedy was recognized as *Aminta* and therefore nobody paid it any attention."

[66] "I would prefer a new comedy, or at least one that is not well known, and I would stay away especially from those that have been printed, though they might be more beautiful. There are two reasons for this: people always like what is new best, and also it seems common that comedies known by the audience are not well received for many reasons. I think the main one is that a performer has to strive as much as he can to take the audience in so that they think that what is on stage happens for real. But if the listeners know in advance what the performer will say and do, what is on stage appears like a silly and obvious lie, and the plot loses the natural quality that must accompany it at all times."

[67] Interestingly, de' Sommi proceeds to liken a dissatisfied audience members to a child who has been tricked and recognizes his inexperience: "l'uditore, quasi schernito, non solo vilipende lo spettacolo, ma disprezza anco se medesimo che come fanciullo si sia lasciato condure a udir, come si dice in proverbio, la novella de l'oca": *Dialoghi*, ed. Marotti, 38 [the listeners are almost insulted and make fun of the show, but they also disparage themselves because like children they let themselves be taken to hear, as the proverb says, a silly old story]. Instead of gathering pleasure and moral teachings, or of sharing in Goffman's "playful unknowingness," in these circumstances the theatergoer would resent his experience as juvenile and demeaning.

[68] "I am content with transforming them, and I avoid transfiguring them. I do my best to make them all look like new people, since when the audience recognizes the performer we take away from them some of the enchantment that they should feel. We should have them believe that each staging is an actual occurrence."

[69] "When a plot goes beyond the natural, it is not fit for comedies, which have to be full of very natural things."

[70] "Through their novelty they corrupt the audience's mind, so that when they go back to the main plot they find it less appealing."

[71] "In tragedies divided into acts and in pastorals stranger occurrences will be allowed. Their very plots include shades, furies, various deities, and extraordinary characters. If the *intermezzi* have something in common with the main plot, then they will be undoubtedly worthy of more esteem, though not everything can be taken from the subject matter of the main plot."

[72] "They do not simply fit with pastorals and comedies, but very much adorn them. Whether similar to or different from the plot, they enrich the show and please the audience."

[73] "La macchineria teatrale rappresenta ambiziosamente una realtà totalizzante, ricca di suggestioni filosofiche sottili e avvincenti; il palcoscenico è diventato una scatola magica abbagliante e mutevole che coinvolge i cinque sensi (non mancano neppure aromi e profumi), in un meccanismo ancora compatto ma fatalmente destinato a dissolversi in una molteplicità di forme meccanica e irrelata: sarà l'apparato barocco del melodramma, dove ormai le mutazioni a vista diventano repertoriali e fini a se stesse": Pieri, *La nascita del teatro moderno*, 97 [stage machinery represents a totalizing reality, filled with subtle, engaging philosophical suggestions. The stage has become a dazzling, ever-changing magical box that involves all five senses (we even have taste and perfumes). This mechanism is still compact, but it is destined to dissolve in a mechanical, non-related multiplicity of forms. This is what the baroque apparatuses of melodrama are: visible set changes are part of a repertory and an end in themselves].

[74] Tasso himself seems to have explicitly condemned the excessive amount of supernatural interventions and *macchine* in a 1575 letter to Luca Scalabrino: "perchè piacque agli spettatori, come a quelli che si dilettano assai del maraviglioso, ed amano la vaghezza della vista, e la magnificenza che appare nella macchina, molti poeti poi troppo vaghi di piacere al popolo con modi non proprj dell'arte loro, affettarono sconvenevolmente sì fatte soluzioni,": *Lettere inedite*, 5 [Audiences liked the marvelous and the beautiful to behold and the magnificence shown by stage machinery. Thus many poets, too desirous to please the people in ways not fitting with their art, put on such solutions in improper ways].

Although this could merely refer to what Fabrizio Cruciani calls "atteggiamento classicista" ("Percorsi critici," 185) [classical-antiquity-bound attitude] found in the *Aminta* text, it is legitimate to perceive in it a conscious attempt at fashioning himself as one of the followers of classical precepts regarding the theater rather than a practitioner caving in to modern taste and to the desires of the audience.

[75] "Fuse the show's continuity, by now called unity of action in the renewed Aristotelian polemic; justify the chronological progression; distract the audience from what the prop masters do on stage; and amuse them during the long, mandatory presence at the theater": "Origini e aspetti della scenografia in Italia," in Nino Pirrotta, *Li duo Orfei* (Torino: ERI, 1969), 371–509, here 449.

[76] de' Sommi praises musical *intermezzi* as reinforcing the chronological frame of a performance: "gl'intermedii di musica . . . sono neccessarii alle comedie, sí per dar alquanto di refrigerio alle menti de gli spettatori, et sí anco perché il poeta . . . si serve di quello intervallo nel dar proporzione a la sua favola": *Dialoghi*, ed. Marotti, 56 [musical *intermezzi* are necessary to comedies to relax the audience's minds and so that the author uses the break to give the right proportions to his plot]. Povoledo does not make this crucial distinction, thus undermining part of her argument.

[77] "If the audience knows that the show has its basis in reality, they will feel more terror and pity towards its terrible, exemplary occurrences. If they are more deeply touched, they will better cleanse their souls of vices and will gain more from those examples as they are reputed real."

[78] See an exhaustive list in Lynn Thorndike, "Newness and Novelty in Seventeenth-Century Science and Medicine," in *Roots of Scientific Thought*, ed. P. Wiener and A. Noland

(New York: Basic Books, 1957), 443–57, which nevertheless disappoints as it does not come to any theoretical or historical conclusion, except that "the new was very much in the consciousness of the men of the seventeenth century" (457).

[79] "Since novelties are well liked, having foreign, uncommon clothes on stage makes for a more pleasant show; thus it occurs that comedies with Greek clothes are considered as the most beautiful."

[80] "It is so unnatural for a room not to have a fourth wall (which would be necessary in a play) that it seems to be an improper solution. I would add that I am not sure that acting in that space could be considered as acting on stage."

[81] "Court, Academy, and Printing House: Patronage and Scientific Careers in Late Renaissance Italy," in *Patronage and Institutions: Science, Technology, and medicine at the European Court 1500–1750*, ed. B. T. Moran (Rochester: Boydell Press, 1991), 25–50, here 38.

[82] H. U. Gumbrecht, "A History of the Concept 'Modern'," in *Making Sense in Life and Literature*, ed. W. Godzich (Minneapolis: University of Minnesota Press, 1996), 79–110, here 106.

[83] "A show is not a repetition but, even within a repeated tradition, is it what is new, surprising, unique": F. Cruciani, "Dietro l'origine del teatro rinascimentale," *Quaderni di teatro* 7 (1985): 14–21, here 16.

[84] The visual arts offer the most obvious and influential examples. Jacob Burckhardt, in his crucial 1860 book *The Civilization of the Renaissance in Italy*, maintained that the rapidly evolving culture of early modern times "needed a guide, and found one in the ancient civilization, with its wealth of truth and knowledge in every spiritual interest" (123). Over eighty years later, in 1944, Erwin Panofsky differentiated three cultural periods: a "Mediterranean phenomenon, arising in Southern France, Italy and Spain" in the twelfth century, usually called proto-Renaissance: "Renaissance and Renascences," in idem, *Renaissance and Renascences in Western Art*, 2nd ed. (New York: Harper and Row, 1969), 42–113, here 55; a contemporary Northern European "proto-humanism" (71); and the Renaissance proper. What set them apart was the awareness of a chronological detachment, resulting in historical distance: "[i]n the Italian Renaissance the classical past began to be looked upon from a fixed distance, quite comparable to the 'distance between the eye and the object' in that most characteristic invention if this very Renaissance, focused perspective. As in focused perspective, this distance prohibited direct contact — owing to the interposition of an ideal 'projection plane' — but permitted a total and rationalized view" (108). For both Burckhardt and Panofsky classical antiquity was a source that reinforced the Renaissance's earliest impulses and deeply fashioned it.

[85] Not all scholars agree with Pirrotta's specific date; however, most presuppose a short transitional period during which opera came fully into its own. Solerti writes that "[c]ol 1608 finisce veramente il periodo delle origini e incomincia quello della diffusione del melodramma in Italia" (*Albori*, 1: 118) [1608 marks the end of the opening period and the beginning of the diffusion of melodrama throughout Italy]. Kimbell's opinion is slightly more nuanced: "[f]or some years after 1600 opera was one of several musico-dramatic genres that might grace a festival. *Intermedi*, *mascherate* and dramatic ballets continued to flourish for many years" (*Italian Opera*, 54); however, in the first decade of the new century "[f]irst in Mantua, then in Rome, the [humanist] spirit of early Florentine opera was compromised — compromised in order to accommodate a more ample supply of virtuosity,

of colour and of spectacle" (61). The only scholar to have put forth an articulate analysis of the issue is Bianconi, who differentiates between court-based and commercial opera, yet does not contest the possibility of firmly establishing "the question of the origins of opera" (*Music in the Seventeenth Century*, 162). It is worth remembering that the same musicians responsible for *Euridice* in 1600 had already composed the score to *Dafne* by Ottavio Rinuccini at least six years before (it was first performed in 1594) (Walker, "Opera," 550–51), but since only fragments are extant scholars generally have neglected the earlier work.

[86] "Protected chastity, made the fierce peaceful, gave courage to the cowards, calmed agitated souls, made minds sharper, filled souls with divine furor, settled the disagreements between peoples, gave birth to good habits among humans, gave hearing back to the deaf, revived lost souls, warded off the plague, made happy and relieved oppressed souls, turned the lustful into chaste, calmed down evil spirits, cured snake bites, appeased the furious and the drunk, repelled the burden of grave worries and toil. Lastly (leaving many more aside), we can say that through the example of actions it freed men from death, in addition to the many admirable works that fill authoritative books": *Dialogo della musica antica e della moderna* (1581) (New York: Broude, 1967), 86.

[87] C. V. Palisca, *Girolamo Mei (1519–1594): Letters on Ancient and Modern Music*, n.p.: American Institute of Musicology, 1960), 11.

[88] *Discorso mandato da Gio: de' Bardi a Giulio Caccini detto Romano sopra la Musica antica, e'l cantar bene* (1578?) in Giovan Battista Doni, *Lyra Barberina*, 2 vols. (Bologna: Forni, 1974): 2: 233–48, here 240.

[89] "My goal is that every time that Licori enters on stage, she is to bring new pleasure by adding new variations in three places; I truly think that I will be able to generate this effect."

[90] The interchangeable usage of "effetti" and "affetti" was by no means restricted to composers, as various letters cited in chapter 3 indicate (for example Mazzi's of 16 November 1627). The dedicatory letter to Luzzasco Luzzaschi's sixth book of madrigals, written in 1596 by the *letterato* Alessandro Guarini, makes the identity of *effetti* and *affetti* more evident, while subordinating music to the words accompanying it: music "[p]iagne, se il verso piagne, ride, se ride, se corre, se resta, se priega, se niega, se grida, se tace, se vive, se muore; tutti questi affetti ed effetti cosí vivamente da lui vengono espressi che quella par quasi emulazione, che propriamente rassomiglianza dee dirsi": Bianconi, "Il Cinquecento e il Seicento," 319 [it cries if the line cries, it laughs, if it laughs; if it runs or stays or prays or says no or shouts or is silent or lives or dies, it expresses all this: affects and effects are so vividly rendered that it looks like emulation or even downright likeness]. Bianconi offers a useful summary of the relationship between music and "the psychological theory of the affections" in *Music in the Seventeenth Century*, 51–54 (the quotation is on 51).

[91] "It does not aim to move the audience in the pit: they are already moved and anxious about Aminta since the end of Act III when he left saying: 'I leave never to come back.' It aims instead to move the main female character on stage."

[92] "On the *Aminta* stage for the first time something happens. It is not a small occurrence, but a sudden, dramatic change in the main female character's behavior. Silvia cries on stage, in front of the audience."

[93] Through a detailed analysis of Tasso's writings on poetics, Accorsi has shown a changing attitude vis-à-vis the relevance of music to poetry. In the dialogue "La Cavaletta"

(completed by early February, 1585, and printed in 1587) Tasso juxtaposes poetry and music with respect to their essence: "[l]a poesia è dialettica nella sua sostanza, è argomentazione . . . mentre la musica inequivocabilmente pertiene alla dolcezza e al diletto, rimane sempre . . . al livello del dolce, del vago, del puro piacere, inferiore al diletto intellettuale del ragionamento": Accorsi, "Musicato, per musica, musicale," 903 [poetry is dialectic, is argumentative in its substance. Music instead belongs to sweetness and entertainment, it remains on the level of what is sweet, vague, purely pleasurable, and inferior to the intellectual entertainment of reasoning]. Later, in the madrigal "Queste mie rime sparte" ("presumibilmente composto tra il luglio 1585 e il marzo 1588 o tra la fine del 1590 e la fine del 1591" [905] [written presumably between July 1585 and March 1588, or between the end of 1590 and the end of 1591]), Tasso avows that "la musica . . . uscita dall'area pura del diletto, può contribuire, insieme alla poesia, alla purgazione delle passioni . . . , compito precipuo della poesia" (905–6) [music, having left the pure area of entertainment, can contribute to purging passions, which is the main goal of poetry]. It is worthwhile stressing that Accorsi underscores an inherently rhetoric-based goal in Tasso's concept of poetry, consistent with Vickers's epideictic indications that I have developed earlier in this chapter.

[94] "With their rustic sets of greenery and costumes prettier than they are lavish, pastorals are well liked by our sense of sight. With their sweet verse and delicate phrasing they are pleasant to the ear and mind. The latter, not incapable of an almost tragic *gravitas*, suffer highly from certain ridiculous comic stagings. Pastorals allow virgins and honest women on stage, which comedies are not allowed to have. Thus they produce noble affects that would not be out of place in tragedies. In sum, they are half-way between the other two genres and generate plentiful entertainment, with or without choruses, with or without *intermezzi*."

[95] "Note sul contributo musicale alla drammaturgia pastorale," in *Sviluppi della drammaturgia pastorale*, ed. Chiabò and Doglio, 101–18, here 102.

[96] "As a point of separation between the culture of the pastoral as a representational genre and pastoral drama as a literary genre that can put forth a new type of staging."

[97] "Respect for the theoretical and formal schemes made firm by tradition;" "support for the creative need for a new genre that would better embody the taste and cultural tendency of the court."

[98] "A staged genre that was not entirely new and yet that could be renewed because it was open to changes in taste and was still waiting for theorization."

[99] D. Smith, "Writers Enchanted by the Freedom of Opera," *New York Times* (28 September 1995): B2.

[100] By *mouvance* Zumthor identifies "le caractère de l'oeuvre qui, comme telle, avant l'âge du livre, ressort d'une quasi-abstraction, les textes concrets qui la réalizent présentant, par le jeu des variantes et remaniements, comme une incessante vibration et une instabilité fondamentale": P. Zumthor, *Essai de poétique médiévale* (Paris: Seuil, 1972), 507 [the character of works that, before the age of the book, enjoy almost an abstraction: the concrete texts that make it real offer something like an incessant vibration and a fundamental lack of stability, through the play of variants and rewritings].

[101] "The birth of modern theater appears from the outset as the synthesis of the cautious exploitation of huge warehouses of ancient materials (both in the field of theater architecture and of staging) and of the mechanisms, general problems, and continuous

process of reinvention, combination and placement of the individual pieces of such an inheritance": "La funzione teatrale nella critica del Manierismo," *Biblioteca teatrale* 23–24 (1979): 1–13, here 4.

[102] "Why Watch It, Anyway?" *New York Review of Books* (16 February 1995): 37–42, here 38–39.

Works Cited

Manuscript Sources

Almerici, Tiberio. *Lettera.* MS oliveriano 390, fols. 92–96. Biblioteca Oliveriana, Pesaro.

Apparati per l'entrata della S[ignor]a Principessa di Urbino. Ducato d'Urbino, classe I divisione B filza X. Archivio di Stato, Firenze.

Armi nelle Chiese, Feste, e Mercati non si tengano. Legazione apostolica di Pesaro-Urbino, decreti 2: 1505–1686, 1535–1651, 1544–1661. Archivio di Stato, Pesaro.

Bonamini, Domenico. *Abecedario architettonico degli architetti Pesaresi civili e militari e Pittori Pesaresi.* MS oliveriano 1009. Biblioteca Oliveriana, Pesaro.

Calandrini, Ippolito. *L'Heroe d'Italia.* MS parmense 737. Biblioteca palatina, Parma.

Calculo Fatto dell'entrate e uscite ordinarie di tutto lo stato fondate sopra quelle degli anni 1573/1574... Ducato d'Urbino, classe I divisione A filza III parte II. Archivio di Stato, Firenze.

Cancelleria ducale, particolari busta 121. Archivio di Stato, Modena.

Cancelleria ducale, particolari busta 123. Archivio di Stato, Modena.

Carteggio farnesiano e borbonico estero, busta 475. Archivio di Stato, Parma.

Casa e corte farnesiane, serie II busta 2 fascicolo 2. Archivio di Stato, Parma.

Casa e corte farnesiane, serie II busta 6 fascicolo 2. Archivio di Stato, Parma.

Casa e corte farnesiane, serie II busta 6 fascicolo 3. Archivio di Stato, Parma.

Casa e corte farnesiane, serie II busta 28 fascicolo 5. Archivio di Stato, Parma.

Casa e corte farnesiane, serie VII busta 51 fascicolo 23. Archivio di Stato, Parma.

Dei Rumori in Feste, e violenza alle Porte dove si Balla. Legazione apostolica di Pesaro-Urbino, decreti 2: 1505–1686, 1535–1651, 1544–1661. Archivio di Stato, Pesaro.

Delle maschere, e provisioni diverse intorno esse. Legazione apostolica di Pesaro-Urbino, decreti dei della Rovere, volume 3. Archivio di Stato, Pesaro.

Ducato d'Urbino, classe I divisione B filza X. Archivio di Stato, Firenze.

Ducato d'Urbino, classe I divisione G filza CCXLII. Archivio di Stato, Firenze.

Gozze, Marco Antonio. *Delle memorie della Città di Pesaro*. MS oliveriano 380, fols. 205–235. Biblioteca Oliveriana, Pesaro.

"Lettere scritte, à Potentati, Principi, e Cav[aliera]ti, per annunci delli sponsali contratti fra'l Ser[enissi]mo Duca di Parma, Don Odoardo, e la Ser[enissi]ma Principessa Marg[heri]ta sorella del Gran Duca di Toscana." Casa e corte farnesiane, serie II busta 6 fascicolo 2. Archivio di Stato, Parma.

Libro dei conti. Ducato d'Urbino, classe III filza XXIII. Archivio di Stato, Firenze.

"Lista delli legnami di Piopa che fano bisogno p[er] il servizio della scena che si fà nel Cortile di S[ua] A[ltezza] Ser[enissi]ma." Teatri e spettacoli di età farnesiana, busta 1 mazzo 1 fascicolo 18 sottofascicolo 4. Archivio di Stato, Parma.

"Lista di legnami, di Piella, che fanno bisogno per la scena over teatro, che si fà nel Cortile di S[ua] A[ltezza] S[erenissi]ma avanti S[an]to Pietro Martire." Teatri e spettacoli di età farnesiana, busta 1 mazzo 1 fascicolo 18 sottofascicolo 5. Archivio di Stato, Parma.

"Liste dela feramenta che fa bisognio per fare il teatro cioe chioderia." Teatri e spettacoli di età farnesiana, busta 1 mazzo 1 fascicolo 18 sottofascicolo 3. Archivio di Stato, Parma.

Manoscritto Antonelli 660. Biblioteca comunale ariostea, Ferrara.

Mediceo del Principato, filza 6075. Archivio di Stato, Firenze.

Mediceo del Principato, filza 6087. Archivio di Stato, Firenze.

Mediceo del Principato, filza 6088. Archivio di Stato, Firenze.

"Memoria deli ordini dato al se[greta]r Spacino per infra[det]ta occas[io]ne dal Ser[enissi]mo Principe." Cancelleria ducale, ambasciatori Parma busta 5. Archivio di Stato, Modena.

Mingucci, Francesco. *Stati, dominii, città, terre e castella dei Serenissimi Duchi, e Prencipi della Rovere tratti dal naturale*. Codice Barberino latino 4434. Biblioteca apostolica vaticana, Roma.

"Nota di Giovan Andrea Cattanio di operai." Teatri e spettacoli di età farnesiana, busta 1 mazzo 1 fascicolo 18 sottofascicolo 1. Archivio di Stato, Parma.

Obbligazione di Pietro e Virginia Vagnoli, musici senesi, di servire nella loro professione Guidubaldo II. Ducato d'Urbino, classe I divisione B filza X. Archivio di Stato, Firenze.

"Ordini per il Magg[iordo]mo." Casa e corte farnesiane, serie VII busta 51 fascicolo 23. Archivio di Stato, Parma.

Pugolotti, Andrea. *Diario parmigiano*. MS parmense 462. Biblioteca palatina, Parma.

Rinalducci, Giovanni Battista. *Notitie Historiche della Città di Pesaro*. MS oliveriano 380, fols. 237–243. Biblioteca Oliveriana, Pesaro.

Raccolta Ronchini. Busta 2 fascicolo 2a. Archivio di Stato, Parma.

Raccolta Ronchini. Busta 4 fascicolo 14a. Archivio di Stato, Parma.

Teatri e spettacoli di età farnesiana, busta 1 mazzo 1 fascicolo 20 sottofascicolo 3. Archivio di Stato, Parma.

Teatri e spettacoli di età farnesiana, busta 1 mazzo 1 fascicolo 20 sottofascicolo 4. Archivio di Stato, Parma.

Teatri e spettacoli di età farnesiana, busta 1 mazzo 1 fascicolo 20 sottofascicolo 5. Archivio di Stato, Parma.

Printed Works

A: Sources

Achillini, Claudio. *Teti e Flora. Prologo della gran Pastorale recitata in Parma nel Maraviglioso Teatro fabricato questo anno dal Serenissimo signor Duca per Honorar l'arrivo della Serenissima Principessa Margherita di Toscana sua moglie . . .* Parma: Seth ed Erasmo Viotti, 1628.

Ariosto, Ludovico. *Orlando furioso*. Trans. Barbara Reynolds. 2 vols. Harmondsworth: Penguin, 1975.

———. *Orlando furioso*. Ed. Cesare Segre. 2 vols. Milan: Mondadori, 1976.

Aristotle. *The "Art" of Rhetoric*. Trans. John Henry Freese. Cambridge, MA: Harvard University Press, 1926.

———. *Poetics*. Trans. Stephen Halliwell. Cambridge, MA: Harvard University Press, 1995.

Barbieri, Nicolò. *La supplica discorso famigliare a quelli che trattano de' comici*. Ed. Ferdinando Taviani. Milan: Il Polifilo, 1971.

Bardi, Giovanni de'. *Discorso mandato da Gio: de' Bardi a Giulio Caccini detto Romano sopra la Musica antica, e'l cantar bene*. (1578?) In Giovan Battista Doni. *Lyra Barberina*. 2 vols. 1763. 2: 233–48. Bologna: Forni, 1974.

Buttigli, Marcello. *Descrittione dell'apparato fatto per honorare la prima solenne entrata in Parma della Serenissima Principessa Margherita di Toscana, Duchessa di Parma, Piacenza, . . .* Parma: Seth ed Erasmo Viotti, 1629.

Castiglione, Baldassar. *Il libro del cortegiano*. Ed. Giulio Carnazzi. Milan: Rizzoli, 1994.

de' Sommi, Leone. *Quattro dialoghi in materia di rappresentazioni sceniche*. Ed. Ferruccio Marotti. Milan: Il Polifilo, 1968.

Fabbri, Paolo, and Angelo Pompilio, eds. *Il corago o vero alcune osservazioni per mettere bene in scena le composizioni drammatiche*. Firenze: Olschki, 1983.

Fabris, Dinko. *Mecenati e musici: Documenti sul patronato artistico dei Bentivoglio di Ferrara nell'epoca di Monteverdi (1585–1645)*. Lucca: Libreria musicale italiana, 1999.

Félibien, André. *Le feste di Versailles*. Ed. Alberto Ausoni. Rome: Salerno, 1997.

Galilei, Vincenzo. *Dialogo della musica antica e della moderna* (1581). New York: Broude, 1967.

Giasone in nove. Comune, busta 625. Archivio di Stato, Parma.

Giustiniani. Vincenzo. "Discorso sopra la musica de' suoi tempi." (1628). In *Le origini del melodramma. Testimonianze dei contemporanei*, ed. Angelo Solerti, 98–128. Torino: Bocca, 1903.

Guarini, Giovanni Battista. *Opere*. 4 vols. Verona: Tumermani, 1737.

Guidotti, Alessandro. "La rappresentazione di *Anima e Corpo* musicata da Emilio de' Cavalieri." (1600). In *Le origini del melodramma. Testimonianze dei contemporanei*, ed. Solerti, 1–39.

Ingegneri, Angelo. *Della poesia rappresentativa e del modo di rappresentare le favole sceniche*. In *Lo spettacolo dall'Umanesimo al Manierismo*, ed. Ferruccio Marotti. 271–308. Milan: Feltrinelli, 1974.

Macrobius. *Commentary on the Dream of Scipio*. Trans. William H. Stahl. New York: Columbia University Press, 1990.

Malipiero, G. Francesco. *Claudio Monteverdi*. Milan: Treves, 1929.

Manso, Giovanni Battista. *Vita di Torquato Tasso* (1621). Rome: Francesco Cavalli, 1634.

Minucci del Rosso, Paolo. "Le nozze di Margherita de' Medici con Odoardo Farnese duca di Parma e Piacenza. Parte I, II, III." *La rassegna nazionale* 21 (16 February 1885): 551–71; 22 (16 April 1885): 550–70; 23 (1 May 1885): 19–45.

Persiani, Horazio. *Contesa d'Apollo, e d'Amore*. Firenze: Zanobi Pignoni, [1628].

Pio di Savoia, Ascanio. *Intermedii recitati in musica dalle più ecc[ellen]ti voci del nostro secolo in uno dei superbissimi Teatri di Parma fabricato dall'Heroica Magnificenza del S[erenissi]mo Duca Odoardo Farnese per honorar l'arrivo della Ser[enissi]ma Principessa Margherita di Toscana...* Parma: Seth ed Erasmo Viotti, 1629.

Reiner, Stuart. "Preparations in Parma — 1618, 1627–28." *Music Review* 25 (1964): 273–301.

Saviotti, Alfredo. "Feste e spettacoli nel Seicento." *Giornale storico della letteratura italiana* 41 (1903): 42–77.

———. "Torquato Tasso e le feste pesaresi del 1574." *Giornale storico della letteratura italiana* 12 (1888): 404–17.

Solerti, Angelo. *Musica ballo e drammatica alla Corte Medicea dal 1600 al 1637.* Firenze: n.p., 1905.

——, ed. *Le origini del melodramma. Testimonianze dei contemporanei.* Torino: Bocca, 1903.

Spennacchi, Enea. *Encomio epitalamico.* Comune, busta 625. Archivio di Stato, Parma.

Tasso, Torquato. *Aminta.* Ed. Bruno Maier. Milan; Rizzoli, 1976.

——. *Gerusalemme liberata.* Ed. Giuseppe Sacchi. Milan: Luigi Sacchi, 1844.

——. *Intrichi d'amore.* Ed. Enrico Malato. Rome: Salerno, 1976.

——. *Delle lettere familiari del signor Torquato Tasso, nuovamente raccolte, e date in luce, libro primo e secondo.* Bergamo: Comino Ventura, 1588.

——. *Lettere inedite.* Ed. Pier Antonio Serassi. Pisa: Niccolò Capurro, 1827.

——. *Opere.* 5 vols. Ed. Bruno Maier. Milan: Rizzoli, 1963.

Ugolini, Filippo. "Diario della ribellione d'Urbino nel 1572 d'ignoto autore." *Archivio storico italiano* n. s. 3 (1856): 37–59.

Vasari, Giorgio. *Le vite de' più eccellenti pittori scultori e architettori nelle redazioni del 1550 e 1568.* 6 vols. Ed. Rosanna Bettarini. Firenze: Studio per edizioni scelte, 1966.

Virgil. *The Aeneid.* Trans. Robert Fitzgerald. New York: Random House, 1983.

——. *Eneide.* Trans. Rosa Calzecchi Onesti. Milan: Mondadori, 1971.

B: Criticism

Accorsi, Maria Grazia. "Musicato, per musica, musicale. Riflessioni intorno ad *Aminta*." In *Torquato Tasso e la cultura estense 3. Il teatro del Tasso*, ed. Gianni Venturi, 881–940. Firenze: Olschki, 1999.

Aercke, Kristiaan P. *Gods of Play. Baroque Festive Performances as Rhetorical Discourse.* Albany: State University of New York Press, 1994.

Allen, John J. *The Reconstruction of a Spanish Golden Age Playhouse. The* Corral del Príncipe *1583–1744.* Gainesville: University Press of Florida, 1983.

Almansi, Guido. "Dov'è la mia fraschetta?" *Panorama* (7 May 1994): 169.

Alonge, Roberto. "Riflessioni sull'*Aminta*." *Il castello di Elsinore* 12 (1999): 5–15.

Anderson, Michael. "The Changing Scene: Plays and Playhouses in the Italian Renaissance." In *Theatre of the English and Italian Renaissance*, ed. J. R. Mulryne and Margaret Shewring, 3–20. London: Macmillan, 1991.

Antaldi, Antaldo. *Notizie di alcuni architetti, pittori, scultori di Urbino, Pesaro e de' Luoghi circonvicini* (1805). Ed. Anna Cerboni Baiardi. Pesaro: Il lavoro editoriale, 1996.

Apollonio, Mario. *Storia del teatro italiano*. 2 vols. Firenze: Sansoni, 1981.

Arcangeli, Letizia. "Atlante genealogico della famiglia Farnese." In *I Farnese. Arte e collezionismo*, ed. Lucia Fornari Schianchi and Nicola Spinosa, 25–48. Milan: Electa, 1995.

Ascari, Tiziano. "Bentivoglio, Enzo." In *Dizionario biografico degli italiani*, 8: 610–12. Rome: Istituto dell'enciclopedia italiana, 1960–.

Attolini, Giovanni. *Teatro e spettacolo nel Rinascimento*. Bari: Laterza, 1988.

Ault, Thomas. "Classical Humanist Drama in Transition: The First Phase of Renaissance Theatre in Ferrara." *Theatre Annual* 50 (1997): 17–39.

Bakhtin, Mikhail. *Rabelais and His World*. Bloomington: Indiana University Press, 1984.

Balestrieri, Lina. *Feste e spettacoli alla corte dei Farnesi (contributo alla storia del melodramma)*. Parma: Donati, 1909.

Barish, Jonas. *The Antitheatrical Prejudice*. Berkeley: University of California Press, 1981.

Bataille, Georges. *Visions of Excess. Selected Writings, 1927–1939*. Ed. Allan Stoekl. Minneapolis: University of Minnesota Press, 1985.

Battistelli, Franco. "Teatri storici nella provincia di Pesaro e Urbino." In *Teatri delle terre di Pesaro e Urbino*, ed. Fermo Giovanni Motta. 23–36. Milan: Electa, 1997.

Beall, Chandler B. *La Fortune du Tasse en France*. Eugene: University of Oregon-Modern Language Association of America, 1942.

Bennett, Susan. *Theatre Audiences. A Theory of Production and Reception*. 2nd ed. London: Routledge, 1997.

Bernardo e Torquato Tasso alla corte di Guidubaldo II e di Francesco Maria II Duchi d'Urbino. Trattenimento accademico che la sera del dì 8 settembre 1843 danno al pubblico... l'accademia dei Nascenti e gli scolari di retorica del collegio dei Nobili d'Urbino. Pesaro: Nobili, 1843.

Besutti, Paola. "Tasso contra Guarini: una rappresentazione con intermedi degli *Intrichi d'amore* (1606)." In *Torquato Tasso e la cultura estense 3. Il teatro del Tasso*, ed. Venturi, 1197–1220.

Beyer, Barbara Ives. "Baroque Representation." *The Journal of Aesthetic and Art Criticism* 12 (1953–54): 360–65.

Bianconi, Lorenzo. "Il Cinquecento e il Seicento." In *Letteratura italiana*, ed. Alberto Asor Rosa, 7 vols. 6: 319–63. Torino: Einaudi, 1982–89.

———. "I Fasti musicali del Tasso." In *Torquato Tasso tra letteratura, musica, teatro e arti figurative*, ed. Andrea Buzzoni. 143–50. Bologna: Nuova Alfa, 1985.

———. *Music in the Seventeenth Century* (1982). Cambridge: Cambridge University Press, 1987.

Blackmer, Corinne E., and Patricia Juliana Smith, eds. *En Travesti. Women, Gender Subversion, Opera*. New York: Columbia University Press, 1995.

Boland, Eavan. "When the Spirit Moves." *New York Review of Books* (12 January 1995): 25–28.

Bosco, Umberto. *Saggi sul rinascimento italiano*. Firenze: Le Monnier, 1970.

Bosisio, Paolo. "Teatro e spettacolo nella corte estense." *Il castello di Elsinore* 7 (1994): 51–70.

Brand, C. P. *Torquato Tasso. A Study of the Poet and of His Contribution to English Literature*. Cambridge: Cambridge University Press, 1965.

Burattelli, Claudia. *Spettacoli di corte a Mantova tra Cinque e Seicento*. Firenze: Le lettere, 1999.

Burckhardt, Jacob. *The Civilization of the Renaissance in Italy* (1860). Harmondsworth: Penguin, 1990.

Burke, Peter. *The Fabrication of Louis XIV*. New Haven: Yale University Press, 1992.

Campori, Giuseppe, and Angelo Solerti. *Luigi, Lucrezia e Leonora d'Este. Studi*. Torino: Loescher, 1888.

Carandini, Silvia. *Teatro e spettacolo nel Seicento*. Bari: Laterza, 1990.

Carducci, Giosué. "Su l'*Aminta* di Torquato Tasso. Saggi tre." (1894–1895). In idem, *Opere. Edizione nazionale*, 30 vols., 14: 137–275. Bologna: Zanichelli, 1962.

Carlson, Marvin. *Places of Performance. The Semiotics of Theatre Architecture*. Ithaca: Cornell University Press, 1989.

Casini, Matteo. *I gesti del principe. La festa politica a Firenze e Venezia in età rinascimentale*. Venezia: Marsilio, 1996.

Castle, Terry. *Masquerade and Civilization: The Carnivalesque in Eighteenth-Century English Culture and Fiction*. Stanford: Stanford University Press, 1986.

Cavallo, Jo Ann. "Tasso's Armida and the Victory of Romance." *Renaissance Transactions. Ariosto and Tasso*, ed. Valeria Finucci, 77–111. Durham: Duke University Press, 1999.

Cavicchi, Adriano. "Ancora sull'*Aminta* del Belvedere." In *Torquato Tasso e la cultura estense 3. Il teatro del Tasso*, ed. Venturi, 1151–63.

———. "Immagini e forme dello spazio scenico nella pastorale ferrarese." In *Sviluppi della drammaturgia pastorale nell'Europa del Cinque-Seicento*, ed. M. Chiabò and F. Doglio, 45–85. Viterbo: Union Printing, 1991.

———. "La scenografia dell'*Aminta* nella tradizione scenografica pastorale ferrarese del secolo XVI." In *Studi sul teatro veneto fra Rinascimento ed età barocca*, ed. Maria Teresa Muraro, 53–72. Firenze: Olschki, 1971.

Cecini, Nando. "Cultura e letteratura dei centri maggiori e minori tra rinascimento e barocco." In *Arte e cultura nella provincia di Pesaro e Urbino dalle origini a oggi*, ed. Franco Battistelli, 333–59. Venezia: Marsilio, 1986.

Chastel, André. "Cortile et théâtre." In *Le Lieu théâtral à la Renaissance*, ed. Jean Jacquot, 41–47. Paris: Centre national de la recherche scientifique, 1964.

Chegai, Andrea. "Musicalità *vs.* musicabilità: l'*Aminta* fra recezione madrigalistica e fortuna critica." *Il saggiatore musicale* 1 (1994): 315–34.

Cherchi, Paolo. "Il re Adone." In *The Sense of Marino*, ed. Francesco Guardiani, 9–33. New York: Legas, 1994.

Ciancarelli, Roberto. *Il progetto di una festa barocca. Alle origini del Teatro Farnese di Parma (1618–1629)*. Rome: Bulzoni, 1987.

Clubb, Louise George. *Italian Drama in Shakespeare's Time*. New Haven: Yale University Press, 1989.

———. "The Pastoral Play: Conflation of Country, Court and City." In *Il teatro italiano del Rinascimento*, ed. Maristella de Panizza Lorch, 65–73. Milan: Edizioni di comunità, 1980.

Croce, Benedetto. "Poesia pastorale." 1945. In idem, *Poeti e scrittori del pieno e tardo Rinascimento*, 3 vols., 1: 326–37. Bari: Laterza, 1958.

Croce, Franco. "La teatralità dell'*Aminta*." In *Sviluppi della drammaturgia pastorale nell'Europa del Cinque-Seicento*, ed. Chiabò and Doglio, 131–57.

Cruciani, Fabrizio. "Dietro le origini del teatro rinascimentale." *Quaderni di teatro* 7 (1985): 14–21.

———. "Percorsi critici verso la prima rappresentazione dell'*Aminta*." In *Torquato Tasso tra letteratura, musica, teatro e arti figurative*, ed. Buzzoni, 179–92.

———. *Lo spazio del teatro*. Bari: Laterza, 1998.

———, and Daniele Seragnoli, eds. *Il teatro italiano nel Rinascimento*. Bologna: Il Mulino, 1987.

Curtius, Ernst Robert. *European Literature and the Latin Middle Ages* (1953). Princeton: Princeton University Press, 1983.

Dalla Valle, Daniela. "L'influence en France de l'*Aminta* du Tasse." In *L'âge d'or du mécénat*, ed. Roland Mousnier and Jean Mesnaid, 305–14. Paris: Editions du Centre National de la Recherche Scientifique, 1985.

d'Amico, Silvio. *Storia del teatro drammatico*. 4 vols. Milan: Garzanti, 1950.

Da Pozzo, Giovanni. *L'ambigua armonia. Studio sull'*Aminta *del Tasso*. Firenze: Olschki, 1983.

———. "Forma allusiva e scenario della mente nel teatro tassiano." In *Torquato Tasso e la cultura estense 3. Il teatro del Tasso*, ed. Venturi, 861–79.

Davis, Tracy C. "Questions for a Feminist Methodology in Theatre History." In *Interpreting the Theatrical Past. Essays in the Historiography of Performance*, ed. Thomas Postlewait and Bruce A. McConachie, 59–81. Iowa City: University of Iowa Press, 1989.

Deierkauf-Holsboer, S. Wilma. *Le Théâtre de l'Hôtel de Bourgogne*. 2 vols. Paris: Nizet, 1968–1970.

"della Rovere, Giulio (Feltrio)." In *Dizionario biografico degli italiani*, 37: 356–57. Rome: Istituto dell'enciclopedia italiana, 1960–.

Della Terza, Dante. "La corte e il teatro: il mondo del Tasso." In *Il teatro italiano del Rinascimento*, ed. Lorch, 51–63.

De Grazia, Marco. "Per una storia del Palazzo della Pilotta." *Parma nell'arte* 4 (1972): 101–49.

De Marinis, Marco. "Dramaturgy of the Spectator." *Drama Review* 31 (1987): 100–14.

de Sanctis, Francesco. *Storia della letteratura italiana*. Ed. Benedetto Croce. 2 vols. Bari: Laterza, 1958.

Di Benedetto, Arnaldo. "L'*Aminta* e la pastorale cinquecentesca in Italia." In *Torquato Tasso e la cultura estense 3. Il teatro del Tasso*, ed. Venturi, 1121–49.

Donadoni, Eugenio. "L'*Aminta*." In *Torquato Tasso. Saggio critico* (1928). 103–25. Firenze: La nuova Italia, 1952.

Donington, Robert. *The Rise of Opera*. New York: Scribner's, 1981.

Donohue, Joseph. "Evidence and Documentation." In *Interpreting the Theatrical Past. Essays in the Historiography of Performance*, ed. Postlewait and McConachie, 177–97.

Durante, Sergio. "The Opera Singer." In *Opera Production and Its Resouces*, ed. Lorenzo Bianconi and Giorgio Pestelli, 345–417. Chicago: University of Chicago Press. 1998.

Eamon, William. "Court, Academy, and Printing House: Patronage and Scientific Careers in Late Renaissance Italy." In *Patronage and Institutions: Science, Technology, and Medicine at the European Court 1500–1750*, ed. Bruce T. Moran, 25–50. Rochester: Boydell, 1991.

———. *Science and the Secrets of Nature. Books of Secrets in Medieval and Early Modern Culture*. Princeton: Princeton University Press, 1994.

Eaves, Morris. "'Why Don't They Leave It Alone?' Speculations on the Authority of the Audience in Editorial Theory." In *Cultural Artifacts and the Production of Meaning. The Page, the Image, and the Body*, ed. Margaret M. J. Ezell and Katherine O'Brian O'Keefe, 85–99. Ann Arbor: University of Michigan Press, 1994.

Falvo, Joseph D. "Urbino and the Apotheosis of Power." *Modern Language Notes* 101 (1986): 114–46.

Fenlon, Iain. "The Origins of the Seventeenth-Century Staged *Ballo*." In *Con che soavità: Studies in Italian Opera, Song, and Dance, 1580–1740*, ed. idem and T. Carter, 13–40. Oxford: Clarendon Press, 1995.

Fenzi, Enrico. "Il potere, la morte, l'amore. Note sull'*Aminta* di Torquato Tasso." *L'immagine riflessa* 3 (1979): 167–248.

Ferrari, Paolo-Emilio. *Spettacoli drammatico-musicali e coreografici in Parma dall'anno 1628 all'anno 1883*. Bologna: Forni, 1884; repr. 1969.

Ferrone, Siro. "Introduzione. Come nasce un copione." In *Seminario sulla drammaturgia*, ed. Luigi Rustichelli, 1–18. West Lafayette: Bordighera, 1998.

———, Claudia Burattelli, Domenica Landolfi, and Anna Zinanni, eds. *Comici dell'Arte. Corrispondenze*. 2 vols. Firenze: Le Lettere, 1993.

Ferroni, Giulio. "La scena, l'autore, il signore del teatro delle corti padane." In *Il teatro italiano del Rinascimento*, ed. Lorch, 537–70.

Firpo, Luigi. *Lo stato ideale della Controriforma. Ludovico Agostini*. Bari: Laterza, 1957.

Flora, Francesco. "Introduzione." In Tasso, *Poesie*, vii–xliii. Milan: Ricciardi, 1952.

———. "L'*Aminta*." In Tasso, *Poesie*, 35–42. Milan: Rizzoli, 1934.

Fontana, Alessandro. "La scena." In *Storia d'Italia. I caratteri originari*, ed. Ruggiero Romano and Corrado Vivanti, 791–866. Torino: Einaudi, 1972.

Fortini, Franco. *Dialoghi col Tasso*, ed. Pier Vincenzo Mengaldo and Donatello Santarone. Torino: Bollati Boringhieri, 1999.

Foucault, Michel. *Les Mots et les choses. Une archéologie des sciences humaines*. Paris: Gallimard, 1966.

Franko, Mark, and Annette Richards, eds. *Acting on the Past. Historical Performance across the Disciplines*. Hanover: Wesleyan University Press, 2000.

Fubini, Mario. "L'*Aminta* intermezzo alla tragedia della *Liberata*." (1947). In idem, *Studi sulla letteratura del Rinascimento*, 200–15. Firenze: La nuova Italia, 1971.

Gamba, Enrico, and Vico Montebelli, eds. *Macchine da Teatro e Teatri di Macchine. Branca, Sabbatini, Torelli scenotecnici e meccanici del Seicento*. Urbino: Quattroventi, 1995.

Gambara, Lodovico. "I teatri minori." In *I teatri di Parma dal Farnese al Regio*, ed. Ivo Allodi, 205–20. Milan: Nuove edizioni, 1969.

Gareffi, Andrea. *La scrittura e la festa. Teatro, festa e letteratura nella Firenze del Rinascimento*. Bologna: Il Mulino, 1991.

Geertz, Clifford. *Negara. The Theatre State in Nineteenth-Century Bali*. Princeton: Princeton University Press, 1980.

Getto, Giovanni. *Interpretazione del Tasso* (1951). Napoli: Edizioni scientifiche italiane, 1966.

Giampieri, Giampiero. *Torquato Tasso. Una psicobiografia*. Firenze: Le lettere, 1995.

Godard, Alain. "La Première représentation de l'*Aminta*: la cour de Ferrare et son double." In *Ville et campagne dans la littérature italienne de la Renaissance, 2: Le Courtisan travesty*, 187–301. Paris: Université de la Sorbonne nouvelle, 1977.

Goffman, Erving. *Frame Analysis. An Essay on the Organization of Experience*. 1974. Boston: Northeastern University Press, 1986.

Graziosi, Elisabetta. Aminta *1573–1580. Amore e matrimonio in casa d'Este*. Lucca: Maria Pacini Fazzi, 2001.

Guarino, Raimondo. *Teatro e mutamenti. Rinascimento e spettacolo a Venezia*. Bologna: Il Mulino, 1995.

Gumbrecht, Hans Ulrich. "A History of the Concept 'Modern.'" In *Making Sense in Life and Literature*, ed. Wlad Godzich, 79–110. Minneapolis: University of Minnesota Press, 1992.

Günsberg, Maggie. *Gender and the Italian Stage from the Renaissance to the Present Day*. Cambridge: Cambridge University Press, 1997.

Gurr, Andrew, and John Orrell. *Rebuilding Shakespeare's Globe*. New York: Routledge, 1989.

Habermas, Jürgen. *The Structural Transformation of the Public Sphere. An Inquiry into a Category of Bourgeois Society*. Cambridge, MA: Massachusetts Institute of Technology Press, 1989.

Hammond, Frederick. *Music & Spectacle in Baroque Rome. Barberini Patronage under Urban VIII*. New Haven: Yale University Press, 1994.

Harbage, Alfred. *Annals of English Drama 975–1700*. 3rd ed. Rev. Sylvia Stoler Wagonheim. London: Routledge, 1989.

Hare, A. Paul, and Herbert H. Blumberg. *Dramaturgical Analysis of Social Interaction*. New York: Praeger, 1988.

Heck, Thomas F., ed. *Picturing Performance. The Iconography of the Performing Arts in Concept and Practice*. Rochester: University of Rochester Press, 1999.

Hughes, Robert. "Why Watch It, Anyway?" *New York Review of Books* (16 February 1995): 37–42.

Huizinga, Johan. "L'elemento estetico delle rappresentazioni storiche." In idem, *Le immagini della storia. Scritti 1905–1941*, ed. Wietse de Boer, 5–31. Torino: Einaudi, 1993.

———. "The Task of Cultural History." In idem, *Men and Ideas. History, the Middle Ages, the Renaissance*, 17–76. Princeton: Princeton University Press, 1984.

L'Imperiale castello sul colle di San Bartolo presso Pesaro già degli Sforza e dei della Rovere oggi de' Principi Albani descritto e illustrato. Pesaro: Federici, 1881.

Jardine, Lisa. *Worldly Goods. A New History of the Renaissance.* London: Norton, 1996.

Kermode, Frank. "Sound and Fury." *New York Review of Books* (16 February 1995): 35–36.

Kimbell, David. *Italian Opera.* Cambridge: Cambridge University Press, 1991.

Lavin, Irving. "Lettres de Parme (1618, 1627–28) et débuts du théâtre baroque." In *Le Lieu théâtral à la Renaissance*, ed. Jacquot, 105–58.

———. "On the Unity of the Arts and the Early Baroque Opera House." In *Art and Pageantry in the Renaissance and Baroque*, ed. Barbara Wisch and Susan Scott Munshower, 518–79. College Park: Pennsylvania State University Press, 1990.

———. "On the Unity of the Arts and the Early Baroque Opera House." *Perspecta* 26 (1990): 1–20.

Lazzaro, Claudia. *The Italian Renaissance Garden. From the Conventions of Planting, Design, and Ornament to the Grand Gardens of Sixteenth-Century Central Italy.* New Haven: Yale University Press, 1990.

Leopardi, Giacomo. *Opere.* 2 vols., ed. Sergio Solmi. Milan: Ricciardi, 1956–1966.

Le Roy Ladurie, Emmanuel. *Carnival in Romans.* New York: Braziller, 1979.

Levin, Harry. *The Myth of the Golden Age in the Renaissance.* Bloomington: Indiana University Press, 1969.

Longman, Stanley. "Esoterismo negli spettacoli della corte dei Farnese." In *Il bosco sacro*, ed. Elémire Zolla and Marina Maymone Siniscalchi, 121–25. Foggia: Bastogi, 1992.

Lotman, Jurij. "Semiotica della scena." *Strumenti critici* 15 (1981): 1–45.

Luisi, Francesco. "Note sul contributo musicale alla drammaturgia pastorale avanti il melodramma." In *Sviluppi della drammaturgia pastorale nell'Europa del Cinque-Seicento*, ed. Chiabò and Doglio, 101–18.

Maggiorotti, Leone Andrea. "Paciotto, Francesco." In *Enciclopedia italiana di scienze, lettere ed arti*, 36 vols., 25: 882. Rome: Istituto dell'enciclopedia italiana, 1929–39.

Malato, Enrico. "Introduzione." In Tasso, *Intrichi d'amore*, ix–lxxi. Rome: Salerno, 1976.

Mamczarz, Irène. *Le théâtre Farnèse à Parme et le drame musical italien (1618–1732). Etude d'un lieu théâtral, des représentations, des formes: drame pastoral, intermèdes, opéra-tournoi, drame musical.* Firenze: Olschki, 1988.

Mamone, Sara. *Il teatro nella Firenze medicea.* Milan: Mursia, 1981.

Maravall, José Antonio. *Teatro e letteratura nella Spagna barocca.* Bologna: Il Mulino, 1995.

Marchini, Giuseppe, ed. *La villa Imperiale di Pesaro.* Pesaro: Cassa di risparmio di Pesaro, n.d.

———, and Nando Cecini. *La villa Imperiale di Pesaro.* Pesaro: Casso di risparmio di Pesaro, 1986.

Marcus, Leah S. "Renaissance/Early Modern Studies." In *Redrawing the Boundaries. The Transformation of English and American Literary Studies,* ed. Stephen Greenblatt and Giles Gunn, 41–63. New York: Modern Language Association of America, 1992.

Marin, Louis. *Portrait of the King* (1981). Minneapolis: University of Minnesota Press, 1988.

Marotti, Ferruccio. *Lo spazio scenico. Teorie e tecniche scenografiche in Italia dall'età barocca al settecento.* Rome: Bulzoni, 1974.

———. *Lo spettacolo dall'Umanesimo al Manierismo. Teoria e tecnica. Storia documentaria del teatro italiano.* Milan: Feltrinelli, 1974.

———. "Teoria e tecnica dello spazio scenico dal Serlio al Palladio nella trattatistica rinascimentale." *Bollettino del centro internazionale di studi di architettura "Andrea Palladio"* 16 (1974): 257–70.

———, and Giovanna Romei. *La commedia dell'arte e la società barocca. La professione del teatro.* Rome: Bulzoni, 1991.

Martufi, Roberta. *Diletto e meraviglia. Le ville del colle San Bartolo di Pesaro.* Pesaro: Nobili, 1992.

McAuley, Gay. *Space in Performance. Making Meaning in the Theatre.* Ann Arbor: University of Michigan Press, 1999.

McClary, Susan. "Construction of Gender in Monteverdi's Dramatic Music," in eadem, *Feminine Endings,* 35–52. Minneapolis: University of Minnesota Press, 1991.

———. "Gender Ambiguities and Erotic Excess in Seventeenth-Century Venetian Opera." In *Acting on the Past. Historical Performance across the Disciplines.* ed. Franko and Richards, 177–200.

McGann, Jerome J. *A Critique of Modern Textual Criticism.* Chicago: University of Chicago Press, 1983.

Mengaldo, Pier Vincenzo. "Premessa." In Franco Fortini, *Dialoghi col Tasso*, ed. Mengaldo and Santarone, 7–15.

Miller, Jonathan. "Doing Opera." *New York Review of Books* (11 May 2000): 12–16.

Millon, Henry A. "I modelli architettonici nel Rinascimento." In *Rinascimento da Brunelleschi a Michelangelo. La rappresentazione dell'architettura*, ed. Henry Millon and Vittorio Magnago Lampugnani, 19–73. Milan: Bompiani, 1994.

Mohler, Frank. "A Brief Shining Moment. An Effect that Disappeared from the Illusionistic Stage." *Theatre Symposium* 4 (1996): 83–90.

Molinari, Cesare. *Le nozze degli dei. Un saggio sul grande spettacolo italiano nel seicento.* Rome: Bulzoni, 1968.

———. "Les Rapports entre la scène et les spectateurs dans le théâtre italien du XVIe siècle." In *Le Lieu théâtral à la Renaissance*, ed. Jacquot, 61–71.

———. "Gli spettatori e lo spazio scenico nel teatro del cinquecento." *Bollettino del centro internazionale di studi di architettura "Andrea Palladio"* 16 (1974): 145–54.

Motta, Fermo Giovanni, ed. *Teatri delle terre di Pesaro e Urbino.* Milan: Electa, 1997.

Nagler, A. M. *Theatre Festivals of the Medici.* New Haven: Yale University Press, 1964.

Nardo, Anna K. *The Ludic Self in Seventeenth-Century English Literature.* Albany: State University of New York Press, 1991.

Newcomb, Anthony. "Antonio Goretti." In *New Grove Dictionary of Music and Musicians*, 2nd ed., 29 vols., 10: 162–63. London: Macmillan, 2001.

Newman, Karen. "The Politics of Spectacle: *La Pellegrina* and the Intermezzi of 1589." *Modern Language Notes* 101 (1986): 95–111.

Newton, Stella Mary. *Renaissance Theatre Costume and the Sense of the Historical Past.* London: Rapp & Whiting, 1975.

Nogara, Gino. *Cronache degli spettacoli nel teatro Olimpico di Vicenza dal 1585 al 1970.* Vicenza: Accademia Olimpica, 1972.

Nuti, Lucia. "The Perspective Plan in the Sixteenth Century: The Invention of a Representational Language." *Art Bulletin* 76 (1994): 105–28.

Nutter, David. "Intermedio." In *New Grove Dictionary of Music and Musicians*, ed. Stanley Sadie, 20 vols., 9: 258–69. London: Macmillan, 1980. Updated in *New Grove*, 2nd ed. (2001), 12: 476–88.

Orgel, Stephen. *Impersonations. The Performance of Desire in Shakespeare's England.* Cambridge: Cambridge University Press, 1996.

——— "The Poetics of Spectacle." *New Literary History* 2 (1971): 367–89.

———. "Shakespeare Imagines a Theater." In *Shakespeare, Man of the Theater*, ed. Kenneth Muir, 34–46. Newark, DE: University of Delaware Press, 1983.

———, and Roy Strong. *Inigo Jones. The Theatre of the Stuart Court*. 2 vols. Berkeley: University of California Press, 1973.

Ortega y Gasset, José. "Meditations on the Frame" (1921). *Perspecta* 26 (1990): 185–90.

Paglioli, Ernesto. *La breve festa del Cardinale Francesco Maria Farnese*. Parma: PPS, 1998.

Palisca, Claude V. *Girolamo Mei (1519–1594): Letters on Ancient and Modern Music to Vincenzo Galilei and Giovanni Bardi*. n.p.: American Institute of Musicology, 1960.

Panofsky, Erwin. "Renaissance and Renascences" (1944). In *Renaissance and Renascences in Western Art*, 2nd ed., 42–113. New York: Harper & Row, 1969.

"Pesaro." In *Enciclopedia italiana*, 26: 917–22.

Petronio, Giuseppe. "Introduzione alla lettura dell'*Aminta*." *La rassegna della letteratura italiana* ser. 4, 41 (1933): 1–17.

Pieri, Marzia. *La nascita del teatro moderno in Italia tra XV e XVI secolo*. Torino: Bollati Boringhieri, 1989.

———. *La scena boschereccia nel Rinascimento italiano*. Padova: Liviana, 1983.

———. "La scena pastorale." *Biblioteca teatrale* 5 (1980): 3–30.

Pinelli, Antonio, and Orietta Rossi. "L'Imperiale nuova di Girolamo Genga." *Storia dell'arte* 6 (1970): 101–19.

Piperno, Franco. "Nuovi documenti sulla prima rappresentazione dell'*Aminta*." *Il castello di Elsinore* 13 (2000): 29–40.

———. "Opera Production to 1780." In *Opera Production and Its Resouces*, ed. Bianconi and Pestelli, 1–79.

Pirrotta, Nino. "The Orchestra and Stage in Renaissance *Intermedi* and Early Opera." In idem, *Music and Culture in Italy from the Middle Ages to the Baroque*, 210–16. Cambridge, MA: Harvard University Press, 1984.

———. "Studies in the Music of Renaissance Theatre." In idem and Elena Povoledo, *Music and Theatre from Poliziano to Monteverdi*, 1–280. Cambridge: Cambridge University Press, 1982.

Povoledo, Elena. "Controversie monteverdiane: spazi teatrali e immagini presunte." In *Claudio Monteverdi: studi e prospettive*, ed. Paola Besutti, Teresa M. Gialdroni and Rodolfo Baroncini, 357–89. Firenze: Olschki, 1998.

———. "Ferrara." In *Enciclopedia dello spettacolo*, 10 vols., 5: 173–86. Rome: Le maschere, 1954–68.

———. "Intermezzo." In *Enciclopedia dello spettacolo*, 6: 572–76.

———. "Origini e aspetti della scenografia in Italia dalla fine del Quattrocento agli intermezzi fiorentini del 1589." In Nino Pirrotta, *Li due Orfei. Da Poliziano a Monteverdi*, 371–509. Torino: ERI, 1969.

———. "Torneo." In *Enciclopedia dello spettacolo*, 9: 991–99.

Praz, Mario. "Tasso in Inghilterra." In *Torquato Tasso*, 673–709. Milan: Marzorati, 1957.

Prodi, Paolo. "Ricerche sulla teorica delle arti figurative nella Riforma cattolica." *Archivio italiano per la storia della pietà* 4 (1965): 121–212.

Quarta, Daniela. "Spazio scenico, spazio cortigiano, spazio cortese." In *La corte di Ferrara e il suo mecenatismo 1441–1598*, ed. Marianne Pade, Lene Wage Petersen and eadem, 301–27. Modena: Panini, 1990.

Raimondi, Luisella. "Villa Imperiale. Pesaro." In *Ville e giardini*, ed. Franco Borsi and Geno Pampaloni, 347–50. Novara: De Agostini, 1984.

Ramat, Raffaello. "L'*Aminta*." In idem, *Per la storia dello stile rinascimentale*, 119–51. Messina: D'Anna, 1953.

Rebhorn, Wayne A. *Foxes and Lions: Machiavelli's Confidence Men*. Ithaca: Cornell University Press, 1988.

Rennert, Hugo Albert. *The Spanish Stage in the Age of Lope de Vega*. New York: Hispanic Society of America, 1909.

Rhu, Lawrence F. *The Genesis of Tasso's Narrative Theory. English Translations of the Early Poetics and a Comparative Study of Their Significance*. Detroit: Wayne State University Press, 1993.

Ricci, Giovanni. *Il principe e la morte. Corpo, cuore, effigie nel Rinascimento*. Bologna: Il Mulino, 1998.

Roach, Joseph R. *Cities of the Dead. Circum-Atlantic Performance*. New York: Columbia University Press, 1996.

———. "Power's Body. The Inscription of Morality as Style." In *Interpreting the Theatrical Past. Essays in the Historiography of Performance*, ed. Postlewait and McConachie, 99–118.

"Roma." In *Enciclopedia italiana*, 29: 589–928.

Ronga, Luigi. "La nascita del melodramma nello spirito della poesia." In *Teatro del seicento*, ed. Luigi Fassò, xxvii–liii. Milan: Ricciardi, n. d.

Rossi, Vittorio. Review of Carducci, "Su l'*Aminta* di Torquato Tasso. Saggi tre." *Giornale storico della letteratura italiana* 31 (1898): 108–16.

Rossi-Pinelli, Orietta. "La villa Imperiale di Pesaro come spazio scenico per la corte urbinate." *Bollettino del centro internazionale di studi di architettura "Andrea Palladio"* 16 (1974): 219–33.

Rousset, Jean. *La Littérature de l'âge baroque en France. Circé et le paon*. Paris: Corti, 1954.

Rudlin, John. *Commedia dell'Arte. An Actor's Handbook*. London: Routledge, 1994.

Ruffini, Franco. *Commedia e festa nel Rinascimento. La* Calandria *alla corte di Urbino*. Bologna: Il Mulino, 1986.

———. *Teatri prima del teatro. Visione dell'edificio e della scena tra Umanesimo e Rinascimento*. Rome: Bulzoni, 1983.

Saslow, James. *The Medici Wedding of 1589. Florentine Festival as* Theatrum Mundi. New Haven: Yale University Press, 1996.

Schechner, Richard. "Behavior, Performance, and Performance Space." *Perspecta* 26 (1990): 97–102.

———. *Between Theater and Anthropology*. Philadelphia: University of Pennsylvania Press, 1985.

Schlegel, August Wilhelm von. *Lectures on Dramatic Art and Literature* (1809). London: George Bell, 1879.

Scorza, Gian Galeazzo. *I della Rovere 1508–1631*. Pesaro: n.p., 1981.

Scrivano, Riccardo. *Finzioni teatrali da Ariosto a Pirandello*. Messina: D'Anna, 1982.

———. "La funzione teatrale nella critica del Manierismo." *Biblioteca teatrale* 23/24 (1979): 1–13.

———. "Tasso e il teatro." In *La norma e lo scarto. Proposte per il Cinquecento letterario italiano*, 209–48. Rome: Bonacci, 1980.

Segre, Cesare. "Il teatro del Rinascimento e la semiotica." In *Il teatro italiano del Rinascimento*, ed. Lorch, 389–401.

Serassi, Pierantonio. *La vita di Torquato Tasso*. Rome: Pagliarini, 1785.

Shergold, N. D. *A History of the Spanish Stage from Medieval Times until the End of the Seventeenth century*. Oxford: Clarendon, 1967.

Smith, Dinitia. "Writers Enchanted by the Freedom of Opera." *New York Times* (28 September 1995): A1, B2.

Solari, Giovanna. *22 storie dei duchi di Urbino tra il Sole e la luna*. Milan: Mondadori, 1973.

Solerti, Angelo. *Gli albori del melodramma*. 3 vols. Torino: Forni, 1903.

———. *Vita di Torquato Tasso*. 3 vols. Torino: Loescher, 1895.

———, and Domenico Lanza. "Il teatro ferrarese nella seconda metà del secolo XVI." *Giornale storico della letteratura italiana* 18 (1891): 148–85.

Southorn, Janet. *Power and Display in the Seventeenth Century. The Arts and Their Patrons in Modena and Ferrara*. Cambridge: Cambridge University Press, 1988.

Sozzi, Bartolo Tommaso. "Nota sui cori e sugl'"intermedi' dell'*Aminta*." *Giornale storico della letteratura italiana* 126 (1949): 426–31.

———. "Nota sull'episodio di Mopso e sull'epilogo dell'*Aminta*." *Giornale storico della letteratura italiana* 127 (1950): 485–86.

———. "Per l'edizione critica dell'*Aminta*." In idem, *Studi sul Tasso*, 11–68. Pisa: Nistri-Lischi, 1954.

Stallybrass, Peter, and Allon White. *The Politics and Poetics of Transgression*. Ithaca: Cornell University Press, 1986.

Stampino, Maria Galli. "Classical Antecedents and Teleological Narratives: On the Contamination between Opera and Courtly Sung Entertainment in the Early Seventeenth Century." *Italica* 77 (2000): 331–56.

———. "Epideictic Pastoral: Rhetorical Tensions in the Staging of Torquato Tasso's *Aminta*." *Theatre Symposium* 5 (1997): 36–49.

———. "Performance, Text, and Canon: The Case of *Aminta*." *Romance Languages Annual* 9 (1997): 351–58.

———. "Publish or Perish: An Early-Seventeenth-Century Paradox." *Romance Languages Annual* 10 (1999): 373–79.

———. "The Space of the Performance: *Aminta*, the Court, and the Theater." *Romance Review* 6 (1996): 7–28.

Starn, Randolph, and Loren Partridge. *Arts of Power. Three Halls of State in Italy, 1300–1600*. Berkeley: University of California Press, 1992.

Sternfeld, F. W. *The Birth of Opera*. Oxford: Clarendon Press, 1993.

"Talassio." In *Harper's Dictionary of Classical Literature and Antiquities*, ed. Harry Thurston Peck, 1521. New York: Cooper Square, 1962.

Tani, Gino. "Moresca." In *Enciclopedia dello spettacolo*, 7: 834–36.

Taviani, Ferdinando. "Bella d'Asia. Torquato Tasso, gli attori e l'immortalità." *Paragone* 408–410 (1984): 3–76.

———. "Teatro di voci in tempi bui (riflessioni brade su 'Aminta' e pastorale)." *Teatro e storia* 9 (1994): 9–39.

———, and Mirella Schino. *Il segreto della commedia dell'arte*. Firenze: La casa Usher, 1982.

Thorndike, Lynn. "Newness and Novelty in Seventeenth-Century Science and Medicine." In *Roots of Scientific Thought. A Cultural Perspective*, ed. Philip P. Wiener and Aaron Noland, 443–57. New York: Basic Books, 1957.

Toffanin, Giuseppe. "Il teatro del Rinascimento." In *Storia del teatro italiano*, ed. Silvio d'Amico, 61–99. Milan: Bompiani, 1936.

Trexler, Richard C. *Public Life in Renaissance Florence*. Ithaca: Cornell University Press, 1980.

Trimpi, Wesley. "Decorum." In *The New Princeton Encyclopedia of Poetry and Poetics*, ed. Alex Preminger, T. V. F. Brogan, Frank J. Warnke, O. B. Hardison, and Earl Miner, 282–83. Princeton: Princeton University Press, 1993.

Trombatore, Gaetano. "L'*Aminta*." In idem, *Saggi critici*, 113–42. Firenze: La nuova Italia, 1950.

Trotti, Anton Francesco. "Le delizie di Belvedere illustrate. Raccolta di documenti editi ed inediti." *Deputazione ferrarese di storia patria. Atti e memorie* 2 (1889): 1–32.

Trovato, Paolo. "Per una nuova edizione dell'*Aminta*." In *Torquato Tasso e la cultura estense 3. Il teatro del Tasso*, ed. Venturi, 1003–27.

Tylus, Jane. "Colonizing Peasants: The Rape of the Sabines and Renaissance Pastoral." *Renaissance Drama* 23 (1992): 113–38.

———. "Purloined Passages: Giraldi, Tasso, and the Pastoral Debates." *Modern Language Notes* 99 (1984): 101–24.

———. *Writing and Vulnerability in the Renaissance*. Stanford: Stanford University Press, 1993.

Valeri, Valerio. "Cerimoniale." In *Enciclopedia*, ed. Ruggiero Romano, 16 vols., 2: 955–67. Torino: Einaudi, 1977–84.

———. "Festa." In *Enciclopedia*, ed. Romano, 6: 87–99.

———. "Rito." In *Enciclopedia*, ed. Romano, 12: 210–43.

Varese, Claudio. "L'*Aminta*." In idem, *Pascoli politico, Tasso e altri saggi*, 91–151. Milan: Feltrinelli, 1961.

Vassalli, Antonio. "Il Tasso in musica e la trasmissione dei testi: alcuni esempi." In *Tasso, la musica, i musicisti*, ed. Maria Antonella Balsano and Thomas Walker, 45–90. Firenze: Olschki, 1988.

Venturi, Gianni. "Picta poësis: ricerche sulla poesia e il giardino dalle origini al Seicento." In *Storia d'Italia. Annali 5. Il paesaggio*, ed. Cesare de Seta, 663–749. Torino: Einaudi, 1982.

———. "Un'isola tra utopia e realtà." In *Torquato Tasso tra letteratura musica teatro e arti figurative*, ed. Buzzoni, 173–178.

Vickers, Brian. "Epideictic and Rhetoric in the Renaissance." *New Literary History* 14 (1983): 497–537.

Vignati, Laura. *Storia delle filodrammatiche negli oratori milanesi dalle origini ai nostri giorni*. Milan: FOM, 1991.

Walker, Thomas. "Opera." In *New Grove Dictionary of Music and Musicians*, [1980] 13: 544–647. Updated by other hands in *New Grove*, 2nd ed. (2001), 18: 416–71.

Whigham, Frank. "Interpretation at Court: Courtesy and the Performer-Audience Dialectic." *New Literary History* 14 (1983): 623–39.

Wiley, W. L. "The Hôtel de Bourgogne. Another Look at France's First Public Theatre." *Studies in Philology* 70 (1973): 1–109.

Wilson, Jean. *The Archeology of Shakespeare*. Phoenix Mill: Sutton, 1995.

Yoch, James J. "'A Greater Power than We Can Contradict:' The Voice of Authority in the Staging of Italian Pastorals." In *The Elizabethan Theatre 8*, ed. George Hibbard, 164–87. Toronto: P. D. Meany, 1982.

——. "The Limits of Sensuality: Pastoral Wildernesses, Tasso's *Aminta* and the Gardens of Ferrara." *Forum Italicum* 16 (1982): 60–81.

Zatti, Sergio. "Epic in the Age of Dissimulation: Tasso's *Gerusalemme liberata*." In *Renaissance Transactions. Ariosto and Tasso*, ed. Finucci, 115–45.

——. *L'ombra del Tasso. Epica e romanzo nel Cinquecento*. Milan: B. Mondadori, 1996.

Zorzi, Ludovico. "Figurazione pittorica e figurazione teatrale." In *Storia dell'arte italiana*, ed. Giulio Bollati and Paolo Fossati, 12 vols., 1.1:419–63. Torino: Einaudi, 1979– .

Zumthor, Paul. *Essai de poétique médiévale*. Paris: Seuil, 1972.

Index

Accorsi, Maria Grazia 19, 254, 282 n. 93
Achillini, Claudio 110, 125, 132, 152 n. 92, 220 n. 59, 222 n. 76, 222 n. 80
Aercke, Kristiaan 147 n. 69, 174, 177, 220 n. 60, 246, 260, 274 n. 30
Aleotti, Giovan Battista 106
Alfonso II d'Este 52, 63, 64, 66, 67, 79
Allen, John J. xviii n. 3
Almansi, Guido 35 n. 35
Almerici, Tiberio 65, 67–79, 87 n. 39, 89 n. 56, 247. 256
Alonge, Roberto 41 n. 69
Aminta and *commedia* dell'arte troupes 18–19, 36 n. 38, 276 n. 43; interpreted in biographical terms 4–7; interpreted within Tasso's poetic production 8–11; interpreted teleologically in the development of Italian literary history 11–14; performance history 14–17, 23–24; printing history 18; selected for performance at Parma 135; supposed *première* on Belvedere Island 16, 17, 36 n. 38, 41 n. 68, 79, 238; text (printed) versions 21–25; at Parma in 1628 182–184, 188, 192–193, 197, 200–201; at Pesaro in 1574 71–79
Anderson, Michael 147 n. 69
Andreini, Giovan Battista 141 n. 37
Andreini, Isabella 73, 276 n. 43
Antaldi, Ciro 63, 64

Apollonio, Mario 8–9, 34 n. 34, 41 n. 69
Arcangeli, Letizia 136 n. 7
Ariosto, Ludovico *Orlando furioso* 3, 145 n. 59, 184–188, 223 n. 83, 224 n. 84, 224 n. 86
Aristotle 27, 250, 251, 252
Ascari, Tiziano 106
Attolini, Giovanni 70, 90 n. 66, 94 n. 102
audience 26, 171–173, 175, 187, 215 n. 35, 225 n. 102, 245–251, 261
Ault, C. Thomas 225 n. 98
Ausoni, Alberto 223 n. 82
Bakhtin, Mikhail 81, 87 n. 38, 94 n. 102
Balestrieri, Lina 148 n. 72, 219 n. 53
Barbieri, Nicolò 141 n. 37, 248
Barish, Jonas 163 n. 155
Bataille, Georges 245, 275 n. 32
Battistelli, Franco 89 n. 55
Beall, Chandler B. xviii n. 5
Bennett, Susan xii, 26, 27
Bentivoglio, Cornelio 204
Bentivoglio, Enzo 106–120, 122–134, 141 n. 37, 142 n. 42, 142 n. 43, 149 n. 76, 150 n. 80, 152 n. 85, 152 n. 93, 157 n. 117, 183, 207, 208, 217 n. 47, 232 n. 174
Besutti, Paola 163 n. 154
Beyer, Barbara Ives 93 n. 92
Bianconi, Lorenzo 35 n. 36, 45 n. 95, 123, 209 n. 1, 263, 264, 267 n. 2, 281 n. 85, 282 n. 90

Blumberg, Herbert H. 27, 272 n. 20
bodies xii, 71, 73, 174, 187, 245–251
Bonamini, Domenico 84 n. 10
Bosco, Umberto 5, 7, 8, 9, 14, 31 n. 12, 34 n. 30, 35 n. 36, 35 n. 38, 40 n. 61, 40 n. 62
Bosisio, Paolo 46 n. 96
Brand, C. P. 30–31 n. 7, 34 n 28, 37 n. 45
Burattelli, Claudia 219 n. 56
Burckhardt, Jacob 281 n. 84
Buttigli, Marcello 105, 165–167, 170–171, 172–173, 175–177, 179–180, 181–182, 184–187, 188–191, 192, 193–196, 197–200, 201–207, 212 n. 10, 224 n. 86, 225 n. 98, 225 n. 102, 228 n. 139, 229 n. 144, 263
Caccini, Giulio 264
Caccini, Settimia 127, 130
Calandrini, Ippolito 100–101, 102–103, 105, 106, 208, 237
Canigiani, Bernardo 213 n. 25
Carandini, Silvia 106, 140 n. 32, 268 n. 6
Carducci, Giosué 4–5, 12, 14–15, 19, 38 n. 51, 38 n. 52, 41 n. 68
Carlson, Marvin 217 n. 45
carnevale 55–61, 66, 81, 85 n. 15, 87 n. 39, 100, 106, 138 n. 21
Casini, Matteo 137 n. 16
Castiglione, Baldassar 52, 74, 77, 215 n. 35, 254
Castle, Terry 86 n. 36
Cattanio, Giovanni Andrea 109, 143 n. 54
Cavallo, Jo Ann 224 n. 90
Cavicchi, Adriano 15, 41 n. 70, 159 n. 128
Cecchini, Pier Maria 141 n. 37
Cecini, Nando 65, 66, 75, 76, 83 n. 6, 84 n. 9, 92 n. 81
Chastel, André 114
Chegai, Andrea 35 n. 36
Cherchi, Paolo 274 n. 31

Chianchi, Vittorio 129, 130, 131, 157 n. 119, 158 n. 124, 160 n. 138
Ciancarelli, Roberto 136 n. 6
Clubb, Louise George 36 n. 40, 254, 271 n. 16
Il corago 153 n. 97, 211 n. 9, 213 n. 25
council of Trent 57, 125–126, 227 n. 125, 251, 253, 277 n. 53
Croce, Benedetto 8
Croce, Franco 264–265, 276 n. 41, 277 n. 55
cross-dressing on stage 91 n. 68, 276 n. 42
Cruciani, Fabrizio xvii n. 3, 16–17, 19, 41 n. 70, 89 n. 53, 89 n. 56, 93 n. 92, 261, 280 n. 74
curtain in front of stage 78, 179, 220 n. 61, 220 n. 63
Curtius, Ernst Robert 277 n. 49
Dalla Valle, Daniela 16, 42 n. 72, 239
d'Amico, Silvio 9, 36 n. 38
Da Pozzo, Giovanni 15–16, 41 n. 70, 42 n. 71, 43 n. 75, 83 n. 8, 238, 239, 273 n. 22
Davis, Tracy 210 n. 5
De Grazia, Marco 141 n. 40, 148 n. 72
Deierkauf-Holsboer, S. Wilma xvii n. 2
Della Terza, Dante 252
De Marinis, Marco 20
Denores, Giasone 30 n. 6, 254
de' Bardi, Giovanni 264
de Sanctis, Francesco 13
de' Sommi, Leone 253, 257–258, 259–260, 278 n. 67, 280 n. 76
Di Benedetto, Arnaldo 277 n. 54
d'India, Sigismondo 123, 124
Donadoni, Eugenio 5, 6, 32 n. 14, 32 n. 19, 278 n. 56
Donington, Robert 263
Donohue, Joseph 20, 23
Durante, Sergio 157 n. 120
Eamon, William 259–261, 267 n. 4

Eaves, Morris 47 n. 109
epideictic rhetoric 251–255
Fabris, Dinko 90 n. 58, 106, 136 n. 10, 141 n. 38
Falvo, Joseph D. 90 n. 66
Farnese bureaucracy 104–105, 113, 138 n. 25, 138 n. 26, 144 n. 55, 147 n. 68
Félibien, André 209, 210 n. 5, 217 n. 47, 223 n. 82
Fenzi, Enrico 278 n. 63
Ferrara 2–3, 8, 67, 106, 226 n. 119, 232 n. 174, 252
Ferrari, Paolo-Emilio 141 n. 40, 165
Ferrone, Siro 17
Ferroni, Giulio 247, 272 n. 19
Fiorillo, Silvio 141 n. 37
Firpo, Luigi 92 n. 81
Flora, Francesco 31 n. 11, 34 n. 28, 35 n. 36, 36 n. 38, 36 n. 41
Florence xi, xii, 19, 137 n. 16, 155 n. 109, 158 n. 122, 167, 214 n. 29, 215 n. 35, 220 n. 63, 230 n. 156, 244, 258, 274 n. 25
Fontana, Alessandro 174
Fortini, Franco 3, 5–6
Foucault, Michel 49 n. 122
frame 75, 92 n. 79, 176, 217 n. 47
Francesco Maria della Rovere 52, 53, 56–61, 84 n. 9, 85 n. 16
Franko, Mark xiv, xvii
Fubini, Mario 278 n. 56
Galilei, Vincenzo 263–264
Gambara, Lodovico 141 n. 40, 147 n. 69, 217 n. 42
Gareffi, Andrea xv, xviii n. 6, 20, 25, 44 n. 77, 49 n. 124, 155 n. 109
Geertz, Clifford 242–243, 245–246
gender on stage and in the audience 72–73, 130, 160 n. 131, 179–180, 247, 250–251, 265
Genga, Girolamo 76, 77
Getto, Giovanni 10, 37 n. 44, 271 n. 16
Giampieri, Giampiero 89 n. 48

Giordani, Camillo 79, 105, 107, 109, 168–169, 170, 177, 178, 184, 206, 209, 219 n. 53
Giulio Cardinal della Rovere 52, 83 n. 4
Giustiniani, Vincenzo 158 n. 123
Godard, Alain 16, 36 n. 40, 41 n. 70, 64, 91 n. 71, 238–239
Goffman, Erving 71, 176, 215 n. 37, 243, 256
Goretti, Antonio 99, 107, 109, 123, 125, 127–135, 142 n. 43, 143 n. 53, 149 n. 76, 152 n. 93, 160 n. 132, 163 n. 156, 207, 213 n. 22
Graziosi, Elisabetta 43 n. 75, 44 n. 79, 137 n. 19
Grimano, Antonio 131, 157 n. 119, 160 n. 138
Guarini, Giovan Battista xviii n. 5, 30 n. 6, 48 n. 115, 254, 278 n. 62
Guarino, Raimondo 20–21, 215 n. 37
Guidubaldo II della Rovere 51, 54, 55–56, 66, 72, 80, 85 n. 14, 89 n. 53, 94 n. 100, 255
Guitti, Francesco 107–109, 114, 117, 120, 124, 126–127, 130, 133–134, 143 n. 53, 152 n. 85, 176, 217 n. 47
Gumbrecht, Hans Ulrich 261, 262
Günsberg, Maggie 73, 91 n. 69, 276 n. 42
Gurr, Andrew xvii n. 3
Habermas, Jürgen 236, 237–238
Hammond, Frederick 159 n. 129, 160 n. 138
Harbage, Alfred xviii n. 5
Hare, A. Paul 27, 272 n. 20
Hoelterhoff, Manuela 266
Hughes, Robert 266–267
Huizinga, Johan 25–26
Ingegneri, Angelo 30 n. 6. 214 n. 26, 253, 258, 265
Inghirami, Luigi 105, 170, 171–172, 176, 177, 178, 179, 180, 181,

182–183, 184, 185, 186, 187, 188, 189–190, 192–193, 194, 196, 197, 199, 200, 201, 203–204, 205, 206, 207, 219 n. 53, 222 n. 71, 226 n. 107, 226 n. 109, 228 n. 137
intermezzi 21–22, 70–71, 91 n. 67, 120–122, 123–124, 145 n. 60, 161 n. 141, 249, 257–259, 263
Jardine, Lisa 139 n. 27
Kermode, Frank 28–29
Kimbell, David 121, 122, 157 n. 119, 281 n. 85
Lavin, Irving 97, 107, 111, 114, 217 n. 42
Lazzaro, Claudia 271 n. 14
Leopardi, Giacomo 7, 33 n. 27, 35–36 n. 38
Le Roy Ladurie, Emmanuel 54, 61, 72, 90 n. 66
Levin, Harry 278 n. 62
London xi, xii
Longman, Stanley 237
Lotman, Jurij 19–20, 21, 95 n. 103
Lucrezia d'Este 52–53, 54, 63, 64, 65, 66, 67, 77, 79, 84 n. 9, 226 n. 119
Luisi, Francesco 265
Luzzaschi, Luzzasco 282 n. 90
Machiavelli, Niccolò 44 n. 77, 94 n. 100
Madrid xi
Maier, Bruno 22
Maggiorotti, Leone 93 n. 88
Magnani 141 n. 40
Malato, Enrico 32 n. 17
Mamczarz, Irène 141 n. 40, 157 n. 117, 175, 183, 214 n. 30, 217 n. 42, 222 n. 73, 230 n. 156
Mamone, Sara 244, 274 n. 25
Manso, Giovan Battista 3, 4, 11, 31 n. 8, 31 n. 9
Mantua 19, 226 n. 119
Maravall, José Antonio 215 n. 37, 244
Marchini, Giuseppe 76, 92 n. 81
Marcus, Leah S. 47 n. 108
Margherita Aldobrandini married Farnese 98, 99, 124, 125–126, 134–135, 136 n. 12, 155 n. 107, 183, 247
Margherita de' Medici 97, 98, 99, 100, 102, 134, 136 n. 12, 167, 181–182; entry into Parma 137 n. 17, 140 n. 32, 168–169, 236, 246–247
Maria Cristina de' Medici 98, 99
Maria Maddalena of Hapsburg married Medici 98, 105
Marin, Louis 237, 245, 246
Marotti, Ferruccio xviii n. 4, 74, 267 n. 1
Martufi, Roberta 76
mask wearing 56–61, 248
Mazzi, Francesco 107, 109–119, 129, 130–131, 145 n. 58, 151 n. 81, 159 n. 128, 175, 177, 220 n. 61
McAuley, Gay xv, 174, 212 n. 10, 215 n. 37, 221 n. 66, 235, 276 n. 37
McClary, Susan 48 n. 112
McGann, Jerome 23
Mei, Girolamo 264
Mengaldo, Pier Vincenzo 3
Miller, Jonathan 48 n. 120
Millon, Henry 151 n. 83
Minucci del Rosso, Paolo 98, 141 n. 40, 210 n. 3, 212 n. 15
Mohler, Frank 228 n. 133
Molinari, Cesare 74, 94 n. 99
Monteverdi, Claudio 24, 99, 122–134, 152 n. 85, 264
moresca 70
Nagler, A. M. 120–121, 141 n. 40, 212 n. 11, 219 n. 53
Nardo, Anna K. 80–81, 94 n. 102, 176, 243, 273 n. 23
Newman, Karen 121
Newton, Stella Mary 90 n. 66
Nogara, Gino 85 n. 15
novelty 70–71, 78–79, 182–183, 255, 256–262, 265
Nuti, Lucia 92 n. 80
Nutter, David 121, 122, 161 n. 141
Oates, Joyce Carol 266
Oddi, Sforza 69–71, 79, 256

Odoardo Farnese 97, 98, 99, 102, 126, 134, 136 n. 12, 167, 181–182, 189, 246–247
opera 262–266
Orell, John xvii n. 3
Orgel, Stephen xvii, 137 n. 19, 215 n. 35, 278 n. 58
Paciotto, Felice 73, 77
Paciotto, Francesco 73, 77
Padua xi
Paglioli, Ernesto 136 n. 7
Palmaroli, Luigi 63
Panofsky, Erwin 281 n. 84
Paris xi
Parma xvi, 26, 28, 97, 169–170
Partridge, Loren 72, 81, 148 n. 71, 179, 215 n. 35
performers at Parma 128–131, 134–135, 184; at Pesaro 67, 69, 72, 78, 81–82, 89 n. 53, 91 n. 70, 247
Peri, Iacopo 263, 264, 281 n. 85
Persiani, Horatio 228 n. 141
Pesaro xvi, 19, 26, 51, 83 n. 2; political troubles of 1572–73 53–54; *carnevale* edicts 55–61; acting tradition 67, 69
Petronio, Giuseppe 5, 6, 13–14, 33 n. 22, 39 n. 59
Pieri, Marzia xvii n. 1, xviii n. 4, 19, 24, 30 n. 6, 73, 183, 220 n. 63, 222 n. 78, 258, 270 n. 11
Pinelli, Antonio 76, 77, 92 n. 81
Pio di Savoia, Ascanio 110, 124, 128, 132–133, 157 n. 117, 222 n. 80, 226 n. 111
Piperno, Franco 43 n. 75, 104, 209 n. 1, 215 n. 37, 217 n. 47
Pirrotta, Nino 122, 141 n. 38, 154 n. 106, 263
Povoledo, Elena 19, 24, 90 n. 58, 121, 158 n. 125, 214 n. 31, 259
Praz, Mario xviii n. 5
Prodi, Paolo 277 n. 53
Pugolotti, Andrea 167
Quarta, Daniela 255, 271 n. 16

Raimondi, Luisella 92 n. 82
Rainaldi, Girolamo 141 n. 40
Ramat, Raffaello 6, 7, 13, 14, 35 n. 36, 36 n. 38, 40 n. 65
Ranuccio I Farnese 98, 101
Rebhorn, Wayne 94 n. 100
referentiality xii, 247–250, 254
Reiner, Stuart 99, 106, 123, 132, 142 n. 43, 145 n. 63, 147 n. 69, 152 n. 92, 212 n. 11, 232 n. 174
Rennert, Hugo Albert xvii n. 3
Rhu, Lawrence 94 n. 98
Ricci, Giovanni 83 n. 8
Richards, Annette xiv, xvii
Rinuccini, Ottavio 263, 281 n. 85
Roach, Joseph 27, 49 n. 123, 61
Romei, Giovanna xviii n. 4
Ronconi, Luca 35 n. 35
Ronga, Luigi 278 n. 56
Rossi, Orietta 76, 77, 92 n. 81
Rossi, Vittorio 38 n. 53
Rousset, Jean 195
Rudlin, John 85 n. 19, 275 n. 35
Ruffini, Franco 114, 140 n. 33, 165, 215 n. 37, 267 n. 1
Sabbioneta xii
Saslow, James xv, xvii, 75, 103, 121, 156 n. 112, 176, 180, 184, 210 n. 2, 214 n. 29, 215 n. 37, 217 n. 47, 223 n. 82
Saviotti, Alfredo 65, 84 n. 11, 91 n. 74, 141 n. 40
Scala, Flaminio 19
Schechner, Richard 176, 215 n. 37, 217 n. 46
Schlegel, August Wilhelm von 27
Scorza, Gian Galeazzo 84 n. 11
Scotti, Fabio 106–110, 112, 124, 129, 133, 143 n. 53, 150 n. 80
Scrivano, Riccardo 9–10, 250, 254–255, 266
Segre, Cesare 215 n. 37
Serassi, Pierantonio 5, 31 n. 11, 61–63, 64
Shergold, N. D. xvii n. 1, xvii n. 3

Solari, Giovanna 65, 75, 84 n. 11
Solerti, Angelo 18, 30 n. 3, 43 n. 75, 52, 65, 66, 83 n. 8, 88 n. 47, 89 n. 52, 93 n. 94, 93 n. 95, 94 n. 97, 154 n. 106, 212 n. 11, 219 n. 53, 238, 281 n. 85
Southorn, Janet 106, 107, 120, 217 n. 47
Sozzi, Bartolo Tommaso 11, 18, 21–23, 24, 47 n. 104, 93 n. 94, 93 n. 95
spaces for performances 73, 108–134, 171–180, 235–245
Spennacchi, Enea 101–102
Stallybrass, Peter 72, 82 n. 1
Starn, Randolph 72, 81, 148 n. 71, 179, 215 n. 35
Sternfeld, F. W. 121, 230 n. 157, 263, 264
Striggio, Alessandro 99, 123, 125
Tani, Gino 70, 90 n. 66
Tasso, Bernardo 52
Tasso, Torquato biographical sketch 1–3; xii, 18, 52, 62–64, 66, 78, 79, 85 n. 17, 280 n. 74, 282 n. 93
Taviani, Ferdinando xviii n. 4, 1, 18, 48 n. 111, 73, 250, 275 n. 33, 276 n. 43
Teatro di San Pietro martire 107–134, 141 n. 40, 240, 241–242
Teatro Farnese 106, 110, 141 n. 39
Thorndike, Lynn 280 n. 78
Toffanin, Giuseppe 12–13, 39 n. 54, 39 n. 55
tournament 214 n. 31; at Parma 202–207; at Pesaro 68–69
Trexler, Richard 71–72, 75, 83 n. 3, 90 n. 60, 169, 238

Trimpi, Wesley 276 n. 44
Trombatore, Gaetano 6–7, 10, 14, 33 n. 26, 37 n. 47, 40 n. 60
Trovato, Paolo 21, 48 n. 111
Tylus, Jane 30 n. 6, 245, 247–248, 274 n. 24
Ugolini, Filippo 84 n. 10
Ugolino, Vincenzo 129, 131, 158 n. 123
Urbino 53–54
Valeri, Valerio 173–174, 176, 215 n. 36
Varese, Claudio 5, 14, 30 n. 5, 32 n. 16, 40 n. 63, 46 n. 103
Vasari, Giorgio 76
Vassalli, Antonio 36 n. 36
Venturi, Gianni 240, 270 n. 12
Vicenza xi, 85 n. 15
Vickers, Brian 252, 253, 254, 277 n. 50
Vignati, Laura 140 n. 36, 278 n. 60
Villa Imperiale 65, 75–77, 92 n. 81, 240, 255
Virgil *Aeneid* 188–192, 226 n. 105, 226 n. 108, 226 n. 111, 228 n. 136
Vittori, Loreto 129, 130, 158 n. 122, 158 n. 124, 160 n. 133
Walker, Thomas 121, 262–263
Warburg, Aby xvii
Whigham, Frank 252–253
White, Allon 72, 82 n. 1
willing suspension of foreknowledge xii, 262
Wilson, Jean xvii n. 3
Yates, William Butler 245
Yoch, James 22, 47 n. 103, 209, 240, 277 n. 46
Zanibelli, Angiola 130
Zatti, Sergio 225 n. 94
Zorzi, Ludovico 273 n. 22
Zumthor, Paul 266, 283 n. 100